Fathers across Cultures

Fathers across Cultures

The Importance, Roles, and Diverse Practices of Dads

Jaipaul L. Roopnarine, Editor

Foreword by Catherine S. Tamis-LeMonda

An Imprint of ABC-CLIO, LLC

Santa Barbara, California • Denver, Colorado

Library of Congress Cataloging-in-Publication Data

Fathers across cultures : the importance, roles, and diverse practices of dads / Jaipaul L. Roopnarine, editor ; foreword by Catherine S. Tamis-LeMonda.
    pages cm
  Includes bibliographical references and index.
  ISBN 978-1-4408-3231-4 (print : alk. paper) — ISBN 978-1-4408-3232-1 (e-book)
1. Fatherhood. 2. Fathers. I. Roopnarine, Jaipaul L., editor.
  HQ756.F38323 2015
    306.874'2—dc23   2015022425

ISBN: 978-1-4408-3231-4
EISBN: 978-1-4408-3232-1

19 18 17 16 15   1 2 3 4 5

This book is also available on the World Wide Web as an eBook.
Visit www.abc-clio.com for details.

Praeger
An Imprint of ABC-CLIO, LLC

ABC-CLIO, LLC
130 Cremona Drive, P.O. Box 1911
Santa Barbara, California 93116-1911

This book is printed on acid-free paper ∞
Manufactured in the United States of America

This book is dedicated to the memory of my father, Fred Lalla Roopnarine, who like so many men of his generation, found unique ways of negotiating provider and caregiving roles.

Contents

Foreword

Catherine S. Tamis-LeMonda

Fatherhood is culturally defined. The views and practices of fathers—from a child's conception forward—are products and expressions of culture. Yet, as is true of most areas of family study and child development, cultural aspects of fathering have long been neglected. Fortunately, this glaring oversight is rapidly changing. A search in Psychinfo for the years 1970–1985 yields a mere 40 peer-reviewed journal articles that contain the keywords "father" and "culture" in their abstracts. Between 1985 and 2000, that number doubled to 81, and a search from 2000 to the present yields 222 articles. Yet even in the presence of this exponential growth in cultural studies of fathering, the field remains fractured. Each cultural study of fatherhood has tended to stand on its own—an isolated silo, like a single frame removed from the backdrop of a complete picture. Consequently, there is need for a coherent, comprehensive, and theoretically grounded integration of studies and perspectives on how cultural context influences men's beliefs about fatherhood, masculinity, men and women's roles, fathers' investments and involvement with children, families, and broader community systems.

Fortunately, Jaipaul Roopnarine's edited volume does just that: It offers the field a much-needed kaleidoscope on the cultural faces of fatherhood that exist across the globe. This thought-provoking collection of chapters showcases the continually evolving and distinct ways that fathering is defined and expressed across cultural communities from geographic regions across the world, how fathering plays out in child and family development, and how historical context, social policies, economic circumstances, and political structures have altered the structural arrangements of families. The various chapters highlight the lives of fathers and families from countries spanning North, Central, and South America, eastern and western Europe, and Asia, and Africa, including a rare portrayal of men in Islamic societies and Israel.

The broad cultural coverage of Roopnarine's volume challenges common conceptions of what it means to be a father and uproots traditional taxonomies that have been used to define and assess father involvement in the U.S. context, in which the majority of research on this topic has been conducted. Moreover, the chapters collectively present an unparalleled window into the full range of fathering possibilities. Indeed, the variability in fathering around the world is striking—ranging from communities in which father participation in direct child care and nurturance is expected, high, and largely shared with mothers to communities in which division of household labor is gendered and fathers engage with their children only minimally. In some cultural settings, fathers live apart from their families and children for economic/employment reasons, making them paradoxically invisible even as they are major influences on the survival of their families.

Yet in the context of this cultural variability, what is notable in this volume is the continual reminders of the shared (dare I say "universal") aspects of fathering that cut across men and families in communities everywhere. Fathers universally care about and seek to ensure the well-being of their children and families, though they do so within the unique constraints and opportunities in their everyday lives. Fathers everywhere confront challenges and barriers to being the types of fathers they hope to be and indeed are expected to be, whether those barriers are economic, psychological, or social. And fathers powerfully affect their children's development through multiple indirect and direct pathways that can no longer be ignored. Thus this book serves as a rewarding, thought-provoking reminder of the key principles of how fathering affects families everywhere and undergird all our work.

Acknowledgments

A number of decades ago, Professor Michael Lamb provided ample opportunities for me to observe human developmental processes up close. To him I owe a lifelong gratitude for taking me on as his first graduate student and for nurturing an intellectual spirit to conduct research on families in diverse cultural communities. On our forays into different cultural settings, my wife, Nancy Beth, offered an emic lens to fathering practices that complimented my etic interpretations of men's behaviors in some cultural settings. I am grateful for her insights, particularly on fathering in Caribbean and Indian cultural settings. My children, Miles, Maya, and India, have helped me tremendously in shaping and reshaping my own cultural scripts about fathering. It is truly a joy to parent such caring children. I greatly appreciate the support of Dean Diane Lyden Murphy in the Falk College at Syracuse University. To my colleagues, near and far, your work has been instrumental in helping me formulate my own research understanding of fathers. Some of you provided a home away from home during my field work. For this I am most appreciative. Kimberly L. Davidson and Elif Dede Yildirim assisted me with the manuscript.

1

Introduction: Toward a Pancultural Understanding of Constructions and Meanings of Fathering

Jaipaul L. Roopnarine

A few primary goals across cultures include eradicating childhood poverty, improving the health conditions of children and women, and providing quality childhood experiences at the family and community levels, all with an eye toward gender equity and human capital development. In this regard, fathering has been identified by several august bodies, governments, nongovernmental and local organizations, policymakers, and research scientists as important for maximizing the life chances of children worldwide. Besides contributing to normative patterns of social and cognitive development in children, fathers have important roles to play in preventing the lost developmental potential of children by enhancing their economic and social welfare, improving their nutritional and health status, and addressing issues of gender inequality. At the same time, the growing global emphasis on child-centered approaches to childrearing and the education of children (e.g., sensitively attuned interactions, age-appropriate practices, availability and guidance throughout childhood and adolescence) can benefit from and be advanced significantly by heightened paternal investment in and involvement with children. This book was conceived in the spirit of these issues by outlining the diverse ways that men construct and carry out fathering roles in a variety of cultural systems and family structural arrangements (e.g., reconstituted, same-sex, living apart) across the world.

As will be gathered, entry into fatherhood and fathering are demonstrated through different pathways, guided by specific beliefs about masculinity, manhood, and women's roles. Their dimensions are constructed and revised in conjunction with other life events, and their particularities are transformative and expressed in cultural settings that are in various stages of economic and social transitions. Accordingly, there is increasing awareness of the need to delineate the importance, roles, and diverse practices of fathers in different cultural communities. This volume documents these diverse belief systems and practices of fathers and provides some evidence of their influence on different dimensions of childhood development in several cultural communities. In line with such broad attention to the importance of fathers for children's development and well-being, this volume provides the reader with windows into the diverse roles of men as fathers and their varied meanings in cultural communities across developing, recently developed, and developed societies.

As is evident from the chapters in this volume, though universally embraced as important for childhood development and family well-being, levels of paternal investment and involvement are far from uniform across cultures. Culturally constructed views of masculinity/manhood and caregiving roles vary a good deal but continue to change and affect childrearing differently across most societies. Additionally, historical experiences, oppressive policies (e.g., apartheid, discrimination, unequal economic opportunities), and political structures (e.g., communism) have all influenced how men construct and enact fathering roles today. A major challenge in the area of fathering research has been to outline inter- and intracultural variations and the cultural–developmental pathways through which paternal involvement influences intellectual, physical, socioemotional, and cultural development in children. This volume begins to address this challenge by presenting the scholarship of a distinguished group of individuals from multiple disciplines (e.g., child development/developmental psychology, family studies, early childhood education, sociology, social work, education, cultural psychology) who are from within the cultures or have conducted groundbreaking work on fathers in different cultural communities around the world.

A presentation of the confluence of studies on fathering from diverse disciplines and cultural communities that fall along different points on economic and human development indices heeds suggestions by scholars for more indigenous voices and better integration of scientific information from the developed and "majority world" (Berry, in press; Kağitcibaşi 2007; Moghaddam & Taylor 1989; Thompson in press). This call for a pancultural understanding of human processes of development is not inimical to attempts to document indigenous perspectives on fathering. Rather, as will become apparent, the construction, expressions, and meanings of fathers' roles within the family and society at large emerge out of sociohistorical experiences and are situated within prevailing cultural practices that are influenced by the ecological niche and the value placed on children. Thus this volume embraces a cultural approach to fathering in everyday settings where men build understandings of their role as fathers out of life's events. In this respect, attempts are made throughout the chapters to discuss how the cultural milieu and conditions and experiences within them influence ideologies about fatherhood and the practices associated with fathering itself.

CONCEPTUALIZING AND DEFINING FATHERS' ROLES ACROSS CULTURES

Until fairly recently, fathering was predominantly conceptualized within Lamb's framework of engagement, accessibility, and responsibility (Lamb, Pleck, Charnov, & Levine 1987). Other conceptualizations of fathering and childhood development have highlighted the emotional and cognitive aspects of father involvement, fathers as resource providers, father identity, father presence, fatherwork, generativity, and responsible fathering (Amato 1998; Doherty, Kouneski, & Erickson 1998; Dollahite, Hawkins, & Brotherson 1997; Palkovitz 1997), as well as the factors that mediate and moderate fathering practices and childhood outcomes (Cabrera, Fitzgerald, Bradley, & Roggman 2007). Despite these advances, cultural psychological frameworks on father–child relationships remain elusive. Admittedly, though the universal goal is to raise children who possess the skills and assets necessary for meeting the demands of life within their cultural community, the pathways to achieving those skills, and the forces that shape them, vary across cultures.

Following perspectives on different developmental pathways to human development (Greenfield, Keller, Fuligni, & Maynard 2003), the chapters in this volume draw from a broad range of frameworks (e.g., autonomous–relational, adaptationist, ecocultural, familism, feminist, collectivistic, men and masculinities, social constructivism, institutional conceptualization of welfare regimes) to situate and anchor fathering practices. In most cases, the theoretical perspectives and conceptual frameworks consider the construction of fathering roles but acknowledge that change in traditional views of fathering is necessary for optimal childhood development. The chapters in this book provide a platform for extending the discussion on conceptual frameworks on the multiple meanings of fathering in a global community marked by changes in parental socialization patterns and expectations of children, migration, and greater attention to human rights. Whereas in some cultural communities a strong case is made for the connection between fathering activities and childhood development, in others, fathers assume a peripheral role as "helpers" amid ambiguity about exactly how they contribute to children's psychological development. In most cultural settings, the emphasis on economic provision for family members dominates and often encourages physical and psychological distance between men and the interior aspects of childrearing.

The theoretical perspectives used by the authors to frame fathering roles and developmental outcomes in children not only lead to greater scientific integration of the fathering literatures from cultural, cross-cultural, and indigenous perspectives, but also invite broadening definitions of fathering beyond traditional conceptions of men's roles. Because a specific feature of fathering is the construction of meaning about roles, there is emphasis on change and continuity. In some instances, change and continuity occur simultaneously. Depending on the approach to and degree of negotiations within families and institutional structures, men hold onto some cultural scripts about fathering while revising or renouncing others. This process is more likely to occur in developed societies in which social policies and laws have forced men to fashion new modes of embracing childrearing and family responsibilities. The face of this much-touted "new fatherhood" is not well defined, for what fathers do in childrearing is measured against women's responsibilities in families and mixes with other life events. Though shifts away from traditional fathering roles are intimately tied to women's and partners' roles and the quality of spousal/partner relationship, the new fatherhood is largely viewed in terms of the equitable distribution of childcare responsibilities across cultures. Obviously, much more clarity is needed about how men revise internal scripts about their roles as fathers in raising children. Because of inconsistency and their self-regulated interpretations across cultures, new meanings of fathering are contested and evolving. It is likely that the very engaged father is deeply engrossed and comes alive in his participation with children where he is at ease with himself.

THE CONTENTS OF THE BOOK

In assembling the chapters for this volume, care was taken to select cultures that are at different levels of economic and technological development and that are from broad geographic regions around the world. The cultural groups discussed in this book also reflect different familial and community or population level sociohistorical experiences (e.g., oppression, marginalization, political domination, progressive policies on fathering) that have influenced the dynamics of family relationships and, in some cases, that have led to spatial and psychological separation and the invasion of cultural space between fathers and families. The first segment of the book covers fathering in groups in Latin America and the Caribbean. A significant practice in African Caribbean families is progressive mating in different unions. Traditional conceptions of masculinity undergird manhood and fatherhood, a pattern noted in South Africa as well. A separation between fathering and partner roles is possible in African Caribbean families. In a similar vein, fathering in Mexico is still largely based in patriarchal traditions, but there is a hint that it is in a state of transition wherein men go through processes of negotiation and interactions with their wives/partners and self-examination of their internal working models of how they were raised. Younger fathers attempt to devise new meanings about family roles and responsibilities that move away from the authoritarian approach to fathering exercised in their fathers' generation. Likewise, Brazil seems to be shedding its patriarchal traditions and practices and has implemented legislation that defines fatherhood (registration at birth to establish paternity regardless of the status of the union) and fathering (partner's rights, socioaffective paternity) in more inclusive and equitable terms. The chapter on Brazil provides some insights into children's and adults' perceptions of fathering and offer a peek into what engaged fatherhood means to some segments of the society.

The section on fathering in North America and Europe is a bit more extensive than the other sections and captures the contrasting realities of life and fathering in European and European-heritage cultures and ethnic/racial groups that have endured long histories of oppression and marginalization or political domination. Clearly, progressive policies have led to the increased participation of men in childcare and household work in Sweden, Portugal, and other western European countries. Whereas Sweden and Portugal are distinguished by their policies on fathers and childcare, few such policy frameworks exist in the United States. Across these regions there is greater agreement that men and women should share childcare and household responsibilities, but women still carry a major share of childcare work. That is, beliefs do not always match practices, and it appears that men's responsibilities as fathers remain firmly planted in economic activities and, as in Portugal, are characterized by a range of participation levels, from engaged fathering to that of helper.

Fathering in eastern European countries (Bulgaria, Georgia, Lithuania, Romania, Russia) was affected (and perhaps still is) by the authoritarian polices of the Soviet Union that created "fatherless" communities. However, the transformations from patriarchal control over women and children to greater autonomy and gender equality in families have introduced multiple forms of paternity and paternal engagement. Family social organization during the communist period has given way to new fertility and reproductive patterns and some changes in ideologies about the division of childcare and household labor. Additionally, economic conditions have contributed to the "anti-nuclearization" of families, and new forms of family traditionalism have emerged. Different rates of transformation from communism to free and independent states, the existence of current policy frameworks on families in different countries, and support for fathers seem to produce heterogeneous patterns of paternal investment in childcare. For example, Lithuania, with its more extensive policy frameworks, resembles western European countries in its paternal practices, whereas Georgia and Russia, with their fewer policies and support for fathering, stand apart from other countries. In a number of the eastern European countries, men display selective and limited involvement in primary caregiving.

In North America, lack of opportunity structures, discrimination, and oppression have had dire consequences for fathering in nondominant ethnic and indigenous groups. In stark contrast to European-heritage groups in North America, African Americans and Latino fathers have been stereotyped as "uninvolved," "macho," or absent from the lives of children and families. Acknowledging variations in family arrangements and belief systems, the chapters on African American and Latino fathers provide strength-based perspectives on men's participation in the cognitive and social lives of children by identifying factors that assist and impede paternal engagement. Employing a similar approach, the chapter on Indigenous fathers in Canada is a grim reminder of the struggles of oppressed peoples to construct and enact fathering roles in the face of economic, social, and structural challenges and inequalities in everyday life.

The section on Asian fathers provides rich excursions into the sociohistorical and cultural roots of fathering in India, China, and Japan—societies that are at different stages of economic development but that have all been influenced by cultural practices now centuries old. In the case of India, Hindu religious edicts (e.g., Laws of Manu) about manhood and fathering responsibilities are still embedded in men's cultural scripts about fathering, dictating how men assume paternal and spousal roles. Despite increasing maternal employment and progressive improvements in India's economic structure, little has changed in men's level of care for children. By contrast, as China has transformed itself into the second-largest economy in the world, fathers have received considerably more attention. As in India, fathering in China is rooted in traditional philosophical and religious traditions. Confucianism was instrumental in guiding collectivistic beliefs about children and childrearing (e.g., the role of parents and the responsibilities of children toward parents). However, China provides a good example of fathering in transition. Fathers must accommodate widespread economic reforms along with changes in family structure, size, and shifts in parenting practices. In Japan, the traditional father role was also based on Confucian principles. Changes in the family system, more equitable beliefs about work and family roles, low fertility rates, and greater social participation of women in different sectors of society have all influenced fathering in Japan. Japanese researchers report that men have increased their involvement with children, albeit modestly, and find deeper meaning in becoming fathers. Time at and dedication to work continue to affect Japanese men's involvement in children's lives.

Despite being the world's second largest religious group, fathers in Islamic (both Arabic and non-Arabic) cultural settings have received scant attention. The fourth section of the book not only discusses the traditional roles of men in Islamic societies, but also delves into fathering in Turkish and Israeli contexts. In the Arab world, fathering roles are closely aligned with the teachings of the Qur'an (Islamic scriptures) and Sunnah (sayings and deeds of Muhammad) and, in non-Arab Islamic societies, with Adat (local customs and cultural norms). Across Islamic societies, fathers' roles are conservative, based on control of family resources. Imported domestic labor is compensating for the lack of paternal involvement in the richer Islamic states (e.g., Saudi Arabia and Kuwait). After its long history of Ottoman rule, Turkey has emerged as a modern secular state. Yet even with industrialization, urbanization, women's increased participation in the labor force, and changes in socialization goals (e.g., movement from collectivism to autonomous–relational self), fathers are viewed as helpers in childrearing. Turkish men and women continue to live a "duo-focal" life of segregation that influences men's roles in families.

If fathering in Islamic societies has remained traditional, fathering in Israeli society is heterogeneous and complex—affected by familism, social inequalities, ethnicity, religion, and national conflict (for Jews the War of Independence; for Palestinians, *el-Nakbah*, "The Catastrophe"). As in other cultural settings, in the new fatherhood, Israeli men try to find a middle ground between the traditional and modern. However, among more Orthodox Jews, religion and economic conditions are driving forces behind conceptions of fathering. For both Jews and Palestinians in Israel, persistent conflicts (e.g., wars) have profoundly affected fathering roles.

Finally, two chapters on fathers in Kenya and South Africa point to the importance of biological fatherhood, economic conditions, and cultural traditions in shaping contemporary fathering in Africa. In South Africa, the segregated and oppressive practices of apartheid are still felt among black men. These men face the daunting task of finding employment away from home to meet their culturally prescribed role as head of the homestead. One consequence is that a majority of black households experience spatial or psychological separation from fathers. Needless to say, non-resident fathering affects family resources, the welfare and well-being of children, spousal/ partner relationships, and men's status in the community

In Kenya, economic activities and cultural traditions also play key roles in men's entrance into fatherhood and fathering responsibilities. Among the Kalenjin, Abagusii, Gikuyu, Luhyia, Luo, and Kamba ethnic groups in Kenya, initiation of boys marks an important transition into adulthood. Traditionally, marriage was a significant event in men's and families lives, and men's roles were primarily situated within the provider and protector roles. But marriage systems, setting up a household, caregiving patterns, and paying bride price are all changing. Increasing numbers of couples choose their own partners, and some engage in "come we stay," or trial, relationships. Although a new marriage act has addressed some aspects of polygyny in Kenya, the roles of men toward children in these relationships are ambiguous. As in other developing societies, far more research is needed about the challenges that men face in the care and education of young children in the diverse cultural communities of the African continent. The adaptive strategies these and other men employ in developing societies (e.g., India, Caribbean, Malaysia, Mexico) reflect a complex interplay of economic conditions, cultural traditions, and the new demands of being a father in a rapidly changing global landscape. Fathers in the majority world have been largely invisible in the literature on parenting.

In summary, a few salient features of this volume include, but are not limited to, the following:

- Considerations of sociohistorical factors and beliefs and practices about men's roles as fathers in cultural settings that are at different levels of economic development
- Diverse conceptual perspectives and frameworks on men's roles as fathers in cultural communities
- Discussions of fathering in the context of transitions; changes in men's internal working models or cultural scripts about fathering, childrearing goals and expectations, and the ethos of the family and childhood
- Current state of fathering research across cultural communities, and possible meanings for childhood development
- Policy implications and future directions for understanding the importance of fathers' roles and their diverse meanings and expressions across cultural communities

From just a decade ago, fathering research across ethnic and cultural groups has increased measurably. Unfortunately, the distribution of studies continues to be uneven, with much of the work conducted in developed and recently developed societies. Nonetheless, within a changing global milieu, the importance of fathers in children's lives in the developing, or majority world is beginning to receive more attention. To reiterate, this volume integrates what we know about men as fathers across diverse settings with two primary goals in mind: to articulate the local and particular in order to understand points of similarities and divergence in men's beliefs and practices and to enhance our understanding of human developmental processes broadly, beyond North America and Europe. In some cultural settings, the pathways between paternal nurturance and childhood development is clear. However, what fathers bring to the childrearing equation above and beyond other socialization agents is far from clear in a number of societies. Much needs to be done to determine what factors moderate and mediate fathers' relationships with children and developmental outcomes.

REFERENCES

Amato, P. R. (1998). *More than money? Men's contributions to their children's lives*. New York: Lawrence Erlbaum Associates Publishers.

Berry, J. (in press). Global, indigenous and regional perspectives on international psychology. In J. L. Roopnarine & D. Chadee (eds.), *Caribbean psychology: Indigenous contributions to a global discipline*. Washington, DC: American Psychological Association.

Cabrera, N., Fitzgerald, H., Bradely, H., & Roggman, L. (2007). Modeling the dynamics of paternal influences on children over the life course. *Applied Developmental Science, 11*, 185–190.

Doherty, W. J., Kouneski, E. F., & Erickson, M. F. (1998). Responsible fathering: An overview and conceptual framework. *Journal of Marriage and Family, 60*(2), 277–292.

Dollahite, D. C., Hawkins, A. J., & Brotherson, S. E. (1997). Fatherwork: A conceptual ethic of fathering as generative work. In A. J. Hawkins & D. Dollahite (eds.), *Generative fathering: Beyond deficit perspectives, 3*, 17–35. Thousand Oaks, CA: Sage.

Greenfield, P. M., Keller, H., Fuligni, A., & Maynard, A. (2003). Cultural pathways through universal development. *Annual Review of Psychology, 54*, 461–490.

Kağitcibaşi, C. (2007). *Family and human development across countries: A view from the other side* (2nd ed.). Hove, Sussex, UK: Psychology Press.

Lamb, M. E., Pleck, J. H., Charnov, E. L., & Levine, J. A. (1987). A biosocial perspective on paternal behavior and involvement. In J. B. Lancaster, J. Altman, A. Rossi, & L. Sherrod (eds.), *Parenting across the lifespan: Biosocial perspectives* (pp. 111–142). Hawthorne, NY: Aldine.

Moghaddam, F. M., & Taylor, D. M. (1989). What constitutes an "'appropriate psychology" for the developing world? *International Journal of Psychology, 21*, 253–267.

Palkovitz, R. (1997). Reconstructing "involvement": Expanding conceptualizations of men's caring in contemporary families. In A. J. Hawkins & D. Dollahite (eds.), *Generative fathering: Beyond deficit perspectives* (pp. 200–216). Thousand Oaks, CA: Sage.

Thompson, A. (in press). Caribbean psychology: Context, imperatives, and future directions. In J. L. Roopnarine & D. Chadee (eds.), *Caribbean psychology: Indigenous contributions to a global discipline*. Washington, DC: American Psychological Association.

Latin America and the Caribbean

2

African–Caribbean Fathers: The Conflict between Masculinity and Fathering

Patricia Anderson and
Camille Daley

In describing the death of his grandson, the aging taxi-driver explained, "Yuh know, when you get yuh first pickney, you want to change what yuh ah do."

His grandson, who had recently welcomed his first child, had rejected the order of the area Don to join his group of "shottas"[1] and had sent the reply "I nah follow man no more." In return, he was gunned down in daylight at a Kingston shopping plaza by two youngsters at the bidding of the same area leader. In this assertion of independence, attempting to separate himself from the life of the gang, Ricardo's brief life ended at age 21, spelling out in tragic clarity the link between fatherhood and manhood.[2]

Though this incident received scant attention in the Jamaican newspapers, being simply another unsolved murder of an unknown youth, it highlights an aspect often overlooked in research on parenting and child development. Namely, fathering is itself a major life change for Caribbean men, requiring them to look beyond themselves and to reconcile the conflicting demands of being masculine and "being responsible." Among African Caribbean males, fathering is not a smooth developmental process, one in which boys are prepared to assume domestic nurturing roles, in the way that their sisters are. Fatherhood is often early and unplanned, frequently occurring outside co-residential unions, and generating economic demands that cannot be easily met. Because the procreative need is quite distinct from the cultural mandate that men demonstrate virility and dominance, and because fatherhood itself opens a door to a new conception of self, men may easily find themselves struggling to balance their images of the person they are supposed to be. The virtual absence of social supports for young fathers helps shift the balance away from making a successful transition to the father role.

This chapter seeks to weave together the threads of an unruly story, one exploring the ideologies of manhood and fatherhood that unite African Caribbean males, their childrearing beliefs and practices, and how fathering involvement is expressed. The extent to which paternal involvement is translated into positive outcomes for children has not yet been established, considering the difficulties in implementing longitudinal studies that systematically map fathering input and developmental outcomes. However, several studies have shown that father presence is correlated with improved child outcomes in Jamaica. In addition, the retrospective assessments of children, some of whom had themselves reached adulthood, provide a basis for suggesting how the quality of fathering affects the lives of children. Our account presents primary data from a study of Jamaican fathers, supplemented by information from other Caribbean countries. This discussion is necessarily limited to males of African descent, in light of the different cultural heritage and family structures of Indo-Caribbean families.

BACKGROUND

Despite the dominance of men in Caribbean society, and the centrality of family studies in early Caribbean sociology, the delineation of men's family roles and perspectives has been fragmented and uneven. Foundation research on the Caribbean family was undertaken by anthropologists, sociologists, and demographers whose primary interests revolved around the structure of households, the cycle of conjugal unions, and the extent to which household composition changed over the lifetime of its members. Men were important actors, though their roles and family involvement varied considerably within different economic contexts. The subsequent movement toward sex role research in the eighties, and the related studies on gender socialization, shifted focus to exploring how men themselves viewed their roles in relation to both women and other males, with examination of the socializing effect of the home, the school, and the street. In this body of research, the sexual attitudes and behaviors of Caribbean males received considerable attention, particularly because these had wide-ranging implications for sexual and reproductive health (Chevannes 1993; Chevannes & Mitchell-Kernan 1982; Dann 1987; Whitehead 1992; Wilson 1969). At the societal level, the increasing levels of violence and the involvement of young males in criminal gang activity (Chevannes 2001; Gayle et al. 2004; Gray 2004; Harriott 2003; Levy & Chevannes 1996), in addition to consistent evidence of academic underachievement (Figueroa 2004; Parry 1996), also highlighted the question of how boys were being socialized both within and beyond family networks. From these studies, men were depicted as driven by the need to establish their claims to strength and virility, with children often being viewed as the proof of manhood. These in-depth accounts did little to modify the image of Caribbean men, derived from earlier family studies, as generally absent from the household or neglectful of their fathering responsibilities.

The emergence of specific work on fathering, which accelerated in the early nineties, corrected some of this imbalance, documenting the active involvement of fathers in the care of their children, even when they did not reside in the same household (Brown, Anderson, & Chevannes 1993; Roberts & Sinclair 1978; Roopnarine et al. 1995; Springer 2010). This gave credence to popular impressions that Caribbean men were indeed becoming more involved fathers. The fact that men were "doing more" than they were generally credited with doing was an important recognition. However it did not address the question of how the two images of men were to be reconciled—that of the wandering "ramgoat" and that of the responsible father. The theoretical imperative to distinguish these two value systems has been identified through a study of Jamaican fathers, drawn from a cross-section of social classes, which explored both gender relations and fathering involvement (Anderson 2009). On the basis of this study, the argument was advanced that values related to fathering should not be subsumed under the same rubric as values related to gender relations, as implied in the western model of a husband–father role. Also critical is the distinction between the procreative need and the commitment to fathering values, although within the existing literature it is not uncommon to find the two dimensions approached as common elements of fathering involvement. Rather, procreative need has been shown to be closely linked to the belief in virility and male dominance, constituting important aspects of masculine identity and gender relations, whereas fathering identity expresses men's commitment to maintaining, nurturing, and socializing children. There is some similarity here to Furstenberg's distinction between "fathers" and "daddies" derived from his interviews with inner-city men and women in Baltimore, though those classifications were based on what men actually did in relation to meeting their commitments to their offspring (Furstenberg 1995). A significant contribution from the Jamaican study is also the light it sheds on fathering behavior across a range of social classes, instead of the familiar focus on low-income communities noted by Roopnarine and Hossain (2013). This chapter shares some of those findings, and relates these to earlier work on masculinity and on fathering, often approached as separate concerns in the literature.

The social context in which fathering occurs for many African Caribbean men is derived from the distinctive family structure in which nuclear units are only one option, for some men, and only for some of the time. Conjugal unions are often first entered on a non-residential basis (the visiting union), and children born within this context are usually absorbed into the mother's household. If the union persists over time, and if resources permit, a common residence may be established and a common-law marriage recognized. Later in life, the common-law union may be formalized, with legal marriage being celebrated. This pattern was documented by the first generation of family researchers, represented by Edith Clarke (1957), Raymond Smith (1957, 1973), M. G. Smith (1962), and George Roberts (1957), among others. It was generally agreed that the stability of this cycle of unions varied with economic context, urban–rural residence and social class (Clarke 1957; Cumper 1958). The persistence in contemporary Jamaica of these alternative conjugal arrangements and varied family patterns may be easily read from the social and demographic statistics collected routinely by government agencies or from large-scale social surveys.

Because the large majority of children are born while parents are in nonlegal unions, in Jamaica, the proportion born out of wedlock is close to 85 percent (Statistical Institute of Jamaica 2012). The age-graduated movement from one conjugal union type to another contributes a familiar pattern to demographic statistics whereby the proportion married increases with age, paralleled by a decline in the proportion in visiting unions. This is illustrated by data from the Reproductive Health Survey, conducted by the National Family Planning Board in 2008 which showed that among young women aged 20–24, only 3.6 percent were in formal marriages, but a quarter (24.6 percent) were in common-law unions (National Family Planning Board 2010). Close to half (49.3 percent) reported being in visiting unions. By the end of the child-bearing period, among women aged 45–49, 32.6 percent indicated that they were married, 18.6 percent remained in common-law unions, and 20.6 maintained visiting relationships. A similar pattern may be discerned for males based on the 2011 census of population, though the census does not distinguish visiting relationships. The 2011 population census showed that among men aged 20–44, the proportion legally married stood at 12.9 percent, while those in common-law unions accounted for 22.4 percent. The category of persons classified as not being in any residential union included both single males as well as those in visiting unions, and this represented 64.7 percent. However men in the older age group, 45 years old or older, were almost three times as likely to indicate that they were legally married, reaching 37.9 percent. Those in common-law unions accounted for 14.8 percent of this older age cohort, with 47.2 percent indicating that they were not in any residential union.

Given the variety of family contexts in which children may be conceived, it is not surprising that large proportions of children do not reside in households with their biological fathers. Data from the Jamaica Survey of Living Conditions (JSLC) showed that in 2010, 34.4 percent of all children 14 years old or younger lived with both of their natural parents, 44.7 percent lived with only their biological mother, and 6.3 percent lived only with their fathers (Planning Institute of Jamaica 2012). In addition, 14.6 percent lived with neither of their biological parents. Among those in the poorest quintile, 33.3 percent lived with both parents, in contrast to 43.8 percent of children in the wealthiest quintile. A further perspective on the availability of father figures for children within Jamaican households is provided through the module on Early Child Development that was attached to the 2010 JSLC. The report noted that for the sample of 845 children who were 8 years old or younger, slightly more than a third (36.3 percent) had no father figure residing within their household. Those who lived with their birth fathers accounted for 41 percent of the sample, whereas 5.1 percent lived with stepfathers. An additional 9 percent interacted with a resident grandfather as their father figure. It is also instructive to compare mother presence and father presence within these households. Whereas birth fathers were present in 41.0 percent of their households, birth mothers were present in 81.8 percent of the households for this birth cohort. From a slightly different perspective, among this cohort, as noted above, 36.3 percent had no father figure in their households, whereas only 2.1 percent of children resided in households without a mother figure (Planning Institute of Jamaica 2012).

In examining this scenario, it is necessary to bear in mind the reality of non-resident fathering in the Caribbean, sometimes referred to as parenting apart. The observation that Caribbean households have permeable boundaries was made by Raymond Smith (1982), who drew attention to the considerable exchanges that take place across household boundaries. These included childcare, cooking, washing, sleeping, sexual relations, and other domestic activities. This pattern, summarized by Smith as "a domestic system which does not confine relations within an easily defined and bounded household" (Smith 1996, p. 87), continues to be characteristic of Jamaican households. This is evident from data on the financial inflows to households for child support, documented by the 2010 JSLC. Child support contributed by persons outside the household was reported by close to a quarter (22.5 percent) of all households, and this contribution ranged from 25.5 percent for households in the poorest quintile to 13.4 percent for those in the wealthiest quintile. Though other family members traditionally help support children, regular child support is usually derived from a parent, whether resident overseas or within the island. These data provide support for the caution voiced by Roopnarine that residence should not be equated with parenting and his observation that "Caribbean living arrangements challenge theoretical frameworks that have emphasized the importance of the biological father and strong male–female emotional bonds as prerequisites for high levels of paternal investment in offspring" (Roopnarine 2013, p. 208).

THE PATH TO MANHOOD

From early in their childhood, Caribbean boys are taught the definitions of masculinity, and they quickly absorb this training. Focus groups conducted in Barbados, Dominica, and Jamaica with different age groups of children, structured to represent different social classes and community contexts, found that between ages 8–9 and 10–11, boys quickly moved from a fairly egalitarian approach to gender definitions and relations toward a more restricted male gender ideology, with an emphasis on antagonism and competition in interpersonal relationships (Bailey et al. 1998). It was observed that by age 10, boys had begun to realize that toughness, physical strength, and sexual dominance were expected of them, and by age 14, youngsters were socialized into an ideology in which boys and girls were expected to be treated differently, with men and women performing different roles. The role of the man as economic provider was clearly articulated, and even in a girlfriend–boyfriend relationship, this expectation was encountered. The authors noted that one of the greatest areas of bitterness expressed by children toward fathers revolved around the nonperformance of this economic role: "My father never try him best. Mi nah tell you lie. My mother play mother and father role" (Bailey et al. 1998, p. 43).

As boys became older, the sexual relationship became "adversarial, aggressive and predatory." It was observed that the entire socialization process conveyed a message to boys that "as they come to manhood, sexual proactivity is a part of their fundamental identity" (Bailey et al. 1998, 57). Multiple partnerships were vigorously advocated by the older teenaged boys as a defensive measure, given the conflict and instability in relationships. It was further reported that in some of the Jamaican inner-city communities, the derisive label of "one-burner" was applied to men who were faithful to one woman. Violence was also shown to be linked to male gender identity, as boys argued that certain challenges to their social and physical power should be met by violence. In this regard, women were expected to heed their partner's instruction and to treat them with respect.

In these focus groups, it was apparent that the DJ (disc jockey) lifestyle itself served as a model for many young boys in inner-city communities in Jamaica and Barbados, as well as that the lifestyle of the "girls-man" was seen as a route to social power. Branche (1998) noted that "As the adolescent stepped out, he saw females and relationships as an area of conflict, as a place where power—psychological, symbolic, material, social and sexual—was necessary to secure for self the required status and values" (Branche 1998, p. 194). This study also observed that while the development of the particular kind of restricted male gender ideology, expressed by the boys in the study, went hand in hand with the challenging urban environment, the deployment of the "tough man" ideology was not particularly Caribbean, and it would be a mistake to overemphasize the class-based nature of this ideological attachment.

Similar focus groups conducted a decade later with inner-city males in Jamaica showed no difference in regard to young men's conception of gender relations (UNFPA 2006). Economic responsibility was an agreed part of fatherhood, but multiple partners were also strongly endorsed. Some participants argued that it was possible to have a stable girl, along with "a whole heap a girl" and that if a man had only one girl, his friends would heckle him about it. The distrust of women and previous experiences of betrayal also served to reinforce this argument. While many young men stated that it was not right to hit a woman, they also argued that at times it was justified if the woman showed disrespect.

These attitudes, expressed by young persons, are congruent with the general body of research on sexual attitudes and gender relations among African-Caribbean men, in which the definitions of masculinity center heavily on dominance and virility and their contribution to men's status (Chevannes 1993; Whitehead 1992; Wilson 1973). However, this focus on virility, and on children as specific proof of virility, has tended to obscure an underlying dimension whereby procreation is the expression of a psychological need. Within the United States, this dimension was highlighted by Marsiglio and elaborated through a series of detailed interviews with fathers (Marsiglio 1998; Marsiglio & Hutchinson 2002).

That Caribbean men do feel strongly about procreation was one of the major findings from a 1993 study of fathering initiated by the Caribbean Child Development Center at the University of the West Indies, which sought to obtain a deeper understanding of men's roles in the family (Brown et al. 1997; Brown & Chevannes 1998). This study, using both in-depth qualitative techniques and community surveys, elicited testimonies from men that they would not feel like men if they did not have children, with many saying that they would feel useless, empty, embarrassed, unbalanced, strange, or irresponsible in such a situation. These somewhat unexpected findings were later pursued in a replication of the first Fathers Study through a 2005 survey of four communities, and the opportunity was taken to design measures to summarize the definitions of masculinity. These comprised the familiar dimensions of virility and dominance, in addition to procreative need (Anderson 2009, 2012). Fathering roles were also explored through direct questions, as well as a series of items, combined into a scale. These findings and the extent to which they varied with social class are discussed below. For brevity, in this chapter we simply refer to this study as the 2005 Fathers Study,[3] as well as to distinguish it from the earlier 1993 study.

DEFINING MANHOOD AND FATHERING

In the 2005 Fathers Study, interviews were conducted in three communities, selected to represent a stable middle class masculinity, a working-class community, and a poor inner-city community. The questions included statements reflecting support for male dominance and virility as well as for procreative need. Although there was a wide body of agreement in regard to the importance of having children, social class location served to moderate the extent to which Jamaican fathers felt that procreation was part of their identity as men. Among middle-income fathers, 13.2 percent scored high on procreative need, as compared with 21.3 percent for those in the working-class community, and 46.1 percent for inner-city fathers.

At least three-fifths of the fathers in the inner-city community believed that a man can tell when a child is his and were certain that they would not marry an infertile woman, that they would not feel like men if they had no children, that in such a situation they would be jealous of other men who had children, and, accordingly, that they would seek to have a child with an outside partner. In the middle-income community, the proportions of fathers who endorsed these views ranged between 30 percent and 45 percent. However, larger proportions of middle-income fathers admitted to being uncertain how they would feel if they had no children and how they would react. Fathers in the working-class community were generally closer to their middle-income counterparts than to the low-income sample in support for these statements, although they expressed more certainty than middle-income fathers that a man could tell when a child was really his biological offspring. This is a common belief in Jamaica but is not limited to this specific culture (Marsiglio & Hutchinson 2002; Springer 2010).

Fathering identification was also found to be strong among a sample of fifty non-residential Barbadian fathers interviewed by Springer in 1998 and reinterviewed in 2007 (Springer 2010).[4] All these working-class respondents claimed to have been emotionally involved and supportive of their "child-mother" during pregnancy and child-birth. The case of a Rastafarian father, aged 40 with an 8-year old daughter, is of particular interest, for he said that the child was planned, and that he wanted the child more than the mother. He referred to the child as a "gift" and explained: "I did more want a child than she—I did want a child. She did not want no child, and she say 'I will breed for you'" (Springer 2010, p. 133).

Although the Jamaican Fathers Study found clear differences across social classes in the intensity to which men held self-images based on dominance and virility,[5] as well as in the extent to which procreative need represented a core value, there was an almost complete lack of variation in regard to definitions of fatherhood. Without hesitation, Jamaican men described a good father as a responsible person, one who provided for his family, a loving man who cared for his children, a man who set an example and gave guidance, and a man who provided emotional support to his family. The individual statements with which fathers were asked to indicate the extent of their agreement served to articulate the characteristics of the ideal father, and they all elicited wide approval from the fathers in the three communities. In light of this general consensus, it was not expected that there would be any major variation by community. It was mainly in regard to church membership that any pattern was observable, with church members expressing stronger fathering commitment.

In overview, the working-class fathers, when compared with both the middle class community and the lower-income community, were shown to gain the strongest sense of satisfaction from their public image as fathers, they being the most likely to agree strongly that they liked to be known as fathers and that they felt good when out in public with their children. The awareness that as fathers they should set an example for their children was strongest among the working-class and middle-income fathers, and these two communities also expressed the greatest commitment to making financial sacrifices to meet the needs of their children. The view that men could be good fathers even if they were unable to contribute financially met with slightly less agreement, but nonetheless the proportions who agreed on this aspect of nurturing accounted for 93.4 percent of middle-income fathers, 95.5 percent of working-class fathers, and 94.5 percent of inner-city fathers. The importance of a father treating his stepchildren in the same way as his own children was also endorsed, though responses tended to converge on "agree" rather than "strongly agree."

Fathering identification was shown to be not simply a good feeling, or the basis for claiming greater community respect, but often linked to the considerable efforts that men made to change their lives. In the middle-income community, 67 percent said that since embarking on fatherhood, they had tried to change their lifestyle, with the working-class community reporting a very similar proportion (69 percent). In the low-income community, roughly three-quarters (77 percent) of all fathers said that they had tried to meet this challenge. The specific changes which fathers sought to make were economic, social, and personal. The economic changes included efforts to increase earning and to improve money management, whereas the social changes included less partying and spending less time on the street, being less promiscuous, and spending more time with children. Personal changes were summed up as "becoming more responsible," and this included becoming less self-centered, becoming a role model, planning for the future, and "moving from boy to man."

In reflecting on his personal transition, a 50-year-old vendor and father of six in the low-income community recalled, "I stopped spending carelessly. I reach home early from work. Bring home little gifts." Others who had been involved in various levels of criminal activity were frank about these changes: "I stop stealing from people up-town by grabbing their bags. I stop rob store," and "I put down the gun thing," said a 31-year-old vendor and father of two children in the inner-city community. Another father simply said, "I got to the stage of thinking of myself last in the house."

The study also explored how far respondents consciously tried to improve on the performance of their own fathers. In this regard, three-quarters of the men in each community said that they did try to be different. The main ways in which these modern-day fathers tried to be different included seeking to play an active role in their children's lives; to provide for children financially; to be homely; to be a family man; to be more loving, kind, and affectionate; to try not to beat kids or be abusive; to communicate more; to have a good relationship with their children; and to show an interest in children's schoolwork.

In light of these findings, we argue that the high and relatively unvarying endorsement of fathering values points to the existence of core cultural elements that define fathering in Jamaica. However, it is essential to note that these two aspects of Caribbean fathering, procreative need and fathering identity, are largely unrelated to each other. Procreative need adheres to definitions of masculinity and is linked to support for virility and female dominance, whereas fathering identity expresses commitment to a set of deeply rooted cultural mandates about parenting. That male gender identity values are quite distinct from fathering values was demonstrated empirically by the lack of any statistical association between the two. The conceptual separation of these two normative dimensions is of critical importance and explains why, indeed, men may be good fathers but bad husbands (Anderson 2009).

Attachment to these two different sets of values, a traditional masculine ideology and strong fathering identification, inevitably generates domestic conflict. The domestic and sexual freedom to which Jamaican men claimed entitlement created jealousies as well as competing financial demands from different households, as they were generally unable to meet their economic responsibilities to different sets of children. The Fathers Study probed the main causes of domestic conflict, as well as the reasons why these men's partners were reported as becoming angry at times. The reasons that men indicated as leading to arguments revolved around infidelity, coming home late at night, money problems, and not spending enough time together. However, in the three communities, infidelity or suspected infidelity was the major source of conflict. It is within this context of frequent domestic conflict, competing demands for economic support, and good intentions that Caribbean fathers try to implement their conceptions of how best to grow their children.

RAISING THE IDEAL CHILD

The wide agreement among Jamaican fathers on their definitions of a good father was paralleled by their consensus on the goals of child-rearing. The most important principles that they agreed should be inculcated were manners, respect, honesty and integrity, being loving, self-discipline, and the fear of God. Other important qualities included learning right from wrong, ambition, working hard, self-confidence, gaining a good education, obedience and respect for parents, and not being "red-eye" (jealous of others).

When specifying particular qualities that they considered to be important for boys or for girls, the responses of fathers in each of the communities reflected the prevailing sex roles for men and women in Jamaican society. Boys were to be encouraged to be manly, and in particular this meant that they should be rough and able to tough it out, to take part in sports, and to be the breadwinners. Almost equal importance was assigned to their being taught not to abuse women, to take care of their sisters, and to love and respect their wives. Other lesser concerns included avoiding homosexuals. Being a good father, protecting the home, and not being promiscuous were also part of the directives for boys. When specific gender roles were indicated for girls, these were directed primarily toward encouraging girls to be ladylike and to delay entry into sexual relationships or to avoid having many boyfriends. Other principles included being neat and tidy and knowing how to dress. Girls were also to be encouraged to be modest and to love their family, to be faithful and obedient, and to behave in such a way as to have men respect them. However, despite this emphasis on traditional values, there was also a marked concern with encouraging girls to be independent, to be able to think for themselves, and to pursue their ambitions. Because many of these fathers were themselves reared by hardworking and independent single mothers, their conceptions of female abilities and roles had been shaped accordingly.

The three main approaches universally endorsed by fathers in bringing up children were to set a good example, to provide guidance, and to spend time and reason with the child. Other important techniques included being around at all times, instilling godly principles, providing education, and being a good friend to the child. When asked to specify how they would convey approval or disapproval, it was observed that the sex role expectations that were articulated for boys and for girls also shaped the type of punishment and rewards that fathers used. There was little gender variation in how fathers showed approval for younger boys and girls (children younger than 10), but there were marked differences in how they showed disapproval. In expressing pleasure, fathers would be equally likely to hug young boys and girls and to tell them they were pleased. When they needed to punish children, their accounts revealed that they were much quicker to use physical punishment for boys than for girls. As children got older, there was an expected shift away from physical punishment toward more talking and reasoning. However, physical punishment was not completely abandoned.

Support for corporal punishment is still fairly widespread in Jamaica (Evans 1989; Evans & Davies 1997; Ricketts & Anderson 2009; Samms-Vaughan, Williams, & Brown 2005; Wint & Brown 2001) and has been explained in terms of a general lack of knowledge among parents about the stages of child development and what should reasonably be expected from children. Though researchers have often classified the Caribbean parenting as authoritarian, relying primarily on punitive measures (Bailey et al. 1998; Crawford-Brown 1999), more recent work by Lipps and colleagues has established that from the perspectives of Caribbean adolescents, parents use a combination of styles, with the main ones being authoritative and neglectful (Lipps et al. 2012).

Data from the Jamaica Survey of Living Conditions 2010 found that among Jamaican children aged 8 or younger, caregivers used a combination of sanctions that included corporal punishment, noncorporal techniques, and psychological aggression (Planning Institute of Jamaica 2012). Corporal methods included slapping, beating with an implement, and pinching, whereas noncorporal methods included removing privileges, timeout, talking about why the action was wrong, ignoring, and reasoning. Psychological aggression included quarreling and shouting, denying food, swearing, and cursing. Corporal punishment accounted for 42.6 percent of all reported punishments, noncorporal punishment for 40.7 percent, and psychological aggression for 16.8 percent. As the child's age increased, there was resort to harsher physical punishment, as well as more noncorporal responses. The report noted that boys were slightly more likely than girls to be subjected to physical punishment, with proportionately more boys being slapped and beaten.

The view that boys should be treated more roughly than girls so that they can themselves become tough has been documented by Brown and Chevannes on the basis of findings from the Gender Socialization Project (Brown & Chevannes 1998). As Chevannes reflected, given the neglect and the very harsh and cruel methods of bringing up boys that their study found, it was difficult to see how grown men were expected to be soft and caring (Chevannes 2001). This belief in harsh treatment was also evident in the 2005 sample of Jamaican fathers, for more than four-fifths of all fathers expressed agreement with the statement "A father has to toughen up his son so that the son can deal with life." This excessive toughening may itself be related to the restricted emotionality earlier observed among Caribbean youth.

OUTSIDE CHILDREN

The outside child, as described by Barrow (2010) was historically the product of a cross-class, cross-race concubinage, dating back to the period of slavery in the Caribbean. The persistence of this pattern of fathering children outside of an established conjugal union was acknowledged "the sexual liberty, multiple partnering and fathering of several children by different women culturally embedded in the Caribbean ethos of masculinity up to today, perpetuates this phenomenon, although many outside children in contemporary society are the product of endogamous class and race relationships" (Barrow 2010, p. 33). It is important to recognize, as the study makes clear, that these children are usually identified as "outside" in relation to their fathers, rather than their mothers. Though these children were socially fatherless within the plantation system, with the status usually connoting paternal neglect, it was pointed out that in the contemporary Caribbean, virtually all outside children will know who their fathers are, and many will be supported by them, as required by law or custom. In the case of the Jamaican elite families, there appeared to be a clear set of rules regarding the economic responsibility for the child, although they were not generally regarded as family (Douglass 1992).

The integration of outside children in existing families is hindered because many of these children are born to women of a lower social standing. In describing the dual marriage system of the Caribbean, Raymond Smith identified one of its characteristics as "[a] mating system which enjoins marriage with status equals, and non-legal unions with women of lower status" (Smith 1996, p. 87). In the life stories recounted by Barrow (2010), the situation of being an outside child appeared to have been associated with discomfort, primarily in cases in which paternity was not acknowledged or in which children experienced neglect. The sense of pain and rejection that these children often experience may be read from the narratives of Olive Senior, in which children fathered by higher-status men were dismissed as being of no consequence (Senior 1986).

The continuation of this pattern may be inferred from the 2005 Jamaican Fathers Study, in which at least a half of the fathers in each of the communities acknowledged that they had children who had not grown with them. This ranged from 50 percent in the middle-income community to 55 percent in the working-class community and reached 72 percent in the inner-city community. All these children would not be classified as outside children, based only on the fact of residence, for their fathers, though living elsewhere, may never have been in a co-residential union. Nonetheless, the earlier 1993 Fathers Study documented clearly that fathers were significantly less likely to spend time interacting and reasoning with those children who lived elsewhere than those who lived under their own roof (Brown et al. 1993).

FATHERWORK WITH CHILDREN

Though an understanding of the role of the father constitutes the foundation on which positive parenting can be built, the translation of this understanding into effective fathering is often difficult for many Caribbean fathers. As summarized by Roopnarine (2013), fatherhood and fathering in Caribbean cultural communities occur in diverse and complex family systems, and accordingly, for many Caribbean men, it is difficult to achieve the family stability needed for children's social and cognitive development. These difficulties relate to "perennial economic hardship, physical separation from children, the desire to be independent, and conflicts with their partners" (Roopnarine 2013, p. 217). In this section, we review the findings from existing research on the inputs made by fathers to children's development, often from the perspective of these offspring, or based on the observation of other participants. Considering the persistence of traditional definitions of the respective roles of fathers and mothers, according to which mothers remain the primary caregivers, we focus particularly on emotional and cognitive inputs and on the extent to which these appear important to their children.

Emotional Exchanges

Despite the characterization of toughness with which Caribbean masculinity is typically defined, it is significant that the Jamaican men in the 2005 Fathers Study spontaneously included being loving and caring in their definition of a father. Furthermore, when they had known their own fathers, they described them as being loving and caring, pleasant and jovial, and positive persons. These descriptions were elicited through the use of emoticons, where respondents were shown a set of smiley faces and were asked which most closely represented their own father when they themselves were about 12 years old. Among fathers in the middle-income community, 9.3 percent said that they had never known their father, whereas 5.8 percent of working-class fathers and 15.5 percent of low-income fathers acknowledged absent fathers. In addition, those who explained that they had not known their fathers well enough to select a face accounted for 13.3 percent in the middle-income community, 10.5 percent in the working-class community, and 7.8 percent in the inner city sample. Whether in selecting a face to represent their own fathers or in selecting one to represent how they believed they were perceived by their own children, there was a consistent choice of icons that they described as loving and caring, pleasant and cheerful, happy and jovial, positive, or pleasant but stern. These descriptions accounted for roughly half the descriptions that they made of their father, as well as two-thirds of the selections that they made for their own fathering persona.

The importance of distinguishing between physical absence and psychological absence has been highlighted by Ramkissoon in her analysis of the effects of father absence on the well-being of a sample of 251 Jamaican secondary school students (Ramkissoon 2005). This study argued that although having a physically absent father served to diminish the quality of the father–child relationship, psychological absence was more detrimental, as it undermined the child's sense of positive well-being. Furthermore, when fathers were physically present but psychologically absent, there was a greater risk of expressive rejection, with negative implications for the child. The study concluded that not all non-resident fathers were marginal and that the stereotype of the marginal father was a better fit for those fathers who were not psychologically present, they being less a companion, an emotional support, a decision-making factor, or a trusted adult, and very often conveying emotional rejection to their children.

The extent to which father involvement appears to be linked to self-esteem among adolescent boys in Trinidad and Tobago has been explored by Awong-Persaud (2003). This study, based on a random sample of 121 boys aged 15–17 from different ethnic groups, did not succeed in establishing a significant relationship between involvement and self-esteem as measured by the Rosenberg Self-Esteem Scale. However, Awong-Persaud found that boys who had higher self-esteem tended to have fathers who relied on an authoritative disciplinary style, encouraged communication with their sons, showed affection freely, including hugging, and were on good terms with the mothers. It was also found that father involvement entailed to varying degrees the roles of caregiver and nurturer, disciplinarian, economic provider, and role model. In regard to the demonstration of affection, only 28 percent of the sample said that they received hugs from their fathers, whereas 38 percent reported that their fathers showed affection by touching or patting on the head, talking, laughing, playing with them or taking them out, or giving them money. The involvement of fathers in school life was to encourage hard work (76 percent), to praise them when they did well (74 percent), to inquire about schoolwork (65.3 percent), to assist with homework (40.5 percent), to attend parent–teacher meetings (28.9 percent), and to speak with teachers (37.2 percent). Though roughly two-thirds of the sample said that they were satisfied with their fathers' performance in regard to their specific roles (caregiving, disciplinarian, provider, and role model), 40 percent said that they would not treat their spouse the way that their father treated their mother. In addition, 42 percent reported a desire for their fathers to be less quarrelsome, 50.4 percent wanted their fathers to show more interest in their activities, 48 percent wanted their fathers to talk with them, 26.4 percent wished their father would spend more time with them, 28.1 percent desired that they would come home early, and 24.8 percent wished that they would express affection by hugging them.

Depression among Caribbean adolescents has also been shown to be linked to home situation and parental interaction. In a random sample of adolescents in Trinidad and Tobago, aged 13–19, Maharaj et al. (2008) established that significantly higher depression levels were reported by students who did not live with both parents, as well as those who admitted that they were physically afraid of their parents. More recent research conducted by Lipps et al. (2012) on the relationship between parenting practices and depression among adolescents reported that in the four countries studied, Jamaica, St. Kitts and Nevis, St. Vincent, and the Bahamas, authoritarian and neglectful parenting practices were associated with the highest levels of depressive symptoms. They noted that although parents were described by their children as using a range of styles, in countries where neglectful parenting styles predominated, adolescents had higher depression scores.

Cognitive Investments

One of the major research undertakings using a longitudinal design to trace developmental outcomes for children is that of the continuing work of Samms-Vaughan and colleagues at the University of the West Indies. These studies have sought to examine the effects of social and environmental factors and child-rearing practices in relation to a range of child outcomes. In general, it was found that Jamaican children whose parents were in a stable co-residential relationship performed better both cognitively and educationally than those in other family structures and that this was not explained by differences in social class (Samms-Vaughan 2000).[6] Children who had no father figure and those who had more than one father figure performed worse on academic and cognitive tests than children who had one stable father figure. This effect was stronger for girls.

The Early Childhood Development module that was attached to the 2010 Survey of Living Conditions has served to provide national data on the extent to which caregivers engage children aged 8 and younger in activities designed to stimulate cognitive and socioemotional development. These include reading or showing books, telling stories and singing songs, playing games, counting, naming or drawing objects, and other special activities. Though there was no information on the relationship of the caregiver to the child, a general pattern was reported whereby a larger proportion of children in the wealthier quintiles engaged in stimulating activities than did children in poorer households (Planning Institute of Jamaica 2012).

The effect of father involvement on the academic performance of high school students has been assessed by Wehby (2005) using the Inventory of Father Involvement Scale (Hawkins, et al. 2002). In this sample of 166 students from urban Jamaica, approximately 40 percent of fathers were resident and 60 percent non-resident. It was noted that roughly three-quarters of non-resident fathers maintained some form of contact with the child. Although the majority of fathers scored as highly involved or very highly involved, these scores were mainly in the areas of economic support and encouraging their children to work hard at school. They were considerably less involved in regard to helping with homework, attending events in which children participated, and taking care of routine daily needs. Academic performance was measured by the score that students had obtained the previous year on a national exam, the Grade 6 Achievement Test (GSAT), which determines assignment to specific high schools. Though Wehby's study, using multivariate analysis, was able to establish that father involvement was positively linked to higher performance, background social class variables had a much greater effect.

Another perspective on the effect of father involvement was obtained from interviews with four primary school teachers who prepared students for the GSAT examination. These primary school teachers were interviewed by one of the authors, with their selection based on their location at two middle-income private preparatory schools and two lower-income government primary schools. Among their 12-year-old students preparing for this important filtering examination, teachers estimated that between a quarter and half had fathers who were actively involved in their schooling. This involvement was expressed through providing transport to school or escorting them along the way, paying for extra lessons, taking them for visits to the doctor, and attendance at some school events. There was agreement between all these teachers that father absence appeared to have a much greater effect on boys than on girls. Boys with involved fathers were described as more "settled" and confident, and more likely to be leaders in their class. One of the teachers based at a government primary school remarked that the boys who were predominantly from low-income families seemed to crave their father's attention and were very happy when he showed up at school events. She also noted that this was sometimes resented by the mothers, who declared that the children were "ungrateful" for their own efforts, as the father was usually absent.

Considerable doubt was also expressed about whether there was any general societal trend toward greater father involvement. For middle-class children, it was suggested that the situation may have deteriorated given increased family breakdown arising from divorce or increased transience in visiting unions. For low-income children, there may be some slight improvement in father involvement, but that generally "the culture has not changed." One of the teachers at a government primary school remarked that some fathers who had provided no financial support for the child's schooling would nonetheless call to inquire about the secondary school where their child had gained acceptance. By contrast, a father who was in prison called every year to ask how his son was doing in school. This son, however, was deemed by his teacher to be the "worst boy" in terms of behavior and academic performance (Daley 2014).

SELF-ASSESSMENT AS FATHER

In the 2005 Fathers Study, fathers in each community were asked to look back at their own experience and to say whether they had been able to be the kind of father they wanted to be. In response, slightly more than half the sample (55.2 percent) said that they were satisfied, while roughly a quarter (24.1 percent) said no, and 20.7 percent said they had partially succeeded. In the low-income community, it was observed that fathers were more likely to express dissatisfaction with their performance, as nearly a third of these fathers (31.1 percent) said they were not satisfied with themselves in comparison to roughly a fifth of the fathers in the other two communities. In general, these self-assessments tended to be quite stable across age groups and education levels. It was also noted that conjugal union status was related to these self-assessments. Fathers who were currently in a co-residential relationship (whether married or common-law), indicated the highest levels of satisfaction with their fathering role, as roughly two-thirds of these groups said that they were satisfied. Those who were not in a current union were the most likely to say that they were not satisfied, with nearly a third (32.2 percent) of the men in this category making a negative assessment.

The reasons why fathers graded themselves positively were as follow:

- Because I gave financial support (43.6% of all reasons)
- Because I have been there for them (20.0 %)
- Because I have been responsible (14.0%)
- Because I provided training in values (10.4%)

Together, these four factors accounted for 88 percent of all the reasons which fathers advanced for their positive self-assessments. Other reasons included their investment in the child's education, their living together, and their having a good relationship. In short, there was a consistent emphasis on the father's economic responsibilities, but considerable emphasis was also placed on emotional support. The spontaneous reference to "being there" for the child was a theme in these three urban communities.

Those fathers who said that they were not completely satisfied with their performance gave reasons centering heavily on the inability to provide adequate financial support, and the separation in domestic arrangements. In the low-income community, economic factors exacted the greatest toll on fathering performance, this being the leading reason given for dissatisfaction. In this community, two-thirds of all fathers gave this as the reason for their dissatisfaction with their role as a father, whereas roughly half of all working-class fathers echoed this feeling. This may be compared with a third of all middle-income fathers who indicated this difficulty. These more secure fathers were more likely to acknowledge that they needed to spend more time with the children, and this may be related to the type of work demands experienced by this middle-class sample. This was mentioned twice as frequently by middle-income fathers than by fathers from the other communities. Separation from the child was a factor over which men often had little control, and in some cases this was related to the child now living overseas. More often, it was the result of different living arrangements, as the child was a product of an earlier union. This reason accounted for 17.7 percent of the explanations given by middle-income fathers, for 19.1 percent of those in the working-class community, and 13.2 percent of those in the inner-city community. Comments from fathers included the following:

> "I would like for her to live with me so I could have more control."
> "I feel I should be living as a family with my child so I could train him."

In some cases, the explanation given by fathers was that they "needed to improve," conveying a view that fathering is a developmental process and that they are embarked on this journey. This theme finds resonance with the argument made by Hawkins et al. (1995)—that fatherhood should be viewed as a developmental task in which men undergo transitions both in their perceptions of themselves and the world and in their behavioral responses.

DISCUSSION

The joy and pride that Caribbean fathers experience on welcoming a new child is without question, and at the outset, their hopes are usually high for the role they expect to play as a father. In reality, the family situation into which this child is born, and the relationship that fathers are able to maintain with their child's mother, will establish the parameters within which they can actually achieve any of these ambitions. Procreation expresses a need that is part of their identity, and Caribbean fathers are very clear about the definition and the responsibilities of a good father. However, child-rearing occurs at the level of a domestic unit, in which men may not reside, where they may eventually become unwelcome, and from which they may either withdraw or be actively excluded. Residential fathers enjoy an undisputed authority, usually as household head, but even in this situation, their closer integration with the set of children living under their roof may be at the expense of marginalizing another set of children to whom they also owe allegiance. These are the inevitable consequences of a cultural framework in which masculinity is defined through multiple sexual unions and childbearing, and in which men still cling to traditional models of dominance.

One requirement for male domestic authority is an adequate financial base if men are to meet the economic responsibilities attached to the husband–father role. When these economic resources do not exist, or are too thinly stretched, the familiar outcome is one in which fathers are located outside their children's households and continue to be visiting partners or visiting fathers. The extent to which low-income men live solitary domestic lives is often not recognized, although within Jamaica, census data and surveys for inner-city communities have consistently documented this pattern. In a typical Jamaican inner-city community, such as Denham Town, the 2001 census showed that single-person households accounted for a quarter of all households, with the majority of these being single males (Anderson 2007). Over time, some of these men will join or establish households with partners as their positions become more secure or as their conjugal relationships strengthen. However, as time goes by, some will also be separated from these units and from their children.

In the studies reviewed on fathering activities, as well as those assessing child development, social class differences have been measured in a variety of ways, and the patterns are quite consistent. There is no socioeconomic difference in regard to how men define the responsibilities of a father, but there are considerable variations across social classes in regard to men's attachment to traditional definitions of masculinity. There are also significant social class differences in relation to how children have fared in terms of economic support, fathering input, and developmental outcomes. The major policy recommendation advanced on the basis of studies of fathering among low-income men is that the economic and labor market issues must be addressed. In reviewing the history of the U.S. concern with the "deadbeat dad," Elizabeth Pleck (2004) pointed out that little attention has been paid to the difficulties fathers faced in securing employment sufficient to pay a family wage; rather, the focus has been on detection and punishment. Similarly, in their cross-cultural review of fathers, fathering, and fatherhood, Seward and Stanley-Stevens (2014) have shown that employment status or lack of paid work is a crucial factor in explaining fathering disparity in large-scale societies. They observed, "In a prosperous and expanding economy, successful involved fathering is more likely. Stable economies support continuity in fathering, but economic downturns tend to undermine men's opportunities to be involved" (Seward & Stanley-Stevens 2014, p. 463). Accordingly, considering the clear role of economic constraints in undermining involved fathering, Roopnarine and Hossain (2013) have stressed the need to increase economic stability for low-income families in the Caribbean.

Though it is reasonable to attribute many of the social class differences in the execution of fathering responsibilities and in child outcomes to the unrelenting hardships faced by low-income males, community influences may also serve to foster an environment in which hypermasculinity is celebrated and even enforced. This is written into much of the popular Caribbean music, which celebrates male dominance and virility—and in particular the songs that are enthusiastically enjoyed at Dancehall gatherings. In an extensive analysis of Dancehall lyrics, Hope (2010) commented that within the context of economic poverty and social deprivation, men resort to claiming status based on the numbers of their "youts" and "baby-mothers" so that "this cycle of ritualistic fathering results in many fatherless children, some of whom become young men, who like their own fathers become 'grilled up' [caged] in a legacy of poverty, promiscuity and posturing masculinity" (Hope 2010, p. 37). There is accordingly a need to counter these partly unconscious influences by programs directed at young males before they enter the adolescent years. Bailey et al. concluded that communication strategies should take account of the differences in the knowledge and orientation of different age groups and that for this to have maximum effect, some cultural re-engineering must take place, with the school playing a significant role in this process of fostering gender equality and fostering a new construct of manhood (Bailey et al. 1998). Our own review of social intervention programs for young men in Jamaica has shown that a major gap exists in relation to pre-adolescent males (Anderson 2009). In this regard, the Program H, initiated by Promundo in Brazil, has met with considerable success in other countries, and could serve as a model for younger age groups.

The involvement of fathers with their children may easily outlast their commitment to the original romantic relationship into which that child was born, and in that situation, fathers may face significant barriers to executing the father role. A similar pattern has been described by Edin, Nelson, and Reed based on their longitudinal study of low-income fathers in New Jersey (Edin et al. 2011). Among these fathers, both black and white, family behaviors were not contingent upon the relationship with the children's mother (often described as "the package deal" following Furstenberg & Cherlin 1991), but instead the father–child relationship was what was viewed as central. Because fathers often gave priority to this relationship, their decisions about maintaining couple relationships were shaped accordingly. Although these fathers outright rejected the "package deal," they realized that their relationship with the mother was their conduit to the child, given the normative and legal practices governing the custody of nonmarital children. The authors concluded that "in the realm of family relations, 'Daddy, Baby; Momma, Maybe' was a fair representation of the worldview" of many of the fathers studied (Edin et al. 2011, p. 87).

Though Caribbean mothers enjoy a relative advantage in maintaining custody and emotional ties to their children, the greater integration of fathers, especially non-residential fathers, will entail the acknowledgement and activation of what Roopnarine and Hossain (2013) have labeled "caregiving alliances." This will, however, require a sustained education campaign, both through the media to increase awareness of men's rights as fathers, and the benefits to children, as well as in regard to the more specific aspects of child-rearing, such as the long-term damage that can result from harsh parenting. Support groups, such as Fathers Incorporated in Jamaica, the Men's Educational and Support Association in Barbados, and the Caribbean Male Action Network in Trinidad and Tobago, if they are able to secure external funding, can also make an important contribution to increasing the profile of Involved Fathering. Other policy initiatives for consideration include legislation for the provision of paternity leave. This has been implemented in several countries and may help to point the way forward for Caribbean fathers.

NOTES

The authors are grateful for the research support provided by colleagues Michael James and Kristin Fox and appreciate the financial support extended by the Human Resource Development Programmes in the Department of Sociology, Psychology and Social Work, the Office of the Principal, UWI, and the Planning Institute of Jamaica. Special thanks are extended to the primary school teachers and to the Fathers who shared their expenses.

1. A "shotta" is the local name for a gunman, working alone or as part of a gang; "don" is the title given to the head of a gang or to the local executive of a political garrison (Gayle & Levy, 2007).

2. This account is based on a conversation between one of the authors and a Kingston taxi driver in January 2014. Attempts to find a report in a local newspaper were not successful.

3. The Fathers Study was conducted in four communities, three urban and one semirural. This paper reports findings from the three urban communities, which included 220 fathers in the middle-income community, 246 from the blue-collar working-class community, and 310 from the low-income inner-city community. In the absence of a random sample, the survey made a complete listing of all fathers in these households to estimate the coverage rate. This was 59 percent for both the middle-income and the blue-collar community and was 66 percent for the inner-city community. These were agreed to be largely representative samples based on census data for these communities (Anderson 2012).

4. This publication is based on the thesis submitted as partial requirement for the master's philosophy at the University of the West Indies, Cave Hill, Barbados, 2008.

5. The general findings in regard to the overall macho scale, and its psychometric properties, are presented in Anderson (2012).

6. Research is currently under way at the University of the West Indies, Jamaica, under the direction of Maureen Samms-Vaughan, professor of child development, to trace the development of a national cohort of children born in 2011. The goal of this project, known as the JA Kids Birth Cohort Study, is to improve the health and well-being of Jamaica's children by tracing the relationships among a wide range of family, school, community, environmental and individual variables. It will also examine the various factors that influence health, disease, and development in young children. Specifically, JA kids will provide national data on maternal health and well-being, pregnancy, paternal well-being and involvement, children's status at birth and at various points thereafter, and children's experiences during early childhood and beyond.

THE CARIBBEAN

www.open.uwi.edu/caribecd/welcome
www.globalchilddevelopment.org
http://blogs.iadb.org/desarrolloinfantil_en/2013/11/25/bad-boys/
www.ecc.gov.jm
www.unicef.org/easterncaribbean/
www.cariman.org

REFERENCES

Anderson, P. (2007). The challenge of housing and community conflict in East and West Kingston. *Social and Economic Studies, 56*(3): 33–70.

Anderson, P. (2009). *The changing roles of fathers in Jamaican family life* (Working Paper No. 10). Kingston, Jamaica: The Planning Institute of Jamaica.

Anderson, P. (2012). Measuring masculinity in an Afro-Caribbean context. *Social and Economic Studies, 60*(1), 49–93.

Awong-Persaud, D. (2003). *The impact of involvement and characteristics of fathers on male adolescents' self-esteem in Port-of-Spain, Trinidad* (M.Sc. thesis), University of the West Indies, St. Augustine, Trinidad.

Bailey, W., Branche, C., McGarrity, G., & Stuart, S. (1998). *Family and the quality of gender relations*. Kingston, Jamaica: Institute of Social and Economic Research.

Barrow, C. (2010). *Caribbean childhoods "outside" "adopted" or "left behind."* Kingston, Jamaica: Ian Randle Publishers.

Branche, C. (1998). Boys in conflict. In W. Bailey (ed.), *Gender and the family in the Caribbean* (pp. 185–201). Kingston, Jamaica: Institute of Social and Economic Research.

Brown, J., Anderson, P., & Chevannes, B. (1993). *The contribution of Caribbean men to the family*. Report to IDRC. Kingston, Jamaica: Caribbean Child Development Centre.

Brown, J., & Chevannes, B. (1998). *Why man stay so*. Kingston, Jamaica: University of the West Indies.

Brown, J., Newland, A., Anderson, P. & Chevannes, B. (1997). Caribbean fatherhood: Under-researched, misunderstood. In J. L. Roopnarone & J. Brown

(Eds.), *Caribbean families: Diversity among ethnic groups.* (85–114). Connecticut: Ablex Publishing Corporation.

Chevannes, B. (1993). Sexual Behaviour of Jamaicans: A Literature Review. *Social and Economic Studies, 45*(1), 1–45.

Chevannes, B. (2001). *Learning to be a man: Culture, socialization and gender identity in five Caribbean countries.* Kingston, Jamaica: University of the West Indies Press.

Chevannes, B., & Mitchell-Kernan, C. (1992). *"How we were grown": Cultural aspects of high risk sexual behavior in Jamaica.* Kingston, Jamaica: Institute of Social and Economic Research, University of West Indies.

Clarke, E. (1957). *My mother who fathered me.* London: George Allen and Unwin.

Crawford-Brown, C. (1999). The Impact of Parenting on conduct disorder in Jamaican male adolescents. *Adolescence, 34,* 417–437.

Cumper, G. (1958). The Jamaican family: Village and estate. *Social and Economic Studies, 7*(1), 76–108.

Daley, C. (2014). *Educational involvement of Jamaican fathers: Observations of grade 6 primary school teachers.* Unpublished manuscript, University of the West Indies, Department of Sociology, Psychology and Social Work.

Dann, G. (1987). *The Barbadian male: Some beliefs and attitudes.* London: McMillan.

Douglass, L. (1992). *The power of sentiment; Love, hierarchy and the Jamaican elite.* Boulder, CO: Westview Press.

Edin, K., Nelson, T., & Reed, J. (2011). Daddy, baby; Momma maybe: Low-income fathers and the "package deal" of family life. In M. Carlson & P. England (eds.), *Social class and changing families in an unequal America* (85–107). Stanford, CA: Stanford University Press.

Evans, H. (1989). Perspectives on the socialization of the working-class Jamaican child. *Social and Economic Studies, 38*(3), 177–203.

Evans, H., & Davies, R. (1997). Overview of issues in childhood socialization in the Caribbean. In J. Roopnarine & J. Brown (eds.), *Caribbean families: Diversity among ethnic groups* (pp. 1–24). London: Apex Publishing Company.

Figueroa, M. (2004). "Male privileging" and "academic underperformance" in Jamaica. In R. Reddock (ed.), *Interrogating Caribbean masculinities* (136–166). Kingston, Jamaica: University of the West Indies Press.

Furstenberg, F. F. Jr., & Cherlin, A. (1991). *Divided families: What happens to children when parents part.* Cambridge, MA: Harvard University Press.

Furstenberg, F. F. Jr. (1995). Fathering in the inner city: Paternal participation and public policy. In W. Marsiglio (ed.), *Fatherhood: Contemporary theory, research, and public policy* (119–147). Thousand Oaks, CA: Sage Publications.

Gayle, H., & Levy, H. (2007). *Forced ripe! A participatory ethnographic evaluation and research (PEER).* Unpublished Paper, Department of Sociology, Psychology and Social Work, University of the West Indies, Jamaica.

Gayle, H., Grant, A., Bryan, P., Yee Shui, M., & Taylor, C. (2004). *The adolescents of urban St. Catherine: A study of their reproductive health and survivability.* Spanish Town, Jamaica: Children First Agency.

Gray, O. (2004). *Demeaned, but empowered: The social power of the urban poor in Jamaica.* Kingston, Jamaica: University of the West Indies Press.

Harriott, A. (ed.). (2003). *Understanding crime in Jamaica: New challenges for public policy.* Kingston, Jamaica: University of the West Indies Press.

Hawkins, A., Bradford, A. K., Palkovitz, R., Christiansen, S., & Day, R. (2002). The inventory of father involvement: A pilot study of a new measure of father involvement. *Journal of Men's Studies*, 10 (2), 183–196.

Hawkins, A., Christiansen, S., Sargent, K., & Hill, J. (1995). Rethinking fathers' involvement in child care: A developmental perspective. In W. Marsiglio (ed.), Research on men and masculinities: *Fatherhood: Contemporary theory, research, and social policy* (41–57). Thousand Oaks, CA: SAGE Publications, Inc.

Hope, D. (2010). *Man vibes: Masculinities in the Jamaican dancehall*. Kingston, Jamaica: Ian Randle Publishers.

Levy, H., & Chevannes, B. (1996). *They cry respect: Urban poverty and violence in Jamaica*. Kingston, Jamaica: Centre for Population, Community and Social Change, University of the West Indies.

Lipps, G., Gillian, L., Gibson, R., Halliday, S., Morris, A., Clarke, N., & Wilson, R. (2012). Parenting and depressive symptoms among adolescents in four Caribbean societies. *Child and Adolescent Psychiatry and Mental Health*, 6(31), 1–12.

Marsiglio, W. (1998). *Procreative man*. New York: New York University Press.

Marsiglio, W., & Hutchinson, S. (2002). *Sex, men and babies: Stories of awareness and responsibility*. New York: New York University Press.

Maharaj, R. G., Alli, F., Cumberbatch, K., Laloo, P., Mohammed, S., Ramesar, A., . . . Ramtahal, I. (2008). Depression among adolescents aged 13–19 years, attending secondary schools in Trinidad. *West Indian Medical Journal*, 57(4), 352–359.

National Family Planning Board. (2010). *Reproductive health survey Jamaica 2008*. Kingston, Jamaica.

Parry, O. (1996). *The educational under-achievement of Caribbean males in Jamaica, Barbados, St, Vincent and the Grenadines: A qualitative study of high school education*. Kingston, Jamaica: Institute for Social and Economic Research, University of the West Indies.

Planning Institute of Jamaica and Statistical Institute of Jamaica. (2012). *Jamaica survey of living conditions 2010*. Kingston, Jamaica: Planning Institute of Jamaica.

Pleck, E. (2004). Two dimensions of fatherhood; A history of the good dad–bad dad complex. In M. Lamb (ed.), *The role of the father in child development* (32–57). Hoboken, NJ: Wiley and Sons.

Ramkissoon, M. (2005). An investigation of the physical and psychological presence of the Jamaican father. *Caribbean Childhoods*, 2, 17–37.

Ricketts, H., & Anderson, P. (2009). *Parenting in Jamaica* (Working Paper No. 9), Kingston, Jamaica: The Planning Institute of Jamaica.

Roberts, G. (1957). *The population of Jamaica*. London: Cambridge University Press.

Roberts, G., & Sinclair, S. (1978). *Women in Jamaica: Patterns of reproduction and family*. Millwood, NY: TKO Press.

Roopnarine, J. (2013). Fathers in Caribbean cultural communities. In D. Shwalb, B. Shwalb, & M. Lamb (eds.), *Fathers in cultural context* (203–227). New York: Routledge.

Roopnarine, J., Brown, J., Snell-White, P., Riegraf, N., Crossley, D., Hossain, Z., & Webb, W. (1995). Father involvement in child care and household work in common-law and single-earner Jamaican families. *Journal of Applied Developmental Psychology*, 16, 35–52.

Roopnarine, J., & Hossain, Z. (2013). African American and African Caribbean fathers. In N. Cabrera & C. Tamis-Lemonda (eds.), *Handbook of father involvement* (223–243). New York: Routledge.

Samms-Vaughan, M. (2000). *Cognition, educational attainment and behavior in a cohort of Jamaican children* (Working Paper No. 5). Kingston, Jamaica: The Planning Institute of Jamaica.

Samms-Vaughan, M., Williams, S., & Brown, J. (2005). Disciplinary practices among parents of six-year olds in Jamaica. *Caribbean Childhoods, 2,* 58–70.

Senior, O. (1986). *Summer lightning and other stories.* London, UK: Longman Press.

Seward, R. R., & Stanley-Stevens, L. (2014). Fathers, fatherhood and fathering across cultures. In H. Selin (ed.), *Parenting across cultures* (459–474). New York: Springer.

Smith, M. G. (1962). *West Indian family structure.* Seattle/London, UK: University of Washington Press.

Smith, R. (1957). *The Negro family in British Guiana.* London, UK: Routledge and Kegan Paul.

Smith, R. (1973). The matrifocal family. In J. Goody (ed.), *The character of kinship* (121–144), Cambridge, UK: Cambridge University.

Smith, R. (1982). Family, social change and social policy in the West Indies. *New West Indian Guide, 56* (3–4), 111–142.

Smith, R. (1996). *The matrifocal family.* New York: Routledge.

Springer, L. (2010). *Fatherhood in the neighborhood.* Maitland, FL: Xulon Press.

Statistical Institute of Jamaica. (2012). *Demographic statistics 2010.* Kingston, Jamaica.

United Nations Fund for Population Activities. (2006). Bringing "Program H" to the Caribbean: Report on focus-groups. Kingston, Jamaica.

Wehby, H. (2005). Father involvement and its impact on academic achievement among grade six students in Kingston, Jamaica (Unpublished M.Sc. research paper). University of the West Indies, Jamaica.

Whitehead, T. (1992). Expressions of masculinity in a Jamaican sugartown: Implications for family planning programs. In T. Whitehead & B. Reid (eds.), *Gender constructs and social issues* (103–141). Chicago: University of Illinois Press.

Wilson, P. (1969). Reputation and respectability: A suggestion for Caribbean ethnology. *Man, 4.* 70–84.

Wilson, P. (1973). *Crab antics: The social anthropology of the English-speaking societies of the Caribbean.* New Haven, CT: Yale University Press.

Wint, E., & Brown, J. (2001). The knowledge and practice of effective parenting. In C. Barrow & R. Reddock (eds.), *Caribbean sociology: Introductory readings* (436–448), Kingston, Jamaica: Ian Randle Publishers.

3

Fathering in Brazil

Ana M. A. Carvalho,
Lucia V. C. Moreira, and Yumi Gosso

The aim of this chapter—to review the literature on fathering in Brazil—faces several challenges. The huge geographic, historical, economic, ethnic, and sociocultural diversity that characterizes the country is expressed in different local cultures and realities with respect to fathers' roles and practices and even to fathers' presence or absence. There is no such thing as a "Brazilian father"—as is also probably the case in many other countries (Shwalb, Shwalb, & Lamb 2013; Tudge 2008). Brazilian research on fathering is relatively recent and very heterogeneous as to methodology (mostly qualitative) and the sociocultural contexts studied are not always clearly described (Bastos et al. 2013). It seems useful, therefore, to offer the reader some background information on Brazilian families to contextualize research findings.

CONTEXTUALIZING FATHERING IN BRAZILIAN FAMILIES

Three aspects of fathering in Brazil are discussed here: historical background, diversity of Brazilian family configurations and life conditions, and evolution of legislation affecting paternity and fathering.

Fathering: A Brief Historical Background

The patriarchal father is probably the oldest and historically more discussed fathering model in western societies, going back to the emergence of the agricultural way of life (Engels 2002). Patronizing a clan or tribe in ancient Middle Eastern civilizations, or a Roman noble family, or a fief in the Middle Ages—or, more recently, from the sixteenth century on, a colonial farm or plantation in Brazilian lands donated by Portuguese kings to occupy their newly conquered territories—the father figure is depicted in basically similar ways. He *owns* and *rules over* both his material property and his dependents—family, servants (or slaves) and other residents of his political area of influence. He has life-and-death rights over his people and answers only to the distant king or other central authority (when there is one). He is usually depicted as a cold, severe, authoritative figure who defines his children's fate, marriages, and education (or lack of) and imposes his decisions, often through harsh and abusive methods (Filgueiras & Petrini 2010).

Gilberto Freyre is the classic Brazilian author who writes about social and family relations during the colonial period and on the dynamics of their evolution in the nineteenth and early twentieth centuries, after the independence and the proclamation of the republic. This history is depicted in his trilogy *Casa Grande e Senzala* (1933), *Sobrados e Mucambos* (1936), and *Ordem e Progresso* (1957).[1] Filgueiras and Petrini (2010) present a useful analytical synthesis of this seminal work. In *Casa Grande e Senzala*, patriarchate emerges as the possible solution for the historical conditions of the colonization process; in a large and acephalous territory, the despotic rule of the patriarchs ensured safety, stability, and continuity. "In that way of life, the family members had strictly defined roles, property was conveniently sacred, heritage warranted the continuity of his authority, and family relations were measured according to the respect paid to him" (Filgueiras & Petrini 2010, p. 30). *Sobrados e Mucambos* analyzes the beginning of the patriarchal father's decline with the strengthening of public power, the development of urban centers and the emergence of a new character, "the doctor," meaning the graduate from a law, medicine, or engineering school, who will compete for political and paternal authority with the ancient landowner patriarch. The rural family, until then mainly responsible for the reproduction of values, is displaced from the rural world toward an urban industrial and capitalist world, "from 'familism' to individualism" (Filgueiras & Petrini 2010, p. 32). The comprehensive roles the patriarchal father performed as an individual will be split between government, church, schools, factories, shops, and banks. Brazilian society will inherit, however, the mark that branded the patriarchal regime: hierarchy.

Finally, in *Order and Progress*, the next stages of this process are analyzed. In 1930, after the political fall of the old rural oligarchy that had ruled the country since the republic was proclaimed in 1889, the incipient industrial development gains strength and creates new sorts of Brazilian citizens—workers, public officers, "doctors"—and an emergent middle class, opposed to the old "rural nobility." Patriarchate comes to be identified with backwardness. Under the influence of European ideals of freedom and individual choice, the family morality changes. Paternal functions are partly transferred to the state, and youngsters claim more freedom to rule their own life. At the public level, however, typical patriarchs have survived in the political arena up to recent times (Filgueiras & Petrini 2010).

As aptly pointed out by the authors, even at its climax, the concept of the patriarchal father did not represent fatherhood across Brazilian society. It referred to patriarchal fathers of aristocratic families in rural areas where they also exerted political power. Thus it cannot be generalized to other social groups such as slaves' families or small urban or semi-urban middle class families, and even less so to indigenous communities that survived the colonization process. However, the patriarchal father "has acquired a symbolic and reference meaning for the comprehension of paternity in the Brazilian society" (Filgueiras & Petrini 2010, p. 24).

Since the 1930s, with the increasing participation of women in the labor market, and particularly since the 1960s, with the spread of feminism and the conquest of sexual freedom for women, men seem to be looking for a new male identity and a new paternal role (Santos et al. 2001). This transition is not smooth for fathers nor families and children. Those who were born in the 1940s and 1950s have often witnessed (and lived with) different experiences of fathering: with their fathers, with their husbands, and now with their sons (Bastos et al. 2013). Thus if the patriarchal model, though symbolically strong, does not describe fatherhood in that less heterogeneous stage of Brazilian society, it is equally not possible to describe a single Brazilian fatherhood in current times. It is thus useful to contextualize the still limited Brazilian literature on fathering in contemporary Brazilian society.

Contextualizing the Researched Families in Contemporary Brazil

The extensive Brazilian territory (more than 8.5 million km^2) is divided into five geographic regions differing significantly with respect to physical characteristics, climate, population density and ethnic origins, cultural heritage, economy, and affluence. South and southeast are the richest and more densely populated regions, followed by the northeast—where, however, economic activity is concentrated in coastal areas; inland areas are predominantly semiarid and very poor. The north region has the more extensive land area and is largely occupied by the Amazon forest and its hydrographic basin; extractive activities are still an important income source. The midwest region, although housing Brasilia, the capital of the country, is predominantly agrarian. Within the north and midwest regions are the largest concentrations of the main indigenous communities' preserved areas. Eighty-four percent of the Brazilian population lives in urban areas, and many of the largest cities are near or in the coastal area (IBGE 2010).

Of approximately 66 million Brazilian households, around 85 percent are nuclear or extended families, of which the largest proportions are parents with children (40%) or with children and other relatives (5%); around 20 percent are couples without children, and around 16 percent are unmarried or separated mothers with children. The remaining households are occupied by single persons or nonrelated mates. Thus the vast majority of Brazilians live in some type of familial arrangement, most frequently parents with children, though the frequency of this arrangement has decreased in the last decade, along with the number of children per mother. There are current trends toward delayed marriage and pregnancy, increasing numbers of informal cohabitation arrangements, judicial and informal separations, official or informal remarriage, and out-of-marriage births. Mono-parental families are usually (around 90% of registered cases) headed by the mother, particularly when the children are younger (younger than 16). All these trends present differences according to socioeconomic status, cultural group, and region (IBGE 2010, 2013).

The literature to be reviewed here refers to very specific segments of this scenery: urban families; fathers living with the family or, in the case of separated couples, keeping in contact with their children; and middle- and upper-middle class families (with the exception of adolescent parents and of studies that included poor families in Salvador, state of Bahia, northeast). Studies on fathering are concentrated in the south and southeast regions, with isolated exceptions in the largest and richest northeast capitals. Whenever available, information on socioeconomic status of the families and region where the study was performed are provided.

Reports on father–child relations in other contexts, such as isolated communities or rural families when available, are episodic and not based on research projects targeting the father. Nonetheless, a brief mention to these reports will be made, for they help enhance the perspective on the links between sociocultural and economic contexts and paternal attitudes and practices.

EVOLUTION OF THE LEGISLATION ON FAMILY AND PARENTING: JURIDICAL CHANGES AFFECTING PATERNITY IN BRAZIL

Along with its history as an independent country (since 1822), Brazil has witnessed the promulgation of seven constitutions. The first, in 1834, established the country as a constitutional monarchy. The others accompanied further historical changes: the proclamation of the republic in 1989 (1891 constitution), the fall of the first republic in 1930 (1934 constitution), the ascent of dictatorial governments (1937 and 1967 constitutions) and their termination with redemocratization processes (1946 and 1988 constitutions). Among these, the 1934 constitution stands out for the introduction of universal vote for literate adults (older than 18), for extending this right to women of age, and for the creation of labor laws such as minimum wage, 13th wage, vacations, regulation of working hours, right to association, and the like. Besides these advances, little else happened in the route to democracy, equality, and other contemporary trends until the 1988 constitution, considered one of the most advanced in the world for civil and political rights and the protection of economically and socially underprivileged segments, minorities, and other targets of discrimination and inequality. The current Brazilian juridical order reflects the changes occurring in society, such as gender equality, lessening of intergenerational hierarchies, and increasing numbers of dissolved marriages. Reciprocally, it also influences social life and relations, for instance with respect to human rights.

Until the 1988 constitution (Brasil 1988), the husband/father was deemed the head of the family and endowed with "paternal power." With the constitution and the new civil code (Act 10.406, as of January 2002), both parents exert together the "family power," defined as the set of rights and duties that parents are endowed and charged with regarding the person and the property of their underage children, which in Brazil means those younger than 18 (Gonçalves 2011). Thus, according to the 2002 civil code, both parents are fundamentally and jointly responsible for ensuring conditions for their children's development at several levels, upbringing, educating, and assisting them in all their needs. Lamenza (2013) indicates that the code also ensures parents' rights, such as keeping their children in their company and demanding obedience and respect from them.

The civil code (art. 1.638) determines that family power may be lost by fathers and/or mothers under certain circumstances: (a) abusive punishment (more recently, even slaps are being criticized in the juridical milieu as unnecessary and inadequate physical punishment); (b) keeping the child in conditions of material, moral, or intellectual abandonment; and (c) practicing actions contrary to morals and customs, such as sexual abuse against children or living with the children in inadequate environments (for instance, whorehouses).

About the parent–child bond, the civil code reviews and rejects the former classifications of filiation as "legitimate," referring to children born to married parents; "illegitimate," referring to those born to unmarried parents; and "natural," when the parents had no conjugal status and were not married to someone else—a classification that was a source of embarrassment and discrimination by being written on the birth certificate. Instead, the civil code (article 1.956) states that "children, whether born from a marriage relationship or otherwise, including adoption, are entitled to the same rights and qualifications, and any discriminatory designations qualifying filiation are from now on forbidden." Furthermore, filiation can also derive from artificial insemination or in vitro fertilization. These practices are increasingly used in the Brazilian context by upper socioeconomic layers of the population that can afford their high costs.

Filiation and birth are proven through a birth certificate registered at a public notary civil office. According to the civil code (articles 50 and 52), the registration must be made by the father within fifteen days of birth; in the absence or impediment of the father, the mother must do so; if she is equally constrained, it can be performed by close relatives, a hospital manager, a physician, or a midwife. When the father does not recognize the child as his, an investigatory lawsuit can determine paternity through a DNA exam. If the father refuses the exam, paternity is presumed. Current debates indicate a trend toward an inversion of this situation: The name of the presumed father should be included in the child's birth certificate, and the father may resort to justice if he believes that the child is not his. Children born to married parents are presumed to be the husband's child unless proven otherwise. Although the Childhood and Adolescence Statute (Act 8.069/1990, as of July 1990) states that the recognition of filiation is a personal, irrevocable and imprescriptible right, the number of persons whose birth certificates do not have the father's name is still significant. The 1988 federal constitution emphasizes the family as the basis of society and ensures the couple's freedom to decide on family planning. The current trend is the reduction of the number of children per family.

With respect to adoption, according to current legal dispositions, the adopted child will be completely detached from his or her natural parents and will be integrated in the adopting family (Lamenza 2013). The Childhood and Adolescence Statute (Act 8.069, article 27) defines, as potential adopters, persons 18 years and older, irrespective of marriage status.

Another relevant issue is the increasing numbers of divorce in the Brazilian context and the implications of marital dissolution on father–child relationships. The long and controversial history of divorce in Brazil is not within the scope of this chapter, but some points are relevant. Since 1890, when the civil marriage was created, some legal regulations were provided to justify, accept, and regulate separation cases. Until the 1970s, judicial separation without marriage dissolution, and thus without the possibility of a new marriage, was the only legal separation condition. This implied a marginal status for those who "remarried" or lived with formerly married partners, with the consequent social costs and lack of marriage rights. The 1988 constitution made several advances in the direction of legal regulation and assurance of partners' rights, particularly for women and children. It endorsed and advanced the 1977 divorce act (Act 6.515, as of December 1977) and created the juridical figure of "stable cohabitation relationships," subject to the same duties and rights as formal marriages, including parenthood.

The main issues resulting from divorce (or other separation conditions) that are targets of juridical decisions are children's custody and the right to visits. According to the current legal order, custody obeys the principle of "the best interest of the child." As pointed out by Pereira (2004), custody is thus given to the parent who presents the best conditions—whereas previously it was given to the "innocent" partner, or the partner who had not caused the separation. When there are serious obstacles to custody being given to either mother or father, it can be transferred to a trustworthy member of one of the parents' families.

The usual form of custody is unilateral custody, where one of the parents (or someone who assumes their role) has custody, and the other is entitled to regulated visits. Since this custody modality deprives the child younger than 18 of daily contact with one of the parents (usually the father), the law encourages the adoption of shared custody, where parents who do not live together exert jointly the family power and thus ensure a close bond between them and their children's education and upbringing (Lamenza 2013). This custody modality tries to avoid parental alienation syndrome (Lyra et al. 2013), an issue that is the target of intense debate in Brazilian juridical and psychological milieus.

The number of reconstructed families is also increasing in Brazil, creating the figures of the stepfather and the stepmother, whose interaction with the children can be either positive or negative. This reality requires further study in the Brazilian context. The juridical milieu is frequently adopting a focus on affective relationships when dealing with parenting and conjugal relations, but the meaning and the importance of what constitutes affective quality are still not clearly stated. Socioaffective paternity is increasingly incorporated by law professionals in this changing scenery of family configurations. Some families have even conquered the legal right to place the names of both the biological father and the socioaffective father in the birth certificate. Besides the stepfather, socioaffective paternity may occur on the part of a grandfather, an uncle, or a close family friend.

Another issue relates to fathers' participation in birth procedures and in the newborn's life. Paternity license is established by law as five working days after the child's birth, whereas the mother's is 120 days, recently extended to six months for public servants. The father's right to escort his wife in the hospital is often hindered by the use of collective lodgings and by other institutional obstacles. There is thus in Brazil a long wait ahead for policies allowing the father's contact with the newborn baby and with his wife at a time when his support is needed (Medrado et al. 2010).

Two apparently contradictory trends are thus present in the recent evolution of Brazilian laws regarding paternity and fathering. On the one hand, the father's power was reduced by the abolition of "paternal power" on behalf of "family power." On the other, the advantages of shared custody of the children by divorced parents and the importance of both parents' frequent interaction with their children are increasingly recognized and valued.

BRAZILIAN RESEARCH ON FATHERING

Until the 1980s, the father was practically absent from the Brazilian literature on child development (Dessen & Lewis 1998), and it was only in the late 1990s that interest on paternal behavior and father–child relationships began to increase (Vieira et al. 2013). Based on the occurrence of the theme in the main science databases from 2000 to 2007, Souza and Benetti (2009) present an estimate of Brazilian and international academic production on paternity. Brazil was one of the three countries with continuous production in the period, with a minimum of six papers per year and a peak of twenty-six in 2006. Adolescent fatherhood and political and social themes stand out in the Brazilian literature in the period, followed by the transition to a "new paternity." These trends contrast with previous decades: From 1960 to 1980, the focus was on the father's absence from family life—either through abandonment or separation/divorce—and its association with negative outcomes for children (Bastos et al. 2013). As pointed out by these authors, the (completely) absent father cannot tell us much about fathering and fatherhood. However, father absence is not necessarily absolute lack of contact between fathers and their children, as in cases of total abandonment. It can mean sporadic contact, as with divorced fathers who have limited opportunities to interact with their children or who neglect using these opportunities (which already configures two different situations). It can also mean that a father is present daily but is uninvolved in his children's lives ("psychological absence")—not to mention fathers whose presence is negative because of abuse or mistreatment. Father absence/ presence is thus a complex gradient involving not only simple dimensions such as number of hours of physical presence or potential interaction, but also the nature and quality of these interactions, as well as fathers' attitudes and feelings with respect to paternity. The concepts of paternal involvement or engagement seem to move toward these qualitative dimensions (Bossardi et al. 2013; Vieira et al. 2013).

Because most studies on fathering are qualitative (Souza & Benetti 2009) and focus on small selected samples that tend to ignore socioeconomic, educational, ethnic, and cultural variations, no general picture about fatherhood and fathering emerges from this literature (Bastos et al. 2013). It is, rather, a collection of portraits of possible fatherhoods, delimited by particular socioeconomic and cultural contexts. However, there is a consensus that a "new father" is (or should be) emerging, in a transition process resulting from macrosocial changes such as women's participation in the labor market, and involving the search for a new model of fathering that can conciliate traditional male roles as provider and authority and the novel expectations for a participative and affective paternal figure—transition that appears to be under way in several other countries (Benetti & Roopnarine 2006). That this transition process is under way in Brazil is suggested by two quantitative studies focusing on perceptions on fathering and mothering by comparatively rare informants: children.

Children's Views on Parenting

Goetz and Vieira (2009) investigated perceptions of children on real and ideal parents using an instrument adapted and validated for the Brazilian context and for their particular sample: 216 10- and 11-year-old middle class children in Florianópolis, state of Santa Catarina, south region. Results showed statistically significant differences between perceptions of ideal and real fathers: In the children's view, to approach the ideal, the father should be more present or active in tasks such as hygiene, feeding, helping with school work, provision of school material and medicine, provision of leisure, guidance on behavior adequacy, playing and expressing affection. The differences occurred in all the analyzed categories, suggesting that the real father's style of parenting should include more direct and indirect care and more instructive and affective social interactions. In contrast, no significant differences were found between the ideal and the real mother with respect to direct care (hygiene, feeding, school and health needs), attention to children's needs, instructive and guidance interactions. But the real mother was deemed more repressive about misbehavior than the ideal mother, and the ideal mother was more available for play, leisure (indirect care), and affective interactions than the real mother. A comparison was also made between children who lived with both parents and children from divorced couples. In both situations, the ideal and the real mother are less distant from one another than the ideal and the real father; the distance between the ideal and real father regarding direct care and interaction was particularly noticeable among children whose parents were divorced (Goetz & Vieira 2008).

A study carried out in the states of São Paulo, southeast region and Bahia, northeast region (Carvalho et al. 2010) investigated perceptions on fathering and mothering with a sample of 120 5- to 11-year-old middle class children, using interviews guided by open-ended questions such as "What is it to be a father/ a mother?" Children's answers were categorized and depicted as percentages in each category, providing a profile of fathers and mothers. The peaks of each profile describe the father as someone who (1) plays, (2) educates, (3) provides, (4) loves his children and (5) offers general care and the mother as someone who (1) offers general care, (2) loves her children (3) educates, (4) takes care of the house, and (5) plays.

Interesting convergences can be detected in these studies and in some trends toward a "new father": It is with respect to direct care and perhaps to attentiveness to children's daily needs that fathers seem to stay behind (whereas mothers could perhaps just play a little more?). Having listened to the children, it is fair to listen also to the targets of these evaluations: mothers and fathers.

Parents' Views on Fathering

To investigate mothers' and fathers' views on ideal and real fathering style, a scale on parenting style adapted to the Brazilian context was used with thirty couples having a mean age of 33 years and at least one child aged 3–6 in Santa Catarina (south region) (Prado et al. 2007) The scale explored three aspects of parenting practices: didactic (offering and participating in opportunities for learning and general development), social (attention and responsiveness to the child's needs and feelings, affective interactions), and disciplinary (teaching conventions and social rules, correcting misbehavior). Furthermore, the parents were asked to estimate the time per week the father was available to interact with the child and his participation in domestic tasks, both ideally and in real terms. No significant differences were found between the conceptions of mothers and fathers on ideal paternal behavior, except with respect to ideal time available and ideal participation in domestic tasks, where mothers had higher expectations and fathers tended to evaluate their real and ideal participation as similar. Both parents considered the ideal father to be distant from the real father with respect to didactic and social interaction, but similar to the real father in the disciplinary domain.

Engaged Fathers

This set of studies focuses on men who perceive themselves as engaged fathers. They are usually qualitative, with semistructured interviews, focus groups, and/or ethnographic observations with young fathers or families who have one or more children in early childhood. It should be pointed out that these samples are subject to bias with respect to the availability of the fathers to participate, for less participative fathers could be less willing to talk about their fathering experiences (Gabriel & Dias 2011; Silva & Piccinini 2007). Thus these studies have no claim to generalization but rather aim to depict men's feelings and experiences in particular segments of the population. Despite these constraints, some trends—and obstacles—do become apparent in the process of construction of a "new father."

Using semistructured interviews, Gabriel and Dias (2011) explored fathers' feelings and experiences with respect to paternity with eight middle/

upper-middle class fathers, aged 28–41, in Santa Maria, state of Rio Grande do Sul (south region). Their children (in every case a first and only child) were younger than 5, and the fathers had stable relationships with the mothers. These fathers describe themselves as present in their children's daily life, with active participation in their education, and sharing caregiving tasks with the mothers—both in pleasant moments such as play and in less pleasant ones such as changing diapers, feeding, taking the child to the doctor for immunization, and scolding and establishing limits. Providing behavior models and education was offered as the most important paternal roles, but there was also a strong emphasis on affective interactions and provision of love and attention. Men felt happy with the experience of paternity and with their own performance as fathers.

Similar trends were found in a qualitative study (Silva & Piccinini 2007) on feelings with respect to paternity and paternal engagement with three middle-class fathers of a young (21–27-month) first and only child in Porto Alegre, Rio Grande do Sul (south region). The fathers' reports coincide in several aspects: strong presence during gestation and childbirth and in the subsequent pediatric follow-up, and sharing basic caregiving tasks, (bathing, changing, feeding, preparing food) since birth, as well as school-related tasks, play, and discipline in the following years (in one case, even more than the mother, who worked more hours and contributed more to the domestic budget). These fathers felt happy with their experiences and felt deeply emotionally engaged with their children. The main difference among them pertained to availability: The two fathers who had a heavier workload (and, in one case, who would be the only provider until his wife completed her college education) complained that they wished for more free time for their children.

In a study carried out in Salvador, state of Bahia (northeast region) (Brasileiro et al. 2010), three middle-/lower-middle-class young men (younger than 30) who were expecting their first child were interviewed at two different moments—during the last three months of their companion's pregnancy and three to six months after the baby was born—aiming to explore meanings attributed to fatherhood, social support networks, expectations for the future, perception of personal changes associated with the transition to paternity, and actions related to the paternal role. The analysis of their narratives highlighted intrinsic characteristics of fatherhood: the complementary nature of the division of tasks—including financial provision—between the parents, effective paternal participation in daily life, and fatherhood as a natural and necessary event in a man's life, a source of personal growth—as well as responsibilities such as the provision of moral and disciplinary support to the children. The fathers report sharing daily tasks such as attending to children during the night and domestic chores but recognized that the mothers (and other females when available) were the main caregivers. They emphasized the importance of the father's presence and effective participation, not only because a division of labor is necessary, but also because it is what will nurture the affective relationship between father and child. They were satisfied with their children and their paternal role but were also concerned and unsure about their personal ability to deal with the commitments and challenges brought about by paternity.

Another research group focused on paternal participation in young children's care in low-income families living in precarious wood or partly built brick houses in an urban neighborhood on the outskirts of Salvador, state of Bahia (northeast region), where there was scarcity of basic services (irregular water and energy supply, deficient health services, and few daycare centers). Poor professional qualification and job and income instability also characterized these families (Bustamante & Trad 2005). The study was based on ethnographic observations during regular visits to the families (two nuclear and four extended families) over nine months and on individual interviews with the fathers and other family members (mothers and two grandmothers from extended families).

This study provides some interesting comparisons with those described earlier, with respect both to concrete possibilities of paternal engagement and to the notion of paternal engagement: these fathers also perceived themselves as engaged, actively demonstrating physical and emotional proximity with their children and valuing paternal presence as necessary to the family and to the children, but how they conceived their role reflects the persistence of traditional gender differences. According to their views, the father's role involves (a) provision of material resources, which is his defining responsibility even when the wife also contributes to the family income and which is also their main concern, as well as the main source of a personal sense of insufficiency as fathers; (b) preservation of the children's physical and emotional integrity, particularly in an environment surrounded by physical risks; (c) education, in the main sense of guidance in behavioral and moral issues, with differential values for boys and girls and, for both sexes, with a conservative notion of unquestionable parental authority (children should obey out of respect, not of fear, and should not "force" the parents to use physical punishment); and (d) presence to inspire respect and impose authority. Daily care, including health attention and particularly physical care, are "women's stuff"; it is improper for men to perform these tasks, especially with daughters. In contrast with these conceptions, in all the families, and particularly in nuclear families in which no other caregivers were available, fathers did take part in daily care while mothers were at work but minimized their role in these tasks, describing themselves as "helpers" and assuming this sort of participation to be always secondary to mothers' participation.

Somewhat similar results are described in a qualitative study with eight (four middle class and four lower class) adolescent fathers aged 16–21. Three of them had married the mother and lived with her and the child as a nuclear family; one lived with his child and partner in his parents' house. In the remaining cases, the children lived with their mothers at their grandparents' house, and father–child contacts took place mainly on weekends—a condition similar to that of many divorced fathers. The study was carried out in Vitória, state of Espírito Santo (southeast region). Using semistructured interviews, the authors investigated changes brought up by paternity in the interviewees' life, meanings of paternity and maternity, and parental practices. The main changes reported were loss of freedom and insertion in the labor market. Traditional models of parenting were prevalent: The mother was the most important person in the child's life and was the person who provided love and care and was willing to sacrifice herself for the child's sake. Fathers' main role was to work and provide for the child's needs, but also to educate and provide attention and affection. Reported father–child interactions were mainly play and leisure. However, there are clear signs of the emergence of significant father–child affective relationships (Trindade & Menandro 2002).

An extreme case of paternal engagement is the solitary father, who is responsible for his children's care with no or little female help. Mono-parental families headed by the father are rare, which is at least partly responsible for the scarcity of studies and the difficulties to access these families. Bittelbrun and Castro (2010) report an interview study with four middle-class fathers in Salvador, state of Bahia (northeast region), which aimed to explore how these fathers came to be responsible for their children's care; how fathering and mothering roles were performed while the mother was part of the family; interviewees' views on the social representation of men, of fathering, and of solitary fathers; and the social network of support to which they resorted. The four fathers had custody of their children for at least three years; two of them took over their sons' custody when they were adolescents (aged 12–16), the third father when the son (aged 9 at the time of the interview) was 4, and the fourth, a widower, since his two sons (9 and 11 years old at the time of the interview) had been in early childhood. The four interviewees reported that they were happy with their current situation and felt they had benefited—as persons and as fathers—from the proximity with their children. They were willing to move away from the traditional father model and deepen their affective bonds with the children. The fathers who had cared for their children since early childhood stated that they enjoyed performing basic caregiving tasks. Social support networks such as relatives, friends, and domestic help were available, but the fathers reported only sporadic resort to these alternative caregivers. The authors interpreted their findings as evidence that fathers are capable of crossing, and willing to cross, gender barriers to caregiving and domestic tasks but suggest that there is a long way ahead until their competence and willingness are socially recognized.

Yesterday and Today Fathers

Some studies offer probed or spontaneous information on the interviewees' experiences with their own fathers. Gabriel and Dias (2011) introduced two specific questions in the interviews: "How would you describe your father as a father?" and "What would you point out as similarities and differences between you and your father as fathers?" The interviewees' reports reveal some degree of ambiguity: The father was a good father but could have been better or different, which nonetheless does not imply that he was not a fathering model or parameter. The main criticisms about fathering style were lack of dialogue and affective expression. These "yesterday fathers" were described as establishing a distant relationship with their children, mostly based on authority. However, this fathering style is attributed to the fathers' personality or to the prevalent social standards at the time when these experiences took place, and it left no hard feelings.

In Silva and Piccinini's study (2007), the interviewees' perceptions of their fathers varied from a negative evaluation of the father's difficulty in establishing limits (a paternal characteristic valued by the interviewee), to positive aspects to be emulated, such as a good relationship with the children, emphasis on the importance of education, being a reliable provider, and being a father who afforded his children the right to express their own points of view. Gomes and Resende (2004) interviewed two middle-class fathers who recognized, with a degree of embarrassment, that their fathers were unable to express the love they certainly felt for their children. This cold relationship led them to aspire to a different fathering style, trying to incorporate affection, sharing, and dialogue in their relationships with their wife and children. The solitary fathers interviewed by Bittelbrun and Castro (2010) consider their own engagement with their children to be very different from their fathers' engagement. In this study there is hardly any mention of paternal caregiving and a clear dominance of female care, either by the mother or by a grandmother or an aunt. Although scarce and episodic, these reports suggest, once more, that the main differential trait of the "today" father as compared to "yesterday" fathers, rests on interactional aspects—dialogue, affective expression, and communication—rather than on provision or education/discipline, which already belonged to more traditional portraits of adequate fatherhood, or on direct caregiving, where fathers are still perceived mainly as coadjutants.

Contextualizing Engaged Fathers

In a study carried out in Porto Alegre, state of Rio Grande do Sul (south region) (Wagner et al. 2005), mothers and fathers from 100 intact middle-class families with school-age children were asked to independently answer a questionnaire on participation (prevalently mother, prevalently father, or both equally) in education-related tasks (discipline, help with school tasks, attending school requests, teaching hygiene habits), affective support, feeding, leisure and financial provision. Except for feeding and help with school tasks, in which mothers were prevalent, the most frequent answers pointed to mothers' and fathers' shared participation. Both mothers and fathers tended to overestimate their own participation compared to the partners' evaluation on the same items. A cluster analysis produced two groups within the sample. In the first group, the mother was the main person responsible for most of the tasks, except for provision, affective support, and leisure, which were shared; the only task in which the father prevailed was financial support. Even when shared participation was the most frequent answer, the second most frequent was the mothers' prevalent participation (varying from around 20% to around 70%), whereas the fathers' position varied from 2 percent to 4 percent. In the second group, most tasks were shared (varying from around 60% to 95% of the answers); mothers still occupied the second position, with slight variations arising from differences between mothers' and fathers' answers. The authors highlight the coexistence of different family models and different rhythms of change toward the "new father" even in a relatively homogeneous sample.

In a survey carried out in Salvador, state of Bahia (northeast region) with 150 lower-class and upper-middle-class stable families, fathers and mothers were separately interviewed on detailed aspects of their participation in early childhood care (from six months to toilet training). Aiming at an intergeneration comparison, half the interviews were retrospective, with parents whose youngest child was at the specified age range at least fifteen years earlier (Castro et al. 2012). Two of the analyses performed on this database are particularly interesting for this discussion. Taking into account the time spent with the child (hours per week and periods—daytime, evening, and weekends) and the diversity and nature of caregiving tasks (which included detailed physical care tasks), Moreira et al. (2012) concluded that irrespective of generation status, mothers were the main caregivers, performing the largest amount and variety of caregiving chores (physical care, leisure/conviviality, education/discipline and outdoor activities), while fathers' participation was more selective (leisure/conviviality, education/discipline, and some outdoor activities) and they were either complementary or peripheral caregivers. Physical care activities (for instance, putting to sleep at night) were performed by a number of fathers when their work commitments allowed it. This trend was more noticeable among younger parents of upper-middle-class families.

Using the same database, Castro and Souza (2012) analyzed who was deemed the head of the family and the main financial provider, as well as parents' representations of their own and their partner's participation in child care and changes in the sexual division of tasks in the domestic realm. Along with a predominantly conservative current situation concerning the participation of mothers and fathers in early childhood care, there were some clues of slight changes in that rigid sexual division of labor when representations are analyzed. Mothers and fathers cherished the ideal of shared responsibilities, both with respect to financial provision and to parental care, and self-evaluated as more prone to shared care than their parents' generation. Nonetheless, actual changes were less evident and seemed to be limited to the realm of representations and to higher socioeconomic and younger segments of society.

Bossardi et al. (2013) report the results of the application of a paternal engagement questionnaire, adapted to the Brazilian context, to fifty fathers of 4–6-year-old children in four cities in the state of Santa Catarina (south region). The questionnaire included fifty-six items covering seven dimensions: emotional support, enhancing the child's access to the world, basic care, physical games, thinking and talking about the child, discipline, and domestic chores. Paternal engagement was considered high according to the instruments' criteria but was not equal across the different dimensions, with the following hierarchy: emotional support, discipline, physical games, thinking/talking about the child, basic care, enhancing access to the world, and domestic chores. This hierarchy suggests a gradual incorporation of previously predominantly female attributions (emotional support and, secondarily, basic care), along with the persistence of traditional male roles (discipline and physical games), possibly indicating that fathering is undergoing transition.

These quantitative data, still limited with respect to fathers' diversity of cultural, educational and socioeconomic background, strongly suggest that "engaged fathering" is still a limited reality, circumscribed by a diversity of interacting factors, from socioeconomic status to personal ideology. It appears to be restricted mainly to some subsegments of the youngest generations (born from the 1970s on) from higher socioeconomic and educational layers of the population.

Some Obstacles to the Emergence of the "New Father"

The studies reviewed here offer some clues about possible obstacles in the pathway toward a "new fatherhood." Low socioeconomic and educational status appears to be an obstacle in at least two ways. Less educated fathers tend to stick to more conservative conceptions of gender roles, which include the notion that the father is expected to be the main (or the only) provider; a father who cannot provide for his children may avoid contact with them out of his bad feelings about his insufficient performance. This was exemplified by one of the interviewees in Bustamante and Trad's study (2005), who recognized that he had no contact with four of his children from two previous marriages because he could not offer them any financial help and felt badly because of it. A very concrete obstacle to more participative fathering lies in work demands. Several fathers, both from higher and lower socioeconomic levels, wished they could have more free time for their children but felt limited by their workload. Similarly, legislation related to fathers' paternity license and obstacles imposed by health services to fathers' participation in prenatal care, birth, and postnatal care can hinder a more expressive engagement in fathering during pregnancy and the first stages of the child's life.

In a qualitative study (Sutter & Bucher-Maluschke 2008) based on a focal group with six middle-class married fathers aged 21–34 having children aged 8 months to 8 years and selected by the criterion of self-perception as engaged fathers, a tension was noticed between willingness to take an active part in childcare and to have deep emotional involvement with their children on one hand and, on the other, the need to preserve a masculine self-image or identity. These fathers searched for some degree of specificity in their own ways of dealing with the child in contrast with maternal ways, "in order not to live fatherhood mirroring the mother" (p. 81). These reports highlight the fact that cultural changes are not passively absorbed and can generate discomfort, even in more educated segments.

This and many other reasons underlie the usually slow process of sociocultural change and the diversity of these processes in different contexts. In the brief review presented here, this can be noticed in differences between generations, socioeconomic/educational levels (changes usually spreading slowly from higher to lower levels) and even between geographic regions with diverse cultural and historical background (Schwalb & Schwalb 2014; Tudge 2008).

As a final note on this issue, paternal involvement seems also to be hindered by lack of daily contact between father and children as a result of separation/divorce. Although many different factors are involved in the quality of fathering in these increasingly frequent conditions, there is some evidence that cohabitation and frequency of father–child contacts (for instance, frequency of visits) are by themselves positively related to paternal involvement, as measured by parental practices inventories and by qualitative indicators (Grzybowski & Wagner 2010a, 2010b). The contextualization of these data would benefit from comparisons between paternal involvement previously and after divorce and also from further evidence about the infrequent cases of fathers' custody and mothers' involvement with the children in the absence of cohabitation.

A Note on Indigenous Fathers

References to children and to upbringing practices of indigenous fathers can be found in the writings of Fernão Cardim, a Jesuit priest who arrived in Brazil in 1583 (Cardim 1980). He reported that as soon as the child was born, the father (or, in the father's absence, another adult male who would be in charge of the child, similarly to a Christian godfather) was the person who lifted the child from the floor and then started to fast until the umbilical cord fell out. Children were cherished and well cared for, took part in their parents' activities from a very young age, and were never punished. Cardim's observations are corroborated by several of his contemporaries (Chaves 2000). To the European mind of that time, it was particularly difficult to understand how "savage" and "uncivilized" people could love their children so tenderly and bring up collaborative and obedient children without any sort of coercion or punishment. In fact, according to these reports, the practice of physical punishment to educate children was introduced in Brazil by the colonizing agents.

Although no recent studies specifically targeted at indigenous fathers are available, the observations of modern researchers on indigenous communities are strikingly similar to those made during the colonial period. Anthropologist David Maybury-Lewis (Maybury-Lewis 1990) reports that when he and his family (wife and a young son) arrived in central Brazil in the late 1950s to live in a *Xavante* village, the presence of his child was a major help to their acceptance by the community. He tells us that *Xavante* men came to the researcher's lodgings early in the morning to wait for the child to wake up and marveled at his blue eyes and blond hair. *Xavante* children took the boy to the brook for a morning dive, and the women used to hide him in their baskets and "kidnap" him to spend some time with them, treating him very carefully and comically. The *Xavante* were very critical of disciplinary attitudes of the father, even when the child was taking advantage of their own children. Men would sometimes look for the researcher by the river or somewhere else to report in detail, with shock and disapproval, that his wife had slapped the boy. As a consequence, the anthropologist decided to stop disciplining his child and to leave him as free as *Xavante* children were, though for he and for his wife the mess in the house was hardly tolerable.

Other reports on indigenous communities in the state of Pará (north region) disclose similar attitudes toward children and their participation in adult activities. A *Xikrin* father whose work is interrupted by a child who seizes his tool will not scold the child or retrieve the tool; he will wait patiently until the child gives it back. Neither will the child be scolded or punished if his or her work when doing adult tasks is not properly done; adults believe that the task will be mastered by the child in due time (Cohn 2002). *Para-kanã* boys were observed playing with bows and arrows made by their fathers. Seven- to eleven-year-old boys were once observed being encouraged by their fathers to help kill, with their small arrows, a wild cat the adults had captured; when they succeeded, the fathers laughed in approval (Gosso 2010). Boys were also observed helping their fathers fish with their hands, and a group of very young children was observed while helping the father to cover the house by preparing the straw to be bundled (Silva 2014, personal communication).

Contemporary indigenous communities' ways of life and subsistence are not very different from their counterparts' in the sixteenth and seventeenth centuries; in turn, they are quite distant from ways of life and subsistence of contemporary families living in large urban centers. The contrast high-lights the intimate relationship between ways of life and cultural values, atti-tudes and practices related to childhood and parenting. Indigenous fathers are not concerned with disciplining, educating, or training their children; they trust them to acquire the knowledge and abilities they will need in adult life through ample opportunities to observe and participate in adult life. Their tolerance and patience with children's needs and limitations do not mean that they love their children better than other fathers do. These attitudes and views are allowed by and compatible with their ways of living and related cultural values.

FINAL REMARKS

An adequate synthesis of the current status of Brazilian research on father-ing is the title of Bastos et al.'s chapter "Fathering in Brazil: a diverse and unknown reality" (Bastos et al. 2013). "Unknown" applies to the limited coverage of Brazilian socioeconomic-cultural contexts and family configura-tions in the literature specifically targeted at fathering. "Diverse" describes differences observed even in similar socioeconomic contexts when some background and contextual aspects are examined, as well as the diversity of methodological options in terms of sampling and research tools.

Despite these limitations, a few general statements can be suggested. A trend toward a new fathering style that moves away from the traditional roles of the father as provider and main authority in moral and economic issues can be identified in the attitudes and practices reported in several studies. The move appears to respond mainly to economic and social changes resulting from women's entrance in the labor market, which disrupted the legitimacy of the separation between the male public space and the female domestic realm and of male economic power as the basis of paternal authority. The contemporary fathering style is still undergoing a process of construction.

There is no prevalent model of a new fatherhood, and in most Brazilian families, there is probably no evidence of change (Cerveny & Chaves 2010). The literature suggests, however, that core characteristics of the new father are affective expression and increased proximity with the child's daily life, besides some availability to share domestic and caregiving tasks.

Similar to what usually occurs with other cultural changes, the emergence of a new fathering model is more noticeable in more educated and affluent segments of society and in the younger generations. In low-income families, parental roles are more traditional than in middle- and upper-middle-class families (Moreira et al., in press). In the particular case of this cultural change that involves gender roles, more resistance would be expected in social environments in which the male identity is often defined by or identified with authority, strength and even violence. It may be recalled here that even some middle-class fathers expressed their difficulties searching for a fathering style that would not mirror mothering (Sutter & Bucher-Maluschke 2008).

Cerveny and Chaves (2010) explicate this concern by asking: "Can the traditional father figure be dismissed without damage to the male identity?" To wit: Changes in fathering styles also involve changes in women's identity, which is so strongly marked by maternity. A young mother whose partner was a very participative father used to complain, half humorously, that all she was needed for was breastfeeding. Although mothers interviewed about their partners' participation in child care may wish more active participation by the father, the extent to which they allow it is ultimately in their hands, as aptly pointed out by Cerveny and Chaves (2010).

The nature of the ideal parents' involvement with the child changes along the developmental stages from basic care in early childhood to education in the school years, to guidance in adolescence and reciprocal help and companionship in adulthood (Cerveny & Chaves 2010). The challenges involved in the move from traditional fathering to a new fathering style seem to rest mainly in participation in physical care in the first years, traditionally performed—and controlled—by female caregivers, and in the interactional style of education and guidance. In every stage, however, attentiveness and affective expression appear as core components of the "new father," and these may also offer some difficulty for the reconstruction of the male identity.

A recurrent issue in the Brazilian literature on fathering is the need for public policies that promote caregiving and affective experiences for men and fathers, particularly with respect to their access to health services related to pregnancy, birth and early childhood, but also to their participation in the child's school life. Cerveny and Chaves (2010) suggest, further, that school curricula could include, equally for both genders, content related to child care and domestic chores as an attempt to restore the value of the domestic universe and modulate the intergenerational transmission of gender roles in the direction of a new model of fathering.

A more participative and affective fathering style not only lessens the mother's workload, but also can reward the father with life experiences of which the traditional paternal model deprives men. Resuming the words of some interviewed fathers, it can make them better persons.

NOTE

1. These books are available in English under the titles *The Masters and the Slaves: A Study in the Development of Brazilian Civilization, The Mansions and the Shanties: The Making of Modern Brazil*, and *Order and Progress: Brazil from Monarchy to Republic*.

REFERENCES

Bastos, A. C. S., Pontes, V. V., Brasileiro, P. G., & Serra, H. M. (2013). Fathering in Brazil: a diverse and unknown reality. In D. W. Schwalb, B. J. Schwalb & M. E. Lamb (eds.) *Fatherhood in Brazil, Bangladesh, Russia, Japan and Australia* (pp. 228–249). New York/London, UK: Routledge.

Benetti, S. P. C., & Roopnarine, J. I. (2006). Paternal involvement with school-aged children in Brazilian families: Association with childhood competence. *Sex Roles, 55*, 669–678.

Bittelbrun, E. E., & Castro, M. G. (2010). Sou pãe! Reflexões sobre os pais que educam/criam sozinhos seus filhos [I am a fa/mo-ther! Reflections on solitary fathering]. In L. V. C. Moreira, G. Petrini & F. B. Barbosa (eds.) *O pai na sociedade contemporânea* (pp. 225–238). Bauru, Brazil: EDUSC.

Bossardi, C. N., Gomes, L. B., Vieira, M. L., & Crepaldi, M. A. (2013). Engajamento paterno no cuidado a crianças de 4 a 6 anos [Paternal engagement in the care of 4–6-year-old children]. *Psicologia Argumento, 31*(73), 237–246.

Brasil (1988). *Constituição da República Federativa do Brasil* [Brazilian Federal Constitution]. Brasília, Brazil: Senado.

Brasileiro, P. G. L., Pontes, V. V., Bichara, I. D., & Bastos, A. C. S. (2010). A transição para a paternidade e a paternidade em transição [Transition to fatherhood and fatherhood in transition]. In L. V. C., Moreira, G. Petrini & F. B. Barbosa (eds.), *O pai na sociedade contemporânea* (pp. 145–165). Bauru, Brazil: EDUSC.

Bustamante, V., & Trad, L. A. B. (2005). Participação paterna no cuidado de crianças pequenas: um estudo etnográfico com famílias de camadas populares [Paternal participation in young children's care: an ethnographic study with low income families]. *Cadernos de Saúde Pública, RJ, 21*(6), 1865–1874.

Cardim, F. (1980). *Tratados de terra e gente do Brasil* [On Brazilian land and people]. São Paulo, Brazil: EDUSP.

Carvalho, A. M. A., Moreira, L. V. C., & Rabinovich, E. P. (2010). Olhares de crianças sobre a família: um enfoque quantitativo [Children's conceptions of family: a quantitative approach]. *Psicologia, Teoria e Pesquisa, 26*(3), 417–426.

Castro, M. G., Carvalho, A. M. A., & Moreira, L. V. C. (eds.). (2012). *Dinâmica familiar do cuidado: afetos, imaginário e envolvimento dos pais na atenção aos filhos* [Dynamics of care in the family: Affects, imagery and engagement of parentes with respect to their children]. Salvador, Brazil: EDUFBA.

Castro, M. G., & Souza, H. P. (2012). O imaginário sobre mudanças na divisão sexual do trabalho doméstico de pais e mães de distintas inscrições socioeducacionais e gerações—Salvador. [Imagery on changes in the sexual division of domestic labor of mothers and fathers from different socioeducational and generation status]. In M. G. Castro, A. M. A., Carvalho & L. V. C. Moreira (eds.), *Dinâmica familiar do cuidado: Afetos, imaginário e envolvimento dos pais na atenção aos filhos* (pp. 267–327). Salvador, Brazil: EDUFBA.

Cerveny, C. M. O., & Chaves, U. F. (2010). Pai? Quem é este? A vivência da paternidade no novo milênio [Father? Who is he? The experience of paternity in the new millenium]. In L. V. C. Moreira, G. Petrini & F. B. Barbosa (eds.), *O pai na sociedade contemporânea* (pp. 41–51). Bauru, Brazil: EDUSC.

Chaves, A. M. (2000). Os significados das crianças indígenas brasileiras (séculos XVI and XVII) [The meanings of Brazilian indigenous children (16th and 17th centuries)]. *Revista Brasileira de Crescimento e Desenvolvimento Humano, 10,* 1–26.

Cohn, C. (2002). A experiência da infância e o aprendizado entre os Xikrin [The experience of childhood and learning among the Xikrin]. In A. L. Silva, A. V. L. S. Macedo & A. Nunes. (eds.), Crianças Indígenas: ensaios antropológicos (pp. 117–149). São Paulo, Brazil: Global.

Dessen, M. A., & Lewis, C. (1998). Como estudar a 'família' e o 'pai'? [How to study the family and the father?]. *Paidéia (Ribeirão Preto),* 8(14–15), 105–121.

Engels, F. (2002). *Origens da família, da propriedade privada e do estado* [Origins of family, private property and state]. Rio de Janeiro, Brazil: Bertrand Brazil.

Filgueiras, M. R., & Petrini, G. (2010). O pai patriarcal segundo Roberto Freyre [The patriarchal father according to Roberto Freyre]. In L. V. C. Moreira, G. Petrini & F. B. Barbosa (eds.), *O pai na sociedade contemporânea* (pp. 23–39). Bauru, Brazil: EDUSC.

Gabriel, M. R., & Dias, A. C. G. (2011). Percepções sobre a paternidade: descrevendo a si mesmo e o próprio pai como pais [Perceptions on paternity: describing oneself and one's father as a father]. *Estudos de Psicologia (Natal),* 16(3), 253–261.

Goetz, E. R., & Vieira, M. L. (2008). Diferenças nas percepções de crianças sobre cuidado parental real e ideal [Children's perceptions of real and ideal aspects of parental care when parents live together or are separated]. *Psicologia, Reflexão e Crítica,* 21(1), 83–90.

Goetz, E. R., & Vieira, M. L. (2009). Percepções dos filhos sobre aspectos reais e ideais do cuidado parental [Childen's perceptions of real and ideal aspects of parental care]. *Estudos de Psicologia (Campinas),* 26(2), 195–203.

Gomes, A. J. S., & Resende, V. R. (2004). O pai presente: o desvelar da paternidade em uma família contemporânea [The present father: Unveiling paternity in a contemporary family]. *Psicologia, Teoria e Pesquisa,* 20(2), 119–125.

Gonçalves, C. R. (2011). *Direito Civil Brasileiro,* vol. 6: *Direito de Família.* [Brazilian Civil Law, vol 6: Family Law]. São Paulo, Brazil: Saraiva.

Gosso, Y. (2010). Play in different cultures. In P. K. Smith (ed.), *Children and Play* (pp. 80–98). New York: J. Wiley.

Grzybowski, L. S., & Wagner, A. A. (2010a). Casa do pai, casa da mãe: a coparentalidade após o divórcio [Father's house, mother's house: co-parenting after divorce]. *Psicologia, Teoria e Pesquisa,* 26(1), 77–87.

Grzybowski, L. S., & Wagner, A. A. (2010b). O envolvimento parental após a separação/divórcio [Parental involvement after separation/divorce]. *Psicologia, Reflexão e Crítica, 23*(2), 289–298.

IBGE [Brazilian Institute for Geography and Statistics] (2010). *Censo Demográfico 2010* [2010 Demographic Census].

IBGE (2013). *Síntese de indicadores sociais: uma análise das condições de vida da população brasileira, 2013* [Synthesis of Social Indicators 2013]. ftp://ftp.ibge.gov.br/ Indicadores_Sociais/Sintese_de_Indicadores_Sociais_2013/SIS_2013.pdf.

Lamenza, F. (2013). Comentários dos artigos 1.591 a 1.688 [Comments on articles 1.591 to 1.688 of the Civil Code]. In C. Machado (ed.), *Código Civil interpretado: artigo por artigo, parágrafo por parágrafo* (pp. 1339–1413). Barueri, Brazil: Manole.

Lyra, J., Medrado, B., & Florêncio, M. C. (2013). Alienação parental: algo novo ou querelas familiares antigas com novas roupagens? [Parental alienation: something new or old family quarrels under new dressings?]. In L. V. C. Moreira (ed.), *Psicologia, Família e Direito: Interfaces e Conexões* (pp. 339–354). Curitiba, Brazil: Juruá.

Maybury-Lewis, D. (1990). *O selvagem e o inocente* [The savage and the innocent]. Campinas, Brazil: Editora da Unicamp.

Medrado, B., Lyra, J., Oliveira, A. R., Azevedo, M., Nanes, G., & Felipe, D. A. (2010). Políticas públicas como dispositivos de produção de paternidades [Public policies as producers of paternities]. In L. V. C. Moreira, G. Petrini & F. B. Barbosa (eds.), *O pai na sociedade contemporânea* (pp. 53–79). Bauru, Brazil: EDUSC.

Moreira, L. V. C., Carvalho, A. M. A., Almeida, V. M. P., & Oiwa, N. N. (2012). A prevalência materna e feminina no cuidado cotidiano de crianças pequenas [Maternal and female prevalence in young children's daily care]. In M. G. Castro, A. M. A. Carvalho & L. V. C. Moreira (eds.), *Dinâmica familiar do cuidado: Afetos, imaginário e envolvimento dos pais na atenção aos filhos* (pp. 1541–204). Salvador, Brazil: EDUFBA.

Moreira, L. V. C., Rabinovich, E. P., & Carvalho, A. B. (in press). A figura do pai: entre declínio e reorganização [The father figure: between decline and reorganization]. In G. Petrini, L. V. C. Moreira, M. A. R. Alcântara, & A. C. S. Bastos (eds.), *Família: recurso pessoal e social. O caso do Brasil.* Curitiba, Brazil: Juruá

Pereira, C. M. S. (2004). *Instituições de direito civil* [Civil Rights Institutions], vol. 5. Rio de Janeiro, Brazil: Forense.

Prado, A. B., Piovanetti, M. R. A., & Vieira, M. L. (2007). Concepções de pais e mães sobre comportamento paterno real e ideal [Fathers's and mothers' conceptions on real and ideal paternal behavior]. *Psicologia em Estudo (Maringá), 12*(1) 41–50.

Santos, M. C., Caldana, R. H. L., & Alves, Z. M. B. (2001). O papel masculino dos anos quarenta aos noventa: transformações no ideário [Male roles from the '40s to the '90s: changes in conceptions]. *Paidéia, 11*(20), 57–68.

Shwalb, D. W., & Shwalb, B. J. (2014). Fatherhood in Brazil, Bangladesh, Russia, Japan, and Australia. *Online Readings on Psychology and Culture.* http://dx.doi.org/10.9707/2307-0919.1125.

Shwalb, D. W., Shwalb, B. J., & Lamb, M. E. (eds.). (2013). *Fathers in cultural context.* New York: Routledge.

Silva, C. E. Personal communication, April 4, 2014.

Silva, M. R., & Piccinini, C. A. (2007). Sentimentos sobre a paternidade e o envolvimento paterno: um estudo qualitativo [Feelings with respect to paternity and
paternal involvement: A qualitative study]. *Estudos de Psicologia (Campinas)*,
24(4), 561–563.

Souza, C. L. C., & Benetti, P. C. (2009). Paternidade contemporânea: levantamento
da produção acadêmica no período de 2000 a 2007 [Contemporary paternity:
academic production from 2000 to 2007]. *Paideia, 19*(42), 97–106.

Sutter, C. C., & Bucher-Maluschke, J. S. N. F. (2008). Pais que cuidam dos filhos: a
vivência masculina na paternidade participativa [Caregiving fathers: The male
experience in participative paternity]. *Psico, 39*(1), 74–82.

Trindade, Z. A., & Menandro, M. C. S. (2002). Pais adolescentes: vivência e sig-
nificação [Adolescent fathers: experiences and meanings]. *Estudos de Psicologia
(Natal), 7*(1), 15–23.

Tudge, J. (2008). *The everyday life of young children: culture, class and childrearing in
diverse societies*. New York: Cambridge University Press.

Vieira, M. L., Crepaldi, M. A., Bossardi, C. N., Gomes, L. B., Azevedo, S. D., &
Piccinini, C. A. (2013). Paternity in the Brazilian context. http://dx.doi
.org/10.57725702.

Wagner, A., Predebon, J., Mosmann, C., & Verza, F. (2005). Compartilhar tarefas?
Papéis e funções de pai e mãe na sociedade contemporânea [Sharing tasks?
Fathers' and mothers' roles and functions in the contemporary society]. *Psicolo-
gia, Teoria e Pesquisa, 21*(2) 181–186.

4

Fathering in México

Alejandra Salguero Velázquez

CULTURAL CONTEXT OF FATHERING IN MÉXICO

As in other cultural communities around the world (see Cabrera & Tamis-LeMonda 2013), fathering in Mexico is diverse. It varies by geographic regions, sociocultural practices, beliefs and meanings related to "being a man," "being a woman," "being a father," and "being a mother," not as natural states of existence but as constructions in the context of gender. Fathering is in constant interaction with diverse forces within the family and community; it is modified and transformed through relationships with different social actors, material conditions of life, sociocultural heterogeneity, and institutional regulations. Thus, instead of talking about "fathering" as a type of predetermined universal relationship of men with their children, this chapter discusses "fatherings" in plural because of the different ways of achieving fathering responsibilities (Keijzer 1998). The view espoused here is that of generalized ideas about fathering situated as cultural practices. Accordingly, a major focus of this chapter is on what men do as fathers in certain contexts, activities, and life paths (Gutmann 2000).

Not unlike research on families and children in many other cultural settings (Georgas et al. 2006), historically, Mexican social scientists have primarily focused on the culture of motherhood and mother–child relationships. Women were presumed to be at the center of children's lives, and even when they perform economic activities and receive remuneration, motherhood, childcare, and homecare are still seen as a major part of their identity (Lagarde 1993; Lamas 1993). At the same time, there is still less importance and social value granted to the participation of Mexican men in childrearing compared to the provider role and professional success. These traditional views were aided by theoretical propositions that emphasized the mother–child bond as the foundation for later childhood development (Chodorow

1984; Bowlby 1993). Simply put, similar to other traditional cultural settings, the father was seen as less important than mothers in influencing children's psychological development in Mexico.

There are other reasons for the comparative lack of sociodemographic and psychological interest in Mexican men as fathers. Figueroa et al. (2006) and Lerner (1998) argue that reproductive behavior has implicitly or explicitly been associated with women, relegating men to a marginal position in the procreation and gestation process. Through a feminized view of reproduction, the presence of Mexican men is assumed to be secondary to fertility, contraception, care, upbringing, and health of their children. A popular view is that men's perceptions about pregnancy and childbirth are inaccurate and misinformed because of the social and psychological distance they tend to maintain from these events (Figueroa 2000). This limited and sometimes erroneous conceptualization of men has led to various forms of exclusion from participation in such events as childbirth, responsibility for family formation, household and family activities, and their relationship and commitment to their partner and children.

That fathering has not been adequately documented among Mexican men does not mean that fathers are not involved in children's lives or that they are ignored in the larger consciousness of Mexican society. Fathering occurs amid changing societal norms, the push for greater equity in gender relations, progressive discourses within families and in society at large about the rights of children and women, and the (re)constructions of expectations of the responsibilities of men toward their children and partners. These topics have received varying degrees of attention by social scientists and policymakers and within families themselves. This chapter is framed within the parameters of some of these issues.

LIFE STRUCTURE AND ORGANIZATION

On the research and policy fronts, interest in fathering in Mexico is relatively recent. At the governmental level, it was not until 2000 that the National Institute of Statistics, Geography and Informatics (INEGI), the agency responsible for generating statistical data nationwide, incorporated indicators to collect information about men and fathering. This move coincided with sociocultural transformations in the 1990s in the roles, meanings, and assessments of the scripts assigned to men and women. Although thin, these types of data are useful in providing general profiles of family formation, conjugal status, and children in different cultural communities in Mexico. For example, declining fertility rates, marriage patterns, and increasing divorce rates all offer a basis for interpreting fathering in Mexico in a changing national social and economic climate. The data presented hereafter are from the 2010 census of National Institute of Statistics, Geography and Informatics (INEGI).

In Mexico there has been a sharp decrease in the overall fertility rate from 6.5 children per family in the 1960s to 2.2 children per family in 2010. This has been attributed to several factors: the amendment to the Constitutional 4° Article, 1973, which established the right to make free, responsible, and informed decisions about how many children a person should have and the time in a person's life when this should occur; the implementation of government and health policies to regulate fertility; and media campaigns that include messages such as "*la familia pequeña vive mejor*" (small families live better) and "*ser pocos para darles más*" (few to give them more), inviting people to regulate their reproduction through the use of contraception. Currently, contraception use among women of childbearing age living with a partner is 72.5 percent.

Men's entrance into relationships and fatherhood are also changing. Although civil or religious marriage, or just civil, dominates, there have been significant changes in marriage patterns in Mexico. Civil and religious marriage has been a practice socially legitimized to bind couples together. This is gradually being replaced by civil marriage or just living together (legalized over time), which doubled from 7.4 percent in 2000 to 14.4 percent in 2010. According to Quilodrán (2001) and Vassallo (2011), "living together" in the Latin American context refers to conjugal union, a way of beginning a family without going through the legal process of civil registry or the church. For most, life as a couple begins at age 20–30. Most men prefer to live with a partner beginning at age 25, with the greatest frequency occurring at ages 35–69. Most women aged 30–74 are either married or cohabiting. About 95.4 percent of this population lives with or shares an apartment with a conjugal partner.

The proportion of couples who are separated or divorced has more than doubled, from 1.9 percent in 2000 to 5.2 percent in 2010, which represents significant transformations in the stability of family life. Differences of gender, age, motivations, and expectations have resulted in different family constellations, such as single-parent families, reconstructed families from a second or third marriage, "living apart together" families in which men and women establish a relationship without taking into consideration shared cohabitation, and same-sex families that are not documented. In November 2006, the Domestic Relationship Law (Ley de Sociedades de Convivencia) was approved, and on December 21, 2009, the Federal District Legislative Assembly approved marriage between people of the same sex in Mexico City. The same-sex marriage law was enforced in March 2010. Little research exists on gay fathers, so father–child relationship in gay men is not considered here.

Despite the emergence of different family forms, there is still a prevalence of nuclear families in Mexico (64.2% of the entire population). The most common family composition is conjugal couples with children. Most (99.8%) of the population younger than 15 live within a family: 74 percent of children live with their mother and father, 16 percent with their mother, 3 percent not with their parents, and only 1 percent with their father. As might be expected, father involvement in different family compositions varies quite a bit across cultural settings (see Carlson & Mclanahan 2010; Roopnarine & Hossain 2013). Unfortunately, we do not know much about these variations in Mexican families.

FAMILY, WORK, AND ECONOMIC ACTIVITIES

In most Mexican homes, there is a highly gendered system of household responsibilities. A majority of men are seen as family heads (56.4%), whereas childcare and household responsibilities are almost entirely assumed by women. Men as heads of their families are predominantly engaged in the breadwinner role; 91 out of 100 perform an economic activity, favoring the production of goods and services. Most men work thirty-five to forty-eight hours a week: 42 percent work forty-eight hours per week. These work patterns keep men away from children and influence when they are involved in childcare and household activities, if any (Bralic et al. 1978; García & Oliveira 2004; Gutmann 2000; Haces 2006; Jiménez 2013). Considering beliefs about Mexican men's roles within families, it is not clear to what extent fathers consider work patterns in the context of responsibility for childrearing. By comparison, 31.2 percent of women engage in economic as well as household activities. Women usually work thirty-five hours per week, permitting them some leeway to perform household activities as well. Most women (68.8%) perform multiple duties that keep the family together; they are primarily responsible for household activities, caring for their homes, and caring for the children.

Overall, different forms of family structural organization still revolve around values such as harmony, solidarity, security, care, and negotiation but are also marked by social hierarchies, manifestations of dominion, authority, and sometimes subordination by gender and age (Rabell 2009; Salles & Tuirán 1998; Ariza & Oliveira 2004; García & Oliveira 2006). The old masculinity prevails in most elements of daily life. Male privilege prevails in the execution of most roles within and external to the family in Mexico.

BELIEFS IN MEN'S ROLE AS FATHER AND THE DIVISION OF ROLES

Though Mexico has been characterized by a long tradition whereby women's role as a mother has been admired and anointed, the father's role has been largely embedded in the provider model. These identity configurations have been enhanced through social control by government, health, education, and religious institutions that have proposed that children's development falls within the domain of women and that any potential problems witnessed in children arise from deviations from these norms or that childhood problems emanate from women's decision to leave their children alone or under the care of third parties. Figueroa (1998) analyzed the results of Encuesta sobre Comportamiento, Actitud y Práctica Anticonceptiva de la Población Obrera (Encapo) (Survey on Behavior, Attitudes, and Contraceptive Practices of the Working Population) and found that men viewed their primary responsibility in the family as offering support to their wife and children; more than half disagreed that women should work outside of the home. Various reasons were given: Women might overlook their household responsibilities, women might be unfaithful, and it was men's responsibility to work and to be the provider. These data coincide with another analysis on family life dynamics provided by Ariza and Oliveira (1999), which indicated that men from different social sectors were still the providers; the economic contribution of women was acknowledged as important to the family but was not socially recognized. The general belief that women who perform activities that depart from those related to their home tend to overlook their responsibilities toward their home and children is still fully entrenched in the Mexican male psyche.

Nationwide coverage of education, women's increased entry into school and productive work have all contributed to changes in the social structure of the family and spousal relationships. Studies show that paid work creates important changes in women's identity as they imbue themselves with greater decision-making power, freedom of movement, and increased autonomy and self-esteem, all of which help transform daily practices between men and women at home (Benería & Roldán 1992; Casique 2004; García & Oliveira 1994). Changes in both women and men include modifications to continuity in gendered cultural patterns, arrangements regarding time, household activities, and care and upbringing of children (García & Oliveira 2006). However, there is a constant. Although gainfully employed, women perform a greater share of household activities while at the same time raising and educating the children (García & Oliveira 1994). This often results in dilemmas and conflicts between women and men, who do not always establish constructive negotiations and make meaningful agreements about family and work responsibilities (Montiel et al. 2008).

Paid work gets women out of the home, and they face the challenge of meeting different and competing commitments at work and in the family. This has led to dynamic shifts in negotiations concerning childcare responsibilities during working hours. In the absence of domestic support, the strategies generated still place most of the childcare responsibilities on women. Though some men hold on to power and control over the family, others have faced the need to change, arguing that they participate in household activities and in the care of the children because their partner was upset or threatened to leave them (García 2007; Salguero & Pérez 2011a). This transition has not been easy, for it represents a different path from the way men learned to be men and fathers in their families of origin (Salguero 2007).

TRANSITIONS, CHANGES, AND CONTINUITIES IN FATHERING

Fathering as a sociocultural practice has evolved over time. Knibiehler (1997, p. 117) states that "in each turn of civilization in the past there were new parents" that incorporated meanings, models, and images of the father, which are part of the social, political and ideological system historically constituted and which conform to the context in which the activity of men as fathers is organized.

In Mexico, the activities and relationships that men establish with their children should be conceptualized within frameworks of change and continuity. Rabell (2009) refers to two models of fathering: the classic patriarchal (authoritarian, rigid and hierarchical) versus the relational (more equitable, democratic, and flexible). There is some movement from patriarchy toward a system based on respect for a more relational approach that is premised on trust and shared gender roles. However, such changes are not comprehensive and do not happen suddenly, so it is more accurate to refer to transitions or displacements in men's roles. Esteinou (2004, p. 253) notes that "when talking about changes we face a difficult task, not only for the different definitions, but for their degree of intensity and direction." In fathering practices, we may find changes in activities and time devoted to children, but they may vary according to generic meanings about women, men, motherhood, fathering, and family dynamics. In some instances, changes and continuities may occur simultaneously. For example, a man may participate in activities with his children and assume little responsibility for household activities. Interaction with children may symbolize a change from the traditional model, but it may underestimate the lack of father involvement as a coparticipant in household activities. Thus, in the face of change, there is permanence and continuity of some traditional roles. Perhaps looking at transitions might better inform us about new patterns of paternal participation in Mexico.

To examine transitions, changes, and continuities in men's activities as fathers, several researchers (Esteinou 2004; Gutmann 2000; Keijzer 2000; Rojas 2000; Salguero 2002; Torres 2002) have examined differences in fathering across generations. Through interviews of men from different socioeconomic levels it was established that in their families of origin, the role structure was traditional—not a surprising outcome considering the belief systems of Mexican parents already described. More specifically, participants' fathers' fathering was very often characterized by a responsible father at work, an economic provider. The relationship between father and child was authoritarian, emotionally and communicatively inexpressive. In other words, authority and discipline were represented by the father, and the mother was responsible for daily relationships, education, care, and upbringing of the children. The father represented responsibility, discipline, and the requirement of meeting goals. But the mother was the one who gave permission for children to go out to play, assisted at children's parties, and organized relationships with children's friends. As children grew into adolescence, the authority of the father was present; he was the one who gave permission to stay out late, to be out with friends, to go to parties or on a trip. The mother acted as a go-between for daughters—negotiating with fathers to obtain permission for daughters to engage in different social activities. Moreover, it was the mother who was involved in everyday disciplinary practices through limit setting and the establishment of rules, constant supervision, and instillation of values through focused care and affection. Most of the time, the means to instill discipline in children was through threats, yelling, scolding, humiliation, guilt, and physical punishment. Against this backdrop of traditional roles in previous generations, transformations in family dynamics and structure have resulted in some role reorganization between men and women in terms of their identity as mother and as father. Because of demands from mothers/partners and children, the authoritarian posture may be changing. Fathers have less latitude to threaten, hit, or impose their will on children today (Salguero 2002). Dialogue and explanations are used more frequently in childrearing. This approach is strengthened by schools that offer conferences and courses on parenting. As part of their program, "school for parents" discusses discipline techniques, the establishment of limits and the follow-up of rules through encouragement and rewards, and acknowledgment of goals and objectives. Negotiation is encouraged. Flexibility and the display of affection in mother–child and father–child relationships are stressed.

Along with changes in parenting practices, transitions are also evident in internal working models of performing fathering. Some men report that they do not want to repeat the story they lived with their fathers. They take strides toward being more flexible and expressive. Being an economic provider is still important, but Mexican men increasingly recognize that being a father also includes communicating with and building a close relationship with children. Respect for adults is not unidirectional, but reciprocal. Equally important is the value placed on children, their needs, opinions, and personal, cognitive, and emotional development. Today, "it is not enough to be a father, it is important to be a good father" (Salguero 2002, p. 201).

COMPLEX IDENTITIES: WIFE/MOTHER/WORKER AND HUSBAND/FATHER/WORKER

By comparing traditional and contemporary ways of conceptualizing roles within families, obvious conflicts have arisen between mothers and fathers. A major source of tensions between partners is negotiating time and responsibility for activities to balance work and family life and at the same time recognize the professional development needs of women and men while taking into account the welfare of the family. Within modernity, this has resulted in some modifications in gender roles and the construction of complex identities as mother/wife/worker and father/husband/worker. The newer roles and identities in Mexican men and women intersect and involve movement in cognitive constructions between them. These shifts are far from uniform and likely reflect diverse modification processes where both men and women pursue pathways that result in different outcomes that range from egalitarianism to the maintenance of traditional roles. In constructing new meanings, the ideal would be that men are able to discover their role as fathers through positive emotional and cognitive engagement with children while fulfilling their economic responsibility toward them.

It is in the arena of the development of internal working models that move away from affirming masculinity and family control to participation in meaningful and equitable relationships with children and partner that new father identities are constructed and articulated. Achieving and attaining a new identity as a father and provider is not automatic and is likely accomplished after several attempts at revising old schemas about men's roles as fathers. This may require concerted effort to be and be there as a man, partner, father, and worker. Admittedly, some men may attribute more significance to work roles, but others may consider it essential to define and incorporate identities that consider it much more important to be with their family and children, and to construct different forms of identity in their practice as men/fathers/workers (Salguero & Pérez 2011a).

THEORETICAL-METHODOLOGICAL FRAMEWORKS FROM WHERE MEN'S ROLES AS FATHERS HAVE BEEN CONCEPTUALIZED

As stated already, the study of what Mexican men say and do as fathers is relatively recent and has its roots in questioning derived from feminist work about generic naturalness and inequality. In social science disciplines, such as anthropology, demography, sociology, and psychology, questions were raised about the generic order "naturally" assigned to women in the private sphere of the home (upbringing and education of children) and men in the public sphere (work and economic provision). It was necessary to point out that historically such order has been a central part of household arrangements and sociocultural practices and that the dichotomous separation generated social inequity. This encouraged research activity on matters related to masculinity and fathering as sociocultural practices from a relational approach to gender (Alatorre & Luna 2000; Figueroa 1999; Fuller 2000; Gutmann 2000; Hernández Rosete 1996; Jiménez 2003; Keijzer 2000; Nava 1996; Núñez 2007; Rojas 2000; Salguero 2002).

An important part of the theoretical–methodological work on Mexican fathers has been derived from masculinity studies. The construction process of male identities includes elements related to power, freedom, sexuality, lack of emotions and feelings, constant worry over the job situation, the possibility of being a father, and of reconstructing an identity as men in shared relationships with children and partner (Gutmann 2000; Salguero 2008; Vivas Mendoza 1996). Historically, the fixed and generalized identity about masculinity of men in Mexico has been characterized by *machismo* stereotypes of male dominance and control (Gutmann 1998). This portrayal has been confronted not only in the academic arena, but also by men who state that "machismo is in the past, now it is different," likely referring to sociocultural changes and ways of being a man and a father in the present.

The predominant theoretical approaches are embedded in constructivism, arguing that fathering is a sociocultural construction with different meanings in different historical moments, differs from culture to culture, and even within the same culture depending on ethnicity or class (Chaudhary 2013; Fuller 2000), or within a man, depending on age, moment, and conditions in which he becomes a father. Thus we cannot speak about fatherhood as being singular, but rather of diverse ways of being a father, alluding to the processural and emergent character of being a man and father (Gutmann 2000; Keijzer 1998; Roopnarine 2013; Salguero & Pérez 2011a). Likewise, eschewing a unified view of masculinity, feminist critical theory (e.g., Clatterbaugh 1997) highlighted diversity in lifestyles and laid the foundation that guided interest and efforts to document not generality but particular conditions that may account for the specificity of ways of acting and living as a man and as a father. The challenge is to document the processural character regarding lifestyles, meanings, activities, dilemmas, and conflicts in doing fathering.

Qualitative methodology has been fundamental to research on Mexican men as fathers. It is a search not for laws or generalizations, but for a sense and meaning that men assign to their actions as a father. In this sense, ethnographic work, deep or semistructured interviews, life stories, and focus groups have been valuable tools to document men's own voices in the socialization and learning processes. This has revealed much needed insights into the difficulty men encounter in living with gender stereotypes acquired from their families of origin and have had to learn once again about roles and relationships from their partner and children about newer meanings about fathering (Jiménez 2013; Gutmann 2000; Núñez 2007; Rojas 2007; Salguero 2007; Salguero and Pérez 2011a).

RESEARCH ON DIVERSE ROLES OF MEN AS FATHERS: SOCIAL-EMOTIONAL AND COGNITIVE INVESTMENT IN CHILDREN'S LIVES

Fathering can be seen as a set of possible relationships that may exist between a father and his children, without relegating it to a biological issue. Relationships can involve the provision of affection, care, and guidance, as well as economic support (Figueroa 2000). Men may assume or move between one or more roles depending on economic conditions, family constellation, and the nature and social agreements about the dynamics in relationships among family members. Whereas in the past children may have lived without the exhaustive care of their mother or father (Ariès 1987), nowadays there is more focus on the way a man lives as a father and the importance given to childhood.

It is from the modern concept of childhood that fathering in Mexico is conceived. Children have come to occupy a central place in the family, educational, and other institutions within society, as their needs, health, and welfare are emphasized. The child-centered focus in socialization highlights optimal experiences and positive developmental outcomes for children which has diversified and expanded the tasks linked to fathering. The sense and meaning granted to childhood, mothering, and fathering are influenced by institutional discourses, even by theories and "expert" opinions, generating a professionalization and technologization of parental functions. The relationship between mother–child and father–child has invited scrutiny from family members, researchers from diverse disciplines (e.g., pediatrics, psychology, sociology), and policymakers, all of whom advocate for a new and engaged fatherhood.

De Mause (1994) has argued that the concept of "child socialization" and "help" comes from the middle of the twentieth century, when it was proposed that the child needed to be taught, trained, and guided in every stage of life. Salinas (2002) and Cillero (2007) further emphasize that in addition to showing interest in children's overall welfare, it was important to recognize two more needs: children's right to develop not only physically, but intellectually, emotionally, and socially, as well as their right to be treated with dignity and respect. With the adoption of the Convention of the Rights of the Child (CRC) in 1989, a culture of childcare has been established and is being spread based on fundamental, civil, and child protection rights agreed on in the Mexican United States Constitution, 4° Art., Law for the Protection of the Rights of Children and Adolescents, 11° Art., and international organizations (CEPAL 2002; UNICEF 2007).

Much of the research literature on fathers in Mexico has targeted men in the process of identity construction as fathers. It was found that they deploy forms of participation beyond a role; men participate and enjoy the close verbal and physical contact with their children, are coparticipants in care activities, perform some household activities, and are economic providers. Researchers (Haces 2006; Jiménez 2003; Nava 1996; Rojas 2006; Salguero 2006) have shown the diverse ways of being and doing fathering in low- and middle-urban areas. They have identified the complexity that represents being a father today. As noted earlier, being a provider and an authority figure is not enough. Fathers must share time and activities with their partner and children, being aware of their needs, being tender, and expressing emotions and feelings. The latter is not easy, because very often men's experiences with their own fathers were not ideal models of fathering. In everyday activities and in their relationship with their children and partner, there are doubts, uncertainties, fears, and contradictions. Men try different ways of being fathers, learning through trial and error. Most of the time, they rely on the feedback they receive from their partners and children about their performance as fathers.

To construct father identity means new responsibilities and commitments, to participate in a constant learning process, creating stories of mutual commitment, shared responsibility, shaping a way of being and living in the new situation as a father of a child, and participating in new activities. Questions are always present, no matter the quantity of information on parenting tips on how to be a good father. The transition to becoming a father leads to a constant search whereby men rehearse and construct ways of fathering, incorporating improvisations based on their experiences and on available cultural resources, and arising in response to the position the person displays in the present (Holland et al. 1998). It involves an effort to find benchmarks that enable them to understand that they are performing in an unknown area most of the time. Regarding new father identities, Salguero and Pérez (2008) introduced the immigrant metaphor to highlight the variety of matters that have to be negotiated to know how to live in such unknown territory. This becomes apparent when men abandon the traditional role of being nothing more than a provider. That is what is being negotiated and produced as identity—an identity improvised with what is at hand.

Father identity is part of a continuous learning process of co-construction. Lave and Wenger (2003) emphasize the opportunities and resources that parents access in practice that enable them to construct identities for themselves. It is through the experiences among father, mother, children, and significant others that identity is constructed and family difficulties are prioritized and solved. In other words, fathering identity is affected not only by how mothers and fathers guide/lead/influence children, but also by how much and in the diverse ways that children influence their parent's development and fathering per se. The daily relationships with children provide a platform for fathers to learn to be tolerant, less demanding, and listening, addressing difficult issues and noting that their children have changed them as fathers.

Attempting to be different from socially accepted norms that are characterized by gender stereotypes regarding what men and women should do in families can invite criticisms. In daring to be "different," mothers and fathers attack established stereotypes, create uncertainty, and question how they are supposed to be, leading to a constant process of negotiating identities as woman/mother/worker and as man/father/worker. Alarcón (2013) notes that the reconciliation of identities becomes necessary, for complex practices as fathering and mothering are designed in terms of being good parents, having a satisfactory relationship with a partner, and being able to remain as individuals having one's own professional, social, and cultural interests. It is a process that generates stress but that at the same time may produce creative approaches to facing and addressing stress. It is necessary to emphasize that there is no single way of accomplishing this; each couple weighs, balances, and decides their own course.

In view of what was said above, it becomes necessary to document the construction process of multiple gender identities, multiple forms of being a father and their complexities. Understanding gender roles involves confronting the homogeneous view of men or fathers in Mexico, placing the point of interest in the processual character, and in the particular conditions in which men live and construct their fathering identities (Gutmann 2000). This requires documenting activities and forms of relationships with children (Esteinou 2004; García & Oliveira 2004; Nava 1996); analyzing the diversity of ways in which men perform as fathers (Figueroa et al. 2006; Keijzer 1998); identifying meaning and practices of fathering (Alatorre & Luna 2000); exploring differences in parenting (Torres 2002); and analyzing particular forms of parenting with children with disabilities (Ortega et al. 2011); determining the links among sexuality, reproduction, and parenthood (Jiménez 2003); being parents, husbands, and children (Figueroa et al. 2006); and assessing dilemmas and conflicts in mothering and fathering (Salguero & Pérez 2011a) among others.

FATHER INVOLVEMENT AND CHILDREN'S DEVELOPMENT

Along with prior exposure to conceptions and practices of parenting, father involvement is constructed as the joint effort with a partner and is influenced by the quality of the relationship between them. For most, this process of paternal engagement begins from the moment the couple thinks about having a child and decides to become pregnant. When pregnancy is confirmed, it represents a very emotional moment, the possibility of achieving what has been expected for some time. More and more Mexican men accompany their partner during initial and follow-up visits to the gynecologist and talk to their child through the abdomen of their partner. They also read books and journals providing tips on how to be fathers.

The birth moment represents an important event in a man's life. In Mexico, private hospitals encourage paternal participation in the birth of children; the public health system does not permit men's assistance during the birthing process, even though its importance has been widely documented (e.g., Astone & Peters 2014; Habib & Lancaster 2006). Thus from the beginning, most Mexican men assume different paths toward paternal involvement. Some directly participate in the baby's care by preparing the milk bottle or in feeding depending on the child's age. They get involved in physical, mental, and emotional activities; express how they feel toward their children by hugging and kissing them; and arrange for children to participate in art and cultural activities. Others are companions to children when they are doing homework and assist in scheduling activities in school (Alatorre & Luna 2000).

Because men devote more time to their jobs, they tend to interact with their children in the mornings when they wake up, during breakfast, when they bring children to school or nursery school, and at night after coming home from work or on weekends. Only a few men are able to share meal time with their children, most being at work. In families in which both parents work, the support from family networks becomes essential. Fathers and mothers rely on grandmothers, aunts, or other relatives for childcare support. Other families use daycare centers when children are young, or enroll older children in private schools that take care of children in the evenings. The private schools promote such services as "support for doing homework" to relieve parents of some of the educational responsibilities they would normally assume after work (Ariza & Oliveira 1999; Esteinou 2004).

Development is a part of increasingly complex interaction processes with socializing agents and multiple sets of relationships that influence physical, cultural, social, emotional, and cognitive development (Baumrind 1983, 1996; Bronfenbrenner & Morris 2006; Leo-Rhynie & Brown 2013; Marlowe 2005; Super & Harkness 2002). Depending on the path, development stage, and gender of the child paternal involvement varies considerably (Torres 2002). For instance, to gain a sense of independence, the activities adolescents share with fathers require less physical presence and more dialogue. This represents a challenge for fathers, as children think they need much more time to be alone but at the same time require parental guidance—perhaps in more silent ways (Hernández Rosete 1996; Nava 1996; Rojas 2000; Parke 1986; Power & Parke 1981; Salguero 2002).

In Mexico, as research on men and their role as fathers is recent, specific data about paternal involvement and links to childhood development are sparse. However, because of insistence from educational institutions and diverse organizations, such as Salud y Género, A. C. (Civil Association Health and Gender) and Colectivo de Hombres por Relaciones Igualitarias A. C. (Coriac) (Civil Association Men's Collective for Equal Relations), which paved the way for the establishment of Viento a Favor in Oaxaca;- Corazonar; Abriendo Senderos hacia la Reconciliación, A. C; Movimiento de Hombres por Relaciones Equitativas y Sin Violencia (Mhoresvi); Hombres por la Equidad, A. C. (Civil Associations as Wind in support to Oaxaca; Opening Paths to Reconcialiation; Mens Movement for Equal Relations and without Violence; Men for Equity) in Mexico City; and Academia Mexicana de estudios de Género de los Hombres (AMEGH) (Mexican Academiy of Gender Studies Men) there is increased attention to research on fathers motivating personal, institutional, and social change in ways of being a man and a father (Ramírez & Cervantes 2013).

Mexican fathers are visualized in children's learning, by inhibiting behaviors that may be unsuitable for themselves and for others, and by encouraging the acquisition of those behaviors that society demands, such as usefulness and consideration for others, self-fulfillment, acceptance of responsibilities, and general acquisition of skills that may facilitate socially proper functioning as children, adolescents, and adults. Through the continuous care, attachment, and emotional support fathers provide, they are considered as having important influences in the social, affective, and cognitive development in the life of their children (see volume by Lamb 2010). The diverse involvement and investment is reflected in better grades in school and lower rates of disciplinary sanctions, and school failure. Furthermore, depending on quality, father presence and involvement have consequences for the psychic and social structure of children, for decreasing addictive behaviors, and for promoting the development of personal limits and the ability to develop social ties (Barker & Verani 2008).

Quality relationships between partners and engagement in constructive negotiations about modes of participation (Figueroa 2000; Pruett 2001) can only bolster involvement with children when behaviors such as empathy, tolerance, and consideration are displayed. Ruiz (1997) conducted a series of interviews in which he found that men situate the fathering process as bidirectional: There is a sense of elation when children express their affection toward their father, feeling proud of him and wanting to be with him. But such patterns of involvement are often mediated by women's participation and insistence that men become more involved with their children in meaningful ways (Gutmann 2000; Haces 2006; Salguero & Pérez 2011b).

FUTURE DIRECTIONS AND POLICY IMPLICATIONS

Some of the commitments established at the International Conference on Population and Development held in Cairo (1994) and the IV World Conference of Women in Beijing (1995) have helped increase the focus on men's roles in families across cultures. The discussions at these conferences established international platforms to involve men in the promotion of gender equity, including greater participation of men in their roles as fathers, insistence on greater assumption of parenting and housework responsibilities by men, and active participation in responsible fathering (Figueroa 1998, 1999; Lerner 1998; Barker & Verani 2008). Clearly, the location of the subject of men in the political agenda highlights the novelty and importance of changes in father's roles as a social matter, and not merely a private issue confined to families.

In the Central American context, the Economic Commission for Latin America and the Caribbean (ECLAC) suggests that with changes in family dynamics and structure in recent decades, the relevance of the traditional model of fathering should be questioned. In Mexico, there is great resistance from government agencies to dealing with subjects related to gender, men, and fathering. Their social relevance is viewed with skepticism, and regulatory frameworks help to perpetuate a traditional model of men's roles. Admittedly, the shift from a father figure focused exclusively on economic contribution and vertical exercise of authority to a fathering conception that includes relationships based on affection and closeness with children occurs slowly and faces cultural, psychological, and social resistance. Nevertheless, there is greater awareness to conduct studies on fathering that generate initiatives in structural public policies in education, health, and work.

Within Mexico, the legal framework refers to "the custom and tradition of the Mexican family" without taking into consideration the diversity of family forms. It does not refer to the international commitments Mexico has subscribed to regarding responsible fathering (children's and women's rights). Instead of meeting international criteria, as commitments acquired by the State, the legal reasoning tends to preserve what is assumed as custom and tradition. Regrettably, the reforms so far included in Mexican legislation are limited and isolated. There are still gender biases in state civil codes regarding responsible fathering. In legal terms, responsible fathering is restricted to maintenance obligations and recognition of filiations. Men as fathers beyond economic procurement and their involvement in the care, attention, and affective relationship with their children are not covered in any Mexican legal construction. Such oversight represents some of the failures in law enforcement in Mexico and constitutes a breach of implementing mechanisms that ensure children's rights and the economic and emotional welfare of Mexican women (CEAMEG, H. Chamber of Deputies 2007).

WORK–LIFE BALANCE

As long as men as fathers are not seen beyond their role as providers and lack benefits related to family care in their places of employment, it would be difficult for them to realize the potential of engaged fathering. The responsibility of caring for children will continue to fall on women. A pending issue is to devise policies in Mexico that assist families to balance work and family responsibilities. For example, flexible work hours and daycare provisions might help to reduce role strain in the family in general and encourage men to become more involved in childcare and household work.

FATHERING LEAVE, FATHERING CARE, NURSERY: A MATTER OF RIGHTS

It should be considered a right for fathers to be granted permission to take care of their children during the newborn period or to take care of older children when a new child arrives in the family. Father involvement in the care of children when a couple enters parenthood not only has implications for father–child relationship but couple relationships and mental health as well (e.g., Treyvaud et al. 2010). Even though it was agreed by the chamber of deputies to grant fathers leave for ten days with pay, there is no obligation under the constitution and federal labor law to recognize this right. In practice, some institutions grant such permits, usually for three to ten days. The relevance of this law lies in the official recognition of men's rights to enjoy their children's birth. There is an obvious need to incorporate paternal leave into the federal labor law for fathers to take care of their children and for couples to make informed decisions regarding time and activities that affect their children's health needs and well-being.

According to federal labor law in Mexico, the right to nursery schools is only granted to working women. Needless to say, similar measures should be taken to grant this right to men to access such services. Even though this service is available in the enterprises that men work in, under the feminized logic of care, only women have this right. The importance of a father leave permit, father care and right to nursery service would most likely lead to responsible fathering and would signal a breakthrough regarding labor laws for men, with a route to gender equity in opportunities and the exercise of family rights (Jiménez 2003; Salguero & Frías 2001).

RIGHT TO FREE, ENJOYABLE FATHERING WITHOUT RISKS

The discussion in terms of family rights, questions gender inequalities that men live when they are excluded from important events in the reproduction and fathering process. Moreover, emphasis on the provider role and the difficulties associated with work limits the focus on the contributions that men make to their families. Work-related challenges can also impinge on fathers' physical and psychological health, which, in turn, can influence men's level and quality of involvement with children (Figueroa 2011; Jiménez & Tena 2007). Unfortunately, in Mexico, there is still a lack of public policies and laws that inspire transformations in the area of family relationships. Efforts are still incipient in the legal system bound to promote a reflexive, responsible, equitable, and democratic exercise of fathering.

In institutional terms, it is essential to promote the generation of public policies aimed at promoting fathers' involvement, participation, and closeness with their children. It is equally important to continue with efforts, beginning from the different actors and sectors of the society, to modify gender stereotypes; to construct more committed, responsible, and participatory father identities that enhance children lives and partner relationship; and to make men able to realize and enjoy optimal fathering through the lens of a shared relationship with their children day by day and moment by moment throughout the lifespan.

Education is an important impetus for change and can transform thinking related to the need to get involved in the care and upbringing of children as shared activities within flexible roles (García & Oliveira 2004). It is essential to challenge the cultural patterns of gender and to demonstrate the cost of generic practices that exclude, stigmatize, and limit women and men to segmented spaces and that deny the exercise of rights. However, it is also necessary to create intervention strategies and public policies. In this regard, campaigns, forums, public debates, workshops, and local, regional, and international collaboration networks can apply pressure to modify laws and legal norms with application to issues such as male identity, sexual, and reproductive health, fathering, definitions of family, gendered division of work, intimate relationships, and gender violence (Ramírez & Cervantes 2013).

Another possibility is to incorporate the gender equality perspective and transversalize it in the different educational, labor, and governmental institutions, so that the practices and spaces historically assigned to men and women are denatured. Ayala (2006) proposes citizen participation in education that leads to awareness about gendered subjects. The project and campaign of fathering performed in 1997, whose objective was to recognize the father figure experienced by children, young individuals, and the experience of fathers, yielded significant outcomes in the generation of working nets to guide fathers and mothers in nonviolent conflict resolution. Programs that focus on engaged parenting can achieve similar results for men in an ever-changing social climate in Mexico.

Much still needs doing with respect to fathering in Mexico. But we have made significant strides not only in regard to questioning men's roles in families, but also in influencing academic study and research and working with men in nongovernmental organization and in different diffused spaces where different ways of being a man and a father can be presented. The academic field has generated important knowledge about the sociocultural practices of men and fathers. However, these advances need to be articulated in terms of the mobilization of men and groups interested in promoting equality and equity, and placed at the governmental level for the generation of public policies. Qualitative studies developed until now are valuable, but it is important to generate quantitative and systemic information on fathers to aid decision-making among those responsible for the design and implementation of public policies that positively affect social and family life.

ASSOCIATIONS PROVIDING ASSISTANCE TO PARENTS AND FAMILIES

Corazonar, A. C. Civil association that provides counseling and psychological support to people in their experience as parents, improving the relationship with their families. www.corazonar.org.

Hombres por la equidad, A.C. (Civil Association Men for Equity). For a responsible, equitable and free from violence to our families fathering. www.hombresporlaequidad.org.mx.

Movimiento de Hombres pos Relaciones Equitativas y Sin violencia MHORESVI (Men's Movement for Equitable Relations and without Violence). mhoresvi.wordpress.com.

Paternidad Responsable. Institute guiding parents who want to help their children, offering counseling, therapeutic care and courses. www.paternidadresponsable.com.mx.

Salud y Género, A. C. Health and Gender Civil Association. Improving the health and quality of life of women and men from the perspective of gender equality and human rights. http://saludygeneroqueretaro.blogspot.mx.

Sistema para el Desarrollo Integral de la Familia del Estado de México (DIF) (System for Integral Family Development of the State of Mexico). http://portal2.edomex.gob.mx/difem/pades_de_familia.

REFERENCES

Alarcón, I. (2013). Volverse adulto en la contemporaneidad: diversificación de senderos [Becoming adult in the contemporary: diversification of paths]. In G. Perez & J. Yoseff (eds.), *Desarrollo psicológico. Un enfoque sociocultural [Psychological development. A sociocultural approach]* (pp. 109–126). Iztacala, México: UNAM, FES.

Alatorre, J., & Luna, R. (2000). *Significados y prácticas de la paternidad en la ciudad de México [Meanings and practices of fatherhood in Mexico City].* PUEG-UNAM: México.

Ariès, P. (1987). *El niño y la Vida Familiar en el Antiguo Régimen [The child and family life in the old regime].* Madrid, Spain: Taurus.

Ariza, M., & Oliveira, O. (1999). *Trabajo, familia y condición femenina: una revisión de las principales perspectivas de análisis [Work, family and status of women: A review of the main perspectives of analysis]* (pp. 89–127). Toluca: Universidad Autónoma de Estado de México.

Ariza, M., & Oliveira, O. (2004). Universo familiar y procesos demográficos [Familiar universe and demographic processes]. In Ariza y Oliveira (eds.), *Imágenes de la familia en el cambio de siglo [Images from family at the turn of the century]* (pp. 9–45). Mexico City: UNAM.

Astone, N. M., & Peters, H. E. (2014). Longitudinal influences on men's lives: Research from the Transition to Fatherhood Project and beyond. *Fathering, 2,* 161–177.

Ayala, G. (2006). De la educación a la política pública [From education to public policy]. In G. Careaga & S. Cruz Sierra (eds.), *Debates sobre masculinidades. Poder, desarrollo, políticas públicas y ciudadanía [Debates on masculinities: Power development, public policy and citizenship]* (pp. 337–352). Mexico City: PUEG-UNAM.

Barker, G., & Verani, F. (2008). *La participación del hombre como padre en la región de Latinoamérica y el Caribe: una revisión de literatura crítica con consideraciones para políticas* [Male involvement as a parent in the Latin America and the Caribbean: a review of critical literature with regards to policies]. Sao Paulo, Brasil: Promundo–Save the Children.

Baumrind, D. (1973). The development of instrumental competence through socialization. In A. D. DIC. (ed.): *Minnesota Symposia on Child Psychology,* vol. 7 (pp. 3–46). Minneapolis: The University of Minnesota Press.

Baumrind, D. (1996). Parenting: The discipline controversy revisited. *Family Relations, 45,* 405–414.

Benería, L., & Roldán, M. (1992). *Las encrucijadas de clase y género. Trabajo a domicilio, subcontratación y dinámica de la unidad doméstica en la ciudad de México [The crossroads of class and gender: Work at home, subcontracting and dynamics of the household in the city of Mexico].* Mexico City: El Colegio de México.

Bowlby, J. (1993). *El vínculo afectivo [The affective bond].* Barcelona, Spain: Paidos.

Bralic, S., Haeusler, I., Lira, M., Montenegro, H., & Rodríguez, S. (1978). Experiencias tempranas y desarrollo infantil [Early experiences and child development]. In *Estimulación Temprana: Importancia del ambiente para el desarrollo del niño [Early stimulation: Importance of the environment for the child's development]* (pp. 38–56). Santiago de Chile: UNICEF.

Bronfenbrenner, U., & Morris, P. A. (2006). The bioecological model of human development. In R. Lerner (ed.), *Handbook of child psychology,* 6th ed. (pp. 793–828). Hoboken, NJ: Wiley.

Cabrera, N., & Tamis-LeMonda, C. (eds.). (2013). *Handbook of father involvement.* New York: Routledge Press.

Carlson, M., & McLanahan, Sara S. (2010). Fathers in fragile families. In Michael E. Lamb (ed.), *The role of the father in child development* (pp. 241–269). New York: Wiley.

Casique, I. (2004). *Trabajo femenino, empoderamiento y bienestar de la familia [Female employment, empowerment and family welfare].* Editado por UCSD Center for U.S.–Mexican Studies. Latin American Studies Association, San Diego, CA: University of California San Diego.

CEAMEG (2007). Colección Género y Derecho. H. Cámara de Diputados, México: Autor, www3.diputados.gob.mx/camara/CEAMEG.

CEPAL (2002). *Propuesta de indicadores de paternidad responsable. Educación reproductiva y paternidad responsable en el Istmo Centroamericano [Proposed indicators of responsible parenthood: Reproductive education and responsible fatherhood in Central America].* Santiago de Chile: CEPAL.

Chaudhary, A. R. (2013). "Franchises." In V. Smith (ed.), *The Sociology of Work: An Encyclopedia.* Thousand Oaks, CA: Sage Publications.

Chodorow, N. (1984). *El Ejercicio de la Maternidad [Motherhood exercise].* Barcelona, España: Gedisa.

Cillero, M. (2007). *El interés superior del niño en el marco de la Convención Internacional sobre los Derechos del Niño [The interests of the child under the International Convention on the Rights of the Child].* www.observatoriosocial.com.ar/proyectos/ proelinteres.pdf.

Clatterbaugh, K. (1997). *Contemporary perspectives on masculinity: Men, women and politics in modern society.* Boulder, CO: Westview Press.

De Mause, L. (1994). La evolución de la infancia [The evolution of childhood]. In *Historia de la Infancia [History for Children].* Madrid, Spain: Alianza.ECLAC (2002). Economic Commission for Latin America and the Caribbean. Indicators proposal of responsible parenthood. http://repositorio.cepal.org/bitstream/ handle/11362/25583/LCmexL542_es.pdf?sequence=1

Esteinou, R. (2004). La parentalidad en la familia: cambios y continuidades [Family parenting changes and continuities]. In M. Ariza & O. Oliveira (eds.), *Imágenes de la familia en el cambio de siglo* (Images of the family in the new century) (pp. 251–281). Mexico City: UNAM.

Figueroa, J. G. (1998). La presencia de los varones en los procesos reproductivos; algunas reflexiones [The presence of men in reproductive processes: some reflections]. In Susana Lerner (ed.), *Varones, sexualidad y reproducción [Men, sexuality and reproduction]* (pp. 163–189). Mexico City: El Colegio de México.

Figueroa, J. G. (1999). Fecundidad, anticoncepción y derechos reproductivos [Fertility, contraception and reproductive rights]. In Brígida García (ed.), *Mujer, género y población en México [Women, gender, and population in Mexico]* (pp. 61–101). Mexico City: El Colegio de México.

Figueroa, J. G. (2000). Algunos elementos del entorno reproductivo de los varones al reinterpretar la relación entre salud, sexualidad y reproducción [Some elements of reproductive males environment to reinterpret the relationship between health, sexuality and reproduction], *Revista Mujer Salud, Santiago de Chile, Red de salud de las mujeres latinoamericanas y del Caribe* no. 3, 60–72.

Figueroa, J. G. (2011). Paternidad, mortalidad y salud: ¿es posible combinar estos términos? [Fatherhood, mortality and health: Is it possible to combine these terms?] In *Estudios sobre varones y masculinidades para la generación de políticas públicas y acciones transformadoras [Studies on men and masculinities for the generation of public policies and transformative actions]* (pp. 71–78). IV Coloquio

Internacional de Estudios sobre Varones y Masculinidades, Montevideo. Montevideo, Uruguay: UNFPA-ONU.

Figueroa, J. G., Jiménez, L., & Tena, O. (2006). Introducción. Algunos elementos del comportamiento reproductivo de los varones [Introduction: Some elements of the reproductive behavior of males]. In Figueroa et al., *Ser padres, esposos e hijos: prácticas y valoraciones de varones mexicanos* (Parenting, husbands and children: Practices and valuations of Mexican men) (pp. 9–53). Mexico City: El Colegio de México.

Fuller, N. (2000). Significados y prácticas de paternidad entre varones urbanos del Perú [Meanings and parenting practices among urban males in Peru]. In Norma Fuller (ed.), *Paternidades en América Latina [Fatherhoods in Latin America]* (pp. 35–90). Pontificia Universidad Católica del Perú, Fondo Editorial.

García, B. (2007). *Cambios en la división del trabajo familiar en México [Changes in the division of family labor in Mexico]* (pp. 23–45). Toluca: Universidad Autónoma del Estado de México.

García, B., & Oliveira, O. (1994). *Trabajo femenino y vida familiar en México [Women's work and family life in Mexico]*. Mexico City: Colegio de México.

García, B., & Oliveira, O. (2004). El ejercicio de la paternidad n el México urbano [The exercise of fatherhood in urban Mexico]. In M. Ariza & O. Oliveira (eds.), *Imágenes de la familia en el cambio de siglo [Images family in change of the century]* (pp. 283–318). Mexico City: UNAM.

García, B., & Oliveira, O. (2006). *Las familias en el México metropolitano. Visiones femeninas y masculinas [The families in the metropolitan Mexico: Male and female views]*. Mexico City: El Colegio de México.

Georgas, J., Berry, J. W., van de Vijver, F. J. R., Kagitcibasi, C., & Poortinga, Y. H. (2006). *Families across cultures: A 30-nation psychological study.* Cambridge, UK: Cambridge University Press.

Gutmann, M. (1998). El Machismo. Masculinidades y Equidad de Género en América Latina [Machismo: Masculinities and gender equity in Latin America]. In Teresa Valdés & José Olavaria (eds.), *Masculinidades* (pp. 238–257). Santiago de Chile: FLACSO.

Gutmann, M. (2000). *Ser Hombre de Verdad en la Ciudad de México. Ni macho ni mandilón [Being a Real Man in Mexico City: Neither male nor mandilón]*. Mexico City: El Colegio de México.

Habib, C., & Lancaster, S. (2006). The transition to fatherhood identity and bonding in early pregnancy. *Fathering, 4*, 235–253.

Haces, Á. (2006). La vivencia de la paternidad en varones del Valle de Chalco [The experience of fatherhood of men of Chalco Valley]. In Figueroa et al., *Ser padres, esposos e hijos: Prácticas y valoraciones de varones mexicanos [Being parents, spouses and children: Practices and ratings of Mexican men]*.Mexico City: El Colegio de México.

Hernández Rosete, D. (1996). *Género y Roles familiares: la voz de los hombres [Gender and family roles: The voice of the man]*. Tesis para obtener el grado de Maestro en Antropología Social. Centro de Investigaciones y Estudios Superiores en Antropología Social. Mexico City: CIESAS.

Holland, D, Lachicotte, W., Skinner, D., & Cain, C. (1998). *Identity and agency in cultural worlds.* Cambridge, MA: Harvard University Press.

Instituto Nacional de Estadística, Geografía e Inormática. (2010). Censo de población y vivienda. www.inegi.gob.mx.

Jiménez, M. L. (2003). *Dando voz a los varones. Sexualidad, reproducción y paternidad de algunos mexicanos [Giving voice to men. Sexuality, reproduction and parenthood of some Mexicans].* Cuernavaca, Morelos, México: UNAM, CRIM.

Jiménez, M. L. (2013). Reflexiones sobre ser proveedor en la crisis económica y del empleo. Impactos desde la perspectiva de género [Reflections on being a supplier to the economic crisis and employment: Impacts from the gender perspective]. In J. C. Ramírez & J. C. Cervantes (eds.), *Los hombres en México. Veredas recorridas y por andar [Men in Mexico. Traveled paths and walking]* (pp. 53–70). Zapopan, Jalisco, México: CUCEA- AMEGH.

Jiménez, M. L., & Tena, O. (2007). *Reflexiones sobre masculinidades y empleo [Reflections on masculinities and employment].* Cuernavaca, Morelos, México: UNAM, CRIM.

Keijzer, B. (1998). Paternidad y transición de género [Fatherhood and gender transition]. In Beatriz Schmukler (ed.), *Familias y Relaciones de Género en Transformación. Cambios trascendentales en América Latina y el Caribe [Families and Gender Relations in Transformation. Major changes in Latin America and the Caribbean]* (pp. 301–325). Mexico City: EDAMEX/Population Council.

Keijzer, B. (2000). Paternidades y transición de género [Fatherhoods and gender transition]. In Norma Fuller (ed.), *Paternidades en América Latina [Fatherhoods in Latin America]* (pp. 215–240). Lima: Pontificia Universidad Católica del Perú.

Knibiehler, I. (1997). Padres, patriarcado, paternidad [Parents, patriarchy, parenthood]. In Silvia Tubert (ed.), *Figuras del padre [Figures of father]* (pp. 117–135). Madrid, España: Ediciones Cátedra.

Lagarde, M. (1993). *Los cautiverios de las mujeres: madresposas, monjas, putas, presas y locas. [The captivity of women: madresposas, nuns, sluts, dams and crazy].* Tlanepantla, Estado de México, México: UNAM.

Lamas, M. (1993). La lucha por los derechos reproductivos [The struggle for reproductive rights], *Fem, 16*(122), 14–15.

Lamb, M. E. (ed.). (2010). *The role of the father in child development,* 5th ed. Hoboken, NJ: Wiley.

Lerner, S. (1998). Participación del varón en el proceso reproductivo: recuento de perspectivas analíticas y hallazgos de investigación [Male involvement in reproductive process: count analytical perspectives and research findings]. In Susana Lerner (ed.), *Varones, Sexualidad y reproducción [Men, Sexuality and reproduction]* (pp. 9–46). México City: El Colegio de México..

Lave, J., & Wenger, E. (2003). *Aprendizaje Situado. Participación Periférica Legítima [Situated learning: Legitimate peripheral participation].* Tlanepantla, Estado de México México: UNAM/FES Iztacala.

Leo-Rhynie, E., & Brown, J. (2013). Child rearing practices in the Caribbean in the early childhood years. In C. Logie & J. L. Roopnarine (eds.), *Issues and perspectives in early childhood education in the Caribbean.* La Romaine, Trinidad and Tobago: Caribbean Publishers.

Marlowe, F. (2005). Who tends Hadza children? In B. S. Hewlett & M. E. Lamb (eds.), *Hunter-gatherer childhoods: Evolutionary, developmental, and cultural perspectives* (pp. 175–213). New Brunswick, NJ: Aldine Transaction Publishers.

Montiel, P., Salguero, A., & Pérez, G. (2008). El trabajo: ¿fuente de conflicto en el ejercicio de la paternidad? [Work: source of conflict in the exercise of parenthood?]. *Psicología y Ciencia Social, 10*(1), 2008, Fecha de Impresión del Volumen 1–2, noviembre de 2009, 26–40.

Nava, R. (1996). Los hombres como padres en el Distrito Federal a principios de los noventa [Men as fathers in Mexico City in the early nineties]. Tesis de Maestría en Sociología. Mexico City: FCPyS UNAM.

Núñez, G. (2007). Vinculo de pareja y hombría: "atender y mantener" en adultos mayores del Río Sonora, México [Link partner and manhood "meet and maintain" in older adults Rio Sonora, Mexico]. In A. Amuchástegui & I. Szasz (eds.), *Sucede que me canso de ser hombre . . . : Relatos y reflexiones sobre hombres y masculinidades en México [It happens that I get tired of being a man . . . Stories and reflections on men and masculinities in Mexico]* (pp. 141–184). Mexico City: El Colegio de México..

Ortega, P., Torres, L., & Salguero, A. (2011). Parenthood and social evaluation of special children. *International Journal of Hispanic Psychology, 3*(2), 283–292.

Parke, R. (1986). *El papel del padre.* Serie Brunner. Madrid, Spain: Ediciones Morata.

Power, T. G., & Parke, R. D. (1981). Play as a context for early learning: Laboratory and home analyses. In Laosa & Sigel (eds.), *Families as learning environments for children* (pp. 147–178). New York: Plenum Press.

Pruett, K. (2001). *El rol del padre. La función irreemplazable [The role of the father: The irreplaceable role].* Buenos Aires, Argentina: Vergara.

Quilodrán, J. (2001). *Parejas conyugales en transformación [Conjugal couples transformation].* Mexico City: El Colegio de México.

Rabell, C. (2009). *Tramas familiares en el México contemporáneo. Una perspectiva sociodemográfica [Frames family in contemporary Mexico. A sociodemographic perspective].* Mexico City: UNAM; El Colegio de México.

Ramírez, J. C., & Cervantes, J. C. (2013). Estudios sobre la masculinidad y políticas públicas en México. Apuntes para una discusión [Studies on masculinity and public policies in Mexico: Notes for a discussion]. In J. C. Ramírez & J. C. Cervantes (eds.), *Los hombres en México. Veredas recorridas y por andar [Men in Mexico: Traveled paths and walk]* (pp. 201–222). Zapopan, Jalisco, México: CUCEA-AMEGH.

Rojas, O. L. (2000). La paternidad y la vida familiar en la ciudad de México, un acercamiento cualitativo al papel desempeñado por los varones en los ámbitos reproductivo y doméstico [Parenting and family life in the city of Mexico: A qualitative approach to the role of men in reproductive and domestic areas]. Tesis Doctor en estudios de población. Mexico City: El Colegio de México, A. C., Centro de estudios demográficos y de desarrollo urbano.

Rojas, O. L. (2006). Reflexiones en torno a las valoraciones masculinas sobre los hijos y la paternidad [Reflections on male judgments about children and parenting]. In Figueroa et al. (eds.), *Ser padres, esposos e hijos: Prácticas y valoraciones de varones mexicanos [Be fathers, husbands and sons: Practices and ratings of Mexican men]* (pp. 95–119). Mexico City: El Colegio de México.

Rojas, O. L. (2007). Criar a los hijos y participar en las labores domésticas sin dejar de ser hombres: un estudio generacional en la ciudad de México [Bringing up children and participate in housework while still being men: a generational study in the city of Mexico]. In Ana Amuchástegui & Ivonne Szasz (eds.), *Sucede que me canso de ser hombre . . . Relatos y reflexiones sobre hombres y masculinidades en México [It happens that I get tired of being a man . . . Stories and reflections on men and masculinities in Mexico]* (pp. 519–562). Mexico City: El Colegio de México.

Roopnarine, J. L. (2013). Fathers in Caribbean cultural communities. In D. Shwalb, B. Shwalb, & M. E. Lamb (eds.), *Fathers in cultural context* (pp. 203–227). New York: Routledge.

Roopnarine, J. L., & Hossain, Z. (2013). African American and African Caribbean fathers. In C. Tamis-LeMonda & N. Cabrera (eds.), *Handbook of father involvement*. New York: Routledge.

Ruiz, R. (1997). La construcción de la paternidad y la maternidad en nuevos padres y madres. [The construction of fatherhood and motherhood new parents]. Tlanepantla, Estado de México: Tesis UNAM. FES-Iztacala.

Salguero, M. A. (2002). Significado y vivencia de la paternidad en el proyecto de vida de los varones [Meaning and experience of paternity in the draft male life]. Tesis Doctoral. Mexico City: Universidad Nacional Autónoma de México.

Salguero, M. A. (2006). Significado y vivencia de la paternidad en algunos varones de sectores socioeconómicos medios en la Ciudad de México [Meaning and experience of paternity in some males of middle socioeconomic sectors in the City of Mexico]. In Figueroa et al. (eds.), *Ser padres, esposos e hijos: Prácticas y valoraciones de varones mexicanos [Be fathers, husbands and sons: Practices and ratings of Mexican men]*. Mexico City: El Colegio de México.

Salguero, M. A. (2007). Preguntarse como ser padre, es también preguntarse como ser hombre: reflexiones sobre algunos varones [Wondering how to parent and how to be a man: Reflections on some men]. In Ana Amuchástegui & Ivonne Szasz (eds.), *Sucede que me canso de ser hombre . . . Relatos y reflexiones sobre hombres y masculinidades en México [It happens that I get tired of being a man . . . Stories and reflections on men and masculinities in Mexico]* (pp. 563–599). Mexico City:: El Colegio de México.

Salguero, M. A. (2008). *Identidad masculina. Elementos de análisis en el proceso de construcción [Masculine identity. Elements of analysis in the construction process]*. Tlanepantla, Estado de Mexico, México: UNAM, FES Iztacala.

Salguero, M. A., & Frías, H. (2001). Reflexiones en torno a la paternidad responsable y la crianza de los hijos [Reflections on responsible fatherhood and parenting]. In J. G. Figueroa (ed.), *Elementos para un análisis ético de la reproducción [Elements for an ethical analysis of reproduction]* (pp. 275–302). Mexico City: Porrúa.

Salguero, M. A., & Pérez, G. (2008). La paternidad en los varones: Una búsqueda de identidad en un terreno desconocido. Algunos dilemas, conflictos y tensiones [Paternity in men: A search for identity in unknown terrain. Some dilemmas, conflicts and tensions]. *Revista Internacional de estudios sobre masculinidades*, 3(4; January–April), 1–18.

Salguero, M. A., & Pérez, G. (2011a). *Dilemas y conflictos en el ejercicio de la maternidad y la paternidad [Dilemmas and conflicts in the exercise of motherhood and fatherhood]*. Tlanepantla, Estado de México, México: UNAM, FES-Iztcala.

Salguero, M. A., & Pérez, G. (2011b). La paternidad en el cruce de perspectivas: El discurso reflexivo de padres y madres [Fatherhood at the intersection of perspectives: The reflexive discourse of parents]. *GénEros*, 18(9)/Época 2, 35–56.

Salinas, L. (2002). *Derecho, género e infancia. Mujeres, niños niñas y adolescentes en los Códigos Penales de América Latina y el Caribe Hispano [Legal claim, gender and childhood: Women, children and adolescents in the Penal Codes in Latin*

America and the Hispanic Caribbean]. Bogotá: UAM-Universidad Nacional de Colombia-UNIFEM.

Salles, V., & Tuirán, R. (1998). Cambios demográficos y socioculturales: familias contemporáneas en México [Demographic and cultural changes: Contemporary families in Mexico]. In B. Schmukler (ed.), *Familias y Relaciones de Género en Transformación [Families and Gender Relations in Transformation]* (pp. 83–126). Mexico City: EDAMEX/Population Council.

Super, C., & Harkness, S. (2002). Culture structures the environment for development. *Human Development, 45,* 270–274.

Torres, L. E. (2002). Ejercicio de la paternidad en la crianza de hijos e hijas [Parenting practices in raising children]. Tesis doctoral. Mexico City: Universidad Nacional Autónoma de México.

Treyvaud, K., Anderson, V. A., Lee, K. J., Woodward, L. J., Newnham, C., Inder, T. E., Doyle, L. W., & Anderson, P. J. (2010). Parental mental health and early socio-emotional development of children born very preterm. *Journal of Pediatric Psychology, 35:* 768–777.

UNICEF. (2007). Presentación de la Convención sobre los Derechos del Niño [Presentation of the Convention on the Rights of the Child]. www.unicef.org/spanish/crc/.

Vassallo, J. (2011). ¿Leyes patriarcales para parejas modernas? La regulación legal de las parejas conyugales en Latinoamérica [Patriarchal laws for modern couples? The legal regulation of marital partners in Latin America]. In Quilodrán (ed.), *Parejas conyugales en transformación [Transformation conjugal couples]*. Mexico City: El Colegio de México.

Vivas Mendoza, M. W. (1996). Vida doméstica y masculinidad [Domestic life and masculinity]. In María de la Paz López (ed.), *Hogares, familias: desigualdad, conflicto, redes solidarias y parentales [Households, families: inequality, conflict, and parental solidarity networks]*. Mexico City: Sociedad Mexicana de Demografía (Somede).

Europe and North America

5

Contemporary Fatherhood in Sweden: Fathering across Work and Family Life

Lars Plantin

Sweden has for a long time been characterized by the implementation of an active and radical gender equality policy, with one manifest intention being that of modernizing Swedish parenting. In the late 1960s, Sweden became the first country in the world to adopt an official policy for equality between the sexes. At the beginning of the 1980s, the first minister with special responsibility for gender equality issues was appointed. The goal of this gender equality work has been not only to strengthen mothers' rights to work and financial independence, but also to create opportunities for fathers to assume a more active responsibility in all areas of the everyday life of the family. This "double emancipation" is thus about ensuring that women and men are given the same opportunities in both work and family life. In order to realize this objective, the Swedish welfare state has assumed a major responsibility and offers a range of different forms of support; first and foremost, today's parents have access to a well-developed and highly subsidized childcare system, as well as to a very generous system of parental insurance.

From an international comparative perspective, there are good grounds for saying that Swedish parents, both mothers and fathers, have been given unique opportunities to strike a balance between individual wishes and needs relating to their working lives and the joint responsibilities associated with having children (Bäck-Wiklund & Plantin 2007; Plantin & Bäck-Wiklund 2009). The Swedish parental insurance system, for example, introduced in 1974, gives all fathers the opportunity to stay at home with their child for eleven months during the period before the child's eighth birthday, as well as to receive compensation amounting to 80 percent of their salary while they do so. This may be seen as constituting a unique political signal marking the reproductive responsibility of the male, and it is something that has greatly influenced the expectations that exist in relation to men's parenting in Sweden. In spite of this, the fatherhood research shows that a shift toward these ideals of improved gender equality is not occurring as quickly as one might expect. The number of parental leave days used by men remains relatively low, and men continue to occupy a more central position than women as providers—and do significantly less household work than mothers (SCB 2014). At the same time, the situation has not remained static, and there are many indications that fathers are gradually moving toward the ideals of greater gender equality and a more caring approach to fathering in both their attitudes and behaviors. The amount of parental leave used by men has more than doubled over the past fifteen years, for example, and they are now devoting more time to their children than they used to (SCB 2012).

There is thus much to suggest that high levels of central government support to parents are important but by themselves may not be sufficient to guarantee change. What, then, influences men's perceptions and experiences of parenthood? How do the attitudes and behaviors of fathers change over time—and, perhaps most important, how can we understand this at the theoretical level? In this chapter, I attempt to provide some answers to these questions in my discussion of fathering in Swedish society. I start out by describing the emergence of fatherhood research in Sweden and how the research focus has shifted over time. After that, I discuss the process of becoming a dad—the different expectations and the careful planning that underpin the decision to become a father. Following this discussion, I present a picture of how fathers combine work and family life with the support of the parental leave system. Finally, I describe men's participation and involvement in internal family work, care of children, and involvement in household work in everyday life.

THE EMERGENCE OF FATHERHOOD RESEARCH IN SWEDEN

The emergence of fatherhood research in Sweden must be understood in the light of Sweden's unique welfare policy context. The gender equality debate that took place in relation to the "double emancipation" of the 1970s and 1980s contributed to directing a major focus on men, masculinity and the traditional fathering role. It was thus not strange that much of the early research on men and fathers was clearly linked to the issue of gender equality. In one of the first, and more extensive, studies of Swedish men, it was noted that a majority were in principle positive toward gender equality, both within the family and at work (Jalmert 1984). It was also noted that men had a clearly negative attitude toward the use of corporal punishment and that they often emphasized the importance of an active, caring form of fatherhood. Strikingly, the men often felt that they were unable to live up to these views for various reasons. Different factors linked to the men's individual situations made it difficult for them to act in accordance with their positive views on gender equality. The author of the study therefore coined the expression "the Swedish in-principle-man," a concept intended to symbolize both the sluggishness of the pace at which men were changing and their ambivalence toward the new expectations being placed on them (Jalmert 1984). Swedish fathers were thus branded as being modern in their rhetoric but traditional in their actions. Talking and doing fatherhood were two different things.

In parallel with this research, there also developed a strong interest in a number of psychological dimensions of fatherhood, particularly those linked to the relationship between fathers and their children (Åström 1990; Hwang 1985; Lamb et al. 1982). In line with this interest, during the 1990s research also came to adopt a more therapeutic approach, discussing the difficulties faced by men in connection with the changes required to move closer to what was often described as a "more androgynous" ideal. The principal concern related to how men would cope with being both "macho" and "velour dads" (Hagström 1996) and how they, faced with the very powerful influence of pro-feminist ideologies, would be able to get in touch with their "true," "natural," and "genuine" masculinity (Högberg 1995). The background to these ideas lay in an intensified debate during the 1980s on the increasing number of divorces, broken homes, and fathers who had no contact with their children. In the wake of the successive development of the feminist movement, conservative men's groups felt that men had experienced a loss of status in family life and that masculinity had become far too feminized. One special area of concern was the way in which young boys were viewed as showing signs of having a fragile gender identity, formed without the guidance of the adult male experience. The growing presence of criminal youth gangs and "hypermasculine" acts of excessive violence were often explained by referring to the absence of a clear frame of reference in the current view of masculinity (Plantin 2001).

This perspective never established a firm foothold in Sweden, however, and quickly became criticized for being essentialist and reactionary from the perspective of gender equality policy. Above all, it was felt that men returning to their "true, natural, and genuine" role within the family involved a risk that this would simply lead to men retaining a patriarchal dominance over women. Instead, a more social constructivist oriented approach to research on fathers emerged, clearly inspired by contemporary studies that discussed the diversity of multiple *masculinities* (Connell 1995). In these studies, fatherhood was viewed not as something predetermined or static, but rather as something that was formed actively and in interaction with both the immediate environment and structural factors (Bangura Arvidsson 2003; Berg & Johansson 1999; Bergman & Hobson 2002; Chronholm 2004; Plantin 2001). Here the focus was directed at emphasizing the differences between fathers in relation to class, age, the family and work situation or the relationship to one's own parents, and at how this generated different fathering practices. This theoretical point of departure has since retained a dominant position in the Swedish fatherhood research to the present day.

Over recent decades, much of the Swedish research on fathers has also had a strong focus on the effects of society's different regulatory and support systems. The research on parental leave, and on how it is negotiated both within the family and at work, is today extensive, as is the research on whether the Gender Equality Act is being implemented in working life (Bekkengen 2002; Haas & Hwang 2000; Haas, Allard, & Hwang 2002; Haas & Hwang 2007). By contrast, there is little research focused on other forms of support, such as how grandparents, siblings, friends or work colleagues constitute sources of support in various ways in the lives of fathers. Thus the questions posed by the research community are greatly influenced by childcare in Sweden being viewed as a shared responsibility between parents and the state. In turn, this has naturally also affected the contents of the following presentation of what we know about today's Swedish fathers.

THE DECISION TO BECOME A DAD—HIGH EXPECTATIONS AND CAREFUL PLANNING

Against the background of the extensive societal changes witnessed over recent decades, with increased demands placed on having a higher education and increasing competition in the labor market, it is relevant to begin by asking the following questions: How do the young men of today view the opportunities for both becoming a parent and simultaneously establishing themselves in the labor market? Do they want to have children? If so, how many?

Studies in this area show that a majority of the young adults in Sweden today have a positive attitude toward having children, even if they are choosing to have them increasingly later in life (SCB 2009; Ungdomsstyrelsen 2003). The average age at which men have their first child is 31, whereas the corresponding age for women is 29 (SCB 2011). The increasingly delayed initiation of parenthood has also meant that the time between the first, second, or third child has become shorter, more or less halved. Thus people are having children later in life and within a shorter period. In spite of this, the Swedish ideal remains that of having two children (Engwall 2005; Socialdepartementet 2001). There are certain sex and class differences in views of when people want to have children, however. Men are generally somewhat less inclined than women to actively develop an attitude toward having children, and parents who are planning a shorter educational career have children earlier than those who are planning to spend more time in education (Schmidt 2008).

The path to becoming a parent appears to follow a partially preplanned course, despite the increased freedom to choose and the individualization associated with life in late modernity. The majority feel that becoming educated, testing different jobs, and becoming established on both the housing and labor market fronts all constitute important prerequisites for having children (Duvander 2000; SCB 2009; Socialdepartementet 2001). Finding a place in the labor market is not entirely easy for today's young people. Statistics show that levels of unemployment are three times higher in this group than they are among adults (Schröder 2010). Similarly, it is becoming increasingly difficult to enter the housing market, and many young people today live with their parents several years after having completed upper secondary education (SCB 2008). It has become increasingly common for young people to continue into higher education and to remain in the education system for longer periods. The so-called establishment age, which specifies when women and men finally enter the labor market, has increased successively over recent decades, from approximately 20 years old at the end of the 1980s to 27 in 2011 (Ungdoms-styrelsen 2012). By extension, this means that the initiation of parenthood is being postponed and that Swedish first-time fathers are becoming correspondingly older. When one finally becomes established in the labor market, and also has children, the difficult balancing act of combining work and family life begins—to be a present parent as well as both a partner and a work colleague.

COMBINING WORK LIFE AND FAMILY LIFE

A fairly extensive body of research in Sweden now describes the everyday life of the family and the balance between work life and family life. One common conclusion drawn from studies in this field is that parents of young children often perceive themselves as finding it difficult to combine family and work. There is not enough time to meet all the expectations, both one's own and others', that are placed on working parents. What is surprising, however, is that Swedish parents who have young children—and also parents in other countries that provide high levels of welfare state support to the "double-income-family," appear to be particularly affected by this pressure (Larsson 2006; Strandh & Nordenmark 2006). In a comparative study of eight European countries, it was found that specifically Swedish parents, fathers as often as mothers, perceived themselves as experiencing more stress than others in relation to the difficulties of combining work and family life (van der Lippe et al. 2006). This might be considered somewhat remarkable, because the welfare state support provided to parents is specifically intended to minimize the conflicts between these two spheres. This argument can be turned on its head. By guaranteeing a high degree of welfare state support with the objective of strengthening the individual's freedom and opportunities both to work and be a parent, the risk that conflicts will arise increases. But what does the situation look like in practice? How do fathers use the support that is offered?

As already noted, Swedish fathers do not use the parental leave to the extent they might. As early as in the 1970s, when parental leave was introduced, it was noted that men only used a small percentage of the leave days available to them; it would take more than fifteen years before this figure rose above 10 percent. Today, 40 years after its introduction, fathers use approximately 25 percent, and mothers 75 percent, of the total number of available parental leave days. This means that Swedish men, after Icelandic men, have the highest takeup of parental leave among the Nordic countries, as well as among European countries (Duvander 2014). But the sluggishness of this trend toward a more equitable use of parental leave has been perplexing for both public sector agencies and researchers. A large number of studies have been conducted to offer plausible explanations for this phenomenon.

One explanation that has been offered refers to the persistence of a *traditional view* of the roles of fathers and mothers in the context of family life. Motherhood is still most commonly linked to the primary parenting role, not least during the child's first years, whereas fatherhood is more often associated with a secondary responsibility of care, with a stronger emphasis on providing for the family's financial and material needs (Gislason & Björk Eydal 2010). This means that many men primarily adopt a position as a "backup" for the family while the children are small. Only later, when the children are older and can play or communicate, do the men recognize a clearer fathering responsibility in relation to their children (Forsberg 2009; Plantin 2001). Another explanation focuses on inequalities in the *economic situation* of men and women. Because men often earn more and have a more firmly established position in working life than women, and because the levels of compensation in parental insurance are related to work incomes, it usually pays families better for the man to work and the *woman* to use parental leave (Plantin et al. 2003; SOU 1998). A number of parents also have difficulty calculating the relevant financial consequences of the situation and therefore do not always have a clear picture of these issues (Gislason & Björk Eydal 2010).

TABLE 5.1 Leave length with income-related compensation in 2010 (weeks)[1]

	Denmark	Finland	Iceland	Norway	Sweden
Maternity leave	18	17.5	(2)[2]	–	(2)[3]
Paternity leave	2[4]	3	–	2[5]	2[6]
Shared parental leave	32/40[7]	26.5	12	27/37[8]	51.5[9]
Father's quota	(3[10])	5[11]	12	10	8.5
Mother's quota	–	–	11	9[12]	8.5

A further explanation targets the *negative attitudes of employers* to men taking parental leave. Swedish work organisations are characterized by traditionally gender-specific norms, and employers often adopt a passive or indirectly reluctant attitude toward encouraging an increase in the extent to which men use parental leave (Haas & Hwang 2000). In times of labor shortages, however, employers tend to become more family-friendly and take more initiatives intended to increase the opportunities for men to use parental leave. This is primarily intended as a means of attracting labor. In recent years, there has been a gradual change in attitudes toward paternal leave and work. A study by Haas and Hwang (2007), for example, found that many Swedish men perceived receiving support from their employers and work colleagues with regard to being able to stay home to care for sick children or not having to work overtime.

The way the *parental insurance system is formulated* also contributes to how women and men use leave. Some argue that the system's flexibility—the way it allows leave days to be transferred between parents—in practice gives men greater opportunities than women to refrain from taking parental leave, for the traditional view of motherhood leads to an expectation that the mother will use a greater part of the available parental leave (Bekkengen 2002; Klinth 2002). With this in mind, changes have been made to the parental insurance system, and today four of the thirteen months of available parental leave can no longer be transferred to the other parent. Two of the months are exclusively to be used by the father, and two by the mother, and if they are not used by the designated parent, they are forfeited. Followups that have examined the effects of this change have shown that this restriction of parents' freedom to choose how to share the available parental leave has dramatically increased the amount of leave used by men (Försäkringskassan 2011).

Finally, there is a range of *demographic explanations* for variations in the use of parental leave. We know, for instance, that mothers and fathers use more parental leave in connection with their first child and that younger fathers and older mothers use longer periods of parental leave than others (Duvander & Eklund 2006). Similarly, immigrant fathers use fewer parental leave days than other fathers (Duvander & Eklund 2006), as do unmarried men by comparison with their married counterparts (Sundström & Duvander 2002).

A majority of these explanatory models discuss the negative influence that male hegemony and patriarchal power structures have on the use of parental leave. The range of the posited explanations, which touch upon all areas of the relational "state–market–family" triangle, shows that the issue of the patterns of parental leave use cannot be understood exclusively on the basis of a structural power perspective. Negotiations about parental leave are often more complex than this and are intimately linked to other factors, such as the economic cycle, the labor market situation, and individuals' levels of education, life experiences, and family situation (Plantin 2001). Furthermore, today we have only a weak picture of how constructions of gender, parenthood and use of parental leave are influenced by other social categories, such as social class and ethnicity (Plantin et al. 2003). Though statistical data indicate that working-class men use less parental leave than men from the middle classes, as well as that fathers who have an overseas background use less parental leave than native-born "Swedish" men (Försäkringskassan 2009; Nyman & Pettersson 2002), we know very little about the factors influencing these relationships at a deeper level.

Parental leave in connection with the birth of a child only constitutes a temporary solution to the problem of striking a balance between work life and family life. When the period of parental leave is over, when the woman or the man is to return to work, there arises a need for new adaptive strategies to combine working life with the life of the family. But in the same way as is the case in connection with the birth itself, the Swedish welfare state provides several different forms of support even here. All children in Sweden are, for example, entitled to municipal childcare provision in return for a low, government-subsidized fee, and all parents are entitled to the so-called temporary parental allowance to stay home and care for a sick child. Once again there are substantial differences between the adaptive strategies adopted by men and women and how they relate to the available welfare state support.

Men appear to adapt their work life to fit their family life to a lesser extent than women, with the majority of fathers of small children continuing to work full-time. Seventy-four percent of children aged 0–17 have a father who works full-time, whereas the corresponding figure among mothers is 42 percent. There is a tendency for fathers to focus on more short-term strategies to resolve conflicts between the demands of work life and family life (Forsberg 2009; Tyrkkö 1997). This may, for example, involve staying at home to look after a sick child, taking time off to accompany children to the dentist, or occasionally leaving work early to collect children from school or the nursery. There is no definitive knowledge of how often or to what extent men regulate their work life or family life in this way. By contrast, women are seen to employ longer-term strategies, in which work life is adapted to the life of the family to a much greater degree. Following parental leave, for example, it is common for women to reduce their working hours to part-time to devote more time to family life (Larsson 2012). Other strategies that have been identified involve working different hours, putting one's career on hold until the children are older, or delaying having children (Kugelberg 2000). These differences in adaptive strategies need not exclusively be related to gender, however, but may also be influenced by other factors, such as an individual's occupational affiliation or the organizational structure at the workplace (Lewis et al. 2009).

Plantin and Bäck-Wiklund (2009) found that an unwillingness on the part of employers to appoint replacement staff in cases of temporary absences had a powerful effect in limiting the opportunities to take part-time parental leave or to stay home for a brief period to care for a sick child. When no replacement is appointed, the individual's work tasks either pile up or spill over and affect the workload of colleagues. Individuals are therefore reluctant to stay home out of consideration of loyalty to colleagues. In the same way, many of the social workers who participated in the study stated that their loyalty to clients in difficult situations contributed to their avoiding staying at home for a number of days even though they are entitled to do so. This was attributed to the lack of replacements at work. The nature of an individual's work tasks and position in the organizational hierarchy has also been found to influence how parents manage the balance between work and family life. Individuals who have predictable, instrumental, and highly regulated forms of work have been shown to find it easier to maintain a distinction between the spheres of work and family, whereas individuals who work in projects, with people, or in different types of management position find it more difficult to make this distinction (Bäck-Wiklund & Plantin 2007).

FATHERHOOD, EVERYDAY LIFE, AND FAMILY-RELATED WORK

In a study of Swedish men conducted more than 30 years ago, it was noted that their attitudes toward paternal involvement in childcare and housework had in many ways changed more quickly than their actual behavior (Jalmert 1984). The Swedish "in-principle-man" was very positive toward becoming more involved in housework and with children but, for various reasons, often found it difficult to actually live up to this ideal. It transpired that women devoted five times as much time as men to housework and child supervision. Though men with children younger than 6 devoted somewhat more time to these areas, there was a substantial difference between men's ideas and their actions. Fifteen years later, at the end of the 1990s, a major inquiry into the gender distribution of economic power and resources was conducted in Sweden and showed that these patterns remained largely the same (SOU 1998). Broadly stated, fathers devoted only half as much time as mothers to cooking, washing dishes, and cleaning. The unequal division of household labor had certainly become less marked, but only one in ten Swedish families that had young children could be characterized as manifesting gender equality in the sense that both parents cooked, washed, and cleaned as often as one another. The move toward a more equal division of household labor between fathers and mothers was more a result of women reducing their share of the housework than it was of men increasing theirs.

The inquiry discussed a range of different explanations for the lack of further progress toward gender equality in family life. First and foremost, a persisting traditionalism was noted in views regarding the division of responsibilities between the sexes, together with an underlying hegemony whereby men actively chose not to involve themselves in certain aspects of work in the family. Men appeared to be engaged in a more limited gender equality project, which was more focused on involvement with children, and which left the responsibility of housework to women (Brandth & Kvande 1998). Björnberg (1994) came to similar conclusions, arguing that fathers tended to participate more in the "fun" aspects of family-related work, whereas the more "tedious" aspects were left to mothers. In a comparative study focused on Sweden and the United States that had been conducted some years earlier (Sandqvist 1992), it was found that Swedish fathers, unlike their American counterparts, experienced less joy and more anxiety in the time spent with their children, because they also participated to a greater extent in regular household chores. The Swedish fathers also expressed feeling more tired and irritable in the context of their parenting than the American fathers.

In the most recent survey of how the Swedish population spend their time, conducted in 2012, it was found that the differences between fathers and mothers have declined further, though the traditional gender patterns continue to persist—Swedish mothers devote more time to housework than Swedish fathers (SCB 2012). According to this study, they also spend more time with their children than fathers. This is largely because fathers spend more time in paid work than mothers. By comparison, time-based surveys showed that playing with children is more evenly distributed between parents. The same is true of reading aloud and attending various leisure time activities. Nonetheless, it should also be emphasized that time-based surveys of parents' behaviors only provide a very limited picture of everyday life. In particular, they do not capture the perceptions, the meaning creation, and the emotional components that sustain relationships among family members. That one parent devotes fewer minutes than the other to the children, for example, says nothing about what this means for the parent's relationship with the child or about how it is perceived by the child. In the following section, I take a closer look at how both fathers and children perceive their relationships with one another.

CHILDREN'S AND MEN'S PERCEPTIONS OF INVOLVEMENT IN FATHERHOOD

There are now a large number of qualitative studies, both in Sweden and internationally, showing that parenthood and family life have a deep emotional significance for today's fathers (Chronholm 2004; Dermott 2008;

Klinth & Johansson 2010; Miller 2010). Many fathers describe parenthood as a maturation process and say that their relationship with their children develops new aspects of their personality—producing greater humility or inner calm or leading them to become more patient. A greater sense of taking responsibility is also often mentioned along with improved receptiveness and empathy (Plantin 2001). Devoting time to one's children, and preferably much more time than one's own father did, is therefore regarded as important by many men (Klinth & Johansson 2010; Plantin 2001). These experiences are also echoed in cross-national studies, wherein Swedish fathers tend to rate themselves higher than other fathers in acceptance and warmth in relation to their preadolescent children (Putnick et al. 2012). Perris et al. (1985) also showed that Swedish fathers were less rejecting toward their children than, for example, Italian and Australian fathers.

These perceptions are also partly confirmed by studies that have examined fatherhood from the child's perspective. Ulf Hyvönen's doctoral dissertation *Om barns fadersbild* (On children's conceptions of the father) shows that although some children, and particularly girls, wished that their father would spend more time at home, the father was, according to the children's descriptions, "not at all a distanced and absent family father in the classic sense" (Hyvönen 1993, p. 60). Quite the reverse: The picture that emerged was one of a father who "clearly participated and was both practically and emotionally involved in the everyday life of his children" (p.139). Similar results also emerged in a large-scale study of children's social relations at age 10–12, wherein both girls and boys stated that their contact with their fathers was good (SCB 2011). Eighty percent of girls and 86 percent of boys in the same survey also stated that their father always, or almost always, had time if they wanted to talk or do something with them. Perhaps a question of greater importance is what significance this involvement on the part of fathers has for children's and youths' health, development, and well-being.

An international literature review conducted by three Swedish researchers found twenty-two large-scale studies that had specifically focused on this question (Sarkadi, Kristiansson, & Bremberg 2004). The conclusions drawn from this review indicate that fathers who involve themselves with their children have a beneficial effect on their children's mental health and social adjustment. A correlation of this kind was found in eight of the nine studies that examined the effects of fathers' involvement while including controls for the family's social background. The same effect was also found in a majority of the studies that had been conducted without the inclusion of controls for the family's social situation. At the same time, the authors emphasize that these studies are not able to clarify whether the positive effects are linked to whether the father is the child's biological parent or even whether he is a man. The same result would probably also be produced by a long-term relationship with another adult, irrespective of the adult's sex. The American fatherhood researcher William Marsiglio (1995) draws similar conclusions:

> Most scholars agree that, although fathers typically interact with their children differently than do mothers, men are not inherently deficient in their ability to parent and a father's gender is far less important in influencing child development than are his qualities as a parent.

A qualitative study of thirty Swedish fathers also asked whether they felt that their involvement with their children differs from that of the children's mothers, and whether they do things that the mothers can't do—that is, what is it that makes the fathers unique (Plantin 2001)? All of the men spontaneously answered that fatherhood was special, but they could not put their finger on what it was that made it unique. Men said that they played more physically with the children, or devoted more time to the children's leisure time activities, but admitted that this was something that both parents could do. Thus identifying aspects of fatherhood that were not socially constructed was difficult for them when they thought about their parenting.

Despite this, it is commonly assumed that young boys need "male role models"—especially young boys who grow up with only their mother. Research shows that the term "male role model" lacks clarity and has different meanings in different contexts (Johansson 2006). A traditional male stereotype of this kind is often characterized by norms, discipline, courage, physical activity and heterosexuality—a manliness that young boys are considered to need to be able to grow up and take themselves out of "the female world of childhood." This viewpoint is linked to ideas of gender differences, where "maleness" is invested with values that seem absent in "femaleness." Sometimes an opposite view of maleness is considered, which views the male as equal, emotionally sensitive, and relationship-oriented. In this discussion, men and women are seen as being alike, a perspective that challenges rather than reinforces the traditional view of gender (Johansson 2006).

CONCLUDING DISCUSSION

The picture of the research base on Swedish fathers presented above shows how fatherhood has become increasingly visible over recent decades, not least in the public and political debate. For more than forty years, Sweden has been implementing an active family policy that has produced positive conditions for parents, both men and women, to combine work and family life. It has also led to an increasing number of fathers using longer periods of parental leave and sharing responsibility for their children and the family in the context of everyday life. There are also a large number of arenas in

Swedish society in which fathers are becoming increasingly visible together with their children, dropping them off and collecting them from the nursery, at the cinema, at the park, pushing the pram in town, in cafés, shops, out in the woods, at work, and during the children's leisure time activities. The mass media are continuously presenting reports about progress or setbacks in the area of gender equality, and there are now lifestyle magazines specifically for fathers. There is thus no doubt that today's Swedish fathers are receiving a great deal of discursive support from their environment to develop a fathering role that is both more caring and more in line with gender equality ideals.

It would be incorrect to argue that these transformed conditions have replaced all the preceding fundamental traditions and structures associated with fatherhood. Society still contains a great many norms, power structures, and values that influence the behavior of both women and men in the context of their parenting. Women continue, for example, to take the primary responsibility for both children and housework in the majority of families, and it is rarer for men to have long-term strategies to adapt their working lives to fit their family lives. It thus seems that within the framework of the modern context of fatherhood, there are a range of contradictory expectations and structures that serve to both facilitate and obstruct change toward a greater degree of gender equality.

The Swedish example also shows how positive welfare state conditions are an important means of supporting fathers, they not being by themselves sufficient to produce rapid change in their attitudes and behaviors toward investment in family life. Ensuring that working life is family-friendly is at least as important, to enable fathers to, in time, become more visible at their workplaces.

NOTES

1. Duvander, A-Z., & Lammi-Taskula, J. (2011). Parental leave. In I. Gislason and G. B. Eydal (eds.), *Parental Leave, Childcare and Gender Equality in the Nordic Countries*. Tema Nord 2011, 562.

2. Obligatory leave after birth.

3. Obligatory leave before or after birth, with or without compensation.

4. Six weeks in the public sector.

5. As of July 1, 2011, the father's quota in Norway has been extended to twelve weeks.

6. Five days of father's quota = a week.

7. With full compensation/reduced reimbursement.

8. With 100% or 80% reimbursement.

9. 390 days (seven days = week). To this, in certain municipalities, can be added the opportunity to receive a childcare allowance until the child turns 3 years old. Municipalities can themselves decide whether they wish to provide childcare allowances; generally, conservative-led municipalities have done so.

10. In the industrial sector.

11. The father receives five bonus weeks if he uses two weeks of the shared portion of parental leave.

12. One might as well call at least six of these weeks "maternity leave," because the mother is not allowed to work.

SWEDISH FATHERHOOD AND GENDER EQUALITY

- https://eng.si.se/areas-of-operation/events-and-projects/equality-and-society-issues/
- www.scb.se/Statistik/_Publikationer/LE0201_2013B14_BR_X10 BR1401ENG.pdf
- https://sweden.se/society/10-things-that-make-sweden-family-friendly/

REFERENCES

Åström, L. (1990). *Fäder och söner. Bland svenska män i tre generationer.* Stockholm, Sweden: Carlsson Förlag.

Bäck-Wiklund, M., & Plantin, L. (2007). "The workplace as an arena for negotiating the work–family boundary—a case study of two Swedish social service agencies." In Crompton, R. (ed.), *Women, men, work and family in Europe.* Hampshire, UK: Palgrave.

Bangura Arvidsson, M. (2003). *Ifrågasatta fäder. Olika bilder av fäder till socialt utsatta barn.* Lund Dissertations in Social Work 13. Lund, Sweden: Socialhögskolan, Lunds universitet.

Bekkengen, L. (2002). *Man får välja—om föräldraskap och föräldraledighet i arbetsliv och familjeliv.* Malmö, Sweden: Liber.

Berg, L-E., & Johansson, T. (1999). *Den andre föräldern. Om deltidspappor och deras barn.* Stockholm, Sweden: Carlssons.

Bergman, H., & Hobson, B. (2002). Compulsory fatherhood: The coding of fatherhood in the Swedish welfare state. In Hobson B. (ed.), *Making men into fathers: Men, masculinities and the social politics of fatherhood.* Cambridge, UK: Cambridge University Press.

Björnberg, U. (1994). "Mäns familjeorientering i förändring" ur Björnberg, U. m.fl. *Janus och Genus.* Stockholm, Sweden: Brombergs.

Brandht, B., & Kvande, E. (1998). Masculinity and child care: the reconstruction of fathering. *The Sociological Review,* 46(2), May 1998.

Chronholm, A. (2004). Föräldraledig pappa : mäns erfarenheter av delad föräldraledighet . Göteborgs universitet, Sociologiska institutionen. Göteborg, Sweden: Sociologiska institutionen.

Connell, R. (1995). *Masculinities.* London, UK: Polity Press.

Dermott, E. (2008). *Intimate fatherhood: A sociological analysis.* New York: Routledge.

Duvander, A-Z. (2000). *Couples in Sweden: Studies on family and work. 2000.* Doctoral dissertation, Swedish Institute for Social Research Dissertation Series 46. Stockholm, Sweden.

Duvander, A-Z. (2014). Män, föräldraledigheten och föräldraförsäkringen. I *Män och Jämställdhet*. SOU 2014:6. Stockholm, Sweden: Fritzes förlag.

Duvander, A-Z., & Eklund, S. (2006). Utrikes födda och svenskfödda föräldrars föräldrapenningsanvändande. I P de los Reyes (red): *Om välfärdens gränser och det vilkorade medborgarskapet*. SOU 2006:37. Stockholm, Sweden: Fritze.

Engwall, K. (2005). *Drömmen om den rätta. Från single till förälder*. Stockholm, Sweden: institutet för framtidsstudier.

Försäkringskassan (2009). *Rapport om uttaget av föräldrapenning I enlighet med regeringens regleringsbrev för försäkringskassan 2009. Svar på uppdrag I regleringsbrev*. www.försäkringskassan.se.

Försäkringskassan (2011). *Föräldrapenning—försäkringsutveckling och analys. Svar på regeringsuppdrag 2011-05-02*. www.försäkringskassan.se.

Forsberg, L. (2009). *Involved parenthood: Everyday lives of Swedish middle-class families*. Tema barn. Linköping, Sweden: Linköpings universitet.

Gislason, I. V., & Björk Eydal, G. (2010). *Föräldraledighet, omsorgspolitik och jämställdhet I Norden*. Tema Nord 2010:595. Köpenhamn, Sweden: Nordiska rådet.

Haas, L., Allard, K., & Hwang, C. P. (2002). The impact of organizational culture on men's use of parental leave in Sweden. *Community, Work and Family, 5*, 319–342.

Haas, L., & Hwang, P. (2000). Programs and policies promoting women's economic equality and men's sharing of child care in Sweden. In Haas et al. (eds.), *Organizational change and gender equity: International perspectives on fathers and mothers at the workplace*. London, UK: Sage.

Haas, L., & Hwang, C. P. (2007). Gender and organizational culture: Correlates of companies' responsiveness to fathers in Sweden, *Gender and Society, 21*(1), 52–79.

Hagström, C. (1996). Becoming a father and establishing paternity. In S. Lundin and L. Åkesson (eds.), *Bodytime: On the interaction of body, identity and society*. Lund, Sweden: Lund University Press.

Högberg, Å. (1995). *En liten bok om konsten att vara pappa*. Stockholm, Sweden: Natur och Kultur.

Hwang, P. (ed.). (1985). *Faderskap*, Antologi, Stockholm, Sweden: Natur och kultur.

Hyvönen, U. (1993). *Om barns fadersbild*, Umeå, Sweden: Umeå universitet., Inst. för socialt arbete.

Jalmert, L. (1984). *Den Svenske mannen* (The Swedish man). Stockholm, Sweden: Tiden Förlag.

Johansson, H. (2006). *Brist på manliga förebilder. Dekonstruktion av en föreställning och dess praktik* (Lack of male role models: Deconstruction of a myth and its practice). Ph.D. dissertation, Göteborg, Sweden: Department of Social Work, University of Göteborg.

Klinth, R. (2002). *Göra pappa med barn. Den svenska pappapolitiken 1960–95*. Umeå, Sweden: Borea.

Klinth, R., & Johansson, T. (2010). *Nya svenska fäder*. Umeå, Sweden: Borea.

Kugelberg, C. (2000). Swedish parents at a multinational conglomerate. In L. G. H. Russell and P. Hwang (eds.), *Organizational change and gender equity: International perspectives on fathers and mothers at the workplace*. London, UK: age.

Lamb, M. E., Frodi, A. M., Hwang C. P., Frodi, M., & Steinberg, J. (1982). Mother-and father-infant interaction involving play and holding in traditional and non- traditional Swedish families. *Developmental Psychology, 18*, 215–222.

Larsson, J. (2006). *Om föräldrars tidspress—orsaker och förändringsmöjligheter.* Forskningsrapport nr 139. Sociologiska institutionen. Göteborg, Sweden: Göteborgs universitet.

Larsson, J. (2012). Studier i tidsmässig välfärd—med fokus på tidsstrategier och tidspolitik för småbarnsfamiljer. Avhandling, Göteborg studies in sociology, no 49. Göteborgs universitet: sociologiska institutionen.

Lewis, S., Brannen, J., & Nilsen, A. (2009). *Work, families and organisations in transitions: European perspectives.* Bristol, UK: The Policy Press.

Marsiglio, W. (ed.). (1995). *Fatherhood: Contemporary theory, research and social policy.* Thousand Oaks, CA: Sage.

Miller, T. (2010). *Making sense of fatherhood: Gender, caring and work.* Cambridge, UK: Cambridge University Press.

Nyman, H., & Pettersson, J. (2002). *Spelade pappamånaden någon roll? Pappornas uttag av föräldrapenning.* RFV analyserar, 2002:14. Stockholm, Sweden: Riksförsäkringsverket.

Perris, C., Arrindell, W. A., Perris, H., van der Ende, J., Maj, M., et al. (1985). Cross-national study of perceived parental rearing behavior in healthy subjects from Australia, Denmark, Italy, the Netherlands and Sweden: Pattern and level comparisons. *Acta Psychiatrica Scandinavica, 72*, 278–282.

Plantin, L. (2001). *Mäns föräldraskap. Om mäns upplevelser och erfarenheter av faderskapet* [Men's parenthood. On men's perceptions and experiences of fatherhood], Ph.D. dissertation. Göteborg, Sweden: University of Göteborg.

Plantin, L., & Bäck-Wiklund, M. (2009). Social service as a human service: between loyalties: A Swedish case. In S. Lewis, J. Brannen, and A. Nilsen, *Work, family and organisations in transition: European perspectives.* London, UK: Polity Press.

Plantin, L., Månsson, S-A., & Kearney, J. (2003). Talking and doing fatherhood: On fatherhood and masculinity in Sweden and Britain. *Fathering, 1*(1), February 2003, pp. 3–26.

Putnic, D., Bornstein, M. H., Lansford, J. E., Chang, L. Deater-Deckard, K., et al. (2012). Agreement in mother and father acceptance–rejection, warmth and hostility/rejection/neglect of children across nine countries

Sandqvist, K. (1992). *Pappor och riktiga karlar. Om mans—och fadersroller i ideologi och verklighet* (Fathers and real men: Ideology and reality behind male and paternal roles). Stockholm, Sweden: Carlsson förlag.

Sarkadi, A., Kristiansson, R., & Bremberg, S. (2004). *Fäders betydelse för barns och ungdomars hälsa: en systematisk översikt av longitudinella studier* (The significance of the father for the health of children and adolescents: a systematic overview of longitudinal studies). Stockholm, Sweden: Swedish National Institute of Public Health (Rapport 17).

SCB (2008). *Ungdomars flytt hemifrån.* Demografiska rapporter 2008, 5. Stockholm, Sweden: Statistiska centralbyrån.

SCB (2009). *Barn eller inte? Resultat från en enkätundersökning om kvinnors och mäns inställning till barnafödande.* Demografiska rapporter 2009, 2. Stockholm, Sweden: Statistiska centralbyrån.

SCB. (2011). Barns sociala relationer. Levnadsförhållanden, rapport 119. www.scb.se.

SCB. (2012). Nu för tiden. En undersökning om svenska folkets tidsanvändning år 2010/11.

SCB. (2014). Statistisk årsbok. www.scb.se.

Schmidt, L (2008). Risk preferences and the timing of marriage and childbearing. Demography, 45(2), 439–460

Schröder, L. (2010). Besvärligt men inte hopplöst — ungdomsarbetslösheten och krisen. Socialförsäkringsrapport 2010, 6. Stockholm, Sweden: Försäkringskassan.

Socialdepartementet (2001). Barnafödandet I focus. Från befolkningspolitik till ett barnvänligt samhälle. SocialdepartementetStockholm: Fritzes.

SOU (1998). Ty makten är din . . . Myten om det rationella arbetslivet och det jämställda Sverige. (For thine is the power: the myth of the rational working life and equality in Sweden). Stockholm, Sweden, Fritzes offentliga utredningar.

Strandh, M., & Nordenmark, M. (2006). The interference of paid work with house hold demands in different social policy contexts: Perceived work-household conflict in sweden, the UK, the Netherlands, Hungary and the Czech Republic. British Journal of Sociology, 57(4), 597–617.

Sundström, M., & Duvander, A-Z. E. (2002). Gender division of child care and the sharing of parental leave among new parents in Sweden. European Sociological Review, 18, 433–447.

Tyrkkö, A. (1997). Anpassning mellan arbetsliv och familjeliv i Sverige och i Finland. In J. Näsman (ed.), Dilemmat arbetsliv—familjeliv i Norden. Köpenhamn, Sweden: Socialforskningsinstitutet 97, 5, Nordiska Ministerrådet.

Ungdomsstyrelsen (2012). Insats med kvalitet—kvalitetssäkring av insatser som erbjuds unga. www.ungdomsstyrelsen.se.

Ungdomsstyrelsen (2003). Dom kallar oss unga. Stockholm, Sweden: Ungdomsstyrelsen

van der Lippe, T., Jager, A., & Kops, Y. (2006). Combination pressure. The paid work–family balance of men and women in European countries. Acta Sociologica, 49(3), 303–319.

6

Fatherhood and Fathering in Eastern Europe

Zhanna Kravchenko and Mihaela Robila

The involvement of women in the workforce in the last century brought up the necessity for men to also increase their involvement in household duties in general and in care in particular (Craig 2006; K. J. Daly 1996). This process, however, has not been linear and straightforward. Often men and women's contribution to household responsibilities becomes more equal not only (or not so much) due to men's increased participation in unpaid work as because the work usually done by women is delegated to a paid person or remains undone (Bianchi, Milkie, Sayer, & Robinson 2000; Craig 2006). A nuanced approach to analyzing men's involvement in caring for children and the practices and norms surrounding them require not only abandoning the traditional view of male participation in care for children as additional form of labor, but also considering it as important as female care work (Marsiglio, Amato, Day, & Lamb 2000). Fathering as a practice includes various kinds of activities and may be analyzed from the point of view of invested resources and time as well as relationship satisfaction (Amato 1998; K. J. Daly 1996; Day & Lamb 2004; Marsiglio 1991; Sayer, Gauthier, & Furstenberg 2004). The current globalization process requires an analysis of normative perceptions of fatherhood from a transnational and global perspective, with multiple centers of powers (e.g., transnational corporations, laws, and networks) and varied paths to and forms of identity.

The aim of this chapter is to examine cross-country variation in attitudes and practices with regard to father's involvement in childcare in eastern Europe. The analysis focuses on five countries—Bulgaria, Georgia, Lithuania, Romania, and Russia. The *Gender and Generation Survey* (Bulgaria and Russia 2004, Romania 2005, Georgia and Lithuania 2006) provided information on normative orientations and everyday care activities. The analysis is based on juxtaposing perceptions of fatherhood as a part of masculinity norm and as a part of parenthood, as well as the implications of paternal involvement for children's well-being, on the one hand, and everyday involvement of fathers in routine care, on the other. Earlier studies about the link between attitudes and behavior have indicated methodological challenges for assuming that attitudes are predictive of practices. First, there is a difference between normative compliance and value-motivated behavior. Second, rather than affect behavior directly, attitudes may affect intentions. Third, though concept operationalizations may lead to discrepancies, individuals' perceptions of certain norms and behaviors as socially desirable may create conformity through self-censure (see Cooper & Croyle 1984 for a comprehensive review). Instead of comparing global attitudes against everyday practices, we examine attitudes that are based on experience and might be considered more accessible and therefore more likely to reflect behavior.

The differences and similarities between the countries, consistencies, and discrepancies between norms and practices are examined against the background of general family patterns and public policy frameworks. Although the scope of general family policy provisions indicates whether the official normative context includes men as caregivers, our analysis does not explain the variation in norms and practices through public efforts aimed at reconciling work and care differences between men and women. Instead, the institutional framework is used as a backdrop for interpretation of norms and practices. We suggest that the normative understanding of the importance of father care does not necessarily imply equality in terms of practical involvement and, as a result, brings into question the conventional understanding of care. Analyzing fathering in categories derived from the analysis of mothering practices might be one of the methodological challenges that produce discrepancies between strong support for father care and relatively low levels of everyday father care among men.

INTERDISCIPLINARY PERSPECTIVES ON FATHERHOOD

Norms and practices associated with fatherhood vary in time and across space, and comparative analysis strives to capture such variation and identify the underlying logic that brings together various aspects of this phenomenon. Earlier research that examined fatherhood and fathering in Eastern Europe can be systematized into several central themes: fatherhood as a part of a larger family system and a factor of demographic processes, fatherhood as a result of influence of overarching economic and political structures, and fatherhood as a normative foundation and everyday practice at the individual level (e.g., Hearn 2002; Therborn 2004).

Family Systems, Demography, and Fatherhood

From a macrosociological perspective, historical institutionalism and social constructivism are usually applied for understanding fatherhood and fathering, revealing the interrelations between institutional structures and individual norms and practices. Among institutional conditions, state regulations with regard to employment and the provisions for cash and care are important, as well as norms around sexual behavior and reproduction, inheritance rules and their effect on family organization and interaction patterns, and, more generally, duties and rights of parents and children, men and women. Hearn (2002) suggests that the "debates about fathers and fatherhood need to be more gendered and more explicitly about power" (p. 245), as well as that "these genderings are partly about changing forms of identity, organizations, welfare, state, nation and global relations" (p. 245). Furthermore, within a macrosociological and historical perspective, the aspect of power in relation to fathers' role and status in society has been perceived through the concept of patriarchy defined as inequality in access to resource and rights and obligations between men and women, parents and children (Therborn 2004).

Eastern European fatherhood, as a part of European family system, entered the twenty-first century through three major transitions: from unconstrained patriarchal control by men over women and children to post-patriarchy with adult autonomy from parents and more gender equality, from universal marriage to more varied patterns of sexual coupling and divorce, and from practice of multiple births to controlled fertility. In contrast to western European countries, however, fathers' roles in eastern Europe were traditionally weaker in large intergenerational households, where it did not directly correspond to *pater familias* (Laslett 1983). During the second half of the twentieth century, the socialist/Soviet gender contract that supported a family model with two breadwinners that severely undermined the conditions for traditional breadwinner model of fatherhood dominated the political agenda, strengthening the separation of conjugal relationships and parenting into independent, sometimes even unrelated social practices (see M. Daly 2005). Furthermore, the authoritarian politics and paternalistic politics of the socialist/Soviet regimes have been considered to have eroded men's status as fathers in society and their status in the family. Adorno's concept of "fatherless society" as applied to the Nazi state has been extended to describe the totalitarian socialist state as well (Ostner 2002).

Systematic scholarship regarding family and various aspects of parenthood in eastern Europe has increased since the fall of communism in the early 1990s (Kravchenko & Grigoryeva 2014; Robila 2004, 2012). Across the region, the family serves as a psychological shelter for the individual and provides the material basis for physical survival. For example, the family is regarded as the most stable social institution, making the post-communist transition period less difficult for the Russian people (Uspenskaya & Borodin 2004). The decreasing birth rates and increasing family dissolution rates are widely discussed by both specialists and policymakers as being associated with the role women play in family and society.

Earlier research largely overlooked men's/fathers' role in the demographic processes in general, as well as in the demographic crisis so widely discussed in the region (see Saarinen 2012 for an exception). Meanwhile, men's fertility behavior becomes increasingly relevant to understanding not only the diversification of family forms, fertility, and nuptuality patterns, but also how individuals and their demographic behavior respond to social, economic, and political changes, beyond the classical female fertility research (Alich 2009). Although systematic comparative research in eastern Europe has not yet been undertaken, evidence from Russia suggests certain similarities and differences between female and male reproductive behavior. Men and women do not differ much in the length of fertile period; men enter parenthood about two years later than women. However, men stay childless more often than women, and their likelihood of becoming fathers is more strongly affected by socioeconomic factors, mainly owing to a reduction in second-order and higher-order births (Alich 2009).

Social Structures and Fatherhood

The role of parenting as an important aspect in the process of (re)production of socioeconomic and gendered division of labor has received special attention in social/family policy studies. Earlier research demonstrated that differences in organization of contemporary welfare states are built around what social rights and obligations are provided for men and women as workers and family members (Crompton 1999; Pfau-Effinger 2005, 2007). Drawing attention to the social repertoire of fathers as a nonmonolithic group whose experience depends on socioeconomic conditions, social capital, and normative orientations, Hobson and Morgan (2002) suggested a theoretical perspective on fatherhood that brings together welfare state institutions, power relations within the family, and everyday practices of parenthood into a system of fatherhood regimes. Inspired by the conventional conceptualization of welfare regimes by Esping-Andersen (1990), the authors suggest a threefold typology based on distribution of fathers' rights and obligations: the *liberal* regime with a strong/moderate set of obligations and moderate set of rights, a *social democratic* regime with a weak set of obligations and a strong set of rights, and *conservative* regime with a weak/moderate set of obligations and rights. Though the typology excludes eastern European experiences, norms, and practices, it becomes an important starting point for a cross-national comparison highlighting the importance of institutional norms. Although systematic cross-national analyses of policy frameworks have not been undertaken so far, it is possible to suggest that a weak model of fatherhood still dominates the east European region (see Rodin & Åberg 2013 for a discussion about Russia).

The upheaval of economic difficulties of the transition toward democracy in eastern Europe had significant influences at the family level. A key aspect of the economic transition in Russia was increased unemployment for both men and women. Ashwin and Lytkina (2004) suggest that men's position in Russian households influenced their ability to deal with employment difficulties. This longitudinal study suggested that unemployed men's labor market problems were compounded by domestic marginalization. Russian men's ability to cope with the economic and labor challenges was affected by their limited involvement in household chores, considered as primarily feminine and women's responsibility. The loss of status as primary breadwinners not only threatened the identity of unemployed men but raised the possibility of double marginalization—from work and from family/household tasks. Performing tasks in the household did not help, but rather threatened, men's self-esteem and sense of competency. The lack of opportunities to develop self-esteem outside paid employment and within the household may have led to the demoralization of men. Although Russian women indicated that they would like men to participate in household tasks, they showed a preference for men to assume "helping" roles and not to have primary responsibility for performing the task. Thus, although women criticized men's disengagement from household responsibilities, in some cases they also contributed to its maintenance (Ashwin & Lytkina 2004).

Social construction of fatherhood, the public discourse, and the legal frameworks that define fathers' roles in the family and their relationships with their children is a complex and changing concept (Gregory & Milner 2011). Policy interventions have focused on two models: the "optimistic" perspective, referring to increasing father involvement in the family and gender equality (referred as "new fatherhood"), and the "pessimistic" perspective on fatherhood, referring to the deficit model, which focused on concerns about the absent parental figure and the lack of financial responsibilities for children (Gregory & Milner 2011). The "new fatherhood" perspective based on greater involvement of fathers at home and a shift toward more egalitarian roles was proposed as an alternative to the old models of masculinity. Data show that policy interventions can help in supporting such a model by shaping practices which organize fathers' rights and responsibilities. In eastern Europe, much as in western European countries, the "new fatherhood" seems to be a middle-class phenomenon that has not been institutionalized into widespread practices, even though norms of active fathering are appealing and easily adapted at the discursive level (Bezrukova 2012).

Normative Ideas about Fatherhood

Attitudes toward childbearing are among the most important variables influencing fertility. At the same time, husbands do not influence wife's childbearing attitudes, even among those husbands who are committed and involved with their families. A study conducted in Croatia examined two types of childrearing attitudes (and their predictors): child rearing as an obligation and as a life joy (Obradovic & Cudina 2011). Women's attitudes were found to be the main factor in making decisions about the number of children couples should bear, which confirms what was determined in previous research (Mackey & Immerman 2002). At the same time, research from Russia demonstrated that there may be discrepancies between the ideal and actual number of children in families, with the former often exceeding the latter, and the general ideal number of children exceeding the personal ideal number, demonstrating a strong two-child norm among women who expect to have or who already have children (Rotkirch & Kesseli 2012). These results resonated with the Croatian study, indicating that the presence/absence of a committed male partner is not a necessary condition for (not) having children.

With respect to personal well-being, the importance of father–child relations on later development has been shown to depend on both the amount of time spent together with the quality of time and the activities performed (e.g., Lamb & Lewis 2004). Quality of early father–child interactions influenced children's later social adjustment through the development of a warm father–child relationship (Webster, Low, Siller, & Hackett 2013). Fathers' involvement in childcare also benefits the quality of the marital relationship. For example, father's contribution to childcare lowered some mothers' aggravation, whereas child fussiness and unpredictability were consistently significant predictors of higher aggravation for both parents (DeMaris, Mahoney, & Pargament 2013). Although this type of research on eastern European fathers is comparatively small, the importance of the quality of family relations for various aspects of individual development and well-being have been brought to light, particularly indicating the importance of early father involvement in childcare.

Losing touch with one's children after separation is not unique to the eastern European experience and may have negative effects on men's and children's well-being—health, psychological development, and adjustment throughout the life course (Amato & Keith 1991a, 1991b; Christopoulos 2001)—but, most important, it is one of the factors that contributes to child poverty in the region (UNICEF 1999). Though it is usually families having many children or families of parents having low incomes and unstable positions in the labor market who find themselves at highest risk for living in poverty, households of single parents (usually headed by mothers) are overrepresented among the poor. One of the reasons behind the higher risks of poverty among single-parent, mother-headed households is that fathers do not fulfill their financial obligations toward their former partners and children (Festi & Prokof'eva 1997).

Fathering Practices

At the individual level, research that mainly focused on western European countries indicated that the increasing breadwinner role of women brought up the need for a renegotiation of time devoted to household and childrearing duties of men and women (Soobedar 2011). Women's time spent performing childcare activities is two to three times that of men's (e.g., Bianchi et al. 2000; Craig 2006; Craig & Killian 2011). Evidence from comparative research shows small differences in gender division of unpaid labor, including care tasks, between eastern and western European countries. For instance, it was shown that although normative ideas about appropriate division of responsibilities between men and women are more traditional in Russia than in Sweden, the patterns of housework are gendered in a similar way, with men engaging in routine care together with their female partners but rarely doing it alone, whereas women in many cases carry their care responsibilities without assistance from their partners (Kravchenko & Motiejunaite 2008). The tasks that parents engage in are also different for mothers and fathers; mothers do more of the routine care, and fathers spend a proportionally larger amount of time playing or doing homework with children (Kravchenko 2008). Moreover, compared to fathering, mothering involves more time commitment, multitasking, physical labor, rigid timetables, time alone with the children, and overall responsibility for managing care—even when women work full-time (Craig 2006).

Research using Doherty's systemic ecological perspective (Doherty, Kouneski, & Erickson 1998), which posits that a complex mix of factors from inside and outside the family affect father involvement, indicates that an additive model of father involvement accounts for the quality of father–child interaction better than a model focused on only one component of the system (Holmes & Huston 2010). A variety of factors was shown to contribute to father involvement in childrearing, such as child characteristics, marital relationship, or demographic characteristics (e.g., father's education level). Spending time with children has been deeply embedded in the discourse about being a good father (K. J. Daly 1996). Though previous generations of fathers have been perceived as not being very aware of this issue, the contemporary generation of fathers reports that spending time with children is profoundly intertwined with beliefs and values about good fatherhood (K. J. Daly 1996). At the same time, empirical evidence from eastern Europe is not unequivocal, as it shows no direct causal relationship between gender and parental norms and caregiving practices among men (Kravchenko 2012).

Studies on time allocation indicate that highly educated mothers and fathers spend more time caring for children because of their awareness of the importance of investment in children's upbringing, because they are highly motivated, and because they might have difficulties finding appropriate substitutes for childcare. However the cross-national effects of education may vary. For instance, education had no effect on father involvement in Norway and had only a weak effect in Germany, suggesting that family policies providing economic support may reduce time constraints on fathers, ameliorating the education effects (Sayer et al. 2004). No effects of education, in particular, and individual sociodemographic characteristics, in general, were shown to influence paternal investment in Russia, suggesting that structural and normative constraints may offset the positive effect of individual attributes (Kravchenko 2012).

To summarize, research on father involvement in childrearing and caregiving from the macrosociological perspective has provided an understanding of the specificities of eastern European fatherhood through the prism of historical, social, economic, and political transformation in the region. Studies have indicated the longstanding trend of attributing fathers with a breadwinning role in the family, consistently excluding them from caregiving and weakening their legal claims. Although "new fatherhood" is being introduced in the region, as microsociological studies illustrate, men are not a monolithic group, and their involvement in childrearing varies based on individual characteristics and access to different resources such as education and employment. Our analysis contributes to the existing theoretical and empirical research on fatherhood by mapping the practices of father involvement in eastern Europe in terms of type and scope and by establishing a relationship between such practices and norms of masculinity, fatherhood, and fathering.

FATHER INVOLVEMENT IN CHILDREARING

Earlier research has outlined an analytical tradition for the analysis of fatherhood and fathering that guides this study. Our analysis begins with an overview of demographic processes that reflect the specificities of family practices in the region and describe the policy framework that affects rights and responsibilities of fathers. We further examine differences and similarities with regard to fatherhood and fathering practices to establish whether normative ideas may influence the degree of men's involvement in child care.

Family Systems and Policy Frameworks

Detailed demographic overviews have demonstrated how markedly the population structures and processes vary between eastern and western European countries with respect to nuptiality, mortality, and migration; eastern Europeans tend to marry earlier (both women and men), die younger, and migrate toward western Europe. Yet overwhelming similarities are observed between the regions with regard to increasing cohabitation, patterns of contraception, and stagnating or declining populations. Moreover, a growing diversity of living arrangements and the different ways that family is conceptualized in policies, practice, and public perceptions suggest a more nuanced perspective on the family within eastern Europe. For instance, demographic statistics indicate that though the age of mothers at first childbirth in most eastern European countries is younger than that of their western European counterparts, a significant number of women in Georgia (37%) give birth between 20 and 24 years old, and in Lithuania—the biggest share of births (35%) skews toward older age and occurs between 25 and 29 years old (UN 2011). Divorce also seems to follow a homogeneous pattern, with most of the divorces occurring after 10 to 14 years of marriage. At the same time, divorce rates vary widely—from 0.7 divorces per 1,000 inhabitants in Georgia to 5.0 divorces per 1,000 inhabitants in Russia in 2008.

Very low fertility rates are registered in countries such as Lithuania (1.29), Bulgaria (1.44), and Romania (1.32). Georgia and Russia have slightly higher rates—1.77 and 1.61, respectively (CIA 2014). Both economic and ideational changes have been associated with influencing fertility changes (Philipov 2006). Public policy debates recognize the double pressure of waged work and care as an important reason for reducing female fertility in the region. The need for female employment is often understood as means of providing economic stability for the family rather than an area of self-realization for women, who are encouraged to withdraw from the labor market if the household can afford it (Rotkirch, Temkina, & Zdravomyslova 2007; Saxonberg & Sirovatka 2007). Economic and ideational turbulence as reflected in decreased support for healthcare and increase in unhealthy practices are also used to explain the devastating increase in morbidity and decline in life expectancy since the early 1990s (Cockerham 1999). Even here the patterns are not homogeneous, with Russia experiencing one of the highest mortality rates in Europe and Asia—399 per 1,000 inhabitants in 2012, compared to Georgia's 176, for instance (WHO 2014).

Demographic research has indicated, among other issues, a diversification of family forms. Surveys on of the intergenerational structures of eastern European families reveal significant differences among countries. The majority of households in all countries examined include respondents with children, with the highest proportion (47%) in Russia, and the lowest (33%) in Georgia. Russia also has the highest share of single-parent households in this category (26%), compared to approximately 12 percent in Bulgaria. Single households and childless couples living separately are rarest in Georgia (8%) and constitute a sizable group of households in Lithuania (33% nuclear and single-parent families combined, 30% childless singles and couples). Two-generation structure, however, is not limited to individuals co/residing with their children; adult respondents living with their parents is not uncommon and varies from 6 percent in Romania to 11 percent in Bulgaria.

Equally interesting is the substantial variation in the number of three- and more-generation households. For example, 28 percent of respondents in Georgia live in households where grandparents, children, and grandchildren coreside.[1] The corresponding share is lower in other countries, with the lowest rate of 6 percent observed in Lithuania. Georgia also has the largest share of households in which adults are living together with their parents and siblings (11%). In Bulgaria, this amounts to 9 percent, in Russia 4 percent, in Romania 5 percent, and in Lithuania 5 percent. Households that combine complex vertical and horizontal structures (grandparents, parents, children, siblings) are very few across the dataset and vary from 6 percent in Georgia to a negligible rate in Lithuania.

As earlier research has indicated, complex household structures often emerge as a result of resource shortage: The economic recession of the 1990s together with an increased housing problem created a process of the so-called anti-nuclearization of the family (Prokofieva 2007). The mechanisms of mutual assistance include joint budgeting, childcare, and in-kind help and often stretch beyond the borders of residence (Kravchenko 2008). However, they are not always sufficient to accommodate all the needs of families. The family support systems, both financial and normative aspects, are important to understand in the context of family in general and of fatherhood or fathering in particular (see Table 6.1).

Welfare policies in eastern Europe have undergone a substantial transformation. As all systems were deeply affected by acute economic downfall, reforms were characterized by a general transition from collective to individualized social security (Fajth 1999). Family allowances were transformed from universal to means-tested benefits (UNICEF 1999). High economic burdens of poverty made dual-employment critical for family survival, despite some decline in female employment (Pascall & Manning 2000). As a result, and despite the curtailment of many programs for social security and provision, most countries maintained their systems of parental leave as introduced during the socialist regime. It is noteworthy that the length of maternity leave is nearly standardized; it is, in many cases, related to medical condition rather

TABLE 6.1 Policy background, 2009

	Bulgaria	Georgia	Lithuania	Romania	Russia
Parental leave (months)	27	34.2*	34	21.9	33.7
maternity leave (weeks)	19	18	18	18	20
paternity leave available (days reserved)	yes (14)	no	yes (30)	yes (7)	yes** (0)
duration of compensation payments (months)	15	0	22	21.9	15.7
compensation level (% of previous income)	50	0	91.8	85	40
Childcare provision (individual entitlement, child younger than 3)	no	yes	no	no	yes
Childcare provision (individual entitlement, child older than 3)	no	yes	no	yes	yes

Notes: * No income compensation is available; ** No statutory right for fathers, but parental leave is formally available to any caregiver, including fathers.
Source: Multilinks database 2014.

than care responsibilities. For instance, in Russia, the procedures and compensation during maternity leave are the same as for sick leave, which is not the case for parental leave.

The understanding of children's care needs and adults' care responsibilities and rights vary considerably among the countries, reflected in the length of parental leave and duration and levels of income replacement. The most striking differences can be observed between Lithuania and Georgia. Though the former provides a lengthy and generous compensation (twenty-two weeks with 91.2% of previous income), the latter reduces provisions to job security during the leave and provides no financial support. The rights of fathers for early childcare are not universally recognized. Georgia has no such provisions, and Russia attributes the right for leave to any relative but has no statutorily assigned leave for fathers. At the same time, Lithuanian parental leave regulations reserve thirty days specifically for fathers; so do Bulgarian (fourteen days) and Romanian (seven days) family policies. Institutionalized childcare provisions have also been reduced substantially. According to Szelewa and Polakowski (2008), Lithuania is one of the few countries that preserved and further developed a system of available and high-quality childcare services, though without statutory individual entitlement. In Russia, official entitlements are not translated into actual public provisions (Teplova 2007).

As the policies outlined demonstrate, neither family processes nor policy frameworks in eastern Europe constitute homogeneous patterns. In some aspects, such as the liberalization of conjugal practices and individualization of responsibility for welfare, many countries of the region distanced themselves from the controlling system of communist collectivity. The transformation, however, has not been uniform. New forms of family traditionalism have emerged (Graff 2009; Zhurzhenko 2004), and retrenchments were accompanied with selective expansions (Cerami 2009). Accordingly, understanding the institutional context of fatherhood and fathering should be considered at the country rather than regional level.

Fatherhood

Norms about parenthood in general, fatherhood and fathering in particular, can be captured in different ways. The *Generation and Gender Survey* contains a battery of questions that reflect various aspects of normative perceptions about gendered division of rights and responsibilities in public and private life. Parenting as a norm and practice is addressed in both men and women and is measured as the degree to which individuals recognize fatherhood as an important part of a man's life fulfillment, masculinity (*"A man has to have children in order to be fulfilled"*), and the extent to which the fathers' presence and active involvement is important for children's well-being (*"A child needs a home with father and mother to grow up happily"* and *"Children often suffer because fathers concentrate too much on work"*).[2] Table 6.2 demonstrates that on average, positive attitudes toward fatherhood and fathering dominate the answers, and there are few differences between men and women, though the variance is substantial.[3]

Earlier research has indicated that a decreased sense of importance of having children in modern societies may contribute to an increase in the number of childless couples (Obradovic & Cudina 2011). The importance of children for one's identification of/with masculinity norms is most pronounced in Georgia (mean = 1.38 and 1.36 for men and women respectively). By contrast, the data on Lithuania demonstrate that the definition of masculinity can be detached from the idea of having children; both men and women have mostly neutral attitudes (mean = 0.25 and 0.17, respectively). Table 6.2 also shows that these attitudes are more positive in Russia and Romania than in Bulgaria.

The idea of fatherhood as an essential part of parenthood is almost universally supported across all countries. The differences in means between genders and countries (although statistically significant with the exception of Bulgaria and Romania) are small enough to suggest that from the perspective of children's well-being, the presence of both parents is essential. This aspect, however, does not specify whether there should be differences or similarities between parents in how they provide for children's welfare. The equal importance of fatherhood and motherhood here does not imply the importance

TABLE 6.2 Attitudes toward fatherhood

	Bulgaria		Russia		Georgia		Romania		Lithuania	
	male	female	male	female	male	female	male	female	male	female
(A) Children and masculinity: "A man has to have children in order to be fulfilled"										
Mean	0.53	0.53	0.92	0.87	1.38	1.36	1.05	1.08	0.25	0.17
SD	1.02	1.04	0.85	0.87	0.68	0.73	0.84	0.89	0.91	0.96
N	5799	6960	4216	7020	4405	5595	5977	6009	4962	4983
(B) Fatherhood/parenthood: "A child needs a home with father and mother to grow up happily"										
Mean	1.47	1.49	1.45	1.43	1.56	1.60	1.45	1.50	1.21	1.22
SD	0.67	0.68	0.59	0.65	0.54	0.53	0.65	0.66	0.76	0.81
N	5809	6964	4221	7035	4405	5595	5977	6009	4979	5019
(C) Fathering: "Children often suffer because fathers concentrate too much on work"										
Mean	0.62	0.68	0.76	0.76	0.81	0.86	0.20	0.23	0.58	0.57
SD	0.94	0.95	0.91	0.91	0.84	0.84	1.00	1.02	0.86	0.89
N	5813	6972	4207	7018	4405	5595	5977	6009	4961	5021

of equality in terms of practical involvement. In fact, with regard to the last question about whether concentrating on work interferes with being a good father, support for this premise is weak, as seen in all questions assessed. This may indicate that concentrating on work allows for better economic provision for children and is not considered an obstacle to, but rather a condition for, fathering. Though access to economic resources is an important factor contributing to men's propensity to become fathers, there is also evidence that men who become fathers are motivated to be better providers by working more hours and earning more money (Dykstra & Keizer 2009). Even in cases of family dissolution, fathers' contribution as breadwinners is quite important. Jennifer Utrata (2008) indicated that with the increased economic pressures and withdrawal of state support, as well as liberalization of legal and social norms, men's ties to families loosened.

Fathering

Fathering as a social practice contains various types of activities and can be analyzed from the point of view of time input, material costs, and levels of satisfaction (Amato 1998; Marsiglio 1991; Sayer et al. 2004). In the next stage of our analysis, we examine the degree to which men are involved in performing various forms of routine childcare: dressing, putting the child to bed, caring during illness, spending leisure time, doing homework, and providing transportation. The survey does not measure the scope of involvement reported by partners in the same households, but it is still possible to conclude that women in all countries tend to report a lower level of fathers' involvement compared to what men report (Table 6.3). The differences are especially prominent in Lithuania and reach as high as 5 percent for leisure activities, homework, and transportation.

Though significant differences in involvement can be observed mostly for Georgia in contrast to other countries, Table 6.3 indicates that Georgian men are least engaged with childcare activities. Dressing, putting to bed, and caring for sick children are chores usually performed by mothers and/or other people in the household, or children themselves. Considering the complex household structures, it is most likely that women of older generations or female siblings of parents share these responsibilities with the mothers. In Lithuania, Romania, and Russia, these activities are reported as being shared more often than performed by men and/or other people. These are also activities that require keeping schedules (dressing before dropping off to school/daycare, putting to bed on time) and taking time from work, all of which are usually normatively assigned to and internalized by women (*cf*. Kravchenko & Motiejunaite 2008). Caring for sick people is a responsibility usually not delegated to other people, and differences between the countries are rather small in this aspect.

TABLE 6.3 Division of parenting responsibilities (% of total N of respondents, by gender)

		Bulgaria		Georgia		Lithuania		Romania		Russia	
		male R	female R	male R	female R	male R	female R	male R	female R	male R	female R
Dressing	men	5.26	1.11	3.50	1.04	4.35	0.87	2.60	2.54	4.86	2.06
	both	15.56	11.66	5.41	3.31	18.77	10.50	19.05	14.85	20.48	11.61
	other*	17.67	19.71	19.73	25.55	13.14	16.41	12.50	12.62	9.14	9.83
Putting to bed	men	4.91	1.54	2.86	0.97	4.23	1.13	2.75	0.93	6.48	2.00
	both	18.81	14.04	3.50	1.10	26.38	15.14	22.54	20.35	32.76	20.87
	other	20.02	23.54	30.55	36.67	14.17	16.97	11.61	14.57	10.29	13.32
Sick care	men	5.29	1.85	4.53	1.45	6.16	2.25	3.49	2.07	5.15	1.03
	both	11.32	8.26	11.93	7.04	12.81	6.74	14.56	11.87	13.44	7.04
	other	7.07	7.62	4.38	6.42	5.38	7.43	5.94	7.66	6.48	10.42
Leisure activities	men	7.18	4.33	5.65	2.90	7.19	2.78	5.53	3.79	6.38	3.21
	both	56.01	46.11	36.83	25.83	61.22	42.58	60.28	52.63	63.71	40.46
	other	12.02	14.21	29.04	39.57	6.30	7.63	8.98	11.36	8.19	14.50
Homework	men	8.98	3.65	5.75	3.30	11.77	4.99	6.59	4.79	9.96	4.55
	both	33.52	28.42	22.76	16.59	37.65	22.99	44.37	38.59	36.27	22.20
	other	15.55	15.32	16.35	17.97	6.34	8.13	4.09	6.71	10.24	14.95
Transportation	men	9.74	6.26	6.65	4.20	10.48	4.29	5.96	5.21	9.28	4.48
	both	27.21	22.88	13.39	9.59	30.33	19.43	29.07	26.69	28.45	17.27
	other	34.34	36.00	47.44	49.57	25.15	27.91	31.20	33.91	28.33	38.01

* This category includes other members of the household, people not coresiding with the family and children themselves. While significant differences in involvement can be observed mostly for Georgia in contrast to other countries[4], Table 6.3 indicates that Georgian men are least engaged with childcare activities. The discussion also draws on Scheffe post hoc multiple comparisons for one-way ANOVA testing for differences in division of responsibilities among the countries, which is not presented here.

Leisure activities and homework engage more men and are often shared by the parents in all countries. Although transportation (from and to day-care, school or other activities) might also require maintaining routines, the relative increase in men performing this chore alone or together with their partners implies that it does not defy the norms of masculinity. It is also note-worthy that transportation is the aspect of everyday life that is delegated to other people more than any other activities in all countries. Dressing and going to bed might also be activities that children start managing on their own before all others. In Bulgaria and Georgia, parents are not engaged with putting children to bed in nearly a quarter and a third of households, respectively.

Much as was the case with earlier research, fathers in our sample engage with childcare mostly together with mothers, and their share of taking main responsibility for everyday routines is selective and limited. Moreover, fathers' involvement does not necessarily lead to a decrease in mothers' involvement; it increases the overall scope and quality of care but is not perceived as alle-viating women's care load. Separation between the genders does not occur in isolation: Other household members and broader social networks become engaged in care. Most activities included in the analysis are not age-specific. In the absence of longitudinal data, it is impossible to discuss how the divi-sion of responsibilities changes over time. Very young children might require more assistance from fathers over a short period of time—for instance, when it comes to putting them to bed, with the father withdrawing after a period of intensive care provision. In comparison, help with homework is usually required at older ages, and the large share of men involved might suggest that they are engaging in activities considered educational rather than car-ing. Studies on how the gender balance changes in terms of work and family responsibilities as children grow indicate that with older children there is more equity in the division of childrearing labor, partly due to how women recalibrate their commitments to work and family and not because domestic labor is redistributed between men and women (Craig & Sawrikar 2009).

Attitudes and Practices: Is There a Relationship?

It is possible to expect some degree of correspondence between the nor-mative ideas of masculinity and fatherhood, and everyday practices. More specifically, we compared levels of fathering across the three norms to see whether normative support for father care translates into greater levels of involvement.[4] The majority of respondents demonstrate positive attitudes toward all three questions. There are small differences among the three nor-mative constructs, with Georgia having the highest coherence among them. When respondents support children-oriented norms and practices, means for the levels of involvement for fathers in the household vary from 1.22 to 1.24. Differences can be seen between various types of attitudes.

It can be argued that there is a relationship between support for children-oriented norms and the levels of involvement for at least two normative aspects. As the results demonstrate (Table 6.4), the more positive the attitudes are toward children's being an important aspect of a man's life and active fathering being beneficial for children, the *less* involved men are in actual care for children. For instance, in Bulgaria, the mean for fathers' aggregated care provision is 1.88 if the respondents demonstrate support for having children as a part of the masculinity norm, 2.22 if they are neutral, and 2.29 if the attitude is negative. This can also be observed for the Romanian sample for the same question and for Bulgaria and Russia with regard to the fathering norm. Turning to the masculinity norm, however, the differences in means are significant between positive and other types of attitudes—i.e., there is no significant relationship between levels of involvement and negative and neutral attitudes. For the fathering norm, it is between the negative and the other types; the direction of the relationship does not change.

There are no statistically significant differences in means of involvement for the fatherhood norm, though it seems that more support for this aspect translates into *more* active fathering. Moreover, the statistically significant relationship is not unambiguous. For instance, in Russia and Georgia, the more positive the attitudes toward the first aspect are, the higher the levels of engagement. This is also true for Lithuania and the question of the importance of father care for a child's happiness. The differences in standard deviation are substantial, indicating that large countries with great socioeconomic and cultural diversity, like Russia, have as much diversity in attitudes and practices as more homogeneous countries such as Lithuania.

The discrepancies observed between normative perceptions and everyday practices indicate that actual household arrangements may have little to do with ideals of family life. Acknowledging the role of fathers in children's upbringing as fulfilling and important for children's well-being may collide with demands from other aspects of individuals' lives, work and other family obligations. Of equal significance is that the content of father care may simply exclude the routines outlined above as feminine. Care includes various forms of physical, intellectual and emotional investment (Davis 1995). The need to separate female and male care as a part of the traditional gender contract in post-communist societies (Temkina & Rotkirch 2003) may require new conceptualizations of father care. The latter is important even in the context of a more equality-oriented gender contract, as it might aim to extend the range of relevant experiences for both men and women.

TABLE 6.4 Degree of involvement in fathering, by attitudes

Country	Attitude	Masculinity norm			Fatherhood/parenthood			Fathering		
		Mean	Std. Dev.	N	Mean	Std. Dev.	N	Mean	Std. Dev.	N
Bulgaria	negative	2.29	2.50	379	1.88	2.16	26	2.36	2.36	368
	neutral	2.22	2.49	547	2.14	3.39	99	2.16	2.60	377
	positive	1.88	2.28	1223	2.04	2.33	2024	1.92	2.32	1404
Russia	negative	1.83	2.35	145	1.48	2.41	27	2.17	2.20	255
	neutral	1.91	2.33	234	1.05	1.90	88	2.10	2.38	302
	positive	2.07	2.32	1316	2.09	2.33	1584	1.96	2.33	1137
Georgia	negative	0.96	1.48	51	0.43	0.79	7	1.39	2.04	197
	neutral	0.84	1.72	74	1.27	1.35	11	1.03	1.44	243
	positive	1.24	2.00	1822	1.22	1.98	1929	1.22	2.04	1507
Romania	negative	2.41	2.17	88	1.92	2.16	25	2.49	2.14	628
	neutral	2.31	2.26	332	1.88	2.16	112	2.13	2.11	514
	positive	2.27	2.19	1678	2.31	2.20	1961	2.22	2.28	956
Lithuania	negative	2.05	2.45	330	1.25	2.00	53	2.07	2.15	219
	neutral	1.99	2.56	541	2.05	2.72	147	2.11	2.58	366
	positive	2.21	2.33	634	2.13	2.42	1307	2.10	2.51	922

Note: Differences between men and women on the three aspects of normative orientation were small and are not included here.

CONCLUSIONS

The overall aim of this chapter was to examine variations in policies, attitudes and practices surrounding men's involvement in care for children in eastern Europe—Bulgaria, Georgia, Lithuania, Romania, and Russia—that experienced rather different trajectories of transformation from socialist regimes. Our analysis does not focus specifically on the experiences of men but instead examines fatherhood and fathering as a phenomenon constructed by both men and women, other significant members of their social networks, and broader policy frameworks.

As has been demonstrated, the region is very heterogeneous in several respects and difficult to conceptualize in terms of differences with western Europe or to identify clear patterns within the region. The latter is also due to the limitation of our analysis of only five countries. The country that stands out in these analyses is Georgia, where family-/father-oriented policies are virtually non-existent, household structures the most complex, fathering practices less active, and yet support for the importance of children for men's fulfillment and of fathers' for children's welfare most significant. A different pattern was evident in Lithuania, which has the most equality-oriented policies, with rather neutral attitudes and widespread practices of fathers and mothers sharing responsibility for the care of children. Bulgaria, Romania, and Russia have less explicit public support for father involvement in childcare, yet there are no particularly large differences in terms of attitudes or practices among them.

Though fathers acknowledge the importance of having children and spending time with them, obstacles exist thanks to factors that are mostly out of the control of families, dependent on workplace-related issues (*cf.* K. J. Daly 1996). For example, though opportunities for flexible working arrangements are more often provided to men than to women (Vandeweyer & Glorieux 2008), an option of part-time work might not always be available due to fathers' bread-winning responsibilities and rigid labor market regulations. Nor can short leave nor longer care-related career breaks offer an incentive for fathers to become more directly involved in the care of children during the most intensive formative years and later, as they grow older.

It seems to reason that policies create an overall normative context that may have an indirect effect on individual attitudes and/or practices. When aims of public policies are formulated, it might also be useful to consider that fathers' involvement does not necessarily lead to relief of responsibilities for mothers. Policies may aim to alleviate the double burden of work and care for women and/or increase father care, but these aims will probably be pursued by separate measures. More specifically, encouraging women to stay at home to have children or developing more comprehensive social services might solve the problem of double workload for women but might not influence fathers' care. If the quality of childrearing is in the center, encouraging more active fathering can be achieved by creating part-time jobs and family-friendly work environments for both men and women. There is support for such measures in some countries in the region, though practical steps are yet to be taken (Obradovic & Cudina 2011). Moreover, policies that actively promote an exaggerated emphasis on and idealization of maternity quite directly decrease the importance of father care, which, coupled with a legacy of matrifocal families in which families rely on cross-generational assistance and caregiving among women, may further promote the estrangement of men from caring for children (Utrata 2008).

Public support for new representations of fatherhood may be helpful in creating more innovative representations of gender relations. Research indicates that despite the recent availability of paternal leave for fathers, in some countries, there is still resistance to use. For example, Estonian parents' division of labor remains conservative, with many fathers deciding not to take parental leave (Pajumets 2010). Governments have the responsibility to introduce and promote legal frameworks to create equal opportunities for men and women and to influence organizational culture and public opinion (Vandeweyer & Glorieux 2008).

NOTES

1. Depending on the family role of the respondent, this category is defined slightly differently in Figure 1: "children and parents" and "children and grandchildren."

2. The answer alternatives varied from "strongly disagree" to "strongly agree" and were coded so that supporting opinions were assigned positive values (1, 2) and rejecting opinions negative values (–1, –2); neutral answers (neither agree nor disagree) were coded 0.

3. A one-way ANOVA was used to test for preference differences among the countries. Attitudes differed significantly across all countries and test variables; the only statistically insignificant values were observed between Romania and Bulgaria with respect to the question on the father's role for the child's happiness.

4. To measure the level of involvement in care, when both partners were being involved the answer was coded 1, if men were carrying out the main responsibility the answer was coded 2, and all others were coded 0. A new variable was subsequently constructed summing the scores for all five categories of activities, thus ranging from 0 to 10.

REFERENCES

Alich, D. (2009). *Fatherhood in Russia between 1970 and 2004: The male perspective of family and fertility behavior in a changing society.* Rostock, Germany: Dissertation zur Erlangung des akademischen Grades doctor rerum politicarum (Dr. rer. pol.) der Wirtschafts—und Sozialwissenschaftlichen Fakultät der Universität Rostock.

Amato, P. (1998). More than money? Men's contributions to their children's lives. In A. Booth & A. C. Crouter (eds.), *Men in families: when do they get involved? What difference does it make?* (pp. 241–278). Hillsdale, NJ: Lawrence Erlbaum Associates.

Amato, P., & Keith, B. (1991a). Parental divorce and adult well-being: A meta-analysis. *Journal of Marriage and Family, 53*(1), 43–58.

Amato, P., & Keith, B. (1991b). Parental divorce and the well-being of children: A meta-analysis. *Psychological Bulletin, 110*(1), 26–46.

Ashwin, S., & Lytkina, T. S. (2004). Men in crisis in Russia: the role of domestic marginalization. *Gender and Society, 18*(2), 189–206.

Bezrukova, O. (2012). Praktiki otvetstvennogo ottsovstva: 'Papa-shkola' i sotsial'nyi kapital. *Vestnik SPbGU, 12*, 266–275.

Bianchi, S., Milkie, M., Sayer, L., & Robinson, J. (2000). Is anyone doing the housework? Trends in the gender division of household labor. *Social Forces, 79*(1), 191–228.

Cerami, A. (2009). Welfare state developments in the Russian Federation: Oil-led social policy and "the Russian miracle." *Social Policy and Administration, 43*(2), 105–120.

Christopoulos, A. (2001). Relationships between parents' marital status and university students mental health, views of mothers and views of fathers: A study in Bulgaria. *Journal of Divorce and Remarriage, 34*(3–4), 179–190.

CIA (2014, June 17). *Total fertility rate, The World Fact Book: Central Intelligence Agency.* https://www.cia.gov/library/publications/the-world-factbook/fields/2127.html.

Cockerham, W. C. (1999). *Health and social change in Russia and Eastern Europe.* New York: Routledge.

Cooper, J., & Croyle, R. T. (1984). Attitudes and attitude change. *Annual Review of Psychology, 35*, 395–426.

Craig, L. (2006). Does father care mean fathers share? A comparison of how mothers and fathers in intact families spend time with children. *Gender and Society, 20*(2), 259–281.

Craig, L., & Killian, M. (2011). How mothers and fathers share childcare. A cross-national time-use comparison. *American Sociological Review, 76*(6), 834–861.

Craig, L., & Sawrikar, P. (2009). Work and family: How does the (gender) balance change as children grow? *Gender, Work and Organization, 16*(6), 684–709.

Crompton, R. (ed.). (1999). *Restructuring gender relations and employment: The decline of the male breadwinner.* Oxford, UK: Oxford University Press.

Daly, K. J. (1996). Spending time with the kids: meanings of family time for fathers. *Family Relations, 45*(4), 466–476.

Daly, M. (2005). Changing family life in Europe: Significance for state and society. *European Societies, 7*(3), 379–398.

Davis, C. (1995). Competence versus care? Gender and caring work revisited. *Acta Sociologica, 38*(1), 17–31.

Day, R. D., & Lamb, M. E. (2004). *Conceptualizing and measuring father involvement.* Hillsdale, NJ: Lawrence Erlbaum Associates.

DeMaris, A., Mahoney, A., & Pargament, K. (2013). Fathers' contributions to housework and childcare and parental aggravation among first-time parents. *Fathering, 11*(2), 179–198.

Doherty, W. J., Kouneski, E. F., & Erickson, M. F. (1998). Responsible fathering: An overview and conceptual framework. *Journal of Marriage and the Family, 60*(2), 277–292.

Dykstra, P. A., & Keizer, R. (2009). The wellbeing of childless men and fathers in mid-life. *Ageing and Society, 29*(8), 1227–1242.

Esping-Andersen, G. (1990). *The three worlds of welfare capitalism.* Princeton, NJ: Princeton University Press.

Fajth, G. (1999). Social security in a rapidly changing environment: The case of the post-communist transformation. *Social Policy and Administration, 33*(4), 416–436.

Festi, P., & Prokof'eva, L. (1997). Alimenty, posobiia i dokhody semei posle razvoda. *Mir Rossii, 4*, 19–24.

Graff, A. (2009). Gender and nation, here and now: Reflections on the gendered and sexualised aspects of contemporary Polish nationalism. In E. H. Oleksy (ed.), *Intimate citizenships: gender, sexualities, politics* (pp. 133–146). London, UK: Routledge.

Gregory, A., & Milner, S. (2011). What is "new" about fatherhood? The social construction of fatherhood in France and the UK. *Men and Masculinities, 14*(5), 588–606.

Hearn, J. (2002). Men, fatherhood and the state: National and transitional perspectives. In B. Hobson (ed.), *Making men into fathers: men, masculinities and the social politics of fatherhood.* Cambridge, UK: Cambridge University Press.

Hobson, B., & Morgan, D. (2002). Introduction: Making men into fathers. In B. Hobson (ed.), *Making men into Fathers. Men, masculinities and the social politics of fatherhood* (pp. 1–21). Cambridge, UK: Cambridge University Press.

Holmes, E., & Huston, A. C. (2010). Understanding positive father–child interaction: Children's, fathers' and mothers' contributions. *Fathering, 8*(2), 203–225.

Kravchenko, Z. (2008). *Family (versus) policy: Combining work and care in Russia and Sweden.* Stockholm, Sweden: Intellecta AB.

Kravchenko, Z. (2012). Muzhchiny v zabote o detiakh: sravnitel'nyi analiz Rossii, Frantsii i Norvegii. *Zhurnal sotsiologii i sotsial'noi antropologii, 15* 65–85.

Kravchenko, Z., & Grigoryeva, I. (2014). Family policy in Russia: Folkways versus stateways revisited. In M. Robila (ed.), *Handbook of family policies across the globe* (pp. 223–238). New York: Springer.

Kravchenko, Z., & Motiejunaite, A. (2008). Zhenschiny i muzhchiny na rabote i doma: gendernoe razdelenie truda v Rossii i Shvetsii. *Journal of Social Policy Studies, 2*, 177–200.

Lamb, M. E., & Lewis, C. (2004). The development and significance of father–child relationships in two-parent families. In M. E. Lamb (ed.), *The role of father in child development.* Hoboken, NJ: Wiley.

Laslett, P. (1983). Family and household as work group and kin group: Areas of traditional Europe compared. In R. Wall (ed.), *Family forms in historic Europe* (pp. 515–563). Cambridge, UK: Cambridge University Press.

Mackey, W. C., & Immerman, R. S. (2002). Cultural variability and gender egalitarianism: An elusive balance yet to be struck. *Journal of Comparative Family Studies, 33*, 475–494.

Marsiglio, W. (1991). Paternal engagement activities with minor children. *Journal of Marriage and Family, 53*(4), 973–986.

Marsiglio, W., Amato, P. R., Day, R. D., & Lamb, M. E. (2000). Scholarship on fatherhood in the 1990s and beyond. *Journal of Marriage and Family, 62*(4), 1173–1191.

Obradovic, J., & Cudina, M. (2011). Child-bearing attitudes in Croatia: A country passing through the modernization process. *Journal of Comparative Family Studies, 42*(1), 77–93.

Ostner, I. (2002). A new role for father? The German case. In B. Hobson (ed.), *Making men into fathers. Men, masculinities and the social politics of fatherhood* (pp. 150–167). Cambridge, UK: Cambridge University Press.

Pajumets, M. (2010). Estonian couples' rationalizations for fathers' rejection of parental leave. *Fathering 8*(2), 226–244.

Pascall, G., & Manning, N. (2000). Gender and social policy: comparing welfare states in central and eastern Europe and the former Soviet Union. *Journal of European Social Policy, 10*(3), 240–266.

Pfau-Effinger, B. (2005). Welfare state policies and the development of care arrangements. *European Societies, 7*(2), 321–347.

Pfau-Effinger, B. (2007). Welfare and families in Europe. *International Journal of Social Welfare, 16*(1), 95–96.

Philipov, D. (2006). Major trends affecting families in central and eastern Europe. 2006(15.08). www.un.org/esa/socdev/family/Publications/mtphilipov.pdf.

Prokofieva, L. (2007). Domokhoziaistvo i sem'ia: osobennosti struktury naseleniia. *SPERO, 6,* 57–68.

Robila, M. (2004). Families in eastern Europe: Context, trends and variations. In M. Robila (ed.), *Families in Eastern Europe* (pp. 1–14). Amsterdam, Netherlands: Elsevier.

Robila, M. (2012). Family policies in eastern Europe: A focus on parental leave. *Journal of Child and Family Studies, 21*(1), 32–41.

Rodin, J., & Åberg, P. (2013). Fatherhood across space and time: Russia in perspective. *Baltic Words, 6,* 21–28.

Rotkirch, A., & Kesseli, K. (2012). "Two children puts you in the zone of misery": Childbearing and risk perception among Russian women. In H. Carlbäck, Y. Gradskova & Z. Kravchenko (eds.), *And they lived happily ever after* (pp. 145–164). Budapest, Hungary/New York: CEU Press.

Rotkirch, A., Temkina, A., & Zdravomyslova, E. (2007). Who helps the degraded housewife? Comments on Vladimir Putin's demographic speech. *European Journal of Women's Studies, 14*(4), 349–357.

Saarinen, A. (2012). Welfare crisis and crisis-centers in Russia today. In H. Carlbäck, Y. Gradskova & Z. Kravchenko (eds.), *And they lived happily ever after: Norms and everyday practices of family and parenthood in Russia and central Europe* (pp. 241–250). Budapest, Hungary/New York: CEU Press.

Saxonberg, S., & Sirovatka, T. (2007). The re-familialisation of the Czech family policy and its causes. *International Review of Sociology, 17*(2), 319–341.

Sayer, L. C., Gauthier, A. H., & Furstenberg, F. F. J. (2004). Educational differences in parents' time with children: Cross-national variations. *Journal of Marriage and the Family, 66*(5), 1152–1169.

Soobedar, Z. (2011). A semiparametric analysis of the rising breadwinner role of women in the UK. *Review of Economics of the Household, 9*(3), 415–428.

Szelewa, D., & Polakowski, M. (2008). Who cares? Changing patterns of childcare in central and eastern Europe. *Journal of European Social Policy, 18*(2), 115–131.

Temkina, A., & Rotkirch, A. (2003). Sovetskie gendernye kontrakty i ikh transfromatsiia v sovremennoi Rossii. *Sotsiologicheskie issledovaniia, 11,* 4–15.

Teplova, T. (2007). Welfare state transformation, childcare, and women's work in Russia. *Social Politics: International Studies in Gender, State and Society, 14*(3), 284–322.

Therborn, G. (2004). *Between sex and power: Family in the world, 1990–2000.* London, UK: Routledge.

UN (2011). *Demographic yearbook 2009–2010.* New York: United Nations. http://unstats.un.org/UNSD/Demographic/products/dyb/dybsets/2009-2010.pdf.

UNICEF (1999). *Ženščiny v perechodnyj period. Regiona´lnyj monitoringovyj doklad No. 6.* Florence, Italy: Meždunarodnyj centr razvitija rebenka, UNICEF.

Uspenskaya, V. I., & Borodin, D. I. (2004). Family relations in 20th century Russia as a projective of popular beliefs, scholarly discourse and state policies. In M. Robila (ed.), *Families in eastern Europe* (vol. 5, pp. 237–248). Amsterdam, Netherlands: Elsevier JAI.

Utrata, J. (2008). Keeping the bar low: Why Russia's nonresident fathers accept narrow fatherhood ideal. *Journal of Marriage and Family, 70*(5), 1297–1310.

Vandeweyer, J., & Glorieux, I. (2008). Men taking up career leave: an opportunity for better work and family life balance? *Journal of Social Policy, 37*(2), 271–294.

Webster, L., Low, J., Siller, C., & Hackett, R. K. (2013). Understanding the contribution of a father's warmth on his child's social skills. *Fathering, 11*(1), 90–113.

WHO (2014, June 18). *World Health Statistics.* World Health Organization. http://apps.who.int/gho/data/node.main.1?lang=en.

Zhurzhenko, T. Y. e. (2004). Staraia ideologiia novoi sem'i: demograficheskii natsionalizm Rossii i Ukrainy. In S. Oushakine (ed.), *Family bones: Models to assemble* (pp. 268–296). Moskva, Russia: Novoe Literaturoe Obozrenie.

7

Fathers in Portugal: From Old to New Masculinities

Karin Wall

Major shifts in gender cultures, policies, and practices in Portugal have brought about substantial changes in fathers' roles and practices over the last few decades. In contrast to a still-strong male breadwinner model in other southern European countries, public policies since the transition to democracy in 1974 have promoted gender equality in employment and in the care of young children. This has made for a public gender culture that has eroded the male provider–female caregiver model, even if the patriarchal ideology of the right-wing dictatorship, in place for five decades until the early seventies, has also left its mark (Aboim & Marinho 2006; Torres 2004; Wall 2011).

Despite recent policy shifts and growing numbers of fathers caring for young children, gender equity in family life remains uneven and proceeds in different ways and rates across families, generations, and social classes. Moreover, culturally, a pathway emphasizing a strong orientation toward children and extended family ties is an important shaping factor of parenting cultures. It produces some normative ambiguity regarding the questioning of female primacy, both of mothers and grandmothers, in the nurturing of young children (Aboim 2010a; Wall & Amâncio 2007; Wall & Gouveia 2014).

The complex nature of the changes that are under way means that our understanding of fathers and fathering in Portugal must carefully examine the processes and factors shaping the new and diverse profiles of fathers. Against a backdrop of changing social and policy contexts, the aims of this chapter are threefold: to describe men in work and family life in Portugal by drawing on existing secondary data, both national and comparative; to present an overview of the research literature on fathers drawing on recent, mostly qualitative, studies to outline the issues and approaches underpinning research; and to examine implications for future research and policy on Portuguese fathers.

MEN IN FAMILIES IN CHANGING SOCIAL AND POLICY CONTEXTS

Portugal is a southern European country with a population of approximately 10 million, predominantly Roman Catholic, ethnically homogeneous (only 4 percent of the total population are foreign-born) and has been a member of the European Union since 1986. It is a highly developed country, with a rank of 41 among UN countries, but with a GDP per capita that is below average in the EU and among the lowest in the seventeen countries of the Eurozone (Eurostat 2014).

Portugal has followed a specific historical and cultural pathway over the last century. After the fall of the monarchy in 1910 and the short period of the first republic (1910–1928, with divorce by mutual consent introduced as early as 1910), it had a right-wing dictatorship that lasted nearly fifty years, which the April Revolution brought to an end in 1974. Thus, in common with some other southern European countries, the transition to democracy was recent. The revolution made for rapid change, particularly in the domains of work–family and gender equality policies.

The contrast in family and gender policies before and after the Revolution in 1974 is of particular importance. During the right-wing Salazar dictatorship (1928–1974), explicit pro-traditional family policies promoted a male breadwinner model emphasizing women's subordinate role and men's role as "head of family" and provider (Torres 2004; Wall 2011). Gender inequality and female responsibility for homemaking were written into the constitution, and the importance of female housework and the care of others was promoted by the state, the church, and female organizations.

Policies after the transition to democracy rejected previous gender cultural models and focused on state responsibilities to support full-time working men and women and a gradual move toward policies that support fatherhood rights and men's involvement in private life. The Portuguese constitution (1976) explicitly forbade gender discrimination in all domains, and gender mainstreaming became a dominant practice in public policies (Ferreira & Monteiro 2014). However, for some time, the spotlight was essentially on women's rights in all areas of public and private life. Men represent a more recent focus both in public debate and in policies, even if the progressive adoption of gender-balanced policies reveals a growing space for new measures and the public voicing of concern regarding men in families (Aboim & Vasconcelos 2012; Perista & Lopes 1999).

To illustrate policy developments, two sets of measures may be identified. The first is the evolving rights of both men and women in balancing work and family life. This has taken place through two main types of measures: making the right to miss work more gender-neutral and promoting measures specifically targeting fathers and their involvement in family life (Wall & Escobedo 2009). By 1995, the right to gender sharing of entitlements had been introduced for the thirty days to care for a sick child younger than 10, the two-hour daily work-time reduction during the first year of the child's life and parental leave (which could be divided between parents by mutual agreement after the first six weeks reserved for the mother). By 1997, the right to work–family balance for all individuals, both men and women, was written into the constitution.

Individual and nontransferable well-paid leave entitlements for fathers were only introduced in the late 1990s: two days of unpaid paternity leave implemented in 1995 was extended to three weeks of fully compensated paternity leave for fathers in 1999 and to four weeks in 2009. Additionally, a "sharing bonus" was introduced with the aim of promoting gender equality in parental care for a young baby: an extra month of fully compensated leave is available if the father takes four weeks or more of parental leave on his own when the mother returns to work. With the new policy measures, fathers' leave periods have become longer, and fathers' use of both paternity leave and parental leave have increased steadily. In 2013, four out of five fathers entitled to leave took paternity leave for at least two weeks, and 24 percent shared the five- to six-month initial parental leave by staying home to care for their child at least one month after the mother returned to work (up from 0.6% of fathers who shared parental leave before the reform) (Wall 2014).

Changes in conjugal and divorce regulation represent a second set of measures seeking to establish equality between partners and between fathers' and mothers' rights. Family law in the late 1970s established equality and mutual obligations between conjugal partners and abolished the husband's power and authority as "head of family" and main provider, as well as the inequality between paternal and maternal authority over children. It also recognized cohabiting couples and eliminated all previous differences in the rights of children born inside and outside of marriage.

Legislative reform since the 1970s has eased the process of divorce and highlighted new concepts such as no-fault divorce and shared parental responsibilities after divorce. The number of divorces has increased steadily since the 1970s, with the crude divorce rate rising above 2 divorces per thousand population since 2002 (2.5 in 2011). Divorce by mutual consent has also increased, with the percentage of litigious divorces dropping from 38 percent in 1980 to 6 percent in 2006. From the point of view of fathers, a major shift in legislation is related to post-divorce parental responsibilities.

Until the late 1990s, the custodial responsibility was usually given to the mother with whom the child lived, but if they wished parents "could agree to share *paternal power*." In contrast, the 1999 law established that *paternal power* must always be shared between both parents, the exception being cases in which the parents do not agree on joint *paternal power*, in which case the court decides to whom custody and power are entrusted. Recent legislation passed in 2008 replaced the concept of shared *paternal power* with the concept of *shared parental responsibilities*. However, it distinguishes between the obligation to share parental responsibility in the case of important decisions regarding the child's life and those concerning "daily life," with the latter considered the responsibility of the parent with whom the child "usually lives." Because the equal alternate residence of the child is not often implemented and the courts tend to consider mothers the primary caregivers and custodial guardians of very young children, this last reform has continued to fuel public debate on the issue of parental equality in postdivorce families. Over the last decade, fathers' associations have been voicing men's difficulties in gaining access to children after divorce, emphasizing that men have to struggle for a place as fathers if they want to share nurturing roles in daily life.

WORK-RELATED ISSUES AND FATHERING

This brief overview of some significant policy developments shows that there has been considerable change over the last few decades in the norms and practices regarding men's roles in families and gender cultural models in general. To capture the main changes, it is important to examine data on men and women in paid and unpaid work in the context of changing labor market dynamics and family living arrangements in Portuguese society.

Table 7.1 shows that the characteristics of male economic activity have changed little over the last few decades. In contrast to the rising activity rates of women, the male activity rate has remained relatively constant; men work full-time and long hours (even if only slightly longer hours than women, thanks to a sharp increase in Portuguese women's full-time employment since the 1970s), and overall they occupy more stable, top-level, and well-paid jobs than women (in 2012, women's average salary was 81.5 percent of men's average salary). Men also tend to have slightly lower rates of unemployment than women, but the recent economic crisis has affected men more than women.

We can also see that in the age groups in which men are more likely to belong to households with dependent children (ages 30–49), men's activity rate is much higher, and working hours also increase for men aged 35–44, who, in 2012, worked an average of forty-three hours per week compared to a weekly average of thirty-nine hours for all men; women's activity rate and working hours are also very high but stay close to the thirty-nine average weekly working hours of the total active population. According to the 2011 census, nearly two-thirds (63 percent) of men aged 30–49 live in simple

TABLE 7.1 Labor market indicators by gender and age group, Portugal, 1991–2012

	1991	2001	2011	2012
Activity rate (%)[1]				
Total (active pop./ total pop.)	48.9	51.5	51.4	51.2
M	57.0	58.1	56.3	55.7
F	41.4	45.4	47.0	47.1
25–34 years, all[2]	85.6	87.6	90.6	90.5
M	93.3	92.2	92.5	91.9
F	78.5	83.0	88.8	89.1
35–44 years, all[2]	84.5	87.2	90.8	90.6
M	96.7	94.8	94.6	93.6
F	73.5	79.8	87.3	87.7
Unemployment rate (%)[1]				
Total	4.1	4.0	12.7	15.5
M	2.7	3.2	12.3	15.6
F	5.8	5.0	13.0	15.5
25–34 years, all	4.9	4.1	14.1	18.1
M	3.0	3.0	13.4	17.7
F	7.0	5.3	14.8	18.5
35–44 years, all	2.8	3.2	11.0	13.3
M	1.7	2.3	10.4	13.1
F	4.3	4.2	11.5	13.5
Average number of weekly working time, all employed[1]	42.4	39.5	39.2	39.2
M	44.1	41.3	40.8	40.8
F	40.2	37.3	37.3	37.4
Difference M–F	3.9	4.0	3.5	3.4
25–34 years, all	42	40	40	40
M	44	42	42	42
F	40	39	39	39
M–F (Difference/%)	4	3	3	3
35–44 years, all	42	40	41	41
M	44	42	43	43
F	40	38	39	39
M–F (Difference/%)	4	4	4	4
Part-time employment[2]				
(% of total employed persons)	5.8	8.2	10.1	11.0
M	2.6	3.7	7.0	8.2
F	9.9	13.7	13.7	14.1

TABLE 7.1 Continued

	1991	2001	2011	2012
Average monthly earnings (€)[3,4]	349.4	687.5	906.1	915.0
M	384.1	747.4	985.2	999.8
F	290.8	601.0	808.4	814.5
M–F (Difference/%)	93.3/75.7%	146.4/80.4%	176.8/82.1%	185.3/81.5%
25–34 years, all	345.3	663.4	964.1	801.4
M	375.6	702.8	1043.5	832.2
F	301.4	613.8	870.0	767.7
M–F (Difference/%)	74.2/80.2%	89/87.3%	173.5/83.4%	64.5/92.2%
35–44 years, all	405	738.1	981.7	972.5
M	440.5	812.5	1099.8	1053.9
F	339.8	634.3	827.3	880.1
M–F (Difference/%)	100.6/77.1%	178.1/78.1%	272.5/75.2%	173.8/83.5%

[1]*Source:* INE: Labour Survey, data available July 30, 2014.
[2]*Source:* Eurostat: EU-LFS.
[3]As there is no information for 2001, the data for this indicator refer to the year 2002.
[4]*Source:* Data for 1991 and 2002 taken from MSESS: GEP: *Quadros de Pessoal*, time series 1991–2006. Data for 2011 and 2012 taken from *INE: Bases de dados*, updated December 3, 2013.

family households of couples with children; only a very small proportion live in lone father families (1.7 percent), and the remainder live in couples (10 percent), alone or in no-family households of various persons (10 percent), and in complex family households (12 percent) (Delgado & Wall 2014). In comparison with men, a higher proportion of women in this age group are living in lone mother households (10 percent) and lower proportions in one-person or no-family households (7 percent).

The growth in lone parent and reconstituted families, alongside the gradual decrease in households of couples with children and the increase in one-person households, is thus a major new trend in family living arrangements. Nevertheless, lone mothers are still the predominant pattern in lone parent families: Lone fathers have increased in absolute numbers but continue to represent only 13 percent of all lone parents. The characteristics of lone fathers having dependent children also reveal some specific characteristics: Compared to lone mothers, lone fathers tend to be older (older than 35), to have one rather than two or more living-in children, and to care more frequently for older children, aged 10–18 (Marinho 2014).

The above mentioned trends have led to a predominant full-time adult worker model in Portugal over the last few decades. Although women have more precarious jobs and the wage gap has persisted over time, the majority of men and women in Portugal work full-time (Table 7.2) and have continuous work trajectories, with the exception of breaks related to parental leave and other breaks, which tend to be short and are taken more by women than men. In contrast with many other European countries, this means that in Portugal, the full-time dual-earner model has become generalized in both norms and practices.

Findings from a national survey in 2002 (Family and Gender Roles Survey—International Social Survey Programme) show that interviewees overwhelmingly agree (93%) that both the man and the woman should contribute to household income and a majority (67%) disagree with the ideal of a housewife supported by a male breadwinner ("a man's job is to earn money, a woman's job is to look after the home and family") (Wall & Amâncio 2007). The proportion who disagree with this gender role model is only slightly higher for women (68%) than men (65%) but is considerably higher for individuals in younger age groups and those belonging to qualified or intermediate occupations (in fact, only 51% of men and 57% of women in manual occupations disagree with this gender role model). In a repeat of this question in a 2010 national survey on family trajectories and the life course, the proportion of those disagreeing with the male breadwinner model had risen to 77 percent.

Practices have followed the same trend. In 2002, 93 percent of couples having at least one child younger than 6 were full-time dual-earner couples (close to proportions in Norway, France, and Denmark). This stands apart from other European countries where the one-earner model is still the prevalent model for families with children (Germany, Luxembourg, Greece, Spain, and Ireland) or those, such as the UK and the Netherlands, where the one-and-a-half earner model is the prevalent form thanks to high levels of female part-time work when children are young (Aboim 2010a).

Norms and practices related to men's roles in the private sphere have changed less and more gradually than women's involvement in paid work over the last few decades. At the normative level, in the 2002 survey, nearly all individuals (85%) agree that men should participate more in household tasks (82% of men and 88% of women) and in the care of young children (82% of men and 90% of women) (Wall 2007). However, agreement with fathers' participation in care is one thing, but agreement with the idea of fathers as equally competent caregivers is another. In this domain, there is considerable hesitation in relation to men's parenting skills: In the 2010 survey, only 30 percent of all individuals agree that a lone father can raise a child as well as a lone mother. The proportion who agree is lowest in the older generation aged 70–75 (22% of men and 18% of women), slightly higher for middle-aged individuals aged 50–55 (28% of men and 26% of women), and much higher (50%) in the younger generation of adults aged 35–40, with 59 percent of men and 45 percent of women agreeing with this statement. Interestingly, the attitudinal gender gap widens as we move across the three generations. It seems to indicate that in the context of a general increase in more favorable attitudes to men's caring skills, there is currently more acceptance on the part of men than of women regarding men's role as a primary caregiver of children.

Nevertheless, there is a difference between expectations and practices. The actual time division of housework and care between men and women is unequal, even if the gender gap has gradually decreased. Measuring weekly hours of housework across the EU, the European Quality of Life Survey shows that employed women in Portugal spend an average fifteen hours on household tasks (down from seventeen hours in 2007), whereas employed men spend eight hours (up from seven hours in 2007) (Table 7.2). The time that Portuguese men allocate to domestic work is slightly below the European average (nine hours), whereas the time allocated by women is slightly higher than the EU average, indicating a still strong norm of female domesticity and dedication to housework.

National surveys have also shown significant differences between occupational groups and levels of education. Women who have low levels of education and who have manual occupations spend the highest number of hours in domestic work, well above the national average, whereas qualified women's hours of housework are well below average and many of them, specifically when they care for young children or dependent elderly persons, are likely to have some paid domestic help (Lyonnette, Crompton, & Wall 2007). A survey on families of couples that have children conducted in 1999 revealed three main patterns of gender division of housework: the female housework pattern (59.2%), in which women do the majority of household tasks; the joint division pattern (30.4%), in which fathers' participation is above average, with 6 percent of couples sharing on an equal basis; and the delegation pattern (10.4%), in which some tasks are carried out by a third person, usually a paid employee. Among couples in which women are highly qualified, one in every two women belongs to the delegation pattern (Wall 2005).

At the same time, men are more involved in childcare, indicating a slow but steady transformation in the ideals and practices of fathering. According to the European Quality of Life survey, employed men in Portugal spend an average fifteen hours caring for children, whereas women spend twenty-two hours (Table 7.2). In a European comparative perspective, the gender gap of seven hours is below the EU average gap of ten hours. As fathers, however, they tend to be more involved than mothers in playing with the child and less in personal care activities. Data from the 1999 time-use survey showed that among those who participate in childcare, men spent fifty-one minutes and women forty-three minutes "playing" with children during the average day, whereas men spent forty-six minutes and women an hour and twenty-seven minutes in activities related to personal or "physical" care.

Recent studies measuring father involvement in Portuguese families using frameworks within developmental and social psychology underline similar trends and some additional findings (e.g., Monteiro, Fernandes, Veríssimo, Costa, Torres, & Vaugn 2010; Arsénio & Vieira Santos 2013). Exploring fathers' perceptions of their level of involvement in five areas of parental care

TABLE 7.2 Hours spent weekly cooking and/or doing household tasks and caring for and educating children, for employed men and women, by country—EU 27 (2011)

	Hours cooking and doing household tasks			Hours caring for and educating children		
	M	F	Difference M–F	M	F	Difference M–F
EU27	9	14	5	18	28	10
Romania	14	15	1	20	24	4
Estonia	12	14	2	19	26	7
Denmark	8	11	3	22	25	3
Sweden	7	10	3	19	30	11
Bulgaria	8	12	4	14	17	3
Slovenia	10	14	4	15	25	10
Finland	7	11	4	20	29	9
France	7	11	4	16	26	10
Italy	8	12	4	13	18	5
Germany	9	14	5	19	22	3
Belgium	8	13	5	14	23	9
Spain	10	15	5	19	31	12
Netherlands	8	13	5	19	30	11
Latvia	10	15	5	19	23	4
UK	9	14	5	26	47	21
Hungary	9	15	6	16	26	10
Ireland	10	16	6	27	44	17
Lithuania	8	14	6	22	26	4
Luxemburg	7	13	6	20	32	12
Poland	9	15	6	19	32	13
Czech Republic	7	13	6	12	20	8
Portugal	8	15	7	15	22	7
Austria	8	16	8	17	24	7
Slovakia	10	18	8	16	29	13
Greece	10	18	8	19	24	11
Cyprus	11	20	9	18	27	9
Malta	10	21	11	17	35	18

Source: Eurostat, European Quality of Life Survey, 2013.

(direct care, indirect care, teaching/discipline, play, leisure outside the home), results show that fathers report participation in all areas but consider that "indirect care" (planning and organization of care routines) is mainly carried out by mothers whereas they themselves participate more in play activities than mothers (Monteiro et al. 2010). The main predictor of fathers' participation in all areas of parental activities was the level of involvement desired by the mother, suggesting the importance of the role of mothers in regulating parental roles. Higher levels of education are associated with higher involvement in the management of care routines and less in play activities. Parenting styles also shape fathers' involvement, with the authoritarian style emerging as a predictor of absence and less time spent with the child and the democratic style as a predictor of father involvement. However, both styles are predictors of fathers' participation in education and discipline (Arsénio & Vieira Santos 2013).

In summary, changing normative and policy contexts have led to a combination of old and new trends in family forms and gender roles. Simple family households of couples and couples with children have decreased but together still represent the predominant family form (61% of all households), whereas lone parent, single person, and reconstituted households have increased. In couples with children, the dual-earner model is the predominant pattern, with almost all men and women in full-time paid work. Female activity rates are high, in particular in the age groups in which the majority of men and women live in households with children, and changes in both the attitudes to and the economic behavior of women have led to the continuing decline of the male breadwinner model. Men's involvement in private life has been much slower to evolve, especially among older age groups and those with lower educational levels. Although, as in midwestern and northwestern European countries, men's participation in unpaid work has increased and women's has decreased, the gender gap is still considerable.

As a result, Portugal displays an average and distinctive overall performance in the European Union Gender Equality Index (Plantenga, Remery, Figueiredo, & Smith 2009): It combines high scores on participation in the labor market, unemployment, and income, with medium scores on political power and low scores on "care intensity" (number of hours spent on providing care for children by men and women aged 20–49), generating a medium score on the overall gender (in)equality index, with a rank of 12 out of twenty-five EU member states. Interestingly, it ranks close to countries such as France and Slovenia but is a clear outlier when compared to other southern European countries, such as Spain and Greece, where public policy underscoring that gender equality must be achieved foremost by women's participation in the public sphere has been less marked.

PAST RESEARCH ON FATHERS: MAIN APPROACHES
AND FINDINGS

There has been a considerable amount of research on men's roles in gender equality, mainly over the last fifteen years, even if, as in policymaking and public discourse, research has been more focused on women rather than on men. An overview of the recent literature shows that the theoretical background draws from different disciplines and combines five main fields of theory: gender studies and feminist thought (e.g., Delphy & Leonard 1992; Walby 1997; Butler 2004); scholarship on men and masculinities, in particular research highlighting hegemonic masculinity in transition and the blurring of gender boundaries and sexualities in a late modern world (Pleck 1981; Morgan 1992; Connell 1995; Hearn et al. 2002); scholarship bridging the issues of gender, work and family, and welfare states, mainly from a comparative social policy perspective (e.g., Hochschild & Machung 1989; Fraser 1994; Orloff 1996; Pfau-Effinger 2000; Gornick & Meyers 2001; Lewis 2001; Crompton 2006); scholarship in the fields of psychology and sociology of fatherhood (e.g., Marsiglio 1995; Bjornberg & Kollind 1996; Coltrane 1996; Palkovitz 1997; Castelain-Meunier 2002; Modak & Palazzo 2002; Hobson 2002; Day & Lamb 2004; Dermott 2008; O'Brien 2013); and family studies highlighting change in family functioning and dynamics, conceptualized within processes such as the pluralization of family interactions and trajectories, individualization, changing intimacies and meanings of family (e.g., Allan 2008; Beck & Beck-Gernsheim 2002; Giddens 1992; Jamieson 1998; Kellerhals et al. 2004; Singly 1996; Widmer 2010).

Different research issues have been raised regarding the role of men in families and gender equality, all revolving around the need to understand how the policy and cultural transformations have paved the way for the emergence of new forms of gender division of labor and, most important, of new models of masculinity and fatherhood underpinned by a renewed vision of the gender contract. The quantitative findings described above reveal the emergence of new attitudes and practices, with men's participation in housework and care responsibilities changing slowly but steadily. This has challenged research to seek to understand the changes from the perspective and lived experiences of men themselves: How are men negotiating old and new masculinities? How are policy changes imprinting how fathers and mothers live and perceive their family lives and care responsibilities? How diverse are the pathways and models of fatherhood? What is the effect of individual agency, of family and conjugal patterns, and of structural and life course factors such as education, employment, religion, or contrasting generational cultures? What is happening to men who live in new family forms such as reconstituted families, lone parent families, transnational families, or same-sex families? Most of this research has relied strongly, though not exclusively, on qualitative methods.

A first important set of findings concerns the changing subjective perceptions and cultural models of fatherhood in Portuguese society. There is a generalized consensus around the ideal of a caring and involved father, as a number of qualitative and quantitative studies with fathers have been able to show (Aboim & Marinho 2006; Monteiro et al. 2010; Wall 2011; Wall, Aboim, & Marinho 2007). Most men vehemently reject the old ideal of a distant and authoritarian father, criticize former generations of fathers, and value the norm of the involved "hands-on" father who participates in the daily responsibilities of parental care, education, and emotional involvement. Fatherhood also emerges as a key dimension in the building of new forms of masculinity. To a great extent, the reconfiguring of the father figure has been a powerful driving force in challenging traditional masculinities in Portuguese society (Aboim & Marinho 2006). Men's discourses and perceptions reveal the enormous centrality of fatherhood in the negotiation of old and new masculinities, with children representing fundamental sources of identity both for women and men.

Moving beyond this general trend, research also shows the social construction of a diversity of fatherhood models and practices (Aboim & Marinho 2006; Monteiro et al. 2010; Wall, Aboim, & Marinho 2007; Wall, Cunha, & Marinho 2013). An exploratory study on men in families of couples with children, drawing on in-depth interviews with twenty-five fathers, revealed findings on the pluralization of fatherhood as well as new results on men's reproductive projects and experiences of work–family stress (Wall, Aboim, & Marinho 2007). Drawing on the analytical linkages between fatherhood, work, and conjugal functioning (e.g., gender models in paid and unpaid work, type of conjugal interactions), seven main profiles of fatherhood were identified: traditional provider, helper, companionship, career-oriented, egalitarian, stay-at-home, appropriative.

"Provider" fathers still identify with female domesticity and traditional masculinity involving male breadwinning and the father's educational role, even if they seek to participate in their children's daily lives more than their own fathers by playing with them or taking them along—particularly their sons—to activities such as sporting events. "Helper" fathers see themselves as secondary, less competent, caregivers who help mothers in the parental routines, relying on their guidance and mediation in parental responsibilities and tasks, whereas "companionship" fathers emphasize the importance of togetherness in conjugal life, seeing themselves as involved fathers who "share," not necessarily on an equal basis, all parenting tasks. Rather than equal parenting, these fathers emphasize the importance of doing things jointly and always being beside/with the mother.

Career-oriented, egalitarian, stay-at-home, and appropriative fathers underscore the importance of gender equality and symmetry in men's and women's roles in both private and public spheres, but their work–family strategies and agency develop along different lines. "Career-oriented" fathers give priority to their professional careers, thereby seeking to be involved in parenting tasks at certain times and through intensive fathering providing "quality time" with children. "Egalitarian" fathers tend to build up their involvement on a more fifty–fifty basis, making a point of being autonomous and competent in all parenting and household tasks. Contrary to expectations, this profile of fatherhood was found in different social classes, not only in highly qualified couples.

"Stay-at home" fathers are those who, constrained by job or career instability, hand over breadwinning to the mother and try to "invent" a new place for men in the domestic sphere, whereas "appropriative" fathers see themselves as more competent than mothers and take on a larger share of household tasks, caregiving, and overall parental responsibility for children's well-being and education. In this case, it is mothers who become secondary housekeepers and caregivers.

A major conclusion is thus that fatherhood is evolving into plurality as there seems to be diversified strands of change. But, as Aboim stresses in her book on plural masculinities (Aboim 2010b), the findings point not only to the hybrid nature of these changes, but also to how some men may be recreating power through these changes. Rather than a continuous and linear movement toward gender equality, the decline of the male breadwinner model has promoted hybrid features combining different values and practices (such as incorporating the ideal of a caring man into the ethics of traditional masculinity), as well as possibly building up new forms of male domination, in particular when men and fathers establish supremacy in the private sphere by appropriating femininity and defining themselves as better at female tasks than women. Following a simple view of hegemonic masculinity, we may say that the latter draws on power as the product of traditional responsibility, breadwinning, and protectiveness. Aboim's perspective helps us to recall that hegemonic masculinity may also be defined as a flexible power structure, thereby challenging research to examine how men are re-creating power when they appropriate or define themselves as better than women.

The aforementioned study (Wall, Aboim, & Cunha 2010) also revealed interesting findings on men's views of family planning and reproduction. Compared to women who, early on in life, know whether and how many children they would like to have (Almeida 2004), men's reproductive ideals seem to develop later in life, usually when they had a stable partnership, and are less well defined regarding the timing of the transition to parenthood. Negotiation of the number and timing of children is perceived as an essential aspect of a balanced and longstanding conjugal relationship, lead-ing men whose wives decided unilaterally to have another child to question the conjugal relationship (Cunha 2010). Building on this point, Cunha's work on the reproductive trajectories of men and women has also shown that despite gender-neutral childbearing ideals (both men and women idealize a two-child family), the trajectories have distinct features; men wish to have children later on in life, postponing the transition to parenthood more than women. In middle adulthood (older than 35), they are highly receptive to being fathers for the first time or having additional children, whereas women tend to begin to withdraw their reproductive intentions. In short, there seems to be a childbearing agenda mismatch in couples today (Cunha 2012).

A second important set of findings concerns men's work–family balance. Several studies have shown that men also feel that work life is acutely affect-ing their role as fathers and have difficulty reconciling family and work when there are young children. In fact, men's work–family stress, not only women's, is particularly high in Portuguese society (Torres 2004). The key factor in men's stress is long working hours and lack of time to be with the family and children, making it difficult for men who feel an obligation and a need to spend more time at home to find their place in parenting and family rou-tines (Aboim & Marinho 2006). Men in manual or low-paid occupations also underscore shift work and the need to put in extra hours to provide a better life for their children. Highly qualified men underscore the ideal of a totally career-invested and time-flexible male worker, thus finding it difficult, particularly in the private sector, to ask for more family-friendly schedules and leaves or to reduce overall work demands. Overall, the findings under-line that employers and families still have strong expectations, despite the predominant dual-earner model, that men in families will assume the role of primary provider and secondary caregiver—meaning that they will be avail-able for work and long hours, less likely to take leave, and more invested in their careers.

Additional findings related to work–family stress emerged in a qualitative study of children's perceptions of family life in times of crisis carried out in 2013 (Wall et al. 2015. Children (aged 8–17) perceived the economic crisis as strongly affecting their parents' work schedules, due to the fear of losing their jobs and pressure from employers to work long hours. They are particu-larly sensitive to new tensions related to money problems, which are revealed in their parents' frequent arguments on these topics and difficulty in talking about other things. They express their wish—not necessarily for more time with parents, for they understand the pressure to work—merely for the social and psychological conditions that would allow mothers and fathers to be able to relax when everyone is at home together, which is what they say makes them happy.

A third set of important findings is related to fathers in specific types of families, such as reconstituted, lone parent, or same-sex families. Owing to the rise in these types of families and new legislation promoting co-parenting and shared parental responsibilities after divorce, men frequently have to negotiate their role as fathers in a postdivorce situation and also to take on the role of stepfather in the care and education of young children (Lobo 2009; Marinho 2011; Atalaia 2012; Correia 2013). Analysis of men's experiences over the last two decades reveals that in many cases, the biological father becomes an absent figure after divorce, sometimes because of conjugal conflict, other times because of maternal gatekeeping and court orders giving him only minimal visiting rights and because of personal life choices or traditional views on fatherhood and motherhood. In many cases, though, men do not want to be absent or distant fathers not actively involved in parenting after a divorce. They sometimes negotiate an active role as fathers in the daily lives of their children, but they may also have had to struggle for a place as fathers, competing with women with a view to sharing the nurturing roles that have traditionally been associated with motherhood.

Many men living in postdivorce situations interviewed in the aforementioned studies on men in families (Aboim & Marinho 2006; Wall, Aboim, & Cunha 2010) expressed their dissatisfaction with the legal arrangements established in court and the forced absence from their children's daily lives. By comparison, fathers living in arrangements involving the alternate residence of children felt that they were involved in the daily lives of their children. Further analysis based on an exploratory qualitative study of fathers in alternate residence families (Marinho 2011) showed that the internal dynamics of fatherhood are shaped by two main social processes in this type of living arrangement, indicating some diversity of fathering styles postdivorce. On the one hand, fathers have to reconfigure their autonomy. Before divorce, they were usually caring fathers who had built up their own parenting skills and individualized relationship with their children. But in postdivorce living arrangements, this autonomy is renegotiated and may move either in the direction of an independent style of fathering, with low levels of interaction with the mother, or toward autonomy embedded in strong interdependency with the mother or reconfigured in the context of support from a new partner. On the other hand, a process of negotiation of the specificity of male parenting may be perceived as similar or equal to that of the mother or may be seen as complementary to or even totally different from the mother's role.

In-depth analysis of men in reconstituted families reveals some diversity in the social construction of their roles as stepfathers. Rather than the dichotomy proposed in the 1980s and 1990s by sociologists of the family between stepfathers who replace the biological father, thus taking on all the responsibilities and activities of a father, and those who build up a complementary role to the biological father (Martin 1997), recent qualitative data reveal a more complex reality and greater diversity. Complementarity may take on various forms, depending not only on the presence or absence of the biological father, but also on the agency and pro-active behavior of the stepfather himself and the attitudes of the mother, who may want to mediate the relationship rather than share the parental role. Thus, besides stepfathers who are "substitute" fathers, there are stepfathers who negotiate their role and the trust of the mother over time; stepfathers who see themselves as secondary parental figures, acting under the guidance of the mother; stepfathers who actively pursue a role as a friend rather than a father figure, investing in relationships with their stepchildren but keeping their distance in relation to parental responsibilities; and frustrated stepfathers who have not succeeded in building up a fathering role, because the mother has occupied the parental space (Atalaia 2012).

The issue of stepfatherhood and the absence of legal regulation regarding the role of stepfathers have also been the focus of recent research on men in same-sex couples with children. Same-sex marriage was legally approved in Portugal in 2010, but adoption was left out of the legal package. In fact, attitudes to adoption and co-adoption by same-sex couples, though changing, are far from reaching a generalized consensus in Portuguese society. Even among younger adults aged 35–40, only 34 percent of women and 37 percent of men (36% for all) in 2010 agreed that "same-sex couples should have the same rights as other couples, including adoption," whereas among the older generations, only 8 percent and 12 percent of all individuals expressed favorable attitudes. A qualitative study that interviewed men in same-sex couples (Aboim & Vasconcelos 2012) highlighted foremost a strong wish for fatherhood and expectations related to future equal rights. Another issue raised by the interviewees was the problem of the recognition of shared parental responsibilities by both partners in same-sex couples. In the absence of legal regulation of adoption and co-adoption, this often leads to situations in which the fathering of the partner's children over many years (e.g., of the partner's biological children from a previous heterosexual marriage) is never recognized, since the stepfather cannot be considered as a parental figure and legally share parental responsibilities.

A fourth set of findings are related to the effects of recent policy developments (2009) in paternity and parental leaves on fathers' experiences in caring for a baby. As mentioned above, in 2009 an extra month of fully compensated leave ("sharing bonus") became available if the father takes at least four weeks of the initial parental leave on his own after the mother goes back to work. Within this changing policy environment, the lived experiences of fathers on "home alone" leave were explored through a qualitative study of fourteen Portuguese fathers who took full-time leave alone for at least thirty days (Wall 2014). Six key social processes related to the experience of leave alone were identified: negotiating, doing activities, learning, bonding, undoing gender roles, and experiencing emotions. Findings reveal social experiences of "fast time," "hard work," and "parental care" rather than "slow time" and "masculine care" focusing on the educational dimensions of fathering. Fathers stressed the strengthening of father–child bonds, the importance of leave alone for enhancing responsibility and autonomy and creating empathy with their partner, and the discovery of new and individualized skills promoting fathers' self-confidence in the interchangeable competences of fathers and mothers when caring for a baby. These two dimensions of lived experiences seem to be uniquely related to taking "home alone" leave. It is in the context of a break with female mediation that the father's self-definition as a capable, independent, or primary caregiver emerges with some strength and puts previous gender roles in question, such as the idea that the mother is the primary and natural caregiver. It is also through being alone with a baby that fathers describe a process of integration of traditionally feminine psychological traits, such as emotional literacy.

The experiences of fathers are not always similar or equally transgressive from a gender perspective. In a profile associated with critical discourses and practices, "innovative–deconstructive" fathers openly question traditional gender role models. At the opposite end of gender undoing, the study revealed profiles in which change is seen as transitional (while the father is on leave). These fathers also see themselves as acquiring new skills and autonomy, with some going through the experience of a "fundamental breakthrough" in conjugal gender roles that seemed unequivocally cemented in inequality. From a policy perspective, the study suggests significant differences between leave policies promoting family time and those encouraging father's time alone with a newborn child.

FINAL REMARKS

A key aim in this chapter was to explore the situation of fathers in Portugal and to understand how changing policies and social contexts are shaping norms and practices related to men's roles in families. An important issue was to understand the current research agenda on this topic and to examine the main findings on the negotiation between old and new masculinities and to what extent they confirm or challenge a traditional model of fatherhood. Drawing on this overview, a further step was to identify some gaps and challenges for future research and to reflect on the policy implications of the analysis.

Overall, as shown in this chapter, we can say that in policies, norms, and practices, fathering in Portugal has evolved from a dominant model emphasizing the role of men in families as distant, provider, and authoritarian father figures toward a model highlighting the role of men as caregiving, close fathers who support or share parental routines and responsibilities. Alongside the new ideal of involved fatherhood and a narrow gender gap in paid work based on a dual-earner model, norms and practices still reveal gender inequalities. The questioning of the primacy of mothers as nurturers and housekeepers is not clear-cut, whereas the opposite also seems to be true—i.e., expectations of a strong investment in breadwinning and protection are still more associated with fathers, when there are young children, and with male workers in general. In conjunction with other shaping factors such as age, occupation, and maternal and paternal agency, this is contributing to considerable pluralization of fathering norms and practices. It also leads to stress and tensions in couples regarding the negotiation of family life and parental roles, and represents important challenges for fathers seeking to incorporate old and new dimensions of masculinity and fatherhood.

Research has focused on these trends by combining different theoretical and methodological approaches. The "undoing" of previous gender cultural models in paid and unpaid work and the reconfiguration and pluralization of fatherhood emerges as the central focus of recent studies. Research on the outcomes of these processes for the social actors themselves has, however, remained underdeveloped. Despite some work on the subjective perceptions and lived experiences of fathers, there is, for example, a gap in research regarding the effects of new fathering norms and practices on children. For some issues, such as the consequences of alternate residence living arrangements in postdivorce families, this gap is making for a heated societal debate that lacks evidence-based research on which to draw. Even case studies of adults who experienced different types of postdivorce living arrangements in their childhood have not emerged. Legal studies are also a missing dimension of research in this area that are important to assessing and reforming existing norms and policies on parental responsibilities as they relate to fatherhood and stepfatherhood in new family forms such as reconstituted families and same-sex families.

Knowledge on the negotiation of fatherhood and motherhood in couples, drawing on interviews with both members of the couple, is also incipient (Wall, Cunha, & Marinho 2013). Methodologically, this type of research design is difficult and lengthy to implement. For the present research agenda emphasizing the complex social processes of negotiation and pluralization, it represents a crucial viewpoint on how the new trends in masculinities and femininities, fatherhood and motherhood, are in the process of reconfiguration and how couples are managing to deal with this.

The effect of the current economic crisis and developments in labor market dynamics driven by high levels of unemployment and new pressures on employees to work long hours or to be flexible about their labor market participation is a third strand of research that has yet to receive more attention. Given the emphasis that is still sometimes given to male primacy in paid work, it is important to understand how pressure in the workplace, as well as increasing precariousness in male employment, may be creating some polarization: between men who become highly involved fathers owing to structural constraints such as unemployment or precarious forms of work and those who, to invest in their careers, build up a weaker involvement in fathering. The recent rise in couples having children in which the mother is the only or main breadwinner signals the importance of such a research agenda.

At the policy level, it is important to recognize and highlight the barriers currently restraining the achievement of gender equality in parenthood and fathers' involvement in family life. They concern the labor market structure; the internal dynamics of family; policies relating to gender, family, and fatherhood; and the persistence of traditional features of masculinity and femininity, not only in families and individuals, but also in social institutions (e.g., family courts, firm and workplace cultures, governmental bodies responsible for ensuring fathers' entitlements, professional groups such as pediatricians).

Raising awareness and debate on how the intersection of these factors generates and reproduces inequality in parental roles, despite the profound changes that have been taking place in Portuguese society, is a first step. For example, the gender structure of the labor market is still an important variable to recognize and take into account. Men tend to work a large number of weekly hours, more so when they are fathers of young children. Professional overload increases among qualified men, especially those who work in the private sector. Thus employment barriers are affecting fathers and are also generating problems of stress in work–family balance. Additionally, leave policy architecture, though promoting the involvement of fathers in leave, does not establish totally gender-neutral entitlements. The acceptance of male employees missing work and taking leave is still difficult to achieve. Furthermore, the decline in the male breadwinner model does not always mean a shift away from former male and female attributes. Financial responsibility, protection, and education are dimensions of good parenting that men and women still often connect primarily to masculinity.

Evaluating existing policies and their effects on fathers and outlining proposals for furthering these policies or ensuring their implementation and consistency are other crucial and necessary next steps. For example, evaluating the difficulties men have taking leave or understanding why the majority still does not share parental leave is as important as analyzing the effects of leave-taking on fathers' involvement in family life. Likewise, assessing consistency and coherence in existing policies is an important objective to keep in view in times of economic crisis and of lessened state support for families. Ideologies and practices, especially in the domain of family life (and fatherhood is not an exception), change slowly and over long periods. Conversely, they may also respond rapidly to inconsistent or weakly defined policy objectives by shifting back to previous cultural models. This is likely to reinforce the over-burdening of mothers in the private sphere and the overburdening of fathers in the public sphere. Policies promoting involved fatherhood thus must strike a delicate balance between the public and private spheres, between policies focusing on fathers and on mothers.

ASSOCIATIONS AND GOVERNMENTAL BODIES DEALING WITH FATHERING ISSUES

Associação para a Igualdade Parental e Direitos dos Filhos (Association for Equal Parenting and the Rights of Children). http://igualdadeparental .org/associados/contactos/.

CITE: Comissão para a Igualdade no Trabalho e no Emprego (Commission for Equality in Work and Employment). www.cite.gov.pt.

Pais para sempre. Associação para a defesa dos filhos dos pais separados (Fathers forever. Association for the Defence of Separated Fathers). www.paisparasempre.eu/.

REFERENCES

Aboim, S. (2010a). Gender cultures and the division of labour in contemporary Europe: A cross-national perspective. *The Sociological Review, 58*(2), 171–196.

Aboim, S. (2010b). *Plural masculinities: The remaking of the self in private life.* Farnham, UK: Ashgate.

Aboim, S., & Marinho, S. (2006). *Men and gender equality: The role of men and fathers in the promotion of reconciliation of work and private life. Report on Portugal.* Portugal, Greece, Norway, Cyprus: CIDM/KEITH.

Aboim, S., & Vasconcelos, P. (2010). *Homens nas Margens. Relatório de Pesquisa.* Lisbon, Portugal: Instituto de Ciências Sociais, University of Lisbon.

Aboim, S., & Vasconcelos, P. (2012). Report on the *Study on the role of men in gender equality in Portugal.* Brussels, Netherlands: European Commission.

Allan, G. (2008). Flexibility, friendship, and family. *Personal Relationships, 15*, 1–16.

Almeida, A. N. (2004). *Fecundidade e Contracepção.* Lisbon, Portugal: Imprensa de Ciências Sociais.

Arsénio, C., & Vieira Santos, S. (2013). Paternidade na infância: Envolvimento paterno e estilos parentais educativos em pais de crianças em idade escolar. In A. Pereira, M. Calheiros, P. Vagos, I. Direito, S. Monteiro, C. Fernandes da Silva, & A. Allen Gomes (eds.), *VIII Simpósio Nacional de Investigação em Psicologia* (pp. 638–648). Lisbon, Portugal: Associação Portuguesa de Psicologia.

Atalaia, S. (2012). *A parentalidade em contexto de recomposição familiar: o caso do padrasto* (Unpublished doctoral dissertation). Lisbon, Portugal: University of Lisbon.

Beck, U., & Beck-Gernsheim, E. (2002). *Individualization.* London, UK: Sage.

Bjornberg, U., & Kollind, A. K (eds.). (1996). *Men's family relations.* Stockholm, Sweden: Almqvist & Wiksell International.

Butler, J. (2004). *Undoing gender.* New York: Routledge.

Castelain-Meunier, C. (2002). The place of fatherhood and the parental role: Tensions, ambivalence and contradictions. *Current Sociology, 2,* 185–201.

Coltrane, S. (1996). *Family man: fatherhood, housework and gender equity.* New York: Oxford University Press.

Connell, R. W. (1995). *Masculinities.* Oakland, CA: University of California Press.

Correia, S. V. (2013). *Conciliação família-trabalho em famílias monoparentais: Uma abordagem comparativa* (Unpublished doctoral dissertation). Lisbon, Portugal: University of Lisbon.

Crompton, R. M. (2006). *Employment and the family: The reconfiguration of work and family life in contemporary societies.* Cambridge, UK: Cambridge University Press.

Cunha, V. (2010). Projectos de paternidade e a construção da fecundidade conjugal. In K. Wall, S. Aboim, & V. Cunha (eds.), *A vida familiar no masculino: negociando velhas e novas masculinidades* (pp. 265–312). Lisbon, Portugal: Comissão para a Igualdade no Trabalho e no Emprego.

Cunha, V. (2012). As decisões reprodutivas na sociedade portuguesa: Elementos para uma reflexão sobre o alcance e os limites das políticas públicas na natalidade. In Casa Civil da Presidência da República (ed.), *Roteiros do Futuro: Conferência Nascer em Portugal* (pp. 131–143). Lisbon, Portugal: Presidência da República/ Imprensa Nacional Casa da Moeda.

Day, R., & Lamb, M. E. (2004). *Conceptualizing and measuring father involvement.* Mahwah, NJ: Erlbaum.

Delgado, A., & Wall, K. (eds.). (2014). *Famílias nos Censos 2011.* Lisbon, Portugal: INE/Imprensa de Ciências Sociais.

Delphy, C., & Leonard, D. (1992). *Familiar exploitation: A new analysis of marriage in contemporary western societies.* Cambridge, UK: Polity Press.

Dermott, E. (2008). *Intimate fatherhood: A sociological analysis.* London, UK: Routledge.

Eurostat (2014). *GDP per Capita.* http://appsso.eurostat.ec.europa.eu/nui/submit-ModifiedQuery.do.

Ferreira, V., & Monteiro, R. (2014). *Trabalho, igualdade e diálogo social: Estratégias e desafios de um percurso.* Lisbon, Portugal: CITE.

Fraser, N. (1994). After the family wage. *Political Theory, 22*(4), 591–618.

Giddens, A. (1992). *The transformation of intimacy: Sexuality, love, and eroticism in modern societies.* Stanford, CA: Stanford University Press.

Gornick, J. C., & Meyers, M. K. (2001). *Families that work: Policies for reconciling parenthood and employment.* New York: The Russell Sage Foundation.

Hearn, J., et al. (2002). Critical studies on men in ten European countries: The state of law and policy. *Men and Masculinities, 5*(2), 192–217.

Hobson, B. (ed.). (2002). *Making men into fathers: Men, masculinities and the social politics of fatherhood.* Cambridge, UK: Cambridge University Press.

Hochschild, A., & Machung, A. (1989). *The second shift.* New York: Avon Books.

Jamieson, L. (1998). *Intimacy: Personal relationships in modern society.* Cambridge/ Oxford, UK: Polity Press.

Kellerhals, J., Widmer, E., & Lévy, R. (2004). *Mesure et démesure du couple : Cohésion, crises et résilience dans les couples contemporains.* Paris, France: Payot.

Lewis, J. (2001). The decline of the male breadwinner model: Implications for work and care. *Social Politics*, 8, 152–169.

Lobo, C. (2009).*Recomposições familiares: Dinâmicas de um processo de transição*. Lisbon, Portugal: Fundação Calouste Gulbenkian/Fundação para a Ciência e a Tecnologia.

Lyonnette, C., Crompton, C., & Wall, K. (2007). Family, gender and work–life articulation: Britain and Portugal compared. *Community, Work and Family, 3*, 283–308.

Marinho, S. (2011). *Paternidades de hoje: Significados, práticas e negociações da parentalidade na conjugalidade e na residência alternada* (Unpublished doctoral dissertation). Lisbon, Portugal: University of Lisbon.

Marinho, S. (2014). Famílias monoparentais: linhas de continuidade e mudança. In A. Delgado, & K. Wall (eds.), *Famílias nos Censos 2011* (pp. 177–195). Lisbon, Portugal: INE/Imprensa de Ciências Sociais.

Marsiglio, W. (ed.). (1995). *Fatherhood: contemporary theory, research, and social policy*. Thousand Oaks, CA: Sage.

Martin, C. (1997). *L'après divorce: Lien familial et vulnerabilité*. Rennes, France: Presses Universitaires de Rennes.

Modak, M., & Palazzo, C. (2002). *Les pères se mettent en quatre !: Responsabilités quotidiennes et modèles de paternité*. Lausanne, Switzerland: EESP.

Monteiro, R., Fernandes, M., Veríssimo, M., Costa, I. P., Torres, N., & Vaugn, B. (2010). Perspectiva do pai acerca do seu envolvimento em famílias nucleares: Associações com o que é desejado pela mãe e com as características da criança. *Revista Interamericana de Psicologia/Interamerican Journal of Psychology, 44*(1), 120–130.

Morgan, D. (1992). *Discovering men*. London, UK: Routledge.

O'Brien, M. (2013). Fitting fathers into work–family policies: International challenges in turbulent times. *International Journal of Sociology and Social Policy, 33*(9/10): 542–564.

Orloff, A. S. (1996). Gender in the welfare state. *Annual Review of Sociology, 22*, 51–78.

Palkovitz, R. (1997). Reconstructing involvement: Expanding conceptualizations of men's caring in contemporary families. In A. J. Hawkins & D. C. Dollahite (eds.), *Generative fathering beyond deficit perspectives* (pp. 200–216). Thousand Oaks, CA: Sage.

Perista, H., & Lopes, M. C. (1999). *A licença de paternidade: Um direito novo para a promoção da igualdade*. Lisbon, Portugal: DEPP/CIDES.

Pfau-Effinger, B. (2000). Conclusion: Gender cultures, gender arrangements and social change in the European context. In S. Duncan & B. Pfau-Effinger (eds.), *Gender, economy and culture in the European Union* (pp. 262–276). London, UK/ New York: Routledge.

Plantenga, J., Remery, C., Figueiredo, H., & Smith, M. (2009). Towards a European Union gender equality index. *Journal of European Social Policy, 19*(1), 19–33.

Pleck, J. H. (1981). *The myth of masculinity*. Cambridge, MA: The MIT Press.

Singly, F. (1996). *Le soi, le couple et la famille*. Bruxelles, Belgium: Nathan.

Torres, A. (ed.). (2004). *Homens e mulheres entre família e trabalho*. Lisbon, Portugal: CITE.

Walby, S. (1997). *Gender transformations*. London, UK: Routledge.

Wall, K. (2007). Main patterns in attitudes to the articulation between work and family life: A cross-national analysis. In R. Crompton, S. Lewis, & C. Lyonnette (eds.), *Women, men, work and family in Europe* (pp. 86–115). London, UK: Palgrave Macmillan.

Wall, K. (2011). A intervenção do Estado: políticas públicas de família. In A. Nunes de Almeida (ed.), *História da vida privada em Portugal: Os nossos dias* (pp. 340–374). Lisbon, Portugal: Círculo de Leitores.

Wall, K. (2014). Fathers on leave alone: Does it make a difference to their lives? *Fathering, 12*(2), 186–200.

Wall, K. (Org.). (2005). *Famílias em Portugal: Percursos, interacções, redes sociais*. Lisbon, Portugal: Imprensa de Ciências Sociais.

Wall, K., Aboim, S., & Cunha, V. (eds.). (2010). *A vida familiar no masculino: Negociando velhas e novas masculinidades*. Lisbon, Portugal: Comissão para a Igualdade no Trabalho e no Emprego.

Wall, K., Aboim, S., & Marinho, S. (2007). Fatherhood, family and work in men's lives: Negotiating new and old masculinities. *Recherches Sociologiques et Anthropologiques, 38*(2), 105–122.

Wall, K., Almeida, A. N., Vieira, M. M., Cunha, V., Rodrigues, L., Coelho, F., Leitão, M., & Atalaia, S. (2015). *Impactos da crise nas crianças portuguesas: indicadores, políticas, representações*. Lisbon, Portugal: Imprensa de Ciências Sociais.

Wall, K., & Amâncio, L. (eds.). (2007). *Família e género: Atitudes sociais dos portugueses*. Lisbon, Portugal: Imprensa de Ciências Sociais.

Wall, K., Cunha, V., & Marinho, S. (2013). *Negotiating gender equality in conjugal life and parenthood in Portugal: A case study* (Working Paper No. WP3-2013.). www.ics.ul.pt/instituto/?doc=31844671217&ctmid=6&mnid=1&ln=p&mm=3.

Wall, K., & Escobedo, A. (2009). Portugal and Spain: Two pathways in southern Europe. In S. B. Kamerman, & P. Moss (eds.), *The politics of parental leave policies* (pp. 207–226). Bristol, UK: Policy Press.

Wall, K., & Gouveia, R. (2014). Changing meanings of family in personal relationships. *Current Sociology, 62*(3), 352–373.

Widmer, E. D. (2010). *Family configurations: A structural approach to family diversity*. London, UK: Ashgate.

8

African American Fathers and Families within Cultural and Historical Perspective

Vivian L. Gadsden, James Earl Davis, and Cleopatra Jacobs Johnson

African American fathers are positioned prominently in research, practice, and policy discussions on fathers, fatherhood, and responsible fathering. There is little question that work in these areas has increased significantly over the past twenty years, with growth in the number of studies, breadth of contexts and populations studied, and depth of analysis. Despite this expanse of research and perspectives, attention to African American fathers continues to focus primarily on low-income fathers. Most often, it is limited to fathers' absence in children's lives, paternity establishment, and financial contributions, as well as to single mother–headed households in African American families. However, not all African American fathers encounter the same parenting obstacles experienced by low-income fathers (Beckert, Strom, & Strom 2006). With a few notable exceptions, research across disciplines has emphasized statistical patterns of behavior and demographic shifts. These studies add to our understanding of issues related to nonmarital births, household composition, living arrangements, economic and emotional support of children, and changes in family life over time (see McLoyd, Hill, & Dodge 2005) but leave open a range of complex questions about how fathers assume and represent their conceptions of fathering.

Relatively absent from research studies and complementary programmatic and policy discussions about families and child well-being is a close examination of the cultural domains of fathering and of fathers themselves (Gadsden, Fagan, Ray, & Davis 2004). Such examinations typically require the deeply analytic, sustained, long-term commitment unique to ethnographic research that interrogates African American fathers' identities and the effects of economic and class differences (see Furstenberg 2007). How, when, and with

what effects African American fathers contribute to their children's well-
being and their own life course trajectories are questions that are likely to
elicit different types of responses depending on the roles fathers assume
in families and communities. In other words, fathering is experienced and
responded to differentially by virtue of a father's age, culture, ethnicity, gender/
masculine identity, race, class, and the contexts (e.g., homes, schools, and
neighborhoods) that influence his development (Bowman & Forman 1997;
Gadsden 1999; Gadsden, Wortham, & Turner 2003). For fathers across racial,
cultural, and ethnic groups, the interplay among these characteristics is complicated for a number of reasons that are biological, psychological, and social,
making attributions to a single demographic or characteristic to explain culture or identity problematic. African American fathers are no exception to
this within-group variability. Not unlike other groups with whom they are
frequently compared, African American fathers share many cultural similarities but demonstrate multiple within-group differences as well.

This chapter focuses on African American fathers in cultural, familial, and
historical perspective. We are interested in the individual and social contexts that inform definitions of fathering, fathering behaviors, and the racial
and economic factors that contribute to or obstruct their engagement with
their children and families. By culture, we are not limited to the longstanding culture versus structure debates to explain African American fathering,
typically debates that are stronger on structural than on cultural analysis (see
Mincy & Pouncy 2007a). We are referring instead to social practices and
beliefs that come to define contexts and the importance of place in determining choices and opportunities. Such work is drawn heavily from developmental psychology, is focused on ecologies of learning and experiencing
the world, points to the significance of context, and increasingly is addressed
in anthropological and sociological research (see Bronfenbrenner 1977;
Burton et al. 1997; Furstenberg 2007; Huston & Bentley 2010; Sampson &
Sharkey 2008). These practices and beliefs are mutable and changing. They
are shaped through interactions in homes and families, embedded in neighborhoods and communities, and affected by societal and political structures.
Numerous scholars (e.g., Gibson 1987; Smedley 1999) have noted that culture is an overarching concept that includes issues related to race, ethnicity, gender, class, and language, all agreed-upon indicators and descriptors of
identity. Hence we are attuned to discussions regarding the degree to which
these indicators and descriptors are implicated in change over time and have
been affected by African American fathers' social locations in existing public
systems, structural hierarchies, and societal shifts.

With this broad definition, this chapter has two aims. First, we examine
the identities of African American fathers as a racially and culturally defined
population in the United States, differing by social history; social class;

familial, cultural, and social practices; education and schooling; and opportunities and options. We draw upon images and data from research as scholarly writings about African American/black families and fathers, both to create an historical context for understanding African American identity and life and to create a fluid composite of the diversity of men who are labeled and/or who refer to themselves as African American fathers.[1] In this way, we aim to understand the ways in which fatherhood is defined, understood, and enacted by African American men in different contexts.

Second, we acknowledge the shifts over the past fifty years in the number of nonmarital births among African Americans and highlight ongoing efforts that focus on low-income, non-residential, noncustodial African American fathers. These men have been studied as a unique subset of all fathers and of African American fathers who do not live with or have custody of their children. They typically are not married (and in most cases have never been married) to the mothers of their children. Many also have another more indelible identity attached to them as "urban," used as an all-encompassing concept associated with limited opportunity and with social problems in cities and large metropolitan areas. The tendency in academic and popular discussions is to link urban-related issues with mother-headed households, poverty, poor schooling, crime, incarceration, and fathering children out of wedlock and to use it as a code or designation for low-income African American and Latino children and families (Gadsden & Dixon-Román, in press; Kirkland 2013). Research on the effects of urban life on African American families has a long history (Du Bois 1899; Frazier 1939; Scanzoni 1977; Wilson 1987; Allen 1995). Although the problems associated with urban conditions are to be found within and across other groups, they appear particularly debilitating for low-income African American and Latino men who experience significant barriers to economic and family well-being.

Throughout this chapter, we take notice as well of the significance of class as a critical determinant of the actions, behaviors, and practices of African American fathers, described consistently in historical and sociological accounts (see Carper 1966; Du Bois 1899, 1909; Frazier 1939; Gans 1965; Rainwater & Yancey 1967). This work has investigated African American family structure and the residual effects of male unemployment and poverty, post-emancipation, on African American families. Comparatively little is written about middle-class African American men who are fathers or about their families (Beckert, Strom, & Strom 2006). The argument for a class difference suggests that middle-class African American fathers' practices diverge from those of low-income African American fathers and implies that middle-class African American fathers engage in practices that are more similar to middle-class white fathers than those of low-income African American fathers.

We do not dismiss this idea, given the detailed analyses in texts dating back to Du Bois (1899) and Frazier. However, we question the idea of normativity—i.e., uniformity and continuity across cultural and social practices among middle-class white fathers, the degree to which middle-class African American father and family practices in fact mirror those of middle-class white fathers and families, and whether and how middle-class African American fathers and families decide to adopt some practices while ignoring others (Weiss et al. 2005). In what ways is the identity of African American fathers tied to racial images? Does class override race as a defining feature of the life experiences and life choices of African American fathers and families? In what ways, if any, are the cultural domains of African American life evident in African American fathering and in the life course of African American families? These questions are among the many unaddressed issues in our field. Although addressing them exceeds the scope of this chapter, they inform and undergird much of the discussion here.

In the next sections of this chapter, we examine the experiences of African American fathers as both broad and nuanced and examine their fatherhood practices as being derived from individual beliefs and shared cultural contexts and familial sociopolitical histories in the United States. We aim to contribute to analyses associated with the following questions: Is there something about African American fathers that makes their experiences and fathering identities different from those of other fathers? What do we know, and how do we know it? We begin by focusing on African American families in historical and contemporary perspective to situate the experiences of African American fathers. We then discuss African American fathers across three time periods, associated with critical points in U.S. political history and the race problem: slavery/post-emancipation through Reconstruction (1640s–1930s), the Civil Rights era (1940s–1970s), and contemporary perspective (1980s–present). We review ongoing discussions about low-income African American fathers in urban settings and cultural dimensions of that identity. We conclude with a few closing considerations, focused largely on challenges to the idea of a single cultural identity for African American fathers and common themes across the experiences of African American fathers within research, practice, and policy.

AFRICAN AMERICAN FAMILIES: CULTURAL AND HISTORICAL CONTEXT

A complex of African cultures in the United States and a series of events related to segregation, integration, and other political events have been linked to African American family formation, structure, and experience. African American families have been studied within three perspectives: their evolution and maintenance; the legitimacy of different family forms; and the degree to which African American families, particularly low-income families, conform to "mainstream" family forms (Billingsley 1968). Typically using comparative models, dominant analyses of African American life examine how African Americans have negotiated the multiple sites of their experience within American society and how they have constructed and revised these contexts to survive and thrive. Although there is agreement that African American culture and the cultures of African American fathers and families are influenced by any number of economic and social factors, African Americans continue to experience racial disparities in access to education, health, employment, and well-being disproportionately to whites (McLoyd et al. 2005; Mickelson 2003; LaVeist 2002). However, disentangling African American culture from the economic and social factors that have dictated the experience of African American families is difficult at best.

The reference to African American culture is itself laden with assumptions. As several researchers (Hill, Murray, & Anderson 2005; Tucker & James 2005) suggest, identifying the features of African American culture is a "moving target" because of the alterable nature of culture and the demographic factors associated with black history in the United States. To the degree that culture can be defined, it may refer to traditions or to adaptations to contextual factors, both of which are reflected in African Americans' experiences. Before increases in immigration to the United States, common references to African American culture were largely traceable to west and central Africa and centered on blacks whose ancestry was linked in some way to slavery. Many of the social practices and beliefs that the enslaved Africans brought to the United States were sustained over time and blended with the social practices and beliefs of African slaves from different countries, European cultures, and Native Americans. Researchers mostly agree that there were "African culturals," referring to beliefs, practices, and values, that slaves brought with them to the United States (McDaniel/Zuberi 1990). These were adapted to accommodate western beliefs and practices in the United States and were modified in response to economic, educational, and social restrictions (Moore 2007).

There is some disagreement about the degree to which current African American traditions are an extension of the practices brought from Africa and their influence on perspectives regarding place and identity. In short, whatever the assumptions about African American culture, it is considered American culture yet distinctive from it (Allen 1995; Du Bois 1899; Frazier 1939; Herskovits 1928; Myrdal 1944; Rainwater 1970; Ruggles 1994). Several practices (e.g., unmarried child-bearing and mother-headed households) that reflect the ways that some African Americans have coped with the restrictions imposed upon them, demands placed on them, and their treatment in the United States are interpreted as unique to African American family culture. However, such practices have been found in other parts of the world as well as where the black slave trade was common (e.g., the Caribbean) and suggest that these practices reflect African traditions and are adaptations or accommodations to the experience of slavery itself (see Roopnarine 2004, 2013).

Who counts as an African American? Research studies largely rely on racial categories that isolate whites and blacks and do not disaggregate country of origin in the count of African American families. For example, the terms *African American* and *black* may be used interchangeably for convenience in some cases and/or to capture cultural practices and social experiences of individuals and families with origins in Africa. Though some of these families were brought by force to the United States and other points in the Americas, others have immigrated from Africa and from colonized and independent countries alike, post-emancipation to the present. The emergence of the term *black* in the 1960s and 1970s was intended to make apparent the diversity of people sharing roots in the United States and in the world and to replace formerly imposed categories of "Colored" and "Negro" with broader conceptualizations of identity tied to the African Diaspora. It was intended to create a new world identity borne out of these shared origins rather than divisive, sociopolitical, national identities borne out of slavery and conquest (Eyerman 2001; Lovejoy 2009). The current uses of African American are by necessity broader, though debates abound about whether an African American must be tied to the U.S. slave trade and whether blacks who are immigrants to the United States also should be included. The residual effects of these debates are reflected in census categories.

Any framing of African American culture may be represented in a range of ways that are being revised constantly. Increasing attention to black immigrants to the United States (see Capps, McCabe, & Fix 2012) will likely demonstrate the inherent problems associated with creating a single narrative and teasing apart African Americans brought to the United States in the 1600s and those who are recent arrivals. Research on blacks in other formerly colonized countries demonstrates the common ethnic and cultural histories of blacks, histories that are as compromised with issues of racism and discrimination as those of African Americans, but that are unique to the colonizers and contexts in which people live (Roopnarine 2004, 2013). Hence a black is not necessarily a black. If we follow the idea that context matters, we can assume that life in Senegal might be different from and similar to life in Martinique or life as a black person in Great Britain, as well as that all or none of it matters if the person now lives in the United States. Some data suggest that problems emanating from racial discrimination cut across western nations that engaged in the black slave trade and in relation to blacks in formerly colonized settings (Roopnarine 2004, 2013). However, these data also point to the nature and salience of context, the slave and conquest histories of the countries, and economies of scale, all of which affect the experiences of blacks in these settings and of power within the societies themselves.

Historians and social scientists alike refer to the critical time known as the Middle Passage, the period between blacks' capture into slavery and their trade in the United States. They make two inextricably tied arguments: (1) that the kinship and bonds forged between and among slaves from different geographic sites and tribes and with different languages, cramped in close quarters and intentional division, translated into transatlantic communities and (2) that these bonds revised African identity and culture, creating new communities based on a common experience as blacks that was carried into life in America (Diedrich, Gates, & Pedersen 1999; Mintz & Price 1992). In addition, laws separating the races, including Jim Crow laws, persisted long after the end of slavery, and African Americans' embrace of long-held traditions resulted in the production of social practices that have come to be called African American culture.

There has been no shortage of studies, social theories, and scholarly writings on black families (see Allen 1995; McLoyd et al. 2005). They share a focus on the problems that black families in the United States have faced; the ravages of slavery, segregation, and ensuing racial discrimination; the issues of poverty and economic hardship experienced by many; the policies that reinscribe poverty and access; and the apparent decline in values such as marriage within black communities and American society more broadly. Allen (1995) argues that there has been uneasiness in the representations of black families, complicated by the representations of "the black family" as a monolith. He notes the inherent problems that have plagued research on black families, in both theoretical and methodological problems that are likely to promote stereotypic portrayals.

African American family structure has shifted over the past hundred years, with increasing nonmarital births among the poor and among African Americans who are disproportionately low-income and working class. Ruggles (1994) observed: "Blacks are far more likely than Whites to become single parents and to reside in extended families" (p. 136). Using microdata to examine birth patterns from 1850 to 1950, he offers two explanations for the origins of the pattern (Ruggles 1994). He suggests, first, that children's residence with one parent may have been a response to the socioeconomic conditions faced by newly freed blacks after the Civil War and free blacks in 1850. Second, he argues, the pattern may reflect a difference in social norms between blacks and whites that may have developed either through the experience of slavery or differences between European and African cultures. The uprooting of families that resulted from slavery, disallowing marriage by pairing men and women to replenish the slave workforce, and undermining kinship patterns are so intertwined that isolating any one factor is rendered impossible (Ruggles 1994; Furstenberg 2007; Cherlin 1981).

In 2011, there were 56 million married-couple households. Black married-couple households constituted 44 percent of these families. Father-only households have grown over time (Vespa, Lewis, & Kreider 2013), as has the proportion of children being raised in same-gender-headed households (Gates 2008; Moore 2011). Research findings also suggest that marital status differences are related to variations in support networks for families and access to economic support (Chatters, Taylor, & Neighbors 1989). Diversity in income and socioeconomic status is linked to differential access to a variety of opportunities for African American families (e.g., employment, housing, and education). Differences in family structure (e.g., single-parent and two-parent households) may be related to housing and neighborhood options and the kinds of experiences to which African American families are exposed (Patillo-McCoy 2000; Sampson, Morenoff, & Gannon-Rowley 2002).

What then has been the pathway for current cultural practices of African American families? Several responses have been offered (Furstenberg 2007). One, as we noted earlier, points to African cultural practices, slavery and discrimination, and persistent poverty that undermined both marriage and marital stability (Du Bois 1939; Frazier 1939; Rainwater 1970). A second singles out the child as the focal point of African cultures and communities and the secondary role of marriage as a defining feature of family (Reiss 1960; McDaniel/Zuberi 1990). Although some arguments have suggested that African American families and communities were more tolerant of premarital sex and nonmarital childbearing, the data suggest that these differences may have been tied to class; they rarely refer to the creation of these families by white slave owners themselves. Whether families were drawing upon African culturals or adapting to American and other western European conquests is relatively unclear. A third response revolves around black families as matrifocal, resulting in part from black women's ability to obtain jobs as servants and other domestics after emancipation and their roles as primary or shared breadwinners. The discrimination that black men faced in the workforce after emancipation often led to marital conflicts and the dissolution of marriages and other unions that then contributed to perceptions of black culture and families as both matrifocal and matriarchal. Such references have persisted, even with increased participation by all women in the workforce, and have directly and indirectly marginalized the roles of African American men in current and past social and public policy formulations that position them as invisible. Some analysts have argued that this invisibility of fathers in policy and in principle has contributed to their absence in low-income communities more broadly, particularly African American and Latino communities, where joblessness and poverty are greatest (Mincy & Pouncy 2007b).

Research on African American family life may be understood within three perspectives, highlighted by Allen (1978). One refers to cultural-deviant perspectives in which African American families who deviate from the qualities of middle-class white families are labeled dysfunctional or pathological. A second focuses on an ecological concept in which differences between African American and white families are attributed to "their respective sociocultural contexts." It acknowledges situational constraints that influence different coping approaches and practices and that result in "the adoption of culturally distinct styles of organization and interaction." In the third perspective, cultural-equivalence, distinctive qualities of African American families are de-emphasized and the common qualities that African American families share with white families emphasized. Allen and others since suggest that the tensions in research have traveled between the conceptual and ideological. In other words, researchers accept terminology, definitions, and assumptions about factors that influence the life course of African American families but differ in their sense of the character and functioning of these families (see Rainwater & Yancey 1967). The conceptualization of the problems in narrow or broad terms, the study of the issues, and the methodological approaches used to understand these families have also dictated our understanding of the role of context and the meaning of culture. Several practices may be attributed to African American family life, among them the role of religion, family and kin networks, childrearing values, racial identity and racial socialization, attitudes about maternal employment, and men's and women's roles as economic providers, to name a few. At the same time, other variables, such as social stressors and poverty also factor into the creation and effects of culture.

The roots of African American families and contemporary practices have been used to explain a range of behaviors and practices, with varying levels of support, for African American fathers. Not surprisingly, increased attention to low-income, non-residential, noncustodial African American fathers in the past twenty years has drawn attention again to African American families and the cultural practices within them. African American fathers are diverse in age, income, number of children, and number of marriages, along with a range of other factors often clustered in groups that reflect variability within and across subgroups. Furstenberg (2007) and others (e.g., Lareau 2003) call for more attention to the role of class, raising the enduring question of how to tease apart the effects of class versus race. How intertwined are different life experiences, and how do we really know how people construct their identities culturally, racially, or socially? There is merit in the idea that middle-class African American fathers probably share several values with

middle-class white fathers, but they do not share the historical or daily experience or reminders of race. Whether and to what degree their values deviate
significantly from all fathers are still debatable. Except in rare cases, Edin and
Nelson (2013) being one, the comparisons are relatively unequal, with practices of low-income African American, non-residential fathers being mapped
against those of middle-class white men for whom issues of employability,
education, and exposure to racial discrimination are small. In an effort to
separate out low-income, non-residential, noncustodial fathers, many recent
discussions have ignored other African American fathers, many of whom are
among the working poor, are married, and live with and support their children. For the most part, the discussion of class differences continues to be
muddled in the binaries of low and middle class, married and never-married,
rural and urban, and black and white.

Both ethnographic studies, which are inherently culture-focused, and
larger quantitative analyses provide a powerful backdrop for understanding
African American families as they have changed over time. These studies
reflect political shifts in the country, the earliest occurring between emancipation through Reconstruction. The second begins in the 1940s and 1950s
and continues throughout the Civil Rights movement and the passage of the
Civil Rights Act. The third runs from the 1980s to the present. We focus
on these three distinctive periods in U.S. history and African American
family life to situate the cultural experiences of African American fathers
and families.

AFRICAN AMERICAN FATHERS BEFORE, DURING, AND AFTER RECONSTRUCTION

The history of African Americans during slavery and the post-slavery
depictions of African Americans in the U.S. South are widely chronicled,
though with different representations and analyses. Several events tell us a
little about how groups of African American men took up the responsibilities
of fathering and commitments to family. For example, shortly after slavery,
former slaves came together in a convention, the Black Men's Convention,
with the clear purpose of determining how they would promote education
and ensure the well-being of their children and families. They aimed to
formulate a position regarding their future in the still uncertain world of
the post-emancipation south. They invoked the language of the Declara-
tion of Independence to claim full rights of citizenship for themselves and
to reduce the danger of new southern laws that were enacted ostensibly to
restrict the movements and employment possibilities of blacks—in other
words, laws created to replace legally the recent constrictions of slavery
(Anderson 1990):

We simply desire that we shall be recognized as men; that we have no obstructions placed in our way; that the same laws which govern White men shall direct colored men; that we have the right of trial by a jury of our peers, that schools be opened or established for our children; that we be permitted to acquire homesteads for ourselves and children; that we be dealt with as others, in equity and justice.

This convention, coupled with a series of activities led by black parents, contributed to efforts toward public education (see Du Bois 1899; Stewart 2013). The residual acts of discrimination to education and social opportunity were overriding the ability of black families to respond to their expectations and hopes. Black men found themselves objects of resistance to change. Bowman and Forman (1997) argue that the African American men's high expectations were aligned with assumptions about men's roles as providers in a society in which black men's ability to support their families was circumscribed, if not eliminated, by frequently revised laws.

Our knowledge and understanding of the lives of African American fathers during Reconstruction and into the 1950s has been drawn largely from historical and sociological analyses about African American families (Hunter 2001). Black families adapted to the move from rural to urban settings and to a different set of demands. In both *The Philadelphia Negro* (1899) and *The Negro Family in the U.S.* (1939), Du Bois described the relationship that existed between the economic demands and exigencies facing black males and females and their effects on family formation, noting that these factors are unique to the context and not to the individual. Du Bois's (1899) analysis in the late 1800s highlighted the diversity in family formation and marriage. In projecting seven family types, ranging from unmarried mothers to two-parent families with children, Du Bois delineates the income available to families with different family compositions. In these descriptions, men are often out of work or working part-time. He refers to their caregiving responsibilities: "The man has work one and one-half weeks in the month as a wire fence maker, when regularly employed, which is about half the time. The rest of the time he takes care of the babies while his wife works at service" (p. 74). We are unable to determine how many fathers served as primary caregivers or the degree to which father caregiving was a common practice. Du Bois (1939) wrote that low wages and the growth in economic standards resulted in the delay of marriage, as women who were able to find jobs (e.g., as domestics) in the city increasingly assumed the provider role, with men staying in the rural areas and kin and other extended families assuming joint responsibility for children. It is likely the case that in urban settings with fewer support or kin systems, men assumed this role and the emotional support and financial support of children and families.

While presenting multiple examples of fathers' role in families during and after slavery, Frazier (1939) paints multiple portraits of men acting in their role as family-caring and responsible fathers and husbands. These men, his account suggests, responded to the moral imperative of the times, often acting upon religious beliefs and values adopted from their owners, and worked to pay for the freedom of their wives and children. These portraits do not speak to their daily contact with their children, in large part, because such daily contact was rare. However, they do represent an image of many African American fathers and their commitment to assuming the provider role. One example is presented in a commentary of a son recounting memories of his father:

> Perhaps no man had a stronger love for his family and his home than my father. In the maintenance of his family he was often away from home during the week working at his trade but always planned to return on Friday nights or during the day on Saturday. On one occasion, when, working in the East part of Baldwin County he came to the river at the week end to go home, he found the ferryman gone and all the boats on the opposite side. There was no bridge across the river. So he saw that the alternatives confronted him: To turn back, or swim the stream. Being a splendid swimmer and knowing that he was expected at home, he plunged boldly into the stream and was soon with those whom he loved. (131–132)

Frazier writes that such family solidarity served as a protective factor against the "disintegrating effects of emancipation," not unlike how we currently describe the protective effects of families on young children (Fantuzzo, Gadsden, & McDermott 2010). The significance of fathers as reliable and trustworthy providers was demonstrative of the ideal of African American men. Such investment did not run throughout all families, but the frequency of references to the importance of men seeking a homestead for their wives and children in Frazier's work adds to the many questions that have been posed about African American men's conceptualization of their roles as fathers and marriage and the significance of religion as a binding force.

Furstenberg (2007), drawing upon Du Bois (1899), Frazier (1939), and Drake and Cayton (1945), among others, argues that class divisions are reflected in family organization among African Americans. This is a plausible argument but does not completely attend to the effects of racial discrimination on the goals, sense of identity, and access available to African American fathers across income levels. Hence an upper-middle-class African American father may have the material trappings of an upper-middle-class white father, but his pathway to that status, the nature of his daily encounters and experiences in the workplace and in society, and his ability to develop a familial trajectory are all affected differently from those of the white father. A black father of any class is more likely to struggle with short-term employment, experience greater likelihood of unemployment, and endure poverty. Frazier also underscores the salience of class and the variability in the significance of marriage. The values that are considered important to the black family are likely reflected in the lives of African American fathers—i.e., religion, provider, kin networks, and the centrality of the child.

SHIFTS IN FATHER PRESENCE AND THE RESHAPING OF FAMILY CULTURES: 1960s–1980s

The Civil Rights Movement, the Civil Rights Act, and the unrest they uncovered are a thorny period for African American fathers and families, as they balanced the promises of opportunity and their continued exposure to inequality. Earlier, in 1954, the *Brown v. Board* decision had introduced the United States to the ensuing efforts for change. The case was brought by an African American father on behalf of his school-age daughter and was emblematic of the steady role and image of African American fathers. The father would likely be described as middle-class in that his stated values appeared to be consistent with those of the middle-class white fathers. The *Brown* decision was the beginning of a series of demonstrations and social unrest to dismantle the restrictive social structures that barred African Americans' access to economic, educational, and social prosperity. Moreover, the decision was among the first to rely heavily on social science research in grounding the arguments (see research from Clark & Clark 1947; Bruner 1956). For more than twenty years, the United States was embroiled in challenges to structural hierarchies that excluded not only African Americans but also numbers of other minorities and women in the United States. As African Americans fought for equality, their communities were flung into increased chaos, and the status of African American men, fathers, and families became more fragile as the critiques of their structures were thrust into the national limelight.

In response, several reports were commissioned. The Moynihan Report, the most often cited of three commissioned reports during that period, offered a stark and controversial analysis of black families as disorganized and dysfunctional. (The other reports were the Kerner Commission Report, 1968, and the Coleman Report, 1966.) Although Moynihan's goals for the report are debated (see Gans 1965), the report was an unforgiving examination of black families in which the growing rates of single, female-headed households, reduction in marriage, persistent male unemployment, and increasing poverty came together for a perfect storm, described by Moynihan as pathology.

Moynihan failed to highlight the regularity of support within the families and institutions that made life for poor blacks possible, points that sociologists such as Billingsley (1968) had identified and that later anthropologists such as Stack (1990) and Hill (1972) noted. Much of the dysfunctionality and disorganization to which Moynihan referred was by his own admission the residual effects of slavery, post-emancipation hardship, and the persistence of discrimination that led to absence of African American fathers in families. During the period between Reconstruction and the 1960s and 1970s, African American fathers' absence resulted in significant increases in single-mother-headed households, particularly among the never married; in divorces; and in growing poverty, as numbers of African Americans continued to move from rural areas into cities, and the vestiges of racial discrimination in employment and education persisted. The culture in the United States had changed as well, with women of all ethnic groups working outside the home, and with greater numbers of divorces.

A notable feature of discussions about African American fathers during this period was that they were never uncoupled from discussions of African American mothers. The quality of life for poor African American families did not change during the thirty years between Frazier and Moynihan's writing or between Moynihan's and more current-day writing. In one response to Moynihan's report, theorists argue that rather than the "disadvantaged position of Blacks [being] the consequence of single-parent families," it was "the cause of them" (see Ruggles 1994). A second argues that the focus on disorganization is overemphasized and fails to provide sufficient attention to the strength of kin ties or the resilience of families in the face of persistent racial discrimination which itself is predicated on the idea of racial differences and the superiority of one group over the other (see Hill 1972). These two explanations are reciprocal in their focus on the deficit orientation of much of the research.

AFRICAN AMERICAN FATHERS IN CONTEMPORARY PERSPECTIVE: THE ISSUE OF CLASS DIFFERENCES

Approximately 41 percent of African American families are headed by a father and mother who are married. The rates of single-mother–headed households have continued to increase with time. Although it is next to impossible to determine whether the shifts are necessarily associated with a shared cultural experience, some would argue that the shifts are yet another example of the survival of African culturals among African American families, most notably the child-focality of African American families (see Edin & Nelson 2013). African American families have different family forms, including legal marriages and cohabiting couples, in which the child serves as the center of the relationship. These shifts do not preclude the importance of kin networks, extended families, and augmented families (see Billingsley 1968).

The arguments regarding child-focality must also be considered within the context of economic declines, men's identity as fathers, and fathers' assessments of whether and with what resources they can contribute to their child's well-being. In other words, is the child still the focal point of relationships among African American fathers, or have the economic declines and intractable inequality negatively affected the conscience and responsibility of young African American men? Edin and Nelson's recent ethnographic research suggests that these questions should be raised for both low-income African American and white fathers alike. The unemployment problems of low-income fathers coupled with relatively high school dropout rates, low levels of school engagement, and continuing decline of urban settings reduce the ability of young fathers to take on the responsibilities of fathering. Low-income, noncustodial, non-residential fathers are in a class of their own, with policymakers focusing considerable attention on child support and (re)engagement. Increased attention to co-parenting reflects the reality that not all men and women will get married but that adult decisions not to marry should not reduce the well-being of children. Although men of all incomes and ethnicities are ostensibly the focus of widespread fatherhood efforts, in principle, the efforts are targeted to poor fathers, mostly minority, in urban centers where the opportunities are fewest and the problems most entrenched. It continues to be telling that the most compelling analyses, with two exceptions, of black families are not to be found in child development or even family studies research but in research on poverty and family dysfunction (see Taylor et al. 1997; McLoyd et al. 2000, 2005).

Research on middle-class African American fathers (married, divorce, and never married) is relatively scant, particularly compared to the many studies and focus on low-income, unmarried fathers. Rhodes, Ochoa, and Ortiz (2005) suggest that there is a tendency to overlook middle-class parents in studies of families and to assign behaviors and practices to class rather than ethnicity (see also Clayton, Mincy, & Blankenhorn 2003). Middle-class African American fathers, Weiss and her colleagues (2005) argue, are faced with problems often significantly different from those faced by low-income men and by other middle-class fathers. Middle-class African American men are more likely to be married, remain in a first marriage, and report greater contentment with their family circumstance than low-income fathers (Gordon, Gordon, & Nembhard 1994) and have been described as providing regular care for their children, sharing in the decision making about childrearing, participating in children's play, and serving as positive influences in socializing their children (Allen 1981; Mirande 1991; Scanzoni 1995). This level of engagement, some assert, is possibly the result of higher incomes, more options around work schedules, education and the exposures that accompany it, and better relationships with their spouses (Kamo & Cohen 1998).

There is a considerable literature base on low-income African American fathers, and there are multiple reasons for the enormous interest in them. The policies regarding child support after 1988 resulted in increased attention to men who were not contributing financially to their children, many of whom were in families receiving public assistance. Second, despite enhancements to child support efforts and welfare reform policies, pregnancies outside of marriage did not decline precipitously among low-income African American fathers, as had been expected. Observers expected that if these fathers became financially responsible for their children, the need for government support to their families would decrease.

Past discussions about African culturals were replaced with discussions about how structural barriers themselves are complicit in limiting employment and education and restricting the well-being of children and families. Both the structural and cultural arguments have resonance, and both have limitations. Motherhood and fatherhood are highly honored familial roles in black communities. Urban, low-income, African American communities represent one kind of setting in which the issues of culture, race, community practices, and intergenerational transfer converge in especially sensitive and important ways to support or militate against the well-being of children and families. Federal welfare policies of the past often encouraged father invisibility, if not absence, by withholding benefits from women whose husband or partners lived at home (Lerman & Sorensen 2000). Many low-income African American fathers became occasional visitors in their children's homes and were removed, or removed themselves, from communities.

Despite barriers to economic and expressive involvement faced by African American fathers, inner-city African American youth tend to acknowledge their paternity informally, and the African American community facilitates the informal establishment of paternity and young fathers' involvement in informal child-support arrangements (Sullivan 1993; Bowman & Sanders 1998). Waller (1999) found that for many young fathers, the breadwinner role was less important than their desire to provide guidance and discipline for their children. The fathers in Waller's study emphasized the need to ensure that their children lived comfortably and that their children's needs were met, either through in-kind informal support or more formal payment arrangements.

Ray and Hans (2001), in an ethnographic study derived from reports by 100 mothers and semi-structured interviews with seventeen fathers, found that more than half the fathers were involved with their children and that the fathers envisioned their role as multidimensional, including teaching, disciplining, and providing moral guidance. Fathers' images of an engaged father included involvement with children's schooling and ensuring that their children felt secure and protected both at home and in the highly vulnerable neighborhoods in which they lived. The study, not unlike other research, was not able to tease apart questions regarding the degree to which environmental stressors contributed to paternal role strain among very involved fathers and whether and how the fathers' sense of responsibility for their children's well-being was affected (for similar findings, see also Hanner 1998).

Though fathering practitioners who work with young, unmarried African American fathers support these assessments, they note the complexity in gauging with consistency the indicators of young fathering and young fathers' willingness to assume responsibility for their children. For example, is the provider role limited to monetary contributions, or is the father's sense of provider role in fact broader than how it has been denoted historically? Carlson and McLanahan (2002), following a birth cohort of children and their families, found the provider role important for unmarried fathers. They argue that the mother–father relationship was crucial to understanding fathers' contributions to their children. When there was a relationship, the likelihood was greater that the fathers would stay involved, though problems related to the continuity of fathers' involvement and the significance of personal and contextual factors, persisted.

Economic factors, few employment options, and low employability limit both African American men's engagement in the lives of their children and their ability to sustain their engagement. Chase-Lansdale, Gordon, Coley, Wakschlag, and Brooks-Gunn (1999) and Coley and Chase-Lansdale (2000), in research on low-income African American fathers, found that employed men were seven times as likely as unemployed fathers to have moved from low involvement to high involvement or to have always been involved. Fathers having at least a high school education were less likely to reduce involvement over time. Paternal age, the child's age, and maternal human capital characteristics were not significant predictors of involvement. Married or cohabiting fathers were more likely to be highly involved than non-residential fathers were, regardless of their involvement at the time of birth. The presence of a new maternal partner or the child's grandmother did not decrease father involvement. Mother reports of emotionally close relationships with fathers increased the likelihood that fathers would be highly involved, regardless of involvement at birth or whether the father lived with the child's mother. The authors suggest that the first few years after the child's birth provide a window of intervention for efforts to increase father involvement. Furthermore, they note that more research is needed to determine the actors that affect a father's ability and inclination to pay child support.

Gadsden, Wortham, and Turner (2003) in a mixed methods study of men in an urban fathering program found that despite potential and real distractions of father absence, poverty, and poor schooling, low-income African American fathers form significant and nurturing bonds with their children and work to negotiate the roles and expectations of parenting with the mothers of their children. They construct possible selves that are based on sometimes limited understanding of their chosen strategies and are constrained in part by the paucity of economic, educational, and societal supports. They seek to support their children in the ways that are presented visually on television and other media and in teachings from their families and the programs in which many participate. In particular, noncustodial, non-residential African American fathers are similar to their peers from other ethnic groups and other social classes who are testing the boundaries of engaged fatherhood and often negotiating these boundaries legally and socially.

These findings are consistent with Miller (1994), who also found that African American fathers, contrary to societal stereotypes, are involved with their children and are attempting to take on responsible roles. Hanner (1998) found that noncustodial fathers placed a greater emphasis on nurturing and caregiving activities than on the role of provider or breadwinner, not unlike fathers in the Ray and Hans (2001) and Waller (1999) studies, and that many fathers sustained their involvement with their children beyond early child-hood. The children ranged in age from 1 to 13, suggesting this involvement was rooted in a commitment to the child's growth and development rather than an infatuation with an adorable infant or toddler. A number of other studies on fathers have pointed to maternal resistance, or maternal gatekeep-ing, as a barrier to father involvement as well (Allen & Doherty 1996; Fagan 2000; Miller 1994; NCOFF *Fathers and Families Roundtable Series, 1995–1997;* Rhein et al. 1997). However, few studies uncouple the different dimensions of maternal gatekeeping or the range of factors contributing to it. Research that explores how fathers' behavior influences maternal resistance to father involvement also is needed.

Several researchers (e.g., Gordon 2000) suggest that the stark discon-nect between current vestiges of fatherhood and historical expectations, perceptions, and practices in African American communities contradict the historical bonds that existed. Bowman and Forman (1997) argue that most African American men have sought to be responsible fathers, at times against incredible odds, and that this evidence collides, in many ways, with popular beliefs and common stereotypes about the persistent tendencies of African American fathers toward irresponsibility. A series of social factors over time have shifted the practices, patterns, and nature of father engage-ment in many African American communities, challenged by the onslaught of high levels of incarceration and social problems and exacerbated since 2008 by the economic downturn.

On one hand, the focus on low-income African American fathers in urban settings is not unwarranted or unnecessary—as a research and practice issue and as a community and social concern. Nowhere is there more urgency about father involvement than in inner-city African American communities. On the other hand, the focus on these communities is much more comfortable when we are able to assign the problems to father absence rather than engage in critical analysis and acts that are necessary to uncover problems of poverty, poor schools, limited employment, subtle forms of racism, social isolation, and vulnerability that reshape the character and culture of these neighborhoods and those who live in them.

Edin and Nelson (2013) write that among the 110 African American and white, low-income, non-residential, noncustodial fathers whom they studied, most contribute little to the financial support of their children. Yet all indicate that good fathers should provide for their children. As they appropriately argue, the meaning of a good provider is broad, including a sense that the father is "all man" and provides for himself and his family. Although not limited to African American fathers, the fathers also had an idealized image of fathers not unlike the images of fathers in 1950s television shows (see Gadsden et al. 2003). The unmarried, low-income African American fathers whom they studied were more involved, they wrote, than the white fathers, but for reasons that have a longer history regarding the nature of conjugal relationships.

The issue of class is deeply ensconced in these discussions of African American fathers. The assumption is, as noted earlier, that middle-class African American fathers look more like white middle-class fathers and are more engaged in the multiple dimensions of fathering. Are they more similar to the fathers drawn from the Frazier text? Do they identify with the images associated with middle-class life or with the cultural dimensions of African American life? Given the similarities between low-income, unmarried African American and white fathers in the Edin and Nelson study, might these same similarities be expected from middle-class African American and white fathers? Furstenberg (2007) writes, "[I]t appears that the emphasis, beginning in the 1960s on the cultural distinctiveness of the black families may be waning, replaced by a somewhat more nuanced blend of structural and cultural analysis anchored in the social position of the family and its responses to its affiliations inside and outside the community" (p. 444).

In a recent report from the Centers for Disease Control and Prevention (Jones & Mosher 2013), father involvement was measured by the frequency with which men participated in a set of activities in the previous four weeks with children who were living with their fathers and with children who were living apart from their fathers. Involvement was measured separately

for children aged 0–4 and children aged 5–18. The analyses were based on
a nationally representative sample of 10,403 men aged 15–44 in the United
States, with father involvement measures based on 2,200 fathers of children
younger than 5 (1,790 who live with their children and 410 who live apart
from their children), and on 3,166 fathers of children aged 5–18 (2,091 who
live with their children and 1,075 who live apart from their children). Findings from the study showed that African American fathers across income
levels and residence with children participated in activities with their children either with as much as or with greater frequency than both white and
Latino fathers. In general, fathers living with their children participated in
their children's lives to a greater degree than fathers who live apart from
their children. Differences in fathers' involvement with their children
reflected the father's age, marital or cohabiting status, education, Hispanic
origin, and race.

    The class arguments have support, on the one hand, as middle-class Afri-
can American fathers like low-income African American fathers, respond to
their contexts. On the other hand, there are multiple accounts of the lives of
African American fathers in the United States, across income levels, being
fraught with remnants of racial discrimination and environmental hazards.
Some men choose to translate their encounters in ways that are amenable
to mainstream values and beliefs; others do not. However, American culture
itself has changed and questions comparative models that ignore the range
of cultural and ethnic groups in the United States. Whether the structural
debates are no longer relevant is contingent upon how race is highlighted as
a dividing feature of U.S. society.

CLOSING CONSIDERATIONS

    Do the behaviors, practices, and experiences of African American fathers
represent African American culture, or is there an African American culture
of fathering? The answer to both is a cautious yes and no and is centered
within discussions of class, age, and the within-group variability to which
we referred at the beginning of this chapter. Have contexts changed significantly enough in the United States to be able to say without qualification
that employment opportunities and access exist to reduce the obstacles to full
engagement and sustainability? Though not post-racial, the current climate
continues to put African American men in general at greater risk for incarceration (Alexander 2012), for unemployment (Young 2007), and for health
problems (Thorpe, Patrick, Bowie, Laveist, & Gaskin 2013). Many of these
men are fathers. Determining whether and how these constraints and liabili-
ties factor into the African American fathers' choices around parenting and

marriage is increasingly complicated. The choices are not simply decisions that are culturally based or sanctioned.

There is no easy approach to bridging the historical context of African American culture with contemporary context. At once, they are different and the same. They are different in that the period from emancipation to the present has seen considerable shifts in access and equality to education and work, but they are the same in that the economic conditions of the past are for many much the same. As findings from Edin and Nelson (2013) and Gadsden et al. (2003) note, television images of fathering are a powerful source of behavioral choices for many young fathers whose own fathers may have been absent in their lives. The effect of television images is notable across class and race, as is the increasingly accessible technology that puts the marital, child-bearing, and child-rearing practices of families around the world within grasp. In other words, are African American fathers engaged in cultural practices that are consistent with African American culture historically, or have they created a hybrid culture representative of a changing country with a changing societal culture?

American culture itself has sent multiple messages to the diverse communities in the United States about the role of parenting, the significance of marriage, and the acceptability of different family forms. In a recent report from the Pew Research Center (Livingston & Parker 2011), the title tells much of the story for both African American fathers and fathers more generally: A Tale of Two Fathers: More Are Active, but More Are Absent. The title and the substance of the report reflect the continual changes in society, making a single research, practice, or policy stance inherently nondescriptive, if not problematic. Not unlike other men who are fathers, African American fathers in determining and enacting their fatherly identities may be drawing from history, their local contexts, and the larger U.S. and international contexts, and responding to the current contexts and opportunities available to them. This suggests that there is no single, unilinear culture of African American fathers, but rather, as is the case with the concept of culture itself, African American men may be formulating their own cultures that are being shaped by shifting expectations, social experiences, and personal goals. These issues are implicated in any research, practice, or policy effort to understand and improve the experiences of fathers, not limited to African American fathers, as they are represented in the variations between and within groups.

NOTE

1. We use the terms black and African American interchangeably throughout much of the chapter.

RESOURCES ON AFRICAN AMERICAN FATHERS AND FATHERING

The list below provides the names of several centers, programs, organizations, and research centers whose work focuses, in some way, on African American fathers. This list is only a partial one. Several other fine resources exist in local and regional settings. For example, we suggest that you consult the Fatherhood Research and Practice Network (www.frpn.org) for additional information regarding programs.

National Centers and Initiatives

- Center for Research on Fathers, Children and Family Well-Being: http://crfcfw.columbia.edu/
- National Center on Fathers and Families: https://workfamily.sas.upenn.edu/archive/links/national-center-fathers-and-families%20
- National Center for Fathering (Shawnee Mission, KS): www.fathers.com
- National Fatherhood Initiative: www.fatherhood.org
- National Fatherhood Leaders Group: www.nflgonline.org
- National Partnership for Community Leadership: www.npclstrongfamilies.com
- National Responsible Fatherhood Clearinghouse: https://www.fatherhood.gov
- Work and Family Researchers Network: http://workfamily.sas.upenn.edu/archive/links/national-center-fathers-and-families%20

Local Centers and Programs

- A Father's Place (multiple locations, South Carolina): www.scfathersandfamilies.com/programs/a_fathers_place/about/
- Center for Fathers and Families (Sacramento, CA): www.fathersandfamilies.com/CFF/Welcome.html
- Center for Urban Families (Baltimore, MD): www.cfuf.org/Home/
- Georgia Fatherhood Program (multiple locations, Georgia): http://dcss.dhs.georgia.gov/community-outreach-programs
- NYC DADS: (multiple locations, New York City): www.nyc.gov/html/hra/nycdads/html/programs/programs.shtml
- Rising above Fatherhood Initiative (Cleveland, OH): www.cdps4u.org/index.php/programs/rising-above
- National Organization of Concerned Black Men (Washington, DC): www.cbmnational.org/fatherhood-initiatives/
- Healthy African American Families (Los Angeles, CA): http://haafii.org/Home_Page.html

WEBSITES

- Black Dad Connection: http://blackdadconnection.org
- Extraordinary Fathers: https://www.extraordinaryfathers.com
- Concerned Black Men National Fatherhood Initiative: www.cbmnational.org/ fatherhood-initiatives/

REFERENCES

Alexander, M. (2012). *The new Jim Crow: Mass incarceration in the age of colorblindness.* New York: The New Press.

Allen, W. D., & Doherty, W. J. (1996). The responsibilities of fatherhood as perceived by African American teenage fathers. *Families in Society: The Journal of Contemporary Social Services, 77*(3), 142–155.

Allen, W. R. (1978). Race, family setting, and adolescent achievement orientation. *Journal of Negro Education, 47,* 230–243.

Allen, W. R. (1981). Mom, dads, and boys: Race and sex differences in the socialization of male children. In L. Gary (ed.), *Black men* (99–114). Thousand Oaks, CA: Sage.

Allen, W. R. (1995). African American family life in societal context: Crisis and hope. *Sociological Forum, 10*(4), 569–592.

Anderson, E. (1990). *Streetwise: Race, class, and change in an urban community.* Chicago: University of Chicago Press.

Anderson, E. (ed.). (2008). *Against the wall: Poor, young, black, and male.* Philadelphia: University of Pennsylvania Press.

Beckert, T., Strom, R., & Strom, P. (2006). Black and white fathers of early adolescents: A cross-cultural approach to curriculum development for parent education. *North American Journal of Psychology, 8*(3), 455–469.

Billingsley, A. (1968). *Black families in white America.* Englewood Cliffs, NJ: Prentice-Hall.

Bowman, P. J., & Forman, T. A. (1997). Instrumental and expressive family roles among African American fathers. In Taylor, T. A., Jackson, R. J., & Chatters, L. M. (eds.), *Family life in Black America* (216–247). Thousand Oaks, CA: Sage

Bowman, P. J., & Sanders, R. (1998). Unmarried African American fathers: A comparative life span analysis. *Journal of Comparative Family Studies, 29,* 39–56.

Bronfenbrenner, U. (1977). Toward an experimental ecology of human development. *American Psychology, 32*(7), 515–531.

Bruner, J. S. (1956). *A study of thinking.* New York: Wiley.

Burton, L. M., Price-Spratlen, T., & Spencer, M. (1997). On ways of thinking about and measuring neighborhoods: Implications for studying context and developmental outcomes for children. In G. Duncan, J. Brooks-Gunn, & L. Aber (eds.), *Neighborhood poverty: Context and consequences for children* (vol. 2, 132–144). New York: Russell Sage Foundation.

Capps, R., McCabe, K., & Fix, M. (2012). *Diverse streams: African migration to the United States.* Washington, DC: Migration Policy Institute.

Carlson, M., & McLanahan, S. (2002). Fragile families, father involvement and public policy. In C. S. Tamis-LeMonda & N. J. Cabrera (eds.), *Handbook of father involvement: Multidisciplinary perspectives* (461–488). Mahwah, NJ: Lawrence Erlbaum.

Carper, L. (1966). The Negro family and the Moynihan report. *Dissent, 13*, 133–140.

Chase-Lansdale, P. L., Gordon, R. A., Coley, R. L., Wakschlag, L. S., & Brooks-Gunn, J. (1999). Young African American multigenerational families in poverty: The contexts, exchanges, and processes of their lives. In E. M. Hetherington (ed.), *Coping with divorce, single parenting and remarriage: A risk and resiliency perspective* (165–191). Mahwah, NJ: Lawrence Erlbaum.

Chatters, L. M., Taylor, R. J., & Neighbors, H. W. (1989). Size of informal help network and mobilizing for a serious personal problem among Black Americans. *Journal of Marriage and the Family, 51*, 667–676.

Cherlin, A. (1981). *Marriage, divorce, remarriage*. Cambridge, MA: Harvard University Press.

Clark, K. B., & Clark, M. P. (1947). Racial identification and preference in Negro children. In T. M. Newcomb & E. L. Hartley (eds.), *Readings in social psychology*. New York: Holt, Rinehart & Winston.

Clayton, O., Mincy, R. B., & Blakenhorn, D. (eds.). (2003). *Black fathers in contemporary American society: Strengths, weaknesses, and strategies for change*. New York: Russell Sage Foundation.

Coley, R., & Chase-Lansdale, P. L. (2000). Fathers' involvement with their children over time. *Poverty Research News, 4*(2), 12–14.

Diedrich, M., Gates, H. L., & Pedersen, C. (eds.). (1999). *Black imagination and the Middle Passage*. New York: Oxford University Press.

Drake, S. C., & Cayton, H. R. (1945). *Black metropolis: A study of Negro life in a northern city*. New York: Harcourt, Brace, and World.

Du Bois, W. E. B. (1899). *The Philadelphia Negro*. Philadelphia: The University of Pennsylvania Press.

Du Bois, W. E. B. (Ed.). (1909). *The Negro American family*. Atlanta, GA: The Atlanta University Press.

Du Bois, W. E. B. (1939). *Black folk then and now*. New York: Henry Holt & Co.

Edin, K., & Nelson, T. J. (2013). *Doing the best I can: Fatherhood in the inner city*. Sacramento: University of California Press.

Eyerman, R. (2001). *Cultural trauma: Slavery and the formation of African American identity*. Cambridge, UK: Cambridge University Press.

Fagan, J. (2000). Head Start fathers' daily hassles and involvement with their children. *Journal of Family Issues, 21*(3), 329–346.

Fantuzzo, J. W., Gadsden, V. L., & McDermott, P. A. (2010). An integrated curriculum to improve mathematics, language, and literacy for Head Start children. *American Educational Research Journal, 48*(3), 763–793

Frazier, E. F. (1939). *The Negro family in the United States*. Chicago, IL: University of Chicago Press.

Furstenberg, F. F. (2007). *Destinies of the disadvantaged: The politics of teen childbearing*. New York: Russell Sage Foundation.

Gadsden, V. L. (1999). Black families in intergenerational and cultural perspective. In M. E. Lamb (Ed.). *Parenting and child development in "nontraditional" families* (221–246). Mahwah, NJ: Lawrence Erlbaum Associates.

Gadsden, V. L., & Dixon-Román, E. (In press). "Urban" schooling and "urban" families: The role of context and place. *Urban Education*.

Gadsden, V. L., Fagan, J., Ray, A., & Davis, J. E. (2004). Fathering indicators for practice and evaluation: The Fathering Indicators Framework. In R. Day &

M. Lamb (eds.), *Measuring father involvement in diverse settings*. Mahwah, NJ: Lawrence Erlbaum.

Gadsden, V. L., Wortham, S. E. F., & Turner, H. M. (2003). Situated identities of young, African American fathers in low-income urban settings. *Family Court Review, 41*(3), 381–399.

Gans, Herbert J. (1965). The Negro family: Reflections on the Moynihan Report. *Commonwealth, 83*, 47–51.

Gates, G. J. (2008). Diversity among same-sex couples and their children. In S. Coontz (ed.), *American families: A multicultural reader*. New York: Routledge.

Gibson, M. A. (1987). The school performance of immigrant minorities: A comparative view. *Anthropology and Education Quarterly, 18*(4), 262–275.

Gordon, E. W. (2000). The myths and realities of African-American fatherhood. In R. D. Taylor & M. C. Wang (eds.), *Resilience across contexts: Family, work, culture, and community* (217–232). Mahwah, NJ: Lawrence Erlbaum.

Gordon, E. T., Gordon, E. W., & Nembhard, J. G. G. (1994). Social science literature concerning African American men. *Journal of Negro Education, 63*(4), 508–531.

Hanner, J. R. (1998). The definition of fatherhood: In the words of never-married African American mothers and the noncustodial fathers and their children. *Journal of Sociology and Social Welfare, 25*(2), 81–104.

Herskovits, M. J. (1928). *The American Negro*. Oxford, UK: Knopf

Hill, N. E., Murray, V. M., & Anderson, V. D. (2005). Sociocultural contexts of African American families. In V. C. McLoyd, N. E. Hill, and K. A. Dodge (eds.), *African American family life: Ecological and cultural diversity* (21–44). New York: Guilford Press.

Hill, R. (1972). *The strengths of black families*. New York: Emerson Hill Publishers.

Hunter, A. G. (2001). The other breadwinners: The mobilization of secondary wage earners in early twentieth-century black families. *The History of the Family: An International Quarterly, 6*, 69–94.

Huston, A. C., & Bentley, A. C. (2010). Human development in societal context. *Annual Review of Psychology, 61*, 411–437.

Jones, J., & Mosher, W. D. (2013). *Fathers' involvement with their children: United States, 2006–2010*. National health statistics reports; no 71. Hyattsville, MD: National Center for Health Statistics.

Kamo, Y., & Cohen, E. L. (1998). Division of household work between partners: A comparison of black and white couples. *Journal of Comparative Family Studies, 29*, 131–145.

Kirkland, D. E. (2013). *A search past silence: The literacy of young black men*. New York: Teachers College Press.

Lareau, A. (2003). *Unequal childhoods: Class, race, and family life*. Berkeley: University of California Press.

LaVeist, T. A. (ed.). (2002). *Race, ethnicity, and health: A public health reader*. New York: Jossey-Bass Publishers.

Lerman, R. & Sorensen, E. (2000). Father involvement with their non-marital children: Patterns, determinants, and effects on their earnings. Marriage & Family Review, 29(2–3), 137–158.

Livingston, G., & Parker, K. (2011). *A tale of two fathers: More are active, but more are absent*. Washington, DC: Pew Research Center.

Lovejoy, P. E. (ed.). (2009). *Identity in the shadow of slavery*. New York: Wellington House.

McDaniel/Zuberi, A. (1990). The power of culture: A review of Africa's influence on family structure in Antebellum America. *Journal of Family History, 15*(2), 225–238.

McLoyd, V. C., Cauce, A. M., Takeuchi, D., & Wilson, L. (2000). Marital processes and parental socialization in families of color: A decade review of research. *Journal of Marriage and Family, 62*(4), 1070–1093.

McLoyd, V. C., Hill, N. E., & Dodge, K. A. (eds.). (2005). *African American family life: Ecological and cultural diversity*. New York: Guilford Press.

Mickelson, R. A. (2003). When are racial disparities in education the result of racial discrimination? A social science perspective. *Teachers College Record, 105*, 1052–1086.

Miller, D. B. (1994). Influences on parental involvement of African American adolescent fathers. *Child and Adolescent Social Work Journal, 11*(5), 363–378.

Mincy, R. B., & Pouncy, H. (2007a). The impoverished "culture vs. structure" debate on the woes of young black males and its remedy. In G. A. Persons (ed.), *The expanding boundaries of black politics*. New Brunswick, NJ: Transaction Publishers.

Mincy, R. B., & Pouncy, H. (2007b). Why we should be concerned about young, less educated, black men. In J. Edwards, M. Crain, & A. L. Kalleberg (eds.), *Ending poverty in America: How to restore the American Dream*. New York: The New Press.

Mintz, S. W., & Price, R. (1992). *The birth of African-American culture: An anthropological perspective*. Boston, MA: Beacon Press.

Mirande, A. (1991). Ethnicity and fatherhood. In E. F. Bozett & S. Hanson (eds.), *Fatherhood and families in cultural context* (53–82). New York: Springer.

Moore, L. M. (2007). *The dispersion of Africans and African culture throughout the world: Essays on the African diaspora*. New York: Edwin Mellen Press.

Moore, M. (2011). *Invisible families: Gay identities, relationships, and motherhood among Black women*. Oakland: University of California Press.

Myrdal, G. (1944). *An American dilemma: The Negro problem and modern democracy*. New York: Harper and Row.

NCOFF Fathers and Families Roundtable Series (1995–1997). *Fathers and families roundtables, 1995–1997: Discussions of the seven core learnings*. Philadelphia: National Center on Fathers and Families, University of Pennsylvania.

Patillo-McCoy (2000). *Black picket fences: Privilege and perils among the black middle class*. Chicago, IL: University of Chicago Press.

Rainwater, L. (1970). Behind ghetto walls: Black family life in a federal slum. Chicago, IL: Aldine Publishing.

Rainwater, L., & Yancey, W. L. (1967). *The Moynihan Report and the politics of controversy*. Cambridge, MA: The MIT Press.

Ray, A., & Hans, S. (2001, April). "Being there for my child": Inner city African-American fathers' perspectives on fathering and sources of stress. Paper presented at the biennial meeting of the Society for Research in Child Development, Minneapolis, MN.

Reiss, I. L. (1960). *Premarital sexual standards in America*. New York: The Free Press.

Rhein, L. M., Ginsburg, K. R., Schwarz, D. F., Pinto-Martin, J. A., Zhao, H., Morgan, A. P., & Slap, G. B. (1997). Teen father participation in child rearing: family perspectives. *Journal of Adolescent Health, 21*(4), 244–252.

Rhodes, R. L., Ochoa, S. H., & Ortiz, S. O. (2005). *Assessing culturally and linguistically diverse students: A practical guide*. New York: Guilford Press.

Roopnarine, J. L. (2004). African American and African Caribbean fathers: Level, quality, and meaning of involvement. In M. E. Lamb (ed.), *The role of the father in child development* (552). Hoboken, NJ: John Wiley & Sons.

Roopnarine, J. L. (2013). Fathers in Caribbean cultural communities. In D. W. Schwalb, B. J. Schwalb & M. E. Lamb (eds.), *Fathers in cultural context* (203–227). New York: Routledge/Taylor & Francis.

Ruggles, S. (1994). The origins of African-American family structure. *American Sociological Review, 59*, 136–151.

Sampson, R. J., Morenoff, J. D., & Gannon-Rowley, T. (2002). Assessing "neighborhood effects": Social processes and new directions in research. *Annual Review of Sociology, 28*, 443–478.

Sampson, R. J., & Sharkey, P. (2008). Neighborhood selection and the social reproduction of concentrated racial inequality. *Demography, 45*, 1–29.

Scanzoni, J. H. (1977). *The black family in modern society*. Chicago, IL/London, UK: The University of Chicago Press.

Scanzoni, J. (1995). *Contemporary families and relationships: Reinventing responsibility*. New York: McGraw-Hill.

Smedley, A. (1999). *Race in North America: Origin and evolution of a worldview* (11–34). New York: Basic Civitas.

Stack, C. (1990). *All our kin: Strategies for survival in a black community*. New York: Basic Books.

Stewart, A. (2013). *First class: The legacy of Dunbar, America's first black public high school*. Chicago: Lawrence Hill.

Sullivan, M. L. (1993). Young fathers and parenting in two inner-city neighborhoods. In R. L. Lerman & T. J. Ooms (eds.), *Young, unwed fathers: Changing roles and emerging policies* (52–73). Philadelphia: Temple University Press.

Taylor, R. J., Jackson, J. S., & Chatters, L. M. (1997). *Family Life in Black America*. Thousand Oaks, CA: Sage.

Thorpe, R. J., Patrick, R., Bowie, J. V., Laveist, T. A., & Gaskin, D. J. (2013). Economic burden of men's health disparities in the United States. *International Journal of Men's Health, 12*(3), 195.

Tucker, M. B., & James, A. (2005). New families, new functions: Postmodern African American families in context. In V. C. McLoyd, N. E. Hill, and K. A. Dodge (eds.), *African American family life: Ecological and cultural diversity* (86–110). New York: Guilford Press.

Vespa, J., Lewis, J. M., & Kreider, R. M. (2013). *America's families and living arrangements: 2012*. Washington, DC: US Government Printing Office.

Waller, M. R. (1999). *Unmarried parents and models of fatherhood: New or conventional ideas about paternal involvement?* Princeton, NJ: Center for Research on Child Wellbeing, Princeton University.

Weiss, H. B., Dearing, E., Mayer, E., Kreider, H., & McCartney, K. (2005). Family educational involvement: Who can afford it, and what does it afford? In C. Cooper, C. Coll, & W. T. Bartko, H. Davis, & C. Chatman (eds.), *Developmental pathways through middle childhood: Rethinking contexts and diversity as resources* (17–39). Mahwah, NJ: Lawrence Erlbaum Associates.

Wilson, W. J. (1987). *The truly disadvantaged*. Chicago, IL: University of Chicago Press.

Young, A. A. (2007). *The minds of marginalized black men: Making sense of mobility, opportunity and future life chances*. Princeton, NJ: Princeton University Press.

9

Latino Fathers: Myths, Realities, and Challenges

Robert P. Moreno and Susan S. Chuang

LATINO FATHERS: MYTHS, REALITIES, AND CHALLENGES

Over the last three decades, research on fathers has grown considerably. Researchers have demonstrated that fathers significantly contribute to the development of their children, above and beyond that of mothers. Fathers have been found to contribute to their children's linguistic, cognitive, and social development (see Cabrera & Tamis-LeMonda 2013; Lamb 2010). Before this research, with the exception of financial support, the role of facilitating children's development was assumed to be solely in the mother's realm. From our current vantage point, the exclusion of fathers almost appears nonsensical. Similarly, despite the established importance of fathers, relatively little attention has been given to ethnic- and racial-minority fathers (Chuang & Moreno 2008, 2013; Downer, Campos, McWayne, & Gartner 2008). This is particularly the case for Latinos, even though they are the largest and the fastest-growing ethnic and racial group in the United States and are projected to grow at an accelerated rate (U.S. Census Bureau 2010). The paucity of research on Latino families is not entirely clear. However, it may be rooted, in part, in historical biases and deficit views of these families.

In this chapter, we draw from existing quantitative and qualitative research to discuss what we currently know about Latino fathers, as well as to illustrate some examples of the historical backdrop that has contributed to the existing stereotypes that have influenced social scientists' perceptions and research regarding Latino fathers and their families. Specifically, we first provide a brief overview on the father involvement literature. Second, we discuss the presence of Latinos in the United States and provide some historical context as well as discuss the diversity of the population. Third, we highlight key cultural values such as familism, masculinity, and *respeto* that guide and influence Latino fathers in their role within the family. Fourth, we discuss the current literature on paternal involvement patterns, with a particular focus on education. Finally, we conclude with some suggestion for future research.

FATHERING AND FATHER INVOLVEMENT

Researchers recognize that theoretical frameworks, models of fathering and father involvement have historically overlooked how developmental processes are shaped by sociocultural contexts (e.g., see Chuang & Moreno 2008; Chuang & Tamis-LeMonda 2009, 2013; Weisner 2002). More recently, research on fathering (as distinguished from "parenting") has gained significant attention, along with conceptual transformations and perspectives on the roles of fathers. As Cabrera and Tamis-LeMonda (2013) eloquently stated, "father involvement is a multidimensional, continually evolving concept—both at the level of scholarship and at the level of cultural awareness" (p. xiii).

As researchers moved to include fathers in the study of parenting, the seminal work of Lamb and his colleagues (1985, 1987) launched and dominated the field on fathering. Rather than building on prior work on parenting, researchers focused on the Lamb et al. (1985, 1987) model, which posited three dimensions of father involvement: accessibility, engagement, responsibility. *Accessibility* refers to the physical availability of the child to the father, regardless as to whether interaction occurs. *Engagement* refers to the actual time spent with the child interacting in caregiving and social activities such as rough-and-tumble play, companionship and learning activities that promote development. *Responsibility* involves the extent to which fathers are responsible for and making decisions about the child's overall well-being when the mother is not around.

Although Lamb and colleagues stressed that the model is not an exhaustive account of ways that fathers are involved and does not capture all the dynamics of fathering, a great deal of research has focused on the "ticks and clicks" of the father involvement model—the temporal and readily observable behaviors (Hawkins & Palkovitz 1999). Over time, researchers refined the father involvement dimension, engagement (which captured the time fathers directly interacted with their children) by focusing on the emotional aspects of the father–child relationship and exploring the quality of the relationship such as fathers' levels of warmth–responsiveness and control (see Pleck 2010).

Many scholars have consistently found that parents' roles in the family have shifted from a distinct division of labor (fathers as breadwinners and mothers as caregivers) to a more egalitarian relationship. This is in line with the family systems perspective, whereby parents and other family members are a part of a system in which each individual will affect and be affected by each other. These roles and responsibilities that parents and other caregivers assume are interconnected and continually negotiated (Tamis-LeMonda 2004). Increasingly, both men and women support egalitarian attitudes toward parenting (e.g., Casper & Bianchi 2002; Chuang, Moreno, & Su 2013), with fathers engaging in increased levels of caregiving, playing, and doing household chores (see Pleck & Masciadrelli 2004 for review).

There are a number of factors associated with paternal involvement. Most directly is the degree to which fathers' attitudes and beliefs emphfasize their importance in their children's development. Freeman, Newland, and Coyl (2008) found that fathers who held strong beliefs about their role in their child's development were more likely to be engaged with their children. Similarly, fathers who held more child-centered parenting attitudes (as opposed to more traditional or authoritarian attitudes) had higher levels of involvement with their children (Fagan & Barnett 2003; Shears & Robinson 2005). Other research has indicated that paternal self-efficacy also plays a significant role in paternal involvement (e.g., Freeman et al. 2008).

However, evidence suggests that mothers have a significant role in facilitating or constraining paternal involvement through their role as "gatekeepers." For example, McBride and his colleagues (2005) found that the relation between fathers' commitment to parenthood and their involvement was tied to mothers' belief that the father's role was important. Similarly, others have found that when mothers frequently criticized their partners, they mitigated the relation between fathers' beliefs and their behavior (Schoppe-Sullivan, Cannon, Brown, Mangelsdorf, & Sokolowski 2008). In addition, the amount and nature of father involvement may vary by the child's gender. Evidence suggests that fathers have less contact with their daughters and tend to be more engaged with their sons (Hosley & Montemayor 1997) and that fathers of boys engaged more frequently in physical play activities, whereas fathers of daughters engaged more frequently in literacy activities (Leavell, Tamis-LeMonda, Ruble, Zosuls, & Cabrera 2012).

LATINOS: DEMOGRAPHIC AND HISTORICAL BACKGROUND

In the United States, Latinos constitute approximately 16 percent of the total population (U.S. Census Bureau 2010). Of those, Mexicans make up the largest single group (63%), followed by Puerto Ricans (9.2%), Cubans (3.5%), and Dominicans (2.2%). All other Latino groups make up the remaining 24 percent (U.S. Census Bureau 2010). The three largest groups, Mexicans, Puerto Ricans, and Cubans, have increased by 54 percent, 36 percent, and 44 percent, respectively. However, new patterns are emerging. For example, Dominican Latinos constituted the largest single increase, approximately 85 percent (U.S. Census Bureau 2010). Based on current and historical socio-political and economic factors, Latinos tend to locate in specific geographic locations in the country, with Mexicans concentrated in the southwest (e.g., Arizona, California, and Texas) Puerto Ricans in the northeast (e.g., New York, New Jersey), and Cubans in the southeast (e.g., Florida).

Before we proceed, it is important to note that although the terms "Latino" and "Hispanic" are often used interchangeably within the social science literature, there has been a long-standing debate over which term is most appropriate and reflective of the Latino community (see Gimenez 1997; Sorris 1992; Taylor, Lopez, Martínez, & Velasco 2012). In this chapter, we use "Latino" for the sake of consistency and clarity. Moreover, it is necessary to be cognizant that *Latino* is a pan-ethnic or umbrella term used to classify peoples who share a common history of Spanish colonization in the Western hemisphere. The term encompasses families that originate from North America (e.g., Mexico), the Caribbean (e.g., Puerto Rico, Cuba, Dominican Republic), and Central and South America (e.g., Colombia, Ecuador, El Salvador, Guatemala, Venezuela)—approximately twenty countries in all. Thanks to their common history, Latinos share many similarities in their cultural values and beliefs. Thus the use of an all-encompassing term provides some utility. At the same time, the use of one term inevitably conceals the vast diversity of the groups that make up the population.

Because of their various histories with respect to Spain, indigenous populations, and the United States, families from Puerto Rico, Cuba, and the Dominican Republic may have more in common than those from Mexico, Guatemala, and Columbia. Indeed, these differences can be seen in various socioeconomic comparisons. Latinos vary across a variety of dimensions, including citizenship, generational status, acculturation, education, English proficiency, and economic standing (Landale, Oropesa, & Bradatan 2006; U.S. Census Bureau 2010). These differences among the various ethnic groups have introduced different opportunities and challenges to family life in the United States.

We argue that existing negative perceptions and stereotypes regarding Latino parenting and family functioning are rooted in a historical deficit orientation commonly associated with involuntary and castelike minorities (see Ogbu & Simons 1998). These groups were viewed as inferior and undesirable immigrants, particularly in comparison to their European counterparts. For example, in the 1921 congressional debate on immigration, Congressman

Martin Madden stated that the bill would "open the doors for perhaps the worst element that comes into the United States—the Mexican peon." Another commented, "I feel that there are very few of you who would be ready to go on record to prove that the Mexican makes a better citizen than the European immigrant" (Betancur, Cordova, & de los Angeles Torres 1993, p. 113). These negative perceptions were subsequently cultivated and legitimized by social scientists, who argued that Latinos were culturally deprived and perpetuated a culture of poverty that was transmitted from generation to generation (Lewis 1961, 1966; Madsen 1973). As a result, research on Latino families has historically been firmly grounded in a deficit orientation according to which behaviors, attitudes, and beliefs that deviated from the mainstream norms.

At the same time, the collectivist orientation of Latinos regarding extended family, familial obligations, and respect was at odds with the mainstream's individualistic focus on the nuclear family, autonomy, and individual growth. These values were viewed as contradictory to the necessary assimilationist trajectory and initially served as risk factors necessitating interventions that would facilitate the acquisition of more appropriate child rearing and family functioning. Despite this bleak history, more recently scholars have called into question past deficit-based conceptualizations of Latino families and have been more forthcoming in acknowledging the proximal and distal cultural practices that foster resilience in challenging environments (see Fuller & García Coll 2010).

LATINO VALUES AND BELIEFS

Latino fathers cannot be understood in isolation from their broader sociocultural milieu. Their roles, responsibilities, and behaviors are influenced by the broader cultural, economic, and political context in which they are immersed (Cabrera, Tamis-LeMonda, Bradley, Hofferth, & Lamb 2000). Among Latinos, values such as *familismo*, *respeto*, and *educación* are particularly salient and provide families with essential cultural scripts guiding and establishing parameters for family members in childrearing.

Familismo. Stemming from a collectivist orientation, one of the most salient and important values distinguishing Latinos from other ethnic groups is their emphasis on *familismo* or familism (McLoyd, Cauce, Takeuchi, & Wilson 2000). *Familismo* embodies a strong sense of family loyalty and connectedness. It involves focusing on the family's best interests over the needs of the individual. It is expressed through the emphasis on cooperation, reciprocity, and obligation to immediate and extended family members. In the case of children, it is important that they maintain the family hierarchy and act in accordance with their role. This involves giving appropriate deference to their parents, extended family members (grandparents, aunts, etc.), and even older siblings (Halgunseth, Ispa, & Rudy 2006). It also involves contributing to the household in the form of maintaining order, assisting family members when needed, and caring for siblings (Ceballo, Huerta, & Epstein-Ngo 2010; Fuligni, Tseng, & Lam 1999).

According to Baca Zinn (1994), familism is a multidimensional construct and comprises four components (demographic, structural, normative, behavioral). *Demographic* familism refers to factors such as family size, *structural* familism involves multigenerational households or extended family systems, *normative* familism relates to the value individuals place on family solidarity and support, and *behavioral* familism refers to the amount of contact among immediate and extended family members. Thus for Latino fathers, high levels of familism may be displayed not only in financial support, but also in activities that promote family togetherness, such as mealtimes, family outings, or cultural celebrations. Familism may also play a role in the higher rates of coresidency observed among Latino immigrants (D'Angelo, Palacios, & Chase-Landsdale 2012).

Respeto.   Latinos place a great deal of value on *respeto* (respect). It serves as a guide for displays of appropriate demeanor in relation to family members and authority figures. Its primacy in social relations has led some researchers to consider it as essential for successful childrearing (Harwood, Leyendecker, Carlson, Asencio, & Miller 2002; Valdés 1996). In part, respeto is signaled by following social conventions such as salutations and courtesies ("good morning," "please," "thank you"). More important, it serves as a script to maintain social order. Family members are expected to show appropriate deference and decorum. Children display respect by following the rules of the household and complying with parental authority (*obediente*); to do otherwise would be considered *falta de respeto* (without respect). Among Latinos, a child who shows disrespect to an adult is not only a sign of ill manner, but it is also considered a reflection of poor parenting.

To be successful in raising a well-mannered child, the parents' authority is paramount. It is imperative that children understand *quien manda*, or who is in charge. Valdés (1996) offers an example of this when she describes a parent's response to her child's demand. In this instance, a child requests that the mother purchase materials for school that she insists she needs for the following day. In an effort to be more persuasive, she adds that she needs the items "because the teacher said so" to which the parent replies, "La maestra no manda aquí" (the teacher is not in charge here). Valdés notes that although Latino parents have great respect for teachers, the teacher's authority has its limits and does not extend into the family sphere. The transgression here is not the request or the needed material; it is the child's attempt to override the parent's authority by invoking that of the teacher.

Bien Educado.   Similar to *respeto*, Latino parents emphasize that their children *son bien educado*. The construct is broad in its meaning and is not well translated into English. Literally translated as "well educated," its meaning extends well beyond academics. It refers to one's entire character and is a sign of good upbringing (Bridges, Cohen, McGuire, Yamada, Fuller, Mireles, & Scott 2012; Ceballo et al. 2010; Valdés 1996). Bridges and her colleagues (2012) describe the construct as a conglomeration of values and corresponding behavior such as respect, self-reliance, appropriate communication, and fulfilling obligations. Thus academic achievement is only a small portion of the entire construct. An academically successful child who lacks respect and is not committed to the family could be characterized as *mal educado* ("poorly educated"). This is as much a criticism of the parents as it is of the child.

In her classic ethnographic account of Mexican immigrant families, Valdés (1996) recalls a conversation between herself and an immigrant mother (Rosario) regarding their respective sons:

Rosario: Lupe, how old is your son?

GV: He's 24.

Rosario: And does he work?

GV: Well, no. That is, yes. Well, the thing is he's studying and his job is to study. When he finishes he's going to get a very good job and what he's got to do now is to dedicate himself to his studies.

Rosario: And he doesn't send you money?

GV: No, but I don't send him money either because he has a very good scholarship and they pay for everything.

Rosario: Oh, I see.

GV: He's a very good son. We miss him a lot.

Rosario: You know Miguel (then 17) is a very good boy too. He always asks us for permission to go places, not like other boys his age. And he works already and helps me out [financially]. Every summer he goes to Dallas to work with his uncle in construction. And when he comes back, he gives me his check. "Here mother," he says, "this is for you." (pp. 184–185)

Embedded in the exchange is a measure of a "good son," stemming from very different value sets. The characteristics included in Rosario's description of her son include employment (self-reliance), financially contributing to the family (*familismo*), and "asks for permission" (*respeto*). Thus a son with these qualities is likely to be viewed as *bien educado*.

MASCULINITY, MACHISMO, AND FATHERHOOD

The notion of masculinity and fatherhood are intertwined and multi-faceted (Pleck 2010). However, for Latino men, the relation between their masculinity and role in the family is more complex. For example, Gutmann (1996) notes that "[i]n social science as well as popular literature the Mexican male, especially if he is from the lower classes, is often portrayed as the archetype of 'machismo,' which however defined invariably conjures up the image of virulent sexism." (p. 223). Thus Latino masculinity is equated with a myopic understudying of machismo; El macho is a womanizer, chauvinistic and misogynistic. He is preoccupied with establishing and maintaining his reputation as a *peleador* (fighter) and is thus prone to physical violence. With respect to women, his manhood is confirmed in his womanizing, as well as his chauvinistic and misogynistic attitudes. As for the household, he is often absent, and when present is emotionally detached, a harsh disciplinarian, neglectful in the caretaking of his children, and rules the house as "lord and master" (Mirandé 1997, 2008). However, there is little empirical evidence to support this longstanding image (Saracho & Spodek 2008).

Taking an emic perspective, qualitative researchers have argued against this unidimensional view of machismo (Gutmann 1996; Mirandé 2008; Taylor & Behnke 2005). For example, in Taylor and Behnke's (2005) study of Mexican and Mexican-origin fathers in the United States, one informant explains, "Machismo means taking care of your family and protecting them. Yes, alcohol and women are often equated with a man's masculinity, but it is also important to provide for your family" (p. 8). Moreover, Gutmann (1996) argues that, much as in the United States, Latino men's roles and responsibilities have changed as a function of economic and cultural factors. In his ethnographic study of families in Santo Domingo (a community adjacent to Mexico City), he notes that as women entered the workforce in increasing numbers, men took on greater responsibilities in household duties including the nurturing and care taking of their children, as well as a corresponding male identity. This is illustrated by one informant (Doña Berta), who describes how a generation ago, her husband would have been ridiculed for participating in household chores and taking care of their children (holding the children, changing diapers), and now "the father who doesn't do these things is more likely to be the one being ridiculed" (p. 226). This finding suggests that shifts from more "traditional" to more "progressive" fathering patterns in household and childrearing duties are less a function of acculturation per se, but driven primarily by economic factors that necessitate a change in family functioning, such as the need for greater maternal employment.

More recently, quantitative researchers have adopted and incorporated this broader notion of machismo, one that embraces the notion of fathers are nurturers, caretakers, and the primary authority figure for their children (Arciniega et al. 2008; Cervantes 2006; Cruz et al. 2011; Mirandé 2008). For instance, in their study of 450 Mexican-origin two-parent families, Cruz and colleagues (2011) found that Latino fathers with higher levels of positive machismo values (also referred to as *caballerismo*) had children who reported higher levels of positive father involvement. In contrast, Glass and Owen (2010) found that the more negative aspects of machismo were associated with lower paternal involvement, and there was no association between *caballerismo* and paternal involvement. One reason for the discrepancy in findings may lie in the sample of the respective studies. Whereas Cruz et al. (2011) used a large, ethnically homogenous Mexican-origin sample, Glass and Owen's (2010) study was based on a relatively small, heterogeneous Latino sample (Mexican, Puerto Rican, Honduran, Cuban, Brazilian, Ecuadorian, El Salvadorian, and Peruvian). Given the variability, direct comparisons are tenuous despite both studies having employed Latino samples.

INVOLVEMENT PATTERNS OF LATINO FATHERS

As indicated earlier, Latino fathers have been characterized as both disengaged and authoritarian in the family. However, both qualitative and quantitative studies have demonstrated a pattern of active paternal participation whereby fathers display warmth and nurturance, and are involved in childrearing. Indeed, studies have suggested that in many ways, Latino paternal involvement is not unlike that of non-Latinos. Similar to European Americans, Latino mothers and fathers spend a disproportionate amount of time on childcare activities, with fathers spending approximately half as much per week as mothers did. Also when compared to African American and European American fathers, Latino fathers spent equivalent amounts of time on caregiving activities (Hossain, Field, Pickens, Malphurs, & Del Valle 1997).

Elsewhere, Latino fathers have been found to exhibit more responsibility for childrearing and less control in comparison to non-Hispanic white fathers (Coltrane, Parke, & Adams 2004; Hofferth 2003). They are also equally or more involved in the monitoring of their children and in direct interactions (e.g., play) and spend more time with them on the weekends than non-Hispanic White and African Americans (Adams, Coltrane, & Parke 2004; Yeung, Sandberg, Davis-Kean, & Hofferth 2001). This pattern of involvement is evident even at the earliest stages of fatherhood. Cabrera and her colleagues (2009a) found that Latino men were already involved in their paternal role before birth. They accompanied mothers to doctor's appointments, participated in viewing sonograms, and caressed the mother's belly in an effort to experience the baby's movements. Moreover, fathers financially supported mothers by purchasing necessary items throughout the pregnancy, and fathers who were involved prenatally tended to continue their involvement as children grew older (Cabrera, Fagan, & Farrie 2008; Cabrera, Shannon, Mitchell, & West 2009a).

CHALLENGES IN EXPLORING LATINO FATHERING

Latinos' particular sociocultural circumstances pose unique challenges for fathers. Factors such as immigration, citizenship, acculturation, levels of education, English proficiency, and economic standing, to name a few, all have an influence on Latino men's ability to effectively engage in their paternal role. Although the choice to immigrate is typically motivated by seeking "a better life for their children" and families often anticipate a relatively short period of separation, the process of extended family separation and reunification can take years (Suarez-Orozco, Todorova, & Louie 2002). As a result, the immigration process alone can have serious ramifications for the father–child relationship.

A common immigration pattern is for the father to enter the United States to seek gainful employment and send remittances to the family. After achieving some degree of financial stability, the father sends for the rest of the family. During the separation, families attempt to maintain contact. Suarez-Orozco and colleagues (2002) noted, "Parents and children [may] maintain contact by phone, letters, and gifts[,] though long-distance communication can be difficult, especially in long-term separations[;] as the children grow up, the parent becomes an abstraction" (p. 635). In some cases, the separation can last an average of five years, for immigrants from the Caribbean (Suarez-Orozco et al. 2002). The social and psychological difficulties associated with separation and reunion are captured in the following interview of a Mexican father with a 13-year-old son:

> My son and my daughter are not warm toward me. They are still mad that I left them and was separated from them for years. Even when I explain to them that I came here for them, they don't hear, they don't understand. My daughter acted strangely when she first got here. She got

jealous when I hugged my wife. She just wanted my attention for herself. Now, that's changed and things are getting back to normal. (p. 635)

Once in the United States, Latino immigrants begin to negotiate and adapt to their new host culture and undergo a process of acculturation (Chuang & Moreno 2013). Briefly, acculturation is the change that occurs when two or more cultures come in contact one another (Berry 1980). Over time, individuals may assimilate (acquire and maintain the values and beliefs of the host culture), maintain their culture of origin, or maintain the values of both cultures (to one degree or another). A fourth possibility is when the culture of origin is lost and there is isolation from the host or dominant culture. Patterns of acculturation have been associated with paternal involvement. In a study of sixty-seven Latino fathers (primarily Mexican and Puerto Rican), researchers found that fathers who were more aligned with Latino culture were more likely to be involved with their children (Glass & Owen 2010). In another study, Mexican parents who reported high levels of disagreements regarding childrearing found that more acculturated fathers (i.e., more oriented to U.S. culture) participated in more caregiving than their less acculturated counterparts (Cabrera, Shannon, & La Taillade 2009b)

In contrast to more static acculturation models wherein the process culminates into one of four types (Berry 1980), Auerbach and colleagues (2008) suggest that acculturation may be more "organic," such that values and behavior patterns of the two or more cultures give rise to new ways of being— a blending or, as they refer to it, *creolization*. In their qualitative study of Mexican, Dominican, and Puerto Rican fathers in New York City, they argue that through creolization, values such as *familismo*, *respeto*, and *machismo* are transformed in such ways that men could maintain their core values but make them more palatable in their new context. As examples, in the interviews, fathers made a distinction between traditional notions like *respeto* ("In Santo Domingo, when the father speaks, everyone listens") and those needed in the new country ("One has to change one's ideas about raising kids in this country. This country makes my role model appear old-fashioned for the life-standard here") (pp. 206–207). Though not abandoning the value of *respeto*, a new form results whereby the father is not entitled to *respeto*. Rather, it needs to be earned or negotiated between the father and his children. As one father states, "Perhaps I haven't earned my daughter's trust . . . . One has to treat children with respect." (p. 207). This more nuanced approach may add much needed insight into the acculturation/creolization *process* and emphasize outcomes that are contextually situated and may not easily align with existing acculturation typologies (e.g., see Berry 1980).

Additionally, when compared to non-Latino families, factors such as low levels of household income, education, and employment disproportionately affect paternal involvement in Latino families. Landale and Oropesa (2001) found that for Puerto Ricans living on the mainland, employment was the single largest predictor of whether fathers contributed financially to the family. It also predicted fathers' levels of involvement in childcare activities such as diapering, feeding, and bathing. This was the case regardless of whether fathers were present in the home, cohabiting, or married.

LATINO FATHERS AND EDUCATION

There has been an enduring negative perception of Latinos regarding their children's education. Academics, school officials, and policymakers have suggested that Latino parents do not care about their children's school success (see Delgado Gaitan 2004; Moreno & Valencia 2011). It has been suggested that this is due in part to the cultural factors inherent in Latino families that preclude academic success (see Moreno & Valencia 2011; Valenzuela 1999). In his *Ethnic America: A History*, Sowell (1981) states, "[T]he goals and values of Mexican Americans have never centered on education" (p. 266). He goes on to suggest that many Mexican Americans find education "distasteful" (p. 267). Still others argue that Latinos once held education in high regard, but it has somehow been lost. This sentiment was expressed by U.S. Secretary of Education Lauro Cavazos (1988–1990) when he said, "Hispanics have always valued education . . . but somewhere along the line we've lost that. I really believe that, today, there is not that emphasis" (Snider 1990, p. 1). Yet others point to the relative lack of parent involvement on school sites as an indicator of a lack of commitment (e.g., classroom volunteering, attending parent–teacher conferences, participation in parent–teacher organizations).

In contrast to this view, other researchers have demonstrated that Latino parents place a high value on education despite the number of barriers they face (Delgado Gaitan 1991; Okagaki & Sternberg 1993; Valdés 1996). Latino parents, particularly immigrants, tend to have limited formal education, lower English-language proficiency, multiple jobs, and inflexible work schedules and are unfamiliar with U.S. schools' expectations. In Mexico and other Latin American countries, for example, school curricula are highly centralized, and the role of the parent is minimal. Rather, the primary role of the parent is to ensure that children act in accordance with school rules and decorum (Delgado Gaitan 2004). As a result of these beliefs and practices, there are disconnects between the existing experiences and expectations of many Latino parents and those held by teachers and administrators in the school systems in the United States.

In the realm of parent involvement in children's education, the focus has almost exclusively been on the mother. But, as already indicated, fathers engage and facilitate their children's development in unique ways such as linguistic development and self-regulatory capacity (Lamb & Tamis-LeMonda 2004; Paquette 2004). These findings, along with the emphasis on the importance of parents' involvement in children education, has led to growing attention directed at fathers' involvement in their children's schooling.

In a recent comparative study on Latino father involvement in children's schooling, Terriquez (2013) found that Latinos differ in their involvement levels by immigrant status. In general, immigrant fathers participate less in their children's school activities when compared to Latino fathers born in the United States. However, further analyses found that these differences were no longer significant when controlling for SES, language preference, and family background. Although informative, the study assessed only father involvement at the school site (e.g., attending a general school meeting, attending sporting event, participating in parent-teacher conference, volunteering at the school); school-related involvement activities in the home were not measured.

Current conceptualizations of parents' involvement in their children's education indicate that parents can be engaged in a number of ways (see Moreno & Valencia 2011; Pomerantz & Moorman 2010). One of the most influential frameworks for understanding parents' engagement with school is that proposed by Joyce Epstein and her colleagues (Epstein 1995; Sheldon & Epstein 2005). According to Epstein, parent involvement should be defined broadly and involve home-based as well as school-based activities. She lists six specific types of involvement: (1) providing a supportive home environment, (2) engaging in and maintaining communication between home and school, (3) volunteering in classroom or schools activities, (4) providing a learning environment in the home, (5) participating in decision making activities and school governance, and (6) facilitating community–school collaborations.

Using this typology, we (Moreno & Chuang 2012) conducted an exploratory study examining Latino fathers' beliefs and behaviors toward their children's schooling. We found that Latino fathers reported strong beliefs about their responsibilities for their children's schooling. But the degree to which fathers held certain beliefs varied as a function of the type of involvement. Fathers' beliefs were highest for more home-based activities such as parenting and learning at home. That is, fathers believed that they should take an active role in meeting their children's needs and provide an overall positive home environment. Fathers also believed it important that they communicate with their child's teacher (be aware of child's progress and school activities) and provide a home learning environment (monitor homework, read to their child). Interestingly, they were less inclined to believe that it is their responsibility to engage in more school-based activities (volunteering, decision making).

In addition to reporting their beliefs, fathers were asked to indicate their level of participation in school-related activities. Fathers reported the highest level of involvement in parenting and providing a learning environment in the home. They were least involved in decision-making activities, such as participating in parent–teacher organizations. It should be pointed out that this home–school distinction is not unique to Latino fathers. Similar results were reported for Latina mothers in California and Chinese immigrant parents in Washington D.C., whose school site involvement was significantly less than home-based activities (Ji & Koblinsky 2009; Moreno 2004).

In the Moreno and Chuang (2012) study, there was a positive association between fathers reported beliefs and involvement behavior in the context of the home. Fathers reported it is their responsibility to provide a learning environment in the home and acted accordingly. Conversely, fathers reported feeling less responsibility for engaging in school–community activities, and corresponding behavior was low. In the areas of home–school communication, volunteering, and school decision-making, there was a discrepancy between beliefs and behaviors. Although fathers reported that it was part of their responsibility to engage in these areas, their reported behavior did not coincide with their beliefs. This was particularly the case for home–school communication. One reason for the disconnect may be language: some Spanish-speaking fathers have difficulty in communicating with English-speaking school personnel.

Though Epstein's parental involvement classification is widely used, others have argued that Latino parents engage in nontraditional forms of school involvement (Campos 2008; Lopéz 2001). For instance, Lopéz (2001) argues that educators' understanding of "involvement" must be broadened and more culturally situated. He illustrates his point in his case study of the Padilla family, wherein the parents demonstrate their involvement and commitment to schooling through their emphasis on the value of hard work. They do this by acquainting their children with the demands of manual labor:

> The Padillas were quite strategic in exposing their children to the world of work, and constantly gave them *consejos* (advice) about the importance of working hard. By giving their children a "choice" to either work hard at school or work hard in the fields, the Padillas recognized that hard work was the foundation of success in any context . . . . (p. 422)

The Padilla father recalls:

> Well, for me, the easy life doesn't count. If there's not a little bit of work, it's not worth much. For example, all my kids know [how to work] the hoe, they know how to pick grapes—various jobs. So they see that

the door is open for them to do more than those types of work. They always told me they were going to stay in school. And it made me happy to hear that, because I taught them how hard it was to work in the fields. (p. 422)

As opposed to the more traditional forms of involvement (as outlined by Epstein), the father of the Padilla family engages in life lessons as a way of extolling the importance of schooling. These examples illustrate that although traditional indicators of involvement may be necessary, they are not sufficient. Rather a broader and more nuanced understanding of involvement is needed.

As in other areas of education, it is important to be cognizant that schools are far from neutral institutions. Their selective use of particular languages, organization structures, and assumptions about home environments, schools "invite" certain practices and segments of the community, and discourage others (Moreno, Lewis-Menchaca, & Rodríguez 2011). In this regard, one way that schools have tried to increase parent involvement is by promoting the notion of *parents as teachers*, a perspective that emphasizes that parents are their child's "first teacher." This view highlights the importance of parents in their child's education, where parents emulate the teacher and the home is an extension of the classroom. When the school culture readily intersects with the home, this orientation operates with little complication. However, when the home and school culture are disparate, as in the case of the Padilla family, the father's role as the "teacher" is only meaningful when viewed through its appropriate cultural lens.

CONCLUSION

It is clear that research on fathers, particularly fathers of color within the United States, has moved beyond oversimplified interpretations based on the presence or absence of fathers or mother–father comparisons. Much of the work discussed here has attempted to provide insight into the specific effect of fathers on their children's development, regardless of residential status. Nonetheless, as Downer and colleagues (2008) note in their extensive review of father involvement on children's early learning, aspects of the fathering research overall still lag behind in compensating for earlier shortcomings both theoretically and methodologically. Although progress has certainly been made since their review, their overall assessment is still relevant. Specifically, there remains a lack of studies that are grounded in culturally situated theoretical frameworks (e.g., developmental niche model, the creolization thesis, critical race theory, colorism, transplantation, and invasion of cultural psyche) that consider sociohistorical experience such as oppression, colonialism, and economic and social inequalities (see Burton, Bonilla-Silva, Ray, Buckelew, & Freeman 2010 for a review of some of these perspectives).

The lack of culturally relevant frameworks and culturally operationalized constructs with respect to different aspects of father investment and involvement with children in Latinos and other ethnic/racial minority groups is a major setback in fathering research. As we have argued, atheoretical comparative studies run the risk of interpreting differences in Latino fathers' behaviors and attitudes along existing stereotypes. Even those who employ an existing theoretical framework may rely on a one ill equipped to identify ways of fathering that are a departure from middle class patterns upon which they are based. A good case in point is Lamb et al.'s (1985) tripartite model. Although a useful guide, the very nature of "accessibility," "engagement," and "responsibility" are culturally bound. Thus the commonly used indices of these constructs on "diverse" populations provide little insight into, perhaps, more fundamental variations. It should be noted, however, that many researchers have moved to using contextual and cultural approaches to ground their work, such as developmental–ecological theory and ecocultural theory (Bronfenbrenner & Morris 1998; Weisner 2002). Yet the utility of cultural–contextual-based models is predicated on more than a superficial understanding of the culture under study. With respect to Latino fathers, a considerable amount of research is needed, using a variety of methods (qualitative, quantitative, mixed method, and longitudinal), in which researchers must give greater attention to the historical, cultural, economic, and geographical diversity among Latinos. Despite these challenges, we believe that continued research on Latino fathers is desperately needed and would be fruitful in expanding both our theoretical and empirical knowledge of fathers across cultures, communities, and contexts in the United States.

REFERENCES

Adams, M., Coltrane, S., & Parke, R. D. (2004). Cross-ethnic applicability of the gender- based attitudes toward marriage and child rearing scales. *Sex Roles: A Journal of Research, 56*, 325–339. doi:10.1007/s11199-006-9174-0.

Arciniega, G. M., Anderson, T. C., Tovar-Blank, Z. G., & Tracey, T. J. G. (2008). Toward a fuller conception of machismo: Development of a traditional machismo and caballerismo scale. *Journal of Counseling Psychology, 55*(1), 19–33. doi:10.1037/0022-0167.55.1.19.

Auerbach, C. F., Silverstein, L. B., Wolderberg, C. Z., Peguero, A., & Tacher, C. (2008). Acculturation via creolization: Constructing Latino American fathering identities. In S. Chuang & R. P. Moreno (eds.), *On new shores: Understanding immigrant fathers of North America* (197–215). Lanham, MD: Lexington Books.

Baca Zinn, M. (1994). Adaptation and continuity in Mexican-origin families. In R. L. Taylor (ed.), *Minority families in the United States: A multicultural perspective* (64–94). Englewood Cliffs, NJ: Prentice Hall.

Berry, J. W. (1980). Acculturation as varieties of adaptation. In A. M. Padillo (ed.), *Acculturation: Theories, models, and some new findings* (9–25). Boulder, CO: Westview Press.

Betancur, J. J., Cordova, T., & de los Angeles Torres, M. (1993). Economic restructuring in the process of incorporation of Latinos into the Chicago economy. In R. Morales & F. Bonilla (eds.), *Latinos and a changing U.S. economy: Comparative perspectives on growing inequality* (109–132). Newbury Park, CA: Sage.

Bridges, M., Cohen, S. R., McGuire, L. W., Yamada, H., Fuller, B., Mireles, L., & Scott, L. (2012). Bien educado: Measuring the social behaviors of Mexican American children. *Early Childhood Research Quarterly, 27,* 555–567. doi:10.1016/j.ecresq.2012.01.005.

Bronfenbrenner, U., & Morris, P. A. (1998). The ecology of developmental processes. In W. Damon (ed.), R. M. Lerner (vol. ed.), *Handbook of child psychology* (5th ed.), vol. 1: *Theoretical models of human development* (993–1028). New York: Wiley.

Burton, L. M., Bonilla-Silva, E., Ray, V., Buckelew, R., & Freeman, E. H. (2010). Critical race theories, colorism, and the decade's research on families of color, *Journal of Marriage and the Family, 72,* 440–459. doi:10.1111/j.1741-3737.2010.00712.x.

Cabrera, N. J., Fagan, J., & Farrie, D. (2008). Explaining the long reach of fathers' prenatal involvement on later paternal engagement with children. *Journal of Marriage and the Family, 70,* 1094–1107. doi:10.1111/j.1741-3737.2008.00551.x.

Cabrera, N. J., Shannon, J. D., Mitchell, S. J., & West, J. (2009a). Mexican American mothers and fathers' prenatal attitudes and father prenatal involvement: Links to mother–infant interaction and father engagement. *Sex Roles, 60*(7–8), 510–526. doi:10.1007/s11199-008-9576-2.

Cabrera, N. J., Shannon, J. D., & La Taillade, J. J. (2009b). Predictors of co-parenting in Mexican American families and links to parenting and child social emotional development. *Infant Mental Health Journal Special Issue: Development of Infants and Toddlers in Ethnoracial Families, 30*(5), 523–548. doi:10.1002/imhj.20227.

Cabrera, N. J., & Tamis-LeMonda, C. S. (eds.). (2013). *Handbook of father involvement: Multidisciplinary perspectives* (2nd ed.). New York: Taylor & Francis.

Cabrera, N. J., Tamis-LeMonda, C. S., Bradley, R. H., Hofferth, S., & Lamb, M. E. (2000). Fatherhood in the twenty-first century. *Child Development, 71,* 127–136.

Campos, R. (2008). Considerations for studying father involvement in early childhood among Latino families. *Hispanic Journal of Behavioral Sciences, 3*(2), 133–160.

Casper, L. M., & Bianchi, S. M. (2002). *Continuity and change in the American family.* Thousand Oaks, CA: Sage.

Ceballo, R., Huerta, M., & Epstein-Ngo, Q. (2010). Parental and schooling influences promoting academic success among Latino students. In J. L. Meece & J. S. Eccles (eds.), *Handbook of research on schools, school, and human development* (293–397). New York: Routledge.

Cervantes, J. M. (2006). A new understanding of the macho male image: Exploration of the Mexican-American man. In M. Englar-Carlsen & M. A. Stevens (eds.),

In the room with men: A casebook of therapeutic change (197–224). Washington, DC: American Psychological Association.

Chuang, S. S., & Moreno, R. P. (eds.). (2008). *On new shores: Understanding immigrant fathers in North America.* Lanham, MD: Lexington Books.

Chuang, S. S., & Moreno, R. P. (2013). Theoretical perspectives on acculturation and immigration. In M. A. Fine & F. D. Fincham (eds.), *Handbook of family theories: A content-based approach* (316–337). New York: Taylor and Francis/Routledge.

Chuang, S. S., Moreno, R. P., & Su, Y. (2013). Moving fathers from the "sidelines": An exploration of contemporary Chinese fathers in Canada and China. In K. B. Chan & N. C. Hung (eds.), *Advances in research in Chinese families: A global perspective* (343–357). New York: Springer Science+Business Media.

Chuang, S. S., & Tamis-LeMonda, C. S. (2009). Gender roles in immigrant families: Parenting views, practices, and child development. *Sex Roles, 60,* 549–558.

Chuang, S. S., & Tamis-LeMonda, C. S. (2013). Current perspectives on gender roles and relationships in immigrant families. In In S. S. Chuang & C. S. Tamis-LeMonda (eds.), *Gender roles in immigrant families* (1–5). New York: Springer Science+Business Media.

Coltrane, S., Parke, R. D., & Adams, M. (2004). Complexity of father involvement in low-income Mexican American families. *Family Relations, 53,* 179–189. doi:10.1111/j.0022-2445.2004.00008.x.

Cruz, R. A., King, K. M., Widaman, K. F., Leu, J., Cauce, A. M., & Conger, R. D. (2011). Cultural influences on positive father involvement in two-parent Mexican-origin families. *Journal of Family Psychology, 25*(5), 731–740. doi:10.1037/a0025128.

D'Angelo, A. V., Palacios, N. A., & Chase-Landsdale, P. L. (2012). Latino immigrant differences in father involvement with infants. *Fathering, 10,* 178–212. doi:10.3149/fth.1002.178.

Delgado Gaitan, C. (1991). Involving parents in the schools: A process of change for involving parents. *American Journal of Educational Research, 100*(1), 20–46.

Delgado Gaitan, C. (2004). *Involving Latino families in schools: Raising student achievement through home-school partnerships.* Thousand Oaks, CA: Corwin.

Downer, J., Campos, R., McWayne, C., & Gartner, T. (2008). Father involvement and children's early learning: A critical review of published empirical work from the past 15 years. *Marriage and Family Review, 43,* 67–108. doi:10.1080/01494920802010264.

Epstein, J. L. (1995). School/family/community partnerships: Caring for the children we share. *Phi Delta Kappan, May,* 701–712.

Fagan, J., & Barnett, M. (2003). The relationship between maternal gatekeeping, paternal competence, mothers' attitudes about the father role, and father involvement. *Journal of Family Issues, 24,* 1020–1043. doi:10.1177/0192513X03256397.

Freeman, H. S., Newland, L. A., & Coyl, D. D. (2008). Father beliefs as a mediator between contextual barriers and father involvement. *Early Child Development and Care, 178*(7–8), 803–819. doi:10.1080/03004430802352228.

Fuligni, A. J., Tseng, V., & Lam, M. (1999). Attitudes toward family obligations among American adolescents from Asian, Latin American, and European backgrounds. *Child Development, 70,* 1030–1044. doi:10.1111/1467-8624.00075.

Fuller, B., & García Coll, C. (2010). Learning from Latinos: Contexts, families, and child development in motion. *Developmental Psychology, 46*(3), 559–565. doi:10.1037/a0019412.

Gimenez, M. E. (1997). Latino/"Hispanic"—Who needs a name? The case against a standardized terminology. In A. Darder, R. D. Torres, & H. Gutiérrez (eds.), *Latinos and education: A critical reader* (225–238). New York: Routledge.

Glass, J., & Owen, J. (2010). Latino fathers: The relationship among machismo, acculturation, ethnic identity, and paternal involvement. *Psychology of Men and Masculinity, 11*, 251–261. doi:10.1037/a0021477.

Gutmann, M. C. (1996). *The meanings of macho: Being a man in Mexico City.* Berkeley, CA: University of California Press.

Halgunseth, L., Ispa, J., & Rudy, D. (2006). Parental control in Latino families: An integrated review of the literature. *Child Development, 77*, 1282–1297. doi:10.1111/j.1467-8624.2006.00934.x.

Harwood, R. L., Leyendecker, B., Carlson, V. J., Asencio, M., & Miller, A. M. (2002). Parenting among Latino families in the U.S. In M. H. Bornstein (ed.), *Handbook of parenting: Social conditions and applied parenting*, 2nd ed. (21–46). Mahwah, NJ: Erlbaum.

Hawkins, A. J., & Palkovitz, R. (1999). Beyond ticks and clicks: The need for more diverse and broader conceptualizations and measures of father involvement. *Journal of Men's Studies, 8*, 11–32. doi:10.3149/jms.0801.11.

Hofferth, S. L. (2003). Race/ethnic differences in father involvement in two-parent families. *Journal of Family Issues, 24*, 185–216. doi:10.1177/0192513X02250087.

Hosley, C. A., & Montemayor, R. (1997). Fathers and adolescents. In M. E. Lamb (ed.), *The role of the father in child development*, 3rd ed. (162–178). New York: Wiley.

Hossain, Z., Field, T., Pickens, Malphurs, J., & Del Valle, C. (1997). Fathers' caregiving in low-income African-American and Hispanic-American families. *Early Development and Parenting, 6*(2), 73–82 doi:10.1002/(SICI)1099-0917(199706)6:2<73::AID-EDP145>3.0.CO;2-O.

Ji, C. S., & Koblinsky, S. A. (2009). Parent involvement in children's education: An exploratory study of urban, Chinese immigrant families. *Urban Education, 44*, 687–709. 10.1177/0042085908322706.

Lamb, M. E. (ed.). (2010). *The role of the father in child development* (5th ed). Hoboken, NJ: Wiley.

Lamb, M. E., Pleck, J. H., Charnov, E. L., & Levine, J. A. (1985). Paternal behavior in humans. *American Zoologist, 25*, 883–894.

Lamb, M. E., Pleck, J. H., Charnov, E. L., & Levine, J. A. (1987). A biosocial perspective on paternal behavior and involvement. In J. B. Lancaster, J. Altman, A. Rossi, & L. Sherrod (eds.), *Parenting across the lifespan: Biosocial perspectives* (111–142). Hawthorne, NY: Aldine.

Lamb, M., & Tamis-LeMonda, C. S. (2004). Fathers' role in child development. In M. E. Lamb (ed.), *The role of the father in child development*, vol. 3. New York: Wiley.

Landale, N. S., & Oropesa, R. S. (2001). Father involvement in the lives of mainland Puerto Rican children: Contributions of nonresident, cohabiting and married fathers. *Social Forces, 79*(3), 945–968. doi:10.1353/sof.2001.0014.

Landale, N. S., Oropesa, R. S., & Bradatan, B. (2006). Hispanic families in the United States: Family structure and process in an era of family change. In M. Tienda & F. Mitchell (eds.), *Hispanics and the future of America* (138–178). Washington, DC: National Academy of Sciences.

Leavell, A. S., Tamis-LeMonda, C. S., Ruble, D. N., Zosuls, K. M., & Cabrera, N. J. (2012). African American, white and Latino fathers' activities with their sons and daughters in early childhood. *Sex Roles, 66*, 53–65. doi 10.1007/s11199-011-0080-8.

Lewis, O. (1961/2011). The children of Sánchez: Autobiography of a Mexican family. New York: Random House.

Lewis, O. (1966). *La vida: A Puerto Rican family in the culture of poverty—San Juan and New York*. New York: Random House.

Lopéz, G. R. (2001). The value of hard work: Lessons on parent involvement from an (im)migrant household. *Harvard Educational Review, 71*, 416–437.

Madsen, W. (1973). *The Mexican Americans of south Texas.* New York: Holt, Rinehart, & Winston.

McBride, B. A., Brown, G. L., Bost, K. K., Shin, N., Vaughn, B., & Korth, B. (2005). Paternal identity, maternal gatekeeping, and father involvement. *Family Relations, 54*, 360–372. doi:10.1111/j.1741-3729.2005.00323.x.

McLoyd, V. C., Cauce, A. M., Takeuchi, D., & Wilson, L. (2000). Marital processes and parental socialization in families of color: A decade review of research. *Journal of Marriage and the Family, 62*, 1070–1093. doi:10.1111/j.1741-3737.2000.01070.x.

Mirandé, A. (1997). *Hombres y machos: Masculinity and Latino culture.* Boulder, CO: Westview Press.

Mirandé, A. (2008). Immigration and Latino fatherhood: A preliminary look at Latino immigrant and non-immigrant fathers. In S. S. Chuang & R. P. Moreno (eds.), *On new shores: Understanding immigrant fathers in North America* (217–229.). Lanham, MD: Lexington Books.

Moreno, R. P. (2004). Exploring parental involvement among Mexican American and Latina mothers. In R. M. De Anda (ed.), *Chicanas and Chicanos in contemporary society*, 2nd ed. (81–97). Lanham, MD: Rowman & Littlefield.

Moreno, R. P., & Chuang, S. S. (2012). Latino fathers and their involvement in their children's schooling. In H. Ho & D. B. Hiatt-Michael (eds.), *Promising practices for fathers' involvement in their children's education* (59–77). Charlotte, NC: Information Age Publishing.

Moreno, R. P., Lewis-Menchaca, K., & Rodríguez, J. (2011). Parental involvement in the home: A critical view through a multicultural lens. In E. M. Olivos, O. Jimenez-Castellanos, & A. M. Ochoa (eds.), *Bicultural parent engagement: Advocacy and empowerment* (21–38). New York: Teachers College Press.

Moreno, R. P., & Valencia, R. R. (2011). Chicano families and schools: Challenges for strengthening family-school relationships. In Valencia, R. R. (ed.), *Chicano school failure and success: Past, present, and future*, 3rd ed. (197–210). New York: Routledge.

Ogbu, J. U., & Simons, H. D. (1998). Voluntary and involuntary minorities: A cultural–ecological theory of school performance with some implications for education. *Anthropology and Education Quarterly, 29*(2), 155–188. doi:10.1525/aeq.1998.29.2.155.

Okagaki, L., & Sternberg, R. J. (1993). Parental beliefs and children's early school performance. *Child Development, 64*(1), 36–56. doi:10.1111/j.1467-8624.1993.tb02894.x.

Paquette, D. (2004). Theorizing the father–child relationship: Mechanisms and developmental outcomes. *Human Development, 47*, 93–219. doi:10.1159/000078723.

Pleck, J. H. (2010). Paternal involvement: Revised conceptualization and theoretical linkages with child outcomes. In M. E. Lamb (ed.), *The role of the father in child development*, 5th ed. (58–93). Hoboken, NJ: Wiley.

Pleck, J. H., & Masciadrelli, B. P. (2004). Paternal involvement by U.S. resident fathers: Levels, sources and consequences. In M. E. Lamb (ed.), *The role of the father in child development* (222–271). Hoboken, NJ: Wiley.

Pomerantz, E. M., & Moorman, E. A. (2010). Parents' involvement in children's schooling: A context for children's development. In J. L. Meece & J. S. Eccles (eds.), *Handbook of research on schools, school, and human development* (398–416). New York: Routledge.

Saracho, O. N., & Spodek, B. (2008). Demythologizing the Mexican American father. *Journal of Hispanic Higher Education, 7*, 79–96. doi:10.1177/1538192707313936.

Schoppe-Sullivan, S. J., Cannon, E. A., Brown, G. L., Mangelsdorf, S. C., & Sokolowski, M. S. (2008). Maternal gatekeeping, co-parenting quality, and fathering behavior in families with infants. *Journal of Family Psychology, 22*(3), 389–398. doi:10.1037/0893-3200.22.3.389.

Shears, J. K., & Robinson, J. (2005). Fathering attitudes and practices: Influences on children's development. *Child Care in Practice, 11*(1), 63–79. 10.1080/1357527042000332808.

Sheldon, S. B., & Epstein, J. L. (2005). School programs of family and community involvement to support children's reading and literacy development across the grades. In J. Flood & P. Anders (eds.), *Literacy development of students in urban schools: Research and policy* (107–138). Newark, DE: International Reading Association.

Snider, W. (1990, April 18). Outcry follows Cavazos comments on the values of Hispanic parents. *Education Week*, p. 1.

Sorris, E. (1992). *Latinos: A biography of the people*. New York: Avon.

Sowell, T. (1981). *Ethnic America: A history*. New York: Basic Books.

Suarez-Orozco, C., Todorova, I. L. G., & Louie, J. (2002). Making up for lost time: The experience of separation and reunification among immigrant families. *Family Process, 41*(4), 625–643. doi:10.1111/j.1545-5300.2002.00625.x.

Tamis-LeMonda, C. S. (2004). Playmates and more: Fathers' role in child development. *Human Development, 47*(4), 220–227. doi:10.1159/000078724.

Taylor, B., & Behnke, A. (2005). Fathering across the border: Latino fathers in Mexico and the U.S. *Fathering, 3*(2), 1–25.

Taylor, P., Lopez, M. H., Martínez, J. H., & Velasco, G. (2012). *When labels don't fit: Hispanics and their views of identity*. Washington, DC: Pew Hispanic Center.

Terriquez, V. (2013). Latino fathers' involvement in their children's schools. *Family Relations, 62*(4), 662–675. doi:10.1111/fare.12026.

U.S. Census Bureau. (2010). The Hispanic population: 2010 census briefs.

Valdés, G. (1996). Con respeto: *Bridging the distances between culturally diverse families and schools*. New York: Teachers College Press.

Valenzuela, A. (1999). Subtractive schooling: U.S. Mexican youth and the politics of caring. New York: State University of New York Press.

Weisner, T. (2002). Ecocultural understandings of children's developmental pathways. *Human Development, 45,* 275–281. doi:10.1159/000064989.

Yeung, W. J., Sandberg, J. F., Davis-Kean, P. E., & Hofferth, S. L. (2001). Children's time with fathers in intact families. *Journal of Marriage and Family, 63,* 136–154. doi:10.1111/j.1741-3737.2001.00136.x.

10

Indigenous Fathers' Journeys in Canada: Turning around Disrupted Circles of Care

Jessica Ball and Sarah Moselle

When Canadian federal government funding for the first nationwide study of Indigenous[1] fathers was announced in a national newspaper, the first author—who was leading the study—was inundated with phone calls from Indigenous men wanting to "tell my story" and from Indigenous communities wanting to become partners in the study.[2] Recurrently, fathers explained, "I just want to shed some light on our journeys to learn what it means for a First Nations man to become a father." They noted that "[a]s far as I know, this is the first time anyone has paid attention to us and wanted to know what it takes for us to learn to be fathers." With initial funding sufficient to interview forty fathers, it became necessary to create a waiting list of men who wanted to contribute to the study. The list grew to more than 130 names. The study ultimately interviewed 80 fathers.

This spontaneous outpouring of enthusiasm for the study was unprecedented and remarkable for two reasons. First, "research" is referred to by many Indigenous people in Canada as a four-letter word. After centuries of overwhelmingly derogatory misrepresentations of Indigenous people in North America by explorers, artists, historians, and social scientists, Indigenous communities are generally reluctant to participate in studies or engage as partners with academics in community-engaged research. Repudiation of standard research practices has led Indigenous scholars to articulate ways to "decolonize" research (Denzin, Lincoln, & Smith 2008) and to require distinctive approaches to negotiating ethical research practice (Government of Canada 2015). Toward that end, researchers working with Indigenous people usually strive to make their research beneficial or meaningful to their community partners. Yet the national study of father involvement was not in a position to offer any tangible benefit in terms of social action or program support. Fathers who asked to be in the study were told they would receive their choice of a children's book authored by an Indigenous writer or a backpack. Repeatedly, fathers explained that it was more than enough to have the chance to be seen instead of hidden "in our dark little holes." Many were motivated "to have this chance to tell other First Nations men there is hope—if I can do it, you can too." A father who was raising his young daughter alone after his partner went missing on Canada's "highway of tears" in northern British Columbia, explained: "I just want people to know what I have to go through to raise this child on my own."

The outpouring of interest by Indigenous fathers to participate in the study was also remarkable because some of the men had a rather tenuous hold on their engagement as fathers. In studies of fathers, it is generally recognized that fathers who volunteer to participate are probably unusually motivated, more established in their relationships with their children, and more connected with resources and services than many fathers. Volunteer father participants may also want to present themselves in a positive light, known to be a potential bias in research. In contrast, many Indigenous fathers volunteering for this study were struggling to sustain a home, sustain connections with their children, sustain their own mental and physical health, and sustain positive communications with the mothers of their children. Yet they all wanted to convey their strong identification with being a father, their desire to be positively involved—whether this was full-time as a co-resident father or in small ways as a father living apart from their child. Their goal was to make their fatherhood journey known to others—to increase the visibility of Indigenous fathers as a whole and to share their vision for a transformation in Indigenous fathers' involvement within circles of care for current and future generations of Indigenous youngsters.

This chapter highlights the findings from this first study of Indigenous fatherhood involvement in Canada. We contextualize the experience of being an Indigenous father within the specific culture and sociohistoric conditions these experiences are embedded in and, in doing so, draw out culturally sensitive ways that family care practitioners and policy makers can better meet the needs of this marginalized population.

GENERAL OVERVIEW OF INDIGENOUS FATHERS AND FAMILIES

This section provides demographic, socioeconomic, historical, and cultural information essential for understanding contemporary First Nations fathers' diverse experiences. Included is a section on the quality of life and emerging trends in Indigenous family life that point to dimensions of continuity and change.

Demographic Features

In 2011, the Canadian census recorded 1,400,685 people who self-identified as Indigenous, representing 4.3 percent of the total population (Statistics Canada 2013a). Among the total Indigenous population, 60.8 percent identify as First Nations, 32.3 percent identify as Métis (mixed First Nations and European heritage), and 4.2 percent identify as Inuit. The largest numbers of Indigenous people live in Ontario and the western provinces. Indigenous people make up the largest proportions of the populations of Nunavut and the Northwest Territories.

The most remarkable trends among Indigenous populations in Canada are the high birth rates and corresponding young age: The median age was 23 years among Inuit, 26 years among First Nations, and 31 years among Métis. Between 2006 and 2011, the overall Aboriginal population in Canada increased by 232,385 people, or 20.1%, compared with a growth of 5.2% of the non-Aboriginal population (Statistics Canada 2011). It is projected that by 2031, the Indigenous population will comprise approximately 4.0–5.3% of the Canadian population (Statistics Canada 2011).

The population of First Nations people living in land-based communities (known by the government as Indian reserves or settlements) is rapidly growing: Of the 637,660 First Nations people who reported being Registered Indians,[3] nearly half (49.3%) live on a reserve or settlement. The last four censuses have also shown a steady migration to urban centers, with more than half of First Nations and Métis people living in cities, predominantly Winnipeg, Edmonton, Vancouver, and Toronto. Indigenous adults are incarcerated at about nine times the rate of non-Indigenous adults. Although Indigenous people make up only 4 percent of the adult population in Canada, they make up 23.2 percent of the inmate population (Office of the Correctional Investigator, 2013). In the authors' meetings with Indigenous men in correctional institutions, all interviewees reported that they are fathers.

Quality of Life

Though some First Nation and Métis families are thriving, poverty and other socioeconomic indicators show that a majority of Indigenous families are struggling, and Indigenous men have the greatest disparities compared to non-Indigenous peoples on virtually every indicator. They have the highest rates of poverty, homelessness, geographic mobility, mental illness, addictions, suicide, and incarceration and the lowest levels of education, employment, and household income (The First Nations Information Governance Centre 2008/10). The average household income of Indigenous families in Canada in 2011 was a little more than a third that of non-Indigenous families. The 2011 census estimated that 41–52.1 percent of Indigenous children live below the poverty line (depending on criteria for defining poverty and whether estimates include children with Indigenous identity or ancestry). One in four First Nations children living in land-based communities lives in poverty, compared to one in six Canadian children as a whole: Approximately 43 percent of First Nations children live in a household with an annual household income of less than $20,000 (The First Nations Information Governance Centre 2008/10). Indigenous unemployment rates exceed the jobless rate of the population as a whole in every province, with rates in Saskatchewan and Manitoba—two provinces having the largest proportion of First Nations and Métis men—more than triple the overall rate. Although educational attainment is improving among Indigenous people, a gap between Indigenous and non-Indigenous education persists, with 48.4 percent of Indigenous adults completing a post-secondary qualification (trade certificate, college diploma, university degree) in 2011, compared to 64.7 percent of non-Indigenous adults (Statistics Canada 2013b). Indigenous children are more likely to be apprehended (primarily for neglect rather than abuse) than non-Indigenous children (Blackstock., Cross, Brown, George, & Formsma 2006).

Combined with social stigma, negative media stories, and pessimistic expectations of their capacity to manage intimate relationships and care for children, First Nation and Métis men face formidable structural and social obstacles to positive involvement as fathers. In the study of Indigenous father involvement, sixty-one of the eighty fathers reported three or more of the aforementioned problems (poverty, homelessness, etc.) as creating difficulties for connecting with their children and playing a role in family life (Ball 2010). Virtually all of the eighty men described past or current challenges with mental health, addictions, or anger management, and a third were struggling to generate a living wage and to secure adequate housing. These factors have been shown in research involving other populations of fathers as deterrents to positive father involvement (Roopnarine, Brown, Snell-White, & Riegraf 1995). Research about non-Indigenous fathers shows significant correlations between father involvement and developmental outcomes for children, mothers, and fathers (Allen, Daly, & Ball 2012; Palkowitz 2002; Sarkadi, Kristiansson, Oberklaid, & Bremberg 2008).

Low Visibility

Indigenous fathers' social exclusion is reflected in their relative invisibility in formal systems such as their child's preschool program, school, health clinic, and recreation programs. Not being seen in their child's world outside the home often generates public perceptions that many Indigenous fathers are "deadbeats" or indifferent toward their children (Claes & Clifton 1998). There is little acknowledgement in family support programs of the unique challenges faced by these men, most of whom have no memories of positive experiences with a father or father figure in their own lives as children and youth. And though there is a trend toward increasing numbers of lone-father–headed households, there are no programs specifically designed to help First Nation and Métis men become effective supports for their children's health and development (Ball & George 2007).

However all of the father participants in the inaugural study reported thinking a lot about their children, even if they saw them rarely, and wishing they could be more involved. Even many of those who were co-resident with their children and reported considerable involvement expressed a goal of being better at caring for their children and being a dad. Some described being invisible to social service and health workers: "My ex-partner had so much support from the Ministry and from parenting and child care programs. She had it all set up for her. But then, when we split up, all that left with her. I went to a parent support program and there were all mothers. Nobody has even tried to talk to me or to me and [my daughter]. They haven't made the effort."

An educator at an Aboriginal Head Start program in one of the partner communities recounted: "I realized that in fact I always asked for the mother when calling or visiting the children's homes. It was understanding that something as simple as this leads to alienating our dads." The pattern of low visibility extends to a lower rate of Indigenous fathers' paternity registration on their children's birth certificates compared to the rate for non-Indigenous fathers (Mann 2005). Indigenous fathers' names and contact information are frequently missing from child protection files, making them virtually invisible to child welfare workers and making it difficult and sometimes impossible for fathers to find or stay in contact with their children (Brown, Callahan, Strega, Walmsley, & Dominelli 2005). Making Indigenous fathers invisible in child welfare pushes men away from being accountable and receiving support from programs and services (Strega, Fleet, Brown, Dominelli, Callahan & Walmsley 2008). As Brown et al. (2005) note, ignoring vulnerable fathers can create risks for children and lost opportunities for Indigenous children and their mothers. Grand Chief Edward John of the British Columbia First Nations Summit provided the impetus for the study of Indigenous fathers when he commented, in 2003, "Aboriginal fathers may well be the greatest untapped resource in the lives of Aboriginal children and youth" (John 2003).

HISTORICAL CONTEXTS OF INDIGENOUS FATHER INVOLVEMENT

Hereditary Chief William Mussell (2005) is the only male Indigenous scholar in Canada who has written specifically about the struggles and healing journeys of First Nations men. He has attributed these struggles to the negative effects of colonization, especially the intergenerational repercussions of

Indian Residential Schools. The devastating effects of colonial government policies in Canada over the past 400 years have been extensively chronicled by the Royal Commission on Aboriginal Peoples (1996), and more recently by the Truth and Reconciliation Commission of Canada (2012). From their earliest encounters, Indigenous Peoples were coerced by European newcomers to change how they managed their families. This was not simply because the newcomers disliked the ways Indigenous Peoples raised their children; rather, Indigenous family systems came under attack because they stood in the way of colonization. Kinship systems supported Indigenous relationships with the land and vice versa. Settlers perceived that all of these relationships would need to be dismantled to get rid of "the Indian problem" and clear a path for them to claim title to the land. Forced relocations of villages, dispersions of clans, unfamiliar combinations of tribes within a system of Indian reservations, along with urbanization and incentives for legally disavowing Indigenous identity, resulted in a shattering of the foundations of Indigenous family life, cultures, languages, and spirituality (Anderson & Ball 2004). Systems of tribal community governance and extended family life were broken down and transmission of cultural knowledge and skills for living on the land disrupted (Smolewsky & Wesley-Esquimaux 2003). Female missionaries were charged by religious organizations supported by the colonial government to convert Indigenous women to Euro-Western norms of conjugality and domesticity (Carter 1997). Indigenous motherhood, the foundation for family decision-making and governance in many Indigenous communities, particularly in the plains of central Canada, came under attack (Anderson 2007). The heteropatriarchal nuclear family was forced upon Indigenous people, disrupting the social, cultural, spiritual, and economic roles of Indigenous fathers and mothers and causing a loss of identity, pride, and knowledge about positive father and mother involvement in caring for children. Referring to a similar process of colonization in the United States, Stremlau (2005) recounts: "Reformers concluded that kinship systems, especially as they manifested in gender roles, prevented acculturation by undermining individualism and social order, and they turned to federal Indian policy to fracture these extended indigenous families into male-dominant, nuclear families, modelled after middle-class Anglo-American households." Persisting high levels of violence toward and within Indigenous communities have been linked to the imposition of a heteropatriarchal family structure and system of community–government relations (Driskill, Finley, Gilley, & Morgensen 2011).

Beginning in 1879 and operating until 1996, Indian residential schools operated by church organizations contracted by the federal government forcibly took over the role of raising Indigenous children. Although they resisted, many communities lost whole generations of children; by 1930, almost 75 percent of First Nation school-aged children were in residential schools (Brown,

Higgitt, Wingert, Miller, & Morrissette 2003). Many children were sent as far as possible from their communities and never returned; those who did return often found themselves alienated from their families and lands, unable to communicate in the language of their parents and Elders. Extensive physical and sexual abuse of children in residential schools has been well documented (Fournier & Crey 1997) and eventually was the subject of an apology made by the federal government in 2008 (Office of the Prime Minister of Canada 2008). After the children, who were the heart of communities, were taken, the wellness of Indigenous people began to deteriorate: Elders had no one to teach, women had no one to care for, and men had no children to provide for and protect (Wemigwans 2002). When residential school survivors became parents, many struggled, because they had not experienced positive parental role modeling (Dion Stout & Kipling 2003). Many lost confidence in their capacity to engage in the kinds of nurturing social interactions with young children that promote attachment and intimate social interaction (Cassidy & Shaver 1999). Through residential schools and foster care and interactions with racist peers and teachers in public school and with professions in health care and child welfare, many Indigenous people learned not to trust others and have recurring difficulties sustaining intimate family relationships. This psychological fallout has been variously described as "historic trauma" (Smolewsky & Wesley-Esquimaux 2003), "the soul-wound" or "postcolonial traumatic stress" passed on from generation to generation of many Indigenous people (Duran, Duran, Brave Heart, & Yellow Horse-Davis 1998).

Today, only half of Indigenous children age 14 or younger (49.6%) are living in a family with both their parents, either biological or adoptive, compared to three-quarters (76%) of non-Indigenous children living with both parents. There is a long-standing and increasing trend toward Indigenous fathers being non-co-resident with their children; the number of Indigenous lone-mother–headed households is high and steadily increasing. About a third of Indigenous children (34.4%) live in a lone-parent family, most often with their mother, compared with 17.4 percent of non-Aboriginal children. The trend toward non-co-residence may reflect in part the extremely high frequency of adolescent motherhood, especially among Inuit and First Nations young women (Guimond & Robitaille 2008). Indigenous adolescents who give birth often live with their parents, who sometimes serve as gatekeepers limiting or even excluding fathers' involvement with children. It could be speculated that non-co-residence is also related to low rates of legal marital unions in the Indigenous population compared to non-Indigenous: historically, legal marriage was not part of Indigenous cultures but was introduced by the colonial government and often linked to retaining custody of children. At the same time, many fathers who are not co-resident with their children and their mother remain involved, including some who take turns being lone caregivers in an often informal custody sharing arrangement, as was found in the study of Indigenous fathers. Extensive involvement of the child welfare systems in each province and territory has resulted in widespread foster placement and adoption into non-Indigenous homes; about half of children in government care are Indigenous (Statistics Canada 2011). Colonialism remains a strong force affecting the lives of many Indigenous people in Canada, particularly those living on reserves. Though some men are doing very well, as Mussell (2005) points out, the repercussions of these experiences are evident in the challenges facing many Indigenous men.

CULTURAL CONTEXTS OF INDIGENOUS FATHER INVOLVEMENT

The foregoing overview of key demographic characteristics and sociohistorical conditions of Indigenous Peoples provides a context for some of the unique experiences of Indigenous fathers that were uncovered in the only study of Indigenous father involvement in Canada, conducted by the author. This inaugural report forms one of seven component parts in the first national study of father involvement in Canada (Ball & Daly 2012). Other components involved community–university partnerships to explore experiences of young fathers, divorced fathers, new fathers, gay fathers, immigrant and refugee fathers, and fathers of children having a chronic health condition. The study of Indigenous fathers involved the author in a collaborative data collection process with First Nations and Métis fathers in five Indigenous communities in the province of British Columbia, Canada. One father from each of the first partnering communities worked with the author to plan, pilot, and implement data collection, involving a questionnaire about family life, a questionnaire about programs and other resources the father had accessed and would like to access, and one-hour, audio-taped, conversational interviews using a set of conversation themes and probes (Ball 2010).

Initially it was intended that all component studies would use the same questionnaire to obtain a basic profile of each father participant, his family context, and care arrangements, including questions on topics such as the number of children in the family, marital status, employment, work–life balance, the division of household labor, forms of involvement in caring for children, and which partner tended to take time from work to care for a sick child. This questionnaire seemed relevant and useful for the other six component studies. However, the questionnaire did not work readily with Indigenous fathers. The five Indigenous collaborating fathers found the generic questionnaire impossible to answer succinctly, including seemingly straightforward questions such as How many children do you have? and How many children live in your household? Moreover, they doubted the relevance, suitability, or comparative importance of many questions, such as about marital status, work–life balance, and partners' division of domestic labor and caring for children—questions typical in studies of father involvement. Questions that were initially closed-ended or that had a limited number of response options were replaced with more open-ended questions and were asked in an interview rather than as a self-administered procedure.

The qualitative, exploratory study involved research team members in a grounded theory analysis of taped and transcribed, semistructured interviews conducted by Indigenous research team members with seventy-two First Nations and eight Métis fathers (all having at least one child younger than 5). Though detailed findings are presented elsewhere (Ball 2010), highlights are presented in this section along with interpretive commentary drawing from Indigenous cultural contexts that contribute to developing understanding of Indigenous fathers' experiences and roles. It should be noted that there are many Indigenous cultures in Canada, having diverse cultures and responses to colonization, but some generalizations are widely understood in Canada as applying to most Indigenous groups. The following discussion focuses on prevalent patterns described in historical accounts and reports by Indigenous fathers in the study. Overall, the fathers' accounts spoke to the unique sociohistorical experiences and cultural features of this population and substantiated the dynamism, flexibility, and challenges of family life for Indigenous fathers consistent with national survey data and context-setting historical accounts.

Colonial Contexts of Fathers' Journeys

Fathers who collaborated on the research insisted that participants not be asked directly about whether or how experiences of residential school, foster care, or adoption had affected their fatherhood journeys. They expressed concern that this could be too overwhelming for some fathers, who might not have talked previously with anyone about their experiences of being a father and who may be struggling with historic trauma. However, they agreed to ask an open-ended question toward the end of each interview, encouraging fathers to share anything else they thought was important. Virtually all eighty participants described their perceptions and experiences of colonial government policies or interventions, direct or indirect effects of the Indian Residential Schools, and/or experience within the child welfare system, either as children or as fathers. Fathers in all five partner communities agreed that the theme of disrupted fatherhood best accounted for challenges they often faced in becoming involved fathers, including for example: learning nonviolent communication; overcoming anger with themselves, partners, and/or children; depression; and not knowing how to be in a family or how to maintain a household. A father commented: "We have lived in the shadow of the Residential Schools and what that took from us as far as knowing how to love our children, how to care for them, how to live harmoniously in families. The government has said it's sorry, but that doesn't fix the harm done." Another father described the lack of emotional care and development experienced in Residential School: "I was in Residential School until I was 18 years old, so I really didn't learn anything. No love and no hugs from the priests or the nuns. I just came out cold." One father commented on the novelty of having multiple generations living together now that the era of Residential Schools is finally over: "Some of the older men in our community were remarking recently on how new it is to have young people in our community. Some of our communities don't have activities or wisdom about how to meet the needs of youth, because we didn't have young people in our communities. They were all in Residential School."

Complex Families

Most fathers had large and complex families. As a group, they ranged from having one to eleven children, including children from different relationships and variously related to them biologically, socially, and in terms of the father's direct involvement as a caregiver. Some fathers were living with their children; some were not co-resident with their children but had formal or informal custody for some periods of time; some had infrequent contact with their children (e.g., when they visited the community where they child resided, when they met for lunch at a community center, when they had supervised visitation). Six of the fathers were lone fathers: Their children's mothers were missing or deceased or had given the father full custody with no visitation. Most fathers were living with one or more adults, including a partner who, in various cases, was the mother of all, some or none of the children living in the home, as well as relatives, most often their own mother, aunt or sister.

Fathers' accounts conveyed the complex, permeable, and mobile nature of many Indigenous families. Although this has often been cast in a negative light, it may also be seen as a strength on which to build. According to the findings of the 2006 Aboriginal Children's Survey, First Nation and Métis children may enjoy the benefit of multiple caregivers and fathers may benefit from being supported by a community, rather than resorting to the nuclear and patriarchal family model imposed by colonial authorities (Statistics Canada 2009). Indigenous Elder Brant Castellano describes how some Indigenous families, particularly in urban settings, are reviving traditional forms of care by knitting together family members and friends to create "families of the heart" (Castellano 2002). Families in urban centers may expand to include more distant relatives from rural or remote communities who come to the city for school, work, or special programs. Families may informally adopt a niece or nephew or even a neighbor. Sometimes an adult family member may leave the family unit temporarily or permanently because of difficulties in the primary-couple relationship, and the remaining parent may welcome a new partner and one or more of his or her children or other relatives. The "open doors" found in many First Nation and Métis families no doubt stem from the traditional extended family structures ubiquitous before colonization.

This kinship model is used in some traditional parenting programs, such as one focused on creative "home making" facilitated by a "grandmother" of the heart, described by Indigenous scholar Arnott (2006). Indigenous scholars Harvard-Lavell and Corbiere-Lavell point out: "Even in its contemporary manifestation, as opposed to the more historical notions of communal tribal living, for most members of the Aboriginal community everyday survival is still dependent on extensive networks of family and friends who support and reinforce one another" (Harvard-Lavell & Corbiere-Lavell 2006).

Between extended families and "families of the heart," there are cultural models for Indigenous fathers to learn and contribute to positive involvement in meetings children's needs as part of a circle of mutual support.

Variable Living Situations

Indigenous fathers often live in complex, rapidly changing households with variable employment patterns. As would be expected based on findings of national surveys such as those highlighted earlier in this chapter, many fathers in the study described persistent housing difficulties and poverty, as well as prevalent health problems, injuries, needs for hospitalization and residential treatment. Among the 80 father participants, four were homeless (living intermittently on the street or as "couch-surfers") and so did not live with their children, three were living away from their children because they had seasonal employment that required temporarily living far from home, and more than half were not currently living with the mother of one or more of their children. Another four did not have contact with at least one of their children because of a legal restraining order or condition of parole.

Interruptions in Father–Child Involvement

Many fathers described having disrupted involvement with their children over time. The most common reason was because of ruptures in their relationship with their child's mother that in some cases were recurrent and in some cases ongoing. For some of these fathers, partner relationships were repaired enough to enable continuous involvement with their child either by being co-resident with the child and the mother or by having visitation or shared custody. Other reasons for disrupted involvement included the father's spending time once or more often in residential treatment programs for problematic substance use or in correctional institutions and the child's spending time in government care. Another reason for changes in a father's involvement in direct care capacities with children was the father's temporary or intermittent participation in employment that required moving away from the community. Across Canada, and especially in rural communities and in the north, many Indigenous communities have far more women than men because men relocate to remote sites for weeks or months at a time to work in extractive industries. Geographic distances put a strain on father–child relationships, especially when combined with lack of funds for telephones, computers, or travel that could help to maintain contact between fathers and children. For a proportion of Indigenous fathers, incarceration also creates monumental challenges to sustaining connections with their children.

Families on the Move

Although Indigenous men are often described in popular Canadian media as having itinerant and unstable lifestyles, from a more strength-focused perspective, father participants in the study conveyed lifestyles characterized by frequent change and adaptation to changing family needs, opportunities, and critical incidents. First Nations living off-reserve and Métis families move nearly twice as often as non-Indigenous families (Statistics Canada 2006). In some cases, Indigenous youth and adults are transient because of family discord and/or homelessness. Mobility may also be due to the need to seek education, employment, or services, including residential school recovery programs and substance abuse treatment programs (Norris & Clatworthy 2006). As described earlier, Indigenous family boundaries tend to be permeable: Family members may transition from one home or town to another or from one set of relationships to another or may divide their time among more than one place that they call home.

Employment

As a group, the fathers in the study could be characterized as having low and atypical patterns of employment. Indeed, in Canada, Indigenous men's participation in the labor force cannot be readily characterized according to the descriptors fitting non-Indigenous men, and this was one area where the demographic questionnaire planned for the Indigenous fathers study was least suitable. Among the eighty fathers in the study, eleven described themselves as "self-employed," including as artists, musicians, groundskeepers, builders, fishermen, farmers, and truck drivers. Many fathers described their employment as "limited," "intermittent," or "seasonal." Many fathers described a pattern of working when, where, and as they were able to find work and were able to accept work depending on their health. Some fathers reported being unable to work because of mental health or substance use problems. Some were unable to work because they lacked a high school diploma or trade certificate.

Work–Life Balance

Questions about work–life balance—typical in studies of parental involvement and domestic labor—did not resonate with Indigenous father participants; in some cases, they were not currently employed or were employed only very part-time, and in some cases, they worked in jobs that required them to be absent from the community intermittently for periods ranging from days to several months. Although the study did not ask specifically about partners' employment, some fathers described their partners' work as similarly irregular and changeable. Another reason why questions about work–life balance did not seem to be the most important questions to ask this population of fathers was that their arrangements for caring for children typically involved several more people than only their primary partner or the child's mother.

PATHWAYS FOR INDIGENOUS FATHER INVOLVEMENT: CONNECTING PAST, PRESENT, AND FUTURE

The theme *cultural reconstruction through circles of care* was superordinate in the analysis of fathers' accounts of their fatherhood journeys. Fathers variously described their efforts to reimagine and enact fatherhood, drawing upon whatever childhood memories they had of fatherhood as well as sources of social support and cultural knowledge of fatherhood available to them through their families, Elders in their communities, and Indigenous organizations. This section expands on this theme, reflecting the histories and experiences of many Indigenous fathers and possibly anticipating the future for a proportion of Indigenous men in caregiving relationships with children and youth.

Web of Extended Family Relationships

As discussed, Indigenous cultures hold that children thrive in an extended web of relationship. Euro-Western models of the nuclear family, in which one father figure (along with one mother figure) is intended to meet all of a child's needs for guidance, discipline, affection, and support, have never characterized traditional Indigenous communities. Historically, Indigenous people lived in extended family groupings that were the core economic and social unit and source of belonging, keepers of traditional cultural and spiritual knowledge such as sacred stories, songs, and medicine (Volo & Volo 2007). Childrearing was typically shared in family groups; traditional Aboriginal communities were the prototypical model of its taking a village to raise a child. Children were raised by siblings, cousins, aunts and uncles, grandparents and great-grandparents, and great-aunts and great-uncles. Although children knew their biological siblings, parents, and grandparents, other members of the extended family could be equally considered a parent, grandparent, or sibling. The names people used to refer to one another are telling in this regard: A child might refer to any elderly person in his or her community simply as "grandmother" or "grandfather." Likewise, Elders would refer to young people in the community as "grandchild" and treat them accordingly. Roles relating to discipline, teaching, and play were distributed in a systematic way among kin so that children received comprehensive guidance and continuity of care across their lifespan and across changing family composition and circumstances. A father in the study recounted: "Our circle has always been like that with our children. Men and women and the whole community pitching in to raise our children."

"Family" meant life itself, as Nuu-chah-nulth hereditary chief Richard Atleo (2004) has expressed:

> In the Nuu-chah-nulth worldview it is unnatural, and equivalent to death and destruction, for any person to be isolated from family or community. Nuu-chah-nulth life, therefore, is founded by creating and maintaining relationships.

Colonial interventions to dismantle Indigenous family systems stripped adults of their culturally prescribed roles in child care. Men's roles as providers and protectors were particularly devastated as the settlers destroyed animal herds, introduced policies restricting Indigenous access to hunting and fishing grounds, architected economic dependencies on the colonial government, and enforced residential schooling as a substitute for family-based care and child welfare systems for child protection. This cultural–historical background contextualizes the trend toward complex and dynamic Indigenous households, as well as ongoing efforts among Indigenous communities to revitalize cultural values and traditions within the context of contemporary life.

A changeable household composition and having multiple caregivers have tended to be seen in a negative light from the perspective of dominant, European-heritage models of the nuclear family and child development. However, families of the heart can afford opportunities for children to experience continuity of care despite changing circumstances, as well as for fathers and mothers to share in learning parenting. A father described how: "Fathers are trying to get more involved with their children. They are trying to get back into the circle. Our circle has been broken for so long and now it is going to make us stronger as a people." In particular, extended circles of care may provide opportunities for fathers who have a tenuous hold on fatherhood to become involved without shouldering more responsibility than they may be ready for. For example, a father said: "I have to give thanks to my partner and my aunties for teaching me how to show care and love to my kids. I learned a lot from my mother and how she parented and duplicated that. Like reading to him and teaching him about different countries, languages and stuff."

Many fathers emphasized the roles of multiple family members, especially women, in helping them step into the role of father and learn parenting skills: "It took a long hard time to mature into becoming a father, long after my kids were born. With 39 years of life behind me, and with the help of my wife, I feel like I'm finally becoming a man. I am finally growing strong spiritually, socially, emotionally, and as a father."

The pattern of complex households and extended family caregiving found in the Indigenous fathers study was one of the most remarkable ways that the original questionnaire planned for the national study could not be readily used to characterize Indigenous fathers' involvement with children and describe care arrangements such as who undertakes which child care tasks according to what schedule, given what work-life balance arrangements, and so on. One father's response to a question asking which partner makes accommodations to care for a child during an emergency seems to weave together several threads sewn through this chapter:

> This question about who takes time from work to take care of an emergency involving one of our kids . . . . You're talking about someone being sick or child getting hurt as an emergency. There is always someone around in our community who can do whatever is necessary. Usually someone is not working, and someone can be there. That's not the kind of emergency, or not the most important one, we're dealing with. The damage from Residential Schools is the real emergency—the crisis—for us, for our families, in our communities, in this country. That's our emergency, and we are all involved in some way in our healing from that.

Generativity

Many of the Indigenous fathers in the study conveyed what Erikson termed "generativity": They were conscious of and concerned about the well-being of the next generation of young people, as well as about the wellness of Indigenous people in general (Erikson 1950). An oft-heard saying among Indigenous people is that it took seven generations to all but destroy Indigenous families and communities and that will take seven generations to heal the "soul wound" (Duran et al. 1998) and rebuild the family—a process widely referred to among Indigenous Peoples in Canada as a "healing journey" (Aboriginal Healing Foundation 2006). Many Indigenous people see the present time as "the turnaround generation." One father remarked: "I look at all these young people experiencing that family life, with fathers involved as much as the rest and I have such a sense of hope. It means we're turning things around."

One father explained: "I stepped up to my responsibilities and am learning all I can about how to be a dad to him so that he will know how to do it when he becomes a dad." Another father commented: "Now I know I do have a family that will help me no matter what, and they are all helping me in raising my girls, and that is good. It's our traditional way. And these girls are seeing that, and I think it will change how they raise their families." These fathers may have been precocious in this regard: Generativity theory and research have usually identified generativity as a preoccupation of adults in midlife (Brotherson, Dollahite, & Hawkins, 2005). Findings from the Canadian national study suggested that fatherhood, including at a young age, can and commonly does shape a more generative self-identity and outlook in men, although through diverse pathways (Pratt, Lawford, & Allen 2012).

Fathers and Children Revitalizing Indigenous Culture

Traditional Indigenous cultures see children as gifts from a creator, on loan to this world from the spirit world (Greenwood 2006). Though intergenerational transmission of knowledge of how to nurture children physically, mentally, emotionally, and spiritually has been interrupted by colonial interventions, this underlying value and knowledge still exists and is often conveyed in teachings by Indigenous Elders. In the study of Indigenous fathers, many expressed their yearning for the kinds of cultural underpinnings that could anchor them and their children and promote their resilience as they navigate through the life cycle, as one father described: "*That* sense of knowing who he is, where he comes from, what his culture is about, his traditions— that will give him strength to face the adversities that will come his way in this society. It will give him pride and resilience. It's a strength he can hold onto and that connects him to me, to his family, to his ancestors going back through time." Developing relationships with Elders is often key for many men to gather culturally based insights and tips for raising their children; most Indigenous communities in Canada have Friendship Centres offering programs and special events to facilitate these intergenerational connections, and many fathers in the study recounted taking their children to cultural events there. One father who did so explained: "I didn't know any of the songs. Now that she likes to Native dance I kind of have to learn the songs so she has something to dance to!" Fathers and their children—young and old—have described setting out on a journey of renewal together. An adult daughter of one of the collaborating fathers in the study explained: "My Dad and I have talked a lot about the upbringing I had and the things that went on in our family and it's been really hard. And our relationship wasn't always good. But now as adults, after a lot of forgiveness and getting the help we needed, we are both on our healing journeys and we are going to potlatches and sharing circles and living our culture together, and we have a tight bond because of what we've faced and where we're headed, together." Indigenous fathers and children have the potential to be significant sources of reciprocal affection and social support in their efforts to be part of the "turnaround" generation for themselves and for Indigenous people.

FUTURE DIRECTIONS AND POLICY IMPLICATIONS

Across Canada and around the world, there is a pressing need to enhance understanding and support for Indigenous fathers who have faced tremendous losses of roles within families, communities, and nations and who continue to face significant barriers to health, education, employment, and social inclusion that limit their capacity to be positively involved as fathers. Policy reforms and program innovations need to promote health and quality of life for Indigenous families and enhanced social inclusion for Indigenous men. Few studies in the English literature have focused specifically on Indigenous fathers. To date, the study by the author remains the only known research study in Canada focused specifically on First Nations and Métis men's experiences of fatherhood. Effective policy and program evaluation identifying meaningful community interventions requires more information and insight about Indigenous fathers' parenting goals, needs, experiences, circumstances, and outcomes.

Though Indigenous fathers face unique difficulties as a result of historical trauma and ongoing colonialism, there are cultural strengths and sources of resilience not commonly reported in research and community programs driven by Euro-Western perspectives. Available information suggests that many Indigenous fathers want to contribute to their children's wellness to a greater extent than might be immediately visible. The study uncovered a strong desire on the part of Indigenous fathers to tell their stories, to be "found" in relationships with both older and younger family members, and to construct a way forward to engaged and sustained fathering. Yet the population of Indigenous men as a whole is only dimly perceived within Canadian society; living on reserves in rural and remote areas, living in poverty, and spending more time in correctional institutions than any other population of fathers, they are no doubt perceived by service workers—if they are seen at all—as a hard-to-reach population. As one service worker explained in the inaugural study: "It's not so much that we have tried and failed, it's more that we haven't tried."

Programming for fathers as a whole is a fledgling field in Canada. A Father Involvement Network in each of three provinces receives provincial government funding for a network coordinator to manage a website, distribute resources, and deliver workshops. Though these may be useful for some Indigenous fathers to some extent, different kinds of support are needed to help Indigenous fathers work through issues associated with their own lost childhoods, to recover psychologically and spiritually, to learn fathering skills, and to achieve balance in their lives and family relationships (Ball & George 2006). Education and training are needed to enhance practitioners' capacity to work with Indigenous men. In the inaugural study, many fathers said they would be more likely to attend an information session or support group if it were facilitated by an Indigenous man. There is no funding in Canada to train men—or anyone—specifically to work with Indigenous fathers. Lack of specific preparation, combined with gendered discourses and practices in health and social services, including parenting education, create challenges to changing practices.

A gathering of Indigenous father outreach programs in 2011 showcased established and emerging programs (". . . With Dad: Showcase on Aboriginal Father Involvement" 2011). One of the longer-running programs is Nēâh Kee Papa (I Am Your Father), offered by the Manitoba Métis Federation since 1999. It is a flexibly structured, eight-session parenting enhancement program covering topics including effective communication, anger management, understanding rights as single parents and in custody relationships, the father's role, and life skills. This program offers Indigenous fathers information and referral to other programs and resources, including counseling, guest speakers, library passes, and peer resource groups. The first province-wide gathering for Indigenous fathers was held in 2013, hosted by the Creating Hope Society, an Indigenous child welfare agency. Discussion at this meeting suggested that grass-roots, community-based efforts to create and implement strategies to support Indigenous fathers' involvement are slowly growing.

In 2013, the Public Health Agency of Canada's Healthy Child Development division supported the authors to conduct a national scan of programs targeting Indigenous father involvement (Moselle & Ball 2013). We surveyed 130 organizations nationwide, yielding descriptions of thirty-five programs that are successful in terms of having been sustained for over one year and having scheduled activities at least once a month with at least a handful of fathers who attend regularly. Many of these successful programs are in the provinces of Ontario, British Columbia, and Saskatchewan and are provided by Aboriginal Head Start programs, the Canadian Prenatal Nutrition Program, Maternal and Child Health, and Child and Family Services agencies. Programs vary in terms of content, frequency, funding sources, leadership, and logistics, ranging from weekly drop-in activity groups to twelve-week violence prevention programs. Despite their diversity, many program coordinators told us that the strength and success of their program was rooted in the program's specific cultural relevance. They described how these programs increase fathers' confidence and direct involvement, strengthen families by fostering healthy relationships, and encourage cultural connectedness. These promising practices warrant further documentation and impact evaluation. Many organizations reported a number of obstacles to initiating and sustaining programming for fathers including difficulties finding and paying capable father outreach workers, as well as challenges attracting fathers or sustaining their involvement over more than one or two sessions. These latter challenges were variously attributed to transportation barriers, underemployment and sporadic/seasonal employment, and residual effects of Indian residential school experiences that make some fathers reticent to engage or stay connected with structured programs, especially if these are located in schools or government offices.

A kit of resources for Indigenous father involvement grew out of the inaugural study, including a documentary featuring six First Nations fathers' journeys. The resources have been used across Canada and in Indigenous communities in Australia, Aotearoa/New Zealand, the United States, and South Africa. The resources aim to inspire and guide less mother-centric and more culturally based forms of engagement of early childhood educators, teachers, child protection workers, and health care practitioners with Indigenous fathers (Ball 2008).[4] Social media may help to increase the visibility of Indigenous fathers. A recent documentary produced by Canada's national broadcasting company, *Blind Spot: What happened to Canada's Aboriginal dads?*, won national acclaim (Canadian Broadcasting Corporation 2012). A current project called *ininiwag dibaajimowag: First Nations Men's Digital Stories on the Intergenerational Experiences of Residential Schools*, conducted by the Canadian Prairie Women's Health Centre of Excellence, aims to encourage public dialogue and understanding of the legacy of residential schools on Indigenous men.[5]

CONCLUSION

Historical and ongoing colonial interventions have created multigenerational challenges for Indigenous men to find their place within circles of care for children, not only in Canada but also in many countries around the world.

Revitalization of culturally congruent ways of living in families and supporting men and women to successfully parent and share their cultures with their
children can promote healing and learning for all Canadians. The pathways
described by Indigenous men in Canada suggest new conceptions of men's roles
in children's lives, as well as sources of resilience that are not often the focus
of family theories or community program models. This is a foundation upon
which to build a program of research that can provide direction for fathers and
families, and for policy decision makers and practitioners focused on families,
in enhancing and making visible the positive contributions that Indigenous
fathers can make to the wellness of children, families, and communities.

NOTES

1. The terms *Indigenous* and *Aboriginal* are used almost synonymously in Canada to
refer to people who identify themselves as descendents of the original habitants of the
land now called Canada. The term *Aboriginal* was coined in the 1800s by the Canadian colonial government as a catch-all label. Some people refrain from using this
term because of its colonial origins. Many people prefer the term *Indigenous* because
of its connection to a global advocacy movement of Indigenous Peoples who use this
term, notably the Maori in Aotearoa/New Zealand. First Nation is a term that can
apply both to individuals and to communities. First Nations communities are culturally distinct, federally registered entities comprised mostly of Status Indians living on
lands reserved for them by the federal government.

2. The research by the authors described in this chapter was supported by funding
from the Social Sciences and Humanities Research Council of Canada, Community-
University Research Alliances program (File No. 833-2003-1002), the Public Health
Agency of Canada, and the British Columbia Ministry of Children and Family Development through the Human Early Learning Partnership. The views expressed here
are those of the author and do not represent the policy of provincial or federal funding
agencies or Indigenous organizations.

The authors thank the Indigenous fathers who participated in the research, as
well as the community partners who made the project possible: Lil'wat Nation, Little
Hands of Friendship and Power of Friendship Aboriginal Head Start Programs in
Prince George, the Terrace Child Development Centre Dad's Group, and Esketemc
First Nation. Important contributions were made by Candice Manahan, Ron George,
Leroy Joe, Ken Moselle, Allison Benner, and colleagues in the Fathers Involvement
Research Alliance of Canada, CURA project, directed by Kerry Daly.

Quotes are from fathers who participated in the project and who gave their written
permission to be quoted.

Address correspondence to Dr. Jessica Ball, School of Child and Youth Care, University of Victoria, Box 1700 STN CSC, Victoria, B.C., Canada V8W 2Y2; Tel: (250)
472-4128 Fax: (250) 721-7218; E-mail: jball@uvic.ca; Web site: www.ecdip.org.

3. Having registered Status under the colonial government's Indian Act, indicating being entitled to federal fiduciary support for basic health, education, and social
services and housing when living on a reserve.

4. Ball, Jessica. *Fatherhood: Indigenous Men's Journeys. Resources to Support Indigenous Men and Community Outreach Workers*. Victoria, BC: Jessica Ball, 2008. www. ecdip.org.

5. For further information, see Wendy McNab, Prairie Women's Health Centre of Excellence: www.uwinnipeg.ca/index/history-teacher-si-mcnab.

RESOURCES AND PROGRAMS FOR INDIGENOUS FATHERS

Aboriginal Head Start Program, Labrador Friendship Centre, Happy Valley-Goose Bay, Labrador. www.lfchvgb.ca/home/26.

Bent Arrow Traditional Healing Society, Edmonton, Alberta. www.bentarrow.ca.

Creating Hope Society, Fathers Sharing Circle, Edmonton, Alberta. www.creating hopesociety.ca.

Daddy Difference Program, Red Lake Indian Friendship Centre, Red Lake, Ontario. http://www.ofifc.org/centres/Red_Lake_Friendship_Centre.php.

Fatherhood: Indigenous Men's Journeys: Guide for practitioners, Guide for Aboriginal Men, DVD, posters, pamphlet, worksheets, and articles. www.ecdip.org/fathers/.

Focus on Fathers Support and Parenting Program, Four Directions Community Health Centre, Saskatoon, Saskatchewan. www.rqhealth.ca/programs/comm_ hlth_centres/four_directions/focus_fathers.shtml.

Full Circle Program Men's Group, Dze L'Kant Friendship Centre, Smithers, British Columbia. www.dzelkant.com/full_circle.php.

Ladysmith Dad's Group, Ladysmith Resources Centre Association, Ladysmith, British Columbia. www.lrca.bc.ca/dads.asp.

Nēâh Kee Papa ("I am your father") Program, Manitoba Métis Federation, Winnipeg, Manitoba. www.mmf.mb.ca.

PRIDE program, Mi'kmaq Confederacy of Prince Edward Island. http://mikmaq familyresources.ca.

Yukon Traditional Parenting Program, Skookum Jim Friendship Centre, Whitehorse, Yukon Territory. http://skookumjim.com/programs/traditional-parenting/.

REFERENCES

Aboriginal Healing Foundation (2006). *Final report of the Aboriginal Healing Foundation*, vol. 3: *Promising healing practices in Aboriginal communities*. Ottawa, ON: Aboriginal Healing Foundation.

Allen, S., Daly, K., & Ball, J. (2012). Fathers make a difference in their children's lives: A review of the research evidence. In J. Ball & K. Daly (eds), *Father Involvement in Canada: Diversity, Renewal, and Transformation* (pp. 50–88). Vancouver, BC: UBC Press.

Anderson, K. (2007). Giving life to the people: An Indigenous ideology of motherhood. In A. O'Reilly (ed.), *Maternal theory: Essential readings* (pp. 761–781). Toronto, ON: Demeter Press.

Anderson, K., & Ball, J. (2004). Foundations: First Nation and Métis families. In D. Long & O. P. Dickason (eds.), *Visions of the Heart: Canadian Aboriginal Issues* (pp. 55–89). Don Mills, ON: Oxford University Press.

Arnott, J. (2006). Dances with cougar: Learning from traditional skills parent-ing programs. In D. M. Lavell-Harvard & J. Corbiere Lavell (eds.), *Until our hearts are on the ground: Aboriginal mothering, oppression, resistance and rebirth* (pp. 94–104). Toronto, ON: Demeter.

Atleo, E. R. (2004). *Tsawalk: A Nuu-chah-nulth worldview.* Vancouver: University of British Columbia Press.

Ball, J., & George, R. (2006). Policies and practices affecting Aboriginal fathers' involvement with their children. In J. P. White, S. Wingert, D. Beavon, & P. Maxim (eds.), *Aboriginal policy research: Moving forward, making a difference,* vol. 3 (pp. 123–144). Toronto, ON: Thompson Educational Publishing.

Ball, J. & George, R. (2007). Policies and practices affecting Aboriginal fathers' involvement with their young children. In J.P. White, W. Wingert, D. Beavon, & P. Maxim (eds.), *Aboriginal Policy Research in Canada, 3,* 123–144). Toronto: Thompson Educational Press.

Ball, J. (2008). *Fatherhood: Indigenous men's journeys—Resources to support indigenous men and community outreach workers.* Victoria, BC.

Ball, J. (2010). Indigenous fathers: Involvement in reconstituting "circles of care." *American Journal of Community Psychology, 45,* 124–138.

Ball, J., & Daly, K. (eds.). (2012). *Father involvement in Canada: Diversity, renewal and transformation.* Vancouver, BC: UBC Press.

Blackstock, C., Cross, T., Brown, I., George, J., and Formsma, J. (2006). *Reconciliation in child welfare: Touchstones of hope for Indigenous children, youth, and families.* Ottawa: First Nation Child and Family Caring Society of Canada.

Brotherson, Dollahite, D.C., & Hawkins, A.J. (2005). Generative fathering and the dynamics of connection between fathers and their children. *Fathering, 3,* 128.

Brown, J., Higgitt, N., Wingert, S., Miller, C., & Morrissette, L. (2005). Challenges faced by Aboriginal youth in the inner city. *Canadian Journal of Urban Research, 14*(1), 81–106.

Brown, L., Callahan, M., Strega, S., Walmsley, C., & Dominelli, L. (2005). Manu-facturing ghost fathers: The paradox of father presence and absence in child welfare. *Child and Family Social Work, 14,* 25–34.

Canadian Broadcasting Corporation. (2012). *Blind spot: What happened to Canada's Aboriginal fathers?* [Video file]. http://curio.ca/en/blind-spot-what-happened -to-canadas-aboriginal-fathers/1441.

Carter, S. (1997). *Capturing women: The manipulations of cultural imagery in Canada's prairie west.* Montreal, QC: McGill-Queen's University Press.

Cassidy, J., & Shaver, P. R. (eds.). (1999). *Handbook of attachment theory and research.* New York: Guilford.

Castellano, M. B. (2002). *Aboriginal family trends: Extended families, nuclear families, families of the heart.* Contemporary Family Trends Series. Ottawa, ON: Vanier Institute of the Family.

Claes, R., & Clifton, D. (1998). *Needs and expectations for redress of victims of abuse at residential schools.* Ottawa, ON: Law Commission of Canada.

Denzin, N. K., Lincoln, Y. S., & Smith, L. (eds.). (2008). *Handbook of critical and Indigenous methodologies.* Thousand Oaks, CA: Sage.

Dion Stout, M., & Kipling, G. (2003). *Aboriginal people, resilience and the residential school legacy.* Ottawa, ON: Aboriginal Healing Foundation.

Driskill, Q., Finley, C., Gilley, B. J., & Morgensen, S. L. (eds.). (2011). *Queer Indigenous studies: Critical interventions in theory, politics and literature*. Tuscon: University of Arizona Press.

Duran, E., Duran, B., Brave Heart, M. H., & Yellow Horse-Davis, S. (1998). Healing the American Indian soul wound. In Y. Danieli (ed.), *International handbook of multigenerational legacies of trauma* (pp. 341–354). New York: Plenum Press.

Erikson, E. (1950). *Childhood and Society*. New York: Norton.

First Nations Information Governance Centre, First Nations Regional Health Survey (RHS) Phase 2 (2008/10) National Report on Adults, Youth and Children Living in First Nations Communities. Ottawa, ON: The First Nations Information Governance Centre.

Fournier, S., & Crey, E. (1997). *Stolen from our embrace: The abduction of Indigenous children and the restoration of Indigenous communities*. Vancouver, BC: Douglas & McIntyre.

Government of Canada (2015). Tri-Council Policy Statement 2: Research involving the First Nations, Inuit and Metis Peoples of Canada. Ottawa: Author. www.pre.ethics.gc.ca

Greenwood, M. (2006). Children are a gift to us: Aboriginal-specific early childhood programs and services in Canada. *Canadian Journal of Native Education, 29* (1), 12–28.

Guimond, E., & Robitaille, N. (2008). When teenage girls have children: Trends and consequences. *Horizons, 10*(1), 49–51..

John, E. (2003). Presentation to the British Columbia Aboriginal Child Care Society, Aboriginal leadership forum on early childhood development. Vancouver: University of British Columbia.

Lavell-Harvard, D. M., & J. Corbiere-Lavell (eds.) (2006). *Until Our Hearts Are On the Ground: Aboriginal Mothering, Oppression, Resistance and Rebirth*. Toronto: Demeter Press.

Mann, M. (2005). *Indian registration: Unrecognized and unstated paternity*. Ottawa, ON: Status of Women Canada.

Moselle, S., & Ball, J. (2013). Aboriginal Father Involvement Program National Scan. Ottawa: ON: Public Health Agency of Canada, Healthy Child Development Section.

Mussell, W. J. (2005). *Warrior–caregivers: Understanding the challenges and healing of First Nations men*. Ottawa, ON: Aboriginal Healing Foundation.

NCCAH (2011). *With Dad: Showcase on Aboriginal Father Involvement*. www.nccah-ccnsa.ca/286/With_Dad__Strengthening_the_Circle_of_Care.nccah.

Norris, M. J., & Clatworthy, S. (2006). *Aboriginal mobility and migration in Canada: Factors, policy implications and responses*. Paper presented at the Second Aboriginal Policy Research Conference, Ottawa.

Office of the Correctional Investigator (2013). Aboriginal offenders—A critical situation. www.oci-bec.gc.ca/cnt/rpt/oth-aut/oth-aut20121022info-eng.aspx.

Office of the Prime Minister of Canada. (2008). Minister offers full apology on behalf of Canadians for the Indian Residential Schools. [Press Release]. http://pm.gc.ca/eng/media/asp?id2149.

Palkovitz, R. (2002). Involved fathering and child development: Advancing our understanding of good fathering. In C. Tamis-LeMonda, & N. Cabrera (eds.), *Handbook of Father Involvement: Multidisciplinary Perspective* (pp. 119–140). Mahwah, NJ: Lawrence Erlbaum Associates.

Pratt, M. W., Lawford, H. L., & Allen, J. W. (2012). Young fatherhood, generativity, and men's development: Traveling a two-way street to maturity. In J. Ball & K. Daly (eds.), *Father involvement in Canada: Diversity, renewal, and transformation* (pp. 107–125). Vancouver, BC: UBC Press.

Roopnarine, J. L., Brown, J., Snell-White, P., & Riegraf, N. B. (1995). Father involvement in child care and household work in common-law dual-earner and single-earner Jamaican families. *Journal of Applied Developmental Psychology, 16*(1), 35–52.

Royal Commission on Aboriginal Peoples (1996). Vol. 3: *Gathering Strength*. In *Report of the Royal Commission on Aboriginal Peoples*. Ottawa, ON: Canada Communication Group.

Sarkadi, A., Kristiansson, R., Oberklaid, F., & Bremberg, S. (2008). Fathers' involvement and children's developmental outcomes: A systematic review of longitudinal studies. *Acta Paediatrica, 97*(2), 153–158.

Smolewsky, M., & Wesley-Esquimaux, C. (2003). *Historic Trauma and Indigenous Healing*. Ottawa, ON: Indigenous Healing Foundation Research Series.

Statistics Canada. (2006). *Census of population 2006*. www.statcan.gc.ca.

Statistics Canada. (2009). Selected Findings from 2006 Aboriginal Children's Survey: First Nations People, Métis in Canada, Inuit in Canada. *Canadian Social Trends* Special Edition (Catalogue no. 11-008). Ottawa, ON: Statistics Canada.

Statistics Canada. (2011). Population Projections by Aboriginal Identity in Canada, 2006–2031 (Catalogue no. 91-552-X). www.statcan.gc.ca/pub/91-552-x/91-552-x2011001-eng.pdf.

Statistics Canada. (2013a). Aboriginal peoples in Canada: First Nations people, Métis and Inuit. *National Household Survey*. www.statcan.gc.ca/nhs-enm/2011/as-sa/99-011-x/99-011-x2011001-eng.pdf.

Statistics Canada. (2013b). The educational attainment of Aboriginal peoples in Canada. *National Household Survey, 2011* (Catalogue no. 99-012-X2011003). http://www12.statcan.gc.ca/nhs-enm/2011/as-sa/99-012-x/99-012-x2011003_3-eng.pdf.

Strega, S., Fleet, C., Brown, L., Dominelli, L., Callahan, M., & Walmsley, C. (2008). Connecting father absence and mother blame in child welfare policies and practice. *Children and Youth Services Review, 30*(7), 705–716.

Stremlau, R. (2005). "To domesticate and civilize wild Indians": Allotment and the campaign to reform Indian families, 1875–1887. *Journal of Family History, 30*(3), 265–286.

Truth and Reconciliation Commission of Canada. (2012). *Canada, Aboriginal Peoples and residential schools: They came for the children*. Ottawa, ON: Government of Canada. www.attendancemarketing.com/~attmk/TRC_jd/ResSchool History_2012_02_24_Webposting.pdf.

Volo, J. M., & Volo, D. D. (2007). *Family Life in Native America*. Westport, CT: Greenwood Press.

Wemigwans, J. (Producer/Director). (2002). *Seven Fires* [DVD]. Toronto, ON: V-Tape.org.

Wendy McNab, Prairie Women's Health Centre of Excellence. www.uwinnipeg.ca/index/history-teacher-si-mcnab.

11

European American Fathers

Rob Palkovitz, Kimberly Dutton, and James W. Hull

OVERVIEW OF EUROPEAN AMERICAN FATHERING

Beginnings matter. We know this from the risk and resilience literature (Matsen 2014). We know that a child who is born with two well-educated, well-functioning, and employed parents has a different developmental prognosis than a child born in the same hospital on the same day who is a small for gestational age infant, addicted to illegal drugs, born into a father-absent household, and residing in a poverty stricken neighborhood (Nair et al. 1997). As these two children develop across time, their outcomes will be evaluated in light of the different beginnings they had and their trajectories forward, for better or for worse, given the opportunities and challenges they faced. This example makes it clear that not all people are born into the same set of resources and opportunity structures (McLoyd 1998).

The same is true of fathers. Every father begins his fathering journey as a man situated in his unique set of developmental and contextual resources. Any assessment of father involvement and the contributions fathers make toward facilitating their children's development is based, at least in part, on the resources they have at their disposal, what they have had to offer to shape the development of their children, and what they have done with those opportunities (Palkovitz, Dutton, & Hull 2014).

Being born a European American (EA) male in the United States typically has associated structural affordances that are incomparable to other demographic statuses as a father, including those associated with being a first-generation European immigrant (Zhou 1997). In reviewing European American fathering, it is thus essential to start with some definitional and conceptual issues that position our understanding of what it means to be a European American father (EAF).

When we discuss EAFs, are we talking primarily about race, class, culture, or, perhaps, ethnicity? How do these factors interact in the lived experience of fathers from European descent who are living in America? How does beginning the developmental journey of being a father differ depending upon the structural affordances characteristically associated with being a father of EA descent? How do these common differences distinguish the opportunity structures that EAFs have from those of equally committed, equally motivated, and lovingly engaged fathers from different ethnic, racial, cultural and class backgrounds? Why is it that EAFs tend to be put forward as the group against which we benchmark the fathering of all other classifications of men (see, e.g., Greenberger & Chen 1996; Varela et al. 2004)?

We submit that the reasons are threefold. First, since the establishment of the United States as a nation, EAFs have represented a majority of fathers. Second, the early research literature on fathering enrolled primarily middle-class EAFs. Finally, in comparison to men characterized by other social addresses, EAFs are, on average, afforded with economic and socially desirable opportunities to positively influence and interact with the development of their children. This is not to mask the great diversity in education, income, and living circumstances within the population of EAFs, or that EAFs are represented in the full range of resources across each of these domains. Our goal in this chapter is to set forth a clear understanding of the structural differences that are correlated because of history, immigration, and distinctions that must honestly be viewed as racism, classism, and other forms of distinction, to more frequently give EAFs, the optimal opportunity structures for fathering positively in comparison to the challenges faced by fathers in other demographic categories. By this analysis, we are not suggesting that EAFs are in any way superior to any other groups of men. In contrast, we assert that there is substantial variability both within and across all groups of fathers as they navigate the resources with which they are afforded and the risk and resilience matrices they navigate through their life course in attempting to be positively involved fathers. An alternative view would suggest that considering the affordances that EAFs enjoy on average, by many socially desirable standards, they have optimal opportunities to engage with their children and positively facilitate their development. Furthermore, we emphasize that this comparative analysis should not lead to determinations of which groups of fathers achieve outcomes that are "better" or "worse" in regard to facilitating child well-being. Rather, we would suggest that the diversity of "beginning points" and associated resources across fathering groups interact with the diversity of fathering within fathering groups in ways that are neither unsystematic nor randomly distributed. Simply stated, on average, EAFs typically benefit from better "starting positions" than men in other fathering categories.

With these perspectives in mind, let us return to the first sentence in this chapter and employ a metaphor to place differential social affordances of fathering in perspective. *Beginnings matter.* As a metaphor, consider being a father limited to foot travel and currently located in the eastern United States. This beginning point precludes the realistic possibility of this father ascending Mount Everest solely by foot. Even if the metaphorical father were fortunate enough to be at base camp on Everest, the journey would still be arduous and fraught with many unforeseen changes in context and condition, including the well-being and skill of his climbing partners, the ever-changing weather, and interactions with conditions on the mountain itself. What should be clear is that someone positioned at base camp cannot assume that he or she will successfully summit out, but the realistic opportunity for achieving that targeted "finish" is considerably different based on their beginning at base camp versus beginning on foot in the eastern United States. So it is with every father in the context the structural affordances that he does and does not have at any given moment and where that places him as a beginning point for striving to achieve his targeted fathering goals. Different beginning points bring different finish points into realistic view.

To contextualize the typical beginning points of EAFs, we need to begin by setting forth operational definitions for terms central to our review. Moreover, understanding historical shifts in the usage and meanings of basic terms will bring clarity to our analysis of EAF involvement patterns.

Operational Definitions in Historical Context

For our purposes, EAFs can be defined as fathers residing in America with ancestry traced to Europe (Merriam-Webster Dictionary). The term was created to emphasize the European cultural and geographical origins of Americans in a way parallel to that used in the cases of African Americans and Asian Americans (American Community Survey 2009). Additionally, the term European American is sometimes used interchangeably with "Caucasian American," "white American," and "Anglo American" in different geographic regions of the United States (Randolph 2007). Though European American ancestral awareness varies across individuals, it is estimated that 90 percent of respondents classified as "white" by the 2000 U.S. census knew some details of their European ancestry (Szucs & Luebking 2006). Ethnic categorization has been both facilitated and complicated since the 2000 census, because respondents have had the option to select "American" as a category to describe their ethnicity. The popularity of the "American" category may result from cases in which the respondent does not perceive that one ancestry is dominant enough to identify with (e.g., a person who is 1/4 German, 1/4 Irish, 1/4 Scottish, 1/8 French, and 1/8 Swedish). However, in 2013, German

Americans (14.6%), Irish Americans (10.5%), English Americans (7.7%) and Italian Americans (5.4%) were the four largest self-reported European ancestry groups in the United States, making up 42.7% of the total population (American Community Survey 2013).

It is important to recognize that categorization of the European American population into subcomponents (e.g., Italian Americans or English Americans) can be a challenging and somewhat arbitrary exercise. Farley (1991) argued that identification of ethnic origins for many whites whose ancestors immigrated from Europe may seem unimportant because numerous generations separate typical survey respondents from their forbears, and the high prevalence of ethnic intermarriage further challenges clear ethnic identity. Farley concluded that "no simple (survey) question will distinguish those who identify strongly with a specific European group from those who report symbolic or imagined ethnicity" (p. 422), highlighting documentation that over 40 percent of respondents to the general population survey changed their self-reported ancestry over the six-month period between survey waves. This finding may be partially explained by the fact that a significant majority of European Americans have lineage that can be traced to a number of different countries, and the response to a single "ancestry" gives little indication of the backgrounds of contemporary Americans. Based on a study of U.S. Census Bureau figures from 1980, 1990, and 2000, statisticians determined that one out of three European Americans is descended from only one European ethnicity; one out of three is descended from two European nationalities; and one out of three is descended from three or more European ethnic origins (American Community Survey 2009).

The picture is further complicated by how far persons are generationally removed from immigration and can accurately trace familial roots to specific European nations. Current data suggest that by the time European Americans are in their second generation, roughly six in ten adults consider themselves to be a "typical American," approximately twice the rate of immigrants who are likely to affirm the same (Pew Research 2013). Particularly as third- and fourth-generation European Americans have assimilated into American culture and have intermarried with persons from various ethnic origins, most people are likely to express their individual ethnic ties sporadically and symbolically and do not consider their specific ethnic origins to be centrally essential to their identity (American Community Survey 2009). Thus a majority of white Americans are more likely to simply view themselves as "Americans," and white fathers may not view their fathering to be significantly shaped by EA roots.

Perhaps it is for all of these reasons that the term "European American" is not in popular use in the United States among the general public, among whom the terms "white" or "white American" are in more common usage

(American Community Survey 2009). In contrast, the popularity of the term EA is growing in the scholarly literature. Specifically, the term, European American Father has increased in frequency of usage from the mid-1990s to the present. A Google Scholar search for "European American fathers" returned twenty-four citations in the 1990s, a figure that more than doubled to 105 in the decade from 2000 to 2010 and that has already appeared forty times in scholarly literature between 2011 and the end of 2014, bringing the total number of occurrences to 170 between 1990 and the present. By comparison, the term "white father" has occurred 8,310 times, "Caucasian fathers" 388 times, and "Anglo fathers" 266 times in the same period. Though specific use of the term European American Fathers has increased in the scholarly literature, the precision of the term is ambiguated by each of the factors already detailed.

Though many scientists view race as an outdated construct (Friedriechs 1996), the racial categorization of fathers is apparently still quite popular. The traditional definitions of race and ethnicity are related to biological and sociological factors respectively (Takaki 1987). In the general population, race is used to refer to a person's physical appearance and characteristics, such as skin color, eye color, hair color, and bone (e.g., jaw) structure (Williams et al. 1997). Ethnicity, on the other hand, is related to cultural factors such as nationality, familial ancestry, language, cuisine, and ideology (Barth 1998; Brubaker & Cooper 2000). The popularity of racial categorization has further contributed to the difficulty of untangling the effects of other important demographic variables like ethnicity, cultural background and social class.

At the most basic level however, EAFs tend to systematically vary from other American fathers across these constructs, especially social class. In the United States, social class represents a controversial construct, having a multitude of competing definitions and models including different numbers of strata and extending to disagreements over its very existence (American Fact Finder 2013). The majority of approaches to social class structure group individuals into various strata according to a combined assessment of wealth, income, education, occupational type, and participation in a specific social network (Kreiger et al. 1997). In America, persons of EA descent are disproportionately represented in the middle and upper strata of social class (McCubbin & McCubbin 1988), further complicating the task of isolating the effects of race, ethnicity, and social class.

Situating the Population of European American Fathers

Currently, approximately 78 percent of all fathers in America could be classified as European American fathers, representing a shrinking majority of contemporary American fathers (American Fact Finder 2013). Though there is great diversity across race, ethnicity, and social class in America, it is typical or normative for particular structural affordances to be associated with being a male from European American descent. In particular, white males are more likely to be married, co-residential with their wife and children, and educated and to have higher gross annual income levels than men of color (Russell & Batalova 2012). Recent demographic statistics substantiate this reality. For example, it is currently the case that more than 70 percent of "African American" children are born outside of marriage, and 67% are likely to reside in a single-parent female-headed household at some time before turning 18. By contrast, 70 percent of European American children are born to married parents, 75 percent live in a two-parent co-residential household at any given time, and 25 percent are likely to spend some portion of their first eighteen years in single-parent families. We know that patterns of father engagement with children vary by co-residence and relational harmony with a co-parent (Palkovitz, Fagan, & Hull 2013). Aponte, Beale and Jiles (1999) have suggested that many characteristics viewed to be cultural differences among families principally arise from structural factors, particularly socioeconomic status, but that prior studies have not been conducted in a manner that offers unequivocal support for this assertion.

Research by Sorensen and Zibman (2001) has also documented that in comparison with higher-SES fathers, poor fathers are not as likely to consistently provide child support. Economically disadvantaged fathers also contend with multiple challenges and barriers to attaining employment because of lower educational attainment, transportation challenges, and criminal records (Sorensen & Zibman 2001). Fathers' sense of efficacy and well-being is associated with ability to adequately fulfill the provider role (Wilson & Brooks-Gunn 2001), and education, employment, and income covary with race and ethnicity. Additionally, as early as 1989, Testa et al. documented that in comparison with unemployed fathers, employed fathers are more than twice as likely to marry the mother of their first child. The emergent pattern is that a majority of white single parents reach that status through divorce, whereas most blacks become single parents through nonmarital childbearing. Blacks also have a younger sexual initiation than whites, on average, and this is associated with differential educational attainment, and subsequent employability and wages. Consequently, the typical EAF has a different beginning point than other groups of fathers. Overall, as the majority group, European Americans have the lowest poverty rate of any racial demographic in the United States (Table 701, U.S. Census Bureau 2012) and rank second to Asian Americans in educational attainment levels, median household income (U.S. Census Bureau 2005) and median personal income (U.S. Census Bureau 2006). Additionally, in two-parent EA families, 69.9% of mothers of children younger than 18 are employed outside the home, increasing family per-capita income and creating cultural expectations for egalitarian parenting (U.S. Department of Labor 2014).

Because of these common economic and social structural affordances, on average, EAFs and their children have better access to goods and services and are more likely to reside with and share parental responsibilities with another adult co-parent, creating a developmental context for higher levels of parental monitoring. Most important, the structural affordances associated with being an EAF create different patterns of accessibility to children, direct engagement with children, and responsibility for children—the most common dimensions of father involvement employed in conceptualizing and measuring patterns of fathering (Lamb 2000; Palkovitz 1997; Pleck 2010).

THEORETICAL FRAMEWORKS USED IN STUDYING EA FATHERS

Evolutions in the marketplace and workforce have shifted parental role sharing significantly over the past fifty years. In particular, women going to college and entering the workforce in large numbers have contributed to family-level transformations in parental expectations and responsibilities for both men and women. Shifts and deviations from the traditional male bread-winner/female homemaker model have resulted in negotiated arrangements between parents in an attempt to balance the demands of the workplace and the home (McFadden & Tamis-LeMonda 2013).

Several fathering scholars have chronicled these macro-level changes in fatherhood over the course of American history (see Lamb 2000; Pleck 1998; Palkovitz 2002 for reviews). The shifts in American fatherhood are neither the purpose nor scope of this paper, but it is noteworthy to mention some of the ramifications of the most recent shift to the "involved father" ideal. Whereas some older Americans spent their lives in egalitarian families, older Americans of most ethnic backgrounds grew up and reared their children in a lineal family with the father as head of the family and the mother as the social–emotional center. As will be discussed later, the effect of this kind of family structure depends on social mobility from one generation to the next and on the degree and kinds of interdependence between generations. Thus the degree to which we can draw conclusions regarding the implications of these shifts across history is weak. Because of disparity in data available during these earlier periods, some have questioned our ability to truly understand the transformations that fatherhood has experienced for all men across time (LaRossa 1997). Specifically there is scant, if any, data available pertaining to variations in fathering role enactments across geographical regions, socioeconomic status, and ethnicity or cultural background. Thus it is difficult to paint a clear picture about particular shifts in involvement patterns or ideology related to specific subgroups of the American population across time. Palkovitz (2002) noted:

> When considering subgroups of fathers, keep in mind that men who may be categorized within the same general classification will have unique histories, varying broadly on variables other than the target variable that triggered their classification into subgroups. (p. 36)

Contemporary fathering scholarship has made strides to curb this issue by studying various subgroups of fathers including minority fathers, at-risk fathers, non-residential fathers, social fathers, primary caregiving fathers, single fathers, gay fathers, and stepfathers, to name a few. However, in light of burgeoning literature on underrepresented subgroups of fathers, groups of men who had traditionally been the target of fatherhood research have seen a diminished presence in the literature. In particular, research on men of white European descent has primarily been for the purposes of comparison or reference. Thus what we currently know about EAFs as a distinct group relates primarily to how they compare or differ from other groups of fathers (e.g., black fathers, Latino fathers, and Asian American fathers). These differences tell us little about how the ideologies and values within the European American subculture have shaped or influenced these observed differences. Though studying differences between groups is beneficial and worthwhile, rigorous inquiry within groups is important as well. The resulting data would lead to a clearer understanding not only of how different groups of men vary across fathering measures, but also of how men within the same group vary on the same constructs.

For years, fathering scholars have set Lamb et al.'s (1985) classic model of father involvement as the benchmark for fatherhood research. The original model consisted of three primary domains of involvement: (1) paternal engagement, (2) accessibility (availability), and (3) responsibility. After its introduction, fatherhood researchers proceeded to apply this model and did so with much variability. Because of the variability in application and interpretation of the classical model, Pleck (2010) proposed a revised conceptualization to account for the wealth of data generated by the original. His reconceptualization refined the original components of engagement, accessibility, and responsibility and included two additional components: indirect care and process responsibility. Thus the reconceptualization of father involvement according to Pleck (2010) is a five-dimensional model: (1) positive engagement activities, (2) warmth and responsiveness, (3) control, (4) indirect care, and (5) process responsibility. Pleck's (2010) rationale for the reconceptualization is in light of recent fatherhood scholarship and lends itself to more relevant investigations of father involvement. He states that the transition from engagement, or total engagement time, toward positive engagement activities reflects fatherhood researchers' increased focus on distinguishing different kinds of engagement time. Warmth and responsiveness, the second component of the revised model, account for the various qualitative-like operationalizations of the original engagement construct. Pleck (2010) argued that because many scholars were including qualitative aspects of fathers' engagement, accounting for these applications was necessary in the reconceptualization. Control is a revised dimension of the original responsibility construct meant to account for all the ways that men monitor and participate in decision making. Indirect involvement includes those things done *for* the child and not *with* the child. Examples could include fathers arranging for childcare, making doctor appointments, or coordinating social activities for their child. Finally, process responsibility, has to do with fathers' taking initiative to recognize what needs to be done or cared for rather than waiting to be told.

Lamb et al.'s (1985, 1987) model remains a staple in the fathering literature, and scholars will likely continue to differ on operationalizing its constructs. As documented earlier, EAFs enjoy structural affordances and social resources that position them to have a greater chance of falling on the higher ends of the involvement continuum, independent of the specific operationalization of involvement employed.

DIVERSITY IN INVOLVEMENT PATTERNS OF EA FATHERS

European American (white) fathers, on average, enjoy the highest levels of income and education and are the second least likely ethnic group to exist in households without married women. White children live in circumstances more conducive to non-resident father involvement (e.g., born within marriage, living in custodial mother households) (Russell & Batalova 2012). There is a lower birth rate among white families, and they tend to wait until later ages to have children in comparison to black and Latino families (Russell & Batalova 2012).

What has been referred to as "the new fatherhood ideal," having a father who works but is also highly involved in the household is most accepted by the educated middle class (Cowan et al. 2007).

Thus this ideal is most frequently adopted by white fathers. This is also true because white women are more likely to attain a higher educational level and obtain jobs outside the household that require the father to become more involved in fathering activities. Crouter, Davis, Updegraff, Delgado, and Fortner (2006) tell us that black marriages are more egalitarian than white marriages and thus that black fathers are more likely than white fathers to be involved in household and child care work. Less educated black men thus are more likely to be involved with their children than less educated white men, but because white men are educated at higher rates, overall it is still more likely that white men will be involved with their children (Crouter et al. 2006).

Hofferth (2003) notes that in comparison to other groups, white children have significantly higher rates of overnight stays with their non-resident fathers and are also more likely to have in-person or phone/letter contact with their non-resident fathers. White adolescents are more likely to participate in sports with their non-resident fathers but are less likely to attend a religious event or work on a school project with their fathers than children of Latino fathers (Hofferth 2003). In general, white fathers have more contact with their children, but minority fathers find diverse ways to be involved in their children's lives (Hofferth 2003).

European American fathers are less likely to be poor, more likely to be fluent in the mainstream language, and have values and practices that are in line with the mainstream culture (Cowan, Cowan, Pruett, & Pruett 2007). These fathers are also more likely to be married to the mother of their child and to live in the same household as their child. All of these factors combined leave EAFs with more resources to be able to provide for their children and thus be more involved than those fathers who are "at risk."

Relationships between Class, Culture, and Fathering

Despite the considerable difference between Italian and American parents' values for their children, social class is related to parental values in much the same way in both countries. Middle-class parents in both Italy and the United States are more likely to value the child's self-direction while working-class parents value the child's conformity to external proscription. In sum: In both classes, men who follow orders at work tend to value obedience, those who have greater degrees of freedom in their work situations are more likely to value self-control for their children (Perlin & Kohn 1966).

EAFs tend to adopt an authoritative style of parenting. Hofferth (2003) tells us that compared to EAFs, black children's fathers display less warmth toward their children but tend to monitor their children more than EAFs. Latino fathers tend to monitor their children less meaning that on a continuum of monitoring, EAFs fall somewhere in the middle, engaging in moderate amounts of monitoring. Research also shows that children of these fathers tend to see them as more strict and authoritarian, whereas fathers themselves tend to view themselves as warm and authoritative (Smetana 1995).

Contemporary research has also supported that although white fathers have structural advantages that allow for potentially greater levels of involvement, they still spend less time in direct caregiving and household activities than mothers. Lang et al. (2014) studied a sample of mostly white (84% mothers, 85% fathers), dual-earner families with newborn infants and found that on average, fathers spent less time than mothers engaged in positive, developmentally appropriate activities over the first nine months of their child's life. Additionally, both fathers and mothers increased their involvement levels over time and did so at similar rates. Consequently, although fathers did increase their time spent in positive engagement over time, their time spent was consistently lower than their partners'.

Employing Lamb et al.'s (1985, 1987) model of involvement, results from Kotila and colleagues' (2013) study of mostly white (86% mothers, 89% fathers), dual-earning, first-time parent families demonstrated that mothers outperformed fathers on most measures of positive engagement and routine child care with their infant at three months and again at nine months. However, the discrepancies between levels of engagement at three months were more profound on nonworkdays. This trend was similar across the responsibility measure that captured such things as child-related planning, wait time medical care, or keeping an eye on the infant. The researchers also found that most mothers and fathers were most equitable in terms of accessibility, meaning total time spent with the infant but not actual involvement occurred.

EA FATHER INVOLVEMENT AND CHILD DEVELOPMENTAL OUTCOMES

Investigations of the roles that men play in the family continue to grow and have received considerably more attention in recent years. The body of evidence that has accumulated suggests that positive developmental outcomes in children are associated with positively involved fathers. In general, research has shown that children who have positively involved fathers demonstrate greater levels of psychological adjustment, tend to perform well in school, display less antisocial behaviors, and grow to have more successful intimate relationships than children with uninvolved fathers (Flouri & Buchanan 2003). Even with large numbers of American children growing up with non-residential fathers, research has also demonstrated that non-resident father involvement can buffer against the negative outcomes typically associated with single-mother families and has positive effects on child well-being (Flouri 2006; Vogt Yuan & Hamilton 2009). Good-quality father–child relationships increase the likelihood of a happy, satisfying adult life (Aquilino 2006). Positive father involvement has been shown to encourage social competence, strengthen interpersonal skills, increase self-esteem levels, promote proper emotional adjustment, and facilitate behavioral regulation (Williams & Kelly 2005).

Interest has grown concerning the developmental outcomes associated with fathers from different ethnic or cultural backgrounds. Because the ethnic and cultural landscape of the United States is continually changing, researchers have increasingly begun to include these variables in their studies of fathers. In doing so, however, contemporary scholarship on fathering has paid scant attention to EAFs and has instead focused heavily on fathers from other ethnic minority groups. The result has been a limited contemporary literature base that elucidates the unique experiences, roles, and scripts associated with fathers from European backgrounds. Although brief, the following studies are a small representation of what we know regarding European American fathers as a subgroup and child developmental outcomes.

Ethnic Differences in European American Fathering

Though a majority of studies focusing on EAFs do not differentiate by specific ethnic identities, a few notable exceptions exist. Specifically, Gambino (1975) details that Italian American fathers tend to be distinguished from other American fathers by being more likely to require lineal respect as opposed to striving for a "buddy" or friendship relationship with their children. Gambino elaborates that Italian American fathers are often viewed as the family's source of authority. In contrast, Greeley and McCready (1972) characterized Irish American fathers as striving for egalitarian relationships with their sons, relationships characterized by common interests and congeniality.

In 2003, Bean and colleagues studied how parental support, behavioral control, and psychological control in European American and African American families influenced adolescent functioning. They found that for European American adolescents, father's behavioral control was significantly related to academic achievement and self-esteem. The same did not hold true for African American fathers and adolescents. Additionally, paternal psychological control was significantly related to self-esteem for both African American and European American adolescents. These findings suggest that similar father–child interactions among these two groups can result in different child outcomes, depending on the dyad. Behavioral control appears to be a positive characteristic of European American father–child dyads resulting in higher levels of adolescent self-esteem and academic achievement, whereas behavioral control does not seem to be a significant factor in predicting these outcomes in African American father–child dyads.

In studying a sample of mostly Caucasian father–son dyads, Morman and Floyd (2002) found that fathers reported having more satisfying, expressive, supportive, and affectionate relationships with their sons than they did with their own fathers. Sons reported similar attitudes and feelings toward their fathers as well. It is difficult, however, to determine whether these findings are an artifact of "Caucasian" father–son dyads and are thus not generalizable to other ethnic or racial groups or whether these findings are evidence of the general changes in the "culture of fatherhood" (LaRossa 1988) occurring in western nations.

In one of the few studies to specifically target a European American-only sample, Putnick and colleagues (2010) argued that because European American adolescents represent a majority of the U.S. population, they should be the focal group of their study. Their study of two-parent families examined continuities and stability in parenting stress across children's transition to adolescence. Their results demonstrated that during the transition to adolescence, fathers and mothers experience similar levels of stress and that the source of stress typically comes from dysfunctional parent–child interactions. The researchers' measure of dysfunctional interactions included a twelve-item scale that asked parents to respond to statement such as "My child rarely does things for me that make me feel good." Though the authors were transparent and provided an argument for studying only European American families, these results are challenging to interpret because of the absence of other ethnic groups for comparison against the European American sample.

Toth and Xu (1999) used Palkovitz's (1997) model of father involvement by operationalizing domains of behavioral, cognitive, and affective involvement. The researchers compared groups of white, Hispanic, and African American fathers and their involvement across these three domains. Their results indicated that white fathers were less likely than African American fathers to monitor and supervise their children's activities (cognitive domain). Moreover, white fathers were less likely than Hispanic fathers to monitor (cognitive), interact (behavioral), and spend time (behavioral) with their children. Thus, according to Toth and Xu, white fathers are less involved from a cognitive perspective with their children compared to African American and Hispanic fathers. These results however, should be interpreted in light of the author's operationalization of "cognitive" involvement. The three items the authors used asked fathers to disclose whether they monitored the amount and type of television programs their children watched and whether they required their children to complete their chores before watching television or going out. It is unclear whether these three items were the only cognitively focused data available or whether there was other psychometric reasoning behind this measurement's operationalization. Though these three items constitute examples of parental monitoring and therefore are consistent with the spirit of Palkovitz's (1997) cognitive domain of involvement, monitoring is one of the many examples and ways in which fathers can be involved and/or experience involvement cognitively. The authors' assertion that "African American fathers invest considerably more energy in the cognitive domain than White fathers" (p. 92) would be better understood had the focus been on parental monitoring rather than cognitive involvement as a whole.

Leidy et al. (2011) studied a sample of Mexican American and European American adolescents and found that fathering acceptance, monitoring, consistent discipline, and interactions were associated with positive adolescent adjustment across both ethnic groups. Furthermore, father rejection was negatively associated with positive adolescent adjustment across both ethnic groups. In this study, European American fathers were less involved and less rejecting than Mexican American fathers, but both groups of fathers were equally accepting. An interesting caveat to this study was that after SES was controlled for, differences in involvement and rejection across European American and Mexican American fathers disappeared. The authors concluded that the observed ethnic differences may be an artifact of different SES levels in Mexican American and European American families. Relatedly, observed differences between European American and Mexican American fathers from Finlay et al.'s (2014) study could likewise be associated with differences in SES, considering that the mean income of European American households was $86,678 compared to $47,514 for Mexican American households in their study. Interpreting these results is difficult as well as other studies that include measures of SES because of the often confounded nature of SES and race/ethnicity in American culture.

Parke et al. (2004) examined how parenting practices were influenced by economic troubles in a sample of European American and Mexican American families. Their analysis demonstrated that European American families and Mexican American families were similarly affected by economic pressures, with economic pressures being related to depressed moods, depressed moods being related to marital problems and increases in hostile parenting, and hostile parenting being related to child adjustment problems. For both groups, only hostile parenting from fathers was related to child adjustment problems. Also, this relationship was stronger in European American families than in Mexican American families. The authors suggest that paternal intensity and infrequency of hostile parenting from European American fathers may partially explain this finding.

These studies represent our limited understanding of the developmental outcomes associated with children with European American fathers. Indeed, more nuanced and contextualized inquiries are necessary to untangle the complicated fathering landscape that blankets the United States. Father involvement is complex, and its associated roles and scripts are myriad. It is evident that one of the more difficult dimensions of fathering to capture is the role of ethnicity and culture in shaping fathering behaviors and attitudes, especially in the United States. Many studies of fathers, including several of those mentioned previously, have been limited in scope in the sense that culture and ethnicity are often used as controls or covariates as to classify men into different, comparable "groups." Thus little is known regarding the true effect of European heritage and culture on fathering as it refers to distinguishable roles and scripts compared to other ethnic and cultural origins in the United States. What characteristics or qualities make a father "European American" versus "American" versus "white American? Indeed, the literature on fathering has been characterized by a much higher prevalence of the use of "white" as opposed to European American or Caucasian. As our review has documented, use of the term "European American Father" is increasing in the scholarly literature, but it is neither clearly linked to categories of ethnic identity available in U.S. census data, nor does it reflect common usage among everyday fathers.

FUTURE DIRECTIONS AND POLICY IMPLICATIONS

When we label a father as European American, it is important to know how centrally his ethnic heritage defines his self-image or identity as a father. It would also be important to know how differentiated his ethnic identity is from his identity as a father, a man, or as a person. Perhaps his personality traits, his perceived strengths and weaknesses, and his parenting style and psychological resources are more (or less) central to him than his ethnic origins. In reality, when we use the term "European American," we do not typically know that the participants are Italian American or Irish American or Greco American, nor what their multiple ethnic roots may be. We also do not typically know how many generations they are removed from the immigration of their ancestors to America, and we know neither the numbers of cultures nor the geographic origins of their maternal and paternal lineages.

Though the term "EA" was created to honor ethnic roots, when applied as a proxy for "White," it does not. Rather, it obscures differences between various ethnicities. In the same way that scholars came to recognize the inappropriate homogenization implied by labeling Mexicans, Cubans, and Puerto Ricans as Hispanics, we must differentiate among the ethnic and cultural roots of diverse European Americans.

Clearly, fathers vary in involvement patterns both within and across groupings organized by labels such as EAFs. Much of the fathering they enact is simultaneously supported and challenged by the structural affordances and social resources they do or do not possess. To date, research on variability between families with different ethnic heritages has been limited by imprecise categorizing of fathers into groups using a few selected labels that routinely confound components of race, class, ethnicity, and culture. Future studies will be enhanced by researchers, allowing participant fathers to describe and elaborate on their identities as fathers. Specifically, if fathers are encouraged to describe themselves as fathers, the extent to which ethnic identity plays a central role in shaping paternal involvement will become more clear.

Our current literature that merely describes similarities and differences between EAFs and varied comparative groups that are defined by a surface distinction on singular or minimalistic clusters of demographic variables does not capture the contributions of ethnic heritage to fathers' lived experiences. Research on variations in fathering contexts, resources and families can help service providers and program planners to understand the perceived needs of diverse fathers. At this time, even the limited research that has been conducted to focus on the developmental cascades experienced by diverse fathers reflects enormous variability in the essence of relationships between fathers and their children. It is our hope that this review will facilitate future researchers in more precisely and thoroughly investigating the richness of the ethnic heritage of European American Fathers.

CONCLUSIONS

Men of every race, ethnicity, and culture must navigate economic issues, and their fathering experiences are situated within real-world structural affordances and limitations (e.g., fathering resources). The current literature does not allow an analysis of the relative contributions of economic and educational capital relative to the influences of race, ethnicity, and culture in regard to father involvement. Though we have reviewed literature that documents differences among different groups of fathers, it is not clear how differences within EA ethnicity shape fathering roles, styles, and patterns of engagement. In most of the literature, inextricable confounds exist between ethnicity, race, and class. Though all groups of fathers manifest diverse differences on multiple variables, disentangling the contributions of those factors to observed patterns of father involvement remains a challenge. What remains as a pivotal question is whether ethnic identity, cultural scripts, or social class carry greater explanatory power in EAFs. It is possible that men who have different ethnic and cultural heritages enact fathering in distinct manners largely obscured by economic resource differences. A comparison of variability in patterns of father involvement by more detailed conceptualizations and measures of social class and ethnicity could begin to elucidate the relative importance of these factors, variables that are richly central to the lived experiences of fathers and typically reduced to broad demographic categorization by researchers. Our lived experiences suggest that beyond economic and structural affordances that differentiate EAFs from other categories of fathers, diverse developmental pathways exist to influence ethnic and cultural expressions of fathering. Future research will be enriched by focusing on the contributions of ethnic and cultural factors as contributors to fathering belief systems, identities, scripts, and involvement patterns.

REFERENCES

American Community Survey. (2009). www.census.gov/acs/www/data_documentation/2009_release/.

American Community Survey. (2013). http://factfinder2.census.gov/faces/tableservices/jsf/pages/productview.xhtml?pid=ACS_13_1YR_DP02&prodType=table.

American Fact Finder. (2013). http://quickfacts.census.gov/qfd/states/00000.html.

Aponte, R., Beal, B. A., Jiles, M. E. (1999). Ethnic variation in the family: The elusive trend toward convergence. In *Hand-book of marriage and the family* (pp. 111–141). New York: Plenum.

Aquilino, W. (2006). The noncustodial father–child relationship from adolescence into young adulthood. *Journal of Marriage and Family, 68*(4), 929–946

Barth, F. (1998). *Ethnic groups and boundaries: The social organization of culture difference*. Long Grove, IL: Waveland Press.

Bean, R. A., Bush, K. R., McKenry, P. C., & Wilson, S. M. (2003). The impact of parental support, behavioral control, and psychological control on the academic achievement and self-esteem of African American and European American adolescents. *Journal of Adolescent Research, 18*(5), 523–541.

Brubaker, R., & Cooper, F. (2000). Beyond "identity." *Theory and Society, 29*(1), 1–47.

Cowan, C. P., Cowan, P. A., Pruett, M. K., & Pruett, K. (2007). An approach to preventing co-parenting conflict and divorce in low-income families: Strengthening couple relationships and fostering fathers' involvement. *Family Process, 46*(1), 109–121.

Crouter, A. C., Davis, K. D., Updegraff, K., Delgado, M., & Fortner, M. (2006). Mexican American fathers' occupational conditions: Links to family members' psychological adjustment. *Journal of Marriage and Family, 68*(4), 843–858.

European American. (n.d.). In *Merriam-Webster Dictionary*. www.merriam-webster.com/dictionary/european%20american.

Farley, R. (1991). The new census question on ancestry: What did it tell us? *Demography, 28*, 411–429.

Finlay, A. K., Cookston, J. T., Saenz, D. S., Baham, M. E., Parke, R. D., Fabricius, W., & Braver, S. (2014). Attributions of fathering behaviors among adolescents: The role of gender, ethnicity, family structure, and depressive symptoms. *Journal of Family Issues, 35*(4), 501–525

Flouri, E. (2006). Non-resident fathers' relationships with their secondary school–age children: Determinants and children's mental health outcomes. *Journal of Adolescence, 29*(4), 525–538. doi: 10.1016/j.adolescence.2005/08.004.

Flouri, E., & Buchanan, A. (2003). The role of father involvement in children's later mental health. *Journal of Adolescence, 26*(1), 63–78.

Friedriechs, D. O. (1996). White collar crime and the race–class–gender construct. In M. D. Schwartz & D. Milovanovic (eds.), *Race, gender and class in criminology* (pp. 141–158). New York: Taylor & Francis.

Gambino, R. (1975). *Blood of my blood*. New York: Anchor.

Greeley, A. J., & McCready, W. (1972). *The transmission of cultural heritages: The case of the Irish and the Italians*. Retrieved from ERIC database. (ED068604)

Greenberger, E., & Chen, C. (1996). Perceived family relationships and depressed mood in early and late adolescence: A comparison of European and Asian Americans. *Developmental Psychology, 32*(4), 707.

Hofferth, S. L. (2003). Race/ethnic differences in father involvement in two-parent families: Culture, context, or economy? *Journal of Family Issues, 24*(2), 185–216.

Kotila, L. E., Schoppe-Sullivan, S. J., & Kamp Dush, C. M. (2013). Time parenting activities in dual-earner families at the transition to parenthood. *Family Relations, 62*(5), 795–807.

Krieger, N., Williams, D. R., & Moss, N. E. (1997). Measuring social class in U.S. public health research: Concepts, methodologies, and guidelines. *Annual Review of Public Health, 18*(1), 341–378.

Lamb, M. E. (2000). The history of research on father involvement: An overview. *Marriage and Family Review, 29* (2–3), 23–42.

Lamb, M. E., Pleck, J. H., Charnov, E. L., & Levine, J. A. (1985). Paternal behavior in humans. *American Zoologist, 25*, 883–894.

Lamb, M. E., Pleck, J. H., Charnov, E. L., & Levine, J. A. (1987). A biosocial perspective on paternal behavior and involvement. In J. B. Lancaster, J. Altaman, A. Rossi, & R. L. Sherrod (eds.), *Parenting across the lifespan: Biosocial perspectives* (11–42). New York: Academic.

Lamb, M. E., Pleck, J. H., & Levine, J. A. (1985). The role of the father in child development. In B.B. Lahey & A.E. Kazdin (Eds.), *Advances in clinical child psychology* (pp. 229–266). New York: Plenum.

LaRossa, R. (1988). Fatherhood and social change. *Family Relations, 37*, 451–457.

LaRossa, R. (1997). *The modernization of fatherhood: A social and political history*. Chicago, IL: University of Chicago Press.

Lang, S. N., Schoppe-Sullivan, S. J., Kotila, L. E., Feng, X., Dush, C. M. K., & Johnson, S. C. (2014). Relations between fathers' and mothers' infant engagement patterns in dual-earner families and toddler competence. *Journal of Family Issues, 35*(8), 1107–1127.

Leidy, M. S., Schofield, T. J., Miller, M. A., Parke, R. D., Coltrane, S., Braver, S., Cookston, J., Fabricius, W., Saenz, D., & Adams, M. (2011). Fathering and adolescent adjustment: Variations by family structure and ethnic background. *Fathering, 9*(1), 44–68.

Matsen, A. (2014). *Ordinary magic: Resilience in development*. New York: Guilford Press.

McCubbin, H. I., & McCubbin, M. A. (1988). Typologies of resilient families: Emerging roles of social class and ethnicity. *Family Relations*, 247–254.

McFadden, K. E., & Tamis-LeMonda, C. S. (2013). Fathers in the U.S. In D.W. Schwalb, B.J. Schwalb & M.E. Lamb (eds.), *Fathers in Cultural Context*, 250–276. New York: Routledge.

McLoyd, V. C. (1998). Socioeconomic disadvantage and child development. *American psychologist, 53*(2), 185.

Morman, M. T., & Floyd, K. (2002). A "changing culture of fatherhood": Effects on affectionate communication, closeness, and satisfaction in men's relationships with their fathers and their sons. *Western Journal of Communication*, 66(4), 395–411.

Nair, P., Black, M. M., Schuler, M., Keane, V., Snow, L., Rigney, B. A., & Magder, L. (1997). Risk factors for disruption in primary caregiving among infants of substance abusing women. *Child Abuse and Neglect*, 21(11), 1039–1051.

Palkovitz, R. (1997). Reconstructing "involvement": Expanding conceptualizations of men's caring in contemporary families. In A. Hawkins & D. Dollahite (eds.), *Generative fathering: Beyond deficit perspectives* (pp. 200–216). Thousand Oaks, CA: Sage.

Palkovitz, R. (2002). Involved fathering and child development: Advancing our understanding of good fathering. In C. Tamis-Lamanda & N. Cabrera (eds.), *Handbook of father involvement: Multidisciplinary perspectives* (pp. 119–140). Mahwah, NJ: Lawrence Erlbaum and Associates, Inc.

Palkovitz, R., Dutton, K., & Hull, J. W. (2014). A resource theory of fathering. Paper presented at the National Council on Family Relations, Baltimore, MD (Nov.).

Palkovitz, R., Fagan, J., & Hull, J. (2013). Co-parenting and children's well-being. In N. J. Cabrera & C. S. Tamis-LeMonda (Eds.), *Handbook of father involvement: Multidisciplinary Approaches*, 2nd ed. (pp. 202–219). New York: Routledge.

Parke, R. D., Coltrane, S., Duffy, S., Buriel, R., Dennis, J., Powers, J., French, S., & Widaman, K. F. (2004). Economic stress, parenting, and child adjustment in Mexican American and European American families. *Child Development*, 75(6), 1632–1656.

Perlin, L. I., & Kohn, M. L. (1966). Social class, occupation and parental views: A cross-national study. *American Sociological Review*, 31, 466–479.

Pew Research. (2013). *Second-generation Americans: A portrait of the adult children of immigrants*. www.pewsocialtrends.org/2013/02/07/second-generation-americans/.

Pleck, J. H. (1998). American fathering in historical perspective. In K. V. Hansen & A. L. Garvey (eds.), *Families in the U.S.: Kinship and domestic politics* (pp. 351–361). Philadelphia: Temple University Press.

Pleck, J. H. (2010). Paternal involvement: Revised conceptualization and theoretical linkages with child outcomes. In M. E. Lamb (ed.), *The role of the father in child development* (pp. 58-93). Hoboken, NJ: John Wiley & Sons.

Putnick, D. L., Bornstein, M. H., Hendricks, C., Painter, K. M., Suwalsky, J. T. D., & Collins, W. A. (2010). Stability, continuity, and similarity of parenting stress in European American mothers and fathers across their child's transition to adolescence. *Parenting: Science and Practice*, 10, 60–77.

Randolph, Gayle. (2007). "Why study European Immigrants?" Iowa State University.

Russell, J., & Batalova, J. (2012). *European immigrants in the United States*. www.migrationpolicy.org/article/european-immigrants-united-states.

Smetana, J. G. (1995). Parenting styles and conceptions of parental authority. *Child Development*, 66, 299–316.

Sorensen, E., & Zibman, C. (2001). Getting to know fathers who do not pay child support. *Social Science Review*, 75, 420–434.

Szucs, D. S., & Luebking, S. H. (eds.). (2006). *The source: A guidebook of American Genealogy*, 3rd ed. Provo, UT: Ancestry.

Table 701 (2012). Median income of people in constant (2009) dollars by sex, race, and Hispanic origin: 1990 to 2009. U.S. Census Bureau.

Takaki, R. T. (1987). *From different shores: Perspectives on race and ethnicity in America.* Oxford University Press, 200 Madison Avenue, New York, NY 10016.

Testa, M., Astone, N. M., Krogh, M., & Neckerman, K. M. (1989). Employment and marriage among inner-city fathers. *Annals of the American Academy of Political and Social Science, 501,* 79–91.

Toth, J. F., & Xu, X. (1999). Ethnic and cultural diversity in fathers' involvement: A racial/ethnic comparison of African American, Hispanic, and white fathers. *Youth and Society, 31,* 76–99.

U.S. Census Bureau. (2005). Median household income newsbrief. http://web.archive.org/web/20060903121511/http://www.census.gov/Press-Release/www/releases/archives/income_wealth/005647.html.

U.S. Census Bureau. (2006). www.census.gov/compendia/statab/2006/2006edition.html.

U.S. Department of Labor. (2014). *Employment characteristics of families summary.* www.bls.gov/news.release/famee.nr0.htm.

Varela, R. E., Vernberg, E. M., Sanchez-Sosa, J. J., Riveros, A., Mitchell, M., & Mashunkashey, J. (2004). Anxiety reporting and culturally associated interpretation biases and cognitive schemas: A comparison of Mexican, Mexican American, and European American families. *Journal of Clinical Child and Adolescent Psychology, 33*(2), 237–247.

Vogt Yuan, A., & Hamilton, H. (2006). Stepfather involvement and adolescent well-being: Do mothers and nonresidential fathers matter? *Journal of Family Issues, 27*(9), 1191–1213. doi: 10.1177/019251306289214.

Williams, D. R., Yu, Y., Jackson, J. S., & Anderson, N. B. (1997). Racial differences in physical and mental health socio-economic status, stress and discrimination. *Journal of Health Psychology, 2*(3), 335–351.

Williams, S., & Kelly, F. D. (2005). Relationships among involvement, attachment, and behavioral problems in adolescence: Examining father's influence. *Journal of Early Adolescence, 25*(2), 168–196. doi: 10.1177/0272431604274178

Wilson, M., & Brooks-Gunn, J. (2001). Health status and behaviors of unwed fathers. *Children and Youth Services Review, 23*(4), 377–401.

Zhou, M. (1997). Growing up American: The challenge confronting immigrant children and children of immigrants. *Annual Review of Sociology,* 63–95.

Asia

12

Indian Fathers:
Traditional with Changes on the Horizon

Jaipaul L. Roopnarine and Mine Göl-Güven

Historically, fathering in India has been situated in traditional religious and cultural scripts. Although these scripts remain a strong force in shaping contemporary family relationships and fathering across India, there is some indication that the nature and quality of paternal responsibility toward children may be changing in some segments of Indian society. Recent economic and technological growth, challenges to the old masculinity and patriarchy, maternal employment, and exposure to representations of more egalitarian relationships and lifestyles in western industrialized societies have all affected Indian men's investment in young children. In this chapter, we examine the family structural dynamics within which fathering occurs, religious and social beliefs about Indian men's involvement with children, and paternal involvement during the early and middle childhood years. An attempt is made to include data from studies conducted on fathers within the growing Indian Diaspora. Because of ethnic and cultural variations in how families approach daily life in the different regions of India and the lack of systematic data on Indian fathers, it is rather difficult to speak of "Indian-ness" and Indian fathers in a uniform voice. Nonetheless, as Chaudhary and Shukla (2015) note, despite this diversity there are some common experiences that Indian families and children share across geographic settings. In this review, we rely heavily on prior papers by the first author (Roopnarine & Suppal 2003; Roopnarine, Krishnakumar, & Vadgama 2013) and research conducted mostly in urban settings. With these caveats in mind, we attempt to present some portraits of Indian fathers within a changing and increasingly globalized Indian economy.

THE STRUCTURAL DYNAMICS OF INDIAN FAMILIES

For Indian men fatherhood and fathering occur within a marriage-based system. Marriage is viewed as a lifelong bond that joins families, castes, and cultural and religious systems. Even though marriage is based on the shared ideal of interpersonal harmony between husband and wife and among members of the household (*samanya dharma* or common agreement), social and economic tensions are not uncommon thanks to structural hierarchies in the family and social inequities between men and women imposed by the traditional ideology of masculinity and the gendered distribution of household responsibilities (Chaudhary 2013). Be this as it may, family boundaries are permeable, fluid, and remain elastic during most social transactions. Husbands and wives raise children within a complex system of horizontal (e.g., hierarchical relationship between fathers and sons) and vertical relationships (e.g., the affective components of relationship between husbands and wives are not always close) (Chaudhary 2013). Even in nuclear family households there is a form of emotional extendedness wherein kinship and nonkinship (e.g., *Aya*, neighbors) members care for children alongside or jointly with parents.

Because childhood is seen as a continuous stage from infancy to adulthood (Sarsawathi 1999; Sarsawathi & Dutta 2010), children are exposed to a barrage of individuals with whom they share activities, living spaces, sleeping arrangements, and the general rhythms of daily life. Thus children are constantly in physical proximity to others, whose care may wax or wane depending on the caregiver and age of the child. To illustrate, in a study conducted in Shanti Nagar outside of New Delhi, multiple caregiving seems to increase after 7 months of age from 38 percent to 61 percent, whereas mother care drops precipitously from 56 percent to 32 percent when infants reach 18 months old (Sharma 2000). This fluctuating pattern was observed for other adults as well: Grandmother care peaked between 7 and 11 months old (15% to 24%) and again at 24 months (14% to 17%), caregiving by aunts (8% to 24%), siblings (5% to 14%), and fathers (5% to 16%) peaked between the second and third year of life, and for uncles, a decline was observed at 11 months (14% to 10%) (Sharma 2000). It is not difficult to see how investment by these diverse caregivers are intertwined with and can influence both levels and patterns of men's contributions to childrearing—a point to which we later return.

Within this extended caregiving system, a preferred living arrangement noted by young men and reflected in a majority of Indian families (Chaudhary 2013; Desai et al. 2010), children learn early in their lives that individuals hold different roles based on gender, age, and social class. For example, traditionally and even today men and sons (son preference) are accorded greater importance than women and daughters, higher-caste families enjoy social privileges that are not accorded lower-caste individuals (e.g., Dalits), and elders command more respect than younger persons (Kakar & Kakar 2007). There are specific kinship terms designated to members of the family.

They denote relationship structure, degree of closeness and responsibility toward children, and the respect that should be shown to different family members. The Hindi terms for father (*bap, pita*), paternal grandfather (*dada*), maternal grandfather (*nana*), paternal uncles (*chacha*), and maternal uncles (*mama*) all signal to children the diverse roles and responsibilities that Indian men, in theory, assume in the family and community at large.

Ideally, fatherhood begins in the householder stage (*grhastha*; 26–50 years old)—one of four stages (*asramas*) in the Hindu life cycle. It is in the householder stage that men marry and become fathers. In addition to their responsibilities to neighbors, friends, society and country, there are strong obligations to one's wife, children, and parents. There is also the expectation that fathers be involved in training children and introducing them to accepted religious and cultural practices (Sriram & Navalkar 2012). The seeds of responsible fatherhood are likely planted in the student stage (*bramacharya*, up to 25 years old) but may evolve into different levels and modes of investment beyond the householder stage as fathers move on to the preparatory renunciation (*vanaprastha*; 51–75 years old), and renouncement (*sanyasa asrama*; 76 years and older) stages. The husband–father is revered and has been portrayed in Indian mythology as both a devoted son (*shravan kumar*) and the provider and protector of his family. The father's duty (*dharma*) is to provide for and nurture the spirit of the child. But, as indicated earlier, this depends on who is present and on the nature of social commerce within the family. Within this mixture of structural and social arrangements grounded in religious beliefs, cultural traditions, and economic changes that followed the 1991 reforms, Indian fathers define and carry out the responsibilities of bearing, raising children, and transacting fathering.

IDEOLOGICAL BELIEFS ABOUT MEN'S AND WOMEN'S ROLES

In a number of developed societies (e.g., Sweden, Japan, United States, England), culture-specific scripts about childrearing and behavioral investment in children have been modified considerably over the last three decades. However, even in these societies, some men/fathers may become more involved in childcare and household labor out of necessity rather than choice. That is, behavioral investment in young children may increase ahead of changes in ideological beliefs about men's roles within the family and work place (see chapter 5 of this volume for a discussion of these issues). Although narrowing in the developed world, a gap still exists in what men articulate they should do "in principle" and what they actually do in relation to childcare and household work (e.g., Devreux 2007). From a modernity perspective, household roles and responsibilities should also be moving toward a more equalitarian distribution in developing societies. However, the provider model remains fully entrenched in a number of traditional societies (Georgas, Berry, van de Vijver, Kagitcibasi, & Poortinga 2006; Kagitcibasi 2006).

Household production theory (Becker 1993) suggests that men and women will maximize their functional utility in their decisions about work, domestic roles, and leisure activities. In much of India's recent history, men have enjoyed greater market earnings and exercise more power in the family than women. According to this theory, Indian men may be expected to devote less time in childcare and household work. At the same time, sociological models have emphasized that gender role beliefs and expectations and traditional masculinity place women in a position in which they adjust work identities and roles to meet household responsibilities and that it does not often occur the other way round. Men do not seem to make such adjustments and thus maintain a strong work identity (Bielby & Bielby 1989). In such situations, there is less tension between fathering and work roles. Quite the opposite occurs for women in the IT industry and newly formed companies in India (Ramadoss 2010).

In Hindusim, *Manusmriti* मनुस्मृति (200 BCE), or the "Laws of Manu," provides a narration of traditional ways of living and has been instrumental in influencing men's and women's roles in Indian society. According to Manu's edicts, men hold an upper hand in the family, and women are supposed to display loyalty and devotion (*pativrata*) to their husbands (Chekki 1988; Dhruvarajan 1990; Shukla 1987). Paradoxically, women are accorded Shakti (power) in their roles as mothers (see Kurtz 1992 for a discussion of mother goddesses). These views still persist in most parts of India, and research findings support this contention. Surveys of ideological beliefs about childcare, filial, financial, and household responsibilities between husband and wife pairs in single- and dual-earner, extended, and nuclear families in New Delhi revealed that family members held traditional beliefs about structural–functional roles and that there was good agreement about who should assume primary responsibility for specific activities (Suppal & Roopnarine 1999; Suppal, Roopnarine, Buesig, & Bennett 1996). Subsequent studies have also reported gendered patterns of involvement in childrearing wherein few mothers shared the care of children with their husbands (Tuli & Chaudhary 2010), and beliefs that women should assume primary responsibility for childcare and household work remain strong in different groups of men (Kapoor 2006; Saraff & Srivastava 2008; Sriram, Dave, Khasgiwala, & Joshi 2006). Among a growing middle class, there is persistence of dominant beliefs about what it means to be masculine or a "real man" (*asli mard*), particularly among young men in Mumbai (Verma, et al. 2006). Similar findings have been reported for Bengali families in Shillong (Dutta 2000).

Despite these findings, there is tremendous vagueness about beliefs regarding roles and responsibilities among Indian couples who choose their own marital partners and who are likely to invest more energy in the emotional aspects of marriage and consider issues of equality than couples who follow a traditional path to marriage (Uberoi 2006). Likewise, there is limited understanding of how beliefs about male–female roles and responsibilities are influenced by caste and social class, educational achievement, rural–urban residence patterns, geography, and family structural arrangements. In other words, in a technologically developing India, the fathering role may be changing in relation to the work patterns, economic aspirations of men and women, and the quality of intimate relationships. There is evidence that women's employment outside of the home affects the selection of marital partners and decision making within the family in some regions of India (Dutta 2000; Singh & Ram 2009). Furthermore, in urban settings (Mumbai, Boroda, and Jaipaur), the ideal father is expected to provide guidance, teach, offer friendship, and assist in fostering health and security in children (Saraff & Srivastava 2008; Sriram & Sandhu 2013), and in dual-earner families, people were less likely to view familial roles and responsibilities in traditional terms irrespective of family structural arrangements (Suppal et al. 1996).

To view the Indian family in solely patriarchal terms, then, would mask some of the ideological and structural adjustments that are occurring in a changing economic system (Chaudhary 2013). Men and women in urban settings seem to be making accommodative shifts in their thinking about traditional male roles in Indian society relative to their own social position and scripted spousal responsibilities (Dutta 2000; Kandiyoti 1988). For instance, there is increased insistence by women that fathers become more involved with children (Kumari 2008; Sriram, Karnik, & Ali 2002) and variations in husband–wife closeness and interactions were observed in families who held more conservative beliefs about the virtues of extended family life and arranged marriages in different regions of India (Derne 1995; Desai et al. 2010).

ECONOMIC PROVISION AND PLANNING FOR CHILDREN

It may be safe to say that economic provision for the family and managerial planning for children are central to Indian fathering. One study (Sriram & Sandhu 2013) found impressive levels of commitment to providing material resources and in arranging activities for children (measured as most of the time or always). Eighty-five percent of fathers provided money for their children's educational and social needs: materials for education (86%), recreation (75%), and sports (72%). Equally important, is that Indian fathers display good managerial skills in relation to children's educational and social activities. Ninety percent of fathers planned for children's future needs by choosing children's school and the type of instruction they should receive, 98% saved for children's education, and 73% were involved in procuring important documents for children (e.g., birth certificates, immigration materials). In addition, 75 percent planned children's vacations, and 56 percent made appointments for children (e.g., with teachers, doctors, and friends).

This level of investment in meeting the economic needs and managing specific aspects of children's lives is not unusual in India. The provider model remains fairly intact and flourishes in Indian society as a whole. Furthermore, as stated earlier, the role of providing for one's family is well defined in Indian scriptures, and data on ideological beliefs about men's roles support this premise. Across six studies, a sizeable number of men and women defined the "ideal father" as one who provides for the child's present and future needs (Sriram & Navalkar 2012). These views were echoed among Bangladeshi Muslim, Pakistani Muslim, Gujarati Hindus, and Punjabi Sikh immigrant men in Great Britain, who also emphasized securing their children's future through financial support (Salway, Chowbey, & Clarke 2009). In the Indian context, financial provision may set the stage for other types of social participation, such as the managerial functions that fathers assume. At the very least, it conveys to children that fathers are around and involved in their lives. An examination of more sustained involvement in the day to day care of children permits a broader gaze of men's roles in India.

FATHERS' INVOLVEMENT IN DAY-TO-DAY CARE OF CHILDREN

With respect to paternal investment and involvement with children, there have been challenges to the father as provider model worldwide. Newer models of fathering consider several dimensions of men's involvement in the family: paternity and economic responsibilities toward children, the emotional support provided to a spouse, the division of childcare responsibilities, and the effects of male investment and benefits to children (Pleck 2010). The involved father model, in which fathers assume more responsibility for basic childcare and emotional and cognitive investment in children has taken front seat in some societies (e.g., Sweden). This has forced men to look at the competing demands of work and childcare responsibilities and there are discourses about morally intelligible fathering where men consider childcare responsibilities relative to the pressures and demands of the work environment (Björk 2013). The extent to which this "new fathering" construct is realized in India has received some attention in studies that have attempted to define what men actually do in families. But there has been little consideration of the "new father" and emotional and physical adjustments in caring for children within the extended family. From the data described below, it is difficult to say whether there are shifts in male parenting, because cohort studies have not been undertaken between the old and new economic order and the possible changes in family roles in India.

In an interview study of men in Mumbai, Saraff and Srivastav (2010) found that only 13 percent of men frequently had sole responsibility for the child, 5 percent frequently changed the child's diaper, 11 percent frequently put the child to bed, 6.3 percent frequently bathed and dressed the child, and 7.4 percent frequently fed the child. Strikingly, 33 percent never had sole responsibility for the child, 16 percent never fed the child, 32 percent never bathed the child, 21 percent never put the child to bed, and 33 percent never changed the child's diaper. These trends were also obtained for nurturing and disciplining children: 75 percent of fathers never or rarely disciplined their children. This is interesting considering that one of the cultural prescriptions is that Indian fathers should offer guidance to children. It is likely that the lack of involvement in physical control on the part of Indian fathers could be an artifact of the greater caregiving involvement of women and other female caregivers who have greater opportunities to attend to child guidance issues. In other cultural settings in Thailand, China, and the Philippines, differences between maternal and paternal rejection–hostility–neglect were negligible (Putnick et al. 2012).

On average, fathers reported spending 2.7 hours in childcare responsibilities (mothers' report on fathers' involvement was 2.8 hours) with older children in Mumbai (Saraff & Srivastava 2010). Higher levels of involvement were found for fathers with preschool-aged children in New Delhi; fathers in single-wage, nuclear families spent 5 hours in primary childcare compared to 4.06 hours for fathers in single-wage, nuclear families, 4.84 hours for fathers in dual-wage, nuclear families, and 4.38 hours for fathers in dual-wage, extended families (Suppal & Roopnarine 1999). In these studies, fathers' socialization responsibility (setting limits, helping children learn, helping children with personal problems), childcare responsibility (e.g., feeding, bathing, dressing, and putting child to bed), decision making regarding discipline and child readiness to try new things, and availability to children (present at home for specified periods) were not significantly different from those of mothers..

A comparison of paternal involvement in the 1990s before the economic transformation and in Mumbai between 2003 and 2007, a period when India's economic growth was impressive showed minor differences in men's behavior over time. With the exception of childcare responsibility, the two groups of fathers appear similar in socialization responsibility, involvement in decision-making, and availability to children. . These samples of men were from urban areas and had high levels of educational attainment and may not be representative of most fathers in India. However, thanks to economic pressures and work patterns, it is in these urban, educated, and "more progressive" families that change in paternal roles is more likely to occur.

An area of research that has received considerable attention across societies is parenting styles. Per Baumrind's parenting typologies, researchers have
examined the prevalence of authoritarian, authoritative, and permissive
styles of parental engagement across cultures (see Lipps et al. 2012; Sorkhabi
2005). Others have employed Rohner's interpersonal acceptance–rejection
theory (IPARTheory) (Rohner & Khaleque 2005; Khaleque & Rohner 2012)
to examine parental acceptance, control, rejection, hostility, and aggression
in different cultural settings as well. Together, these two related bodies of
work have shown that the construct parental warmth and responsive is linked
to positive childhood outcomes, whereas detached and harsh behaviors are
related to negative childhood outcomes (e.g., internalizing and externalizing behaviors). Again, data of this nature are nonexistent in Indian cultural
communities. Nevertheless, it has been suggested that Indian parents adopt
a "traditional parenting style" where parental control is seen as caring, not
an imposition. Saraswathi and Dutta (2010) characterize Indian parenting as
the "greater use of power assertion among the lower classes and more use of
induction in the middle and upper classes." The meager findings on Indian
fathers' parenting practices indicate that men do engage in limit setting,
implementing rules and guiding children in following them, and monitoring
children's behaviors (Sriram & Sandhu 2013). The emotional qualities of
these exchanges are not known.

One may reasonably assume that cultural scripts about childrearing may
change when families move from traditional to less traditional societies
where more egalitarian roles are highly valued. Two studies conducted on
Indian immigrant men in the United States are instructive in this regard.
Among young children (18–44 months) of East Indian immigrants in the
United States, fathers were classified as "caretaker," "engaged," and "disengaged." The group designated "engaged" showed higher levels of involvement in disciplining (guidance, teaching manners, praising appropriate
behavior, and prohibiting and punishing inappropriate ones) and teaching
children (reading, building, labeling objects) than caretaker and disengaged
fathers. Caretaker fathers engaged in more basic caregiving activities than
the other groups. Not surprisingly, disengaged fathers were low in all levels
of father involvement assessed. Fathers who were the least acculturated and
maintained a high level of traditionalism were the least involved with children; those who were better acculturated to U.S. cultural practices were more
involved with children (Jain & Belsky 1997).

In a sample of Indian immigrant parents and adolescents living in Houston,
Texas, mothers were more apt to socialize their children toward "American
values" than fathers were; fathers were more likely to maintain traditional
values and instill them in their children. For instance, traditional fathers of
girls were more likely to stress politeness, manners, and deference to adults

and less likely to stress competence and effectiveness than "modern" fathers. There was a lack of association between modernity in fathers and competence and effectiveness in boys. Interestingly, these traditional fathers were low on modernity but high on acculturation to American mainstream values. Modernity was positively related to reasoning and persuasion and negatively to psychological control used by parents during socialization (Patel, Power, & Bhavnagri 1996). Another study of Indian immigrants in England showed that social support was linked through paternal negativity to children's internalizing behaviors (Atzaba-Poria & Pike 2005).

These findings on immigrant fathers paint a more complex picture than the one we constructed for men in the Indian context. While the role of modernity and traditionalism seems to influence Indian immigrant fathers' level and quality of participation with children, the roles of fathers and mothers seem to evolve in different directions. Fathers adopt of more active stance in maintaining continuity in socialization beliefs and practices that are consonant with the natal culture whereas mothers did not (Patel et al. 1996; Salway et al. 2009). Away from the Indian context, women may find the freedom to instill competence and effectiveness in daughters than fathers who may still believe in the protection of daughters. Alternatively, it may take longer for Indian men to revise their traditional ideological beliefs about roles in the family that, in the past, have been beneficial to them.

FATHERS' EMOTIONAL INVESTMENT IN CHILDREN

The emotional distance between Indian fathers and children has been discussed by several leading figures of Indian psychology. For example, using psychoanalytic interpretations and Indian mythology, Kakar (1992) and Kurtz (1992) stress the importance of maternal figures (*Uma, Sarsawati, Lakshmi*) and the peripheral role of fathers in the young child's life. A few (Kakar 1992) went so far as to say that the Indian child has an exclusive attachment to the mother and that the father did not figure prominently in children's lives during the early childhood years. Are these claims about the centrality of female caregivers and the peripheral role of Indian fathers justified in contemporary India?

A voluminous attachment literature points to the importance of the early mother-child bond for setting the stage for children's early and later social and cognitive development (Ainsworth 1989; Ainsworth, Blehar, Waters, & Wall 1978). In recent years, this body of work has benefited from insights provided by studies of father–child attachment and the qualitative aspects of father–child relationships (see volumes by Cabrera & Tamis-LeMonda 2013; Lamb 2010). For instance, research shows that in European and European-heritage groups, most men will witness the birth of their children, mothers and fathers display equal levels of sensitivity to infants during the first year of life (Schoppe-Sullivan et al. 2008), the relationship between paternal attachment representation and father–infant attachment is moderately good (De Wolff & van Ijzendoorn 1997), and fathers engage in qualitatively different types of interactions and play activities with children compared to mothers (Lamb 1977, 2010). Furthermore, the primacy of parents' warmth and responsiveness to children's social cues and overtures for childhood development has been demonstrated across several cultures (see meta-analysis by Khaleque & Rohner 2012).

Comparable work in the Indian context is rare, but some survey and observational studies have provided useful insights into the nature of the support offered by fathers to their wives during pregnancy and on the frequency of early father-child social interactions. One study (Singh & Ram 2009) conducted in rural Ahmadnagar, India assessed (a) the presence of men during prenatal visits and childbirth, (b) support provided during pregnancy, and (c) involvement in decision making with respect to where the delivery should occur and by whom. Husbands indicated that 92 percent of the wives made prenatal visits (63 percent during the first trimester), in 81 percent of the cases both husbands and wives decided jointly to access prenatal care, and 81 percent of the men accompanied their wives on prenatal visits. Higher levels of education and egalitarian attitudes seem to increase men's involvement in prenatal visits. More than half of the men (52%) were present at the birth of their last child; men in nuclear households, those with higher educational attainment (above high school), those with a good standard of living, and those who were older than 34 and who had more than two living children showed a greater likelihood of being present at the delivery. However, only 25 percent of husbands (18% of wives reported receiving support) reported offering emotional support and assistance to their wives during pregnancy. The effect of such investment during pregnancy on later father–child attachment and relationship is not known at this point.

In a rather interesting display of interest in the birth process, fathers in a southern Indian group go through a series of ritualistic practices. Among the Erickala-Vandu, as soon as the woman goes into labor, she tells the father, who then wears the woman's clothes and lays in a bed in a dimly lit room covered with a long sheet. After the baby is born and cleaned, it is placed on a cot next to the father (as described in Parke 1996). The subsequent involvement of these men in early basic caregiving is not clear. Another study (Karande & Perkar 2012) did show that Indian fathers had very favorable attitudes toward breast-feeding during the first year of life and their attitudes were significantly correlated with maternal attitudes toward breast-feeding. Attitudes toward breast-feeding were related to several aspects of infant care and development such as optimal nutritional value, digestion, mother–infant bonding, and the long-term health of the infant. Paternal attitudes were not related to duration of breast-feeding (Karande & Perkar 2012).

A study by Roopnarine and his colleagues (Roopnarine, Talukder, Jain, Joshi, & Srivastava 1990) examined patterns of social interactions between fathers and one-year-old infants in New Delhi, India. Of importance here are the findings on holding, sensitively attuned caregiving, and social–affiliative behaviors, all considered important for the development of attachment relationships to parents. During in-home observation periods, fathers held their infants about 25 percent as much as mothers did (on average 1.15 minutes compared to 4.65 minutes for the mother during 60 minutes of observations). This level of paternal holding by Indian fathers (2 percent of the time observed) is similar to those assessed for Taiwanese fathers (2 percent) (Sun & Roopnarine 1996) but lower than those of Aka foragers (22 percent).

Contrary to prior assertions about the lack of an emotionally close relationship between Indian fathers and young children, fathers were equally as likely to display physical affection (hugging and kissing) to infants as mothers did and, on average, expressed similar frequencies of social–affiliative behaviors, such as smiling, vocalizing, offering, and accepting objects from infants. For their part, infants approached and touched their fathers and mothers about equally. However, infants did smile and vocalize to their mothers more than they did to their fathers. In other cultural settings in Asia such as Taiwan (Sun & Roopnarine 1996) and Thailand (Tulananda & Roopnarine 2001) observational data showed that fathers also displayed as much affection to infants and preschoolers as mothers did, and in a study of kangaroo care, Indian fathers who carried their babies in skin-to-skin contact received higher sensitivity scores than fathers who did not (Verla et al. 2014). However, self-reports of parental warmth indicated that Chinese and Thai but not Filipino fathers expressed less warmth to 7- to 10-year-old children than mothers did (Putnick et al. 2012). Nonetheless, the display of warmth was high among Thai and Filipino fathers. These data begin to question popular characterizations of the emotional distance that fathers in India and other Asian societies display toward young children.

Parent–child play is heralded as important for the development of a variety of social and cognitive skills in children (see Pellegrini 2011) and has been the focus of a few investigations in India. Play interactions between Indian fathers and infants were relatively low when compared to self-reports of how many Indian fathers (38%) played indoors and outdoors with older children (Sriram & Sandhu 2013) and to rates of play between fathers and children in North American and European communities (see Roopnarine 2011 for a review). Notably, the physical play that is so characteristic of early father–child interactions in some societies (see Paquette 2004; Tamis-LeMonda 2004) was observed at low frequencies between Indian men and infants.

So too, were frequencies of peek-a-boo and object-mediated play. Low levels of play were also witnessed in the interactions between fathers and children in Taiwan and Thailand, and Kadazan mothers in Malaysia exceeded fathers in total levels of play with young children (Hossain, Roopnarine, Isamel, Menon, & Sombuling 2008; Sun & Roopnarine 1996; Tulananda & Roopnarine 2001). In some of these societies, fathers may use other mechanisms, such as storytelling and general conversations, to provide social and cognitive stimulation to young children. Play may not be as viable an avenue through which children form close emotional relationships with fathers as they do in communities in North America. Rather, parental socialization goals (allocentrism) and expectations for children (relational goals) in the Indian cultural milieu may have a greater hand in determining what behavioral mechanisms are salient for the development of close relationships with fathers (Keller, Borke, Chaudhary, Lamm, & Kleis 2010).

FATHERS' INVOLVEMENT IN CHILDREN'S EDUCATION

There is a high premium placed on educational achievement (*gaan* or knowledge) at the local and societal levels in India. The Vedas (Hindu doctrines) outline the importance of education and suggest that learning and the acquisition of knowledge begins in childhood (*Balya*). These beliefs are further reinforced by worshipping and paying respect to the importance of *Saraswati*, the goddess of learning and knowledge, as a path to enlightenment. As already indicated, in Hindusim, the *dharmasastra*, or religious scriptures, confer on the father the role of teacher. In keeping with this emphasis, our consideration of paternal investment in children's cognitive development here is restricted to involvement in academically-related activities.

In their study of fathers in Mumbai, Saraff and Srivastava (2010) reported that 50 percent of fathers assisted children with homework (58% of mothers did) and 51 percent helped children learn (47% of mothers did) sometimes or frequently. Basically identical findings on educational investment were obtained in another study (Sriram & Sandhu 2013) of older children, some of whom were adolescents, from Baroda, Gujarat. Forty-four percent of fathers arranged study times for children, 57 percent attended parent–teacher meetings and school activities, 53 percent monitored the child's progress in school, and 74 percent exposed children to literature and books most of the time.

Data on immigrant fathers in North America and Europe also shed some light on Indian fathers' engagement in educational training. Given their high success in educational achievement in North America, it is possible that first generation Indian immigrants strive to maximize the potential for success in North America through hard work and sacrifice. Accordingly, it might be argued that Indian immigrant fathers would be keen in investing in the future of their children. In a study conducted in the northeastern United States, Sanghavi (2010) examined fathers' and mothers' levels of involvement in academic socialization with children at home and their level of parent–school engagement. A goal of the study was to explore whether cultural identity influenced parents' involvement on these two constructs. Mothers and fathers were classified as either bicultural (blending natal and U.S. cultural values and beliefs) or as having maintained their Indian identity after migrating (on average 12.6 years for fathers and 11.1 years for mothers) to the United States. Mothers were significantly more likely to engage in academic work (e.g., homework, checks work brought home from school), extracurricular activities (e.g., participate in games, takes child to playground), and educational activities (e.g., growing plants, takes child to library) with children outside of school and were more involved with their children's school than fathers were. However, there were no differences on these measures between mothers and fathers as a function of cultural identity. That is, a greater identification with natal culture values did not influence maternal or paternal involvement in these activities at home (Sanghavi 2010); in other work, parental stress and social support did not, either (Londhe 2014). The levels of investment by these immigrant fathers in the United States were far greater than those determined for Bangladeshi Muslim, Pakistani Muslim, Gujarati Hindus, and Punjabi Sikhs residing in Great Britain (Salway, Chowbey, & Clarke 2009).

In short, in a few communities in India and the United States, well-educated, economically secure mothers and fathers were highly involved in the academic socialization of their grade school children who excelled on standardized measures of academic performance (Sanghavi 2010). Among Bangladeshi Muslim, Pakistani Muslim, Gujarati Hindus, and Punjabi Sikh families in Great Britain, who were not as economically privileged, fathers appeared preoccupied with other family responsibilities (e.g., family economics and security) and spoke less about the educational needs of children. This could possibly be attributed to differences in acculturation where the effect of immigrant drive may fade in subsequent generations. Some of the fathers in Great Britain were second-generation immigrants, whereas all the fathers in the United States were first-generation immigrants.

MULTIPLE CAREGIVING: THE FATHER IS IN THE PICTURE

In several societies around the world, multiple caregiving is a distinct feature of early childhood socialization. For example, in Trinidad and Tobago, 44.2 percent of care interactions originated with mothers, 17.6 percent with grandparents, 16.3 percent with siblings, 10.3 percent with fathers, 7.2 percent with distant kin and nonrelatives, and 4.5 percent by aunts and uncles, and in South Africa, children refer to uncles (father's younger brother (*ubaba omncane*) or older brothers (*ubaba omkhulu*)) as their own father (see chapter 18 of this volume; Hunter 2006). These childrearing alliances are seen in North America as well (e.g., among African Americans; Fouts, Roopnarine, Lamb, & Evans 2012). Yet much of the theorizing and research on fathers across the world has focused on the two-parent heterosexual model and co-parenting (see Pleck 2010). Maternal gatekeeping has also been introduced by some researchers as an impediment to father involvement (Schoppe-Sullivan, et al. 2008). The relevance of these conceptual frameworks for paternal engagement in Indian society at this time is undetermined.

Multiple caregiving among Indians and the levels of investment by multiple caregivers were introduced at the beginning of this chapter. In view of the emphasis placed on mother goddesses and women in childrearing (Kakar 1992; Kakar & Kakar 2007) and blood ties in surrogacy that bind caregivers and children (Pande 2009), are Indian fathers' levels of involvement with children influenced by these other female caregivers in the family? Does this shared practice of caregiving produce conflict and confusion? Accepting the premise that most Indian children grow up within a system of kinship and nonkinship caregivers, it is not difficult to see that in favorable situations most men/fathers work directly or indirectly with others to promote the general welfare and psychological well-being of their children. Despite cultural childrearing scripts about the primary role of mothers and other female caregivers in meeting children's daily needs, it is our contention that in the Indian context, fathers are not "squeezed out" of the childrearing situation by female caregivers.

According to Roopnarine et al. (1992), in households in which relatives were present (grandparents, aunts, uncles, and siblings, among others), East Indian mothers and fathers were more likely to pick up, smile at, and vocalize to infants than were relatives. But there were no significant differences in other areas of participation, such as play, soothing, and the display of affection between mothers, fathers, and relatives. Similarly, infants were more likely to smile at, approach, follow, touch, and offer objects to mothers than relatives and to touch and smile at fathers more than they did relatives. These findings suggest that the care of relatives did not necessarily supplant the care offered by fathers.

Among the Ongees of the Little Andaman Islands in the Bay of Bengal, the general belief is that children should interact with all members of the family (Pandya 1992). Young Ongee boys and girls address all men as fathers (*omoree*) and nonmaternal figures as *maikuta* (maternal relatives). After marriage boys refer to other men as *inerare* (not an outsider). Children are presented with a myriad of social opportunities to interact with different men with the potential of forming social bonds with one or more of them. More specifically, boys engage in play with different men with whom they have close social ties. Such relationships are not inimical to the ones they develop with their fathers or, for that matter, female caregivers. Children seem to profit from exposure to different paternal models, none of whom resents the child.

Not unlike the Ongees, we propose that Indian children are in close contact with multiple male figures who in most cases collaborate with female caregivers in meeting their emotional, cognitive, religious, and cultural needs. Along with female caregivers, fathers and male relatives lay a foundation for children to navigate, process, and incorporate different elements of their social worlds. This is not an automatic or seamless process. Depending on beliefs, the number of caregivers in the extended family, economic conditions and modes of production, among other factors, the contributions of fathers may be of primary or secondary importance at different times and situations. Fathers may not always have access to the interior aspects of care or may simply relinquish basic care during the early childhood years to mothers and other female caregivers. Likewise, tensions may exist between male and female caregivers about the socialization goals and practices regarding sons and daughters. Nonetheless, the Indian father's presence is felt or invoked even when other caregivers are administering to the child. In this sense, the father does not compete but cooperates with other caregivers in a collective responsibility of raising the Indian child. The Indian father's presence in the family is grossly underestimated.

GENDER OF CHILD AND PATERNAL INVOLVEMENT

It would be a gross oversight if we did not consider paternal involvement and the differential treatment of boys and girls in India. Cultural beliefs bemoan the benefits that boys bring by inheriting the family name (son preference) and caring for parents in old age, and it is well documented that overall, boys are treated better than girls. Girls have differential access to schooling and medical care, have higher mortality rates, and are given less resources during economic downturns (see Das Gupta & Li 1999; Lundberg 2005 for a discussion of son preference). More concretely, in the Mewat region of Haryana, boys were more likely to be cared for by mothers-in-law and older siblings (75% of boys received adequate care compared to 44% of girls) and to be breastfed exclusively during the first six months than were girls (84% versus 64%). Boys were given additional food sooner and were weaned later than were girls (16 versus 11 months of breastfeeding) (Jatrana 2010). Parallel findings have been reported on the greater length of breastfeeding offered to boys and the growth advantage this has on boys' height and weight (Barcellos, Carvalho, Lleras-Muney 2014). Does this type of treat-ment extend to boys during father–child social contacts?

From the small number of studies on the caregiving interactions of fathers in India and the diaspora, child sex differences were hardly visible during the early childhood years. In the New Delhi infant study discussed earlier, moth-ers and fathers engaged in similar rates of social interactions with boys and girls across a range of social behaviors (Roopnarine et al. 1990 1992), and in Sanghavi's (2010) study of Indian immigrant families with children in the middle childhood period, no significant differences were found in academic socialization and school engagement between mothers and fathers of boys and mothers and fathers of girls. As can be gathered from the previous sec-tion, this changed when assessments were done on older children (Patel et al. 1996). The differential socialization of boys and girls are deeply entrenched in the psyche of the Indian people, and much more needs doing to unmask these socialization practices in contemporary Indian society.

FUTURE DIRECTIONS AND POLICY IMPLICATIONS

In Indian scriptures and mythology, men and fathers are accorded quite a bit of attention. The *Ramanaya* celebrates the devotion of father to son (e.g., Lord Rama), the *Shastras* discuss the differentiated roles and responsibilities of men and women, and taking care of one's family is viewed as one's *dharma* (duty). Yet in this old civilization of more than 1 billion people, fathers have received little attention in scholarly circles. This overview is based on a relatively small number of studies. To build on this slim body of work, studies on Indian fathers have to be considered in the context of cultural, social, environmental, and religious factors and the effects of these factors on spousal relationships, parental roles, and parent–child interaction patterns (Roopnarine et al. 2013). Although ideological beliefs about masculinity, ideal men, household roles and responsibilities in India are often predeter-mined by religious and cultural traditions, Indian men and women who are parents of young children are in the process of forging new partnerships and becoming more involved and caring parents. This is particularly so among younger urban, educated men. A fruitful step would involve augmenting the research literature with additional studies on marital relationships, men's support of their wives during pregnancy and childbirth, and father–infant relationships across socioeconomic and religious groups, family constella-tions, and regions, not to mention the changing nature of the work lives of men and women (Ramadoss 2010). As Saraswathi and Dutta (2010) have surmised, participants in psychological research in India "are urban, middle-class, school or college-going children and youth who represent approxi-mately 40% of the population. The remaining 60%, who constitute the less privileged (rural, poor, tribal, nonschooled)" (p. 467), rarely participate in research studies.

At the policy level, both grassroots and national initiatives must target men's internal working models or ethnotheories about caring for young children. This is no easy task, for fatherhood and fathering are braided by religious doctrines, a history of patriarchy that continues to this day, and the oppression of women. Untangling the existence of these different elements in the daily lives of Indian families must be done in the context of a human rights perspective and in accordance with an examination of women's roles and aspirations within a changing economic climate. The economic and emotional control that men exercise within the family often disregards the changes that women have marshaled and continue to marshal to address parenting, spousal, and work roles. At the national level, policies need to focus on marital rights, paternal leave (currently India has a twelve-week leave period for women only), and more precise definitions of paternal responsibilities (e.g., child-centered approaches to parenting) within an economic feasibility model. Some of the other BRIC countries have passed laws focusing on family rights that have defined paternal responsibility in diverse family systems (see chapter 3, this volume). At the local level, community-based programs such as Manav Sadhana of the Gandhi Ashram in Ahmedabad, Gujarat, and India's vast early childhood education infrastructure can be used as a conduit for information about the influences of fathers in children's lives during the formative years, the need to become involved in pregnancy and prenatal care, and the role of fathers in the early care and education of children. In both cases, electronic media can be used to highlight and send messages to men about the important roles fathers play in the lives of children not to mention their rights to optimal parenting.

WEBSITES

www.unicef.org/infobycountry/india_statistics.html
www.in.undp.org/content/india/en/home/mdgoverview/overview/mdg3/
www.un.org/esa/socdev/family/docs/men-in-families.pdf

REFERENCES

Ainsworth, M. D. S. (1989). Attachments beyond infancy. *American Psychologist, 44*, 709–716.

Ainsworth, M. D. S., Blehar, M. C., Waters, E., & Wall, S. (1978). *Patterns of attachment: A psychological study of the strange situation*. Hillsdale, NJ: Erlbaum.

Atzaba-Poria, N. & Pike, A. (2005). Why do ethnic minority (Indian) children living in Britain display more internalizing problems than their English peers?

The role of social support and parental style as mediators. *International Journal of Behavioral Development, 29*, 532–540.

Barcellos, S. H., Carvalho, L. S., & Lleras-Muney, A. (2014). Child gender and parental investments in India: Are boys and girls treated differently? *American Economic Journal: Applied Economics, 6*(1), 157–189.

Becker, G. (1993). *Human capital: A theoretical and empirical analysis, with special reference to education*, 3rd ed. Chicago: University of Chicago Press.

Bielby, W. T., & Bielby, D. D. V. (1989). Family ties: Balancing commitments to work and family in dual earner households. *American Sociological Review, 54*(5), 776–789.

Björk, S. (2013). Doing morally intelligible fatherhood: Swedish fathers' accounts of their parental part-time work choices. *Fathering, 11*(2), 221–237.

Cabrera, N. J., & Tamis-LeMonda, C. S. (2013). *Handbook of father involvement: Multidisciplinary perspectives*, 2nd ed. New York: Routledge.

Chaudhary, N. (2013). The father's role in the Indian family. In D. Shwalb, B. Shwalb, & M. E. Lamb (eds.), *Fathers in cultural context* (pp. 68–94). New York: Routledge.

Chaudhary, N., & Shukla, S. (2015). "Children's work is to play": Beliefs and practices related to childhood play among Indians. In J. L. Roopnarine, M. Patte, J. E. Johnson, & D. Kuschner (eds.), *Children's play in international perspective*. London: Open University Press/McGraw-Hill.

Chekki, D. A. (1988). Recent directions in family research: India and North America. *Journal of Comparative Family Studies, 19*, 171–186.

Das Gupta, M., & Li, S. (1999). Gender bias in China, the Republic of Korea, and India 1920–90: Effects of war, famine, and fertility decline. Policy Research Working Paper Series 2140, The World Bank.

Derne, S. (1995). *Culture in action: Family life, emotion, and male dominance in Banaras, India*. Albany, NY: SUNY Press.

Desai, S., Dubey, A., Joshi, B., Sen, M., Sharrif, A., & Vannenman, R. (2010). *Human development in India: Challenges for a society in transition*. New York: Oxford University Press.

Devreux, A. M. (2007). "New fatherhood" in practice: Domestic and paternal work performed by men in France and in the Netherlands. *Journal of Comparative Family Studies, 37*, 87–103.

De Wolff, M., & van IJzendoorn, M. (1997). Sensitivity and attachment: A meta-analysis on parental antecedents of infant attachment. *Child Development, 68*, 571–591.

Dhruvarajan, V. (1990). Religious ideology, Hindu women and development in India. *Journal of Social Issues, 46*, 57–69.

Dutta, M. (2000). Women's employment and its effects on Bengali households of Shillong, India. *Journal of Comparative Family Studies, 31*(2), 217–229.

Fouts, H., Roopnarine, J. L., Lamb, M. E., & Evans, M. (2012). Infant social partners and multiple caregivers: The importance of ethnicity and socioeconomic status. *Journal of Cross-Cultural Psychology, 43*(2), 328–348.

Georgas, J., Berry, J. W., van de Vijver, F. J. R., Kagitcibasi, C., & Poortinga, Y. H. (2006). *Families across cultures: A 30-nation psychological study*. Cambridge, UK: Cambridge University Press.

Hossain, Z., Roopnarine, J. L., Isamel, R., Menon, S., & Sombuling, A. (2008). Fathers' and mothers' reports of involvement in caring for infants in Kadazan families in Sabah, Malaysia. *Fathering, 5*, 58–78.

Hunter, M. (2006). Father without amandla: Zulu-speaking men and fatherhood. In L. Richter & R. Morell (eds.), *Baba: Men and fatherhood in South Africa* (pp. 99–107). Cape Town, South Africa: HSRC Press.

Jain, A., & Belsky, J. (1997). Fathering and acculturation: Immigrant Indian families with young children. *Journal of Marriage and the Family, 59*, 873–883.

Jatrana, S. (2010). Indian fathers: Family dynamics and investment patterns. *Psychology and Developing Societies, 25*(2), 223–247.

Kagitcibasi, C. (2006). Theoretical perspectives on family change. In J. Georgas, J. W. Berry, F. J. van der Vijver, C. Kagitcibasi & Y. H. Poortinga (eds.), *Families across cultures: A 30-nation psychology study* (pp. 72–89). Cambridge, UK: Cambridge University Press.

Kakar, S. (1992). *The inner world.* New Delhi, India: Oxford University Press.

Kakar, S., & Kakar, K. (2007). *The Indians: Portrait of a people.* New Delhi, India: Viking.

Kandiyoti, D. (1988). Bargaining with patriarchy. *Gender and Society, 2*, 274–289.

Kapoor, S. (2006). Alternate care for infants of employed mothers. Unpublished doctoral dissertation of the Department of Child and Family Development, Lady Irwin College, University of Delhi, India.

Karande, S., & Perkar, S. (2012). Do fathers' attitudes support breastfeeding? A cross-sectional questionnaire-based study, Mumbai, India. *Indian Journal of Medical Sciences, 66*(1), 30–39.

Keller, H., Borke, J., Chaudhary, N., Lamm, B., & Kleis, A. (2010). Continuity in parenting strategies: A cross-cultural comparison. *Journal of Cross-cultural Psychology, 41*(3), 391–409.

Khaleque, A., & Rohner, R. P. (2012). Transnational relations between perceived parental acceptance and personality dispositions of children and adults: A meta-analytic review. *Personality and Social Psychology Review, 16*, 103–115. doi:10.1177/1088868311418986.

Kumari, A. (2008). Father involvement as children view it. Unpublished master's dissertation, Department of Human Development and Family Studies, Maharaja Sayajiaro University of Baroda, Boaroda, India.

Kurtz, S. N. (1992). *All the mothers are one: Hindu India and the cultural reshaping of psychoanalysis.* New York: Columbia University Press.

Lamb, M. (1977). Father–infant and mother–infant interaction in the first year of life. *Child Development, 48*, 167–181.

Lamb, M. E. (ed.). (2010). *The role of the father in child development,* 5th ed. New York: Wiley.

Lipps, G., Lowe, G. A., Gibson, R. C., Halliday, S., Morris, Clarke, A. N., & Wilson, R. N. (2012). Parenting and depressive symptoms among adolescents in four Caribbean societies. *Child and Adolescent Psychiatry and Mental Health,* 31

Londhe, R. (2014). Acculturation of Asian Indian parents: Relationship with parent and child characteristics. *Early Child Development and Care.* doi:10.1080/0300 4430.2014.939650.

Lundberg, S. (2005). Sons, daughters, and parental behavior. *Oxford Review of Economic Policy, 21*(3), 340–356.

Pande, A. (2009). It may be her eggs but it's my blood: Surrogates and everyday forms of kinship in India. *Qualitative Sociology, 32*, 379–397.

Pandya, V. (1992). Gukwelonone: The games of hiding fathers and seeking sons among the Ongee of Little Andaman. In B. S. Hewlett (ed.), *Father–child relations: Cultural and biosocial contexts* (pp. 263–279). New York: Aldine De Gruyter.

Paquette, D. (2004). Dichotomizing paternal and maternal functions as a means to better understand their primary contributions. *Human Development, 47*, 237–238.

Parke, R. (*1996*). *Fatherhood*. Cambridge, MA: Harvard University Press.

Patel, N., Power, T. G., & Bhavnagri, N. (1996). Socialization values and practices of Indian immigrant parents: Correlates of modernity and acculturation. *Child Development, 67*, 302–313.

Pellegrini, A. D. (ed.). (2011). In *The Oxford Handbook of Play* (pp. 19–37). New York: Oxford University Press.

Pleck, J. H. (2010). Paternal involvement: Revised conceptualization and theoretical linkages with child outcomes. In M. E. Lamb (ed.), *The role of the father in child development*, 5th ed. (pp. 67–107). New York: Wiley.

Putnick, D. L., Bornstein, M. H., Lansford, J. E., Chang, L., Deater-Deckard, K., Di Giunta, L., . . . Bombi, A. S. (2012). Agreement in mother and father acceptance–rejection, warmth, and hostility/rejection/neglect of children across nine countries. *Cross-cultural Research, 46*, 191–223.

Ramadoss, K. (2010). Job demand, family organizational culture and positive spillover from work-to-work among families in the information technology enabled services in India. *International Journal of Business and Social Science, 22*, 33–41.

Rohner, R. P., & Khaleque, A. (eds.). (2005). *Handbook for the study of parental acceptance and rejection*, 4th ed. Storrs, CT: Rohner Research Publications.

Roopnarine, J. L. (2011). Cultural variations in beliefs about play, parent–child play, and children's play: Meaning for childhood development. In A. D. Pellegrini (ed.), *The Oxford Handbook of Play* (pp. 19–37). New York: Oxford University Press.

Roopnarine, J. L., Krishnakumar, A., & Vadgama, D. (2013). Indian fathers: Family dynamics and investment patterns. *Psychology and Developing Societies, 25*, 223–247.

Roopnarine, J. L., & Suppal, P. (2003). Kakar's psychoanalytic interpretation of Indian childhood: The need to emphasize the father and multiple caregivers in the socialization equation. In D. Sharma (ed.), *Childhood family and sociocultural change in India: Reinterpreting the inner world* (pp. 115–137). New Delhi, India: Oxford University Press.

Roopnarine, J. L., Talukder, E., Jain, D., Joshi, P., & Srivastav, P. (1990). Characteristics of holding, patterns of play and social behaviors between parents and infants in New Delhi, India. *Developmental Psychology, 26*, 667–673.

Roopnarine, J.L., Talukder, E., Jain, D., Joshi, P., & Srivastav, P. (1992). Personal well-being, kinship tie and mother-infant and father-infant interactions in single-wage and dual-wage families in New Delhi, India. *Journal of Marriage and the Family, 54*, 293–301.

Salway, S., Chowbey, P., & Clarke, L. (2009). *Parenting in modern Britain: Experiences of Asian fathers in the UK.* York, UK: Joseph Roundtree Foundation.

Sanghavi, T. (2010). *Factors influencing Asian Indian American children's academic performance* (Unpublished doctoral dissertation), Syracuse University.

Saraff, A., & Srivastava, H. C. (2008). Envisioning fatherhood: Indian fathers' perceptions of an ideal father. *Population Review, 47*(1), 45–59. http://muse.jhu.edu/journals/population_review/v047/47. L.saraff.pdf.

Saraff, A., & Srivastava, H. C. (2010). Patterns and determinants of paternal involvement in childcare: An empirical investigation in a metropolis of India. *Population Research and Policy Review, 29*(2), 249–273. doi: 10.1007/s11113-009-9139-4.

Saraswathi, T. S. (Ed.). (1999). *Culture, socialization, and human development: Theory, research, and applications in India.* New Delhi, India: Sage.

Saraswathi, T. S., & Dutta, R. (2010). India. In M. Bornstein (ed.), *Handbook of cultural developmental science* (pp. 465–483). New York: Psychology Press.

Schoppe-Sullivan, S. J., Cannon, E. A., Brown, G. L., Mangelsdorf, S. C., & Sokolowski, M. S. (2008). Maternal gatekeeping, co-parenting quality, and fathering behavior in families with infants. *Journal of Family Psychology, 22*(3), 389–398.

Sharma, D. (2000). Infancy and childhood in India: A critical review. *International Journal of Group Tensions, 29,* 219–251.

Shukla, A. (1987). Decision making in single- and dual-career families in India. *Journal of Marriage and the Family, 49,* 621–629.

Singh, A., & Ram, F. (2009). Men's involvement during pregnancy and childbirth: Evidence from rural Ahmadnagar, India. *Population Review Publication, 48*(1), 83–102.

Sorkhabi, N. (2005). Applicability of Baumrind's parent typology to collective cultures: Analysis of cultural explanations of parent socialization effects. *International Journal of Behavioral Development, 29,* 552–563.

Sriram, R., Karnik, R., & Ali, R. (2002). *Social construction of fatherhood and motherhood: A view from within families.* [Research Report] Mimeo. Baroda, India: Women's Studies Research Centre, Maharaja Sayajiaro University of Baroda.

Sriram, R., & Navalkar, P. G. (2012). Who is an "ideal" father? Fathers', mothers' and children's views. *Psychology and Developing Societies, 24*(2), 205–237.

Sriram, R., & Sandhu, G. K. (2013). Fathering to ensure child's success: What urban Indian fathers do? *Journal of Family Issues, 34*(2), 161–183.

Sriram, R., Dave, P., Khasgiwala, A., & Joshi, A. (2006). Women and families in households in Gujarat. In P. Dave (ed.), *A profile of women in Gujarat* (pp. 195–218). Vadodara, India: Women's Studies Research Centre, Maharaja Sayajiaro University of Baroda.

Sun, L., & Roopnarine, J. L. (1996). Mother–infant and father–infant interaction and involvement in childcare and household labor among Taiwanese families. *Infant Behavior and Development, 19,* 121–129.

Suppal, P. (1998). Correlates of child care in single-wage and dual-wage nuclear and extended families in New Delhi, India. Unpublished doctoral dissertation, Syracuse University.

Suppal, P., & Roopnarine, J. (1999). Parental involvement in child care as a function of maternal employment in nuclear and extended families in India. *Sex Roles*, 40(9/10), 731–744.

Suppal, P., Roopnarine, J. L., Buesig, T., & Bennett, A. (1996). Ideological beliefs about family practices: Contemporary perspectives among north Indian families. *International Journal of Psychology*, 31, 29–37.

Tamis-LeMonda, C. S. (2004). Conceptualizing fathers' role: Playmates and more. *Human Development*, 47, 220–227.

Tulananda, O., & Roopnarine, J. L. (2001). Mothers' and fathers' interactions with preschoolers in the home in northern Thailand: Relationships to teachers' assessments of children's social skills. *Journal of Family Psychology*, 14, 676–687.

Tuli, M., & Chaudhary, N. (2010). Elective interdependence: Understanding individual agency and interpersonal relationships in Indian families. *Culture and Psychology*, 16(4), 477–496.

Uberoi, P. (2006). *Freedom and destiny: Gender, family, and popular culture in India*. New Delhi, India: Oxford University Press.

Verla, N., Munoz, P., Tessier, R., Palta, S., & Charpak, N. (2014). Indian fathers and their premature baby—an early beginning: A pilot study of skin-to-skin contact, culture, and fatherhood. *Fathering*, 2, 211–217.

Verma, R. K., Pulerwitz, J., Mahendra, V., Khandekar S., Barker, G., Fulpagare, P., & Singh, S. K. (2006). Challenging and changing gender attitudes among young men in Mumbai, India. *Reproductive Health Matters*, 14(28), 135–143.

13

Fathering in Chinese Culture: Traditions and Transitions

Xuan Li and Michael E. Lamb

The Chinese family, for its embodiment of distinctive cultural traditions and representation of rapid social changes, has sparked considerable interest from social scientists and members of the public. Though Chinese mothers—often (mis)represented as "tiger moms"—have inspired scholars to reconceptualize child development, parenthood, and the culturally determined assumptions behind them, their male counterparts have remained relatively invisible in international academia.

The underrepresentation of Chinese fathers in existing literature does not mean that Chinese men are insignificant in the lives of their children; nor are the fathers themselves unaware of their roles and identity. On the contrary, Chinese fathers today receive unprecedented attention, face complicated challenges, and experience profound cultural shifts as active and indispensable members of their families. This chapter aims to provide a brief introduction to the sociocultural contexts in which Chinese fatherhood is embedded, a review of major conceptual frameworks and empirical findings regarding the parenting behavior and influence of contemporary Chinese fathers, and suggestions for future research.

Before further discussion, it is worth pointing out that the working definition of "Chinese" used in this chapter connotes ethnicity instead of nationality and refers to people of Chinese ancestry residing in mainland China, Taiwan, Hong Kong, and Macau, a total population of 1.39 billion ("China Population 2014," http://worldpopulationreview.com/countries/china-population/)—as well as those living outside the Greater China Area, either as temporary expatriates or as long-term immigrants, totaling 50 million ("Overseas Chinese," http://en.wikipedia.org/wiki/Overseas_Chinese). Though this chapter focuses on fathers of Chinese descent living in mainland China, home to the largest and fastest growing subgroup among the Chinese population, totaling 1.39 billion ("China Population 2014," http://worldpopulationre-view.com/countries/china-population/), the literature review also examines the scholarly literature dealing with Chinese fathers and families around the globe.

CHINESE FATHERS: CULTURAL TRADITIONS

The Chinese culture, regarded as one of the oldest in the world, has been shaped by the joint influences of Confucianism, Daoism, and Buddhism, as well as by a variety of regional cultures and customs from ethnic minorities (Tang 1992). It is believed that many of the core traditional values have been retained in contemporary Chinese communities and continue to influence the everyday lives of hundreds of millions of Chinese (Sim 2005). Because of the wide geographic extension and the large population, as well as the innumerable societal changes that have taken place throughout its long history, Chinese civilization has involved a bewildering variety of sociopolitical landscapes, means of subsistence, and kinship structures, some discussed later in this chapter.

Within this complexity, it is nevertheless possible to identify some features that characterize major Chinese societies. One of the most deep-seated cultural traditions that fundamentally distinguishes the Chinese from Europeans and North Americans is collectivism. It has been widely acknowledged that in contrast to the individualistic cultures of western Europe and North America, the Chinese value the group over the individual (Bond 1993; Xinyin Chen et al. 1998; Chen, Kennedy, & Zhou 2012; Friedlmeier, Corapci, & Cole 2011; Markus & Kitayama 1991; Wu et al. 2002). Unlike European and North American cultures, which tend to advocate self-assertion, the Chinese culture endorses interpersonal harmony for the sake of the collective good and expects individuals to restrain themselves within social norms to secure and maximize group interest. Individuals are encouraged to carefully regulate the expression of their agency and subjectivity, for instance by masking their feelings (xǐ nù bù xíng yú sè, 喜怒不形於色, literally "not show joy or anger on the face," *Book of Rites* (Lǐjì, 《禮記》) and confining the inevitably aroused pleasure, anger, sorrow and joy in "the due degree" (fā ér jiē zhōng jié, 發而皆中節, (Lǐjì, 《禮記》). Chinese people, in contrast to Europeans and Americans, thus appear more introverted and reserved (Chuang 2009; Tsai & Levenson 1997; Yang 1986) and their interpersonal interactions less charged with passion.

Consistent with the emphasis on social harmony, the concrete social rules for everyday behavior largely depends on position in the social network. The patriarchal traditions of Chinese societies, institutionalized in the form of hierarchical interpersonal relationships and a preference for males over females, set the behavioral expectations for individuals based on their age, gender and social roles. Confucius and his followers, for instance, suggested that the 'basic' human relationships—those between father and son, between sovereign and subordinate, and between husband and wife—are by nature hierarchical. Despite the varying degree of intimacy and interpersonal distance, all these relational dyads involve superior and inferior parties with unequal rights and obligations; the latter are expected to follow the guidance of the former. Among these dyads, the father–son relationship (which also represents other parent-child combinations) is the prototype for all social relationships within and beyond the family.

Apart from interpersonal hierarchy, the Chinese culture portrays males as superior to females, a tradition that probably stems from the agrarian origin of Chinese civilization, with male heirs advantageous as potential laborers and economic assets (Li & Lamb 2013; Lu & Chang 2013; Strom, Strom, & Xie 1995). The unequal gender power has been codified in the Chinese language and further consolidated through later laws and morality: The Chinese character for "woman," 女(nǚ), has its hieroglyphic origin in the image of a kneeling, submissive woman: 𠨰. Further, a proposal by the prominent Han Dynasty scholar Dǒng Zhōngshū (董仲舒, 179–104 BC) that women should be guided by their male relatives (particularly elderly ones) was ardently advocated by many subsequent scholars, including the influential Neo-Confucian scholar Zhū Xī (朱熹, AD 1130–1200) (Zhang 2007). Chinese males are thus expected to behave in closer conformity to the personhood idea than their female counterparts, as well as to demonstrate higher levels of self-mastery and emotional reserve (Louie 2002). In everyday practice, men are assigned the role of family heads, taking responsibilities for providing, decision making, and handling "external affairs" while their wives cover the "interior chores" (e.g., nán zhǔ wài, nǚ zhǔ nèi, 男主外, 女主內) (Shek 1998).

The Traditional Chinese Family: Living Arrangements, Parental Roles, and Variation by Child Characteristics

The aforementioned cultural values have long been translated into practical arrangements in traditional Chinese families, as well as into concrete expectations of everyday parenting practices for fathers and mothers.

The traditional Chinese family is patrilocal, with the married couple residing with the groom's family and the bride becoming part of their lineage. Procreation is of core importance for marriage and family life. Adult males assume the responsibility of extending and expanding their family lineages through the production of offspring. Fatherhood is thus a default part of a man's life path that he must embrace to demonstrate respect for his ancestors and to avoid being accused of being unfilial.

Chinese parents, as members of a collectivistic culture, primarily emphasize their children's adjustment to the group. Unlike Euro-American parents, who are keen to foster their children's agency, traditional Chinese parents want their children to fit into, rather than exert their own will over existing orders, as well as to maintain smooth, interdependent social relationships, especially within the family (Chen 2010; Wu et al. 2002). This tendency might have been further reinforced in communist and reformed socialist eras, when compliance with and dedication to group needs were further emphasized (Way et al. 2013).

The day-to-day parenting in Chinese families is executed within the context of a hierarchical yet highly intertwined parent–child relationship: Chinese parents have authority over their children, which continues even after the children reach adulthood, often making co-resident grandparents the de facto heads of multigenerational households. Parents are expected to maintain emotional distance from them so as to consolidate their dominance and to use strict discipline to instill in children the appropriate conduct. Such power requires close supervision (guǎn, 管), genuine kindness, immense devotion, and voluntary sacrifice for children (Chao 1994, 2001; Chao & Tseng 2002; Xu et al. 2005): Chinese parents are encouraged to embody benevolence (rén, 仁, a highly regarded virtue in Confucianism) during everyday interactions with their children and to act with a warm and concerned, yet proper, demeanor (fù zǐ yǒu qīn, 父子有親) (Hwang 2001). Parental love should be displayed subtly, preferably in implicit ways that do not undermine parental authority. Children, on the other hand, are taught to reciprocate parental love by acting in an obedient, respectful manner, following principles of filial piety (xiào, 孝), so as to reinforce deep, interdependent relationships with their parents (Chao & Tseng 2002; Xinyin Chen, Liu, & Li 2000; Chuang 2009; Hwang 2001).

Chinese fathers and mothers, having culturally prescribed gender expectations, are assigned different parental roles. Whereas mothers are in charge of the childcare chores, the main responsibilities of fathers are those of providers and disciplinarians. Chinese fathers, much like their counterparts in many other societies, need to secure the family income to support their wives and children, if not also elderly parents. Fathers are also held responsible for their children's behavior as part of their obligation to maintain the reputation of the family lineage, as reflected in widespread idiomatic expressions (e.g., yǎng bú jiào, fù zhī guò. 養不教，父之過, literally "to feed but not teach the child, the dad's fault indeed") (Chang, Chen, & Ji 2011). To make sure that family honor is not tainted by children's misbehavior, Chinese fathers are particularly aware of their disciplinary role (Ho 1987). Furthermore, the father's presumed moral and intellectual superiority make him the more appropriate educator and role model within the family. In contrast to the mother, who nurtures children both physically and emotionally, the father is expected to parent strictly within the boundary of kindness (Chao & Tseng 2002; Xinyin

Chen et al. 2000; Kim & Wong 2002) and not display excessive affection to his children (fùzǐ zhī yán, bù kěyǐ xiá; gǔròu zhī ài, bù kěyǐ jiǎn, 父子之嚴, 不可以狎; 骨肉之愛, 不可以簡; literally "the father should be strict with the son and not improperly close; the love for one's own blood should not be spared," *Admonitions for the Yan Clan* (*Yánshì Jiāxùn*, 《顏氏家訓》).

As summarized by the extensively documented "strict father, kind mother" model (yánfù címǔ, 严父慈母) (Chang et al. 2011; Ho 1987, 1989; Li & Lamb 2013; McHale, Rao, & Krasnow 2000; Shek 1998; Shwalb, Nakazawa, Yamamoto, & Hyun 2010), a father who strongly adheres to Chinese cultural traditions should be proactive in childbearing and invested in the provision of family resources. Although not directly involved in everyday childcare, he should complement the mother's role by disciplining and educating his children and striving to maintain a smooth yet distant father–child relationship, expecting his child to hold him in high regard and reverential awe.

According to Chinese cultural traditions, however, not all children are to be treated in the same way. The male superiority leads to a preference for sons over daughters, for instance. A well-known piece of folklore included in the *Book of Poetry* (*Shījīng*, 《詩經》), one of the major Confucius classics, accurately presents the different expectations for sons and daughters: Whereas parents "put their boys to sleep on couches, clothe them in robes," and aspire for them to become "future kings and princes," they "put girls to sleep on the ground, cloth[ing] them with wrappers" in the mere hope that they do not become troublemakers. Sons are clearly favored and are granted more resources and rights (e.g., in patrilineal inheritance of family properties) than daughters (Berndt, Cheung, Lau, Hau, & Lew 1993; Ying Wang & Fong 2009) but are treated with greater parental strictness and control in reflection of higher expectation and standards. Besides, boys are also more likely to be treated with emotional reserve in everyday parent–child interactions as part of gender role socialization. Girls, because of lowered parental expectations, are treated with more lenience, indulgence, and affection, because parents do not expect much more than obedience from them.

Apart from being gender-sensitive, Chinese fathers and mothers adjust their parenting styles based on their children's age. Many scholars have noticed the stark contrast in the affective climate of parent–child interactions in Chinese families before and after the child reaches "the age of reason" (Chuang & Su 2009; Jankowiak 1992; Putnick et al. 2012; Wolf 1978). Despite the absence of an exact cutoff point, it is generally believed that the transition takes place around the time that children start school (approximately age 6) (Fung 1999; Ho 1989). Preschool children are treated with considerable affection and indulgence within the boundary of propriety, especially by their mothers and other female caregivers (Chuang & Su 2009; Kim & Wong 2002; McHale et al. 2000; Putnick et al. 2012). At this stage, fathers have less contact with their children and are likely to be tolerant when they do engage with them. As children grow older, however, fathers begin to assume roles as strict teachers and disciplinarians (Chuang & Su 2009; Wang & Chang 2010). Although both mothers and fathers are aware of age-appropriate parenting, Chinese fathers are particularly conscious about demonstrating a marked shift in parenting style from early lenience to later harshness.

CHINESE FATHERS: SOCIAL TRANSITIONS

Many scholars have argued that traditional parenting styles might have shifted in reaction to the drastic changes in social, economic, and cultural contexts of family life in China (Chang et al. 2011; Chuang 2009; Ho 1989; Li & Lamb 2013; Department of Economic and Social Affairs [DESA] 2011; Strom et al. 1995; Way et al. 2013; Ying Wang & Fong 2009). More specifically, recent economic reforms, gender equality, and family planning policies have challenged the patriarchal family system by deconstructing traditional living arrangements, decreasing average family size, and altering the power dynamic between males and females. Accordingly, the related childrearing goals, the division of childcare chores, and the patterns of interaction between parents and children have undergone profound changes, with new role expectations set for Chinese fathers.

Social Transitions in Contemporary China: Economic Reform, Gender Equality, and Family Planning Policy

China, despite its outstanding economic advancement in the past decades, is a rather recent player in the global economy. The country's "Open and Reform" policy (gǎigé kāifàng, 改革开放), which began in 1978 with the aim of catching up with developed countries, dismantled the centralized planned economy and replaced it with a capitalistic market economy (Chang et al. 2011; Fong 2007). Within three decades, China has quickly risen to become the world's second-largest economy, with a 23-fold increase in GDP per capita (World Economic Outlook 2014, www.imf.org/external/country/CHN/index.htm).

Together with general improvements in average income and living standards, economic reforms brought about sweeping changes in China's social structures. The end of the "iron rice bowl" (tiěfànwǎn, 铁饭碗) era, when private life was organized around lifetime employment in the "work unit" (dānwèi, 单位) to which workers were allocated after training or education, led not only to greater freedom and flexibility in career choice and family arrangement, but also to fierce professional competition (Xinyin Chen et al. 2010). The workplace in today's China, as in many industrialized countries, has become a source of both profound enjoyment and tremendous stress (Chang et al. 2011; Jankowiak & Li 2014).

The enormous wealth generated by economic reform is unevenly distributed across social classes and geographic areas, resulting in rapidly widening social gaps and unbalanced regional development, as indicated by China's rocketing Gini coefficient (Chang et al. 2011; World Bank 2013, http://data.worldbank.org/indicator/SI.POV.GINI.). There is a particularly stark contrast between the rural and urban areas. As in other developing countries, rural China lags behind the urban areas in economic growth, family resources, living conditions, and information accessibility (Chang et al. 2011; Ho 1989; Powell, Taylor, & Smith 2008; Quah 2003; Survey and Research Center for China Household Finance, Southwestern University of Finance and Economics, China, 2012, www.chfsdata.org/detail-19,21-28.html). Such disparities have been further exacerbated by the current household registration system (hùkǒu zhìdù, 戶口制度), which continues to stratify urban and rural families by allocating different educational resources, career opportunities, and welfare schemes. Because of poorer job prospects and the lack of social security, rural dwellers (especially young males) are more likely than their urban compatriots to experience economic pressures that force many to join the 211 million–strong "floating" population (liúdòng rénkǒu, 流動人口) as migrant workers, leaving their spouses and children behind (Li & Lamb 2013).

The changing labor market has also changed the roles of Chinese men and women both within and beyond the family. The egalitarian policies, vividly captured in the slogan "Women can hold up half of the sky" (fùnǚ néng dǐng bànbiān tiān, 婦女能頂半邊天), have granted Chinese women equal legal rights since 1954. The gender-equal principle, together with the "One-Child Policy," instituted in 1978, encourages women to pursue educational opportunities and careers to become cocontributors to the country's modernization (Fong 2002; Nolan 2010). Nowadays, 64 percent of Chinese females participate in paid labor; they constitute 44.8 percent of the Chinese labor force (Institute of Social Science Survey, Peking University 2010; Strom et al. 1995; World Bank 2013, http://data.worldbank.org/indicator/SL.TLF.CACT.FE.ZS). These figures put China (rank 69) ahead of its East Asian neighbors such as Japan and Korea (ranks 105 and 111, respectively) in gender equality and comparable to other major emerging nations such as Mexico and Brazil (rank 68 and 62, respectively) (Hausmann, Tyson, Bekhouche, & Zahidi 2013).

The extent to which the well-intended gender equality legislation has been effective is unclear, however. Messages from the media clearly indicate that traditional beliefs about men's and women's different rights, obligations, and competencies linger (To 2013). Overt or covert discrimination against women in hiring, payment, promotion, and education has even increased in brutally competitive economic times (Fong 2002; Kim et al. 2013; Nolan 2010; Strom et al. 1995). Many Chinese men, still assuming their traditional role as family providers, now feel both compelled and motivated to devote a great proportion of their time and energy to (ideally lucrative) career development (Yeung & Alipio 2013), leaving housework and childcare chores to their wives.

One other policy closely linked to economic reform and gender equality is the enforcement of family planning (jìhuàshēngyù, 計劃生育). The "One-Child Policy," proposed in the early 1970s and legally instituted in 1978, aims not only to slow population growth, but also to accelerate China's modernization process by producing generations that have better "quality" (sùzhì, 素質) (Ying Wang & Fong 2009; Way et al. 2013). In principle, each married couple is allowed to have only one child, with exemptions for ethnic minorities, families who give birth to disabled firstborns, and rural families whose first child is a girl, among others (Li & Lamb 2013). Unlike the gender equality regulations, the birth control policy was forcefully carried out through a mixture of education, persuasion, and coercion, leading initially to strong resistance and much controversy (Fong 2007; Strom et al. 1995). More than three decades later, however, the policy is well accepted, at least by urban citizens (Fong 2007; Strom et al. 1995). As a result of the policy, the fertility rate of Chinese women has shrunk from 5.8 births per woman in the 1970s to 1.6 births per woman in 2010; the average family size, which was 4.41 people per household in 1980, is now 3.10 (Ma 2011). Official statistics estimate that at least 90 million children were born as singletons under the family planning policy, and as many as 400 million births were prevented ("90m Chinese growing up as only children," *China Daily*, www.chinadaily .com.cn/china/2007-01/20/content_788315.htm; "400 million births prevented by one-child policy," *People's Daily*, http://english.peopledaily.com. cn/90882/7629166.html).

The Contemporary Chinese Family: Changing Social Contexts and Parenting Ideals

The ecology of fatherhood in Chinese families has thus been transformed by the aforementioned policies in fundamental ways. First of all, the ideal of a traditional patrilocal family, in which several generations reside under the same roof, is shattered by the increasing mobility brought by the vibrant market economy. A surging demand for independence by members of the younger generations, coupled with increased employment-driven mobility, makes it undesirable and barely possible for married couples to maintain traditional patrilocal residences or to stay within reachable proximity of (paternal) grandparents and other members of the extended families for childcare

(Li & Lamb 2013). Mass female participation in the labor force, triggered by both the ideological shift and financial pressures, has made dual-earner families the norm, with both parents employed full-time. The rise of nuclear families and the high maternal employment rate have made some men more cautious about the timing of having children or whether to have children at all, prompting others to assume greater paternal responsibility for childcare (Berndt et al. 1993; Strom et al. 1995). Together with the increasing workload, however, comes autonomy: Without the interference of conservative grandparents, Chinese fathers now enjoy greater freedom to negotiate the division of childcare work, set their own parenting goals, and adopt the parenting strategies they prefer (Chuang & Su 2009; Li & Lamb 2013).

Many have argued that the socialization goals of contemporary Chinese parents may have shifted from collectivism toward individualism under the joint influence of the market economy and the one-child policy (Chang et al. 2011; Xinyin Chen & Chen 2010; Xinyin Chen et al. 2010; Chuang 2009; Chuang & Su 2009; Ho 1989; Kim et al. 2013; Naftali 2009; Strom et al. 1995; Way et al. 2013; Xu et al. 2005). Chinese parents, though not without conflicts and confusion, increasingly realize that the competitive market economy demands from their children traits such as creativity, individual initiative, self-governance, competitiveness, and assertiveness, which stand in stark contrast to the traditionally endorsed obedience, conformity, and modesty (Chuang 2009; Fong 2007; Naftali 2009; Way et al. 2013). Most couples' inability to have more than one child further personalizes the child as an individual having rights and agency instead of merely being part of the family lineage (Naftali 2009). It is thus not surprising that parents in today's China are adjusting their childrearing strategies to foster children's autonomy and self-assertion and nurturing more equal parent–child relationships, much like their counterparts in industrialized societies (Chang et al. 2011; Chuang 2009; Friedlmeier et al. 2011; Ho 1989; Naftali 2009; Way et al. 2013).

The child's socioemotional well-being, as a critical component of the child's individuality, has become a new focus of socialization especially among urban, well-educated Chinese parents. Strong emphasis on the child's conduct and academic performance certainly persists, perhaps as a result of both the cultural traditions and new anxiety about children's success in the market economy (McHale et al. 2000; Naftali 2009; Wang & Chang 2010). However, Chinese parents increasingly recognize children's "individual consciousness" and tend to tolerate, if not encourage, children's expressions of their ideas and emotions (Naftali 2009). Such awareness is amplified by parental realization that their children are the only ones whose welfare and happiness need to be ensured, as well as that children will become a source of their postretirement support. For both affective and pragmatic reasons, the parent–child relationship needs to be reaffirmed, even by using nontraditional means such as overt affection display and indulgence, in an era when the traditional binding forces between parents and children are challenged (Fong 2002; Ho 1989; Strom et al. 1995; Way et al. 2013). In addition to these strong motives, the absence of multiple offspring makes it possible for parents to focus their resources and energy on the psychological and emotional needs of single children (Liu, Lin, & Chen 2010).

These drastic social changes, which constantly redefine masculinity and femininity, have reshaped the norms of fatherhood and motherhood. Not only do Chinese men anticipate shouldering childcare tasks, but more flexibility is allowed in and higher expectations set for their emotional engagement and self-expression as parents (Chang et al. 2011; Jankowiak & Li 2014). Contemporary Chinese fathers are encouraged to exhibit less authority and more nurturance in family life in general than their predecessors, and they behave in a warmer, more responsive, and more affectionate manner toward their children (Engle & Breaux 1998; Yan 2006).

The ever-blurring gender roles, together with the one-child policy, promote the equal treatment of sons and daughters. Extensive state-sponsored propaganda programs criticizing the preference for sons, touting the indispensable economic and labor contribution of women to their families, and highlighting women's rising growing power in day-to-day family decision-making have led parents to realize that "daughters are at least as good as sons" (shēng nán shēng nǔ yīyàng hǎo, 生男生女一样好) (Fong 2002). In addition, contemporary Chinese parents, whose singleton children are their "only hope," can no longer choose to favor sons over daughters and invest all their material and emotional resources in their children, regardless of sex (Fong 2002; Ying Wang & Fong 2009). Chinese daughters born after 1978, though benefiting from better family resources and empowered by their status as the sole focus of parental attention, face increased parental expectations for their independence, self-reliance, and excellence (Ying Wang & Fong 2009). Also, today's Chinese daughters, like sons, are seen as potential post-retirement supporters of their parents even after marriage, an event that used to symbolize the termination of the bride's responsibilities to her natal family. It is likely that Chinese fathers and mothers will have ambivalent attitudes toward the socialization of their children as gendered beings and become both more invested in and stricter with their daughters.

Within Chinese society, it is reasonable to assume that the vast rural–urban disparity in lifestyle will be reflected in fathering behavior. Chinese rural families, like their counterparts worldwide, are regarded as reservoirs of traditional values and practices for being less exposed to the modern market economy (Xinyin Chen et al. 2010; Ho 1989; Powell et al. 2008). Rural fathers are thus more likely than their urban counterparts to adopt the emotionally reserved roles of traditional Chinese fathers as financial providers and disciplinarians. In the particular context of China's uneven economic development, underprivileged rural Chinese fathers are more likely to suffer job insecurity and work–life imbalance and have other aspects of their parenthood, such as caring, nurturing, communicating, and playing, "swallowed" by the heavy burden of providing (Powell et al. 2008). Similar patterns can also be expected of fathers in affluent coastal areas and those in underdeveloped inland provinces.

In summary, Chinese fathers, under the influence of patriarchal traditions, were motivated to build harmonious, hierarchical, and emotionally distant relationships and were thus expected to adopt a more group-oriented, power-assertive, controlling, emotionally inexpressive, and gender-discriminative posture as strict disciplinarians during everyday interactions with their children. However, rapid changes in economic climate, social development, and family policies in contemporary China have instilled in parents an individualistic, child-centered, gender-equal parenting philosophy, encouraging them to behave in warmer and more affectionate ways. With the ongoing economic development and continuity in gender and birth-control policies, there is reason to believe that contemporary Chinese males, in pursuit of their children's socioemotional well-being and father–child intimacy, will further depart from the image of stern, aloof, traditional fathers and embrace a more engaged, more nurturant, and emotionally demonstrative ideal of fatherhood.

TABLE 13.1 Chinese parenting: past and present

	Traditional	Contemporary
Living arrangement	Patrilocal; co-residence with extended family	Neolocal; nuclear family
Socialization goal	Collectivistic, emphasizing social norms	Individualistic, focusing on child well-being
Parent–child relationship	Hierarchical	Democratic
Father/mother divergence	Differentiation between paternal and maternal roles; "strict father, kind mother" model	Convergence between paternal and maternal roles
Son/daughter differentiation	Preference for sons; more resources and attention for sons; higher standards, stricter control, and less warmth for sons	Diminishing preference for sons; equal resources and attention for sons and daughters Higher standards, stricter control, and less warmth for sons
Social class	No specific information	Stark rural/urban and coastal/inland contrasts

EXISTING LITERATURE: FATHER INVOLVEMENT, INTERACTIVE STYLE, AND INFLUENCE

Empirical research on Chinese fathers, a growing subfield of developmental psychology and family studies that took off less than two decades ago (Li & Lamb 2013), has yet to become a full-fledged field having unique, well-conceptualized frameworks. In recent years, theories, evidence, and policies on fathers from developed societies have gradually been introduced to Chinese scholars, and many empirical studies have been carried out to investigate different aspects of fatherhood in today's Chinese societies. Reports of research on Chinese fathers that were often published in nonacademic media or nonprestigious journals, are starting to appear in higher-tier academic publications (both in English and Chinese), particularly since 2010.

As in developmental psychology as a whole, research on Chinese fathers draws heavily on theories and methodological tools imported from the west. A detailed examination of twenty-six review or overview papers published by Chinese scholars between 2000 and 2004 suggested that father involvement, among all aspects of fatherhood, attracted the most attention. Theories that are most frequently referred to include Lamb, Pleck, Charnov, and Levine's (1987) tripartite model of father involvement (Pu & Lu 2008; Song 2009; Sun 2013; Jingzhi Wang, Wang, & Wu 2012; Wang 2005); Hawkins and colleagues' (2002) nine factors of fathering (Pu & Lu 2008; Sun 2013; Jingzhi Wang et al. 2012); and Amato's (1998) conceptualization of fathers as resource providers (Sun 2013; Teng, Xing, & Yang 2010; Jingzhi Wang et al. 2012; Xu & Zhang 2008). Dollahite, Hawkins, and Brotherson's (1997) seven types of generative "father work"; Palkovitz's (1997) fifteen categories of father involvement; Doherty, Kouneski, and Erickson's (1998) definition of "responsible fathering"; and Krampe's (2009) conception of "father presence" were also cited. Discussions of father involvement are often embedded in the contexts of Bronfenbrenner's (1986, 1997) ecological model and Belsky's (1984) process model of the determinants of parenting, with emphasis on father characteristics (e.g., father's personality and role identity), child characteristics (e.g., child gender and temperament), and spousal support for father involvement.

Most reviews or studies of fathering styles are built on Paquette's (2004) activation theory that differentiates between father–child and mother–child relationships, with further support from Lamb's early emphasis on the different features of father–infant and mother–infant play. With a few exceptions (e.g., Wang 2005; Zhou & Zhang 2004; Zhou & Yang 2007), these theories are often followed by statements about gender differences that derive from (largely westernized) intuitive beliefs about males and females. A strong tone of "father essentialism" is also present in reviews concerned with the father's influence on child development: Children's sex-typical gender identity is the most commonly mentioned area of paternal influence, followed by children's "personality" development (as an umbrella term including children's moral development and problem and criminal behavior), social competence, cognitive development and academic achievement, and physical development.

Nearly all researchers have pointed out cultural and societal differences between China and "western" countries and have called for caution when applying the aforementioned theories in the Chinese contexts. Culturally specific folk theories about fathers' and mothers' roles, such as ideas about "men working outside [the family], women taking care of interior chores" or the "strict father, kind mother" model, are recurrent themes in the literature on Chinese fatherhood. Few scholars have actually attempted to conceptually unpack Chinese fatherhood. Indigenous theories about Chinese fathers, mostly developed in Taiwan, are still scarce (see C. Wang 2000 and T. Wang 2000 for exceptions) and have yet to be widely cited.

Empirical Evidence: Father Involvement

Considering China's lingering patriarchal tradition, it is not surprising that Chinese women are still significantly more involved in household chores and more devoted to their parental roles than their husbands (Kim et al. 2013; Li & Lamb 2013), and breadwinning is still seen as the father's role rather than the mother's, even in families in which wives earn more (Yeung & Alipio 2013). Survey data suggest that mothers remain primary caregivers within families, especially in terms of everyday physical care (Xu 2004; Xu & Zhang 2007, 2008). In a sample of 360 families in northeastern China, 30.6 percent of the fathers having preschoolers and 31.2 percent of those having school-aged children admitted that they spent no time or less than one hour per day with their children (Liu & Zhao 2006). Chi (2013) also found in her sample of sixty families with kindergarteners that father–child communication was shorter, less frequent and more opportunistic than mother–child communication. Similar findings have been obtained in studies using Taiwanese samples. During naturalistic observations of Taiwanese parents with infants, Sun and Roopnarine (1996) found that fathers "feed, smile at, vocalize to and engage in object play" less than mothers do. Ho and colleagues (2010), on the basis of reports by fathers and mothers in twenty-six Taipei families, concluded that contemporary Taiwanese fathers were less involved in most daily childcare tasks than their wives; Hsu et al. (2010), using Taiwan Education Panel data, found that Taiwanese mothers even outperformed their husbands on involvement in children's academic development, a domain often considered the father's specialty.

Chinese fathers, some willingly and others reluctantly, are becoming more involved in their children's lives, albeit slowly: Whereas urban fathers in northern China in the early 1980s were barely involved in childcare (Jankowiak 1992), they were taking care of their children "with pride and affection" a mere ten years later (Engle & Breaux 1998); 83.6 percent of modern Shanghainese fathers acknowledged fathers' responsibilities for infant care, compared to 61.8 percent in the grandparental generation, and 87 percent actually helped with childcare tasks, compared with 60.4 percent of their own fathers (Liu 1995). Xu and Zhang's (2007) multi-informant survey of Shanghai families further indicated that fathers—though not yet so much as mothers—actively helped prepare for childbirth, engaged in daily childcare, and accompanied and guided their children. Chuang and Su (2009), too, suggested that Beijing fathers not only participated in joint decisions about childcare when their children were still infants and toddlers, but also devoted an average of forty-five minutes per day (in contrast to thirty-two minutes per day among American fathers with young children) to childcare.

Assistance with children's school work remains a focus of paternal involvement (Strom et al. 1995; Xu 2004). Although fathers might not sit alongside their children during homework hours, especially when the children are young, they assume an active role in children's academic development by shouldering "managerial" responsibilities, such as making decisions about school choice (Xu & Zhang 2008). Fathers also contribute to semi-educational activities by taking their children to museums and exhibitions or simply recounting aspects of family and ethnic history more than mothers do (Ho et al. 2010). Other areas of father involvement include spending leisure time with their children (Wu, Zhu, & Liu 2012), and providing material rewards to compensate for the time when they are not able to be with their children in person (Cai 2014).

Though some fathers are still deeply concerned about their children's academic performance and conduct (Cai 2014; Ho et al. 2011), others have started to openly acknowledge that other areas of father involvement are just as important. Beijing participants in Chuang and Su's (2009) study, for instance, provided a multidimensional (re)construction of fatherhood that included child care and playing, while reports by 400 Shandong fathers with children aged 3–7 suggested that these fathers valued their responsibilities to act as expressive parents and to support their children indirectly more than their obligations to encourage children in their schoolwork, supervise children's conduct, and set behavioral boundaries.

Some scholars have attempted to assess possible determinants of father involvement in Chinese families. As might be expected, socioeconomic background significantly influences paternal involvement. Xu and Zhang (2007) compared urban and rural fathers and found that the content of father involvement was often affected by fathers' work commitment. Rural fathers, who face less fierce career competition than their urban counterparts, devote more time to accompanying their wives to prenatal checks and day-to-day child care, whereas urban fathers spend more time in direct engagement with their children, taking children to educational or entertainment activities, providing emotional support, and initiating father–child intimacy. Better-educated fathers, in spite of their longer working hours, spent more time with their children because they appeared to better internalize multifaceted paternal roles. In another study, Chen and Liu (2012) compared the frequency and amount of father–child interaction experienced by 1,016 children of migrant workers and 446 children from local families. They concluded that children from migrant families spent less time interacting with their fathers, and did so less frequently, than did their counterparts in local families.

As far as child characteristics are concerned, the effect of child age seems to be eroding now that Chinese fathers are involved in the care of children earlier than their predecessors. Yan Xu, Ji, and Zhang (2006) found that fathers of kindergarteners and first-graders were equivalently involved in most domains of childcare except discipline. At the same time, the impact of child gender on paternal involvement is not evident in studies of fathers with young and adult children (Xu, Ji, & Zhang 2006; Pu, Lu, Ling, & Cao 2012), though little is known about father involvement in families with adolescents.

Other factors, such as fathers' work commitment, appear to place external constraints on fathers' availability for childcare, whereas father's perceived marital satisfaction and social support are positively correlated with involvement in childcare (Xu 2010). In the same vein, Chi (2013) found that fathers whose wives were more invested in parent–child interaction spent more time communicating with their preschool children. These findings underline the importance of proximal family processes in affecting paternal involvement with children.

Empirical Evidence: Interaction Styles

Though it is difficult to offer a precise account of historical and current parenting styles of Chinese fathers, a few patterns can be identified from the literature. Using reports of children of different age groups from different regions in China, researchers have consistently found strong correlations between fathers' and mothers' parenting styles in Chinese families (Chen, Ni, & Yang 2007; Wang 2013; Yang & Hou 2014; Zhou & Ma 2008). However, the "strict father, kind mother" model has received wide support as well. Wolf's (1978) and Jankowiak's (1992) ethnographic accounts, collected more than two decades ago from relatively undeveloped areas of Chinese societies (rural Taiwan and Inner Mongolia), portrayed Chinese fathers as deeply concerned yet emotionally reserved disciplinarians and inept caregivers of their infant children, whereas mothers played nurturing, affectionate roles. Similarly, Lau, Lew, Hau, Cheung, and Berndt (1990), Berndt and colleagues (1993), and Shek (1998), using retrospective reports by adolescents and adults in Mainland China, Taiwan, and Hong Kong, all found fathers were perceived as less warm, less indulgent, less responsive, less concerned, harsher, and more controlling than mothers.

Subsequent studies of college students in Hebei Province, north China, suggested that young Chinese adults remembered their fathers as harsher; less warm, interventive, protective, and loving; and more punitive than their mothers (Li & Fang 2007) and noted that father–child communication was not as good as mother–child communication (Chen & Liu 2012).

The disciplinary image of the traditional father still persists to some extent (DESA 2011; McHale et al. 2000): 16.61 percent of early adolescents in Shaanxi Province, midwest China, disclosed that their fathers had never praised them (Dai, Wang, & Gao 2003). But there has been increasing evidence that Chinese fathers—beginning with well-educated men—have begun to adopt warm, nurturing personae and to value father–child intimacy (Engle & Breaux 1998; Jankowiak & Li 2014). Among fathers who have preschool children, 46.3 percent reported that they frequently praised and encouraged their children (Cai 2014), and Shanghai children viewed fathers as involved, warm, and indulgent (Xinyin Chen et al. 2000). A survey of urban Beijing families found that fathers enjoyed playing with their children and discussing feelings and ideas with them (Strom et al. 1995). Moreover, despite low levels of self-reported emotional support, Shanghai fathers comforted distressed children better than their predecessors had (Xu & Zhang 2008).

Parenting styles vary considerably in relation to father characteristics such as educational attainment, rural/urban background, and profession. There is strong evidence that urban fathers are more affectionate than their rural or migrant counterparts, though it is debatable whether they are also less rejecting, intrusive, and overprotective (Hao & Li 2008; Lu 2009; Pan, Jin, Yang, Wang, & Chen 2005; Yang 2010; Yang, She, & Zhang 2005; Zeng 2009; Zhang 1997). For instance, fathers who are permanent urban residents are better at communicating with their children than are those who are migrant workers (Chen & Liu 2012), but Yan Xu's (2008) rural or unemployed fathers were less expressive than blue-collar workers or (semi-)professionals. Fathers' gender roles also seem to influence their parenting behavior: Xu, Ji, and Zhang (2006) found that Chinese fathers who were higher on masculinity tended to be more controlling and were involved in more disciplining and moral training, whereas those who were higher on femininity engaged in more interactive activities with children (such as talking and providing reading and homework support).

Ethnographic data consistently show that Chinese boys receive more severe parenting from fathers than girls did across developmental stages (Ho 1989; Kim & Wong 2002; Strom et al. 1995). In southern Chinese families, fathers of preschool children tended to be harsher with boys than with girls (Chang, Schwartz, Dodge, & McBride-Chang 2003) and mainland Chinese college students retrospectively reported that their fathers had been less warm toward sons than daughters (Lau et al. 1990). This finding is corroborated by those obtained in several other studies (e.g., Han et al. 2004; Li & Fang 2007; Li 2001; Li & Zhao 2007; Peng et al. 2011; Shen, Wu, & Zhao 2006; Wang et al. 2005; Yang 2010; Yang & Hou 2014; Yuqin Yang & Zhao 2010; Zhang 1997; Zhou & Ma 2008).

Fathers also exert more control over their sons. A study of Shanghai families with preschool children demonstrated higher paternal control over boys than over girls, though parents were equally warm and indulgent with sons and daughters (Xinyin Chen et al. 2000). Pre- and early adolescent girls reported significantly less perceived control than boys (Xinyin Chen et al. 2000) as did adolescent girls (Li & Zhou 2008). Elevated paternal control for sons was also found in Yang and Zou's (2008) study of parent–adolescent communication: Fathers were more sternly interrogative when talking to sons than when talking to daughters. Some of these differences may be attributed to the interaction between child gender and fathers' rural/urban backgrounds (Lu 2009; Yuqin Yang et al. 2005).

The moderating effect of child age has not received as much scholarly attention as child gender. Wolf's (1978)s remark that father–child affection in rural Taiwanese families "deteriorates into paternal lectures" after the child reaches the age of reason was further supported by more recent evidence comparing Chinese fathers with preschool and school-aged children (Xu et al. 2006). Interestingly, Yunyun Yang et al. (2005) and Yang and Zou (2008) found that although urban fathers became more rejecting and less communicative with their early adolescent children, rural fathers exhibited more warmth and understanding toward adolescents than primary school pupils, presumably because rural teenagers demanded autonomy less. Other studies concerned with children within narrower age ranges have failed to reveal substantial age-of-child effects on paternal behavior (Chi 2013; Pu et al. 2012).

Empirical Evidence: Influences of Father Involvement on Child Development

Much scholarly effort has been devoted to identifying the associations between Chinese fathers' investment and engagement with their children and different domains of child development. Because the findings of many of the early studies of Chinese fathers and childhood outcomes have been included in previous overviews (such as Shwalb et al. 2010 and Li & Lamb 2013), the main focus here is on studies published after 2005.

MENTAL AND PHYSICAL HEALTH

The availability of translated, revised, and standardized child-report measures of parenting behavior and psychopathology, and other child-report measures such as EMBU (Egna Minnen av Barndoms Uppfostran [My memories of upbringing]; Perris, Jacobsson, Lindstroem, Von Knorring, & Perris 1980), Symptoms Checklist (SCL-90-R) and Mental Health Test (MHT) have made it easy for Chinese researchers to quickly obtain large quantities of cross-sectional data on paternal behavior and child mental health. Strong correlations have been found between paternal warmth and positive child mental health across age, gender, and social groups: Shen, Wu, and Zhao (2006), who surveyed early adolescents in Hangzhou, southeast China, found that harsh, punitive, intrusive, rejecting, and overprotective fathering practices were related to children's mental health symptoms, as did Zhang, Zhang, Xie, and Li (2010); Yu, Liang, Zhao, Lin, and Yang (2005); and Yin, Li, and Su (2013), all of whom reached the same conclusions with samples from different regions and age groups using various outcome measures. Fathers' intrusive and overprotective behaviors were positively related to high school students' test anxiety (Liu et al. 2005) and to fifth- and sixth-graders' social anxiety (Ge & Zhang 2007). Paternal warmth can have a buffering effect on these associations (Sun, Lu & Dong 1998; Huang & Li. 2012).

Though empirical studies have repeatedly demonstrated that Chinese fathers who act in an accepting, supportive manner can contribute positively to their children's mental health, very little attention has been given to fathers' influences on children's physical health. Zhu and colleagues (2009) examined many residents of Hubei Province, mid-south China and found that better educated men tended to have preschoolers who were physically better developed, as well as that such benefits increased with child age. However, fathers seem to play a minor role in early adolescents' transition to puberty, apart from telling their sons about personal hygiene (Wu et al. 2010). The dearth of such research is presumably because Chinese fathers are not yet fully involved in physical childcare.

PROBLEM BEHAVIOR AND OVERALL ADJUSTMENT

Many scholars believe that aversive father–child interaction is responsible for undesirable behaviors in Chinese children. Guo and Wang (2009); Xu, Bao, and Zheng (2004); and Shen, Wu, and Zhao (2006), using samples of preschoolers, primary school students and early adolescents, respectively, discovered that fathers' punitive, rejecting, overprotective parenting style contributed to children's problem behavior. Paternal rejection, punishment, control, and intrusion reportedly increased the risk of externalized problems in preschool children (Zhang et al. 2008), as well as enhanced implicit aggression (Chen & Du 2006), inclination toward violent video games (Li, Zhou, & Zhu 2007), and engagement in criminal activities in adolescents (Deng, Fang, Li, & Wan 2006). Internet addiction, a growing concern of Chinese parents and teachers, appears to result from undesirable fathering, too: Perceived fathering style was a stronger predictor of Internet addiction among young adults than was perceived mothering style (Xie, Zhang, & Li 2009); among Shanghai adolescents, those with intrusive fathers were more likely to indulge themselves in video games (Li, Zhou, & Zhu 2007).

As in several other studies around the world (Khaleque & Rohner 2011), paternal warmth and support appears to ameliorate children's behavior and promote their general well-being. The more time fathers spent communicating with their early adolescent children, the fewer behavioral problems their children exhibited (Wang, Lei, & Liu 2004); adolescents who had warm, understanding fathers reported higher levels of subjective well-being (Yang 2010), and college students who reported more physical interaction with fathers and higher perceived father presence in their lives rated themselves as more persistent, more optimistic, and, overall, more resilient (Pu et al. 2012; see also Ju, Liu, & Fang 2011).

When fathers and mothers have well-coordinated parenting strategies, they both make unique contributions to their children's overall adjustment in the family and at school (Liu & Tan 2003). Encouraging fathers were found to buffer the negative effects of maternal depression (Liu & Li 2013), and better attachment quality with fathers was related to children's enhanced self-efficacy, which, in turn, lowered children's depressive symptoms (Lu & Zhang 2008). Da (2002), Lu (2009) and Li, Zou, and Zhao (2008) also provided evidence of a link between nurturant fathering and college students' self-confidence, self-esteem, self-efficacy, and self-perceptions. Li et al. (2010) further revealed that father's parenting style had strongly affected college students' avoidance and concern for social life, as well as their feelings of loneliness.

COGNITIVE DEVELOPMENT AND ACADEMIC ACHIEVEMENT

With fathers often deemed to be children's first educators in Chinese families, many scholars have sought to verify the link between fathering and children's cognitive development. The latest studies show that Chinese fathers indeed make significant contributions to the cognitive foundations, allowing children to acquire further knowledge and skills: Liang and his team (2013), looking at the developmental trajectory of children's effortful control, found that encouraging, accepting fathers promoted the development of effortful control, whereas rejecting, punitive fathers impeded such development. Moreover, they found that warm fathering also predicted the faster development of effortful control later in childhood, whereas warm mothering slowed it down. Similarly, Nie and Lu (2014) found that preschool children, especially boys, with more involved fathers—in terms of engagement, accessibility and responsibility—performed better in delayed gratification tasks, after the effects of child characteristics and mother involvement were controlled for. Another study (Xu & Liu 1999) highlighted the influence of fathers on school-age girls' self-control. In late childhood and adolescence, the benefit of warm, understanding fathering manifests itself in children's greater interest in learning and higher diligence (Xu & Zhang 2008), better learning strategy (Li & Fang 2005) and greater creativity (Jisheng Wang & Ding 2003). Pu, Lu, and He's (2012) study of college students provided further evidence that fathers' influence extends into their children's adulthood: College students who reported higher paternal presence and better between-parent relationships reported higher motivation to achieve.

It is noteworthy that some studies have yielded contradictory results: Liu and Chen (2005), for instance, examined the respective contributions of child temperament and parenting to children's language development. Their results suggested that paternal strictness (rejection, punishment, and encouragement of independence) positively predicted better language development. Yang, Wang, Teng, and Yu (2008), too, found that Chinese children who were insecurely attached to their fathers achieved more academically. These counterintuitive conclusions were attributed to Chinese children's perceptions of the ideal father as a strict parent who expects academic success.

SOCIOEMOTIONAL DEVELOPMENT

The paternal role in children's socioemotional development has been assessed in relation to a variety of benchmarks, often in comparison to the maternal role. Most of the recent evidence is congruent with the results of earlier studies (e.g., Zeng et al. 1997; Chen et al. 2004) which indicated that fathers have at least as much influence as mothers on children's socioemotional development. Li et al. (2004), who observed fifty-five 6- to 8-year-old children's social behavior during playtime, found that children whose fathers encouraged their independence and achievement tended to have richer play behavior and that children whose fathers were less rejecting initiated social interaction with peers more. Gu and Zhou (2008), too, found that children who had warm, understanding, nonpunitive fathers showed more competence and creativity in social contexts. Father involvement, mediated by father–child attachment, positively influences children's prosocial behavior (Li et al. 2012), and fathers who spend more time communicating with their adolescent children tended to have offspring who had better peer relationships (Song & Hao 2005; Wang, Lei, & Liu 2004).

Other empirical data seem to imply that fathers have less effect than mothers on children's developing socioemotional competence, as well as that such paths of influence are not straightforward. Ma, He, and Chen (2005), for instance, found that fathers' expression of negative emotions, when accompanied by mothers' expression of positive emotions, predicted children's secure attachment, implying that the "strict father, kind mother" ideal might still be at work. Liang, Zhang, Chen, and Zhang (2012), however, came to the opposite conclusion: Although both fathers' and mothers' emotional coaching contributed to better social skills, the best outcomes were achieved when fathers displayed more positive emotions and suppressed their negative emotions.

L. Liu et al. (2013) showed that father involvement, but not positive parenting styles, were linked to better cooperativeness and social skills in children and could buffer the negative impacts of harsh mothering. Zhang (2013), after carefully examining the bidirectional relationship between father–child interaction and children's social competence, found that the two factors predicted each other over a nine-month period in the first year (but not second year) of children's preschool lives. Taken together, these complicated and inconsistent results underline the need for more nuanced and better contextualized research on the role and effects of Chinese fathers.

SUMMARY AND FUTURE DIRECTIONS

The literature already reviewed clearly demonstrates growing awareness of the paternal role in China. Fathers are increasingly included in research on child development, and leading theories, existing research evidence, and standardized instruments are better known by Chinese scholars, who have started systematic research on fathers in Chinese families. Because fatherhood has only begun to attract academic and public attention in China and elsewhere, much remains unexplored about Chinese fatherhood. First, in-depth investigations are needed to better understand the culture of fatherhood in contemporary China. For instance, qualitative analyses of current public discourses of fatherhood, and its relation to constructs such as parenthood and masculinity, should be pursued to provide further information on what it means to be a father in Chinese societies today. At a time of globalization, one may ask how the Chinese people today perceive fathering relative to its incarnation in other cultures. How do Chinese men decide to become fathers, and what personal and societal factors are at work during the negotiation process now that the family planning policy has been relaxed in some provinces?

Having said that, the overreliance on theories and measures developed in the West and the paucity of indigenous approaches make it difficult to disentangle the cultural specificity of fathering in China from universal patterns of fathering. Although a growing body of evidence has shown similarities between Chinese fathers and their counterparts in other cultures and societies (such as the significance of warm, supportive fathering), the question "What is the Chineseness of Chinese fathers?" remains unanswered.

Second, it is necessary to thoroughly examine actual fathering conduct in contemporary Chinese families, ideally using representative samples (especially those including rural, inland, and ethnic minority populations and other understudied Chinese subgroups), multi-informant designs, and improved measures. Though "conventional" families can provide "baseline" data about the overall patterns of father involvement and father–child interaction, it is also crucial to study nonconventional and emerging family forms, such as migrant families and families with "long-distance" fathers, single fathers, and nonbiological fathers. Longitudinal data are of particular importance for establishing causal links between fathering behavior and childhood outcomes and for understanding the contributions of contextual variables such as father characteristics (e.g., fathers' education attainments, employment patterns and personality), child characteristics (e.g., child age, gender, physical and mental health), and family background (e.g., socioeconomic status) to father–child relationships.

Third, more research is needed on how father–child interactions are embedded in the wider interpersonal web, such as in relation to marital relationships and intergenerational contacts beyond the nuclear family. This is particularly relevant to Chinese societies considering the rapid social changes that are redefining various domains of public and personal life. For example, how are different relational dyads (parent–child, husband–wife, and parent–grandparent) (re)organized and evaluated in Chinese families? This begs for a family system perspective in studying fatherhood that takes into consideration the interconnection and mutual influences between the father–child dyad and other critical relationships in the family and beyond.

Whereas most existing studies of fathers focus on the child, researchers have much to explore regarding fathers' own experiences of parenthood and the influence of fatherhood on men themselves. This could be accomplished by looking at father's own accounts of their subjective feelings in day-to-day parenting and by identifying the effects of timing and quality of parenthood on men's lifespan development.

REFERENCES

Amato, P. R. (1998). *More than money? Men's contributions to their children's lives*. New York: Lawrence Erlbaum Associates Publishers.

Belsky, J. (1984). The determinants of parenting: A process model. *Child Development, 55*(1), 83–96.

Berndt, T., Cheung, P. C., Lau, S., Hau, K.-T., & Lew, W. J. F. (1993). Perceptions of parenting in mainland China, Taiwan, and Hong Kong: Sex differences and societal differences. *Developmental Psychology, 29*(1), 156–164.

Bond, M. H. (1993). Emotions and their expression in Chinese culture. *Journal of Nonverbal behavior, 17*(4), 245–262.

Bronfenbrenner, U. (1986). Ecology of the family as a context for human development: Research perspectives. *Developmental Psychology, 22*(6), 723–742.

Bronfenbrenner, U. (1997). Ecological models of human development. In M. Gauvin & M. Cole (eds.), *Readings on the development of children*, 2nd ed. (pp. 37–43). New York: Freeman.

Cai, C. (2014). Chengzhen ertong chengzhang zhong fuzhicanyu de xianzhuan ji sikao [Father involvement in the growth of urban suburban children]. *Journal of Inner Mongolia Normal University (Educational Science), 27*(4), 62–64.

Chang, L., Chen, B. B., & Ji, L. Q. (2011). Attributions and attitudes of mothers and fathers in China. *Parenting: Science and Practice, 11*(2–3), 102–115. doi: 10.1080/15295192.2011.585553.

Chang, L., Schwartz, D., Dodge, K. A., & McBride-Chang, C. (2003). Harsh parenting in relation to child emotion regulation and aggression. *Journal of Family Psychology, 17*(4), 598–606. doi: 10.1037/0893-3200.17.4.598.

Chao, R. K. (1994). Beyond parental control and authoritarian parenting style: Understanding Chinese parenting through the cultural notion of training. *Child Development, 65*(4), 1111–1119.

Chao, R. K. (2001). Extending Research on the Consequences of Parenting Style for Chinese Americans and European Americans. *Child Development, 72*(6), 1832–1843.

Chao, R. K., & Tseng, V. (2002). Parenting of Asians. In M. H. Bornstein (ed.), *Handbook of parenting* (2nd ed.), vol. 4: *Social conditions and applied parenting*, 59–84). Mahwah, NJ: Lawrence Erlbaum Associates, Inc.

Chen, C., Ni, H., & Yang, J. (2007). Xiaoxue Gaonianji ertong qizhi dui fumu jiaoyangfangshi de yingxiang [Influences of fourth and fifth-grade children's temperament on their parental parenting styles]. *Journal of Nanjing Normal University (Social Science), 2007*(3), 107–113, 160.

Chen, H., Zhang, H., Yin, J., Cheng, X., Wang, M. (2004). Father's rearing attitude and its prediction for 4–7-year-old children's problem behaviors and school adjustment. *Psychological Science, 27*(5), 1041–1045.

Chen, L., & Liu, Y. (2012). Liudong ertong qinzi goutong tedian jiqi yu xinli jiankang de guanxi [The characteristics of migrant children's communication in comparison with urban children and its relation to mental health]. *Chinese Journal of Special Education* (139), 59–64.

Chen, S. H., Kennedy, M., & Zhou, Q. (2012). Parents' expression and discussion of emotion in the multilingual family: Does language matter? *Perspectives on Psychological Science, 7*(4), 365–383. doi: 10.1177/1745691612447307.

Chen, Xin, & Du, J. (2006). Fumu jiaoyangfangshi yu neiyingongjixing de guanxi yanjiu [The relationship between parenting style and implicit aggression]. *Psychological Science, 29*(4), 798–801.

Chen, Xinyin (2010). Socioemotional development in Chinese children. In M. H. Bond (ed.), *Handbook of Chinese psychology* (pp. 37–52). New York: Oxford University Press.

Chen, Xinyin, Bian, Y., Xin, T., Wang, L., & Silbereisen, R. K. (2010). Perceived social change and childrearing attitudes in China. *European Psychologist, 15*(4), 260–270. doi: 10.1027/1016-9040/a000060.

Chen, Xinyin, & Chen, H. (2010). Children's socioemotional functioning and adjustment in the changing Chinese society. In R. K. Silbereisen & X. Chen (eds.), *Social change and human development* (pp. 209–226). London, UK: Sage Publications Ltd.

Chen, Xinyin, Hastings, P. D., Rubin, K. H., Chen, H., Cen, G., & Stewart, S. L. (1998). Child-rearing attitudes and behavioural inhibition in Chinese and Canadian toddlers: A cross-cultural study. *Developmental Psychology, 34*(4), 677–686.

Chen, Xinyin, Liu, M., & Li, D. (2000). Parental warmth, control, and indulgence and their relations to adjustment in Chinese children: A longitudinal study. *Journal of Family Psychology, 14*(3), 401–419. doi: 10.1037//0893-3200.14.3.401.

Chi, L. (2013). You'er jiating fuzi goutong zhuangkuang yanjiu [Father–child communications in families with preschoolers]. *Journal of China Women's University* (3), 107–112.

China population 2014. (n.d.). http://worldpopulationreview.com/countries/china -population/.

Chuang, S. S. (2009). Transformation and change: Parenting in Chinese societies. In J. A. Mancini & K. A. Roberto (eds.), *Pathways of human development: Explorations of change* (pp. 171–190). Plymouth, UK: Lexington Books.

Chuang, S. S., & Su, Y. (2009). Says who? Decision-making and conflicts among Chinese–Canadian and mainland Chinese parents of young children. *Sex Roles, 60*, 527–536. doi: 10.1007/s11199-008-9537-9.

Da, H. (2002). Fumu jiaoyangfangshi yu haizi de zixin, zixun, ziwoxiaoneng ji xinlijiankang shuiping de xiangguan yanjiu [Relationship of upbringing given by parents to self-confidence, self-esteem, self-efficacy and mental health of their children]. *Chinese Journal of Health Education, 18*(8), 483–486.

Dai, F., Wang, F., & Gao, X. (2003). Zhongxuesheng de xinlijiankang zhuangkuang jiqi yingxiang yinsu yanjiu [Mental health of high school students and its predictors]. *Occupation and Health, 19*(5), 99–101.

Deng, L., Fang, X., Li, Y., & Wan, J. (2006). Fumu jiankong yu qingshaonian de wenti xingwei [Parental monitoring and adolescent problem behaviors]. *Chinese Journal of Applied Psychology, 12*(4), 305–311.

Department of Economic and Social Affairs, U. N. (2011). Men in families and family policy in a changing world. New York: United Nations.

Doherty, W. J., Kouneski, E. F., & Erickson, M. F. (1998). Responsible fathering: An overview and conceptual framework. *Journal of Marriage and Family, 60*(2), 277–292.

Dollahite, D. C., Hawkins, A. J., & Brotherson, S. E. (1997). Fatherwork: A conceptual ethic of fathering as generative work. In A. J. Hawkins & D. Dollahite (eds.), *Generative Fathering: Beyond Deficit Perspectives*, 3, 17–35. Thousand Oaks, CA: Sage.

Engle, P. L., & Breaux, C. (1998). Fathers involvement with children: Perspectives from developing countries. In N. G. Thomas (ed.), *Social Policy Report*, vol. 12 (pp. 1–24). Ann Arbor, MI: Society for Research in Child Development.

Fong, V. L. (2002). China's one-child policy and the empowerment of urban daughters. *American Anthropologist, 104*(4), 1098–1109.

Fong, V. L. (2007). Morality, cosmopolitanism, or academic attainment? Discourses on "quality" and urban Chinese only children's claims to ideal personhood. *City and Society, 19*(1), 86–113. doi: 10.1525/city.2007.19.1.86.

Friedlmeier, W., Corapci, F., & Cole, P. M. (2011). Emotion socialization in cross-cultural perspective. *Social and Personality Psychology Compass, 5*(7), 410–427. doi: 10.1111/j.1751-9004.2011.00362.x.

Fung, H. (1999). The moral child: The socialization of shame among young Chinese children. *Ethos, 27*(2), 180–209.

Ge, M., & Zhang, H. (2007). Gaonianji xiaoxuesheng fumu yangyufangshi, gexing yu shejiaojiaolv de guanxi [Relationship among the parental rearing behaviors and personality and social anxiety of pupils]. *Chinese Journal of Primary Care, 21*(9), 33–34.

Gu, C., & Zhou, Z. (2008). Xiaoxuesheng shehuichuangzaoxing qingxiang yu fumu yangyufangshi de guanxi [On the relationship between social creative tendency and parenting styles among primary school students]. *Psychological Development and Education, 2008*(2), 34–38.

Guo, Z., & Wang, J. (2009). Fumu jiaoyangfangshi yu youer xinlijiankang de guanxi yanjiu [The relationship between parenting styles and mental health of preschoolers]. *Journal of Cangzhou Teachers' College, 25*(2), 72–73.

Han, J., Yu, Y., Yang, S., & Li, W. (2004). 365 Ming Yixuesheng de fumu jiaoyangfagshi yu qi xinlijiankang guanxi de yanjiu [The relationship between parental rearing styles and mental health among 356 medical students]. *Chinese Journal of School Health, 25*(5), 524–526.

Hao, Y., & Li, J. (2008). Xi'an shi chengxiang fumu jiaoyangfangshi dui gaozhongsheng xinlijiankang de yingxiang [The impact of urban/rural parental rearing pattern on the mental health of senior high school students of Xi'an]. *China Journal of Health Psychology, 16*(2), 201–203.

Hausmann, R., Tyson, L. D., Bekhouche, Y., & Zahidi, S. (2013). The global gender gap index *Insight Report*. Geneva, Switzerland: World Economic Forum.

Hawkins, A. J., Bradford, K. P., Palkovitz, R., Christiansen, S. L., Day, R. D., & Call, V. R. (2002). The inventory of father involvement: A pilot study of a new measure of father involvement. *The Journal of Men's Studies, 10*(2), 183–196.

Ho, D. Y. F. (1987). Fatherhood in Chinese culture. In M. E. Lamb (ed.), *The father's role: Cross-cultural perspectives* (pp. 227–246). Hillsdale, NJ: Lawrence Erlbaum Associates, Inc.

Ho, D. Y. F. (1989). Continuity and variation in Chinese patterns of socialization. *Journal of Marriage and Family, 51*(1), 149–163.

Ho, H.-Z., Chen, W.-W., Tran, C. N., & Ko, C.-T. (2010). Parental involvement in Taiwanese families: Father–mother differences. *Childhood Education*, 86(6), 376–381. doi: 10.1080/00094056.2010.10523173.

Ho, H.-Z., Tran, C. N., Ko, C.-Tt., Phillips, T. M., Boutin-Martinez, A., Dixon, C., & Chen, W.-W. (2011). Parental involvement: Voices of Taiwanese fathers. *International Journal about Parents in Education*, 5(2), 35–42.

Hsu, H. Y., Zhang, D., Kwok, O. M., Li, Y., & Ju, S. (2010). Distinguishing the influences of father's and mother's involvement on adolescent academic achievement: Analyses of Taiwan Education Panel Survey data. *Journal of Early Adolescence*, 31(5), 694–713. doi: 10.1177/0272431610373101.

Huang, Y., & Li, L. (2012). Jiating jiaoyangfangshi dui liushouertong xinlijiankang de yingxiang [Influence of family education style on stay-at-home children]. *Health Medicine Research and Practice*, 9(2), 31–34.

Hwang, K.-K. (2001). The deep structure of Confucianism: A social psychological approach. *Asian Philosophy, 11*(3), 179–204. doi: 10.1080/095523601 20116928.

Institute of Social Science Survey, Peking University (2010). *Chinese Family Dynamics 2010*. Beijing: Peking University Press.

Jankowiak, W. (1992). Father–child relations in urban China. In B. S. Hewlett (ed.), *Father–child relations: Cultural and biosocial contexts* (pp. 345–363). New York: Walter de Guyter.

Jankowiak, W., & Li, X. (2014). The decline of the chauvinistic model of Chinese masculinity: A research report. *Chinese Sociological Review*, 46(4), 3–18. doi: 10.2753/CSA2162-0555460401.

Ju, X., Liu, X., & Fang, X. (2011). Qingshaonian fumu, tongban yilian yu shehui shiyingxing de guanxi [Research on adolescent parents and peer attachment in relation to self-esteem and social adaptation]. *Psychological Development and Education, 2011*(2), 174–180.

Khaleque, A., & Rohner, R. P. (2011). Pancultural associations between perceived parental acceptance and psychological adjustment of children and adults: A meta-analytic review of worldwide research. *Journal of Cross-cultural Psychology, 43*(5), 784–800. doi: 10.1177/0022022111406120.

Kim, S. Y., Wang, Y., Orozco-Lapray, D., Shen, Y., & Murtuza, M. (2013). Does "tiger parenting" exist? Parenting profiles of Chinese Americans and adolescent developmental outcomes. *Asian American Journal of Psychology, 4*(1), 7–18. doi: 10.1037/a0030612

Kim, S. Y., & Wong, V. Y. (2002). Assessing Asian and Asian American Parenting: A review of the literature. In K. Kurasaki, S. Okazaki & S. Sue (eds.), *Asian American mental health: Assessment methods and theories.* ,New York: Kluwer/ Plenum Publishers.

Krampe, E. M. (2009). When is the father really there? A conceptual reformulation of father presence. *Journal of Family Issues, 30*(7), 875–897. doi: 10.1177/0192513x08331008.

Lamb, M. E., Pleck, J. H., Charnov, E. L., & Levine, J. A. (1987). A biosocial perspective on paternal behavior and involvement. In J. B. Lancaster, J. Altmann, A. S. Rossi & L. B. Sherrod (Eds.), *Parenting across the lifespan: Biosocial dimensions* (pp. 111–142). New York: A. de Gruyter.

Lau, S., Lew, W. J. F., Hau, K.-K., Cheung, P. C., & Berndt, T. J. (1990). Relations among perceived parental control warmth, indulgence, and family harmony in Chinese in mainland China. *Developmental Psychology, 26*(4), 674–677.

Li, D., Cui, L., Cen, G., Zhou, J., & Chen, X. (2004). Peer interaction of children aged 6–8 and its relation to paternal nurturing styles. *Psychological Science, 27*(4), 803–806.

Li, D., Zhou, Z., & Zhu, D. (2007). Diannaoyouxi yu qingshaonian wentixingwei, jiating ge yinsu de guanxi yanjiu [The interrelation among adolescent behavior problems, computer game playing and family factors]. *Psychological Science, 30*(2), 450–453.

Li, G., & Fang, P. (2007). A cognition research on parental rearing patterns of undergraduates. *Psychological Exploration, 103*(3), 61–65.

Li, J., & Zhou, H. (2008). Zhongxuesheng fumu jiaoyangfangshi, yingduifangshi de guanxi ji yingxiang yinsu [The Correlations between Parental Rearing Style and Coping Styles of the Middle School Students]. *China Journal of Health Psychology, 16*(12), 1382–1385.

Li, W., Zou, H., & Zhao, X. (2008). Daxuesheng tongyixing fazhan jiqi yu qinziyilian de guanxi yanjiu [College students' identity development and its relationships with parental attachment]. *Journal of Capital Normal University (Social Sciences Edition)* (180), 113–119.

Li, Xiuhong, Guo, L., Jing, J., Chen, Y., Lei, L., Wu, Y., & Lu, W. (2010). Daxuesheng gudu yu renzhifangshi yu fumu jiaoyangfangshi de xiangguanxing fenxi [Survey on the influence of cognitive style and parental rearing patterns on loneliness among undergraduates]. *Chinese Journal of School Health, 31*(12), 1456–1458.

Li, Xuan, & Lamb, M. E. (2013). Fathers in Chinese culture: From stern disciplinarians to involved parents. In D. Shwalb, B. Shwalb, & M. E. Lamb (eds.), *Fathers in cultural contexts* (pp. 15–41). New York: Routledge.

Li, Y., & Fang, P. (2005). Fumu jiaoyangfangshi yu zhongxuesheng ziwotiaojian xuexi de guanxi [Research of the relationship between parenting style and self- regulated learning in middle school students]. *Psychological Exploration, 25*(3), 40–45.

Li, Y., & Zhao, J. (2007). Fumu yangyu fangshi, fumu liyi dui gaozhongsheng xinlijiankang zhuangkuang de yingxiang [The influence of the parental rearing pattern and the divorce of parents to the mental health of high middle school] students. *China Journal of Health Psychology, 15*(10), 898–900.

Li, Zhihua, Yin, X., Cai, T., & Su, L. (2012). Fuqin canyujiaoyang chengdu, fuzi yilianguanxi dui ertong qinshehui xingwei de yingxiang [Role of father–child attachment in effects of father involvement on children's prosocial behavior]. *Chinese Journal of Clinical Psychology, 20*(5), 705–707.

Li, Zuoshan. (2001). Zhuanxingqi chuzhongsheng xinlijiankang yu fumu yangyufangshi de yanjiu [Mental health of junior high school students and parenting styles]. *Psychological Science, 24*(4), 445–448, 511.

Liang, Z., Zhang, G., Chen, H., & Zhang, P. (2012). Fumu yuanqingxu linian, qingxu biaoda yu ertong shehuinengli de guanxi [Relations among parental meta-emotion philosophy, parental emotion expressivity, and children's social competence]. *Acta Psychologica Sinica, 44*(2), 199–210. doi: 10.3724/sp.j.1041.2012.00199.

Liang, Z., Zhang, G., Deng, H., Song, Y., & Zheng, W. (2013). A multilevel analysis of the developmental trajectory of preschoolers' effortful control and prediction by parental parenting style. *Acta Psychologica Sinica, 45*(5), 556–567. doi: 10.3724/sp.j.1041.2013.00556.

Liu, Jinhua. (1995). An intergenerational comparison of paternal child-rearing attitudes and ideas in Shanghai. *Psychological Science* (4), 211–215, 255.

Liu, Jintong, Meng, X., Xu, Q., & Zhang, Y. (2005). Gaozhong xuesheng kaoshi jiaolv yu jiating yinsu de guanxi fenxi [An analysis of test anxiety and its family related factors in senior high school students]. *Shandong Archive of Psychiatry, 18*(3), 129–132.

Liu, L., & Li, Y. (2013). Muqin yiyu he chengfa dui ertong zaoqi wentixingwei de yingxiang ji fuqin de baohu zuoyong [The detriment of mother's depression and punishment on preschooler's problem behaviors and the protecting father]. *Psychological Development and Education, 2013*(5), 533–540.

Liu, L., Li, Y., Lü, Y., & Li, Y. (2013). Fuqin canyujiaoyang zhuangkuang dui xueqian ertong shehuijineng de zuoyong [The effects of father's involvement and parenting on children's early social skills]. *Psychological Development and Education, 2013*(1), 38–45.

Liu, R. X., Lin, W., & Chen, Z. Y. (2010). School performance, peer association, psychological and behavioral adjustments: A comparison between Chinese adolescents with and without siblings. *Journal of Adolescence, 33*(3), 411–417. doi: 10.1016/j.adolescence.2009.07.007.

Liu, X., & Zhao, N. (2006). Fuqin juese touru yu ertong de chengzhang [The role of the father and child development]. *Studies of Foreign Education, 33*(197), 13–18.

Liu, Z., & Chen, H. (2005). Qisui ertong yuyanbiaoda de yingxiang yinsu [The influencing factors of seven-year-old children's language expression]. *Psychological Science, 28*(5), 1126–1130.

Liu, Z., & Tan, Q. (2003). Gaozhongsheng de fumu yangyufangshi, tongbanguanxi yu qi ziwogainian de guanxi yanjiu [The study on relationship between parental rearing styles, companionship and self-concept in senior middle school students]. *Health Psychology Journal, 11*(4), 245–248.

Louie, K. (2002). *Theorising Chinese masculinity: Society and gender in China.* Cambridge, UK: Cambridge University Press.

Lu, H. J., & Chang, L. (2013). Parenting and socialization of only children in urban China: An example of authoritative parenting. *Journal of Genetic Psychology, 174*(3), 335–343. doi: 10.1080/00221325.2012.681325.

Lu, Q. (2009). Chengxiang fumu yangyufangshi yu daxuesheng ziwogainian de youguan yanjiu [Relationship between parenting style and self-concept of college students from city and countryside]. *Psychological Exploration* (129), 78–83.

Lu, Y., & Zhang, Y. (2008). Chuzhongsheng yiyu yu yilian, ziwoxiaonenggan de guanxi yanjiu [Researches into the relationships among attachment, general self-efficacy and depressive symptoms in junior middle school students]. *Psychological Development and Education, 2008*(1), 55–60.

Ma, Jianhong, He, X., & Chen, M. (2005). Jiating qingxuqifen dui ertong yilianxingwei leixing de yingxiang [Style of attachment of children and the emotional expression of parents]. *Chinese Mental Health Journal, 19*(10), 672–675.

Ma, Jiantang. (2011). Press release on major figures of the 2010 National Population Census. www.stats.gov.cn/english/newsevents/201104/t20110428_26448.html.

Markus, H. R., & Kitayama, S. (1991). Culture and the self: Implications for cognition, emotion, and motivation. *Psychological Review*, 98(2), 224–253.

McHale, J. P., Rao, N., & Krasnow, A. D. (2000). Constructing family climates: Chinese mothers' reports of their co-parenting behaviour and preschoolers' adaptation. *International Journal of Behavioral Development*, 24(1), 111–118. doi: 10.1080/016502500383548.

Naftali, O. (2009). Empowering the child: Children's rights, citizenship and the state in contemporary China. *The China Journal*, 61, 79–103.

Nie, J., & Lu, Y. (2014). Fuqin canyu dui ertong yanchimanzu nengli de yingxiang: Ertong xingbie de tiaojie zuoyong [Fathers' involvement and children's delay of gratification: The moderating role of gender]. *Psychological Development and Education*, 2014(2), 121–128.

Nolan, J. (2010). Gender and equality of opportunity in China's labour market. In M. F. Ozbilgin & J. Syed (eds.), *Managing gender diversity in Asia: A research companion* (pp. 160–182). Cheltenham, UK: Edward Elgar Publishing Limited.

Overseas Chinese. (n.d.). http://en.wikipedia.org/wiki/Overseas_Chinese.

Palkovitz, R. (1997). Reconstructing "involvement": Expanding conceptualizations of men's caring in contemporary families. In A. J. Hawkins & D. Dollahite (eds.), *Generative fathering: Beyond deficit perspectives* (pp. 200–216). Thousand Oaks, CA: Sage.

Pan, Y., Jin, X., Yang, Q., Wang, J., & Chen, X. (2005). Fumu jiaoyangfangshi yu xiaoxue zhonggaonianji xuesheng gudugan de diaochayanjiu. [A Survey on the relationship between parents' teaching methods and three-six graders' loneliness]. *Journal of Wenzhou Normal College*, 26(6), 108–113.

Paquette, D. (2004). Theorizing the father–child relationship: Mechanisms and developmental outcomes. *Human Development*, 47, 193–219. doi: 10.1159/000078723.

Peng, Y., Niu, C., Chen, X., Li, J., & Zhang, H. (2011). Zhongzhisheng fumu jiaoyangfangshi de yanjiu [Study on the Parental Rearing Patterns among the Secondary Vocational School Students]. *China Journal of Health Psychology*, 19(4), 433–434.

Perris, C., Jacobsson, L., Linndström, H., Knorring, L. V., & Perris, H. (1987). Development of a new inventory for assessing memories of parental rearing behaviour. *Acta Psychiatrica Scadinavica*, 61(4), 265–274.

Powell, M. A., Taylor, N., & Smith, A. (2008). Rural childhoods: Literature review. Childwatch International Study Group.

Pu, S., & Lu, N. (2008). Fuqin jiaoyang de yanjiu jinzhan [New progress in research on paternal nurturance]. *China Journal of Health Psychology*, 16(10), 1194–1197.

Pu, S., Lu, N., & He, J. (2012). Daxuesheng fuqin zaiwei yu chengjiudongji de guanxi [Relationship between father presence and achievement motivation of college students]. *Journal of Southwest China Normal University (Natural Science Edition)*, 37(6), 193–197.

Pu, S., Lu, N., Ling, Y., & Cao, Y. (2012). Daxuesheng fuqin zaiwei de tedian fenxi [Characteristics to father presence of Chinese college students]. *Journal of Preventative Medical Information*, 28(8), 591–593.

Putnick, D. L., Bornstein, M. H., Lansford, J. E., Chang, L., Deater-Deckard, K., Di Giunta, L., . . . Bombi, A. S. (2012). Agreement in mother and father acceptance–rejection, warmth, and hostility/rejection/neglect of children across nine countries. *Cross-cultural Research, 46*(3), 191–223. doi: 10.1177/1069397112440931.

Quah, S. R. (2003). Major trends affecting families in east and southeast Asia (D. o. S. P. a. Development & U. N. Department of Economic and Social Affairs, trans.) *Major trends affecting families: A background document* (pp. 78–105). New York: United Nations.

Shek, D. T. (1998). A longitudinal study of the relations between parent–adolescent conflict and adolescent psychological well-being. *Journal of Genetic Psychology, 159*(1), 53–67. doi: 10.1080/00221329809596134.

Shen, J., Wu, H., & Zhao, M. (2006). Fumu yangyufangshi dui ertong xingwei he xinlijiankang yingxiang de yanjiu [Study of the effect of parental rearing pattern on the children's behavior and mental health]. *Chinese Journal of Children's Health, 14*(2), 133–135.

Shwalb, D. W., Nakazawa, J., Yamamoto, T., & Hyun, J.-H. (2010). Fathering in Japan, China and Korea. In M. E. Lamb (ed.), *The role of the father in child development* (5th ed.). Hoboken, NJ: John Wiley and Sons.

Sim, B.-W. T. (2005). *The dynamics of family relationships in male adolescent drug rehabilitation.* Ph.D. dissertation, Hong Kong University, Hong Kong.

Song, G., & Hao, B. (2005). Xuesheng shejiaohuibi xingwei, kunao tiyan zhuangkuang jiqi yu fumu jiaoyangfangshi guanxi de yanjiu [Relationship between social avoidance, distress experience and parented educational modes of college students]. *Chinese Journal of Health Psychology, 13*(2), 133–135.

Song, L. (2009). Qianxi fuqin zai ertong xingbiejuesehua guocheng zhong de yingxiang [Father and children's sex-role development]. *Journal of Lingcant Teachers' College, 18*(3), 66–69.

Strom, R. D., Strom, S. K., & Xie, Q. (1995). The small family in China. *International Journal of Early Childhood, 27*(2), 37–46.

Sun, L.-C., Roopnarine, J. L. (1996). Mother–infant, father–infant interaction and involvement in childcare and household labor among Taiwanese families. *Infant Behavior and Development, 19,* 121–129.

Sun, Yongming, Lu, Y., & Dong, Q. (1998). Fumu jiaoyu xingwei de jiegou jiqi yu xiaoxue ertong jiaolv qingxu de guanxi [The relationship between the structure of parenting and pre-school children's anxiety]. *Psychological Development and Education, 1998*(3), 14–18.

Sun, Yuanyuan (2013). Fuqin canyu dui peiyang you'er shuangxinghua renge de yingxiang [The influence of fathers' involvement on training infants' androgyny]. *Educational Psychology* (4), 197–198.

Tang, N. M. (1992). Some psychoanalytic implications of Chinese philosophy and child-rearing practices. *Psychoanalytic Study of the Child, 47,* 371–389.

Teng, Q., Xing, Y., & Yang, X. (2010). Fuqin de jiaoyangfangshi jiqi dui zinv jiaolv de yingxiang [Paternal parenting style and its influence on the anxiety level of children]. *Journal of Ningbo Radio and TV University, 8*(1), 66–70.

To, S. (2013). Understanding Sheng Nu ("leftover women"): The phenomenon of late marriage among Chinese professional women. *Symbolic Interaction, 36*(1), 1–20. doi: 10.1002/SYMB.46.

Tsai, J. L., & Levenson, R. W. (1997). Cultural influences on emotional responding: Chinese American and European American dating couples during interpersonal conflict. *Journal of Cross-cultural Psychology*, 28(5), 600–625. doi: 10.1177/0022022197285006.

Wang, C.-K. (2000). An exploratory study on the formation of child-rearing fatherhood. *Research in Applied Psychology* (6), 1–40.

Wang, Jingzhi, Wang, X., & Wu, J. (2012). Fuqin canyu dui ertong zaoqi xinli fazhan de yingxiang tanjiu [Paternal participation in the early mental development]. *Journal of Hebei Normal University (Educational Science Edition)*, 14(1), 89–92.

Wang, Jisheng, & Ding, X. (2003). Zhongxuesheng chuangxin xinlisuzhi yu xiangguanyinsu de zonghe yanjiu [A study on the relevant factors in the innovative diatheses of secondary school students]. *Psychological Science*, 26(4), 599–602.

Wang, L. (2005). Guowai fuqin jiaoyangfangshi yanjiu de xianzhuang he qushi [The history, present condition and trend of the research on fathering pattern in the western]. *Advances in Psychological Science*, 13(1), 290–297.

Wang, Q., & Chang, L. (2010). Parenting and child socialization in contemporary China. In M. H. Bond (ed.), *The Oxford Handbook of Chinese Psychology* (pp. 53–68). New York: Oxford University Press.

Wang, S. (2013). Fuqing jiaoyangfangshi yu muqin jiaoyangfangshi de guanxi yanjiu [The relationship between fathers' and mothers' parenting style]. *Journal of Jining University*, 34(2), 45–48.

Wang, T.-W. (2000). "Fuzhi canyu" huo "Canyu qinzhi de fuqin"? [Father involvement or involved fathers?]. *Applied Psychology Research* (7), 12–18.

Wang, Yijun, Zhang, H., Lu, X., Chen, S., Xia, W., Qiao, M., & Li, H. (2005). Zhongxuesheng kaoshijiaolv biaoxian de xingbie chayi [Gender difference of test-anxiety in secondary school students]. *Chinese Journal of Clinical Recovery*, 9(40), 24–26.

Wang, Ying, & Fong, V. L. (2009). Little emperors and the 4:2:1 generation: China's singletons. *Journal of the American Academy of Child and Adolescent Psychiatry*, 48(12), 1137–1139. doi: 10.1097/CHI.0b013e3181bc72f8.

Wang, Z., Lei, L., & Liu, H. (2004). Qinzi goutong dui qinshaonian shehui shiying de yingxiang: Jianji putong xuexiao he gongdu xuexiao de bijiao [Parent–child communication and adjustment: A comparative study]. *Psychological Science*, 27(5), 1056–1059.

Way, N., Okazaki, S., Zhao, J., Kim, J. J., Chen, X., Yoshikawa, H., . . . Deng, H. (2013). Social and emotional parenting: Mothering in a changing Chinese society. *Asian American Journal of Psychology*, 4(1), 61–70. doi: 10.1037/a0031204.

Wolf, M. (1978). Child training and the Chinese family. In J. Guillemin (ed.), *Anthropological realities: Readings in the science of culture* (123–138). Palo Alto, CA: Stanford University Press.

Wu, H., Zhu, M., & Liu, W. (2012). You'er fuqin canyu fuzhijiaoyu de yiyuan he zu'aiyinsu diaocha ji xiangguan sikao—Yi Wuhan Shi weili [Investigation and reflections on willingness to take fathering education and the hindering factors—taking Wuhan as an example]. *Early Childhood Education (Educational Sciences)* (555–556), 61–64.

Wu, P., Robinson, C. C., Yang, C., Hart, C. H., Olsen, S. F., Porter, C. L., . . . Wu, X. (2002). Similarities and differences in mothers' parenting of preschoolers in

China and the United States. *International Journal of Behavioral Development*, 26(6), 481–491. doi: 10.1080/01650250143000436.

Wu, W., Wang, L., Zhou, Y., Yang, H., Yang, S., & Han, J. (2010). Wuhan Shi mouxiao chuzhongsheng shengzhiweisheng zhuangkuang jiqi yingxiang yinsu fenxi [Reproductive health and its predictors among junior high school students in Wuhan]. *Chinese Journal of School Health* (12), 1512–1513.

Xie, J., Zhang, H., & Li, X. (2009). Fumu jiaoyangfangshi, ziwogainian yudaxuesheng wangluochengyin de guanxi [The relationship among parenting styles, self-concept and internet addiction among university students]. *Studies on Ideological Education* (163), 47–50.

Xu, A. (2004). Nvxing de jiawu gongxian he jiating diwei. In X. Meng (ed.), *Zhuanxing shehui zhong de zhongguo funv* [Chinese women in social transitions]. Beijing: China Social Sciences Press.

Xu, A., & Zhang, L. (2007). Fuqin canyu: Hexie jiating jianshe zhong de shanghai chengxiang bijiao [Father involvement: A comparison between rural and urban families during the construction of harmonious families]. *Youth Studies* (6), 41–48.

Xu, A., & Zhang, L. (2008). Nongcun fuqin de qinzhi canyu yiyuan, xingwei yu tiyan: Shanghai jiaoxian de jingyan yanjiu [Rural father's will, acts and experience of parenting—Experienced researcher of Shanghai's suburb]. *Bulletin of Social Science, Hunan Normal University* (3), 72–76.

Xu, S., & Liu, J. (1999). Ertong ziwokongzhi shuiping yu fumu jiaoyuguannian jian guanxi de yanjiu [The relationship between children's self-control and parental child-rearing attitudes]. *Psychological Development and Education*, 1999(2), 23–26.

Xu, Y. (2008). Guanyu fuqin canyu ertong jiaoyang de diaochayanjiu: Fuqin canyu jiaoyang zai shehuijingjidiwei shang de tedian [A survey of father involvement: Father involvement and its relationship to socioeconomic status]. *Bulletin of Shandong College of Educational Sciences*, 128, 15–19.

Xu, Yan. (2010). Fuqin de hunyin manyidu ji shehuizhichi dui qi canyu ertong jiaoyang de yingxiang [The effects of satisfactory about marriage and social support on fathers' involvement]. *Bulletin of Shangdong College of Educational Sciences* (137), 115–118.

Xu, Yan, Ji, L., & Zhang, W. (2006). Chengshi fuqin canyu ertong jiaoyang de tedian jiqi yu xingbiejuese de guanxi [Urban fathers' involvement in children's parenting and its relationship with gender roles]. *Psychological Development and Education* (3), 35–40.

Xu, Yiyuan, Farver, J., Zhang, Z., Zeng, Q., Yu, L., & Cai, B. (2005). Mainland Chinese parenting styles and parent–child interaction. *International Journal of Behavioral Development*, 29(6), 524–531. doi: 10.1177/01650250500147121.

Xu, Z., Bao, S., & Zheng, W. (2004). Shanghai Shi xueling ertong xingwei wenti yu qinzi guanxi xiangguan yanjiu [A correlation study on the behavioral problem and parent–child (P-C) relationship of school children in Shanghai]. *Psychological Science*, 27(2), 404–406.

Yan, Y. (2006). Girl power: Young women and the waning of patriarchy in rural north China. *Ethnology*, 45(2), 105–123.

Yang, A., Wang, D., Teng, F., & Yu, Z. (2008). Gaozhongsheng dui fumu de yilian yu xueyechengjiu he zizun de guanxi [Relationship between attachment to parents with perceived academic achievement and self-esteem in high-school students]. *Chinese Journal of Clinical Psychology, 16*(1), 55–58.

Yang, B., & Hou, Y. (2014). Zinv xingbie yu fumu jiaoyangfangshi zhijiande guanxi yanjiu [The relationship between children and parental rearing styles]. *Journal of Weinan Normal University, 29*(3), 58–61.

Yang, G. (2010). Fumu jiaoyangfangshi dui zhongxuesheng zhuguan xingfugan de yingxiang [The impact of parents' upbringing modes on senior high school students' subjective well-being]. *Journal of Wuxi Institute of Technology, 19*(1), 93–96.

Yang, K.-S. (1986). Chinese personality and its change. In M. H. Bond (ed.). *The Psychology of the Chinese People* (pp. 106–170). New York: Oxford University Press.

Yang, X., & Zou, H. (2008). Qingshaonian qinzi goutong de tedian yanjiu [Characteristics of parent–adolescent communication]. *Psychological Development and Education, 2008*(1), 49–54.

Yang, Yunyun, She, C., & Zhang, L. (2005). Ertong qingshaonian fumu jiaoyangfangshi de chengxiang bijiao [A comparative study on children and adolescents parenting styles between rural and urban China]. *Journal of Shandong Normal University (Humanities and Social Sciences), 50*(6), 152–155.

Yang, Yuqin, & Zhao, Z. (2010). Guanyu mou bianjiang diqu fumu dui zinv jiaoyangfangshi de diaocha [A survey about parents' training children in some border area]. *The Border Economy and Culture* (84), 130–131.

Yeung, W. J. J., & Alipio, C. (2013). Transitioning to adulthood in Asia: School, work, and family life. *The Annals of the American Academy of Political and Social Science, 646*(1), 6–27. doi: 10.1177/0002716212470794.

Yin, X., Li, Z., & Su, L. (2013). Fuqin yilian yu ertong qingxu xingwei fazhan de yuce guanxi: Yinian zhuizongyanjiu [Father attachment and children's emotional and behavioral development: A one-year follow-up]. *Chinese Journal of Clinical Psychology, 21*(6), 1036–1038.

Yu, Yyingyi, Liang, X., Zhao, G., Lin, Z., & Yang, X. (2005). Jiangmenshi Xinhuiqu gaozhongsheng xinlijiankang zhuangkuang diaocha ji yingxiang yinsu fenxi [Investigation of mental health status and influencing factor analysis in senior middle school students in Xinhui district of Jiangmen city]. *Chinese Journal of Clinical Rehabilitation, 9*(40), 22–24.

Zeng, Q., Lu, Y., Zou, H., Dong, Q., & Chen, X. (1997). Fumu jiaoyufangshi yu ertong de xuexiaoshiying [Parenting styles and children's school adjustment]. *Psychological Development and Education, 1997*(2), 46–51.

Zeng, S. (2009). Liudong ertong fumu de jiaoyangfangshi jiqi dui ganyu de qishi yiyi [Parenting styles of migrant children and their significance to interventions]. *Journal of Educational Development* (5), 25–28.

Zhang, G. (2007). Lun tangdai jiating zhong fumu de juese jiqi yu zinv de guanxi [Relationship between parents and children in the Tang Dynasty]. *Journal of Chinese Literature and History* (3), 207–249.

Zhang, L., Zhang, G., Xie, S., & Li, Y. (2010). Chuzhongsheng xinlijiangkang zhuangkuang yu fumu jiaoyangfangshi de yanjiu [Relationship between mental health status and parental rearing styles in junior high school students]. *China Journal of Health Psychology, 18*(3), 288–291.

Zhang, W. (1997). Chengxiang qingshaonian fumu jiaoyufangshi de bijiao yanjiu [A comparative study of parenting styles of rural and urban adolescents]. *Psychological Development and Education, 3*, 44–49.

Zhang, X. (2013). Bidirectional longitudinal relations between father–child relationships and Chinese children's social competence during early childhood. *Early Childhood Research Quarterly, 28*(1), 83–93. doi: 10.1016/j.ecresq.2012.06.005.

Zhang, X., Chen, H., Zhang, G., Zhou, B., & Wu, W. (2008). Qinziguanxi yu wentixingwei de dongtai xianghuzuoyong moxing: Dui ertong zaoqi de zhuizongyanjiu [A longitudinal study of parent–child relationships and problem behaviors in early childhood: Transactional models]. *Acta Psychologica Sinica, 40*(5), 571–582.

Zhou, B., & Zhang, Z. (2004). Meiguo ertong fazhan zhong fuqin yingxiangzuoyong yanjiuzongshu [Review of research on the influence of fathers on child development in the United States]. *Dangdai Qingnian Yanjiu [Contemporary Youth Research]* (2), 47–51.

Zhou, J., & Ma, Z. (2008). Dui Wenzhou diqu gaoyi xuesheng fumu yangyufangshi de diaochayanjiu [Survey study on the parenting styles of senior high school freshmen in Wenzhou]. *Journal of Chifeng University (Social Sciences), 29*(2), 9–12.

Zhou, L., & Yang, X. (2007). Xitonglun shiye xia de fuqin jiaoyangfanghi yu ertong qizhi de guanxi tanxi [The relationship between fathers' parenting styles and children's temperament, analyzed with the view of system theory]. *Journal of AShanxi College for Youth Administrations, 27*(4), 21–23.

Zhu, M., Fan, J., Luo, Q., & Huang, Q. (2009). Fuqin shoujiaoyu chengdu yinsu yu youer tizhi shuiping de guanlianxing [Research on the relationship between fathers' education and level of the children's body constitution]. *Journal of Hubei Sports Science, 28*(4), 28.

14

Fathering in Japan

Jun Nakazawa

CULTURAL OVERVIEW OF JAPANESE FATHERING

"I will go back home now. My baby may be crying. His mother may also be waiting for me." (Manyoshu, Vol. 3, #337)

"Silver, gold, and jewels are all treasures. However, they never equal the greater treasure that is a child." (Manyoshu, Vol. 5, #803)

These are traditional *waka* (Japanese poems) by Okura Yamanoue (728) in the *Manyoshu*. His poems showed that a Japanese father cared and loved his child more than 1,300 years ago. Centuries after the *Manyoshu* in 1563, Portuguese missionary Fróis visited Japan and wrote, "We whipped our son as a form of discipline, but do not observe any whipping in Japan. Instead, the Japanese only scold verbally (Fróis 1585)." Three hundred years later, American biologist Morse (1917) wrote similarly that "Japan is a paradise for children. The children in this country are not only treated kindly, but they also have more freedom than children in other countries." Thus, permissive parenting based on loose parent–child relations was a traditional folk discipline in Japan.

The Japanese traditional father role was based on Confucianism, a system of ethics derived from Chinese culture in the sixth century. In the seventeenth and eighteenth centuries, a patriarchal *Ie* (family) system governed Japanese life. The *Ie* system put a higher value on boys than on girls and on the eldest son than on younger ones. The eldest son became the head of the extended family and controlled the whole family as a patriarch. Confucianism emphasized *Kou* (filial piety), and parents adhered to a *Genpu Jibo* (Strict father and gentle mother) parenting style in which fathers guided their children strictly and mothers gave protective nurturing care. Fathers had all responsibility for the discipline and education of children.

The most famous childrearing guidebook in the Edo Era was the *Wazoku-Douji-Kun* (Kaibara 1710). Kaibara wrote this book for fathers and indicated that the father's childrearing should be strict and that children should be filial (loyal) toward parents. Maternal childrearing tended to be overprotective and was thought to spoil children. Mothers were to raise children under the guidance of fathers. However, Kojima's (2001) analysis of samurai journals showed that samurai fathers were actively involved in childrearing and nurtured their children with love. Thus the formal role of strict fathers coexisted with an informal tradition of permissive fathering.

Although Japan westernized after the Meiji Era (1868), the virtues of Confucianism were stressed in the Japanese legal system. In addition, after the Meiji Era, modern family gender roles in which fathers worked outside the home and mothers stayed at home and were in charge of household work and childrearing gradually diffused through Japanese society. Childrearing became the mother's work, and fathers were deprived from the experience of childrearing.

After World War II, the *Ie* system was repealed and Confucian virtues separated from the political system. The father's role became that of a breadwinner, a responsible worker in the era of postwar economic reconstruction. From the 1950s to the 1980s, the Japanese work system prioritized work over home life. In return for this commitment, companies provided housing and lifelong employment. The childrearing pattern in which mothers took care of children and fathers were not involved with children appeared the same as in the prewar era.

Changes in Marriage and Family Systems

In the *Ie* system, marriage meant connections in each *Ie* (family) and marriage was for the sake of the family. Arranged marriages prevailed. After World War II, the Japanese view of marriage changed from that of connections primarily between families to connections both between families and between individuals, based more on the will of the young couple. The number of arranged marriages decreased (percentages of arranged marriages and love-based marriages were, respectively, 69.0% and 13.4% for 1930–1939, 49.5% and 41.1% for 1960–1964, and 5.3% and 88.0% for 2005–2009; National Institute of Population and Social Security Research 2010).

Because of the collapse of the *Ie* system and urbanization, the trend toward nuclear families accelerated. The percentage of nuclear families among those with children was 69.9% in 1975 and increased to 80.5% in 2010 (National Institute of Population and Social Security Research 2014). The percentage of spouses who lived with their parents was 37.8 percent in rural areas but only 17.2 percent in urban areas in 2008 (National Institute of Population

and Social Security Research 2008). This made it difficult for urban parents to depend on grandparents for assistance with childrearing. Moreover,
because the Japanese view childrearing as parents' responsibility, the use of
babysitters and housemaids is uncommon. Accordingly, childrearing relies
on parents and formal childcare institutions such as day nurseries (Shwalb,
Shwalb, Sukemune, & Tatsumoto 1992).

Employment and Economic Conditions Related to Fathering

The post–World War II growth of the Japanese economy faded from the
1990s. In succession, a lengthy recession in the context of failed economic
policies in the 1990s, the Kobe Earthquake of 1995, the international financial
crisis of 2008, and the Tohoku earthquake, tsunami, and nuclear plant failure of 2011 all severely affected Japan's economy and industrial system. These
changes brought the demise of the Japanese employment system—i.e., accepting policies such as outsourcing, performance-based pay, and increasingly temporary employment in Japanese workplaces. As a result, the family income
gap is widening. To support family income, maternal employment continues
to grow even as fathers' involvement in childrearing is increasingly necessary.

Social Structural Changes Related to Fathering

Low fertility.   The number of Japanese children is now rapidly decreasing,
and the number of newborn children in 2012 (1.04 million) was less than half
what it was in 1949 (2.70 million). The total fertility rate of 1949 was 4.32,
but it had decreased to 1.41 by 2012 (Ministry of Health, Labor and Welfare 2013). This decrease in the number of children may be a major reason
for increasingly protective childrearing and raised expectations for fathers'
involvement in childrearing.

Along with low fertility, Japanese society is characterized by a rapidly
aging population. The percentage of aged people (older than 65) was only
4.9 percent in 1950 but increased to 25.1 percent by 2013 (Cabinet Office,
Statistics Bureau 2014).

Women's social participation.   The notion of gender equality after World
War II, the popularization of higher education among women (the college-
university entrance rate of women is 55.5 percent and that of males is 50.8
percent; Ministry of Education, Culture, Sports, Science & Technology
2013) and women's increased participation in society has made women a
huge factor in the workforce. For example, the percentage of women who
agreed with the survey statement that staying at home is the ideal life course
for women was 34 percent in 1987 but only 19.7 percent in 2010. Meanwhile,

the percentage of women who reportedly wanted to get married and have children while continuing to work was 19 percent in 1987 and increased to 30.6 percent in 2010 (National Institute of Population and Social Security Research 2010). The percentage of women who actually continue to work after their first baby's birth is higher among university graduates (45.7%) than among those having a high school diploma (27.5%) (National Institute of Population and Social Security Research 2008).

Maternal workforce.   Japan faces a labor shortage and difficulty in maintaining its economic system because of decreasing fertility and the aging population. These factors, women's motivation to participate in society, and the long recession have all contributed to the expansion of maternal employment. Comparing the female work rate between 2002 and 2012, there was stability for unmarried women (aged 25–29: 91.4–90.9%; aged 30–34: 89.1–89.2%). However, there was an increase during this decade of about 10 percent among married women (aged 25–29: 45.5–55.5%; aged 30–34: 46.7–55.6%) (Ministry of Health, Labor and Welfare 2012). The social need for the continuation of maternal employment has promoted fathers' childrearing involvement, as most people believe that husbands in dual-earner families should perform a share of housework and be more involved with childrearing activities in support of the mothers' employment.

Social discourse about father absence.   Children's problem behavior and maladjustment such as school nonattendance, bullying, suicide, and homicide increased from the 1980s to the 1990s. At that time, social discourses appeared in the mass media suggesting that father absence (or noninvolvement in childrearing) was a main contributing factor to these problems. These discourses also influenced men's thinking about childrearing activities—i.e., that they should attend, more to and actively interact with, their children (Shwalb, Imaizumi, & Nakazawa 1987).

The Father's Role in Japan

Paternal involvement in childrearing.   As the number of working mothers increased, childrearing has become the shared task of mothers and fathers. Chuochosasha's (2012) research, in which about 1,300 people older than 20 were interviewed about the father's participation in childrearing, reported increasing levels of agreement with the statement that "Both father and mother actively share and participate in childrearing." This rate (45% in 2012) has gradually increased year to year (34.7% in 2010; 39.1% in 2011), whereas agreement that "Fathers should concentrate on work, and mothers should concentrate on childrearing" was only 8.5 percent in 2012.

Magazines for fathers. Societal interest in father involvement has also brought about the publication of several magazines for fathers since 2000. Tendo and Takahashi (2011) analyzed the contents of two of these magazines, *Nikkei Kids+* and *President Family*. Based on page ratios, "study and learning" (13.3%), "entrance examination for prestigious schools" (12.0%), and "ways of childrearing and discipline" (9.4%) were the dominant themes of articles. These two magazines provide educational and childrearing information and emphasize the father's responsibility to bring out the child's innate talents in support of the child's pursuit of higher education and higher income. However, they do not focus on the societal needs for shared childrearing between working parents.

JAPANESE FATHERS' ROLE AND CHILDREARING INVOLVEMENT

Japanese fathering research has been described in several book chapters (Shwalb, Imaizumi, & Nakazawa 1987; Shwalb, Nakazawa, Yamamoto, & Hyun 2004, 2010; Nakazawa & Shwalb 2013). In the following section, I will describe recent fathering research in the context of Japan's major economic and social transitions.

Becoming a Father

What kind of psychological changes do men experience by becoming fathers? Sasaki (2009) examined fathers' feelings before and 1.5–2 months after the first child's birth. In her sample, reports of "Actually feeling like a father" and "Happiness" increased after the birth of the child. She also found that a good marital relationship was positively related to "Actually feeling like a father," "Happiness," and "Confidence," and negatively related to "Economic constraints and loss of freedom."

One common Japanese setting for childbirth is delivery in the maternal parents' hometown, a custom called *satogaeri shussan*. In this context, the mother benefits from parental support and can be relieved of some of her anxiety before delivery. Kimura et al. (2003) examined pairs of pregnant wives and husbands before *satogaeri shussan* delivery and four months after delivery. There were no differences in women's feelings about being mothers between those who did or did not deliver in their hometowns. But the intensity of men's feelings about being a father and their participation in taking care of the baby were lower among those whose wives delivered in the hometown rather than with the husband's support. This study suggested that involvement at the time of delivery and early contact with the baby may affect father's subsequent attitudes and behavior.

In another study, Morishita (2006) found that fathers' childrearing involvement with kindergarten children influenced the following psychological changes among men: "Increased love for his family," "Responsibility," "A broader perspective," and "A new way of looking at the past and future." Takahashi and Takahashi (2009) also found several psychological changes in parents of kindergarten children, such as "A wider perspective," "Flexible thinking," "Gaining a reason for living," "Strength of self," "Integrative vision of past and future," and "Loss of freedom." They further noted that satisfaction with the spousal relationship influenced the father's psychological development and that his childrearing participation influenced the mother's psychological development.

Oshima (2011) examined the psychological development of fathers of adult children (20- to 30-year-old children) and identified two aspects of these fathers' psychological development: "A wider perspective" and "Deepening of his own life." These two elements appeared to be influenced and enhanced by interactions with children.

These studies of the father's own development showed overall that participation in childrearing and the spousal relationship are important factors influencing the psychological development as a father. Thus becoming a father provides a man with a good opportunity to gain a new view of his own life.

Father–Child Involvement

Data from the national government's cabinet office (2013a) showed that fathers of children younger than age 6 on average spent only sixty-seven minutes daily in household activities in 2011, including thirty-nine minutes in childrearing. This was an increase of seven minutes daily from 2006, but it was significantly less than comparable data from three other countries in this international study (U.S. household time = 171 minutes, including sixty-five minutes of childrearing; U.K. household time = 166 minutes including, sixty minutes of childrearing; Sweden household time = 201 minutes, including sixty-seven minutes of childrearing).

The research by Chuouchosasha (2012) provided some reasons for this low level of childrearing involvement among Japanese fathers. The first reason they gave was "Difficult to take time for childrearing because of hard work" (71.5%), followed, in frequency of reporting, by "Childrearing is a woman's work" (37.2%), "Lack of governmental support to promote a father's childrearing involvement" (34.4%), "Lack of knowledge of childrearing methods" (31.4%), and "childrearing is bothersome" (17.5%). This research also asked about critical factors that would improve men's participation in childrearing. In order of frequency, participants chose the following alternatives: "Father recognizes himself more as an agent of childrearing" (56.4%), "Improvement of the work environment, including shorter work hours" (52.3%), "Government support to encourage fathers' participation in childrearing" (40.7%), and "Changing the mentality that childrearing is women's work" (32.7%).

Though Japanese people have come to recognize that the father's participation in household work and childrearing is important for both spousal relationships and childhood development, both the workplace environment and governmental support have not yet evolved in this direction.

DETERMINANT FACTORS OF THE FATHER'S INVOLVEMENT WITH CHILDREN

According to Matsuda's (2006) analysis of national survey data from the Japan Society of Family Sociology, both longer maternal work time and shorter paternal work time were related to more childcare and play with children by fathers. Elsewhere, Hirata (2003) examined the determinants of fathers' involvement with junior high school children. Highly involved fathers were more likely to report that they had "fathers who were involved with them when they were high school students" and who showed "cooperation with their wives."

Sugawara's longitudinal study (Sugawara 2005; Sugawara et al. 1999) showed the father's involvement with the care for their young children was a determinant of the wife's love for the husband eleven years later. In addition, Ogata (2011) found that university students whose fathers were highly involved with their family had more positive family identity (awareness of being the family member which exists in one's mind with uniformity and continuity, as approved by other family members) than did students with fathers who were not involved. This relationship was stronger among working parent families than in the case of students who had stay-at-home mothers or part-time working mothers. Finally, according to Ogata's data fathers' involvement with work had no effect on the student's family identity (identification as a member of one's own family).

Influence of Father's Absence on the Family

Psychological absence. In the Tokyo metropolitan area, some fathers have to spend much time commuting to and at work. For example, many go to work before their children wake up in the morning and return home after their children go to bed in the evening. Does this absent weekday father–child interaction time reduce fathers' influence on their children? Ishii-Kuntz (1993) examined the effects of fathers' absence for work and commuting. It was apparent that in the case of fathers who were absent in the home, mothers compensated for this absence by emphasizing to the children that the fathers were important and authorities in the family. This was also observed more than fifty years ago in Ezra and Susan Vogel's observations of Tokyo families, and it still provides men with a psychological presence and a sense of balance in families (Vogel 1996).

Long-term effects of father's absence often occur when a Japanese father's job transfer requires him to live alone in a different city, away from his family (called *tanshinfunin*). Because of children's schooling, home mortgages, and the need to care for elderly parents, it can be difficult for the wife and children to accompany the father. In a longitudinal study of families of adolescents (fifth- to twelfth-graders), five or more years of continuous father absence by *tanshinfunin* led to higher boredom and loneliness among their adolescent children. Here the lengthy lack of fathers as models of work and the authority who set rules of discipline for the family weakened family cohesiveness and lowered children's morale toward work and school (Tanaka & Nakazawa 2005).

Physical absence. Yoda and Hayashi (2010) examined the data of the National Survey of Social Stratification and Social Mobility, which has been conducted every ten years since 1955, comparing differences of academic careers and jobs between people who had a father at age 15 and those who did not. In terms of academic career, father-absent individuals who attended college or beyond achieved less than those who had fathers present, and this difference became more notable in recent years. Among men born between 1956 and 1975, father-present individuals tended to take white-collar jobs, but those who had absent fathers tended to get blue-collar jobs. Binary logistic analysis showed that economic affluence at age 15 positively affected the probability of becoming a white-collar worker in a big company, and even statistically controlling for this affluence, father absence had a negative effect on the probability of becoming white-collar workers in a big company. This result indicated that father absence had not only economic, but also psychological, influences on offspring—e.g., lack of a male role model and psychological stress.

EFFECT OF FATHERS ON CHILD DEVELOPMENT

Children's Social Development

Social development. Kato, Ishii-Kuntz, Makino, and Tsuchiya (2002) showed that fathers' childrearing participation was positively related with the social abilities of their 3-year-old children. Kato and Kondo (2007) observed the play behavior of parents with their 3-year-old children and found that children whose parents "provide structure and set limits," show "respect for the child's autonomy," and "respond sensitively to children's talk" showed high emotional regulation at age 4.

Nakamichi (2013) also examined the self-regulation behavior (self-assertion and self-repression) of kindergarten children. As to self-assertion, the authoritarian and authoritative fathers' sons were more assertive than the permissive fathers' sons, but there were no such differences among daughters. There were no differences in self-repression according to fathering style, but mothers' authoritativeness promoted children's self-repression.

In sum, father involvement with children has been shown to relate to children's social development. In particular, an authoritative childrearing style (high in both construction and limitation setting as the control dimension and the sensitivity dimension) was related to the emotional and behavioral self-regulation of children.

Fathers' influence on self-identity and job selection. How do Japanese fathers influence the formation of adolescents' sense of self? Identification with the father may have an effect on the adolescents' job selection, which is one of the most important decisions in life. Tanaka and Ogawa (1985) asked their sample of fathers who were professionals, such as elementary school teachers, university professors, and architects, about their children's occupations. Fathers tended to have children who took the same kind of jobs (elementary school teacher: son 20.7%, daughter 57.6%; university professor: son 14.8%, daughter 5.6%; architect: son 45.1%, daughter 10.2% taking the same job as their father). The presence of a father clearly had a great effect on their children's occupational selection. It would be interesting to examine whether such job selection trends continue even in the context of contemporary changes in economics and parent–child relations.

Takahashi (2009) asked female university students about past parent–child communications about their choice of university. Students' self-identity correlated positively with parental encouragement and negatively with parental suppression of discussion. Student's moratorium status correlated negatively with fathers' expression of his own opinions. Here fathers' expression of their own opinions supported the identity formation of adolescents.

Ohtaka and Karasawa (2011) examined the father's effect on adult-age (mean age 33) offspring's internal political efficacy, the feeling that people can have a real influence on real politics. The participants talked with mothers about important things and problems, and they talked with fathers about politics and work. The more they discussed politics with their fathers, the higher their internal political efficacy, and higher internal political efficacy was related to more active participation in politics. In contrast, discussion about politics with mothers had no such effects. This result supported the proposition of Parsons and Bales (1955) that fathers had the role of connecting the family to the wider society.

Children's Cognitive Development

Ishii-Kuntz (2007) found that highly educated fathers had children who had high school morale and good peer relations. These educated fathers also had sons who evaluated themselves positively and who had a clear image of their future careers. Highly educated fathers may emphasize the value of education and learning in their childrearing.

Mimizuka (2007) examined causal factors of mathematics achievement in the national examination data of sixth-grade children. In the Tokyo area, where competition for secondary school entrance is intense, mathematics achievement was affected by attendance at cram schools, learning time in the home, and the father's academic background. Children whose fathers were university graduates had scores that were 10–20 percentile points higher than those of children whose father did not attend a university. Out-of-school expenses per month were positively related with math achievement scores. The achievement scores of children with an out-of-school expense of ¥0 was 35.3 (maximum = 100), and the achievement scores of children with ¥50,000 expenses was 78.4. Family income was also related positively with children's mathematics achievement. The average achievement scores of children whose family income was less than ¥5 million was 41.9, while the mean score of children whose family income was more than ¥10 million was 65.9. Thus, among family background characteristics, these economic factors (out-of-school expenses and family income) were important for children's achievement according to multiple regression analysis (other significant factors were parental expectation of high education and mother's educational background). In areas outside Tokyo, where competition for secondary schools and beyond is not so strong, children's mathematics achievement was also influenced by the father's academic background, but attending or not attending a cram school had no influence.

Matsuda (2007) found that study time was positively related with school achievement in fourth- to sixth-grade children. In addition, he showed that fathers' academic background was positively related with children's study time (for children of high school graduate fathers, fourth- to sixth-graders studied 0.9 hours/day and seventh- to ninth-graders studied 0.8 hours/day; for fathers with degrees from university/graduate school, fourth- to sixth-graders studied 1.2 hours and seventh- to ninth-graders 1.4 hours/day).

Higher education among fathers was also associated with higher family income. These fathers may have a high value for education and provide educational support to their children. This was an important factor in children's achievement gap and may contribute to the economic gap of the next generation.

Children's Mental Health

Psychological health. One other aspect of paternal influence is the mental health and adjustment of children. Oshima (2013) found that adolescents whose mothers were highly reliable toward their husbands and perceived their father's supportive involvement for them had more positive psychological health (high self-affirmation and low depression).

Internal problem behavior. School nonattendance coincident with nearly complete social withdrawal (a pairing called *hikikomori* in Japan) is a common internal problem behavior among Japanese youth. Igarashi and Hagiwara (2004) found that the nonattendance of junior high school children related positively with "distrust/refusal" attachment to the opposite-sex parent. Hanashima (2007) asked university male students and *hikikomori* males (who refused social interaction with others for at least more than six months by their late 20s), about the personality of their father and about their relationships with the father. The personalities of fathers of *hikikomori* males were described as more "strict and inflexible" and less "intimate," "respectful and trusting," "emotionally understanding," "feeling loved," and "interactive" than that of control group students. The more the father was "strict and inflexible" and the less "intimate," "interactive," and "respectful and trusting," the longer the period of *hikikomori*. These data were collected after the problems occurred, so that it is difficult to determine the causal direction of these relationships. Causal analysis and longitudinal developmental research on this mental health issue is required in follow-up studies on this topic.

External problem behavior. Nakamichi and Nakazawa (2003) found that children of authoritarian fathers were rated as more aggressive by kindergarten teachers than were the children of authoritative and permissive fathers. Meanwhile, there were no such differences among mothers' parenting styles. Ogata, Miyashita, and Fukuda (2005) reported that young children whose fathers communicated less with their children and wife showed higher levels of aggressiveness.

Obokata and Muto (2005) examined the delinquent behavior of junior high school children. Children (seventh- to ninth-graders) who had intimate father–child relations showed higher inhibitions against delinquent behavior.

Inhibitions of mother–child relations on delinquency were only apparent for seventh-graders. Thus fathers may be more influential than mothers on early adolescents' external problem behavior.

FUTURE DIRECTIONS AND FATHERING-RELATED POLICIES

In the wake of a rapidly declining total fertility rate, the Japanese government has started to adopt childrearing friendly policies and to promote fathers' involvement in household work and childrearing. The caption of the first such campaign poster in 1999 was "A man who does not participate in childrearing is not called a father." Policies favoring father involvement have continued since that time.

The Japanese Children and Child Rearing Vision, a 2010–2014 policy, was based on an ideological shift from family and parental responsibility to societal responsibility for childrearing (Ministry of Health, Labor and Welfare 2010a). As a profathering policy, the childrearing allowance provides for single-father families; this benefit formerly was paid only for single-mother families. It emphasized promotion of the father's participation in childrearing through childcare leave for men and of changing men's attitudes toward housework and childrearing. The Japanese government set 2014 as the target year for the following goals: (1) The rate of the company workers working more than 60 hours/week would decrease from 10 percent in 2010 to 5 percent, and (2) the time fathers spend with children younger than 6 would increase from sixty minutes in 2010 to 150 minutes (the degree to which these goals were met will be known in 2015).

The Ministry of Health, Labor and Welfare (2010b) initiated the "*Ikumen* project." *Ikumen* (childrearing men) is a word coined to combine the Japanese word *iku* (rearing) and the English word "men," and *ikumen* are thus men who enjoy childrearing and fulfill themselves through childrearing. The motto of this project is "Childrearing men change families and society." The numerical goal of the Ikumen Project is to increase the percentage of fathers who take childcare leave from work from 1.23% in 2008 to 10% by 2017 and to 13% by 2020.

The Japanese government also decided in June 2013 that urgent measures were needed to counter the falling birth rate (Cabinet Office 2013b). These measures were as follows: (1) enhancement of childrearing support (acceleration of solutions to the *taikijidou* problem by which many children cannot enter nursery school because of limited capacity at such facilities), financial support for the multiple-child family, and promotion of childrearing in the community and workplace; (2) fostering changes in work behavior (support for a balance between work and family life, appointment and promotion of women in the workplace, presentation of women in upper management positions as role models, and reexamination of men's way of working); and (3) support of marriage, pregnancy, and childbirth (enhancement of community-based health care and for fertility treatment). Thus the Japanese government is pursuing policies to promote work–life balance in society, as well as to support the father's participation in childrearing and household tasks. Many local government and nonprofit groups have developed fathering classes to support these policies.

Nonprofit organizations (NPOs) actively support the government's "Children and Child Rearing Vision" policy. There are now two such powerful organizations—the "Ikujiren: Let's take time for childrearing, both males and females!" which was founded in 1996 (www.eqg.org/index-e.html), and the newer "Fathering Japan," founded in 2006 (www.fathering.jp). The webpage of Fathering Japan says: "Being a father is joyful. We're not trying to make 'good Dads,' but we want to fill society with 'smiling Dads.'" These NGOs organize many fathering classes and also actively present fathering policy proposals.

New Fathers

There are now many new fathers who take childcare leave or become househusbands. According to the cabinet office (2013c), men who want to take childcare leave tend to have parents who think men should take part in housework and childrearing. Saito (2012) interviewed a sample of twenty-one fathers who took childcare leave and found that they had flexible attitudes toward gender roles. They also had household skills such as cooking, washing, and cleaning up before marriage. Their wives had flexible gender roles and were open to the husband's taking a domestic role and the wife's taking the role of wage earner. Their desire to be independent of parental support, and the husband's willingness to take responsibility for childcare, led to men's choice to take childcare leave. However, they were not received positively among coworkers in their companies for doing so. Another line of interview research about new fathers who took childcare leave reported that such men valued their shared time with the family and the wife's point of view but also experienced the monotony of routinized childcare, childcare anxiety, feelings of deprived contact with outer society, and loneliness (Kikuchi & Kashiwagi 2007; Yagi 2009). These studies showed that fathers had the same household and childcare capabilities as mothers and that they also experienced feelings of isolation when they committed to raising children alone like stay-at-home mothers.

SPECULATION AND CONCLUSION: FUTURE OF JAPANESE FATHERING

Japan faces a decrease in its population of children, and parents may become more protective in their attitudes toward the fewer children. Because of economic and social changes in recent years, maternal employment has increased so that fathers need to share more in housework and childrearing. The Japanese government should promote a more childcare-friendly society, making it easier for fathers to take childcare leave; shorten men's work hours; and increase the capacities of childcare facilities. It appears that Japanese childcare will change from maternal care to multiple caregiving by mothers, fathers, and institutional daycare, placing younger Japanese fathers in a double bind: They want to attend to childrearing as *ikumen*, which has the support of mothers, the government, and NPOs. And they want to be more involved with their fewer children. But they continue to have difficulties taking part in childrearing because of hard economic times. This dilemma may be more challenging to new fathers than was the situation in past generations, when fathers took the role of breadwinner mainly and could leave childrearing to mothers. Nevertheless, Japanese fathers' involvement with children continues to grow, and the cultural tradition of high concern for children will continue to support this movement toward active fathering.

Acknowledgement: The author thanks Dr. David W. Shwalb of Southern Utah University for his careful editing and valuable comments on different drafts of this chapter.

WEBSITES

"Fathering Japan." www.fathering.jp.

"Gender Equality Bureau, Cabinet Office." www.gender.go.jp/english_contents/index.html.

"Ikujiren: Let's take time for childrearing, both males and females!" www.eqg.org/index-e.html.

"National Institute of Population and Social Security Research." www.ipss.go.jp/index-e.asp.

REFERENCES

Cabinet Office. (2013a). *Gender equality white book in 2013*. www.gender.go.jp/about_danjo/whitepaper/h25/gaiyou/index.html.

Cabinet Office. (2013b). *Society with fewer children white book in 2013*. http://www8.cao.go.jp/shoushi/shoushika/whitepaper/measures/w-2013/25pdfhonpen/pdf/s2-3.pdf.

Cabinet Office. (2013c). *Prompt report of research on work and life balance*. wwwa.cao.go.jp/wlb/research/wlb_h2511/follow-up.pdf.

Cabinet Office, Statistics Bureau. (2014). *Demographic records of 2010*. www.stat.go.jp/data/kokusei/2010/index2.htm#kaisetu.

Chuouchosasha. (2012). *Research about fathers' participation in childrearing*, Report No. 659. www.crs.or.jp/backno/No659/6592.htm.

Fróis, L. D. (1585). *Tratado em que se contem muito susintae abreviadamente algumas contradições e diferenças de custumes antre a gente de Europa e esta provincial de Japão*, trans. A. Okada (1991), Tokyo: Iwanamishoten.

Hanashima, H. (2007). The father–son relationships that are seen from Hikikomori males and their fathers. *Japanese Journal of Family Psychology, 21*, 77–94.

Hirata, H. (2003). Fathers' relating behaviors to their children in early adolescence. *Japanese Journal of Family Psychology, 17*, 35–54.

Igarashi, T., & Hagiwara, H. (2004). Junior high school students' tendency toward non-attendance at school and attachment in early childhood. *Japanese Journal of Educational Psychology, 52*, 264–276.

Ishii-Kuntz, M. (1993). Japanese fathers: Work demands and family roles. In J. C. Hood (ed.), *Men, work, and family* (pp. 45–67). Newbury Park, CA: Sage.

Ishii-Kunz, M. (2007). Fathers' effects on their adolescent children's development: How do fathers effect on children's social development? In H. Mimizuka & K. Makino (eds.), *Academic achievement and the crisis of transition* (pp. 125–142). Tokyo: Kaneko Shobo

Kaibara E. (1710). *Wazoku Douji Kun*. In M. Yamazumi & K. Nakae (eds.), *Koso-datenosho 2* (1976). Tokyo: Heibonsha.

Kato, K., Ishii-Kuntz, M., Makino, K., & Tsuchiya, M. (2002). The impact of parental involvement and maternal childcare anxiety on sociability of three-year-olds: Two cohorts comparison. *Japanese Journal of Developmental Psychology, 13*, 30–41.

Kato, K., & Kondo, K. (2007). A comparison between fathers and mothers in a play situation with three-year olds. *Japanese Journal of Developmental Psychology, 18*, 35–44.

Kikuchi, F., & Kashiwagi, K. (2007). Father's child rearing: fathers who took a child-care leave. *Journal of the Faculty of Human Studies, Bunkyo Gakuin University, 9*, 189–207.

Kimura, K., Tamura, T., Kuramochi, K., Nakazawa, C., Kishida, Y., Oikawa, Y., Aramaki, M., Morita. C., & Izumi, H. (2003). Comparison of marital relationship of the couple who had their first childbirth in relation to their perinatal visits to the family of origin. *Bulletin of Tokyo Gakugei University: Section 6, 55*, 123–131.

Kojima, H. (2001). *Visiting traditional childrearing*. Tokyo: Sinyosha.

Matsuda, S. (2006). Change of father's involvement in household and childrearing. *Quarterly Research on Household Economics, 71*, 44–53.

Matsuda, S. (2007). Parents teach their children: Fathers' motivate on learning make differences between children's academic achievement differences. *LifeDesign REPORT, 9–10*, 28–35.

Mimizuka, H. (2007). Who can make the academic success? In H. Mimizuka & K. Makino (eds.), *Academic achievement and crisis of transition* (pp. 3–23). Tokyo: Kaneko Shobo.

Ministry of Education, Culture, Sports, Science and Technology. (2013). *Basic research about Japanese school in 2013*. www.mext.go.jp/b_menu/toukei/chousa01/kihon/kekka/k_detail/1342607.htm.

Ministry of Health, Labor and Welfare. (2010a). *Vision of children and child-rearing*. www.mhlw.go.jp/bunya/kodomo/pdf/vision-zenbun.pdf.

Ministry of Health, Labor and Welfare. (2010b). *The outline of Ikumen Project*. www.mhlw.go.jp/bunya/koyoukintou/ikumen_shiryou/dl/ikumen_gaiyou.pdf.

Ministry of Health, Labor and Welfare. (2012). *Fact-finding of working women in 2012*. www.mhlw.go.jp/bunya/koyoukintou/josei-jitsujo/12.html.

Ministry of Health, Labor and Welfare. (2013). *Research on demographics in 2012*. www.mhlw.go.jp/toukei/saikin/hw/jinkou/kakutei12/index.html.

Morishita, Y. (2006). The effect of becoming fathers on men's development. *Japanese Journal of Developmental Psychology, 17*, 182–192.

Morse, E. S. (1917). *Japan day by day*. Boston, MA: Houghton Mifflin.

Nakamichi, K. (2013). Effects of childrearing styles on young children's self-regulation. *Bulletin of the Education Faculty, Shizuoka University, 63*, 109–121.

Nakamichi, K., & Nakazawa, J. (2003). Maternal/paternal childrearing style and young children's aggressive behavior. *Chiba University Faculty of Education Bulletin, 51*, 173–179.

Nakazawa, J., & Shwalb, D. W. (2013). Fathering in Japan: Entering an era of involvement with children. In D. W. Shwalb, B. J. Shwalb., & Ml. E. Lamb (eds.), *Fathers in cultural context* (pp. 42–67). New York: Routledge.

National Institute of Population and Social Security Research. (2008). *National family research in 2008*. www.ipss.go.jp/ps-katei/j/NSFJ4/NSFJ4_gaiyo.pdf.

National Institute of Population and Social Security Research. (2010). *The 14th national basic birth research, 2010*. www.ipss.go.jp/ps-doukou/j/doukou14/doukou14.asp.

National Institute of Population and Social Security Research. (2014). *National demographic data in 2014*. www.ipss.go.jp/syoushika/tohkei/Popular/Popular2014.asp?chap=0.

Obokata, A., & Muto, T. (2005). Regulatory and preventive factors for mild delinquency of junior high school students: Child–parent relationships, peer relationships, and self-control. *Japanese Journal of Developmental Psychology, 16*, 286–299.

Ogata, K. (2011). Exploring links between father's view of work–life balance, mother's working patterns and family identity in adolescence. *Bulletin of Aichi University of Education, 60*, 97–101.

Ogata, K., Miyashita, K., & Fukuda, K. (2005). Exploring links between father's cooperation with family chores, mother's feelings of mother-role and wife-role attainment, child's aggression and father's stress coping styles. *Japanese Journal of Family Psychology, 19*, 31–45.

Ohtaka, M., & Karasawa, K. (2011). Association between political conversation with fathers and children's internal political efficacy. *Hougakuronshu: The Yamanashi Gakuin Law Review, 68*, 391–411.

Oshima, K. (2011). Positive recollection of childcare from middle-aged fathers' point of view. *Japanese Journal of Family Psychology, 25*, 135–147.

Oshima, K. (2013). Parents' marital trust, positive parenting, and young adults' mental health. *Japanese Journal of Developmental Psychology, 24*, 55–65.

Parsons, T., & Bales, R. F. (1955). *Family, socialization and interaction process.* Glencoe, IL: Free Press.

Saito, S. (2012). Empirical research on the awareness of fathers who took the paternal level. *Journal of Ohara Institute for Social Research, 647–648*, 77–88.

Sasaki, Y. (2009). Factors influencing the development of fathers' roles before and after the birth of the first baby. *Japanese Journal of Maternal Health, 50*, 413–421.

Shwalb, D. W., Imaizumi, N., & Nakazawa, J. (1987). The modern Japanese father: Roles and problems in a changing society. In M. E. Lamb (ed.), *The father's role: Cross-cultural perspectives* (pp. 247–269). Hillsdale, NJ: LEA.

Shwalb, D. W., Nakazawa, J., Yamamoto, T., & Hyun, J-H. (2004). Fathering in Japanese, Chinese and Korean cultures: A review of the research literature. In M. E. Lamb (ed.), *The role of the father in child development*, 4th ed. (pp. 146–181). Hoboken, NJ: Wiley.

Shwalb, D. W., Nakazawa, J., Yamamoto, T., & Hyun, J-H. (2010). Fathering in Japan, China, and Korea: Changing context, images, and roles. In M. E. Lamb (ed.), *The role of the father in child development*, 5th ed., (pp. 341–387). Hoboken, NJ: Wiley.

Shwalb, D. W., Shwalb, B. J., Sukemune, S., & Tatsumoto, S. (1992). Japanese non-maternal childcare: Past, present and future. In M. E. Lamb, K. Sternberg, C-P. Hwang, & A. G. Broberg (eds.), *Childcare in context* (pp. 331–353). Hillsdale, NJ: Erlbaum.

Sugawara, M. (2005). Maternal employment and child development in Japan: A twelve-year longitudinal study. In D. W. Shwalb, J. Nakazawa, & B. J. Shwalb (eds.), *Applied developmental psychology: Theory, practice, and research from Japan* (pp. 225–240). Charlotte, NC: Information Age Publishing.

Sugawara, M., Kitamura, T., Toda-Aoki, M., Shima, S. Sato, T & Mukai, T. (1999). Development of problem behavior: A longitudinal study of externalizing problems from infancy to middle-childhood. *Japanese Journal of Developmental Psychology, 10*, 32–42.

Takahashi, A. (2009). Identity and communication with parents of young women during the period of career decisionmaking. *Japanese Journal of Personality, 17*, 208–219.

Takahashi, M., & Takahashi, M. (2009). Development of becoming fathers and mothers. *Bulletin of Tokyo Gakugei University. Educational Sciences, 60*, 209–218.

Tanaka, K., & Ogawa, K. (1985). The influence of parental occupation's on children's career choice: The case of school teachers, college professors and architects. *Japanese Journal of Educational Psychology, 3*, 173–178.

Tanaka, Y., & Nakazawa, J. (2005). Job-related temporary father absence (Tanshin-funin) and child development. In D. W. Shwalb, J. Nakazawa., & B. J. Shwalb (eds.), *Applied Developmental Psychology: Theory, practice, and research from Japan* (pp. 241–260). Charlotte, NC: Information Age Publishing.

Tendo, M., & Takahashi, H. (2011). Subjection of child-rearing fathers: Child-rearing strategies and discourse analysis of parenting magazines. *Japanese Journal of Family Sociology, 23*, 65–76.

Vogel, S. H. (1996). Urban middle-class Japanese family life, 1958–1996: A personal and evolving perspective. In D. W. Shwalb & B. J. Shwalb (eds.), *Japanese childrearing: Two generations of scholarship* (pp. 177–200). New York: Guilford Press.

Yagi, T. (2009).Being a househusband as an alternative lifestyle of the family: A qualitative study on the consciousness of househusbands. *Annals of Family Studies, 34*, 91–108.

Yoda, S., & Hayashi, Y. (2010). Father absence and children's socioeconomic status attainment. *Annual Reports of the Tohoku Sociological Society, 39*, 63–74.

Turkey, Israel, and Arab and Non-Arab Islamic Societies

15

Fathering in Turkey

Aysegul Metindogan

Over the last century, perceptions of fathering and fathers' contribution to children's development have changed "from moral teacher and disciplinarian, through breadwinner and later gender-role model and 'buddy', to the new nurturing, co-parenting father" (Sarkadi, Kristiansson, Oberklain, & Bremberg 2007). At the same time, research in North American and European cultural communities has shown that fathers contribute positively to nearly all areas of childhood development and that father involvement in child care has positive effects on the quality of the relationship with the mother, which, in turn, moderates and mediates developmental outcomes in children (Allen & Daly, 2007; Cabrera & Tamis-LeMonda 2013; Cabrera, Tamis-LeMonda, Bradley, Hofferth & Lamb, 2000; Garbarino, 2000; Harris, 2014; Lamb 2010). Despite some changes in family life within the more traditional developing countries, or "the majority world" as Kağıtçıbaşı (2005, 2007) puts it, improvements in fathers' involvement in caregiving responsibilities seem to be lagging behind those in developed societies. In the majority world, it appears that fathers participate in caregiving responsibilities out of necessity, or due to demands made by spouses and their work patterns (Gürmen & Rohner 2013; Roopnarine, Krishnakumar, & Vadgama 2013). This chapter provides a glimpse into fathering in Turkey. The focus is on the sociocultural context of fathering, family structure and living arrangements, patterns of father involvement and factors that influence them, links between father involvement and childhood outcomes, and future directions and policy implications.

TURKISH CULTURAL CONTEXT

Turkey is a geographical bridge between Asia and Europe. Its population of nearly 82 million people is fairly equally divided by sex (CIA Worldfactbook,

2014). Turkey is a direct descendent of the Islamic Ottoman Empire, which spanned more than 600 years. In this secular society, a majority (98%) of the Turkish people are nonetheless Muslim (Pew Forum on Religion & Public Life 2009; Oktem 2002). Of the Muslim population, the major denominations are Sunni, followed by Alevi. The Alevi denomination practice an Anatolian interpretation of Islam, in which adherents do not follow certain major Islamic tenets; Alevis do not fast during Ramadan, go on the Hajj, or perform the five daily prayers (Balkanlioğlu 2011; Oktem 2002). The majority ethnic group is made up of Turks. Kurds are the largest ethnic minority group (about 20%), and Armenians, Greeks, Sephardic Jews, Circassians, gypsies (known as Roma), Laz, Syriacs, Arabs, and others make up 2 percent of the population.

Turkey has transformed itself into a more modern, egalitarian, industrial, urban state over the years (Sunar & Fisek 2005). Today, 70 percent of the population lives in cities; 26.2 percent works in the industrial sectors, 48.4 percent in the service sectors, and about 25 percent in agriculture. With a growth rate of 8.5 percent in 2011 (Koçak 2004), Turkey has become the sixteenth-largest economy in the world and the sixth-largest in Europe (Ministry of Foreign Affairs, 2014; OECD, 2014). Along with such steady economic growth have come significant changes in family structure and organization. For example, compared to previous decades, there has been a steady increase in women's participation in the labor force (30% compared to 71.8% for men) and an increase in the divorce rate (TÜİK, 2012). Moreover, urban life and women's employment outside of the home have introduced changes in paternal and maternal involvement in child care and household responsibilities (Koçak 2004).

After going through some political turmoil—including a few military coups in its recent history—Turkey seems to be a durable republic. Women have had the right to vote since 1934, and the mandatory length of education is now twelve years. Turkey's progress as a developing country and being a candidate to enter the European Union aside, there are some troubling societal trends that directly affect the lives of men, women, and children. High rates of domestic violence and spouse (typically after a divorce or separation) and honor killings of women (murder of women increased 1400 percent within the last nine years [Türk Üniversiteli Kadınlar Derneği 2014]); problems with access to schooling in rural areas, specifically for girls; forcing children, mainly girls, into marriage; and a less democratic climate and harsh governmental reactions to any opposition in the social and political domains (European Commission 2014) all conspire against the safety and well-being of families.

Since 2002, Turkey has been governed by the Justice and Development Party, a socially conservative political party. The conservative and religious roots of this party have informed the government's views on fertility patterns, family relationships, and issues of social equality between men and women (Haberturk, Kadın ve erkeğin eşit olması mümkün değil 2010. A view often espoused is that men are supreme to and have power over women, and that women are responsible for rearing children. Studies indicate that many Turkish families are still traditional and that beliefs regarding men's roles in most social domains have changed little (Demren, 2001; Koçak 2004). It is important to note that perceptions of manhood are directly related to men's roles as fathers and affect how men's roles and responsibilities within the family are experienced and transmitted to future generations (Boratav, Fisek, & Ziya 2014).

FAMILY STRUCTURES AND LIVING ARRANGEMENTS

Marriage is a primary basis for entry into fatherhood and fathering. Historically, family life has been highly valued in Turkey. According to the Turkish Statistical Institute's (TurkStat) 2013 national data, 83.4 percent of females and 70.4 percent of males marry by age 30. However, the average age of first marriage is 26.8 for males and 23.6 for females. In 2007, the crude marriage rate (people per thousand) was 0.909 percent, which dropped to 0.802 percent in 2011. The divorce rate was 0.190 percent in 2011 (TÜİK Haber Bülteni 2013). With few exceptions, women are stigmatized after a divorce. By comparison, men seem to have no problem remarrying after divorce and rebuilding their married lives. Marriage remains a strong institution in Turkey (Sunar & Fisek 2005).

Turning to family structures, in 2013, only 8.6 percent of households included a single person, and 13.5 percent of households were extended, including three generations living in the same unit (TÜİK 2013). Among families, 15.8 percent were childless, 7.8 percent included a single parent, and 54 percent were couples with children. Of the single parent-families, most (84.9%) were headed by mothers, and 15.1 percent were headed by fathers. A nationwide study of family life in Turkey showed that the average household size was 3.59 people in 2011 (T.C. Ministry of Family and Social Policies 2014), suggesting that a typical Turkish family is nuclear, with two parents and children living in the same dwelling. Turkish families are functionally extended. That is, extended families are a "cultural ideal," but most households are "structurally nuclear," yet "functionally extended" (Kağıtçıbaşı, Ataca, & Diri 2005, p. 99). Couples live close to extended family members, receive support, and come together often to receive help from grandparents and aunts in raising children. Married couples feel that they are responsible for the well-being of parents, siblings, and children of siblings and are culturally pressured to keep close family ties. Children remain with their parents until they get married, and social ties do not weaken after marriage. As a result, children in a Turkish household continuously interact with their kin from both their mother's and father's side of the family and grow up in a "culture of relatedness" (Kağıtçıbaşı 1996; Kağıtçıbaşı, Ataca, & Diri 2005).

Kağıtçıbaşı's famous nationwide study of "The Value of Children" (VOC) that began in the mid-1970s investigated "the values attributed to children, motivations for childbearing and the fertility outcomes" (Kağıtçıbaşı, Ataca, & Diri 2005, p. 104). Findings showed that children were valued in three different ways: "economic/utilitarian," "psychological" and "social" (p. 104). Furthermore, this thirty-year study revealed that children's psychological value, wherein they are seen as the family's joy, source of happiness, and companionship, increased, whereas economic/utilitarian values of children, seeing the children as old-age security and depending on them as sources of material support, decreased over time. As a reflection of these changes, the preference of families to have male children, who are typically considered as the sources of material support, decreased as well (Kağıtçıbaşı, Ataca, & Diri 2005).

FATHERHOOD IN THE HISTORICAL CONTEXT OF TURKEY

Turks, now the ethnic majority in Turkey, entered Anatolia in 1071, their roots going back to central Asia. There have been many civilizations in the land that is modern Turkey, including that of the Seljuk Turks. Of these civilizations, the most recent and powerful one was the Ottoman Empire. Family life of the Ottomans contains some of the early semblances of current beliefs and practices concerning family dynamics and the roles men play as fathers and husbands in modern Turkey.

FAMILY LIFE AND FATHERS DURING THE OTTOMAN ERA

The Ottoman Empire was diverse, hosting many religions, nations, and ethnicities. Even though the different cultural groups lived side by side for hundreds of years, they rarely mixed, managing to preserve their own traditions and lifestyles, including family life. Thus cultural transitions and changes evolved separately in the different groups. Although the majority culture of the Ottomans was mainly defined by Islam, there were many minorities, such as Armenian Gregorians, Catholics, and Protestants, living within the empire. These minority groups carried out their own cultural traditions and expressed their own religious beliefs while, of course, paying their taxes to the Ottoman Empire (Ortayli 2010).

Family life during the Ottoman era was not limited to the household. Entire neighborhoods and villages acted as family environments, with three-generation households residing within a dwelling and courtyard. As a cultural unit, kinship was always important for both Muslims and non-Muslims. Extended family units were the norm in the Ottoman Empire and probably aided survival. Though Muslim women were required to marry within-group, Muslim men were given the right to marry a woman from a different religion, with the woman usually converting to Islam. Still, interreligious marriages were not very common, and both Muslims and non-Muslims tried to keep marriages within their own communities. Men typically had a single wife, and polygamy was not well received in the communities. Only men of higher status and income could marry more than one wife, and in different reports, the rates of polygamy ranged from 2 percent to 5 percent of all marriages (Ortayli 2001; Ortayli 2010). However, it is difficult to make proper estimations, for census reports only included adult men at home, not women or children (Ortayli 2010). Although divorce was not very common, men were given the privilege over women to seek a divorce (Kayra 2008). Religious leaders were in charge of the social order in these communities.

Ottoman fathers were the legal custodians of their children. Childrearing and education were the responsibilities of mothers and grandmothers. The father's main role was in educating his children about "morals," and he often used fear when disciplining children (Bayam 2010). Fathers essentially owned their daughters, and a man transferred responsibility for his daughter to another man through marriage, but only after he received a dowry. Men and women had completely segregated lives in terms of socializing, entertainment, and otherwise. When families and neighbors came together, men and women used separate areas, with children playing next to their mothers. Women prepared food for everyone, but stayed away from the areas occupied by men. After they came home from work, men would leave after dinner and socialize with other men while the women stayed home with their children (Ortayli 2001, 2010). Some of these practices are still applicable to modern Turkey, where urban, more educated, men and women still tend to socialize separately, and in rural areas men and women have gender-segregated lives.

TURKISH REPUBLIC

When the Turkish Republic was founded, the country went through dramatic changes that affected both the social and economic lives of families (Kağıtçıbaşı, Ataca, & Diri 2005). Several reforms were passed that reflected attempts to move the society toward modernization. Of the reforms, perhaps the one most relevant to the present discussion was the end to religious governance by the Ottoman Empire and the start of a secular republic (Kağıtçıbaşı, Ataca, & Diri 2005). Reforms increased the legal marriage age to 18, ended the husband's ultimate ownership of his wife, and acknowledged marriages and divorces as official. Because of a depleted population as the result of many wars, suggestions were made to levy a tax on any man who did not get married after age 25 without an excuse. The so-called "celibacy tax" (Ozer 2013; Semiz 2010) was brought up repeatedly in the Turkish parliament between the 1920s and 1940s. Finally in 1949, a bill was passed to increase the tax rate for unmarried men aged 25–45, and to decrease the tax rates for men who had children (Ozer 2013; Semiz 2010). Though it is unclear whether the passing of these bills did in fact increase the population size (Ozer 2013; Semiz 2010), we can speculate that it may have influenced the cultural emphasis on the idea that men should be married, have children, and provide for their family.

Family life in the early years of the republic varied by whether families were living in Istanbul as the elite descendants of Ottoman autocracy; whether they were of the middle class, which comprised merchants, government workers, and lower-rank army officials; or whether they were Anatolians, who were peasants and agriculturalists (Shaw 2007). Westernization had already been in place for the first group, but for the others, and especially for the Anatolians in the villages of eastern Turkey, modernization was a very slow process. This, coupled with ethnic, religious, and geographic differences, makes it impossible to generalize about family life or the respective roles of mothers and fathers in Turkey (Boratav, Fisek, & Ziya 2014; Sunar & Fisek 2005). But one traditional aspect of Turkish families that has survived through the generations is the authority that fathers and men exercise in the home. (Kiray, 1985). Both Islam and patriarchal traditions have contributed to the position of men as superior to women and children (Boratav, Fisek, & Ziya 2014; Erkal, Çopur, Doğan & Şafak, 2007; Sunar & Fisek 2005). It was not until 2002 that a law was passed indicating that the husband and wife together share the responsibility of heading a household.

THE ROLE OF FATHERS IN TURKISH CULTURE

As measured by TurkStat's recent survey in 2013, people in Turkey are fairly happy (59%) and somewhat hopeful (77%). When it comes to the source of happiness, the family (73%) was a key source. Money, success, and job combined constitute only 15 percent of sources of happiness, whereas health (68%) takes the lead (TÜİK Haber Bülteni 2014). Looking at these statistics, and considering what was said earlier about the emphasis placed on social ties, one may reasonably surmise that Turkey falls within a collectivistic orientation that entails relatedness and heteronomy as opposed to separateness and autonomy, considered more an individualistic orientation. Kağıtçıbaşı (2005) suggested that it is very simplistic to consider cultures as falling on either end of this fairly popular continuum (Kağıtçıbaşı 1996,

2005; Kağıtçıbaşı & Ataca 2005). In her autonomous–relational–self family model, she argues that cultures, as well as families within any culture, can value both autonomy and relatedness, because these behavioral constructs constitute different dimensions of each individual's life. Both are important and essential for fostering support and togetherness among family members. In Turkey, relatedness is valued across socioeconomic groups, but in rural areas, families are more heteronomous and enmeshed, and urbanized and more educated families seem to value relatedness and autonomy within the family (Ozdikmenli-Demir & Sayıl 2009). An important question that goes largely unanswered is what roles and responsibilities fathers assume in this family socialization framework.

Fathering research is relatively new in the Turkish context. The existing research has mainly used conceptual frameworks (e.g., Lamb et al. 1987), constructs, and scales used in North America and Europe, ignoring the heterogeneity of meanings attributed to fathering across cultures (Bocknek, Hossain, & Roggman 2014). Moreover, there are virtually no observational studies on father–child interactions and few studies during infancy and the middle childhood years and on children with disabilities (Meral & Çavkaytar, 2012; Şahin & Demiriz 2014; Tan & Waldhoff, 1996). There is an increasing interest in adolescent–father relationships. For the most part, studies have concentrated on fathers' time investment during the preschool years, possibly out of a focus on early childhood educational development and schooling effects across the world (Çarkoğlu & Kalaycıoğlu 2014; Durmuşoğlu-Saltalı & Arslan, 2012; Gürşimşek, Kefi & Girgin 2007; Izci 2013; Özgün & Honig 2004, Sabırlı-Ozışıklı, 2008; Şahin & Demiriz 2014;). Little effort has been made to explore the qualitative aspects of father–child relationships (Bocknek, Hossain, & Roggman 2014).

Childcare is a woman's job in Turkey. Although this statement comes across as quite a bold generalization, across socioeconomic groups and throughout its history from the Ottoman era on, fathers can be termed "helpers" when it comes to childcare; mothers are the primary caregivers to children (Çarkoğlu & Kalaycıoğlu, Türkiye'de aile 2014). Results of a recent survey of 1,555 household members aged 18 or older sampled randomly by TSI showed that 42 percent of the participants indicated that a man's job is to earn money and a woman's to be responsible for the care of children. As in so many other traditional cultural settings, the Turkish father's main responsibility is to work outside of the home to financially support the family, regardless of whether he lives in an urban or rural setting and whether the mother works outside the home. Historically, because men worked outside the home, they were the main element connecting the family to the outside world. Mothers not only took care of children, but they also cooked, cleaned, and worked to create a peaceful environment at home among family members. In short, a woman's main role was mothering and caring for her husband (Koçak 2004; Sunar & Fisek 2005; Nacak, Yagmurlu, Durgel, & van de Vijver 2011; Şahin & Demiriz 2014).

As noted above, studies focusing on infant–father relationships are very rare in Turkey, and one reason for this is the perception that infant care is a woman's task (Kuruçırak 2010). In addition, pregnancy, childbirth, and societal expectations prepare mothers to be more involved in infant care (Kuruçırak 2010). Kuruçırak (2010) assessed father involvement in child care activities with infants aged 4–12 months in families from low and high socioeconomic backgrounds. Congruent with historical depictions, fathers were mostly helpers in infant care. Fathers accompanied their wives when they took the infant out for fresh air, monitored the infant's growth and development, and talked with the infant. They almost never gave the infant a bath, took the infant alone to the doctor for shots, or told stories to the infant. When fathers' responses were examined based on the general domains of involvement, play had the highest scores, followed by health and physical care (Kuruçırak 2010). Fathers of higher socioeconomic backgrounds whose wives were working in higher-status jobs and had higher educational attainment, who lived in city centers, who came from the west and north of Turkey, and who had fewer children were more involved in the infant caregiving activities and had more positive perceptions of their roles as fathers than fathers in families having other sociodemographic characteristics.

One of the earliest studies (Evans 1997) conducted of father involvement and perceptions of fathering in Turkey used Lamb's taxonomy of involvement. The fathers, who were from the Ankara area, saw a wage earner role as best fitting a father but also expressed that providing love and affection were responsibilities of a father. They thought that mothers' roles were strictly associated with childcare. Interestingly enough, though the perceptions of fathers seem to be different based on whether the mother was employed or not, with the fathers of working mothers having slightly more egalitarian beliefs concerning who is responsible for household tasks, actual caregiving behaviors did not seem to have changed much (Evans 1997). Most of the fathers did not play with or become involved in the physical care of their children.

A recent qualitative study (Ozgün, Çifti, & Erden 2014) that included twenty-one police fathers and their preschool-aged children examined the meaning of fatherhood as perceived by both fathers and their children (Ozgün, Çifti, & Erden 2014). Most of the men had stay-at-home wives and were the only financial provider for the family. Drawings were used to collect data on children's perspectives on fathering, whereas fathers were directed to write on paper about the type of father they thought they were, with no restrictions on page limit. As in the other studies, findings indicated that

both children and fathers perceived a father's role to be that of financial provider followed by being a play partner and a disciplinarian (Ozgün, Çifti, &
Erden 2014). A majority of fathers and children described outdoor activities
as part of play engagement.

Both children and fathers saw fathers as disciplinarians, but their descriptions of "disciplinarian" were different. While children reported fathers as
using harsh discipline, yelling and scolding children when they misbehaved,
basically describing fathers' use of power assertion, fathers reported that they
were educators and role models. Half the fathers reported that they used
power assertion with their children and the other half reported using "reasoning, modeling, and reinforcement" (Ozgün, Çifti, & Erden 2014, p. 017).
Neither fathers' nor children's reports included fathers as caregivers. The
researchers interpreted this as an indication of the traditional aspects of the
environment in which the children were being raised. As far as emotional
involvement in children's lives is concerned, fathers reported that they loved
and cared for their children and showed affection (Ozgün, Çifti, & Erden
2014), but heavy investment at work prevented them from being as involved
as they wished. By contrast, almost all children reported that most of the
time their fathers were "emotionally distant and unavailable" (Ozgün, Çifti,
& Erden 2014, p. 016).

Similarly, findings in a study of Turkish family life indicated that a major
share of the household chores, such as cooking, cleaning, washing dishes, and
doing the laundry, were completed by the mother with the help of female
children. Fathers did chores such as fixing and maintaining the home, paying
the bills, and doing the shopping. In actuality, it was mothers who completed
these tasks, at rates ranging from 88 percent to 95 percent. Only a few fathers
participated in household chores, helping set the table (9.9%) and serving
the tea at night after dinner (7.4%). Men's contribution to other chores was
minimal (5%). Male children did not contribute much to doing household
chores, either (T.C. Ministry of Family and Social Policies 2014). In homes
with very young children, mothers were the sole primary caregivers, with
rates as high as 88 percent in urban areas and 94.3 percent in rural areas (T.C.
Ministry of Family and Social Policies 2014). These distinct role responsibilities notwithstanding, mothers and fathers reported that they were happy in
their relationship (T.C. Ministry of Family and Social Policies 2014).

If we consider fathers' involvement in their children's lives globally, a common finding is that they avail themselves as playmates to children despite
some contradictory findings from cultures like India (Roopnarıne 2010, 2013;
Roopnarine & Jin 2012; Roopnarine, Krishnakumar & Xu 2009). In Turkey,
fathers seem to be more involved in play—not necessarily more than mothers,
but more than their involvement in childcare activities (Kuruçırak 2010). A
study conducted to identify the factors involved in parent involvement in

child play found no parent sex differences in terms of academic and learning games and encouragement of play (İvrendi & Işıkoğlu 2008) However, mothers and fathers were different in their involvement in active play and play that involved sociodramatic activities. Similar to involvement in other domains, fathers who had fewer children and who had higher levels of income and education were more involved in play (İvrendi & Işıkoğlu 2008). Income and education effects were also reported in a more recent study on father involvement in play (İvrendi & Işıkoğlu 2008). In addition, fathers seemed to differ on whether they engaged more in unconstructive play based on their socioeconomic background. Possibly because they viewed play to be more for entertainment, low-income fathers tended to engage in unconstructive play more than other income groups.

In sum, the traditional belief about men's roles as a provider persists in Turkey. Fathers' role in caregiving can be defined more in terms of being a "helper." It also appears that fathers remain somewhat emotionally distant from children. Some evidence indicates that income and education seem to temper these beliefs and involvement patterns. Turkish fathers navigate a complex landscape in attempting to bridge concepts that they learned from their fathers with the demands of contemporary, urban life that encourage greater involvement in childcare and household responsibilities. In essence, Turkish fathering may be in a state of transition.

FATHERING IN TRANSITION

Kağıtçıbaşı (1982, p. 34) writes that western families are categorized as either modern, where husband–wife relationships are egalitarian and there is a "high degree of communication and companionship between spouses" with "joint decision making," or traditional, with "rural, non-industrialized, and technologically simple . . . and not highly differentiated in the occupational, social or political sense." Such a characterization further implies that family roles "evolve" from traditional to modern. This dichotomy has been applied to Turkish families because they are often considered traditional and are perceived to be extended and as having highly segregated roles and lives. In fact, Turkish families of the Republic have never been extended in a traditional sense, and they are not necessarily moving toward "modernization" when gauged by western standards. Instead, as Kağıtçıbaşı (1982) argues, Turkish families are more in line with Elizabeth Bott's "social network" model. In this model, husbands and wives have separate roles, yet their roles and responsibilities are complementary. Kağıtçıbaşı (1982) proposed that a "Duofocal Family Structure" model captures the unique dynamics of Turkish family life, for mothers and fathers indeed have highly segregated lives and are structurally nuclear. This way of constructing fathering roles contradicts current understanding of father involvement (Lamb 2000; Lamb, Pleck, Charnov, & Levine 1985) and introduces complexities and challenges for understanding the dynamics of father involvement and for encouraging fathers to become more involved in their children's lives in Turkey. Many men and women hold on to the cultural script that childcare is a woman's job (Çarkoğlu & Kalaycıoğlu & ,Turkiye'de aile 2013; Izci 2013; Ozgün, Çifti, & Erden 2014), which, no doubt, has contributed to the invisibility of Turkish fathers in children's lives.

Fatherhood in Turkey is in transition (Boratav, Fisek, & Ziya 2014). Men who are currently fathers seem to constantly struggle with finding a new model of fatherhood for themselves such that they can implement the positive experiences they had with their fathers to their relationships with their children and at the same time discard the negative ones and integrate new and more modern experiences into parenting (Boratav, Fisek, & Ziya 2014; Unlu 2010; Yalçınöz 2011). Today's Turkish fathers were raised by men who were emotionally unavailable, distant, authoritarian, and restrictive (Boratav, Fisek, & Ziya 2014; Unlu 2010; Yalçınöz 2011). In their attempts to be more involved, more playful, more understanding, and more authoritative in their relationship with their children, contemporary fathers are likely to blend past parenting practices with those evolving in the immediate present. As Roopnarine, Krishnakumar, and Vadgama (2012) suggested about Indian fathers, as families go through structural and social changes, fathers find ways to increase the time and effort they put on "behaviorally investing" in their children before their cultural ideologies about fathering begin to change.

Boratav et al. (2014) conducted a study in which married fathers were interviewed with a focus on their experiences with their own parents, children, and wives. The researchers reported that modern views about fathering, men's experiences with their own fathers, and what they desire to do and what they cannot do in terms of involvement in their children's lives bring contradictions and dilemmas to childrearing. Most men reported that their fathers were not emotionally involved in their lives. "Respect" was important, but "fear, distance, and restriction" also emerged in these men's definition of their relationships with their fathers (p. 306). The men also reported that they were aware of the importance of father involvement and that they wished to be more involved in their children's lives by being "less authoritarian, more loving and involved," than their fathers, but they also seemed to be unsure where to draw the line (p. 308). Highly educated fathers who lived in urban areas seem to struggle more in defining and living their current roles as fathers than did less educated fathers. Paradoxically, these fathers indicated that they were investing more in their children's emotional well-being and trying to be more connected and open with them but failed to mention that they assumed more responsibility for caregiving. One interpretation is that they adhere to being a father who is cognizant about "children's welfare" and who has a "nurturant concern." They are far from a father who takes on some of the traditional mothering roles (Boratav, Fisek, & Ziya 2014, p. 317).

Two other studies compared fathers' assessments of paternal involvement across generations. Fathers in Yalçınöz's (2011) study complained that their fathers were distant and authoritarian but said that they themselves were closer with their children (Yalçınöz 2011). Likewise, Unlu (2010) compared levels of men's involvement with their children and their fathers' involvement with them when they were children. Current fathers were more involved in their children's lives than their own fathers had been (Unlu 2010). Moreover, those fathers who had more involved fathers were also more involved as fathers themselves in the domains of child care traditionally carried out by mothers.

FACTORS INFLUENCING FATHER INVOLVEMENT IN TURKEY

Research on factors that influence fathers' involvement at home—and particularly at school—has produced mixed results (Şahin & Demiriz 2014; Gürşimşek, Kefi & Girgin 2007; Izci 2013; Ozgün & Honig 2005). One study (Şahin & Demiriz 2014) that examined 650 highly educated fathers' perceptions of their roles as fathers, their involvement in their preschool-aged children's schooling, and their participation in parent involvement programs delivered at their children's schools (Şahin & Demiriz 2014) revealed that when fathers had higher levels of education, or if the target child was the firstborn, the fathers perceived themselves to be more competent and had positive perceptions of fatherhood. Additionally, older fathers perceived themselves to be more competent and were more involved in their children's home-based programs. As might be expected, when fathers perceived themselves as more competent, they were more involved in their children's schools' parent involvement programs (Şahin & Demiriz 2014). Fathers preferred home–school conferencing as best fitting for their involvement, followed by home-based school involvement. The educational level of the father was also a significant contributor to the school-involvement of fathers. This is consistent with another study that showed a relationship between maternal and paternal education and involvement with children's school (Kotaman 2008).

In a similar study, Gürşimşek, Kefi, and Girgin (2007) investigated factors associated with fathers' involvement in their children's early childhood education in the west of Turkey, in Izmir—a city traditionally known to be more forward-thinking. Fathers' educational level or age was not related to their involvement levels in early education (Gürşimşek, Kefi, & Girgin 2007). Time spent with children, perceptions of the importance of early childhood education, and fathers' involvement were all related. Finding enough time or other general issues related to "time" were problems for fathers independent of whether the school implemented parent involvement programs. Not knowing how to contribute was an important challenge for fathers to be involved in their children's education, especially if their children were attending schools that did not support family involvement (Gürşimşek, Kefi, & Girgin 2007). Other challenges included transportation, difficulty interacting with the teachers, not knowing how to communicate with other parents, and and thinking it is mothers' responsibility to be involved in children's early childhood education. When fathers felt their children benefited highly from attending the preschool program, they showed higher levels of involvement (Gürşimşek, Kefi, & Girgin 2007).

In a comparable study (Çatıkkaş 2008), though no significant relationship was found between fathers' age, marital status, and occupation and overall involvement in preschool-aged children's schools, fathers who had higher educational attainment were more likely to engage in school-based activities and were less likely to engage in home-based activities when there were larger numbers of children in families. Kuruçırak (2010) also found that fathers having higher levels of education and income seemed more involved in their children's care and development. Child sex had no effect on father involvement in early schooling (Çatıkkaş 2008; Şahin & Demiriz 2014; Yılmazçetin 2003). Division of labor was an important factor determining whether fathers were involved in their children's lives. When the roles of fathers were more traditional at home, fathers engaged less in childcare activities and they were not as involved in their children's schooling. However, as fathers stayed longer in a marriage, their roles as husbands at home and the overall well-being of the family seem to improve (Çelik 2007). Marital satisfaction of the mothers is often discussed as a factor positively affecting child development. It is argued that when fathers are more involved in child and home care, mothers feel more satisfied, and consequently children benefit from these positive relationships. In the same vein, when fathers are satisfied at home and feel supported by their wives, they seem to be more involved in their children's lives (Unlu 2010). This changes if fathers are surrounded by extended family members. Their involvement declines. In a nuclear family setting, fathers are more involved in their children's lives (Çelik 2007; Poyraz 2007).

Finally, enrollment in father training programs seems to influence paternal involvement with young children. Recently several father training programs were implemented in Turkey (see AÇEV 2004) that taught topics related to fathering and child development: importance of fathering in child development; ways that fathers can be involved in childcare; positive discipline; children's development in social, emotional, and cognitive domains; effective communication; activities appropriate for the age of children; games and books; problem solving strategies; and sex education (Koçak 2004; Kocayörük

2007; Taşkın & Erkan 2009; Ünüvar & Senemoğlu 2010). There were also a few programs specifically designed for fathers of infants to improve breast-feeding rates and attachment (Ozluses & Celebioglu 2014) and even some for fathers of unborn children to improve reproductive health knowledge and behaviors, infant health, feeding, and communication and support between spouses (Turan, Nalban, Bulut, & Sahip 2001). In short, findings of all these father training programs seemed to have positive effects on fathers in terms of their involvement, knowledge, and behavior (Koçak 2004; Kocayörük 2007; Turan, Nalbant, Bulut, & Sahip 2001; Taşkın & Erkan 2009; Özlüses & Çelebioğlu 2014). Fathers who participated in these training programs were more satisfied with their own roles as fathers and fathering behaviors after the training in comparison to how they were before they entered the program. However, the effects of these training programs are strong soon after the training but fade thereafter (Kocayörük 2007). A shortcoming is that studies only assessed the effects of such training programs once after the training is finished. The training may have "sleeper effects" on later paternal involvement.

LINKS BETWEEN TURKISH FATHERS' INVOLVEMENT AND CHILDHOOD DEVELOPMENTAL OUTCOMES

From such a small body of work focusing mostly on levels of paternal involvement and factors influencing involvement, it is difficult to make strong statements about the influence of fathers on childhood development in Turkey. Nevertheless, a handful of studies provide some insights into the links between father involvement and various child development outcomes. The findings are largely in the direction of those found in several other cultural communities (see Lewis & Lamb 2010).

In the developed world, particularly in the United States, many studies focus on the effects of father's presence and residential status on childhood development (e.g., Carlson & Mclanahan 2010). There is scant research in this area in Turkey. Low divorce rates and societal disapproval of having children out of wedlock may be factors responsible for the lack of interest in these associations by Turkish researchers. Özdal and Aral (2005) compared levels of anxiety in 10- and 11-year-old children who are from two parent families and those who do not have a father around. Children whose fathers were no longer with them had higher levels of anxiety than children from two-parent families. Children who had the highest levels of anxiety were those whose fathers had abandoned them, followed by those whose fathers had divorced and those whose fathers had died (Özdal & Aral 2005).

The relationship between paternal involvement and children's school achievement has received some attention as well (Erdoğan 2011; Vatansever

Bayraktar 2012). Erdoğan (2011) assessed the relationship between parent involvement and eighth-grade children's academic achievement in Turkish Cypress. In this sample, more than half the fathers indicated that they attended parent conferences "sometimes," less than half attended parent–child association meetings and visited their children's schools, and a majority checked their children's homework often. Overall, mothers were more involved in their children's schooling than fathers, and both mothers and fathers were more involved with school-related activities at home than at school. Levels of mothers' and fathers' involvement and children's academic achievement as measured by their cumulative GPA were positively correlated.

In a longitudinal study assessing developmental ecologies in Turkey, Alici (2012) assessed preschool- and kindergarten-age children's adaptive social behavior, externalizing behaviors, mathematical skills, receptive language skills, and school readiness at two waves. Results revealed that mothers were more involved with children than fathers, and nearly 85 percent of the mothers were highly involved, whereas only half the fathers were identified as highly involved. Paternal availability at age 5 was positively associated with adaptive social behaviors and negatively associated with externalizing problems but positively associated with adaptive social behaviors, mathematical skills, language skills, and school readiness. Similarly, paternal involvement at age 5 was also positively associated with adaptive social behaviors, mathematical skills, language skills, and school-readiness at age 6. Along with wealth, paternal and maternal education, as well as paternal involvement but not maternal involvement positively predicted language skills and school readiness at age 5. At age 6, children's school adjustment was negatively associated with maternal dissatisfaction with father's lack of care and support and positively associated with children's school-readiness and their language skills at age 5. These findings suggest that fathers may make unique contributions to children's overall development and well-being.

A number of studies have investigated father involvement and the social and emotional well-being of adolescents (Arcan, 2006; Gunuc & Doğan 2013; Gürmen & Rohner 2013; Karacan, 2014; Kocayörük, 2007, 2010; Kuzucu & Özdemir 2013; Yaban, Sayıl, & Kindap Tepe 2013; Sirvanli Ozen 2009). For example, Kuzucu and Özdemir (2013) examined the association between self-reports of maternal and paternal involvement and adolescents' levels of depression, aggression, life satisfaction, and self-respect. Levels of maternal and paternal involvement were negatively associated with adolescent aggression and depression and positively associated with measures of adolescent life satisfaction and self-respect (Kuzucu & Özdemir 2013). Another study revealed that perceived father support was positively associated with positive peer relationships as well as adversely related to bullying the adolescent faced and to negative peer relationships. It was also found that father support improved peer relationship quality, which, in turn, affected whether the adolescent faced bullying. Father support mediated the associations between maternal support and bullying and between mother support and peer relationship quality. These results show that perceived father support and having a close relationship with one's father were important indicators of adolescent well-being in a peer context (Yaban, Sayıl, & Kindap Tepe 2013). In yet another study (Sirvanli Ozen 2009), paternal acceptance played a mediating role between maternal acceptance and adolescent self-image, and father acceptance mediated the effects of mother acceptance on self-image for both male and female adolescents. However, the strength of the mediating effect was higher for female adolescents than male adolescents. Maternal and paternal acceptance were positive predictors of better adolescent self-image (Sirvanli Ozen 2009).

In summary, this small but growing body of work is largely correlational. As the later studies show, maternal and paternal factors can mediate and moderate the relationships between paternal investment and involvement in children and childhood outcomes. Factors such as belief systems about roles, prior relationships with one's father, the quality of spousal relationships, and parenting styles—among many other factors—may all act as mediators and moderators of the influence of involved fathering and childhood outcomes.

FUTURE DIRECTIONS AND POLICY IMPLICATIONS

Both researchers and policymakers in Turkey should focus on the diversity of ways that fathers' investment and involvement in the family influence spousal relationship and childhood development. There seems to be strong research evidence that Turkish fathers from middle to higher socioeconomic backgrounds are more involved, whereas lower-income fathers are less involved in their children's lives. A few of the factors that impinge on father involvement seem to be a lack of time, inadequate skills, being primary wage earners, and the comfort that extended family members provide to fathers when they are involved in childcare. Traditional roles and perceptions of men in society seem to also contribute to traditional roles in the home. Accordingly, researchers and policy makers need to consider the range of family proximal (e.g., marital relationship, communication strategies) and distal factors within specific developmental niches in Turkey to study fathers and develop policies to improve the roles of fathers in childhood development.

Fathering in Turkey is in transition, as is research investigating the effects of parenting on child development outcomes. To develop a better understanding of the dynamics of this transition and identify culture-specific factors aiding and abetting it, studies should focus on fathers of children from different age groups and from different socioeconomic backgrounds and regions in

Turkey. This would require moving away from general involvement-focused research to assessments of the quality of different dimensions of father–child interactions at home, at school, and in the community at large and determining their relationships with children's health, safety, and cognitive, social–emotional, and language development. Needless to say, diverse methodologies and assessment and observational techniques would provide much-needed information that could better inform policies on families and children in Turkey.

Fathering programs seem to impart positive effects on paternal involvement across cultures (see AÇEV 2004; Downer, Campos, McWayne, & Gartner 2008; Lundahl, Tollefson, Risser, & Lovejoy 2008; McBride 1990). Increasing fathers' awareness of the importance of their involvement with children, including special needs children, providing child development information to fathers and families, and introducing strategies for increased engagement with children of all ages can do much to improve father–child relationships in Turkey. To sustain gains made by attendance in father education and training programs, every attempt should be made to keep in touch with fathers periodically (e.g., using technology to text messages about parenting) to provide support and encouragement for optimal parenting after the initial program goals are achieved.

WEBSITES

www.acev.org/en/kaynaklarimiz/arastirmalarimiz-ve-yayinlarimiz

www.global-womens-network.org/wiki/Mother_Child_Education_Foundation_(ACEV),_Istanbul,_Turkey

http://www.haberturk.com/polemik/haber/537849-kadin-ve-erkegin-esit-olmasi-mumkun-degil

REFERENCES

AÇEV [Mother Child Education Foundation]. (2014). AÇEV 2013 Faaliyet Raporu, İstanbul. www.acev.org/docs/faaliyet-raporlar%C4%B1m%C4%B1z/acev_faaliyet_raporu_tr2013.pdf?sfvrsn=2.

Alici, C. (2012). *Paternal contributions to children's cognitive functioning and school readiness* (Unpublished master's thesis). Istanbul: Koc University.

Allen, S. M., & Daly, K. J. (2007). The effects of father involvement: An updated research summary of the evidence. Centre for Families, Work & Well-Being, University of Guelph.

Aral, N., Gürsoy, F., Özdal, F., & Dizman, H. (2008). A study of depression levels in children from single-parent and two-parent families. In L. S. Woodcock (ed.) (2008), *Change and challenge in education* (pp. 253–261), Athens, Greece: Atiner.

Arcan, K. (2006). *Özel okullara giden lise düzeyindeki ergenlerin, akademik başarıları ile algıladıkları anne baba tutumları arasındaki ilişkilerin incelenmesi* (Unpublished doctoral dissertation). Istanbul: Boğaziçi University.

Balkanlıoğlu, M. A. (2011). *Influence of Alevi–Sunni intermarriage on the spouses' religious affiliation, family relations, and social environment: A qualitative study of Turkish couples* (Unpublished doctoral dissertation). Denton, TX: University of North Texas.

Bayam, Ö. Ç. (2010). *Anne-babaların öz-yeterlik inançları ile çocuklarının problem davranışlarına yönelik algıları arasındaki ilişkinin incelenmesi* (Unpublished master's thesis). Ankara, Turkey: Ankara University.

Bocknek, E. L., Hossain, Z., & Roggman, L. (2014). Forward progress of scientific inquiry into the early father–child relationship: Introduction to the special issue on very young children and their fathers. *Infant Mental Health Journal, 35*(5), 389–393.

Boratav, H. B., Fisek, G. F., & Ziya, H. E. (2014). Unpacking masculinities in the context of social change internal complexities of the identities of married men in turkey. *Men and Masculinities, 17*(3), 299–324.

Cabrera, Natasha J., and Catherine S. Tamis-LeMonda (2013). *Handbook of father involvement: Multidisciplinary perspectives.* London: Routledge.

Cabrera, N. J., Tamis-LeMonda, C. S., Bradley, R. H., Hofferth, S., & Lamb, M. E. (2000). Fatherhood in the twenty-first century. *Child Development, 71*(1), 127–136.

Carlson, Marcia J. and McLanahan, Sara S. (2010). Fathers in fragile families. In M. E. Lamb (ed.). *The Role of the Father in Child Development (5th ed.)* (pp. 241–269), Hoboken, NJ: Wiley & Sons.

Çarkoğlu, A., & Kalaycıoğlu, E. (2013). *Türkiye'de aile, iş ve toplumsal cinsiyet* (Unpublished report). İstanbul Politikalar Merkezi. Sabancı Üniversitesi. http://ipc.sabanciuniv.edu/wp-content/uploads/2013/11/Aile-2012-ISSP-Family-Survey-final.pdf.

Çatıkkaş, K. T. (2008). *Okul öncesi eğitime babaların katılım düzeyleri ile ilgili değişkenlerin incelenmesi* (Unpublished master's thesis). Istanbul: Yeditepe University.

Çelik, S. B. (2007). Family function levels of Turkish fathers with children aged between 0– 6. *Social Behavior and Personality: An International Journal, 35*(4), 429–442.

Central Intelligence Agency. (2014). *World Factbook Download 2014.* https://www.cia.gov/library/publications/the-world-factbook/geos/print/country/countrypdf_tu.pdf.

Demren, Ç. (2001). *Ataerklik ve erkeklik biçimlerinin karşılıklı ilişkileri ve etkileşimleri* (Unpublished master's thesis). Ankara, Turkey: Hacettepe University.

Downer, J., Campos, R., McWayne, C., & Gartner, T. (2008). Father involvement and children's early learning: A critical review of published empirical work from the past 15 years. *Marriage and Family Review, 43*(1–2), 67–108.

Durmuşoğlu-Saltalı, N., & Arslan, E. (2012). Ebeveyn tutumlarının anasınıfına devam eden çocukların sosyal yetkinlik ve içe dönüklük davranışını yordaması (Parent's attitudes as a predictor of preschoolers' social competence and introverted behavior). *Elementary Education Online, 11*(3), 729–737.

Erdoğan, Y. (2011). *An investigation of the relationship among parental involvement, socio-economic factors of parents and students' academic achievement.* Unpublished doctoral dissertation, Eastern Mediterranean University (EMU), Northern Cyprus.

Erkal, S., Çopur, Z., Doğan, N., & Şafak, Ş. (2007). Examining the relationship between parents' gender roles and responsibilities towards their children (a Turkish example). *Social Behavior and Personality: An International Journal, 35*(9), 1221–1234.

European Commission. (2014). *Turkey 2013 Progress Report.* http://ec.europa.eu/ enlargement/pdf/key_documents/2013/package/brochures/turkey_2013.pdf.

Evans, C. (1997). *Türkiyeli babaların babalık rollerine yönelik tutum ve katılımları: Düşük sosyo-ekonomik ortamdan bir örneklem [Turkish fathers' attitudes to and involvement in their fathering role: a low socio-economic sample]* (Unpublished master's thesis). İstanbul: Boğaziçi University.

Garbarino, J. (2000). The soul of fatherhood. *Marriage and Family Review, 29*(2–3), 11–21.

Gunuc, S., & Doğan, A. (2013). The relationships between Turkish adolescents' Internet addiction, their perceived social support and family activities. *Computers in Human Behavior, 29*(6), 2197–2207.

Gürmen, M. S., & Rohner, R. P. (2013). Effects of marital distress on Turkish adolescents' psychological adjustment. *Journal of Child and Family Studies,* 1–8.

Gürşimşek, I., Kefi, S., & Girgin, G. (2007). Okul öncesi eğitime babaların katılım düzeyi ile ilişkili değişkenlerin incelenmesi. *Hacettepe Üniversitesi Eğitim Fakültesi Dergisi (HU Journal of Education), 33,* 181–191.

Habertürk. (July 31, 2010). Kadın ve erkeğin eşit olması mümkün değil. *Habertürk.* www.haberturk.com/polemik/haber/537849-kadin-ve-erkegin-esit-olmasi -mumkun-degil.

Harris, R. D. A. (2014). *Meta-analysis on father involvement and early childhood social-emotional development.* http://steinhardt.nyu.edu/opus/issues/2010/spring/father_ childhood_development.

İvrendi, A., & Işıkoğlu, N. (2010). A Turkish view on fathers' involvement in children's play. *Early Childhood Education Journal, 37*(6), 519–526.

Izci, B. (2013). *An exploratory study of Turkish fathers' involvement in the lives of their preschool aged children* (Unpublished master's thesis). Florida State University.

Kağıtçıbaşı, Ç. (1982). *Sex Roles, Family and Community in Turkey.* Bloomington, Indiana: Indiana University Turkish Studies Series: 3.

Kağıtçıbaşı, Ç. (1996). *Family and human development across cultures: A view from the other side.* Hillsdale, NJ: Erlbaum.

Kağıtçıbaşı, Ç. (2005). Autonomy and relatedness in cultural context implications for self and family. *Journal of Cross-cultural Psychology, 20*(10), 1–20.

Kağıtçıbaşı, Ç. (2007). *Family, self, and human development across cultures: Theory and applications,* 2nd ed. Mahwah, NJ: Lawrence Erlbaum Associates.

Kağıtçıbaşı, Ç., & Ataca, B. (2005). Value of children and family change: A three-decade portrait from Turkey. *Applied Psychology, 54* (3), 317–337.

Kağıtçıbaşı, Ç., Ataca, B., & Diri, A. S. (2005). The Turkish family and the value of children: Trends over time. In G. Trommsdorff & B. Nauck (eds.), *The value of children in cross cultural perspectives: Case studies from eight societies* (pp. 91–120). Lengerich, Germany: Pabst Science Publishers.

Karacan, E. (2014). Timing of parenthood and generativity development: An examination of age and gender effects in Turkish sample. *Journal of Adult Development, 21*(4), 1–9.

Kayra, C. (2008). *Osmanlı'da fetvalar ve günlük yaşam*. İstanbul: Boyut Kitapları.

Kiray, M. B. (1985). Metropolitan city and the changing family. In *Family in Turkish society* (pp. 79–89). Ankara, Turkey: Turkish Social Science Association.

Koçak, A. A. (2004). *Baba destek programı değerlendirme raporu*. İstanbul: AÇEV.

Kocayörük, E. (2007). *The effects of father involvement training (FIT) on family functioning and peer relationships of 9th grade high school students* (Unpublished master's thesis). Ankara, Turkey: Middle East Technical University (METU).

Kocayörük, E. (2010). Ergen gelişiminde aile işlevleri ve baba katılımı. *Türk Psikolojik Danışma ve Rehberlik Dergisi, 33*(4), 37–45.

Kotaman, H. (2008). Türk ana babalarının çocuklarının eğitim öğretimlerine katılım düzeyleri. *Uludağ Üniversitesi Eğitim Fakültesi Dergisi, 21*(1), 135–149.

Kuruçırak, Ş. (2010). *4-12 aylık bebeği olan babaların, babalık rolü algısı ile bebek bakımına katılımı arasındaki ilişki* (Unpublished master's thesis). Antalya, Turkey: Akdeniz Üniversitesi.

Kuzucu, Y., & Özdemir, Y. (2013). Ergen ruh sağlığının anne ve baba katılımı açısından yordanması. *Education and Science/Egitim ve Bilim, 38*(168), 96–112.

Lamb, M. E. (2000). The history of research on father involvement: An overview. *Marriage and Family Review, 29*(2–3), 23–42.

Lamb, M. E. (2010). *The role of the father in child development*, 5th ed. Hoboken, NJ: John Wiley & Sons.

Lamb, M. E., & Lewis, C (2010). The role of parent-child relationships in child development. In M. H. Bornstein & M. E. Lamb (eds.), *Developmental science: An advanced textbook* (6th ed., pp. 469–517). New York: Taylor and Francis.

Lamb, M. E., Pleck J. H., Charnov, E. L., & Levine J. A. (1987). A biosocial perspective on paternal behavior and involvement. In J. Lancaster, J. Altman, A. Rossi, et al. (eds.), *Parenting across the lifespan: Biosocial perspectives* (pp. 11–42). New York: Academic Press.

Lundahl, B. W., Tollefson, D., Risser, H., & Lovejoy, M. C. (2008). A meta-analysis of father involvement in parent training. *Research on Social Work Practice, 18*(2), 97–106.

McBride, B. A. (1990). The effects of a parent education/play group program on father involvement in child rearing. *Family Relations, 39*(3), 250–256. doi: 10.1177/1049731507309828.

Meral, B. F., & Çavkaytar, A. (2012). Fathers' involvement in childrearing practices of their children with intellectual disabilities. *Journal of Education, 1*, 91–106.

Turan, J. M., Nalbant, H., Bulut, A., & Sahip, Y. (2001). Including expectant fathers in antenatal education programmes in Istanbul, Turkey. *Reproductive Health Matters, 9*(18), 114–125.

Nacak, M., Yagmurlu, B., Durgel, E., & van de Vijver, F. (2011). Metropol ve Anadolu'da ebeveynlik: Biliş ve davranışlarda şehrin ve eğitim düzeyinin rolü [Parenting in metropole and Anatolia samples: The role of residence and education in beliefs and behaviors]. *Türk Psikoloji Dergisi, 26*(67), 85–104.

Oktem, N. (2002). Religion in Turkey. *Brigham Young University Law Review*, 2, 371–404.

Ortaylı, İ., (2001). *Osmanlı toplumunda aile*. Timaş.

Ortaylı, İ., (2010). *Osmanlı toplumunda aile*. Timaş.

Özdal. F. & N. Aral, (2005) Baba yoksunu olan ve anne babası ile yaşayan çocukların kaygı düzeylerinin incelenmesi, *Gazi Üniversitesi Kırşehir Eğitim Fakültesi Dergisi*, 6(2), 255–267.

Özdikmenli-Demir, G., & Sayıl, M. (2009). Individualism-collectivism and conceptualizations of interpersonal relationships among Turkish children and their mothers. *Journal of Social and Personal Relationships*, 26(4), 371–387.

Özer, S. (2013). Cumhuriyet'in ilk yıllarında bekârlık vergisi'ne ilişkin tartışmalar. *Gazi Akademik Bakış*, 6(12), 173–191.

Özgün, O., Çifti, M. A., & Erden, Ş. (2013). The meaning of fatherhood as perceived by Turkish police fathers and their young children. *Educational Research and Reviews*, 8(21), 1966–1978.

Özgun, Ö., & Honig, A. S. (2005). Parental involvement and spousal satisfaction with division of early childcare in Turkish families with normal children and children with special needs. *Early Child Development and Care*, 175(3), 3259–3270. doi:10.1080/0300443042000235749.

Özlüses, E., & Çelebioglu, A. (2014). Educating fathers to improve breastfeeding rates and paternal-infant attachment. *Indian pediatrics*, 51(8), 654–657.

Pew Forum on Religion and Public Life. (October 2009). *Mapping the Global Muslim population*. www.pewforum.org/files/2009/10/Muslimpopulation.pdf.

Poyraz, M. (2007). *Babaların babalık rolünü algılamalarıyla kendi ebeveynlerinin tutumları arasındaki ilişkinin incelenmesi* (Unpublished master's thesis). Ankara, Turkey: Gazi Üniversitesi.

Roopnarine, J. L. (2010). Cultural variations in beliefs about play, parent-child play, and children's play: Meaning for childhood development. In A. Pellegrini (Ed.), *Oxford encyclopedia on play*. Oxford: Oxford University Press.

Roopnarine, J. L. (2013). What is the state of play. *International Journal of Play*, 3.

Roopnarine, J. L., & Jin, B. (2012). Indo Caribbean immigrant mothers' and fathers' beliefs about play: Do they moderate the relationship between preschoolers' time in play and early academic performance? *American Journal of Play*, 4, 441–463.

Roopnarine, J. L., Krishnakumar, A., & Vadgama, D. (2013). Indian fathers: Family dynamics and investment patterns. *Psychology and Developing Societies*, 25(2), 223–247.

Roopnarine, J. L., & Krishnakumar, A., & Xu, Yi-Li (2009). Beliefs about mothers' and fathers' roles and the division of childcare and household labor in Indo Caribbean immigrants with young children. *Cultural Diversity and Ethnic Minority Psychology*, 15, 173–182.

Sabırlı-Ozışıklı, I. (2008). *A Study of parent involvement in the Boğaziçi University Preschool Center* (Unpublished master's thesis). İstanbul: Boğaziçi University.

Şahin, H., & Demiriz, S. (2014). Beş altı yaşında çocuğu olan babaların, babalık rolünü algılamaları ile aile katılım çalışmalarını gerçekleştirmeleri arasındaki ilişkinin incelenmesi. *TSA*, 18(1), 273–294.

Sarkadi, A., Kristiansson, R., Oberklaid, F., & Bremberg, S. (2007). Fathers' involve-ment and children's developmental outcomes: a systematic review of longitudi-nal studies. *Acta Paediatrica, 97*(2), 153–158.

Semiz, Y. (2010). 1923–1950 Döneminde Türkiye'de nüfusu arttırma gayretleri ve mecburi evlendirme kanunu (Bekârlık Vergisi). *Selçuk Üniversitesi Türkiyat Araştırmaları Dergisi, 27,* 423–469.

Shaw, W. (2007). Museums and narratives of display from the late Ottoman Empire to the Turkish Republic. *Muqarnas, 24,* 253–279.

Şirvanlı-Özen, D. (2009). Ergenlerde anneden algılanan kabul/ilgi ile benlik-algısı arasındaki ilişki: Babadan algılanan kabul/ilginin aracı rolü. *Türk Psikoloji Yazıları, 12* (24), 13–23.

Sunar, D., & Fisek, G. (2005). Contemporary Turkish families. In U. P. Gielen & J. L. Roopnarine (eds.), *Families in global perspective* (169–183). London: Pearson.

Tamis-LeMonda, C. S., & Cabrera, N. (eds.). (2002). *Handbook of father involvement: Multidisciplinary perspectives*. Mahwah, NJ: Lawrence Erlbaum Associates.

Tan, D., & Waldhoff, H. P. (1996). Turkish everyday culture in Germany and its prospects. *Turkish Culture in German Society Today,* 137–156.

Taşkın, N., & Erkan, S. (2009). The influence of father education programs on the levels of father involvement with children: An experimental study. *Hacettepe University Journal of Education, 37,* 136–148.

T. C. Ministry of Foreign Affairs (2014). *Economic Outlook of Turkey.* www.mfa.gov.tr/turk-ekonomisindeki-son-gelismeler.tr.mfa.

T. C. Ministry of Family and Social Policies (2014). Türkiye'de aile yapısı araştırması 2011. Ankara. www.cocukhaklariizleme.org/wp-content/uploads/turkiyenin-aile-yapisi-arastirmasi-20111.pdf.

The Organisation for Economic Co-operation and Development (OECD). (2014). *OECD Better Life Index.* www.oecdbetterlifeindex.org/countries/turkey/.

TÜİK (2013). Turkey in Statistics 2012. Ankara. www.amasyaplanlama.gov.tr/ortak_icerik/amasyplanlama/ISTATISTIKLERLE%20TURKIYE%202012.pdf.

TÜİK (Türkiye İstatistik Kurumu) [Turkish Statistical Institute] Haber Bülteni. (2012). *Evlenme ve Boşanma İstatistikleri 2011 [Marriage and Divorce Statis-tics 2011].* Publication No. 10844, June 15, 2012. www.tuik.gov.tr/PreHaber Bultenleri.do?id=10844.

TÜİK Haber Bülteni (2013). *Evlenme ve Boşanma İstatistikleri 2012 [Marriage and Divorce Statistics 2012].* Publication No. 13469, March 28, 2013. www.tuik.gov.tr/PreHaber Bultenleri.do?id=13469.

TÜİK Haber Bülteni (2014). *Yas,am Memnuniyeti Aras,tırması 2013,* Publication No. 16052, March 11, 2014. www.tuik.gov.tr/Kitap.do?metod=KitapDetay&KT_ID=11&KITAP_ID=15Yılmaz.

Türk Üniversiteli Kadınlar Derneği. (2014). *Kadın Cinayetleri.* www.tukd.org.tr/basinhaber07.asp.

Unlu, Ş. (2010). *Being fathered and being a father: Examination of the general pattern of Turkish fathers' and their own fathers' involvement level for children between the ages of 0-8* (Unpublished master's thesis). Ankara, Turkey: Middle East Technical University.

Ünüvar, P., & Senemoğlu, N. (2010). Babaların 3–6 Yaş grubu çocuklarıyla geçir-dikleri zamanın niteliğini geliştirme [Developing the quality of the time period fathers spend with their children at 3–6 years old]. *Pamukkale University Journal of Educational Faculty, 27*, 55–66.

Vatansever Bayraktar, H. (2012). *İlköğretim 5. sınıf öğrencilerinin öğretmeni ve ebeveyni ile olan iletişimleri ile Türkçe dersi konuşma becerileri arasındaki ilişki* (Unpublished master's thesis). Istanbul: Marmara University.

Yaban, E. H., Sayıl, M., & Kındap Tepe, Y. (2013). Erkek Ergenlerde Anne Babadan Algılanan Destek ile Akran Zorbalığı Arasındaki İlişkide Arkadaşlık Niteliğinin Rolü. *Türk Psikoloji Dergisi, 28*(71), 20–32.

Yalçınöz, B. (2011). *From being a son to being a father: An intergenerational comparison of fatherhood in Turkey* (Unpublished master's thesis). Istanbul: İstanbul Bilgi University.

Yılmazçetin, C. (2003). *Babanın katılımı ve ergen öncesi çocukların davranış problemleri arasındaki ilişki* (Unpublished master's thesis). Istanbul: Boğaziçi University.

16

Fathers in Israel:
Contextualizing Images of Fatherhood

Roni Strier

Israel is a very challenging ground for researching fathers. In this heterogeneous and complex society, it is not surprising that Israeli fatherhood is a fragmented and contested construct. Understanding the myriad of faces of fatherhood in Israel requires distinct attention to Israel's historical background as well as to the national, ethnic, religious and social class diversity characterizing Israeli society. The aim of this chapter is to provide a contextual framework for a deeper understanding of fathers in Israel. The chapter analyzes shared processes (westernization, familism, increasing inequalities, and the national conflict) and divides (national, religious, ethnic and social class) that significantly affect the construction of fatherhood in Israel.

The study of fathers as a distinctive area of research is only now beginning to take shape in Israel. Despite the large number of courses dealing with family and gender issues in academic institutions in Israel, only two universities have taught specific courses on fatherhood, and the first academic conference on fathers was held in 2014. Conceptualizing fatherhood in Israel involves untangling its unique historical background and walking through its heterogeneous social composition and its cultural, social, and gender clashing orientations. Even though Israel is a very small country, smaller than Lake Michigan and about half the size of Switzerland, any attempt to define an essential Israeli fatherhood would be a terrible mistake. Talking about a shared Israeli fatherhood is an invitation to commit oversimplifications, for this would ignore the uneven texture of Israeli society. Thus navigating the multiplicity of Israeli fatherhoods means both pinpointing common processes and identifying main differences that affect the experience of fatherhood in Israel.

ISRAELI FATHERHOODS: MAIN SHARED PROCESSES

Before discussing issues of diversity, I will first address four main processes that I believe strongly affect the experiences of fathers in Israel, irrespective of differing affiliations. First, Israel is part of the world's most developed economies, and much as in other postindustrial societies, families have undergone huge transformational processes, including the privatization of the family sphere and the individualization of family life. Families, which in the past were constructed around serving the community and family needs, are now seen as foremost fulfilling the needs of their members as individuals. As result, there is a diversification of family structures, including two-career families, second families, single-parent families, extended families, and same-sex families. Besides, fathers in Israel are exposed to the effects of globalization, modernization, fast-paced technological growth, and digital communication. For educated and urban Israeli fathers, ideals of fatherhood tend to fit such western standards as those that stress breadwinning, providing security and protection in addition to care roles that include the emotional and cognitive aspects of children's development (Geva 2003).

Although studies suggest that fatherhood in Israel is constantly changing, these changes are slow and are not uniform across and within different sectors. Shapira (2013) indicates a tendency of Jewish fathers to have greater involvement in children lives than in the past, more equality in the division of household roles, and an attempt to challenge old standards of fatherhood. These "new fathers" look for a middle way between traditional fatherhood views and images of a more involved fatherhood consistent with studies that show a change in attitudes and beliefs regarding traditional fathers' roles among primary caregiver fathers (Gonet 2007; Sagiv 2003). At the same time, Khativ Abed El-Hai (2011) states that Israeli fathers, both Jewish and Palestinian, are more involved in childcare activities than their fathers, who basically performed breadwinner roles. Most of them defined their fathers as estranged and authoritarian figures involved in physically punishing children.

Second, alongside the cultural orientation toward westernization, Israel remains a highly traditional family and child-centered society. Israel has made impressive progress in gender equality. Women's participation in the labor market is quite high (44% of the workforce), and gender educational gaps have been radically narrowed. In 2013, women obtained 60 percent of master degrees (Central Bureau of Statistics 2013). However, women's overall status in Israel is still low in many areas such as wages, managerial roles, and political representation. According to Perez (2011), the reason for the continued gender inequality is the lack of changes at the family sphere. In other words, the changes in labor participation and education are not followed by an increase in men's participation in the family area, wherein the division of family labor has remained relatively steady with the final responsibility of the household and childcare burden being carried by women.

According to Fogiel-Bijaoui and Rutlinger-Reiner (2013), familism is a main cultural code in Israel, an orientation that takes for granted the centrality of family in the private and public sphere and secures the role of women as wives and mothers as the main pillars of family life. Marriage, a central element in the construction of familism, is still considered by most Israelis the only legitimate frame for fertility. These traditional orientations have maintained the privileges of men and also prevented significant changes in fathers' traditional roles. Lavee and Katz (2003) confirm that Israeli families in general have undergone two simultaneous, yet opposing processes, one pulling them toward westernization, the other, toward traditionalism. These opposing trends are also reflected in dominant gender views wherein gender equality discourses coexist with traditional views of the gendered division of family roles (Hertzog & Barude 2009). These clashing orientations, modernization and westernization in the midst of a highly familistic and child-centered society, have generated inner tensions and confusion between conflicting views of old and new fatherhood in Israel (Ogny 2014).

Third, Israel is among the countries having the highest income inequality, surpassed only by Chile, Mexico, the United States, and Turkey (OECD 2013). Israeli society is undergoing deep transformations from a welfare state and egalitarian society to a highly socially polarized, market-based, and competitive one (National Insurance Institute 2014). Israel's labor market and social policies have not managed to expand the middle class, which has decreased in numbers, its share in the distribution of income having dropped by 14 percent in the last decade (Dagan-Buzaglo & Konor-Attias 2013). The shrinking middle class is one of the expressions of a highly polarized society. Statistics show that the Israel middle class is one of the smallest among industrialized countries (Pressman 2007). In addition to the middle class economic vulnerability, Israel has the highest index of poverty among the OECD countries. Israel maintains a poverty rate of 20.9 percent—nearly twice the OECD average of 11.3 percent (OECD 2013).

The increasing economic insecurity of the middle class and the pauperization of the low working class all negatively affect fathers. Research documents the centrality of the breadwinner role as a component of hegemonic masculinities and dominant views of fatherhood across industrialized nations (Connell 2005; Nelson 2004; Nonn 2007). Studies indicate that working fathers face significant challenges in proving their economic self-sufficiency, which is traditionally achieved by holding a decent job (Baxandall 2004). The increasing neoliberalization and privatization of the Israeli economy have both generated a climate of economic vulnerability in many Israeli families. Thus it comes as no surprise that poverty is a menace to the psychological well-being of Israeli fathers from the working and lower middle classes (Strier et al. 2014).

Fourth, transcending national and ethnic differences are all affected by the existence of the Israeli–Palestinian/Israeli–Arab conflicts that have deeply affected the lives of millions of fathers and families in the region. Studies confirm the gendered nature of armed conflicts and the effects of war on the construction of fatherhood (Cockburn 2010; LaRossa 2011). Countless wars and decades of violence and losses have changed the course of both Jewish and Palestinian families and fathering (Simon 1999). The negative effects of war on children and mothers have been well documented (Garbarino 2008; World Health Organization 2003). Although less documented, fathers are no less affected by the harmful physical and psychological influences of war (Baaz 2009; Shepard 2000). Fathers are engaged in the conflict as exposed civilians, as soldiers, and as fathers of children and soldiers. As traditionally responsible for the physical security of families, communities and property, war is a permanent threat to fathers in Israel.

These four trends taken together expose Israeli fathers to unique challenges and dilemmas such as promoting individualism and yet maintaining family cohesion, enhancing children's group identity (national, religious, ethnic) and promoting child integration in society, and finally protecting the physical security of their children and families, and keeping a high level of father involvement while still remaining a successful provider. All of this occurs in the context of a competitive, highly unequal neoliberal market-based economy in the midst of conflict. These challenges surmount the different national, religious, and ethnic segmentations of fathers and families, making Israel a unique setting in which to observe fatherhood as a complex and dynamic construct. As asserted above, alongside these common particularities, Israeli fatherhood is also a highly fragmented construct, mirroring the diversity of Israeli society itself. In the following section, I analyze four main diversity axes (national, religious, ethnicity, social class).

The National Divide: Jewish–Palestinian Fathers in Israel

The Israeli father population is basically comprised of two main national groups: Jewish and Palestinian. The history of these distinctive father groups is rooted in the narrative of both national collectives. Israel was established as an independent state in 1948 in the context of a war between the Jews established in Palestine and Arab countries. Around the same time, the United Nations launched a Partition Plan meant to put an end to the British Mandate and to subsequently create two nation-states, one Jewish and one Palestinian. The UN Partition Plan was accepted by the Jewish leadership, who saw the resolution as recognition of the Zionist goal to establish an independent Jewish state (Morris 2008). This was not true for the Arab countries, which rejected the plan, seeing in it the loss of Palestine, their homeland, part of the Arab territory. This difference led to the war called by the Jews the War of Independence and by the Palestinians, *el-Nakbah*, the Catastrophe. The war resulted in the defeat of the Arab armies, the establishment of Israel, and the dispersal of the Palestinian population (Kimmerling & Migdal 2003).

Almost seven decades later, after several wars and endless hostilities, the conflict still has a strong effect on the lives of Jewish and Palestine fathers and families in Israel and in the region as a whole (Shavit 2013). Fathers being the protector of the family, house, and community, the violent conflict represents a real threat to men's roles. This threat is aggravated because both national collectives have experienced the traumatic shadow of war and exile in their families and communities. On one side, the history of Judaism is deeply embedded in a narrative of persecution and multiple exiles in which Israel is seen as the answer to a life in exile (Shapira 2013). On the Palestinian side, Zionism and Israel are seen as the cause of exile and disruption of Palestinian history (Said 1992).

For the majority of Jews in Israel, the Israeli state is the realization of Zionism, a Jewish national movement established in the last decade of the nineteenth century in Europe as a viable solution to the growing anti-Semitism and persecutions of Jews in Europe. Zionism was inspired by the effervescent national political climate of the European Enlightenment. The rise of European national feelings ignited the national imagination of some sectors of the Jewish population, who looked for a territorial national solution to the "Jewish question." For its founders, Zionism was the historical answer to the anti-Semitism of the European continent that had seen centuries of Inquisition, persecutions, and the systematic extermination of half of the Jewish population by the Nazi regime and their allies in World War II. The Zionist movement called for the settlement of Jewish pioneers in the Jewish homeland, Israel.

The call for the "normalization" of Jewish life also has a specific gendered aspect, the promotion of a new image of the Jewish man and father, a counterimage to the diasporic and submissive image of the Jewish father. In the Zionist social imagery, the new Jewish father was an autonomous, productive, strong, physical male, free from the Jewish vulnerability that characterized the common image of subjugated masculinities of Jewish men (Boyarin 1997). Fathers as traditionally responsible for the physical security of their families experienced anti-Semitism with a sense of male failure. Zionism proposed a new archetype of Jewish fatherhood: a father of work and war who can both provide and protect the family (Kaplan 2003, 2007). Zionism proposed a new Jewish fatherhood project, unknown to previous Jewish history, a fatherhood model more biblically entrenched than informed by the diasporic, defeated, and emasculated image of Jewish males (Ben-Ari & Dardashti 2001).

In a sense, Israel may be seen as a project of Jewish fatherhood's liberation from their devaluated masculinities (Kamir 2009 2011). Under this prism, Israel emerges as the creation of a safe domain for Jewish fatherhood away from the threats of the precariousness of the diasporic Jewish fatherhood (Anabi 2012). Thus the new and successful father should be foremost a productive provider, a warrior totally committed to the security of his offspring and his country, producing offspring who will be soldiers themselves (Sasson-Levy 2011). Hollander (2012) criticizes this construction of masculinity and suggests that scholars of Israeli masculinity must move beyond binary models (old versus new Jewish masculinities). Essentially, such models limit complex social processes to either a total rejection of past behavioral models or facile imitations of new ones and overlook internal differences among Jewish fathers.

On the other side, the Palestinian fatherhood in Israel is to no lesser a degree shaped by the course of the Palestinian history and the Israel–Palestine conflict. However, whereas the new Jewish fatherhood narrative seems to be one of "normalization," the narrative of the Palestinian fatherhood is one of "resilience." The historical context has left a deep mark in the life of Palestinian communities and no doubt has affected the lived experiences of Palestinian fathers. Palestinian masculinity, as a central category in Palestinian patriarchal culture, provides a perspective from which Palestinian fatherhood in Israel can be understood (Monterescu 2006). In the eyes of Palestinian historiography, the process of Jewish colonization, massive land acquisition and appropriation, and the rapid transformation of the rural Palestinian society all overwhelmed the Palestinian collective (Samih & Naseer 2006). For Palestinians, the British mandate was a regime of political and military oppression, the cover of a secret alliance between western imperialism and Jewish colonization. Under the British domination, Palestine was economically, politically, and psychologically crushed (Farsun & Aruri 2006).

The establishment of Israel resulted in hundreds of thousands of Palestinian refugees, the loss of main cities such as Haifa, Lod, Acre, and Jaffa and the region of eastern Galilee. The war disintegrated Palestine. Israel took over most of the Jewish historical territory, and Arab countries such as Egypt and Jordan occupied some of the former Palestinian territories (Gaza and the West Bank). In a matter of weeks, the Palestinian fate was disrupted. The Palestinian population became divided in three main separated groups: Palestinians who remained in their homes and became Israeli citizens, Palestinians who remained in the territories defined as part of a future Palestinian State under the temporary control of Jordan (West Bank and east Jerusalem) and Egypt (Gaza), and a refugee population temporarily staying in the refugee camps in central Palestine, Gaza, and Arab countries (Lebanon, Jordan, and Syria). The aftermath of al-Nakbah saw the displacement of more than half of the Palestinian population. Later, after the 1967 war, more than 400,000 Palestinians emigrated from the Palestinian areas in the West Bank and Gaza to other countries (Dowty 2012).

Since 1948, the Palestinian–Israeli father population underwent multiple processes (Qumsiyeh 2011). Many men left rural agriculture, thought to be the traditional lifestyle and economy, to be integrated into the national labor market. Fathers, traditional breadwinners in a patriarchal society, lost their self-confidence. According to Sa'ar and Yahya-Younis, Palestinian fathers who were meant to provide moral, spiritual, and social guidance to their children and protect their families in the context of the conflict, had to cope with the post el-Nakbah. Palestinian masculinity was a masculinity in crisis (Sa'ar & Yahya-Younis 2008). Monterescu suggests that this crisis has triggered simultaneously both a loosening and tightening of patriarchy. The new masculinity loosened the grip of patriarchy grounded in the pre-Nakbah old social order. But in a paradoxical way, the new post-Nakbah masculinity tends to preserve patriarchy because it is seen as part of the national legacy to be secured, a vestige of Palestinian pride. This insecurity evolved into a masculine defense mechanism of tighter control over the wife and children.

In a study of the effects of house demolition in East Jerusalem, Khsheiboun (2013) found that Palestinian fathers whose houses were demolished by Israeli authorities felt guilty for allowing their families to experience the loss of homeland and loss of the real home. For some Palestinian fathers, the humiliation in front of their extended family, neighbors, and friends stirred emotions of shame and disgrace. Today, Palestinian citizens in Israel are a very heterogeneous community in terms of level of education, residence (rural or urban), religiosity, and income. They also differ in their level of Israelization, or integration into Israeli society (Smooha 2010). They enjoy full civil citizenship rights but as a national minority group experience different levels of discrimination, including inequity in the labor market, and low accessibility to social services and to other important social and economic areas.

According to Hawari, the discrimination of Palestinian men in Israel has severed Palestinian conceptions of masculinity (Hawari 2004). In a way, Palestinian masculinity was reduced to the man's capacity to provide for his family's subsistence needs (housing, food, water). The ideal normative Palestinian father is the resilient father, one who could provide for his family, build a house, and marry off his children. Today, Palestinian fatherhood in Israel is shaped by the battle for daily sustenance, which became the primary domain of struggle and resistance (Shimony 2013). Remaining in the country became in and of itself a measure of steadfastness. In this complex historical and social context, Palestinian fathers confront multiple dilemmas and challenges such as transmitting a Palestinian identity while encouraging a full integration into Israeli economy and society, preserving father authority while exposing their families to egalitarian family values or maintaining Arab culture and still being exposed to western values (Peleg & Waxman 2011). Young Palestinian fathers defined their main role as setting limits and cultural socialization and described multiple conflicts in their fatherhood, between traditional and modern norms and between continuity and change (Khativ Abed El-Hai 2011). They ascribe high significance to values such as continuity, respect for family values, and discipline. According to Shalhoub-Kervokian and Daher-Nashif (2013), the culture of control characterizing Palestinian fathers in Israel is partly a response to the aforementioned politics of exclusion.

In short, the national conflict and the interplay between local views of masculinity and conceptions of fatherhood are both critical in understanding the complexity of fatherhood in Israel.

The Religious Divide: Secular and Religious Fathers

Religion and religiosity play a central role in Israeli society. Israel hosts several religions (Jewish, Muslim, Christian, Druze, Bahai). The Jewish group is divided into subgroups of varying levels of religiosity: ultra-Orthodox, Orthodox, Conservative, and Reform Jews. Most Israeli Jews identify themselves as belonging to one of four social–religious groups: the secular (44–51% of the population); the traditional, who respect religious authority but only partially observe religious law (Halacha) as dictated by Orthodox rabbis (30–39%); the Religious Zionists (10–15%); and the ultra-Orthodox (7–9%) Central Bureau of Statistics 2011). The Muslim community is mostly Sunni, also characterized by different levels of religiosity varying from the very religious to modern Islamists. Among the Arab Muslim population, 8 percent describe themselves as very religious, 47 percent as religious, 27 percent as not very religious, and 18 percent as not religious.

Religion permeates all spheres of life such as politics (Jewish religious parties, Islamic political organizations), family (absence of civil marriage or civil divorce), law (Jewish and Muslim religious courts), economic life (enforced religious prohibition of work on Shabbat), immigration policy (Law of Return), and even transport (restricted public transportation on Shabbat). The discussion around the separation of state and religion is one of the ongoing, provocative political debates in Israel.

Religion also impinges on gendered conceptions of family roles. One of the most differentiated groups of fathers according to religiosity level is the ultra-Orthodox. The definition of ultra-Orthodox or *Haredi* (religious, observant, pious) is far from clear (Ben-Bassat et al. 2013; Gottlieb 2007). Heilman defines four lines of differentiation between the Haredi community and the general population of Israel: physical (geographical segregation), institutional (separated educational system), social (distinct lifestyle), and political (ultra-Orthodox political parties) (Heilman 2000). The ultra-Orthodox family is clearly different from other families in Israel. The ultra-Orthodox community segregates itself for the sake of upholding unique values and institutions based on adherence to Jewish law, alongside the rejection of modern values and a lack of trust in the external, dominant secular society (Freund & Band-Winterstein 2012). The ultra-Orthodox society in Israel has established a thick net of community organizations that attend to the community's basic needs.

Rabbinical authorities represent the political, economic and spiritual leadership of the community. Judaism assigns a central role to parents in general and to fathers in particular. The Jewish religion in its more orthodox version is a highly male-centered tradition giving men a dominant position. Men hold most roles in religious institutions. Fathers are meant to be leaders of the family, to conduct religious rites, and to take responsibility for Jewish continuity by taking roles of religious socialization. *Kaddish*, the prayer of funerals and mourning of a father is recited by the eldest son. For example, men and only men hold the babies in the circumcision rite; only men can perform the act itself (Bilu 2000). However, Jewishness, according the *Halacha* (Jewish law), is inherited by the mother. In this manner, Judaism protects biological fatherhood.

Ultra-Orthodox fathers differ from other groups in five main areas. First, they have low levels of participation in the labor market. Men's level of labor participation is 68.6 percent, whereas the average of working men in the ultra-Orthodox community is very low, around 32 percent (Ben-Bassat et al. 2013; Gottlieb 2007; Klein, 2000). Second, ultra-Orthodox fathers are generally poorer than non–ultra-Orthodox fathers. As prescribed by ultra-Orthodox values, material life should be very modest. In this sense it is not surprising that 56 percent of the ultra-Orthodox community lives below Israel's poverty line (Feferman & Malchi 2010). The main causes of poverty rates in the ultra-Orthodox society are culture and value-related: high birth rates and education not oriented toward skills needed in the labor market (Gottlieb 2007). Ultra-Orthodox men who do enter the labor market tend to be much older and thus receive a lower income (Ben-Bassat, et al., 2006). Even though poverty in the ultra-Orthodox society has been researched at the macro level, the study of the ultra-Orthodox father working population has been marginal. Klein (2000) found that between 1982 and 1995, the rate of poverty among ultra-Orthodox children increased by 40 percent and found a clear correlation between the parents' lack of participation in the labor force and the rate of children living under the poverty line. Strier (2005) examined perceptions of poverty among low-income ultra-Orthodox fathers and found that these men do not define themselves as poor. They prefer to identify themselves through their collective religious belonging than through their poverty-stricken lifestyle.

Third, they have larger families, with the number of children in the ultra-Orthodox sector almost double that of the number in two-parent families in the rest of the Jewish population (Hleihel 2011). The ultra-Orthodox mother has an average of 7.7 children, as opposed to 2.6 children among secular Jews. Families having ten or more children are quite common. The number of children per family in this society reflects a cultural preference, rather than the number of years of education or level of income (Gottlieb 2007).

Fourth, ultra-Orthodox men do not participate in compulsory military service (Hakak 2009). Eighty percent of non–ultra-Orthodox men serve in the military and do reserve work, whereas less than 30 percent of the ultra-orthodox serve in the military. Despite the compulsory nature of the military service in Israel, ultra-Orthodox men have the right to stay in religious institutions and postpone their enrollment until they receive an age or parental exemption. Recently, this distinction has raised political discussion, and new laws have been established to increase the number of ultra-Orthodox men in the Army. However, these new regulations have generated violent ultra-Orthodox protests against changes in the status quo.

Fifth, ultra-Orthodox fatherhood offers a counternarrative to dominant views of fatherhood (Aran et al. 2008). As opposed to the view of fathers as providers, this community prioritizes men's dedication to holy studies (Blumen 2007). In 2010, around 87 percent of ultra-Orthodox men declared that they study in religious institutions. It presents itself as a singular case in which patriarchy is detached from the traditional role of breadwinner but secured by religious lifestyle. The ultra-Orthodox preference is for women to enter employment. The burden of women to financially support the family and the high level of fertility enforce multiple changes in the lifestyle of ultra-Orthodox fathers. El-Or states that the ultra-Orthodox subordination of women rests on their contribution to the collective effort to maintain the society of male scholars and sharing a western ideal of equal partners (El-Or 2002). Stadler (2009) notes that the feminist discourse has infiltrated ultra-Orthodox society. More ultra-Orthodox men and women are enrolled in new higher education programs especially established for this religious community. Women are becoming increasingly employed, so the level and patterns of father involvement are subsequently changing. In addition, the exposure to secular modern Israel is felt in the lifestyle of many families, which brings about difficulty in trying to describe a "typical" ultra-Orthodox family.

These changes aside, studies show that patriarchy patterns have not essentially changed (Sztockman 2011). Stadler describes several ways that young men in particular are contemplating and bringing about changes to help reconcile them with Israeli society (Stadler 2009). Fathers are much more engaged in household chores; they come home to prepare lunch for their children and usually stay later in the house after women leave for work (Blumen 2007). These unique characteristics affect the construction of ultra-Orthodox fatherhood, which is grounded in a discourse based on humility, frugality, commitment, and devotion to religiosity but that is still exposed to changing westernized, individualist, competitive, industrialized society perspectives. The ultra-Orthodox father is an ambivalent father trapped in contradictory orientations. These clashing processes create a sense of duality that "stems from the complexities of trying to implement dogmatic isolationism in the context of a modern, open Jewish society and from the odd situation of being economically and militarily dependent on a State the existence of which their ideology opposes" (Finkelman 2014, p. 264).

The Ethnic Divide: Immigrant Fathers

Immigration is a central component of Israeli society. Since 1948, Israel has received more than 3.5 million immigrants. Immigration is a crucial transition period for fathers (Chuang & Moreno 2008). The study of the effects of immigration on fathers and fathering practices shows the nature of fatherhood as both a socially and culturally negotiated construction (Roopnarine 2013). Immigration has shaped the ethnic structure of Israeli society. From its foundation, Israel has defined Jewish immigration as a main goal. From its independence in 1948 to the end of 1964, Israel absorbed 1,213,555 immigrants, of whom 648,160 (53%) were from Muslim countries, divided between 294,722 who came from Asia and 353,438 from North Africa. Asian Jews (mostly from Yemen, Iraq, and Iran) arrived in the first few years of statehood, settled in or close to the urban centers, and enjoyed better social services, whereas North African Jews (mostly from Morocco, Libya, and Tunisia) arrived later, were directed to the periphery, many to provisory tent camps, and were given poorer resources. Sephardic mass immigration of the 1950s evolved as a new permanent ethnic group owing to its concentration in the lower classes (Ayalon & Shavit 2004).The gap between Sephardic and Ashkenazi regarding access to Israel's structure of opportunities has been extensively discussed (Mizrachi & Herzog 2012).

The full absorption of the immigrant into the new Jewish society was conditional on radical personal transformation and adoption of the model of the new Jew. Studies show that the status of the Sephardic fathers was devastated by the transition from more traditional societies to Israel. These fathers lost their authority, and the western orientation of Israel left them culturally irrelevant to their children. Much Israeli research has demonstrated that social inequality between Sephardic and Ashkenazi endures in the second, third, and even fourth generation (Haberfeld et al. 2011). Today, most Ashkenazi families belong to the middle and upper classes, whereas a majority of Sephardic families belong to the working and lower classes. Although there is nearly equal representation of Ashkenazi and Sephardic populations in the political and military elites, there is only a limited Sephardic presence in the economic, managerial, cultural, and academic elites (Cohen et al. 2007).

The largest Russian immigration brought to Israel more than 1 million immigrants, who currently represent more than a fifth of the total population (Central Bureau of Statistics 2013). The majority of former Soviet Union (FSU) immigrants were professionals, highly educated, and secular who have formed small nuclear families. Most immigrants came married, and the rate of those married on arrival is higher among male immigrants than among female immigrants (Weiss et al. 2012). Even immigrants who came from the FSU at ages 15–18 and who married mostly in Israel are married to spouses from the FSU. Thus it might be expected that fathers from FSU imported their own cultural views of fatherhood.

An examination of the private culture of the Jews living in the former Soviet Union against the background of Soviet public culture reveals a context within a context (Remennick 2005). As a cultural minority group in the FSU, Jews were not allowed to practice their religion. Thus the transmission of Jewish culture took place within the family. In their public culture, as communists, they valued work and were educated to believe that all types of work were equally important, accessible to both women and men. However, in the private culture, Jews maintained fostering intelligence and academic achievement for their children, as well as a conservative and highly gendered perception of family roles. Russian immigrants to Israel were also found to have a basic trust in their families but a deep mistrust toward Israeli institutions and services.

Nonetheless, new immigrants to Israel found promise as well. Strier and Roer-Strier (2005), in a comparative study of former Soviet Union and Ethiopian immigrant fathers in Israel, found that in both groups, immigration was perceived as an opportunity to give new meanings to traditional roles and to reinterpret previous definitions of fatherhood. In a comparative study of immigrant fathers from ten different cultural backgrounds in Canada and Israel, Roer-Strier et al. (2005) found that fathers, regardless of their cultural background, stressed the new opportunities and resources the new countries offered them and their children and were optimistic about their families' possibilities and future. Immigrant fathers who escaped from countries with political dictatorship regimes stressed the positive experience of living safely in a democracy, and others found in immigration the "opportunity to re-invent themselves as fathers and men" (Roer-Strier et al. 2005, p. 323). Research on Russian and Ethiopian immigrant fathers in Israel warns us against binary, unidimensional, and essentialist analysis for interpreting the effects of immigration on the identity of immigrant fathers and instead suggests an appreciation of hybridity, dislocation, and multiplicity.

The Social Class Divide: Poor and Rich Fathers

Fatherhood is a class-based category (Catlett & McKenry 2004). Israel, despite its impressive economic growth of the last decades and its well-developed welfare and public health systems, has become one of the most unequal societies among the developed countries in the world. The rise of the index of inequality is the fastest in the world. In a few years, Israel will become more unequal than Mexico and the United States. Having been established as a welfare state and a quasi-socialist society, Israel has through its last governments embraced neoliberal policies resulting in one of the highest levels of poverty among children in industrialized societies. The incidence of poverty among families in Israel has become one of the highest among developed countries (OECD 2013). The net income of approximately 20.5 percent of families falls below the poverty line. The rate of poverty among nonworking families rose from 68.9 percent in 2006 to 75 percent in 2012 (National Insurance Institute 2013). Furthermore, there is a consistent rise in the rate of poor working families in general and of poor families with one earner in particular. Around 14 percent of working families live under the poverty line. In 2012, families with at least one working parent represented 46.4 percent of the families living in poverty (National Insurance Institute 2013).

In various studies of Israeli fathers, Jewish and Palestinian, working and nonworking, Strier found that poverty represents a challenge to fatherhood, a call to come to terms with threatened masculinities. Along with the national, religious, and ethnic divide of Israeli fatherhood, the widening socioeconomic divide that characterizes Israeli society propels the creation of class-based narratives of fatherhood. Studies show that fatherhood identities are highly vulnerable to poverty and exclusion (Lamb 2004, 2010; Roy 2006). These have been sharpened by social inequality that has linked gendered images of successful fatherhood to economic success (Strier 2005).

DISCUSSION

Walking the Israeli fatherhood labyrinth means rediscovering fatherhood as a highly changing and multifaceted construction (Shwalb et al. 2013). The Israeli case confirms the dynamic nature of fatherhood (LaRossa 1997, 2007). Fatherhood trajectories (Zionist, ultra-Orthodox, and Immigrant Jewish, as well as the Palestinian) already reviewed help us disclose the fluctuating character of fatherhood as a historical, cultural, and class-based construction. The Israeli case also questions the validity of a possible essential Israeli fatherhood and suggests the need to discuss changing fatherhoods in Israel—fatherhood as facing shared processes (westernization, familism, growing inequalities, and national conflict) and huge divides.

Of equal importance is the recognition of the complexity of the fatherhood experience as a multilayered phenomenon in which gendered images of masculinity interact with changing views of fatherhood. The Israeli case study presents fatherhood as a puzzle of internal tensions and external constraints. This frame helps us to acknowledge the contributions and shortfalls of the nation-state to grasp the changing and dynamic nature of fatherhood as a historical construction (Oechsle et al. 2012). Finally, the Israeli case calls on fatherhood scholars to keep examining the impact of war and political violence on the well-being of fathers and families (LaRossa 2011). In a more broad, global scope, the experience of fatherhood in Israel should call for a new discourse of fatherhood that includes the respect for human rights, the repudiation of any form of violence and injustice, and the pursue of political goals through nonviolent means (Hayward 2001).

REFERENCES

Anabi, O. (2012). *Between army and fatherhood perceptions of masculinity of combat fathers in the IDF* (MA Thesis). Department of Sociology and Anthropology. Ramat Gan, Tel Aviv District, Israel: Bar Ilan University.

Aran, G., Stadler, N., & Ben-Ari, E. (2008). Fundamentalism and the masculine body: The case of Jewish ultra orthodox men in Israel. *Religion, 38*, 25–53.

Ayalon, H., & Shavit, Y. (2004). Educational reforms and inequalities in Israel: The MMI hypothesis revisited. *Sociology of Education, 77*, 103–120.

Baaz, M. E. (2009). Why do soldiers rape? Gender, violence and sexuality in the DRC armed Forces. *International Studies Quarterly, 53*, 495–518.

Baxandall, P. (2004). *Constructing unemployment: The politics of joblessness in east and west*. Aldershot, UK: Ashgate.

Ben-Ari, E., & Dardashti, G. (2001). Tests of soldierhood, trials of manhood: Military service and male ideals in Israel. In D. Maman, Z. Rosenhek & E. Ben-Ari (eds.), *Military, state and society in Israel: Theoretical and comparative perspectives* (pp. 239–269). New Brunswick, NJ: Transaction Publishers.

Ben-Bassat, D., Dahan, M., & Kermnitzer, M. (2013). A proposal for integrating the Ultra-orthodox into the IDF "Shall your brethren go to war, and shall you sit here?" Jerusalem, Israel: The Israel Democracy Institute.

Bilu, Y. (2000). From circumcision to circumcision: A psycho-cultural analysis of male identity construction in childhood ceremonies within the Haredi community. *Alpayim, 19*, 16–46 (in Hebrew).

Blumen, O. (2007). The gendered display of work: The midday scene in an ultra-Orthodox street in Israel. *Nashim: A Journal of Jewish Women's Studies and Gender Issues, 13*, 54–123.

Boyarin, D. (1997). *Unheroic conduct: The rise of heterosexuality and the invention of the Jewish man*. Berkeley: University of California Press.

Catlett, B. S., & McKenry, P. C. (2004). Class-based masculinities: Divorce, fatherhood and the hegemonic ideal. *Fathering, 2*, 165–190.

Central Bureau of Statistics (2011). Israel in figures. Central Bureau of Statistics. Israel.

Central Bureau of Statistics (2013). *Women and men in Israel*. Israel. http://www1.cbs .gov.il/www/statistical/mw2013_e.pdf.

Chuang, S. S., & Moreno, R. P. (eds.). (2008). *On new shores: Understanding immigrant children*. Lanham, MD: Lexington Books.

Cockburn, C. (2010). Gender relations as causal in militarization and war. *International Feminist Journal of Politics, 12*, 2, 139–157.

Cohen, Y., Haberfeld, Y., & Kristal, T. (2007). Ethnicity and mixed ethnicity: Educational gaps among Israeli-born Jews. *Ethnic and Racial Studies, 30*, 896–917.

Connell, R. W. (2005). *Masculinities*, 2nd ed. Berkeley/Los Angeles: University of California Press.

Dagan-Buzaglo, N., & Konor-Attias, E. (2013). *Who are we talking about when we refer to "the middle class"? The state of the middle stratum in Israel, 1992–2010*. Israel: Adva Center.

Dowty, A. (2012). *Israel/Palestine*, 3rd ed. Cambridge, UK: Polity Press.

El-Or, T. (2002). *Next year I will know more: Identity and literacy among young Orthodox women in Israel*. Detroit: Wayne State University Press.

Farsoun, S. K., & Aruri, N. H. (2006). *Palestine and the Palestinians: A social and political history*. Boulder, CO: Westview Press.

Feferman, B., & Malchi, A. (2010). *The characteristics of employment in the Haredi Sector and government tools for promoting employment in this sector*. Administration of Research and Economy, Ministry of Industry Trade and Labor. Jerusalem (in Hebrew).

Fogiel-Bijaoui, S., & Rutlinger-Reiner, R. (2013). Rethinking the family in Israel. *Israel Studies Review, 28*, 7–12.

Freund, A., & Band-Winterstein, T. (2012). Between tradition and modernity: Social work-related change processes in the Jewish ultra-orthodox society in Israel. *International Journal of Intercultural Relations, 37*(4), 422–433.

Garbarino, J. (2008). *Children and the dark side of human experience: Confronting global realities and rethinking child development*. New York: Springer.

Geva, N. (2003). *There is no substitute for a father: Israeli custodial fathers—perceptions of the father roles* (MA Thesis). Department of Behavioral Sciences. Beersheba, Israel: Ben Gurion University of the Negev.

Gonet. R.(2007. Is daddy at home? Factors affecting father's engagement. *Megamot, 45*(1),103–120 (in Hebrew).

Gottlieb, D. (2007). *Poverty and labor market behavior in the ultra-Orthodox population in Israel*. Jerusalem: Van Leer Institute (in Hebrew). www.vanleer.org.il/econsoc/ pdf/1_research_mdiniut4.pdf.

Finkelman, Y. (2014). The ambivalent Haredi Jew. *Israel Studies, 19*, 264–293.

Haberfeld, Y., Cohen, Y., Kalter, F., & Kogan, I. (2011). Differences in earnings assimilation of immigrants from the former Soviet Union to Germany and Israel during 1994–2005: The role of observed and unobserved immigrants' attributes. *International Journal of Comparative Sociology, 52*, 6–24.

Hakak, Y. (2009). Haredi male bodies in the public sphere: Negotiating with the religious text and secular Israeli men. *Journal of Men, Masculinities and Spirituality*, 3, 100–122.

Hawari, A. (2004). Men under the military regime. *Adala's Review*, 4, 33–44.

Hayward, R. (2001). Needed: A culture of masculinity for the fulfillment of human rights. *Development*, 44, 48–53.

Heilman, S. (2000). *Defenders of the faith. Inside ultra-Orthodox Jewry*. Berkeley, CA: University of California Press.

Herzog, H., & Braude A. (eds.) (2009). Untangling modernities: Gendering religion and politics. New York: Palgrave Macmillan.

Hleihel, A. (2011). *Fertility among Jewish and Muslim Women in Israel, by Level of Religiosity, 1979–2009*. Jerusalem: Israel Central Bureau of Statistics.

Hollander, P. (2012). Contested Zionist masculinity and the redemption of the schlemiel in Levi Aryeh Arieli's "Allah Karim!" *Israel Studies*, 17, 92–118.

Kamir, O. (2009). Masculine Zionist utopia between Jewish honor and dignity in Herzl's Alteneuland and in contemporary Israel. In Stern, Y., Sagi, A., and Mandel. *Herzl. Then and Now. An old Jew or a new person?* (209–256). Bar-Ilan University and Hartman Institute. (In Hebrew).

Kamir, O. (2011). Zionism was a male liberation movement. *Zionism*, 4, 443–470.

Kaplan, D. (2003). *Brothers and others in arms: The making of love and war in Israeli combat units*. New York: Harrington Park Press.

Kaplan, D. (2007). *The men we loved: Male friendship and nationalism in Israeli culture*. New York: Berghahn Books.

Khativ Abed El-Hai, M. (2011). *Viewpoints of fathers and professionals regarding the challenges of fatherhood in a multicultural society* (MA thesis). Early childhood graduate studies, Swartz program. Jerusalem: Hebrew University.

Khsheiboun, S. (2013). *The meaning of home and the impact of its loss on the Palestinian family in East Jerusalem* (Doctoral thesis). School of Social Work. Jerusalem: Hebrew University.

Kimmel, M. (2010). *Misframing men: The politics of contemporary masculinities*. New Brunswick,,NJ: Rutgers University Press.

Kimmerling, B., & Migdal, J. S. (2003). *The Palestinian people: A History*. Cambridge, MA: Harvard University Press.

Klein, S. (2000). Poverty among children in Israel 1982-1995. *The Economic Quarterly*, 47, 510-534 (in Hebrew).

Lamb, M. E. (2004). Developmental theory and public policy: A cross-national perspective. In H. Goelman, S. Ross, & S. Marshall (Eds.), *Multiple lenses, multiple images: Perspectives on the child across time, space and disciplines* (pp. 122–146). Toronto: University of Toronto Press.

Lamb, M. E. (ed.). (2010). *The role of the father in child development* (5th ed.). Hoboken NJ: Wiley.

LaRossa, R. (1997). *The Modernization of fatherhood: A social and political history*. Chicago: University of Chicago Press.

LaRossa, R. (2007). The culture and conduct of fatherhood in America, 1800 to 1960. *Japanese Journal of Family Sociology*, 19, 87–98.

LaRossa, R. (2011). *Of war and men: World War II in the lives of fathers and their families*. Chicago: University of Chicago Press.

Lavee, Y., & Katz, R. (2003). The family in Israel. *Marriage and Family Review, 35,* 193–217.

Mizrachi, N., & Herzog, H. (2012). Participatory destigmatization strategies among Palestinian citizens, Ethiopian Jews and Mizrahi Jews in Israel. *Ethnic and Racial Studies, 35,* 418–435.

Monterescu, D. (2006). Stranger masculinities: Gender and politics in a Palestinian–Israeli "third space." In L. Quzgane (ed.), *African Masculinities* (pp. 123–142). London, UK: Zed Books.

Morris, B. (ed.). (2008). *Making Israel.* Ann Arbor, MI: University of Michigan Press.

National Insurance Institute. (2014). *Poverty and social gaps.* Annual Report. Jerusalem.

Nelson, T. J. (2004). Low-income fathers. *Annual Review of Sociology, 30,* 427–451.

Nonn, T. (2007). Hitting bottom: Homeless, poverty and masculinity. In B. A. Arrighi (ed.), *Understanding Inequality* (pp. 281–288). Lanham, MD: Rowman and Littlefield.

OECD (2013). *Economic Survey of Israel.* OECD Publications. www.oecd.org/eco/surveys/Israel.

Ogny, M. (2014). *Self-employed Israeli fathers and the ideal of a new fatherhood* (MA thesis). Haifa, Israel: University of Haifa (in Hebrew).

Peleg, I., & Waxman, D. (2011). *Israel's Palestinians: The conflict within.* Cambridge, UK: Cambridge University Press.

Perez, N. (2011). *Making fathers care: Parental leave for fathers in Israel—policy recommendations.* Jerusalem: Taub Center for Social Policy Studies in Israel.

Pressman, S. (2007). Cross-national comparisons of poverty and income inequality. *Journal of Economic Issues, 41,* 181–200.

Oechsle, M., Müller, U., and Hess, S. (eds). (2012). *Fatherhood in late modernity. Cultural images, social practices, structural frames.* Opladen, Germany: Barbara Budrich Publisher.

Qumsiyeh, M. (2011). *Popular resistance in Palestine: A history of hope and empowerment.* London: Pluto Press.

Remennick, L. (2005). Immigration, gender, and psychosocial adjustment: A study of 150 immigrant couples in Israel. *Sex Roles, 5,* 847–863.

Roer-Strier, D., Strier, R., Este, D., Shimoni, R., & Clark, D. (2005). Fatherhood and immigration: Challenging the deficit theory. *Child and Family Social Work, 10,* 315–329.

Roopnarine, J. L. (2013). Fathers in Caribbean cultural communities. In D. Shwalb, B. Shwalb, & M. E. Lamb (eds.), *Fathers in cultural context* (pp. 203–227). New York: Routledge.

Roy, K. (2006). Father stories: A life course examination of paternal identity among low-income African American men. *Journal of Family Issues, 27,* 31–54.

Sa'ar, A., & Yahya-Younis, T. (2008). Masculinity in crisis: The case of Palestinians in Israel. *British Journal of Middle East Studies, 35*(3), 305–323.

Sagiv, D. (2003). *Fathers' role salience, gender attitudes, essentialist perceptions and socialization: Comparing primary caregivers fathers to non-primary caregiving fathers* (MA thesis). Department of Gender Studies. Ramat Gan, Tel Aviv District, Israel: Bar Ilan University.

Said, E. (1992). *The question of Palestine.* New York: Vintage Books.

Samih, K. F., & Naseer, H. A. (2006). *Palestine and the Palestinians: A social and political history*. Boulder, CO: Westview Press.

Sasson-Levy, O. (2011). Research on gender and the military in Israel: From a gendered organization to inequality regimes. *Israel Studies Review, 26*, 73–98.

Shalhoub-Kervorkian, N., & Daher-Nashif, S. (2013). Femicide and Colonization: Between the politics of exclusion and the culture of control . *Violence against Women, 19*, 295–315.

Shapira, A. (2013). *Israel: A history—The Schusterman Series in Israel Studies*. Waltham, MA: Brandeis University Press.

Shapira, N. (2003). *Fathers talk about fatherhood: How does the modern father experience his fatherhood?* (MA thesis). Department of Labor Studies. Tel Aviv, Israel: Tel Aviv University.

Shavit, A. (2013). *The triumph and tragedy of Israel*. New York: Random House

Shepard, B. (2000). *A war of nerves: Soldiers and psychiatrists in the twentieth century*. London, UK: Jonathan Cape.

Shimony, B. (2013). Shaping Israeli–Arab identity in Hebrew words. *Israel Studies, 18*, 146–169.

Shwalb, D., Shwalb, B., & Lamb, M. (eds.). (2013). *Fathers in cultural context*. New York: Routledge.

Simon, C. (1999). *The place of the father in life stories of young adult sons and daughters post military service in Israel: A narrative study* (MA thesis). Faculty of Education. Haifa, Israel: University of Haifa.

Smooha, S. (2010). *Arab-Jewish relations in Israel. Alienation and rapprochement*. Washington, DC: United States Institute of Peace.

Stadler, N. (2009). *Yeshiva fundamentalism: Piety, gender, and resistance in the ultra-Orthodox World*. New York, NY: University Press.

Strier, R. (2005). Gendered realities of poverty: Men and women's view of poverty in Jerusalem. *Social Service Review, 79*(2), 344–367.

Strier, R., & Roer-Strier, D. (2005). Fatherhood and immigration: Perceptions of Israeli immigrant fathers from Ethiopia and the former Soviet Union. *Families in Society, 86*, 121–133.

Strier. R., Sigad, L., Eisikovits, Z., & Buchbinder, E. (2014). Masculinity, poverty and work: The multiple constructions of work among working poor men. *Journal of Social Policy, 43*, 331–349.

Sztockman, E. M. (2011). *The men's section: Orthodox Jewish men in an egalitarian world*. Waltham, MA: University Press of New England.

Weiss, Y., Cohen Goldner, S, & Eckstein, Z. (2012). *The immigration from the former Soviet Union to Israel: Evidence and interpretation*. Discussion Paper. The Pinhas Sapir Center for Development. Tel Aviv, Israel: Tel Aviv University.

World Health Organization. (2003). *Mental health in emergencies: Psychological and social aspects of health of populations exposed to extreme stressors*. Geneva, Switzerland: World Health Organization.

17

Fathers across Arab and Non-Arab Islamic Societies

Ziarat Hossain and Rumaya Juhari

FATHERS ACROSS ARAB AND NON-ARAB ISLAMIC SOCIETIES

It is widely accepted that sociohistorical and cultural factors play instrumental roles in defining fathering in many cultural communities (see Shwalb,
Shwalb, & Lamb 2013). For example, hegemonic models of masculinity and
religious beliefs about men's and women's roles have helped define fathering in traditional societies. In Islamic societies, the Qur'an and *Sunnah* and
longstanding traditions continue to shape several aspects of fatherhood and
fathering. Whereas the Qur'an is the divine book revealed to the prophet
Muhammad, *Sunnah* is the sayings and deeds of Muhammad. The Qur'an and
Sunnah work in concert to construct the Islamic religious laws and values that
all Muslims are expected to follow in both private and public life (Al Mutair,
Plummer, O'Brien, & Clerehan 2014). In view of contemporary socioeconomic changes in women's roles in Muslim societies, the globalized context of
family life, and the paucity of data on Muslim fathers, a discussion of fathers'
levels of involvement in Islamic societies can help further untangle men's
roles in a large and an often ignored segment of the world's population. A primary focus of this chapter is to consider how religious views and sociocultural
constructs jointly work to articulate fathers' roles in a few Islamic societies,
such as Bangladesh, Egypt, Kuwait, Malaysia, and Saudi Arabia. The chapter
elaborates on the following themes: (1) ecology and demographic profile of
fathers in Islamic societies, (2) beliefs and sociocultural contexts of men's
roles in the Islamic world, (3) economic practices and gender roles, (4) men's
roles as fathers and husbands, (5) fathering and childhood development, and
(6) future research directions and policy issues.

ECOLOGY AND DEMOGRAPHIC PROFILE OF
FATHERS IN ISLAMIC SOCIETIES

Numbering about 1.6 billion people, Muslims are the second-largest religious group in the world (Pew Research Center 2012). The leading countries with Muslim populations are Indonesia, Pakistan, India, Bangladesh, Nigeria, Egypt, Iran, and Turkey (see Table 17.1). Although Muslims reside on all continents save Antarctica, the majority are found in the Asia–Pacific, the Middle East, and sub-Saharan and north Africa. The Islamic world started in Saudi Arabia in 610, when Muhammad received the *Nabuate* (revelation through the Angel Gabriel that Muhammad was the last prophet for the Abrahamic religion). Because Muhammad was born in Mecca in 570 CE, Saudi Arabia is considered the homeland of Islam. After the death of Muhammad in 632, the four caliphs (successors of Muhammad) established the Islamic world within and beyond the Arabian Peninsula.

The rapid and vast growth of the non-Arab Islamic world (Africa, southern Europe, and south and east Asia) happened during the eighth to eleventh centuries. Arab conquerors and traders brought Islam to the Indian subcontinent, including to Bangladesh (Bengal), in the eighth century. In most cases, lower-caste Hindus embraced Islam to realize economic prosperity and new social identity in society. Indian, Chinese, and Arab Muslim traders brought Islam to the Malays in Malaysia around the twelfth century. Islamic values took root in Malaysia and became an integral part of Malay families and their cultural practices (Von der Mehden 1987). A recent estimate (Pew Research Center 2009) indicates that about 80 percent of Muslims reside in the non-Arab world, and about 20 percent of all Muslims reside in countries such as India, China, and Russia, where Islam is not the major religion (Table 17.1). The contemporary Arab world includes twenty-two countries located in two continents: Asia (e.g., Saudi Arabia, Kuwait, Qatar, Jordan) and Africa (e.g., Egypt, Tunisia, Algeria, Sudan). These countries have formed a political and economic cooperative bloc known as the Arab League.

Islamic societies are largely divided into Arab and non-Arab geopolitical and cultural worlds. The Arab world typically includes Middle Eastern and north African Muslim societies, and the non-Arab world spreads throughout Asian and African territories. Islamic societies in the Arab world have a common cultural and Arabic linguistic identity. The non-Arab Islamic societies have diverse linguistic and cultural characteristics. For example, Muslims in Bangladesh (Bengali) and Malaysia (Malay) live in very different ecologies and have their own cultural identities and languages. Muslims in Saudi Arabia, Kuwait, and Egypt derive from various tribal assemblies; they live primarily in desert ecologies and speak the same language (i.e., Arabic). Also, there are several sects of the Islamic religious denominations (e.g., Sunni, Shiite)

TABLE 17.1. Muslim Population across Societies (2014)

	Population (millions)	% Muslim	% of World Muslims
Indonesia	203	88	13
Pakistan	175	96	11
India	1002	13	10
Bangladesh	166	90	9
Egypt	79	95	5
Nigeria	78	51	5
Iran	74	99	4.7
Turkey	74	98	4.7
Algeria	34	98	2.2
Malaysia	30	60	1.1
Saudi Arabia	26	99	1.7
Kuwait	3.5	77	<1
Russia	142	12	1.1
China	1355	1.8	1.6

across societies. Even though Sunnis (e.g., Hanafi, Shafi, Maliki, Hanbali schools of jurisprudence) and Shiites (e.g., twelvers, Ithna Asharis, Ismailis, Zaydin, Alawites) are divided over the leadership succession after the death of Muhammad, they faithfully observe the five pillars of Islam: *sahada* and the Prophet Muhammad (faith), *salat* (prayer), *zakat* (charity), *swam* (fasting), and *hajj* (pilgrimage). Broadly speaking, about 12 percent of Muslims are Shiites, concentrated primarily in Iran, Bahrain, Iraq, and Lebanon. A major factor binding Muslims across Arab and non-Arab realms is the Islamic religious identity. Such a phenomenon is often termed as the transnational Islamic community (see Moghadam 2004).

The wide geographic distribution of the Muslim population adds tremendous cultural, economic, and ecological variation to lifestyles and childrearing practices. While some nations still remain subsistence and agro-based (e.g., Mali, Western Sahara) and have high poverty rates (e.g., Bangladesh), others have achieved remarkable growth in the economic, technological, and industrial sectors and enjoy high standards of living (e.g., Malaysia, Saudi Arabia, Kuwait) comparable to those in some western countries. There may be more homogeneity in cultural practices among Arab Muslims (e.g., Saudi Arabia, Kuwait, Qatar, Egypt), but non-Arab Muslims are very diverse, and their childrearing practices are influenced by the socialization beliefs and goals of other ethnic groups with whom they share a common cultural space (e.g., India, Malaysia). Thus Muslim parents in the non-Arab world have to navigate both Islamic religious and various indigenous cultural norms in their parenting roles. This aside, subscription to and practice of Islamic beliefs keep all Muslims under one set of religious precepts that may impart common influences on family processes and functioning across geographic locations. It is possible that fathers' roles are similar across Arab and non-Arab Islamic societies in that they are built on a common set of religious principles, but they may reflect diverse cultural pathways to childrearing and childhood development in different settings.

Demographic indicators such as income, literacy, infant mortality, urbanization, and life expectancy vary significantly across the Arab nations and are also linked to fathers' roles in the family (Table 17.2). Similarly, contemporary factors such as labor migration, media, imported domestic maids, and the overall westernization process (e.g., exposure to democratic modes of parenting, more equitable distribution of household roles) exert influences and add complexities to paternal practices in Arab families. For example, international labor migration takes men from families in low-income Islamic countries (e.g., Egypt) to high-income Islamic countries (e.g., Kuwait, Saudi Arabia). It is estimated that 65 percent of the current Kuwaiti population is expatriate foreign workers. The lion's share of the 300,000 Egyptians who currently work in Kuwait are male workers. Many of these migrants are fathers who leave their children and families in their countries of origin and do not see them for years at a time (Ahmed 2013; Hossain 2013). Such cross-boundary labor migration promotes father absence that undermines fathers' caregiving roles in many Arab countries and in the sending Islamic societies as well.

Along with individual demographic factors, the structural properties of family such as age at first marriage, age difference between husband and wife, and marriage partner (i.e., endogamous vs. exogamous) vary between the Arab and non-Arab world and influence birth rates and early parenting (see Jones 2010). In Saudi Arabia, the average age at first marriage for men is about 29 and about 17 for women; in Kuwait the average age at first marriage for both men and women is 27; in Malaysia the average age at first marriage is 26–28 years; and in Bangladesh, the average age at first marriage for men

TABLE 17.2. Sociodemographic Characteristics of Selected Islamic Societies (2014)

	Saudi Arabia	Kuwait	Bangladesh	Malaysia
Birth Rate	1.9	2.3	2.2	2.0
Age Structure (0–25 year %)	47	40	51	46
Urbanization (%)	82	98	28	73
Major Ethnicity	Arab 90%	Kuwaiti 36%	Bengali 98%	Malay 51%
Life Expectancy	75	78	71	75
GDP per Capita (USD)	26,000	56,000	900	11,000

is 24 and 18 or younger for women (www.quandl.com). The age discrepancy between husbands and wives across most Islamic societies likely affects the variant sequence of parenting tasks and the distribution of power within the family. Likewise, limited cross-sex socialization outside close family relatives usually results in a higher rate of consanguineous marriages in the Arab world than in the non-Arab world and influences the control that men exercise over women. It is important to state that such patrilineal parallel cousin marriages are slowly being replaced by inter-Arab marriages. Furthermore, compared to the Arab world (e.g., Saudi Arabia and Kuwait), the tradition of polygamy is less pronounced in non-Arab Muslim societies (e.g., Albania, Malaysia, Kosovo, Bangladesh).

Regardless of ethnic or cultural differences, Muslim fatherhood is constructed within a marital relationship (i.e., *nikah*) commonly viewed as a sacred bond. A family is typically defined as a marital union between a man and a woman and includes their children and extended family members. In other words, fatherhood starts within a religiously approved legal heterosexual union, because premarital and extramarital sexual relations and the birth of a child outside of a marital union are prohibited in Islam. The role of an adoptive father is highly limited in Islamic practice, indicating the importance of paternal biological descent and the genealogy of the child (Kabir & az-Zubair 2007). Islam treats a breastfeeding foster and/ or adoptive mother as equal to the biological mother of an infant. From the current globalized world view, formation of nuclear families, women's education and participation in the paid labor force, increasing numbers of divorce and female-headed households, and smaller family size characterize growing numbers of contemporary Muslim families across geographic regions.

BELIEFS AND SOCIOCULTURAL CONTEXTS OF FATHERS' ROLES IN THE ISLAMIC WORLD

It is often difficult to separate religious beliefs from the cultural aspects of parenting in Islamic societies. Religious values synchronize cultural and social mores regarding parenting and childrearing tasks and ultimately work as an integrated force that shapes paternal roles and parenting in Islamic societies. A primary source of Islamic beliefs and practices about fathers is embedded in *Sharia*. According to this concept, Islam is the complete code of life and all Muslims are expected to abide by *Sharia* for their daily conduct. Additionally, *Adat* (local customs and cultural norms) transcends non-Arab Muslim societies and non-Muslim communities, particularly in south and southeast Asian countries such as Malaysia and Bangladesh (Kling 1995). Hegemonic cultural belief structures about masculinity identify the father as the family patriarch, and the mother must practice domesticity, purity, and assume a submissive role in the family (Noor 1999). The father or grandfather acts as the supreme authority figure in the family. The traditional norm of a joint and/or extended family system is still practiced. However, such practices are less common in modern urban families in Islamic societies (Ahmed 2013; Hossain 2013).

The principles of *Sharia* and *Adat* ask a Muslim father to care for, educate, protect, give his daughter(s) away in marriage and to provide for his family and children. As the head of the household, the father is expected to inculcate Islamic values of reverence, truthfulness, shyness, loyalty, and benevolence in his children. It is his sacred obligation to raise children with good moral character, to educate and treat sons and daughters equally, and to protect the welfare of the family. Children inherit social and religious identities from the father. The child must be god-fearing, pious, and a good citizen of the community. In turn, children's rights to enter heaven are mostly based on the extent to which they respect and take care of their parents, especially their mother. Their parents' salvation also depends on their prayers and good deeds.

Perhaps the most important source of Islamic beliefs about fatherhood and fathering derives from *Hadith*, the sayings and deeds of Muhammad himself. Muhammad's closest followers (e.g., *al-Bukhari*) claimed to have chronicled his sayings and family interactions as they happened. In keeping with Islamic beliefs that children are sacred and are a blessing from the divine power, Muhammad was portrayed as always warm to children, carrying them in his arms, and kissing and hugging them (Giladi 2014). As a father, Muhammad demonstrated wisdom and compassion toward his children and instilled values of freedom, morality, spirituality, gender equality, and fairness in them. He inquired about his children's welfare, shared meals, and engaged in play activities with them, strongly encouraging his growing daughter Fatimah to assume a community leadership role. Muhammad also actively contributed to family decisions to arrange marriages for his daughters and acted as a counselor for his daughters and their husbands. Overall, these historical accounts align well and are compatible with what contemporary family scholars term commitment to children's well-being as engaged fathers (see Lamb 2004).

The tradition of female seclusion and domesticity, veiling, and male guardianship over women introduced earlier is still widely practiced in the Arab world especially in Saudi Arabia (Dwairy, Achoui, Abouserie, Farah, Sakhleh, Fayad, & Khan 2006). However, the Qur'an clearly echoes an egalitarian and emancipatory voice for women that embrace the ideals of complementary roles between the husband and wife and shared parenting. Banking on these egalitarian messages, contemporary Islamic feminists and groups (e.g., Sisters of Islam in Malaysia) are actively involved in a transnational effort to establish justice and peace across societies (Moghadam 2004). Although Muslims generally subscribe to gender segregated socialization, not all Islamic societies (e.g., Bangladesh) observe this tradition with the same level of fervor seen in the Arab world. Regardless whether in a monogamous or a polygamous marriage, the Muslim father is expected to provide for children and their biological or foster suckling-mother (The Qur'an, *surat* Al-Baqra, v. 233) and meet their psychological and emotional needs. Fathers are expected to respect their children's rights to paternal affection, protection, provision, and care (Giladi 2014). In terms of discipline, fathers are permitted to use physical punishment so long as it does not harm sensitive body parts such as the head, spine, vision, hearing, and sexual organs. Furthermore, the Qur'anic verses elucidate the importance of the father's positive engagement activities, gender-neutral treatment of children, children's education and welfare, and cordial father–child relationships (Chaudhry 2009; Oweis, Gharaibeh, Maaitah, Gharaibeh, & Obeisat 2012). In agreement with the portrait provided of Muhammad, these instructions and practices suggest that fathers must be available and engaged, raising their children with good moral and religious values.

Although Islamic views about maternal and paternal roles in the family are similar across Islamic societies, parenting goals and expectations are expressed in unique terms specific to the particular cultural group. As an example, the Malaysian and Bangladeshi value system of *Adat* in parent–child interactions underscores the cultural and religious importance of children's loyalty to the family and father in particular. At the same time, many pre-Islamic sociocultural customs (e.g., veiling and segregation of women, son preference, honor killing, control over women's sexuality), including Bedouin tribalism (e.g., male superiority, blood money), have been modified and the reformulations tacitly incorporated into Arab Islamic family practices (Abudabbeh 2005; Mernissi 1987). A few other male practices have also been affected by modernity, but somewhat modestly. Take the case of multiple wives: A Muslim man can have a second wife only if his first wife gives consent to it without any coercion and if the man has sufficient psychological and economic resources to treat both women equally (see Al-Ati 1995; Mashhour 2005; *Surat An-Nisai*, 4:3). However, anecdotal data suggest that disregarding these conditions, a polygamous Muslim man often takes multiple wives under the guise of patriarchy, economic power, and social domination (see Al-Ati 1995; Mernissi 1987). Among Islamic societies, only Tunisia has banned polygamous marriages. One of the sociocultural implications of multiple wives is that it excuses fathers from childcare responsibilities and pushes them to continue to adopt the breadwinning role for the family.

In summary: Muslim fathers are expected to socialize their children and act within the beliefs of the five pillars of Islam. Fathers are responsible for instilling *Akhlaq* in their children, another core Islamic belief that espouses responsible parenting and raising respectful children (Tamuri 2007). Within the interrelated nature of social and religious values of parenting in Islamic cultural groups and collectivistic caregiving systems, fathers forge partnerships with family agencies, community programs, and schools to instill Islamic and universal human values in young children (Selvarajah & Meyer 2008). Muslim parents—especially fathers—are responsible for providing for the family and investing their utmost resources in children's education. The complementary roles between husbands and wives in family matters, fathers' kindness (affection) toward children, and older siblings' responsibility to elderly parents are resolute and paramount Islamic values. Muslim parents believe that economic hardship, individual shortcomings, and physical disabilities in humans caused by predetermined genetic and/or physiological traits can be improved and/or rectified through giving/charity, prayer, and devotion to the divine power. Unlike the Christian belief, but similar to Hinduism, Muslim childhood is considered a period of innocence, and children are usually allowed to live a carefree life (i.e., no sin is recorded for any activity) until age 12.

ECONOMIC PRACTICES AND GENDER ROLES IN ISLAMIC SOCIETIES

For the most part, premodern peasant society in the Islamic world was based on subsistence agriculture and was largely structured through the patrifocal kinship system. Even though in some Islamic communities the equitable distribution of labor between men and women was somewhat similar to that which existed between men and women among indigenous hunter–gatherer (e.g., Batek) and hill tribes in Malaysia (Endicott 1992), and although Islamic religious beliefs recognize both men's and women's economic contributions to the family, the prevailing social and political systems kept women under men's authority and social status. A man's authority position as a husband and father in the home derives from his social status outside the home, professional standing, and political and economic power. The cultural practice of gender hierarchy subdued women's economic authority and excluded women from the religious order and political power in society. Instead of duly recognizing premodern women's economic contributions to the family, female subordination made women subservient to their husbands and saddled them with household chores. The separation of unpaid housework and paid employment outside the home led fathers to maintain economic responsibilities and resource ownership in the family. Thus childcare was perfunctory to Islamic men's roles in the past.

Far from egalitarian, men's investment in the family as caregivers has increased considerably in the last three decades in western developed societies (see Cabrera & Tamis-LeMonda 2013; Lamb 2010). Arguably, it is also true that paternal and maternal roles are changing in many Muslim nations (e.g., Malaysia, Kuwait, Saudi Arabia) as they transform their historically agriculture-based economic practices into modern and industrial employment sectors. But these changes have not affected men's roles as caregivers appreciably across Islamic societies. A case in point is Malaysia, a country that has transformed its traditional economic structure toward a modern system of production. Today only 8–11 percent (as compared to 75 percent in 1980) of the Malaysian labor force is based in the agricultural sector. This means that a large portion of the labor force is currently employed in the service and industrial sectors. Unfortunately, such an enormous change in the economic and employment structures has been working insidiously to sustain the existing gender gap in parental involvement in childcare in Malaysia and other Islamic societies. The low-paid service sectors (clerical, tourism, restaurant and so on) are highly populated by women, and the highly paid management positions are occupied by men. The occupational distribution has created income differentials that uphold men's authority and provisioning roles in the family.

In contemporary Islamic societies, women continue to provide primary childcare as they did during the agriculture-based economy. Additionally, imported domestic labor in Malaysia and the Arab countries such as Saudi Arabia and Kuwait is heavily compensating men's caregiving roles in the family. Data suggest that compared to rural families, there was less differentiation between mothers' and fathers' involvement in childcare in urban families in Malaysia. It was not that the urban father contributed more time to child care; rather, other women provided childcare as a paid nanny or domestic maid that decreased women's time with children in the family (Hossain 2013). This scenario may also apply to Kuwait and Saudi Arabia. In essence, a crucial factor determining gender dynamics in parental childcare involvement in contemporary Muslim families is economic conditions, such as the ownership and control of resources in the family.

MEN'S ROLE AS HUSBANDS AND FATHERS

As this volume indicates, research on fathers in different cultural communities has increased over the last two decades (Lamb 2010; Roopnarine 2013; Shwalb, Shwalb, & Lamb 2013). However, most research findings in the field still derive from western and non-Muslim families. Empirical research on fathers' involvement with children in Arab societies such as Saudi Arabia and Kuwait is virtually nonexistent. Furthermore, available research findings are in Arabic and are mostly based on a few Arab nations (Hossain 2013; Hossain, Roopnarine, Masud, Muhamed, Baharudin, Abdullah, & Juhari 2005; Juhari, Yaacob, & Abu Talib 2013). Drawing on examples of men's involvement with children in selected Arab and non-Arab communities, we attempt to illustrate men's roles as fathers in Islamic societies. This brief outline relies on a review by Ahmed (2013), an Egyptian psychologist who translated the Arabic literature on fathers, and our own research in Bangladesh and Malaysia.

As can be gathered from what has been said so far, fatherhood and fathering in most Islamic cultural communities, Arab and non-Arab (e.g., Bangladesh and Malaysia), are steeped in patriarchy and strong kinship networks wherein men have control over women and wives. Adhering to principles outlined by *Sharia* and *Adat* and other local practices, husband-wife roles follow a traditional path; within an interdependent collectivistic system, men are foremost providers and protectors and women caregivers. What men do as fathers and husbands is largely a function of the age-old cultural tradition of claiming paternity and patriarchal authority in the family. In this structural dynamic, the father is seen as crucial to the overall welfare of the family, and his death or marital dissolution threatens old Islamic perceptions of family harmony and economic stability. It is safe to say that the Islamic view of shared parenting and involved fathering is still an illusion, as much of the childrearing tasks are routinely delegated to women in Arab families.

Examining the links between contemporary socioeconomic changes and parenting in Arab societies, scholars argue that many Arab fathers lack positive parenting skills to raise children (Ahmed 2013). This notwithstanding, the birth of a child brings a sense of completeness to a man's life. A Muslim father starts his journey of paternal responsibility by saying the *azan* (Islamic call for prayer) into the ears of the newborn child. He publicly declares his fathering role by calling the newborn to follow the path of Islam in life. The father is expected to arrange and bear expenses for follow-up events such as *Namakaran* (name giving) and *Akika* (inviting relatives and community members to a feast of gratitude for having a child). After these initial activities, the Islamic father's level of involvement with children during the immediate postbirth period and during the early childhood years is largely unknown.

Based on Ahmed's (2013) recent overview on Islamic fathers, it appears that most studies typically focused on children's and mothers' perceptions of parental behavior in the family. Thus few studies have focused on what Islamic men do in families. Furthermore, social changes in some Arab families have altered men's access to children in some Islamic communities. As already indicated, low-income Egyptian fathers are often absent from home when they become migrant workers, and high-income Saudi or Kuwaiti fathers hire maids to care for their children. What little data exist on Arab fathers indicate that Egyptian and Kuwaiti fathers are more flexible in their interactions with their children than Saudi fathers, and urban Arab fathers show more flexibility in their parenting role than rural (Bedouin) fathers. However, rural Egyptian fathers interact more with their children than urban fathers. It is possible that the greater flexibility in Kuwaiti and Egyptian fathers is linked to greater openness of these societies compared to Saudi Arabia.

A few studies have focused on paternal warmth and hostility and abuse toward children. A recent study showed that Jordanian fathers and mothers did not differ in levels of warmth displayed to young children, as measured by the Parental Acceptance–Rejection Questionnaire (PARQ), and that paternal warmth and maternal warmth were significantly correlated. The Jordanian fathers showed high levels of warmth that were comparable to those of fathers in developed societies (e.g., Italy and the United States). In the same study, paternal and maternal rejection/hostility/neglect were also quite similar and highly correlated (Putnick, Bornstein, Lansford, Chang, Deater-Deckard, Di Giunta, & Bombi 2012). It appears that paternal abuse of children is more prevalent among less educated and lower-income families in Iraq, Algeria, and Bedouin communities in the Arabian Gulf states, including Saudi Arabia, compared to other Arab countries. We should point out that the study on Jordanian fathers marks a significant departure from most of the research on Arab fathers that has largely focused on the difficulties associated with fathering rather than the range of activities in which men engage with their children inside and outside the home (e.g., moral guidance, recreational). It also focused on the sensitive aspects of parenting—constructs having implications for attachment relationships and social adjustment (Khaleque & Rohner 2012).

Data from children's perceptions of paternal roles provide additional insights into Arab fathers' investment in children. Egyptian children viewed their fathers as negligent and psychologically abusive, especially toward their daughters (Hashem 2001, cited in Ahmed 2013), and college-age Egyptian males perceived their fathers as more accepting, whereas females perceived their fathers as controlling, hostile, stern disciplinarians (Abou-el-Kheir 1998, cited in Ahmed 2013). Although the father is traditionally viewed as the power symbol in Arab societies, the majority of Kuwaiti adolescent girls see mothers as more powerful than fathers (Ibrahim 2010, cited in Ahmed 2013).

In non-Arab communities in Malaysia, wives in urban, professional Chinese and Malay families spent more time in childcare and other household tasks than their husbands did (Noor 1999). Our findings from both rural and urban Malay families in Malaysia also revealed that mothers spent more time in childcare activities such as feeding, cleaning, and playing with their young children than fathers did. Mothers and fathers in rural families spent more time (11.91 vs. 4.16 hours) than mothers and fathers in urban families (5.41 vs. 2.56 hours) during a typical weekday, and the discrepancy between levels of maternal and paternal involvement was higher in rural families than in urban families (Hossain 2013; Hossain et al. 2005). That is, rural mothers were more likely to engage in activities such as physical care, feeding, bedtime routines, and playing than their husbands were. Both mothers and fathers in Malay families reported spending more time playing with their children than caring for them, which contradicts propositions in western theory about the role of play as a major activity between fathers and children (Paquette 2004).

The primacy of maternal care in Malay families could be attributed to eco-logical factors and cultural practices associated with childcare. Fathers' and mothers' differential level of involvement in childcare is more in line with Malay cultural norms of patriarchy than Islamic principles of shared parent-ing. Although rural fathers reported spending more time than urban fathers in Malay families, the difference perhaps results from activities and work pat-terns in the two ecological settings. During our field work, we observed that rural parents either held or kept their children within arm's length while working in the kitchen, vegetable garden, and rice fields. Unlike clearly demarcated home and work environments in urban settings, such an intimate rural ecology often makes it difficult to draw clear boundaries between par-ents' work environment and childcare involvement. We speculate that rural parents who participated in our study may have included the time they held their children while working as part of caregiving involvement.

Kadazan fathers in Malaysian Borneo, of whom a significant proportion were Muslim, spent far less time in basic childcare than their spouses did (Hossain, Roopnarine, Ismail, Hashmi, & Sombuling 2007). More specifi-cally, Kadazan fathers reported spending about 30 percent as much time as mothers did in early childcare in the family. Findings from another study showed that although both maternal and paternal involvement in childcare was necessary, Kadazan mothers tended to be more affectionate and were more loving than were fathers (Rosnah 1999). Relatedly, fathers' roles in Thai Muslim families were largely limited to performing cultural and religious rituals during childbirth, a pattern observed in Arab families. Men were not usually allowed in the birthing room. But after birth, fathers were expected to recite the *azan* into the baby's ears and burn or bury the placenta to protect the baby from malevolent spirits (Merli 2011).

In Bangladesh, fathers in middle-class families spent fewer than four hours per week with their children in childcare activities such as playing, reading, or talking to them (Jesmin & Seward 2011). Mothers' estimates of fathers' involvement in these activities were slightly higher than fathers' estimates of their own involvement. Mothers in both rural and urban Bengali families spent more time in school-age children's care and academic work than fathers did (Hossain 2013). Whereas rural fathers spent 43 percent as much time (21.8 hours) as mothers did in children's care and academic work each week, urban fathers spent about 59 percent as much time (57.28 hours) as their spouses did in these activities. Both urban and rural fathers showed similar levels of involvement with their sons and daughters. These findings suggest that mothers remain the primary caregivers for their children in Bengali Muslim families.

It is clear that compared to mothers, most fathers in the Islamic world spend less time with their children and are primarily responsible for financially supporting the family. Despite increasing attention to women's rights, higher educational attainment, delayed marriage, urbanization, and rising divorce rates, mothers still perform the majority of childcare tasks across Islamic societies. At the same time, contemporary educated and urban Islamic fathers in non-Arab societies show levels of involvement with young children that are in line with men in other cultural communities. It is estimated that 40 percent of the time spent in taking care of children is done by the father in most cultures (Pleck & Masciadrelli 2004). Whereas Black Carib fathers spend little to no time with their children (Munroe & Munroe 1992) and Batek fathers in Malaysia spend as much time as their wives do in childcare (Endicott 1992), non-Arab Muslim fathers are moderately involved in childcare compared to Arab Muslim fathers. These patterns of involvement hardly match the ideals of Islamic fathering discussed earlier.

There are some inconsistencies regarding whether the gender of the child makes a difference in maternal and paternal involvement. Kadazan, Malay, and Bengali fathers and mothers were equally involved with male and female children (Endicott 1992; Hossain et al. 2007; Hossain et al. 2005). In the face of such lopsided involvement between mothers and fathers and the social norms of patriarchy and economic practices in Islamic societies, the lack of gender of child differences in paternal involvement is rather surprising. However, it is in line with Islamic expectations that instruct parents to be involved with and treat their sons and daughters equally. The differential treatment of children has added significance for children's access to health and schooling in patriarchal societies and deserves far more research attention. Future research should focus on how sociocultural and religious factors influence parent–child interactions in Islamic nations.

FATHER INVOLVEMENT AND CHILDHOOD DEVELOPMENT

Using Baumrind's parenting framework (Baumrind 1967) and Rohner's (Rohner & Khaleque 2005) acceptance–rejection theory, it has been shown that positive father–child interactions are associated with favorable social and cognitive developmental outcomes across cultural communities (Khaleque & Rohner 2012; Lamb 2010). Comparatively little exists in the way of research on paternal involvement and childhood outcomes in Islamic societies. Nonetheless, what findings have emerged parallel those found in other societies. In the social development realm, children in many Arab societies perceive their fathers' behaviors as psychologically abusive and emotionally distant, and this has negative consequences for psychological adjustment (Ahmed 2013). It has been found that parental pressure and strictness are related to children's aggressive behaviors. Research on Saudi and Kuwaiti children suggests that paternal rejection was positively correlated with adolescent's maladaptive behavior at home (Ahmed, Rohner, & Carrasco 2012). The Saudi data further indicate that fathers' parenting style was positively linked to college-age children's internal locus of control (Al-Nefie 1997, cited in Ahmed 2013). Also, Egyptian children of absent fathers seem to lack appropriate social skills, demonstrate maladaptive behaviors in school, and develop depressive symptoms, and the rising divorce rate in many Arab communities is linked to childhood aggression and depression (Ahmed 2013).

Turning to children's cognitive skills, data from Malaysia and Bangladesh reveal that fathers' educational level has a positive association, whereas family size and fathers' work hours have negative associations, with children's school work (Hossain 2013; Hossain et al. 2005). Urban fathers' availability and level of encouragement (e.g., asking about school and teacher, attending school activities, arranging a tutor) are positively associated with school-age children's test scores on national exams in Bangladesh. Findings from Egyptian and Kuwaiti families suggest that father acceptance positively influences adolescent children's language development, academic curiosity, and creative thinking (Al-Reguieb 1996, cited in Ahmed 2013). The same study reported that father neglect and overprotection had negative associations with children's intellectual development.

CURRENT CHANGES, POLICY IMPLICATIONS, AND LOOKING INTO THE FUTURE

Western-style democratic social exchanges, economic practices, and parent–child interactions have the potential to slowly reshape old customs and traditions in Islamic societies. Modernization is contributing to a greater prevalence of single-parent families, increased divorce rates, and higher literacy in families compared to a few decades ago (Ahmed 2013; Stivens 2006). Different levels of changes are evident in women's roles and in the traditional aspects of childrearing (e.g., *Adat*, *Akhlaq*), especially in non-Arab Muslim families (Baharudin, Krauss, Yacoob, & Pei 2011). But sharp gender-demarcated roles and responsibilities remain in much of the Muslim world. In situations in which women have entered the "modern" sector and have made vast strides in education and in white-collar employment (Noor, Gandhi, Ishak, & Wok 2014; Stivens 2006), contemporary Islamic families are using commercial childcare centers, extended kin, paid servants, and maids to assist in childcare. How this affects fathers' involvement in childcare is largely undocumented. Future research may want to shed light on the extent to which these alternative childcare practices are influencing paternal involvement with children, husband–wife relationships, and childhood development.

Increased industrialization and urbanization encourages women across Islamic societies to pursue higher education, to enter the paid labor force as both workers and entrepreneurs, and to work longer hours outside the home (Mellström 2009; Yusof & Duasa 2010). Women's current employment in the paid sectors bolsters economic development and personal growth in modern families (Elias 2011; Stivens 2006). In view of changes in women's roles, Islamic societies need to develop childcare policies for working parents. It appears that children older than 4 have near universal enrollment in preschool, especially in wealthy Islamic societies. However, there is a lack of adequate, affordable, and accessible childcare facilities for infants and toddlers in most Islamic societies. For example, the majority of Malaysian workers desire greater flexibility in their places of employment and express a lack of support for child and elder care (Elias 2011; Subramaniam & Selvaratnam 2010). Also, college-going contemporary Malaysian women who intend to enter the paid labor force believe that they will have to provide the majority of care for their offspring and assume most housekeeping duties while working outside the home (Mellström 2009). Furthermore, young employed Muslim women are becoming the "sandwich generation," expected to work and care for their elderly parents and young children. Today and in future Islamic societies, there will be a generation of young mothers responsible for balancing ever-increasing workloads in the family and places of employment (Norzareen & Nobaya 2010). This makes us wonder whether the increased modernization of Islamic societies will force working mothers to embrace a "second shift" (Hochschild 2003) or fathers will be pressed to become more involved in childcare ahead of ideological changes about manhood and fatherhood.

Although most Islamic societies have undergone various levels of modernization, including a high rate of economic growth since the 1980s (Stivens 2006; UNDP 2008), parenting behaviors still revolve around religious rituals and the traditional social norms of patriarchy and *Adat*. The dual pathways of maintaining a patrilineal social structure and women's entry into education and paid employment create a clearly visible conflict in modernized Islamic societies. Because of this cultural–religious dualism in parenting roles, many mothers and fathers must deal with parenting in a multifarious and different light. The availability and use of inexpensive live-in domestic maids from other societies have removed direct responsibility of children away from mothers and fathers and consequently made parenting roles more complex in affluent Islamic societies. Some fear that modernization and relegating caregiving roles to paid helpers will diminish the social values of family harmony and increase social delinquency and increase other serious issues, such as immorality, family violence, child abuse, and corruption (Amin, Yusof, & Haneef 2006).

Progressive thinkers and feminist scholars point out that there are some national level policies and efforts to debunk such fears of moral decay. For example, with the support from the Ministry of Women, Community and Development, the National Population and Family Development Board (LPPKN) in Malaysia initiated a campaign called the "Malaysia Nation of Character" (MNOC). This campaign stresses that the solution to these anticipated social and family problems in Malaysia, and possibly in other Islamic societies, can be resolved by encouraging mothers and fathers to become more involved with their children and by raising them with democratic values of equality, resilience, and ethics. These western democratic values are compatible with the Islamic ideals of shared and involved parenting between men and women, respecting children's rights, treating boys and girls equally, and investing in their education. In this regard, there is need to address the role of ill-trained religious leaders and their uninformed preaching, poverty and unemployment, illiteracy, lack of parenting and early childhood development programs, lack of scientific innovations, and business and administrative corruption. The "Arab Spring" movement has provided much essential impetus to establish equal and democratic societies in the Islamic world. It seems likely that paternal roles will follow suit.

As a part of civil society, Islamic parents need to understand that changes in social norms are inevitable. If they fail to adapt and equip themselves with appropriate parenting skills, then the family as an institution and overall family functioning will be at risk of difficulties (Stivens 2006). Across Islamic societies, there are suggestions to systematically strengthen programs for early paternal involvement in prenatal care and the birthing process (Faruque, Ahmed, Ahmed, Islam, Hossain, et al. 2008; Jesmin & Seward 2011). National policies can be developed and implemented through prenatal programs, especially in poorer nations such as Bangladesh (e.g., doctor's visits, childbirth education classes). These programs can target fathers' understanding of the health and emotional well-being of the mother and the developing fetus, mother–father relationship, fathers' relationship with the unborn child, and fathers' involvement in childcare during the immediate postbirth period, when the formation of a bond between father and child is critical for later social and cognitive development (Lamb 2010; Lupton & Barclay 1997).

Finally, there is a visible lack of research on links between father involve-ment and developmental outcomes in Islamic societies. Research findings in this area have the potential to inspire scholars to revisit aspects of skills, tech-niques, and strategies for successful parenting that may or may not resonate across Muslim populations. In view of increasing modernization of Islamic soci-eties, more attention should be paid to early childhood development and par-enting policies and programs that specifically focus on Islamic fathers who live in different settings and who hail from different socioeconomic backgrounds. It is incumbent upon these programs to target traditional conceptions of mascu-linity and ideological beliefs about the diverse dimensions of fathering.

ISLAMIC VALUES AND MUSLIM FAMILIES

www.fiqh.org
www.onislam.net
www.islamreligion.com
www.ing.org
www.ezsoftech.com
www.familylinks.org.uk
www.alrawiya.org
www.chaplaincyinstitute.org
www.pewforum.org
www.ispu.org
Note: *The authors of this chapter are not linked to any of the aforementioned websites.*

Acknowledgement: This chapter was supported by a research grant, awarded to the first author, from the College of Education in cooperation with the Office of the Provost, University of New Mexico.

REFERENCES

Abudabbeh, N. (2005). Arab families: An overview. In M. McGoldrick, J. Giordano, & N. Garcia-Preto (eds.), *Ethnicity and family therapy* (pp. 423–436). New York: The Guilford Press.

Abou-el-Kheir, M., M., S. (1998). Perceived father figure image and self-esteem among college students. *Psychological Studies*, 8, 419–453 (in Arabic).

Ahmed, R. A. (2013). The father's role in the Arab world: Cultural perspectives. In D. W. Shwalb, B. J., Shwalb, & M. E. Lamb (eds.), *Fathers in cultural context* (pp. 122–150). New York: Routledge.

Ahmed, R. A., Rohner, R. P., & Carrasco, M. A. (2012). Relations between psychologi-cal adjustment and perceived parental, sibling, best friend, and teacher acceptance among Kuwaiti adolescents. In K. J. Ripoll, A. L. Comunian, & C. M. Brown (eds.), *Expanding horizons: Current research on interpersonal acceptance* (pp. 1–10). Boca Raton, FL: Brown Walker Press.

Al-Ati, H. A. (1995). *The family structure in Islam*. Plainfield, IN: American Trust Publications.

Al Mutair, A. S., Plummer, V., O'Brien, A. P., & Clerehan, R. (2014). Providing culturally congruent care for Saudi patients and their families. *Contemporary Nurse*, 46, 254–258.

Al-Nefie, A. A. (1997). The relationship between styles of parental treatment and locus of control in a sample of male and female students at Umm el-Qura University, Mecca, Saudi Arabia. *Journal of the Faculty of Education* (Al-Azhar University, Egypt), 66, 281–314 (in Arabic).

Al-Reguieb, Y. A. F. (1996). *Parental warmth and its relation to personality traits and creativity in a sample of primary school children in Kuwait and Egypt* (Unpublished doctoral dissertation). Minia, Egypt: Minia University (in Arabic).

Amin, R. M., Yusof, S. A., & Haneef, M. S. (2006). Values, social problems and balanced development in Malaysia. *Journal of Socio-Economics*, 35, 151–163.

Baharudin, R., Krauss, S. T., Yacoob, S. N., & Pei, T. J. (2011). Family processes as predictors of antisocial behaviors among adolescents from urban, single-mother Malay families in Malaysia. *Journal of Comparative Family Studies*, 42, 509–522.

Baumrind, D. B. (1967). Child care practices anteceding three patterns of preschool behavior. *Genetic Psychology Monographs*, 75(1), 43–88.

Cabrera, N., & Tamis-LeMonda, C. S. (eds.). (2013). *Handbook of father involvement: Multidisciplinary perspectives*, 2nd ed. New York: Taylor & Francis.

Chaudhry, M. H. (2009). *A code of the teachings of Al-Qur'an*. Delhi, India: Adam Publishers.

Dwairy, M., Achoui, M., Abouserie, R., Farah, A., Sakhleh, A. A., Fayad, M., & Khan, H. K. (2006). Parenting styles in Arab societies: A first cross-regional research study. *Journal of Cross-Cultural Psychology*, 37, 230–247.

Elias, J. (2011). The gender politics of economic competitiveness in Malaysia's transition to a knowledge economy. *Pacific Review*, 24, 529–552.

Endicott, K. M. (1992). Fathering in an egalitarian society. In B. S. Hewlett (ed.), *Father–child relations: Cultural and biosocial context* (pp. 281–295). Hawthorne, NY: Aldine de Gruyter.

Faruque, A. S. G., Ahmed, A. M. S., Ahmed, T., Islam, M. M., Hossain, M. I., Roy, S. K., et al. (2008). Nutrition: Basis for health children and mothers in Bangladesh. *Journal of Health, Population Nutrition*, 26, 325–339.

Giladi, A. (2014). The nurture and protection of children in Islam: Perspective from Islamic sources. *Child Abuse and Neglect*, 38, 585–592.

Hashem, S. M. M. (2001). A study of determinants of parental child maltreatment. *Faculty of Arts Journal* (Menoufia University, Egypt), 44, 249–307 (in Arabic).

Hochschild, A. R. (2003). *The second shift*. New York: Penguin.

Hossain, Z. (2013). Fathers in Muslim families in Malaysia and Bangladesh. In D. W. Shwalb, B. J. Shwalb, & M. E. Lamb (eds.) *Fathers in cultural contexts* (pp. 95–121). New York: Routledge.

Hossain, Z., Roopnarine, J. L., Ismail, R., Hashmi, S. I., & Sombuling, A. (2007). Fathers' and mothers' reports of involvement in caring for infants in Kadazan families in Sabah, Malaysia. *Fathering*, 5(1), 58–72.

Hossain, Z., Roopnarine, J. L., Masud, J., Muhamed, A. A., Baharudin, R., Abdullah, R., & Juhari, R. (2005). Mothers' and fathers' childcare involvement with young children in rural families in Malaysia. *International Journal of Psychology,* 40(6), 385–394.

Ibrahim, M. A. (2010). *Effects of parents' power and prestige on children's psychological adjustment.* Paper presented at the 3rd International Congress on Acceptance and Rejection, University of Padua, Italy, July 28–31.

Jesmin, S. S., & Seward, R. R. (2011). Parental leave and fathers' involvement with children in Bangladesh: A comparison with United States. *Journal of Comparative Family Studies, 42,* 95–112.

Jones, G. W. (2010). *Changing marriage patterns in Asia.* Working Paper Series No. 131. Singapore: Asian Research Institute, National University of Singapore.

Juhari, R., Yaacob, S. N., & Abu Talib, M. (2013). Father involvement among Malay Muslims in Malaysia. *Journal of Family Issues, 34,* 208–227.

Kabir, M., & az-Zubair, B. (2007). Who is a parent? Parenthood in Islamic ethics. *Journal of Medical Ethics, 33,* 605–609.

Khaleque, A., & Rohner, R. P. (2012). Transnational relations between perceived parental acceptance-rejection and personality dispositions of children and adults: A meta-analytic review of worldwide research. *Personality and Social Psychology Review, 16,* 103–115.

Kling, Z. (1995). The Malay family: Beliefs and realities. *Journal of Comparative Family Studies, 26,* 43–66.

Lamb, M. E. (ed.). (2004). *The role of the father in child development.* Hoboken, NJ: Wiley.

Lamb, M. E. (ed.). (2010). *The role of the father in child development.* Hoboken, NJ: Wiley.

Lupton, D., & Barclay, L. (1997). *Constructing fatherhood: Discourses and experiences.* London, UK: Sage.

Mashhour, A. (2005). Islamic law and gender equality: Could there be a common ground? A study of divorce and polygamy in shariah law and contemporary legislation in Tunisia and Egypt. *Human Rights Quarterly, 27,* 562–596.

Mellstrom, U. (2009). The intersection of gender, race, and cultural boundaries; or, why is computer science in Malaysia dominated by women? *Social Studies of Science, 36,* 885–907.

Merli, C. (2011). Patrescence in southern Thailand: Cosmological and social dimension of fatherhood among the Malay–Muslims. *Culture, Health and Sexuality: An International Journal for Research, Intervention and Care, 13,* 235–248.

Mernissi, F. (1987). *Beyond the veil: Male–female dynamics in modern Muslim society.* Bloomington: Indiana University Press.

Moghadam, V. M. (2004). *Towards gender equality in the Arab/Middle East region: Islam, culture, and feminist activism.* Occasional paper of the United Nations Development Program. New York: UNDP.

Munroe, R., & Munroe, R. (1992). Fathers in children's environments: A four-culture study. In B. Hewlett (ed.), *Father–child relations: Cultural and biosocial contexts* (pp. 213–229). New York: Aldine de Gruyter.

Noor, N. (1999). Roles and women's well-being: Some preliminary findings from Malaysia. *Sex Roles, 41,* 123–145.

Noor, N. M., Gandhi, A. D., Ishak, I., & Wok, S. (2014). Development of indicators for family well-being in Malaysia. *Social Indicators Research, 115,* 279–318.

Norzareen, M., & Nobaya, A. (2010). Women of the sandwich generation in Malaysia. *European Journal of Social Sciences, 13*, 171–178.

Oweis, A., Gharaibeh, M., Maaitah, R., Gharaibeh, H., & Obeisat, S. (2012). Parenting from a Jordanian perspective: Findings from a qualitative study. *Journal of Nursing Scholarship, 44*, 242–248.

Paquette, D. (2004). Theorizing the father–child relationship: Mechanisms and developmental outcomes. *Human Development, 47*, 193–219.

Pew Research Center (2009, October). Mapping the global Muslim population. www .pewforum.org/2009/10/07/mapping-the-global-muslim-population/.

Pew Research Center (2012, December). The global religious landscape. http://www .pewforum.org/2012/12/18/global-religious-landscape-muslim/.

Pleck, J., & Masciadrelli, B. (2004). Paternal involvement by U.S. residential fathers: Levels, sources, and consequences. In M. E. Lamb (ed.), *The role of the father in child development* (pp. 222–271). Hoboken, NJ: Wiley.

Putnick, D., Bornstein, M. H., Lansford, J. E., Chang, L., Deater-Deckard, K., Di Giunta, L., & Bombi, A. S. (2012). Agreement in mother and father acceptance–rejection, warmth, and hostility/rejection/neglect of children across nine cultures. *Cross-Cultural Research, 46*, 191–223.

Rohner, R. P., & Khaleque, A. (eds.). (2005). *Handbook for the study of parental acceptance and rejection*, 4th ed. Storrs, CT: Rohner Research Publications.

Roopnarine, J. L. (2013). Father–child involvement in English-speaking Caribbean countries: Links to childhood development. In J. Pattnaik (ed.), *Father involvement in young children's lives* (pp. 183–200). New York: Springer.

Rosnah, I. (1999). *Family quality of Kadazandusan*. Kota Kinabalu, Malaysia: Universiti Malaysia Sabah.

Selvarajah, C., & Meyer, D. (2008). One nation, three cultures: Exploring dimensions that relate to leadership in Malaysia. *Leadership and Organization Development Journal, 29*, 693–712.

Shwalb, D. W., Shwalb, B. J., & Lamb, M. E. (eds.). (2013). *Fathers in cultural contexts*. New York: Routledge.

Stivens, M. (2006). "Family values" and Islamic revival: Gender, rights, and state moral projects in Malaysia. *Women's Studies International Forum, 29*, 354–367.

Subramaniam, G., & Selvaratnam, D. P. (2010). Family-friendly policies in Malaysia: Where we are? *Journal of International Business Research, 9*, 43–55.

Tamuri, A. H. (2007). Islamic education teachers' perceptions of the teaching of akhlaq in Malaysian secondary schools. *Journal of Moral Education, 36*(3), 371–386.

UNDP (2008). *Capacity development: Empowering people and institutions—annual report*. New York: United Nations Development Program.

Von der Mehden, F. R. (1987). Malaysia: Islam and multiethnic politics. In J. L. Esposito (ed.), *Islam in Asia: Religion, politics, and society* (pp. 177–201). New York: Oxford University Press.

www.quandl.com (2014). The age at first marriage. www.quandl.com/c/society/age-at-first-marriage-male-by-country.

Yusof, S. A., & Duasa, J. (2010). Household decision making and expenditure patterns of married men and women in Malaysia. *Journal of Family Economic Issues, 31*, 371–381.

Africa

18

Black Fathers in South Africa

Tawanda Makusha and Linda Richter

Black fathers in South Africa are absent from two-thirds of homes in which children live (Statistics South Africa 2011). Among South African children younger than 15, in 2009, about 30 percent had a father present in the home compared to 53 percent of colored children, 83% of white children, and 85 percent of Indians. There is also a higher prevalence of father absence in urban than rural areas (43% and 55% respectively) (Holborn & Eddy 2011) and in homes with low disposable income (fewer than 400 Rand per month) (Desmond & Desmond 2006). A smaller number of maternal orphans (28%) live with their biological fathers, whereas 83% of paternal orphans live with their biological mothers (Wollard, Buthelezi, & Bertscher 2012). Comparable rates of father absence were noted in waves 1 (2008) and 2 (2010–2011) of the National Income Dynamics Study (NIDS 2008, 2010–2011) as well. Father absence among black men in South Africa has strong implications for the health, safety, and welfare of children and results from a number of factors: cultural practices promoting collective involvement of the extended family in looking after children; ideological beliefs about men and fathering; dual forces of migration, separation, divorce, and repartnering; related changes in social and residential arrangements; and the high rate of paternal deaths thanks to the HIV epidemic and other causes of early male mortality (Eddy, Thomson-de Boor, & Mphaka 2013; Hosegood & Madhavan 2012; Hunter 2006; Mkhize 2006).

Whereas marriage is a basis for entry into fatherhood in a number of societies (see chapters 12 and 17 this volume), the marriage rate among black South Africans is low and is frequently delayed until men have fathered one or more children, potentially by different women (Posel, Rudwick, & Casale 2011). An estimated 37 percent of black South Africans aged 30–34 years are married, and the figure increases to 51 percent for men aged 35–39 (Richter, Chikovore, & Makusha 2010). A similar pattern of entry into fatherhood and mate shifting has been observed in African Caribbean men, who tend to have children first in visiting relationships before progressing to common-law living arrangements and eventually marriage once they become more economically secure (see chapter 2, this volume). These men have children from several "baby mothers," and the level of contact and support offered to children from prior unions are unpredictable. About 59 percent of the men never had contact with biological children (Anderson 2007).

The growing diversity of father–child residency patterns in South Africa and in other societies has raised a new awareness about fathers' roles, as well as the recognition that an increasing proportion of all children do not live with their biological fathers (Makusha et al. 2012; Richter et al. 2010), nor is the two-parent resident model ideal for examining father–child relationships in Black South African families. As in other African cultural communities (e.g., Hadza, Bofi, Efe, Aka), children are raised by multiple caregivers who contribute to the health, safety, and well-being of children (see Fouts 2013; Hewlett & Mcfarlan 2010; Marlowe 2005). In this chapter we explore a few salient factors influencing father involvement among blacks in South Africa. More specifically, we provide a sociohistorical context for understanding current fathering practices, examining the biological meaning of fatherhood, non-resident fathering, and the effects of fathers on children and the family and discussing some policy implications for fathering in South Africa.

HISTORY OF FATHERHOOD IN SOUTH AFRICA

Fatherhood in South Africa has been shaped by the country's complex social, historical, political, and economic processes, including the socially disorganizing and discriminating effects of apartheid (Hosegood & Madhavan 2010). Hunter (2006) argues that in the precolonial and early colonial era, black men were seen to be successful by the amount of agricultural labor that they controlled. A man who fathered many children tended to be a respected household head and was able to draw on his large family for labor to increase agricultural output (Chikovore, Richter, & Makusha 2013; see also chapter 19). Fathering centered on men's ability to build a homestead through marriage, having children, continuing the patrilineal lineage through a male heir (Hunter 2006), and representing the family in public matters (Epprecht 2007). With fathering and fatherhood also came *inhlonipo* (respect), whereby men who had fathered a child or were supporting children were held in high regard in their family and community (Hunter 2006).

With the implementation of apartheid—which strengthened the economic and political power of the ruling white minority and enforced racial segregation through oppressive laws, these constructions of fatherhood shifted (Mathews, Jewkes, & Abrahams 2011). Richter and Morrell (2006) contend that in the apartheid era, different experiences of work fundamentally shaped what was possible for black, colored, Indian, and white fathers.[1] Apartheid affected and continues to influence African fathers and patterns of fatherhood in South Africa. Many black men are fathers in households in which some or all of the children may be neither their biological offspring nor co-resident (Chikovore et al. 2013).

This scenario arises from various factors, including historical dynamics around apartheid legislation and volatile resistance to it. Families, relationships and family connections have been disrupted by the apartheid migrant labor system, which separated reproduction and production (Burawoy 1976). Townsend and colleagues (2006) argue that although the Pass Laws, which were introduced by the apartheid regime to control the location and movement of black South Africans, were eradicated in 1986, and although independence in 1994 removed the last vestiges of formal legal segregation, the separation of opportunities for earning an income from the sites of family life has remained a prominent and distinguishing feature of life for many black South Africans (Spiegel & Mehlwana 1997).

Economic and land dispossession and the introduction of government taxes on black people made it difficult for fathers to provide for their families and forced them to seek work on farms and in towns (Lesejane 2006). Policies of racial separation restricted black people to "Bantustans" or "Homelands," which were remote, rural, and impoverished (Mathews et al. 2011). This disempowerment led men, who were only allowed to migrate from their "Bantustans" for the sake of labor, to leave their homes to work on annual labor contracts in mines, factories, and commercial farms. These men left their wives and children at home only to return during Christmas holidays or when their contracts expired (Townsend et al. 2006).

In a study on the conceptualization of fatherhood among mineworkers, men who lived in bare and demeaning single-sex hostels saw economic support for children as being core to what it meant to be a "good father" (Rabe 2006). Most stated that they only undertook dangerous work underground so that they could support their children (Rabe 2006). During this period, fatherhood was enacted within the constraints of paid employment (Henwood & Procter 2003). Labor migration became the main cause of the low rate of co-residence between fathers and their children in South Africa as the financial muscle power of fathers became exclusively important in determining and measuring "good" fathers (Kaufman, Maharaj, & Richter 1998; Lesejane 2006). Employed fathers who provided financially for their families were held in high regard, because men came to be judged only by their ability to provide (Lesejane 2006). During this period, some migrant fathers were portrayed as responsible because they sent remittances to support the homestead and made occasional visits back home (Hunter 2006). At the same time, other migrant fathers were labeled irresponsible because they did not send money back home or had relationships and children with other women in town, abandoning and neglecting their children from previous unions (Townsend et al. 2006).

Men who left their homesteads in search of work became what has been termed "shadowy" heads of households, who were "symbolically important" but with "little actual importance in children's lives" (Roy 2008, p. 99). Later, women also sought work away from the rural homestead, with children remaining in the care of older relatives or siblings. Many households functioned as "stretched" residential units (Spiegel, Watson, & Wilkinson 1996), with family members "dispersed" between different households for reasons of work, care, support, and housing. These patterns have become entrenched and continue to influence contemporary domestic and labor environments in South Africa even after independence and democracy.

NEW FATHERHOOD AMONG BLACKS IN SOUTH AFRICA

The advent of democracy in South Africa has witnessed the introduction of father-friendly policies and programs by government and nongovernmental organizations (NGOs). The South African constitution provides for modest paternity leave and acknowledges the need to increase this in order to facilitate greater involvement of men in children's lives. By law, South African fathers are currently entitled to three days of paid family responsibility leave (Human Sciences Research Council 2006). NGOs such as Sonke Gender Justice advocate for male involvement in HIV prevention, reproductive health, and the stamping out of gender-based violence (Chikovore et al. 2013). The introduction of policies and programs promoting involved fatherhood has led some black men to embrace what is referred to as the "new fatherhood." These fathers now practice direct childcare work, spend more high-quality time with their children, attend their children's school functions, and provide financially for their children and families. Grubb (2010), for example, highlights how fathers are now more involved in family and children's lives:

> If you look around you, you must have seen them. They are in the local supermarkets. They are dropping their children at school every morning and sneaking out at lunch time to pick them up again. They are bathing them every evening, and reading them bedtime stories . . . . They are even seen running and yelling supportively at school sports activities, not just on weekends, but in the middle of a work-day afternoon. They are proud South African fathers—and they are becoming more and more involved in their children's lives. (Grubb 2010, p. 137)

Although this is taking place in middle-class black families, it has not been possible for most poor black fathers and children, because "the spatial separation of employment and family has remained a fact of life for many South Africans" (Madhavan et al. 2008). There are still many children in low socioeconomic contexts who do not coreside nor receive financial support from their fathers, because their fathers have moved to look for work or take employment somewhere, or for a variety of other reasons (Madhavan, Gross, Richter, Norris, & Hosegood 2012). In fact, the number of black children having non-resident fathers increased during the postapartheid period (1996–2009) from 45 percent to 53 percent. During the same period, it also increased for colored children from 34 percent to 41 percent and from 13 percent to 15 percent for whites (Holborn & Eddy 2011).

It appears that the spatial separation influences fathers' social contact and support of children. According to data collected in wave 2 of the NIDS (2010–2011), the level of father contact and support varied considerably: 28 percent of black non-resident fathers "never" saw their children, compared to 35 percent of colored, 33 percent of Indian, and 11 percent of white families. Only 7 percent of black South African non-resident fathers saw their children daily. Most (47%) saw their children several times a month or several times a year. Men in rural areas were more likely to display these limited patterns of contact than urban men. There was also a significant association between men who saw their children and the support offered to them. Seventy-four percent of fathers who saw their children daily provided support to them, compared to 5 percent who never saw their children. Regardless of ethnic background, a majority of fathers had limited contacts with children. What is not clear is the level of disengagement by men from their children's lives and the degree to which children kept absent or low-contact fathers psychologically present when they were not around. Among African Caribbean families who practice mate shifting and non-residential fathering, there is a reasonably good degree of psychological presence of fathers in children's lives (see Ramkissoon 2002).

THE IMPORTANCE OF BIOLOGICAL FATHERHOOD AMONG BLACKS IN SOUTH AFRICA

As in several other cultural communities (e.g., African Caribbean; see chapter 2, this volume), biological fatherhood is an integral element in the construction of masculinity and a stamp on manhood. Hunter (2006) emphasizes the importance of paternity and fathering in men's identity in South Africa. The mere fact of having a child is sometimes used to claim the status of manhood. In black South African society, a biological father is a highly visible and respected member of society who is also often the acknowledged head and central authority for his family (Hunter 2006). Within this frame-work, biological fathers also have an ascribed status rather than an achieved one and are often viewed as symbols and guardians of ultimate power and responsibility in the family and in the community (Lesejane 2006). In the African tradition, a man who neither marries nor biologically fathers a child may be seen as having failed to build a homestead, an essential aspect of masculinity (Hunter 2006). However, until he pays *inhlawulo* (damages for impregnating a girl) or *lobola* (bride wealth), a biological father may not be recognized as the father of a child, especially by the family of the child's mother, and he may be restricted from visiting his child at the mother's family homestead.

Even though many children grow up in households where their biologi-cal fathers were absent, and were in the care and support of multiple adults, biological fatherhood in African settings—similar to South Africa—remains very important, having cultural, as well as social and personal, significance. In South Africa, as in other African societies, married black biological fathers provide a child with the "family or clan name," and this represents a signifi-cant source of social capital (e.g., ancestral traditions) and status for children, linking them to resources and other people in the communities in which they live (Eddy et al. 2013; Madhavan & Roy 2011; Morrell 2006). Biological fatherhood is very important in transmitting cultural values to children and in promoting identity development, because children and families identify with the biological father even when he is absent from the household (Mad-havan & Roy 2011).

Biological fatherhood in black communities is defined by the powerful role accorded to men and fathers as acknowledged heads of households, based on a traditional patriarchal system (Morrell 2006; Richter et al. 2011). The bio-logical father is seen as an authoritative figure who is consulted on important household decisions even in his absence (Hunter 2006). He is viewed as a provider of economic and emotional support, who brings the family together and assumes leadership (Richter et al. 2011). This is well validated by the symbolic attachment between a married man and his homestead even when he spends most of his time away from home; such a man is usually referred to as "the father of the house" (Hunter 2006). Long spells of absence from the household aside, the man is still viewed as the one in charge of the household.

The significance of paternal links for children is highlighted by Ramphele (2002). Boys who did not know their fathers would rather run away from home to avoid the deep shame that came from not knowing their father's name when they went for initiation. Zwang and Garenne (2009) concur with Ramphele and acknowledge that in the Shangaan culture, children who are born outside wedlock are highly stigmatized and often referred to as *goyas* (wild cats) (p. 104). These children suffer social vilification, seen as intruders who do not belong in the formal family. Likewise, in certain ethnic groups in Kenya, even if the man is not present, he confers a sense of legitimacy to the family, and children have traditionally enjoyed higher status and felt less shame and guilt in married than in single-parent families (Lasser, Fite, & Wadende 2011).

For all the positive things that men do for children in families, biological fathers are not always an asset to households in South Africa. Levels of substance abuse among South African men, as well as neglect of and violence toward female partners and children, are unacceptably high (Jewkes, Sikweyiya, Morrell, & Dunkle 2011). Even though female-headed households are invariably worse off in terms of resources than male-headed households, female heads are much more likely to invest in children's well-being, including in health and education. Some fathers neglect their obligation to support their children financially (Lloyd & Blanc 1996). In a recent grim testimony of the destructive role of fathers, Polela (2012) recounts how his father murdered his mother and then turned his back on him and his sister (at the time aged 3 and 5). The story, set in KwaZulu-Natal in the 1980s, is an account of heartlessness and indifference to the welfare of children as well as a callous disregard for the legal obligations of care (Richter et al. 2012).

THE ROLE OF NON-RESIDENT BIOLOGICAL FATHERS AMONG BLACKS IN SOUTH AFRICA

As stated earlier, South Africa has one of the highest rates of father absence in Africa, after Namibia (Posel & Devey 2006), with only about a third of black preschool children coresiding with their fathers (Statistics South Africa 2011). But considering the nature of extended family relations, having children living apart from fathers, especially due to migrant labor does not automatically mean that the children are being neglected or that the men are irresponsible, nor does it equate to a break in social connectedness between a father and child (Makusha et al. 2012). Father's physical location and child involvement are two separate dimensions of fathers' connection to their children (Madhavan et al. 2008). In South Africa, as in many other countries, some non-resident fathers can make substantial contributions to families and children, as well as to children who are not biologically their own, through remittances, social visits, and telephone contacts (Makusha et al. 2012; see also Marlowe 1999 for a discussion of provisioning to nonbiological children).

Interviews of South African male mineworkers, including men who are separated from their children, suggest that they highly value their status as fathers (Rabe 2007). They express deep affection for their children and often endure extreme hardship in work and through separation from their families to be able to provide financial support for their children. In one case, a mine worker said, "I found myself bound to work for a contractor although it pays so little because I could not face my children and tell them I had no job, and that is why I could not provide them with clothing and food" (Rabe 2006, p. 262). The importance of the work role was also echoed in a focus-group study conducted of "absent fathers" in Gauteng, South Africa; difficulty in meeting the economic needs of the family was seen as a major barrier to achieving successful fathering. In another study (Eddy et al. 2013) of fathers (40% had children residing elsewhere) in four communities (Alexandra, Doornkop, Thembisa, and Devland) in South Africa, the paternal role meant an obligation to provide material resources to family members, whereas it was the "natural" responsibility for mothers to care for children. With such emphasis on the provider role, there is the possibility of a conceptual separation between the provider and caregiving roles. Men's internal scripts or ethnotheories placed caregiving primarily within the domain of women (Mavungu 2013). These roles were seen "as deterministic and static phenomena" even though some fathers saw their investment in caregiving as potentially enhancing the parent–child bond (Eddy et al. 2013, p. 19).

Although images of fathers as caring and loving people exist (Mkhize 2006), deep shame and alienation is experienced by men who cannot secure employment and who are unable to live with and support their families, which can affect other aspects of personal and family functioning (Ramphele & Richter 2006; Wilson 2006). For example, a study conducted in the Mpophomeni area in KwaZulu-Natal on the long-term effects of unemployment indicated that parental depression and family disruption were not uncommon among men. One participant stated: "If you are not working you are not a genuine father. You are a father because you work. My children do not love me as they used to. I sometimes get angry with my wife when she asks me whether I am searching for a job. I have lost my status as the man of the house" (Mkhize 2006, p. 185). This statement conveys that the absence or inadequacy of men's financial support for children is a regular source of conflict within and between families and has been identified as a major contributor to the increase in domestic violence. These outcomes are not uncommon in men in some developing societies (e.g., Jamaica) where partner conflicts and domestic violence increase with unstable economic conditions (e.g., Anderson 2007).

Makusha, Richter, and Chikovore (2013) argue that because of high poverty and unemployment rates, many South African men suffer damage to their sense of identity, masculinity, self-esteem, and confidence to act as fathers to their children, because they are not able to provide financial support to their children and families. Morrell (2006) and Eddy et al. (2013) concur that "providing" is a deeply entrenched part of masculine identity and being unable to command financial and material resources undermines men's involvement in families, both practically and psychologically. Poor men may try to avoid criticism by distancing themselves from their children (Hunter 2006). Furthermore, Spiegel and Mehlwana (1997) were also able to demonstrate that non-resident black fathers in South Africa who were in stable relationships perceived themselves as worthless or as "failures" if they were not able to send money to their families. They also noted that wives and children would become angry at them if they were not able or willing to provide for the family's economic needs. In some cases fathers were prevented by wives/partners from carrying out other paternal responsibilities. But in other situations mothers insisted that fathers see their children "with or without money" (Mavungu 2013, p. 74).

In sum, evidence from South Africa suggests that employment status and income now largely discriminate between men who are able to get married and coreside with their children and those who are not able to marry and coreside with their children (Desmond & Desmond 2006). Employed men in higher income categories are several times more likely to be living with their wives and children than men in the lowest income category or those who are unemployed (Desmond & Desmond 2006). Additionally, cultural norms, such as *lobola*, compounded by family dispersal also frequently contribute to the social and residential separation of biological fathers from their children (Townsend et al. 2006). The majority of young children born to unmarried parents live with their mothers, often in extended households headed by maternal kin. Such living arrangements persist until the parents can conclude the interfamily marriage negotiations and afford a wedding.

SOCIAL FATHERHOOD AMONG BLACKS IN SOUTH AFRICA

Though it is universally acknowledged that biological father–child involvement is very important, research and data on fatherhood should not be restricted only to them. Throughout Africa and many other parts of the world, there is recognition that the person fulfilling the role of father may not always be the child's biological father. Men may experience fatherhood through varying relationships with children (Rabe 2007; Richter et al. 2011). In South Africa, a man may father children with whom he may never reside, or he may marry and reside with a woman and support the woman's children fathered by another man, while supporting his brothers' and sisters' children in different households, thereby providing father care and support for children who may not be his biological offspring (Hosegood & Madhavan 2010; Mkhize 2004).

As in some other groups in Africa, namely the Nso in northwestern Cameroon (Nsamenang & Lamb 1995; Verhoef 2005) and the Bofi, Hadza, Efe, and Aka people in central Africa (Fouts 2013; Hewlett & Mcfarlan 2010;

Marlowe 2005), fatherhood in black families in South Africa is a collective responsibility in keeping with traditionally extensive patterns of family formation and kinship network that seek to meet the needs of children (Hosegood & Madhavan 2012; Hunter 2006; Mkhize 2006). In such families, which include men, children are exposed to multiple adult figures who may participate in childrearing to a greater or lesser extent (Marlowe 1999, 2005; Mkhize 2004). The spirit of communalism (*Botho/Ubuntu*) is characterized by the connectedness of people and their commitment to the common good, including one's descendants and one's ancestors (Chikovore, Richter, & Makusha 2013; Lesejane 2006; Roy 2008).

The importance of other male relatives in children's lives in South Africa and other African communities is reflected in the manner in which some children and adults refer to children's uncles (father's younger brother [*ubaba omncane*] or older brother [*ubaba omkhulu*]) as the child's father. Similarly, black children in the African context also refer to their mother's sisters as "junior mother" (*umama omncane*) or "senior mother" (*umama omkhulu*) depending on whether they are younger or older than the biological mother (Hunter 2006). In this regard, Richter and Morrell (2008) argue that "the African notion of father, then, is a man who enacts the responsibility of caring for and protecting a child" (p. 152). In other words, even when the child's biological parents are alive and co-resident in a household, the child may also have other men and women he or she calls "father" and "mother" (a child may have more than one father and mother) (Mkhize 2006). The degree to which co-resident father involvement is affected by these other caregivers is yet to be determined for black South African fathers.

This characterization of a family denotes kinship, long-term commitment, and security (Mathambo & Gibbs 2009). Even where there have been shifts from the traditional co-resident extended families to nuclear families, relatives continue to maintain close ties among each other in the extended family system (Hunter 2006; Morrell 2006) and may jointly make decisions regarding where and how members live and what families prioritize and what they put resources toward and how they deal with major life events such as marriage, childbirth and naming, and death (Chikovore et al. 2013). This interdependence of relatives is fostered through marriage, collaboration in social and economic activities and mutual dependencies between working adults who send home remittances and recipient households who care for children, the aged, and other dependents (Chikovore et al. 2013; Chirwa 2002; Fouts 2013; Hosegood & Madhavan 2012; Hunter 2006; Mkhize 2004, 2006; Morrell 2006; Richter et al. 2011). These bonds include not only biologic family of origin, but also extended family ties, which may include cousins, aunts, uncles, grandparents, related kin and clan members, close friends, and neighbors (Chirwa 2002; Verhoef 2005).

BARRIERS TO FATHERING

Apart from the overwhelming effect of economic factors on fathering in South Africa, there are some other barriers within men themselves and their experiences as children that seem to affect fathering in South Africa. It has already been introduced that cultural practices such as bride wealth (*ilobolo*) and damages (*intlawulo*), still quite common in urban areas of South Africa, are known to be deterrents to marriage. But other factors are rooted in men's experiences with their own fathers that hold clues to their current behaviors. In the qualitative accounts provided by Eddy et al. (2013), men seem to lack basic knowledge about parenting young children and on "how a father should behave." Many did not have father figures in their lives, or if they did, they may not have been viable models of engaged fathering. This points to intergenerational stability in poor fathering practices, particularly those that pertain to abandonment and disengagement.

Not everyone agrees with male essentialism. In fact Silverstein and Auerbach (1999) cogently argue that having men around can be detrimental to the well-being of women and children. Others (Eddy et al. 2013) propose instead that with such high rates of father absenteeism, exposing men to good fathering models might contribute in meaningful ways to improving the present state of fathering among Black South Africans. An often ignored issue in contexts in which biological fatherhood is highly emphasized is the skills that men bring to bear in their role as fathers. Would improving parenting skills in general improve men's investment and relationships with children? Can men collaborate with women who are good mothers to improve parenting skills?

FATHER INVOLVEMENT AND CHILD DEVELOPMENT AMONG BLACKS IN SOUTH AFRICA

Not much research in South Africa has determined the association between black father involvement and childhood development. Children in South Africa and other parts of the world live in families where men are generally unacknowledged sources of support for children. Popular perceptions and the media frequently cast black South African men as perpetrators of violence, oppressors of women and children—absent and uninvolved in children's lives and generally uncaring and disengaged (Richter, Manegold, Pather, & Mason 2004). Nevertheless, studies in several cultural communities around the world have shown relationships between different levels of father involvement, parenting styles, and economic investment and different aspects of children's development (see volumes by Cabrera & Tamis-LeMonda 2013; Lamb 2010; Shwalb, Shwalb, & Lamb 2013).

A growing body of research across cultural communities in North America, Europe, China and some studies from South Africa indicate that accessible, supportive, engaged, and responsible fathers give girls self-confidence and help boys develop healthy masculinity (see Lamb & Lewis 2010; chapter 13, this volume). One of the biggest effects of an involved father is that he gives credibility and encouragement for educational achievement. Children stay longer in school and achieve more if their fathers support them in education (Carlson & McLanahan 2004; Carlson 2006; Flouri & Buchanan 2003; Richter et al. 2011; Schacht, Cummings, & Davies 2009), have higher self-esteem, and, for girls, are more secure in their relationships with partners of the opposite sex (Carlson & McLanahan 2004; Carlson 2006; Flouri & Buchanan 2003; Richter et al. 2011; Schacht, Cummings, & Davies 2009). By contrast, lack of father involvement has been linked to a wide range of detrimental effects such as risk of internalizing or externalizing behavior, stigmatization, risky sexual behavior—including early sexual debut, and substance abuse (Carlson & McLanahan 2004; Omar 2010).

Men's presence and involvement in large part determine the social resources of the household (Richter & Morrell 2006). Households with men in South Africa are likely to be better off economically (Desmond & Desmond 2006), whereas households without men are worse off, more so when affected by HIV and AIDS (Denis & Ntsimane 2006; Richter et al. 2010). In addition, men usually have access to other community resources that may not be available to women, including loans, mutual support, and influence. Accordingly, children are not necessarily disadvantaged by the absence of their father, but they are disadvantaged when they belong to a household without access to the social position, labor, and financial support provided by men (Townsend 2002). Moreover, in households where men are available, children and women may be more secure from predatory behavior of men from outside the household (Guma & Henda 2004).

Women who are supported in stable partnerships with men experience lower levels of family stress, are less likely to suffer mental health problems, and derive greater satisfaction from their roles as mothers (Richter et al. 2011). Importantly, supportive men not only contribute to women's well-being and happiness, but their investment in the family has been found to buffer against the effects of neglectful or harsh parenting by a distant, demoralized, or overburdened mother (Martin, Ryan, & Brooks-Gunn 2010; Richter et al. 2012). This has particular relevance for black South African fathers because of the employment patterns of men, which keep them away from their families, and because of the different unions within which men father children. Mate shifting and child shifting have negative consequences on children's cognitive performance and social behaviors in African Caribbean families in which men have fathered children in visiting and common-law unions (see Samms-Vaughan 2005).

Despite this evidence, father involvement among black South Africans remains a matter of choice rather than obligatory, mainly because most fathers do not coreside with their children and other relatives play an important role in supporting children (Madhavan et al. 2012; Mkhize 2006). The importance of social fathers and other female caregivers in buffering any potential negative consequences of extended paternal absence and relationship instability between partners remains largely unexplored. Furthermore, the effects of psychological presence and the significance attributed to having a father around even intermittently in South Africa should not be underestimated.

DIRECTIONS FOR FUTURE RESEARCH, POLICY, AND PRACTICE

How men behave in South Africa is strongly influenced by dominant ideals of masculinity, including norms related to binge drinking and being strong and tough, which often translates into being insensitive, unemotional, and even aggressive. However, it is possible to challenge negative and harmful forms of masculine identities, and this is being done by many voluntary associations and networks of men, who work to promote nurturing and other positive images of men. Formal education as it is provided in schools, training institutions, and places of higher education, and informal education provided through media channels and in the work of government, NGOs, and community-based organizations (CBOs) are key areas in which to display, model, and communicate representations of positive fatherhood and masculinity.

Local leaders, church elders, and influential men in communities are also being encouraged to stand up and promote good fathering practices and to resist complicity in the abusive behavior of other men. Establishment of men's forums that share knowledge and skills important to fatherhood is also an important development. These help reduce the pressures on men to conform to rigid and sometimes dangerous forms of masculinity while focusing on the positive experiences that men generally report as they become more involved in caregiving and family relationships.

Several South African government policies and programs run by civil society organizations (CSOs) aim to assist men to become and stay engaged with their children over the course of their life (e.g., the Brothers for Life campaign). Stable father–mother relationships, father–child coresidency and well-functioning marriages are considered to be important for the protection and well-being of children. However, in the South African context, where marriage rates are low and many families are separated, efforts have to be made to promote healthy father–child relationships and facilitate greater social and cultural willingness to enable fathers to be more involved economically and socially in their children's lives regardless of the parents' relationship or coresidency status. A start to this is improved registration of births which establishes the legal tie between children and their fathers in nonmarital relationships.

Government and CSOs should introduce programs encouraging men to be more involved in their children's lives during the first important 1,000 days (from conception to the end of the second year), enabling men to participate positively in the decision to have a child, support women during pregnancy and at birth, care for and protect their child, and stay involved with their children over the course of their development. Information needs to be made available to men about childcare and protection, hygiene, disease prevention, recognition, and treatment of child illnesses, nutrition, and access to health services. This will help new fathers learn more about child care and protection and solidify the father–child bond.

Relatives, friends, and mothers must support father–child involvement, as their lack of support may discourage men who want to be involved in child care and protection. Fathers must be made aware of the importance of their engagement and availability, care, and protection of children regardless of their financial capacities. Men can be encouraged knowing children think fathers' love, affection, care, presence, and affection are as important as financial support. Despite men's inability to provide financially, children still need their fathers to be involved in other ways and to be their role models.

CONCLUSIONS

In South Africa, we are often struck by the portrayal of men as extremely brutal, violent, and abusive, but if we are going to change anything, we will have to change these men. We also know that not all men are violent and abusive. Most men we know are kind, loving, and nurturing. Despite high levels of father absence, and despite reported violence and neglect by men, the role of caring fathers in the lives of children and families is undisputed. Children in families having caring and loving men benefit from their economic support, care, and protection. Besides providing care and support to children in their homes, these caring men protect children in their neighborhood, at school, and in the community.

Policies and programs in South Africa need to promote positive male and fatherhood roles. Children need to be safe around men. All men need to be engaged and encouraged to be good and protective fathers, even to children who are not biologically their offspring. Tougher jail sentences for perpetrators of violence, neglect, and abuse toward children also need to be introduced to deter potential perpetrators of child abuse and neglect.

NOTE

1. These are all apartheid appellations. None is a "neutral" adjective.

FATHERHOOD IN SOUTH AFRICA

www.genderjustice.org.za
www.fathers.co.za
https://www.facebook.com/fatherhoodsa
www.f4j.co.za
www.men-care.org/Africa/South-Africa.aspx

REFERENCES

Anderson, P. (2007). *The changing roles of fathers in the context of Jamaican family life*. Kingston, Jamaica: Planning Institute of Jamaica and the University of the West Indies.

Burawoy, M. (1976). The functions and reproduction of migrant labor: Comparative material from southern Africa and the United States. *American Journal of Sociology, 81*(5), 1050–1087. doi: 10.2307/2777555.

Cabrera, N., & Tamis-LeMonda, C. (eds.) (2013). *Handbook of father involvement*. New York: Routledge Press.

Carlson, M. J. (2006). Family structure, father involvement, and adolescent behavioral outcomes. *Journal of Marriage and Family, 68*(1), 137-154. doi: 10.1111/j.1741-3737.2006.00239.x.

Carlson, M., & McLanahan, S. (2004). Fathers in fragile families. In M. Lamb (ed.), *The Role of the Father in Child Development*, 5th ed. (pp. 241–269). New York: John Wiley and Sons.

Chikovore, J., Richter, L., & Makusha, T. (2013). Father involvement in young children's care and education in southern Africa. In J. Pattnaik (ed.), *Father involvement in young children's lives*, vol. 6 (pp. 261–278). Houten, Netherlands: Springer.

Chirwa, W. (2002). Social exclusion and inclusion: Challenges to orphan care in Malawi. *Nordic Journal of African Studies, 11*, 93–113.

Denis, P., & Ntsimane, R. (2006). Absent fathers: why do men not feature in stories of families affected by HIV/AIDS in KwaZulu-Natal? In L. Richter & R. Morrell (eds.), *Baba: Men and fatherhood in South Africa* (pp. 237–249). Cape Town, South Africa: HSRC Press.

Desmond, C., & Desmond, C. (2006). HIV/AIDS and the crisis of care for children. In L. Richter & R. Morell (eds.), *Baba: Men and fatherhood in South Africa* (pp. 226–236). Cape Town, South Africa: HSRC Press.

Eddy, M. M., Thomson-de Boor, H., & Mphaka, K. (2013). "So we are ATM fathers": A study of absent father sin Johannesburg, South Africa. Centre for Social Development in Africa. University of Johannesburg and the Sonke Gender Justice.

Epprecht, M. (2007). Review of Ouzgane, L., & Morrell, R. (eds.), African masculinities: Men in Africa from the late nineteenth century to the present. *Postcolonial Text, 3,* 2–6.

Flouri, E., & Buchanan, A. (2003). The role of father involvement in children's later mental health. *Journal of Adolescence, 26,* 63–78.

Fouts, H. (2013). Fathering in central and east Africa: Cultural and adaptationist perspectives in small-scale societies. In D. Shwalb, B. Shwalb, & M. E. Lamb (eds.), *Fathers in cultural context* (pp. 151–172). New York: Routledge.

Grubb, L. (2010). Fathers ruling the roost. *Mamas and Papas, 2,* 137–140.

Guma, M., & Henda, N. (2004). The socio-cultural context of child abuse. A betrayal of trust. In L. Richter, A. Dawes & C. Higson-Smith (eds.), *Sexual abuse of young children in southern Africa* (pp. 95–109). Cape Town, South Africa: HSRC Press.

Henwood, K., & Procter, J. (2003). The "good father": Reading men's accounts of paternal involvement during the transition to first-time fatherhood. *British Journal of Social Psychology, 42,* 337–355. doi: 10.1348/014466603322438198.

Hewlett, B. & McFarlan, S. J. (2010). Fathers' roles in hunter-gatherer and other small scale societies. In M. E. Lamb (ed.), *The role of the father in child development,* 5th ed. (pp. 413–434). Hoboken, NJ: Wiley.

Holborn, L., & Eddy, G. (2011). *First steps to healing the South African family.* Johannesburg, South Africa: African Institute of Race Relations.

Hosegood, V., & Madhavan, S. (2010). Data availability on men's involvement in families in sub-Saharan Africa to inform family-centred programmes for children affected by HIV and AIDS. *Journal of the International AIDS Society, 13,* S5.

Hosegood, V., & Madhavan, S. (2012). Understanding fatherhood and father involvement in South Africa: Insights from surveys and population cohorts. *Fathering: A Journal of Theory, Research, and Practice about Men as Fathers, 10*(3), 257–273. doi: 10.3149/fth.1003.257.

Human Sciences Research Council. (2006). The Fatherhood Project Newsletter, No. 24.

Hunter, M. (2006). Father without *amandla*: Zulu-speaking men and fatherhood. In L. Richter & R. Morell (eds.), *Baba: Men and fatherhood in South Africa* (pp. 99–107). Cape Town, South Africa: HSRC Press.

Jewkes, R., Sikweyiya, Y., Morrell, R., & Dunkle, K. (2011). The relationship between intimate partner violence, rape and HIV amongst South African men: a cross-sectional study. *PloS One, 6,* e24256.

Kaufman, C., Maharaj, P., & Richter, L. (1998). *Children's schooling in South Africa: Transitions and tensions in households and communities.* Paper presented at the Annual Meeting of the Population Association of America, Chicago.

Lamb, M. E. (ed.). (2010). *The role of the father in child development,* 5th ed. Hoboken, NJ: Wiley.

Lamb, M. E., & Lewis, C. (2010). The development and significance of father-child relationships in two-parent families. In M. E. Lamb (ed.), *The role of the father in child development 5th ed.* (pp. 94–153). Hoboken, NJ: Wiley.

Lasser, J., Fite, K., & Wadende, A., P. (2011). Fatherhood in Kenyan ethnic communities: Implications for child development. *School Psychology International, 32*(1) 49–57. doi: 10.1177/0143034310396613.

Lesejane, D. (2006). Fatherhood from an African cultural perspective. In L. Richter & R. Morell (eds.), *Baba: Men and fatherhood in South Africa* (pp. 173–182). Cape Town, South Africa: HSRC Press.

Lloyd, C., & Blanc, A. (1996). Children's schooling in sub-Saharan Africa: The role of fathers, mothers, and others. *Population and Development Review, 22*, 265–298.

Madhavan, S., Townsend, N., & Garey, A. (2008). 'Absent breadwinners': Father-child connections and paternal support in rural South Africa. *Journal of Southern African Studies, 34*, 647–663.

Madhavan, S., Gross, M., Richter, L., Norris, S., & Hosegood, V. (2012). *Fathering across the early life course in urban South Africa*. Paper presented at the Annual Meetings of the Population Association of America, San Francisco, CA.

Madhavan, S., & Roy, K. (2011). Securing fatherhood through kinwork: A comparison of black fathers and families in South Africa and the U.S. *Journal of Family Issues, 33*, 801–822.

Makusha, T., Richter, L., & Bhana, D. (2012). Children's experiences of support they receive from men in the context of HIV/AIDS and poverty in rural KwaZulu-Natal as reported by men, women and children. *Africa Development, Special Issue on Parent's Involvement in Children's Lives in Africa, 37*, 129–154.

Makusha, T., Richter, L., & Chikovore, J. (2013). Fatherhood and masculinities in South Africa. In D. Glennrich (ed.), *Men and masculinities in South Africa*. Pietermaritzburg, South Africa: PACSA and Sonke Gender Justice Network.

Marlowe, F. (1999). Showoffs or providers? The parenting effort of Hadza men. *Evolution and Human Behavior, 20*, 391–404.

Marlowe, F. (2005). Who tends Hadza children? In B. Hewlett & M. E. Lamb (eds.), *Hunter–gatherer childhoods*. (pp. 177–190). New Brunswick, NJ: Aldine Transaction.

Martin, A., Ryan, R. M., & Brooks-Gunn, J. (2010). When fathers' supportiveness matters most: Maternal and paternal parenting and children's school readiness. *Journal of Family Psychology, 24*, 145–155.

Mathambo, V., & Gibbs, A. (2009). Extended family childcare arrangements in a context of AIDS: collapse or adaptation? *AIDS Care, 21*, 22.27.

Mathews, S., Jewkes, R., & Abrahams, N. (2011). 'I had a hard life': Exploring childhood adversity in the shaping of masculinities among men who killed an intimate partner in South Africa. *British Journal of Criminology, 51*, 960–977. doi: 10.1093/bjc/azr051.

Mavungu, E. M. (2013). Provider expectations and father involvement: Learning from experiences of poor "absent fathers" in Gauteng, South Africa. *African Sociological Review, 17*, 65–78.

Mkhize, N. (2004). Who is a father? *ChildrenFirst, 56*(July/August), 3–8.

Mkhize, N. (2006). African traditions and the social, economic and moral dimensions of fatherhood. In L. Richter & R. Morrell (eds.), *Baba: Men and Fatherhood in South Africa* (pp. 183–198). Cape Town, South Africa: HSRC Press.

Morrell, R. (2006). Fathers, fatherhood and masculinity in South Africa. In L. Richter & R. Morrell (eds.), *Baba: Men and fatherhood in South Africa* (pp. 13–25). Cape Town, South Africa: HSRC Press.

Nsamenang, A. B., & Lamb, M. E. (1995). The force of beliefs: How the parental values of the Nso of Northwest Cameroon shape children's progress toward adult models. *Journal of Applied Developmental Psychology, 16,* 613–627. doi: http://dx.doi.org/10.1016/0193-3973(95)90007-1.

Omar, S. (2010). A study of child-on-child sexual abuse of children under 12 years: An analysis of the phenomenon. Johannesburg, South Africa: Teddy Bear Clinic.

Polela, M. (2012). *My father, my monster.* Johannesburg, South Africa: Jacana.

Posel, D., & Devey, R. (2006). The demographics of fatherhood in South Africa: An analysis of survey data, 1993–2002. In L. Richter & R. Morell (eds.), *Baba: Men and fatherhood in South Africa* (pp. 38–52). Cape Town, South Africa: HSRC Press.

Posel, D., Rudwick, S., & Casale, D. (2011). Is marriage a dying institution in South Africa? Exploring changes in marriage in the context of ilobolo payments. *Agenda, 25*(1), 102–111. doi: 10.1080/10130950.2011.575589.

Rabe, M. (2006). Being a father in a man's world: The experiences of goldmine workers. In L. Richter & R. Morrell (eds.), *Baba: Fathers and fatherhood in South Africa* (pp. 250–264). Cape Town, South Africa: HSRC Press.

Rabe, M. (2007). My children, your children, our children. Fathers, female partners and household structures. *South African Review of Sociology, 38,* 161–175.

Ramkissoon, M. W. (2002). *The psychology of fathering in the Caribbean: An investigation of the physical and psychological presence of the Jamaican father.* Unpublished Masters Thesis. Mona, Jamaica: The University of West Indies.

Ramphele, M. (2002). Steering by the stars: Being young in South Africa. Cape Town, South Africa: Tafelberg.

Ramphele, M., & Richter, L. (2006). Migrancy, family dissolution and fatherhood. In L. Richter & R. Morell (eds.), *Baba: Men and fatherhood in South Africa* (pp. 73–81). Cape Town, South Africa: HSRC Press.

Richter, L., Chikovore, J., & Makusha, T. (2010). The status of fatherhood and fathering in South Africa. *Childhood Education, 86,* 360–365.

Richter, L., Chikovore, J., Makusha, T., Bhana, A., Mokomane, Z., Swartz, S., & Makiwane, M. (2011). Fatherhood and families. In Department of Economic and Social Affairs (ed.), *Men in families and family policy in a changing world* (pp. 49–84). New York: United Nations.

Richter, L., Desmond, C., Hosegood, V., Madhavan, S., Makiwane, M., Makusha, T., Morrell, R., & Swartz, S. (2012). *Fathers and other men in the lives of children and families.* Paper presented at the Strategies to overcome poverty and inequality: Towards Carnegie III, University of Cape Town, South Africa.

Richter, L., Manegold, J., Pather, R., & Mason, A. (2004). Harnessing our manpower. *ChildrenFIRST, 8,* 16–20.

Richter, L., & Morrell, R. (2006). Introduction. In L. Richter & R. Morell (eds.), *Baba: Men and Fatherhood in South Africa* (pp. 1–12). Cape Town, South Africa: HSRC Press.

Richter, L., & Morrell, R. (2008). Fathering: The role of men in raising children in Africa—holding up the other half of the sky. In M. Garcia, A. Pence & J. Evans (eds.), *Africa's future, Africa's challenge: Early childhood care and development in sub-Saharan Africa.* Washington, DC: World Bank.

Roy, K. (2008). A life course perspective on fatherhood and family policies in the United States and South Africa. *Fathering: A Journal of Theory, Research, and Practice about Men as Fathers, 6,* 92–112.

Samms-Vaughan, M. (2005). The Jamaican pre-school child: The status of early childhood development in Jamaica. Kingston, Jamaica: Planning Institute of Jamaica.

Schacht, P., Cummings, E., & Davies, P. (2009). Fathering in family context and child adjustment: A longitudinal analysis. *Journal of Family Psychology, 23,* 790.

Shwalb, D. W., Shwalb, B. J., & Lamb, M. E. (eds.) (2013). *Fathers in cultural context.* New York: Routledge.

Silverstein, L. B., & Auerbach, C. F. (1999). Deconstructing the essential father. *American Psychologist, 54,* 397–407.

Southern Africa Labour and Development Research Unit. National Income Dynamics Study 2010–2011, Wave 2 [dataset]. Version 2.2. Cape Town: Southern Africa Labour and Development Research Unit [producer], 2014. Cape Town: DataFirst [distributor], 2014.

Spiegel, A., & Mehlwana, A. (1997). Family as social network: Kinship and sporadic migrancy in the Western Cape's Khayelitsha. Cape Town: Human Sciences Research Council.

Spiegel, A., Watson, V., & Wilkinson, P. (1996). Domestic diversity and fluidity among some African households in Greater Cape Town. *Social Dynamics, 22,* 7–30. doi: 10.1080/02533959608458599.

Statistics South Africa. (2011). General Household Survey 2010: Statistical release P0318. Pretoria, South Africa: Statistics South Africa.

Townsend, N. (2002). Cultural contexts of father involvement. In C. Tamis-LeMonda & N. Cabrera (eds.), *Handbook of father involvement multidisciplinary perspectives* (pp. 249–277). Mahwah, NJ: Lawrence Erlbaum Associates, Inc.

Townsend, N., Madhavan, S., & Garey, A. (2006). Father presence in rural South Africa: Historical changes and life-course patterns. *International Journal of Sociology of the Family, 32,* 173–190.

Verhoef, H. (2005). "A child has many mothers": Views of child fostering in north-western Cameroon. *Childhood, 12,* 369–390.

Wilson, F. (2006). On being a father and poor in southern Africa today. In L. Richter & R. Morrell (eds.), *Baba: Men and Fatherhood in South Africa* (pp. 26–37). Cape Town, South Africa: HSRC Press.

Woolard, I., Buthelezi, T., & Bertsher, J. (2012). Child grants: analysis of the NIDS Wave 1 and 2 datasets. *NIDS Discussion Paper 2012/7, 84.*

Zwang, J., & Garenne, M. (2008). Social context of premarital fertility in rural South-Africa. *African Journal of Reproductive Health, 12*(2), 98–110.

Zwang, J., & Garenne, M. (2009). Social context of premarital fertility in rural South-Africa. *African Journal of Reproductive Health, 12,* 98–110.

19

Fathering in Kenya

Teresa Mwoma

Kenya has more than forty-two ethnic groups from different cultural and linguistic backgrounds. As might be expected, there is tremendous variation among these groups in levels of paternal investment and involvement with children based on economic conditions, modes of production, geographic region, urbanization, and exposure and interaction with neighboring ethnic groups. Despite this variability, ethnic groups in Kenya are largely patrilineal, and rituals and inheritance are transferred from one generation to the next through males from father to son (Oburu 2011; Watson 2000). Moreover, as Oburu (2011) observed, certain sociodemographic factors and cultural practices have helped usher in some similarities among ethnic groups in Kenya, key among them interethnic marriages, formal employment, improved access to education, and better opportunities for trade. Even so, it would be a mistake to ignore intracultural variations in family beliefs, rituals, and socialization patterns across ethnic groups. Bearing this in mind, this chapter provides a general overview of fathering in specific Kenyan communities.

In conceptualizing fatherhood in Kenya, two types of fathers come to mind: fathers in the traditional context and fathers in a contemporary world. Though this dichotomy suggests two distinct groups of men, there are those fathers who straddle the past they grew up with and a contemporary world that demands much more of them as fathers (e.g., emotional support to family members). This tension between the past and present can cause quite a bit of dissonance in terms of how men define masculinity and fathering identities. Furthermore, it has implications for the negotiation of roles, rituals, and childrearing responsibilities and practices in both rural and urban areas. For traditional societies, the distance between the old and emergent ways of doing fathering can be wide.

Historically, Kenyan fathers were the providers and protectors of their families and the community at large. In the hierarchy of family relationships, the father was the head, followed by the eldest son and other male relatives, with women and children relegated to lower status and social positions. The father was the ultimate symbol and custodian of power and responsibility in the family and community (Ratemo, Ondigi, & Kebaso 2007). Men in different ethnic groups married several wives with the purpose of producing many children who would inherit property, land, and livestock. Being appointed in leadership positions, such as being a chief of a community also contributed to polygyny and a man having many children. The prevailing wisdom was that if a man was capable of provisioning for and managing many wives and children, then he was qualified to be appointed a chief. A large number of offspring was seen as a source of pride and an emerging work force.

Though the hegemonic model of the Kenyan father as provider and protector was paramount and foremost among different ethnic groups, another major responsibility of men/fathers in the patriarchal social system was to induct young boys into male-related social and economic activities in preparation for adult life. In this process, boys accompanied their fathers while they engaged in subsistence activities, which provided ample opportunities for them to learn naturally about the adult provider roles, guidance from fathers being handy and available when needed. By contrast, girls mainly stayed around mothers and other women and were introduced to domestic chores and responsibilities early in their lives. These modes of participation with parents are synonymous with what Gaskins and Paradise (2010) term "open attention" to the many activities of mothers and fathers that occur simultaneously in the family and community.

With increased urbanization, modernization, and population growth, fathers roles have changed noticeably in Kenya over the last twenty years (Ratemo et al. 2007). Many fathers migrate from rural to urban areas in search of gainful employment; many work in businesses, different organizations, and government agencies. Others work in tea, sugarcane, coffee, and sisal plantations, and some still engage in small-scale farming and casual labor. These employment patterns have separated fathers from their families and changed the face of father–child activities. Unlike in the past, when children accompanied their fathers to engage in subsistence and trade activities, today children spend a good deal of time in school. These changes have affected the customary induction of boys into adult male activities and interrupted the processes that provided opportunities for children to learn male responsibilities and behaviors through direct observation.

In this chapter, I provide a descriptive account of few dimensions of fathering in Kenyan men: living and marriage arrangements as entry ways into fatherhood and fathering, the role of the father in the family, beliefs about fathering, and fathers' involvement in children's lives. In this effort, I weave together information on fathers in six ethnic groups: the Kalenjin, Abagusii,

Gikuyu, Luhyia, Luo, and Kamba. The Kalenjins are from the rift valley, the Luos and Luhyias live near Lake Victoria in the western part of Kenya, the Abagusii live in the highland regions of former Nyanza Province, and the Kamba are from eastern Kenya. Before proceeding with a discussion of the aforementioned issues, I first present a brief overview of what we know about fathers in a few neighboring African countries. Information presented on the different ethnic groups in Kenya is aided by survey data I gathered from university students about traditional and contemporary aspects of fathering in Kenyan cultural communities.

FATHERS IN A FEW OTHER AFRICAN SETTINGS

Psychological research on African fathers is rather thin. Using cultural and adaptationist theoretical perspectives, the ethnographic work of anthropologists has provided insights into the caregiving patterns of men in hunter–gatherer, pastoralist, and farming communities (Fouts 2013; Hewlett & McFarlan 2010; Marlowe 2005). Basically, the adaptationist perspective takes into consideration the changes in men's roles as fathers relative to economic, demographic, social, and political conditions within the immediate environment. The cultural perspective incorporates ideological beliefs about masculinity and men's roles within and external to the family (Super & Harkness 1997, 2002) and internal working models about parenting practices, such as when children display common developmental milestones and breastfeeding and weaning schedules (Hewlett & McFarlan 2010). These two perspectives capture some of the larger nuances of fathering roles in some African communities with long, adaptive histories and are relevant for the discussion that follows in the next section on fathering among the Kalenjin, Abagusii, Gikuyu, Luhyia, Luo, and Kamba ethnic groups.

Of particular interest here are the paternal investment and involvement patterns among the Aka and Bofi, who live in the Central African Republic and who are foraging and net-hunting groups; the Efe, a foraging and bow-hunting people who live in the Democratic Republic of the Congo; and the Hadza, nomadic foragers who live in northern Tanzania. Among these groups, Aka fathers are exceptional in that they are, arguably, the most intimate fathers observed to date. They adopt a permissive parenting style, rarely punish their children, hold their infants 22 percent of time observed, and keep their infants within reach about 47 percent of the day (Hewlett 1991). By comparison, Efe fathers hold their infants about 2.6 percent of the time, and low rates of holding were observed among Bofi foragers (1.9% with 18–35-month-olds) and the Hadza (2.5% with infants) (Fouts 2013; Marlowe 2005). Levels of holding and physical proximity have implications for developing attachment bonds to fathers (Ainsworth 1989) and provide opportunities for different types of social engagement between fathers and infants.

Direct care by fathers varied quite a bit among foraging groups with higher levels of involvement more characteristic of the Aka, who display egalitarian tendencies in husband–wife roles. Aka rarely engage in rough stimulating play (one incident during 264 hours of observations) with infants—an activity that has been emphasized as having significance for the development of attachments to fathers and for children's later social development in western industrialized societies (Paquette 2004). Furthermore, Aka fathers soothe and display affection to children more often than do mothers (Hewlett 1991). Bofi fathers were more distant from caregiving activities and engaged in direct childcare a paltry five minutes per daylight hours. Among the Hadza, children younger than 8 were seen interacting with fathers about 15.52 percent of the time, with mothers about 36.29 percent of the time, with older sister 13.37 percent of the time, with older brother about 9.77 percent of the time, and with maternal grandmother about 9.18 percent of the time. As in other cultural settings (e.g., Trinidad and Tobago, Flinn 1992; Roopnarine 2013; Sharma 2000) other women, such as grandmothers and the mother's sisters, and siblings provide much of the care to children in foraging groups.

In the sympatric communities of Efe foragers and Lese farmers, fathers appear similar in their involvement with children. Efe forager fathers were within proximity (three meters) of their young children about 40 percent of the time, significantly lower than the time forager mothers were in proximity to their children. Lese fathers were within three meters of their children 15 percent of the time, was also far less than the time mothers were near children. Although forager fathers spent more total time with children than farmer fathers, time in individual activities with children were quite similar, with the exception of play. In both groups, significant time was spent as targets of children's attention and in sharing with them. A striking finding was that children were more likely to have forager boys as social partners compared to other males. In the farmer group, boys were similar to fathers and men in social engagement with children. There was a moderate amount of time in play between fathers and children (Morelli & Tronick 1992).

These qualitative and quantitative data suggest that levels of father involvement in some foraging groups are equivalent to or exceed those in developed societies (Hewlett & McFarlan 2010). Role sharing and kinship networks influence men's direct involvement with young children. The availability of men and boys in the community has some bearing on paternal investment among the Efe and Lese. In the same vein, siblings and relatives provide direct care to young children in conjunction with fathers in these cultural groups. These patterns of care do not fit neatly into existing models on fathering in western industrialized societies and call for conceptual frameworks that separate out the relative contributions of multiple caregivers to child development outcomes. Additional insights into fathering in African cultural communities can be found in several volumes (Hewlett 1992; Hewlett & Lamb 2005; Richter & Morell 2006; Shwalb, Shwalb, & Lamb 2013).

FATHERS IN KENYA

Not unlike other cultural groups in developing societies (see Hewlett & McFarlan 2010; Roopnarine 2013; Shwalb, Shwalb, & Lamb 2013), living arrangements, selecting a mate and marriage arrangements, belief systems, and economic modes of production influence paternal investment and involvement with children in Kenyan cultural groups. In many African cultural groups, rituals such as circumcision mark important life transitions in preparation for parenthood, and marriage may mean negotiating the terms of bride price and service. Thus, on the journey to becoming a man, emphasis is placed on severing ties with mothers, establishing separate living arrangements, and heeding the advice of other men.

LIVING ARRANGEMENT AND ENTRANCE INTO FATHERHOOD

For many African cultural groups, initiation was a transition period from childhood to adulthood and marked a separation from parents in preparation for entry into mating and establishing a family (Watson 2000). Although variations exist in the transition process to becoming an adult and father in Kenya, the rituals of two ethnic groups, the Gikuyu and Abagusii, aptly exemplify the paths to becoming a man. Male circumcision in the Gikuyu and Abagusii signaled readiness for separate living quarters (Monyenye 2004; Watson 2000; Worthman & Whiting 1987). After initiation, young men were compelled to live in separate huts (*thingira* for Gikuyu and *esaiga* for Abagusii)) a few meters away from their parents' house, being deemed young adults. However, initiations included not only the rites of circumcision, but also exposure to the cultural rituals and customs of the particular group as well (Miller et al. 2009). Among the Luo, initiation into manhood involved removing six lower teeth; in the Gikuyu, the initiation ceremony was combined with a course in Gikuyu history and customs with lessons in sexuality and skills for adulthood; young Abagusii initiates would meet with older men in their huts (*egesarate*) for advice on manhood that presumably included paternal responsibilities. An initiated Gikuyu adult gains social respect and is recognized for his reproductive potential (Watson 2000; Davison 1996). After marriage, a Gikuyu man would build his own house on his father's homestead; he would also build houses for his wives. Each wife would take turns to visit the husband for conjugal rites (having sex). But this was influenced by the age of the youngest child and successful weaning, which indicated the woman's readiness to have another child. The conjugal rites were a little different for the Abagusii, among whom the man would visit his wives for sexual relations and then return to his hut (Mwoma 2014).

MARRIAGE ARRANGEMENTS AND ENTRANCE INTO FATHERHOOD AND FATHERING

Whether marriage occurs between same or different ethnic groups, it has been and continues to be a basis for fatherhood and fathering in much of Kenya. Legally, five kinds of marriages are recognized in Kenya: Christian marriages, civil marriages, customary marriages, Hindu marriages, and Islamic marriages (Republic of Kenya 2014). Christian, Hindu, and civil marriages are monogamous, whereas customary and Islamic marriages are presumed to be polygamous or potentially polygamous.

Lasser, Fite, and Wadende (2011) assert that even if a man hardly gives any support to his family, in marriage, he plays an important role by confirming the legitimacy of the family and children in the eyes of society. Legitimacy as a social construct in Kenya inspires the confidence needed for children to face life and be successful when compared to children from single-mother families who at times are swamped with feelings of rejection. In traditional Kenyan society, children from women who are married and remain in stable marriages enjoyed higher status than those from single mothers. Today, however, there is greater acceptance of diverse family constellations, and such a status attributed to marriage does not carry the same meaning, as many single mothers are able to sustain their families and support their children's educational attainment and other achievements.

Marriage, being a very important rite of passage among Kenyan ethnic groups, is carefully organized to ensure that a man obtains the right wife from a good family. Marriage is not a single event. It is a series of events accompanied by rituals that bring together two clans or two ethnic groups and their extended families. Thus marriage becomes a form of contract between two lineages, not mainly a direct commitment between husband and wife. Marriage is cemented by the payment of bride price as a sign of appreciation to the bride's family for the good care they provided to their daughter. Bride price among many ethnic groups in Kenya is negotiated between adult males of the groom's and the bride's family, though women are involved in the negotiation process in some ethnic groups. Bride price is negotiated based on the perceived value of the woman to be married. It is negotiated in the form of cows and goats but can be paid in monetary equivalent of the negotiated animals.

Usually, payment of bride price was an ongoing process that could conceivably take an entire lifetime, depending on the particulars of the agreement between the two families (Worthman & Whiting 1987).

Traditional marriage patterns and the process of entry into fatherhood varied somewhat among different ethnic groups in Kenya. But some similarities exist in macro-level approaches to obtaining a mate and becoming a father. To illustrate, among the Kalenjins there was no courtship leading into marriage, and in most cases the groom chose a bride to marry without her knowledge and with little information provided to her about himself. In some instances, the bride was taken without consent to the groom's home, after which the groom's family would arrange a visit to the bride's parents' home to organize to pay a bride price. Similarly, among the Luo, there was no courtship between the bride and the groom. Instead an aunt/elder acted as a go-between to identify a good bride who was hard-working and who would make a good wife. In other cases, young women were married by force when they were grabbed on their way to the marketplace or while fetching firewood or water (Mwoma 2014).

In the Abagusii ethnic group, men married a few years after circumcision. The mate was chosen by the man's parents through a suitor (go-between), who identified a hard-working woman from a "good" family, usually from a neighboring clan. Bride price was fully settled before a traditional wedding was organized. The agreement was sealed by tying rings (*ebitinge*) on each leg of the bride. This signified that the woman would never marry another man— that only death could separate her from her husband. After having children, the first wife would find a second wife for her husband. The second wife was a helper to the first wife. This kind of arrangement would continue when the second wife got a third wife for her husband, and so on (Mwoma 2014).

Slightly different selection methods were involved in the prelude to marriage in the Gikuyu and Luhyia ethnic groups. The man's parents would arrange to visit the woman's parents and make known their son's intention to marry their daughter and arrange for bride price payment. Gikuyu men have to accumulate bride price for marriage as a first step toward the establishment of a household and participation in ruling council (Watson 2000). The payment of substantial bride price hinders the accumulation of wealth by a single family, and brothers may end up marrying with the bride price given for their sisters (Watson 2000; Shaw 1987). Before marriage, Gikuyu women and men engaged in an intense social life organized around cycles of dances and male competitions of prowess (Watson 2000). Among the Luhyia, after a good bride was identified for marriage, elderly women were sent to visit the young woman's family to discuss the proposition with her parents. In turn, a visit was made by a delegation from the woman's family (usually women) to the man's home to express their acceptance or denial of the marriage proposal.

After discussions between the man's father and other community members, dowry payment was made to the bride's family, and thereafter, the bride officially was married and moved to live with the groom's family (Mwoma 2014).

In short, marriage was a significant event for becoming a father among different ethnic groups in Kenya. It was a communal activity, involving families from different clans and ethnic groups, and was supported by members of the community to ensure that the bride/groom found the right partner from the right family. In contemporary Kenyan society (Mwoma 2014), young people choose their own partners, meet in social places and engage in a courtship process, and—depending on the type of marriage—may or may not introduce their partners to their parents before marriage. In some ethnic groups, such as the Gikuyu, the man identifies the woman he wants to marry, they get introduced to the parents, and bride price payment is arranged, followed by a church wedding. Marriage ceremonies also occur on a civil basis, whereby a mate is identified, dowry is paid, and the wedding is legalized at an attorney's office. Others marry on a "come we stay" basis (trial marriage) whereby the couple lives together and has children, then pays the bride price later on. Reasons for trial relationships are various: inability to raise bride price on the part of the groom, wedding expenses and the many arrangements involved in preparing for a wedding, premarital sex leading to pregnancy, and fear of the groom's moving on to another relationship. Increasingly, religion plays an important role in guiding and counseling young people intending to marry, and they receive social support during the marriage process (Mwoma 2014).

ECONOMIC ACTIVITIES OF FATHERS

According to the ecocultural model (Whiting & Whiting 1975), challenges/opportunities within the near environment, the history of people, modes of production, the learning environment of the child (e.g., settings, caregivers), behavioral tendencies and beliefs of adults, and religion and ideology all influence parenting. That is, the cultural practices and belief systems of the group influence roles and responsibilities within the family (Lasser et al. 2011; Super & Harkness 1997, 2002). Moreover, parents may prioritize certain parenting goals to ensure the health and survival of the child. They employ specific strategies that are consonant with the demands of the environment and that have been proven to be of adaptational advantage (LeVine 1974).

In traditional, patriarchal Kenyan communities, a key role of men and fathers was provisioning for the family (e.g., providing resources, taking care of kinship members). Fathers in the Kalenjin ethnic group engaged in hunting of wild animals, herding animals (cows, goats, and sheep), and growing crops such as maize, wheat, and vegetables. They also engaged in barter, trading animals for grains (e.g., goats for bags of maize or millet). The Abagusii fathers engaged in farming, growing maize, sweet potatoes, bananas, and beans; hunted; carved; gathered food such as fruits and mushrooms; participated in iron blacksmith work; and practiced traditional medicine. Gikuyu fathers participated in farming, barter (exchange of animals for foodstuffs), hunting, food gathering, and animal husbandry, whereas Luhyia fathers engaged in hunting, fishing, farming, and mining. Luo fathers engaged in fishing, weaving, hunting, farming, and barter, and Kamba fathers engaged in herding, long-distance trade, agriculture, carving stones, blacksmith work, and barter (Mwoma 2014).

These economic activities of fathers were influenced by geography, subsistence opportunities, and local ecological conditions (Mwoma 2014). For instance, Luos and Luhyias, who live near Lake Victoria, practice fishing; the Abagusii, from the highlands, practice farming and cattle rearing; the Kalenjins, from Rift Valley, herd animals and practice large-scale farming; and the Kamba, from eastern Kenya, practiced long-distance trade and carving. In a number of these ethnic groups, children were an integral part of subsistence activities, either observing or assisting fathers. As hinted earlier, these means of production and provision for families and children are changing as men move away from homesteads in search of employment in urban areas or on larger farms. It is not clear whether, or for how long, fathers are separated from families, nor how this affects the allocation of care to children. Nonresident fatherhood has severe implications for black South African men who leave their families behind to work in the mining and other industries (see chapter 18, this volume).

CONCEPTIONS OF THE ROLE OF THE FATHER IN THE FAMILY

Scholars across disciplines have proposed that the cultural meaning of manhood has become elusive and that men continue to seek ways to (re) define their masculinity and roles in the family in a globalized world (see chapters 4 and 5 this volume). Simultaneously, women's employment and increased earning power, sometimes eclipsing men's, have contributed to the reconceptualization of the traditional provider role once solely assumed by men. This does not necessarily mean that fathers in patriarchal societies have entirely abandoned their ideologies about traditional masculinities or that increased investment and involvement with children is changing ahead of ideologies. Rather, it may be that at the moment, men are forced to increase their paternal responsibilities and engage in more childcare as their wives assume ever greater responsibilities at home and in the workplace. Put differently, increased paternal involvement in many traditional societies may be a result of women working outside of the home instead of changes in internal working models about childcare responsibility. Accordingly, "if a father's ideal is to be involved in his children's lives, he may engage in generative behaviors that match his perceptions of his ideal self. If dissonance between the real self and ideal self is too great, a father may flee from involvement and discard the ideal" (Shaw 1987; Watson 2000).

As stated already, in traditional Kenyan communities, the father was the one having ultimate authority and responsibility for the family. In the Abagusii and Gikuyu ethnic groups, men were viewed as superior to women, and in the Abagusii, Kamba, Gikuyu, and Luo, women were expected to remain quiet when men/fathers spoke. Essentially, they were not permitted to challenge male authority. Across ethnic groups, fathers (Ratemo et al. 2007) were expected to go out and fend for their families while mothers remained at home doing household chores such as cooking, caring for children, and fetching water and firewood. In some ethnic groups (e.g., Gikuyu), fathers were not supposed to enter the kitchen or cook food, and in many ethnic groups, fathers received food before children and others in the family. Apart from their breadwinning role and providing security, fathers were also in charge of disciplining their children, wives, and other persons who were judged to have disregarded the rules and regulations of the community. Fathers were advisors and mentors to young men and boys in the community and ensured that family disputes were settled amicably. Women were the advisors to girls. Invariably, children belonged to their father and the father's side of the family. Children were expected to strictly obey their father (Mwoma 2014).

Male superiority and privilege was expressed in other ways as well. The Kalenjins believed that only fathers should own/inherit land from their parents. The same was true for Abagusii men and boys, who inherited land from parents and grandparents (Mwoma 2014). Inheritance was not limited to property. According to Oburu (2011), a unique aspect of Luo customs and traditions dictated the marriage of widows. Remarriage for women (also known as wife inheritance, or *tero*) was expected to occur within families between close relatives because of brothers' and close relatives' affinity to the social norms within the group and perceived responsibility for taking care of the interest of vulnerable widows and children. Luo men would inherit a brother's wife after death to sire children for the departed brother (Oburu 2011).

With modernity, Christianization, and the perceived links of *tero* (act of inheriting) to HIV/AIDS-related mortalities, these traditional beliefs and practices about men as fathers are changing. Women now have a constitutional right to own/inherit land from parents. However, the extent to which male dominance and the provisioning role are giving way to emotional functions among fathers/men is not known. Furthermore, it is not clear how newer practices such as care of children by institutions outside of the family affect men's ideologies about husband–wife roles. Evaluation of the personal against ideal fathering roles may be an impetus for change, but, again, it is unclear how this is working out among Kenyan men.

FATHERS' INVOLVEMENT IN CHILDREN'S LIVES

A popular framework proposed by Lamb, Charnov, Pleck, and Levine (1985, 1987) indicates that paternal involvement contains three major components: engagement (direct care, playing etc.), accessibility (being around and available to a child), and responsibility (knowing the child's needs and responding to them). Furthermore, Lamb et al. (1985, 1987) outline four factors important for understanding variations in paternal involvement: motivation, skills and self-confidence, support, and institutional practices. It is argued that motivation alone cannot ensure increased paternal involvement: Skills and self-confidence are also necessary. Ostensibly motivated men often complain that a lack of skills prevents increased involvement with children (Lamb 1987). Support in the form of encouragement and reinforcement from mothers is also critical in paternal involvement. Newer models of father involvement have emphasized the cognitive and emotional aspects of paternal involvement and the factors that mediate and moderate the effects of father involvement on child development outcomes (Cabrera, Fitzgerald, Bradely, & Roggman, 2007; Pleck 2010) and suggest that fathers may serve a protective function when family processes are disrupted through marital dissolution and political and social violence across cultural communities (Cowan, Cowan, & Heming 2005; Cowan, Cowan, Pruett, Pruett, & Wong 2009; Lasser et al. 2011).

In the precolonial tradition, Kenyan fathers did not play much of a role in young children's socialization. They were background forces that influenced the child's life through mothers by providing for the family as dictated by culturally ascribed duties (Lasser et al. 2011). It was rare for Kenyan men to be directly involved with young children through interactions such as play or in their education. This was left to women and female extended family members. Among the Kipsigis, men were almost never the designated caregivers of infants and children, and cultural traditions prevent the father from seeing the newborn during the first month. Kipsigis fathers were never observed to "carry the infant outside the house, dress, feed, or bathe the infant, or take charge of it in the mother's absence" (Harkness & Super 1992). Caregiving was the responsibility of mothers and siblings (Harkness & Super 1992). Ocholla-Ayayo in Oburu (2011) noted that "fathers' care giving roles primarily involved adjudicating family disagreements, passing on skills to their sons aged over seven years and providing advice and guidance to family members. Fathers traditionally left other parenting roles to their wives, daughters aged over seven years, and grandmothers" (Oburu 2011, p. 156). However, they were involved in disciplining children and in teaching them moral values. A study by Ratemo et al. (2007) revealed that 60 percent of working fathers that they interviewed in Nairobi did not take the initiative to practice their roles as fathers. At the same time, most (60%) indicated that they would rather work extra hard to provide for their families than getting involved in the caregiving of children. However, 40 percent of the men interviewed expressed a passion for a better family, possibly indicating the intention of a shift toward greater paternal involvement with children.

In keeping with the conceptualization of "cultural training" (Whiting & Edwards 1988), traditionally, Kenyan fathers introduced boys into male-associated activities and work. As examples, the Kalenjin trained boys in herding, hunting, and in the construction of structures like houses and cattle pens. They showed their sons the best places for herding, taught them times for watering animals, digging farms together, weeding crops, harvesting and storing farm produce, and worked together in planning, buying, collecting construction materials, and building structures. Abagusii fathers engaged their children in farming, carving, and masonry (building houses, roofing, grass thatching and making furniture) and the Luhya trained young boys how to fish and harvest crops and exposed them to marketing and shopkeeping (buying and selling of goods) activities. Luo fathers trained children to know the best times for fishing, especially at night, and inducted young boys into the construction of homesteads by preparing building materials and selecting the position of a child's hut (*simba*). Kamba fathers instructed their children in constructing dams and roads, planting trees, and soil conservation. Fathers taught children how to inspect these activities and often financed and provided materials for them (Mwoma 2014).

Across ethnic groups, Kenyan fathers got involved in several cultural practices that included the naming of children, initiation ceremonies, the negotiation and payment of dowry for their sons and daughters, and the burial of departed loved ones. Naming a child can be an involved cultural practice. Children are named in several ways. Some children are named after the dead, whereas others are given names because of particular strengths. Abagusii fathers named children according to time, place, and ancestors. Watson (2000) reports that in the Luhya ethnic group, the father of the child consults a wise man of the village who talks to the dead to know whom among the dead wants his name given to the child. The wise man and the grandfather of the child preside over the ceremony. A big feast and animal sacrifice to the ancestors follow (Watson 2000). Perhaps of equal importance is that fathers decide the age at which a child should be initiated (circumcision) and guide him accordingly for entry into adulthood. Abagusii fathers participate in preparing boys for circumcision through informal teachings and making arrangements for circumcision and in advising young initiates about how to behave as young adults after circumcision. They also take part in planning and organizing marriage ceremonies for their children and negotiating bride price for their sons and daughters. These practices are witnessed in Gikuyu, Luo, and Luhyia fathers as well, among whom men act as models and mentors to young boys.

With respect to involvement in educational activities, Mwoma (2014) noted that Kalenjin, Abagusii, Luo, Kamba and Gikuyu fathers paid school fees and bought educational materials (books, uniforms, and stationeries) for their children. The Abagusii fathers attended school academic days, the Gikuyu fathers attended school functions and assisted children in doing homework, and Lou fathers checked on children's academic progress. In a comparative study of the activities of parents and children in Kenya, Korea, Russia, Estonia, and the United States, Tudge et al. (2000) provide additional insights into the activities of Luo fathers in Kenya. They were far less likely to engage in academic activities (e.g., spelling, counting, learning about shapes and colors, etc.) with preschoolers than mothers did, and this did not change even after the degree of presence was taken into consideration. This was also true when other learning activities (e.g., etiquette, religious knowledge) were offered to children. As in so many other traditional societies, it may be that men engage in diverse educational activities in these ethnic groups, but far less than women.

Mwoma (2013a) found that the type of school a child attended was related to fathers' involvement in children's education: Fathers whose children were enrolled in private preschools were more involved in their children's education than fathers whose children were enrolled in public preschools. In the Abagusii, fathers' educational level was related to involvement in children's education. Those having postsecondary education were more involved with children's education than those with no formal education and those who reached the seventh and eighth grade (Mwoma 2013b). This is consistent with another study that found that fathers with better educational attainment were more directly involved in their children's literacy activities than fathers who were not educated (Maina 2010). It should be pointed out that in a number of ethnic groups (e.g., Abagusii, Kalenjin), storytelling was practiced by fathers that conveyed language to children.

It has been argued that men avail themselves as playmates to children above caregiving activities (see Roopnarine 2011). Although this is changing and women have been shown to engage in the same levels of play with young children as fathers in Malaysian, Canadian, and Brazilian families, it still is a major activity between fathers and children (Benetti & Roopnarine 2006; Hossain, Roopnarine, Ismail, Hashmi, & Sombuling 2007; Laflamme, Pomerleau, & Malcuit 2002). Luhyia men participate in community sports (e.g., running, playing football, bullfighting, cockfighting) and music festivals (e.g., church concerts, singing, drama). Luo fathers participate in social recreational activities, such as wrestling, hockey, and dancing, organizing venues for these recreational activities and encouraging children to participate in them. Kamba fathers also take their children to recreational activities, provide play materials, and play with them, and the Abagusii induct children into community festivals such as *ribina* (a traditional dance to attract rain). Again, data on the Luo show that fathers played far less with preschool children than did mothers (Tudge et al. 2000) and in the Kipsigis, fathers rarely played with 1-year olds and occasionally played with 2–3-year-olds (Harkness & Super 1992).

A recent study (Putnick et al. 2012) of parental acceptance and rejection across nine countries and ten communities indicated that paternal warmth was high among fathers in Kisumu, Kenya (3.37, Range 1–4), was equivalent to maternal warmth (3.35), and was close to mean rates reported for other cultural groups (China = 3.37; Jordan = 3.57; Philippines = 3.69; United States = 3.79; Thailand = 3.50). Maternal and paternal warmth was significantly correlated in Kenyan families. In terms of hostility/rejection/neglect, again mothers exceeded fathers in the display of these behaviors. Paternal hostility among Kenyan fathers in Kisumu was below those of mothers but well within the range of fathers in other societies. These findings based on 7–10-year-olds are inconsistent with the caregiving distance recorded of Kenyan fathers during the early childhood years (e.g., Harkness & Super 1992) and may be due to cohort differences. Alternatively, they may reflect some of the changes that are possibly occurring among fathers in certain areas of Kenya.

It is difficult to draw any strong conclusions from the work on fathers in Kenya. What emerges is that fathers in traditional Kenyan cultural communities and ethnic groups followed cultural scripts that endowed them with specific roles tied to economic production, headship, moral guidance, and mentorship primarily to boys and to young men when they made the transition to adulthood. Fathers' investment in the emotional lives of children is not well defined, and they seem to maintain considerable distance from the socialization and education of daughters. Moreover, at least among the Kipsigis, the care that fathers offer to young children may be minimal but continue to increase as children age and become more involved in chores and make the transition to young adulthood (see Putnick et al. 2012). These modes of paternal involvement in children are seen in several cultural groups in the developing world (e.g., India, Caribbean, Arab world), among whom men are more protective of daughters and become managers and offer guidance to children as they enter late childhood and adolescence (Georgas et al. 2006).

FUTURE DIRECTIONS AND POLICY IMPLICATIONS

As is the case elsewhere, with modernity, there is a sense that the dominant masculine approach to fathering may be changing in Kenya. To what degree and in what manner would require more extensive investigations on different dimensions of father involvement with children in rural and urban environments and from different family constellations. For example, beyond paternal involvement, researchers need to tease out how children fare emotionally and cognitively in polygynous, monogamous, and trial relationships. Furthermore, there should be more focus on the effects of sociodemographic factors, health conditions, family and environmental stressors on father–child relationships and the factors that mediate and moderate these relationships. African researchers have also called for more indigenous theoretical perspectives on African patterns of childrearing and early education to better understand the cultural beliefs and practices central to addressing the needs of African families (Nsamenang 2008). This begs for the development of models that incorporate paternal risk and resilience factors associated with African cultural communities.

At the policy level, two issues, circumcision and marriage, central to becoming fathers in Kenya have been better defined. Because male circumcision is widely practiced in Kenyan communities (an estimated 84% of males are circumcised), the Kenyan government, through the Ministry of Health, has provided guiding principles on male circumcision with the goal of both respecting traditions and reducing HIV and other sexually transmitted infections (Republic of Kenya 2008). The focus is on safety, cultural sensitivity, well-trained practitioners, informed consent and confidentiality, provision of support and accurate information about health-related issues, and monitoring and evaluation. An obvious goal is to reduce HIV transmission to female partners and to improve the quality of family life and relationships and preserve certain traditions associated with journey into manhood and fatherhood.

As discussed in a previous section, marriage is central to men's entrance into fatherhood and carries heavy symbolic meaning and provides a context for understanding fathering in Kenya. In several communities, polygyny is practiced, and obtaining additional wives is now included under the new Marriage Act of 2014. The act defines marriage as a voluntary union between a man and woman, whether in a monogamous or polygamous union, that is registered in accordance with the Marriage Act (Republic of Kenya 2014). The act also states that a person should be 18 years old to marry.. It will be of interest to determine how this new law affects the selection of a husband/wife and men's entrance into fatherhood, husband–wife relationships, and the distribution of resources to women and children. Although it is more explicit in its definition, the Marriage Act by itself is unlikely to improve the quality of father–child relationships. Policies that define the social—emotional and cognitive responsibilities of men in relationships with children have far-reaching implications for human capital development.

KENYAN FAMILIES AND POLICIES

Legal/statutory marriage in Kenya: www.infotrackea.co.ke/articles/index.php?option= com_content&view=article&id=74%3Alegal-marriage-in-kenya&catid=42% 3Asemapa&Itemid=74&showall=1https://www.icrc.org/applic/ihl/ihl-nat.nsf/ a24d1cf3344e99934125673e00508142/95bcf642e7784b63c1257b4a004f95e8/ $FILE/Children%27s%20Act.pdf
Historical development of family laws in Kenya: www.kenyalawresourcecenter.org/ 2011/07/historical-development-of-family-laws.html
Gender and family law: http://kenyalaw.org/family/statutes.php
Family roles: https://megansteele.wordpress.com/2010/03/08/family-roles/
The people of Kenya and way of life: http://www.countriesquest.com/africa/kenya/ the_people_of_kenya/way_of_life.htm
Kenya and culture: http://www.everyculture.com/Ja-Ma/Kenya.html
The concept of marriage and the family Kenya: http://family.jrank.org/pages/1014/ Kenya.html

REFERENCES

Ahmed, R. A. (2013). The father's role in the Arab world: Cultural perspectives. In D. W. Shwalb, B. J., Shwalb, & M. E. Lamb (eds.), *Fathers in cultural context* (pp. 122–150). New York, NY: Routledge.
Ainsworth, M. (1989). Attachments beyond infancy. *American Psychologist, 44,* 709–716.
Benetti, S. P., & Roopnarine, J. L. (2006). Paternal involvement with school-aged children in Brazilian families: Association with childhood competence. *Sex Roles, 55,* 669–678.
Cabrera, N., Fitzgerald, H., Bradley, R., & Roggman, L. (2007). Modeling the dynamics of paternal influences on children over the life course. *Applied Developmental Science. 11(4),* 185–190.
Cowan, P. A., Cowan, C. P., & Heming, G. (2005). Two variations of a preventative intervention for couples: Effects on parents and young children during the transition to elementary school. In P. A. Cowan, C. P. Cowan, J. Ablow, V. K. Johnson & J. Measelle (eds.), *The family context in parenting in children's adaptation to elementary school.* Mahwah, NJ: Erlbaum.
Cowan, P. A., Cowan, C. P., Pruett, M. K., Pruett, K., & Wong, J. J. (2009). Promoting fathers' engagement with children: Preventative intervention with low-income children. *Journal of Marriage and the Family, 71,* 663–679.
Davison, J. (1996). *Voices from Mutira: Change in the lives of rural Gikuyu women, 1910–1995.* Boulder, CO: Lynne Rienner Publishers.

Flinn, M. (1992). Paternal care in a Caribbean village. In B. Hewlett (ed.), *Father–child relations: Cultural and biosocial perspectives* (pp. 57–84). New York: Aldine De Gruyter.

Fouts, H. (2008). Father involvement with young children among the Aka and Bofi foragers. *Cross-Cultural Research, 42,* 290–312.

Fouts, H. (2013). Fathering in central and east Africa: Cultural and adaptationist perspectives in small-scale societies. In D. Shwalb, B. Shwalb, & M. E. Lamb (eds.), *Fathers in cultural context* (pp. 151–172). New York: Routledge.

Gaskins, S. and Paradise, R. (2010). Learning through observation. In D.F. Lancy, J. Bock, and S. Gaskins (eds.) *The anthropology of learning in childhood* (pp. 85–117). Lanham, MD: Alta Mira Press.

Georgas, J., Berry, J. W., van de Vijver, F. J. R., Kagitcibasi, C., & Poortinga, Y. H. (2006). *Families across cultures: A 30-nation psychological study.* Cambridge, UK: Cambridge University Press.

Harkness, S., & Super, C. M. (1992). The cultural foundations of fathers' roles: Evidence from Kenya and the United States. In B. S. Hewlett (ed.). *Father–child relations: Cultural and biosocial perspectives* (pp. 191–211). New York: Aldine De Gruyter.

Hewlett, B. & McFarlan, S. J. (2010). Fathers' roles in hunter-gatherer and other small scale societies. In M. E. Lamb (ed.), *The role of the father in child development,* 5th ed. (pp. 413–434). Hoboken, NJ: Wiley.

Hewlett, B. S., & Lamb, M. E. (eds.) (2005). *Hunter–gatherer childhoods: Evolutionary, developmental, and cultural perspectives* (pp. 175–213). New Brunswick NJ: Aldine Transaction Publishers.

Hewlett, B. S. (1991). *Intimate fathers: The nature and context of Aka Pygmy paternal infant care.* Ann Arbor, MI: University of Michigan Press.

Hewlett, B. S. (ed.) (1992). *Father–child relations: Cultural and biosocial perspectives* (pp. 57–84). New York: Aldine De Gruyter.

Hewlett, B. S. (1992). Husband-wife reciprocity and the father-infant relationship among Aka Pygmies. In B. S. Hewlett (ed.), *Father–child relations: Cultural and biosocial perspectives* (pp. 153–176). New York: Aldine De Gruyter.

Hossain, Z., Roopnarine, J. L., Ismail, R., Hashmi, S. I., & Sombuling, A. (2007). Fathers' and mothers' reports of involvement in caring for infants in Kadazan families in Sabah, Malaysia. *Fathering, 5*(1), 58–72.

Laflamme, D., Pomerleau, A., & Malcuit, G. (2002). A comparison of fathers' and mothers' involvement in childcare and stimulation behaviors during free-play with their infants at 9 and 15 months. *Sex Roles, 47,* 507–518.

Lamb, M. E. (1987). Introduction: The emergent American father. In M. E. Lamb (ed.), *The fathers' role: Cross-cultural perspectives* (pp. 3–26). Mahwah, NJ: Lawrence Erlbaum Associates Inc.

Lamb, M. E. (ed.) (2010). *The role of the father in child development,* 5th ed. Hoboken, NJ: Wiley.

Lamb, M. E., Pleck, J. H., Charnov, E. L., & Levine, J. A. (1985). Paternal behavior in humans. *American Zoologist, 25,* 883–894.

Lamb, M. E., Pleck, J. H., Charnov, E. L., & Levine, J. A. (1987). A biosocial perspective on paternal behavior and involvement. In J. B. Lancaster, J. Altman, A. Rossi, & L. Sherrod (eds.), *Parenting across the lifespan: Biosocial perspectives* (111–142). Hawthorne, NY: Aldine.

Lasser, J., Fite, K., & Wadende, A., P. (2011). Fatherhood in Kenyan ethnic communities: Implications for child development. *School Psychology International*, *32*(1), 49–57. doi:10.1177/0143034310396613.

LeVine, R. (1974). Parental goals: A cross-cultural view. *Teachers College Record, 76*, 226–239.

Maina, A. (2010). Factors relating to fathers' direct and indirect involvement in the early childhood literacy in Thika District. Saarbruken: VDM Publishing House Ltd.

Marlowe, F. (2005). Who tends Hadza children? In B. S. Hewlett & M. E. Lamb (eds.), *Hunter–gatherer childhoods: Evolutionary, developmental, and cultural perspectives* (pp. 175–213). New Brunswick, NJ: Aldine Transaction Publishers.

Miller, A., N., Golding, L., Ngula, K., Wambua, M., A., Mutua, E., Kizito, M., N., Teti, C., Booker, N., Mwithia, K., & Rubin, D. (2009). Couples communication on sexual and relational issues among the Akamba in Kenya. *African Journal of AIDS Research*, 8(1): 51–60. doi:10.2989/AJAR 2009 8.1.6.719.

Monyenye, S. (2004). Rites of passage. Controversy over the role of initiation ceremonies for cultural identity among some Kenyan societies: The Case of the Abagusii community of South Western Kenya. In J. M. Bahemuka & J. L. Brockington (eds.), *East Africa in transition images, institutions and identities* (pp. 245–266). Nairobi, Kenya: University of Nairobi Press

Morelli, G. A., & Tronick, E. Z. (1992). Male care among Efe-foragers and Lese farmers. In B. S. Hewlett (ed.). *Father–child relations: Cultural and biosocial perspectives* (pp. 231–261). New York: Aldine De Gruyter.

Mwoma, T., B. (2013a). Type of preschool an important factor in determining fathers' support for their children's education. *Journal of Education and Practice*, 4(17), 190–193.

Mwoma, T., B. (2013b). Are educated fathers more involved in their children's education? Research findings on fathers' involvement in Gucha District Kenya. *Prime Journal of Social Sciences, 2*(1), 185–190. www.primejournal.org/PJSS.

Mwoma, T., B. (2014). Fathering among different communities in Kenya. Nairobi, Kenya: Unpublished research findings.

Nsamenang, A. B. (2008). (Mis)Understanding ECD in Africa: The force of local and global motives. In G. Marito, P. Alan and J. L. Evans (eds.), *Africa's future, Africa's challenge: Early childhood care and development in sub-Sahara Africa* (pp. 135–146). Washington, DC: The World Bank.

Oburu, P., O. (2011). Attributions and attitudes of mothers and fathers in Kenya. *Parenting in science and practice, 11*, 152–162.

Paquette, D. (2004). Theorizing the father–child relationship: Mechanisms and developmental outcomes. *Human Development, 47*, 193–219.

Pleck, J. (2010). Paternal involvement revised conceptualization and theoretical linkages with child outcomes. In M. E. Lamb (ed.), *The role of the father in child development*, 5th ed. Hoboken, NJ: Wiley.

Putnick, D., Bornstein, M. H., Lansford, J. E., Chang, L., Deater-Deckard, K., Di Giunta, L., . . . Bombi, A. S. (2102). Agreement in mother and father acceptance-rejection, warmth, and hostility/rejection/neglect of children across nine cultures. *Cross-Cultural Research, 46*, 191–223.

Ratemo, L., Ondigi, A., & Kebaso, J. (2007). Is There Time for the Family? Working Men in Nairobi, Kenya. www.womenofthemountains.org.

Republic of Kenya (2008). National guidance for voluntary male circumcision in Kenya. Ministry of Health National AIDS/STD Control Programme. www .malecircumcision.org/programs/documents/KenyaMCguidance.pdf.

Republic of Kenya (2014). The Marriage Act No. 4 of 2014: Special Issue. Kenya Gazette Supplement No. 62. http://kenyalaw.org/kl/fileadmin/pdfdownloads/ Acts/TheMarriage_Act2014.pdf.

Richter, L., & Morell, R. (eds.). (2006). *Baba: Men and fatherhood in South Africa*. Cape Town, South Africa: HSRC Press.

Roopnarine, J. L. (2011). Cultural variations in beliefs about play, parent-child play, and children's play: Meaning for childhood development. In A. Pellegrini (ed.), The *Oxford of the development of play* (pp. 19–37). New York: Oxford University Press.

Roopnarine, J. L. (2013). Fathers in Caribbean cultural communities. In D. Shwalb, B. Shwalb, and M. E. Lamb (eds.), *Fathers in cultural context* (pp. 203–227). New York: Routledge.

Sharma, D. (2000). Infancy and childhood in India: A critical review. *International Journal of Group Tensions*, 29, 219–251.

Shaw, C. M. (1987). *Colonial inscriptions: Race, sex and class in Kenya*. Minneapolis: University of Minnesota Press.

Shwalb, D. W., Shwalb, B. J., & Lamb, M. E. (eds.). (2013). *Fathers in cultural contexts*. New York: Routledge.

Super, C., & Harkness, S. (1997). The cultural structuring of child development. In J. Berry, P. Dasen, T. Saraswathi (eds.), *Handbook of cross-cultural psychology*, vol. 2: *Basic processes and human development* (pp. 1–39). Needham, MA: Allyn & Bacon.

Super, C., & Harkness, S. (2002). Culture structures the environment for development. *Human Development*, 45, 270–274.

Tudge, J., Hayes, S., Doucet, F., Odero, D., Kulakova, N., Tammeveski, P., Mettsas, M. & Lee, S. (2000). Parents' participation in cultural practices with their preschoolers. *Psicologica Tenria e Pesquisa*, 16, 1–11

Watson, M. A. (2000). Rites of passage: Birthing, naming, coming of age, marriage, elderhood, widowhood, death. In M. A Watson (ed.), *Modern Kenya: Social issues and perspectives* (pp. 245–273). Boston, MA: University Press of America Inc.

Whiting, B. B., & Edwards, C. P. (1988). *Children of different worlds: The formation of social behavior*. Cambridge, MA: Harvard University Press.

Whiting, B. B., & Whiting, J. W. (1975). *Children of six cultures: A psycho-cultural analysis*. Cambridge, MA: Harvard University Press.

Worthman, C., M. and Whiting, J. W. M. (1987). Social change in adolescent sexual behavior, mate selection, and premarital pregnancy rates in Kikuyu community. *Ethos*, 15(2), 145–165.

20

Conclusion

Jaipaul L. Roopnarine

As in most of the psychological sciences, our knowledge base and conceptual frameworks on father–child relationships emerge out of and are largely situated in a rather small segment of the world's population. As Lamb's (2010) popular volume on the father's role in child development suggests, there is now a sizeable body of work on fathers, but most fathering research is based on European and North American families. This has led to a limited understanding of the broader cultural influences on fathering and childhood development in the rest of the world. This volume approaches fathering from a pancultural or universal perspective while highlighting the local and particular about men's roles as fathers in specific cultural communities. As such, the volume attempts to integrate an emerging scientific literature on fathering that is rooted in different conceptual frameworks and addresses the need to understand the beliefs, practices, and processes that govern fathering from a global perspective. Berry (in press) notes that this "universalist view asserts that basic psychological processes are common to our species, while their development and expression are culturally-shaped."

Despite policy frameworks on fathering in several of the societies considered in this volume, there is a constant when it comes to fathering especially in developing societies. The provider role still seems integral to how men define themselves as fathers in families. In most societies, men have greater latitude to negotiate work and family roles, and it appears that women, not men, are the ones who make the necessary accommodative shifts to balance parenting, spousal/partner, and work roles. To be fair, in a number of societies, men are beginning to examine their internal scripts or working models about manhood and fathering that they inherited from their fathers and that were, and continue to be, influenced by the political, social, and religious institutions in their societies. Men report that they aspire to be highly nurturing fathers, but often the shifts that occur in fathers' attitudes and behaviors come at the insistence of wives/partners and children for more paternal engagement. Not surprisingly, then, there is much more ambiguity surrounding men's roles as caregivers and nurturers in several cultural settings. Currently, men's roles are being defined and redefined in the context of economic conditions, household composition, and diverse social structures.

Borrowing from the vast parenting literature, it is fairly well established that sensitively attuned, consistent, reciprocal and predictable parent–child activities that incorporate the child's needs and interests are hallmarks of good parenting (Baumrind 1967). These attributes of authoritative parenting have been shown to have positive influences on childhood development across cultures. For example, the construct of warmth and responsiveness is linked to favorable outcomes in children, whereas high levels of control, rejection, hostility, and neglect are associated with negative developmental outcomes across societies (see meta-analysis by Khaleque & Rohner 2012). These patterns of parenting and outcomes appear universal, though their expressions and pathways of associations may vary a bit. There is no reason to believe that when displayed by fathers these behavioral tendencies would not produce the same social and cognitive outcomes across cultures. Indeed, in several chapters in this volume in which such data are discussed, the developmental outcomes appear quite similar and begin to point to the shared meaning of certain paternal childrearing practices for childhood development. Of course, other mechanisms within cultures may work in different ways to influence fathering and children's development. Notably, the cultural pathways through which beliefs about gender roles, socialization practices and goals, the quality of spousal relationships, economic conditions, and history of parenting in one's own father, among other things, may directly or indirectly influence fathering outcomes across cultural settings. As yet, there is minimal work on how children influence fathering in a majority of cultures.

In these rich descriptive accounts of fathering across cultures, an overarching theme was to consider fathers' roles and their relevance for childhood development in terms of context and experience—a goal of cultural and cross-cultural psychology and human development. In both these subdisciplines, there has been greater acceptance of cross-comparative analysis and the indigenizing of our understanding of human development. The search continues for differences and commonalities in human behaviors, experiences, and developmental processes across cultures and disciplines (see Berry, Poortinga, Breugelmans, Chasiotis, & Sam 2011). Presenting fathering in diverse cultural settings side by side permits readers to make their own comparisons and inferences about what is universal and what is local or culture-specific. However, much more research is needed on fathering across cultures to achieve a more balanced scientific view of the importance of fathers in the developed and majority world. Along with international and regional organizations in the psychological sciences and human development, this volume joins efforts under way among researchers and policymakers to understand fathering and developmental processes in a global community marked by increasing intercultural contacts, academic collaborations across geographic regions, and rapidly changing social and economic systems.

REFERENCES

Baumrind, D. (1967). Child care practices anteceding three patterns of preschool behavior. *Genetic Psychology Monographs, 75*, 43–88.

Berry, J. (in press). Global, indigenous and regional perspectives on international psychology. J. L. Roopnarine & D. Chadee (eds.), *Caribbean psychology: Indigenous contributions to a global discipline*. Washington, DC: American Psychological Association.

Berry, J. W., Poortinga, Y. H., Breugelmans, S. M., Chasiotis, A., & Sam, D. L. (2011). *Cross-cultural psychology: Research and applications*, 3rd ed. Cambridge, UK: Cambridge University Press.

Khaleque, A., & Rohner, R. P. (2012). Pancultural associations between perceived parental acceptance-rejection and psychological adjustment of children and adults: A meta-analytic review of worldwide research. *Journal of Cross-Cultural Psychology, 43*, 784–800.

Lamb, M. E. (ed.). (2010). *The role of the father in child development*, 5th ed. Hoboken, NJ: Wiley.

About the Editor and Contributors

JAIPAUL L. ROOPNARINE (Ph.D., University of Wisconsin) is Jack Reilly professor of child and family studies at Syracuse University, Syracuse, New York. He has 35 years' experience conducting observational and survey studies around the world on father involvement and childhood development (e.g., India, Malaysia, Taiwan, Brazil, United States, Jamaica, Trinidad and Tobago, Thailand). Along with colleagues at Syracuse University and the University of the West Indies, St. Augustine, he recently conducted a national study of childrearing, mental health, and family belief systems and childhood outcomes in Trinidad and Tobago. He was a consultant to the Roving Caregiver Program, an intervention for parents and children, implemented in several Caribbean countries, and helped revise the Guyanese national early childhood curriculum. He was Fulbright scholar to the University of West Indies, was recently awarded a distinguished visiting Nehru chair at M. S. Baroda University, Gujarat, India, is the current editor of the journal *Fathering*, and has published extensively in the areas of family relationships, childhood development, and early childhood education.

PATRICIA ANDERSON was appointed professor of applied sociology at the Mona campus of the University of the West Indies, Jamaica. She holds a B.Sc. in sociology from the University of the West Indies, Mona, and an M.A. and Ph.D. in sociology and demography from the University of Chicago. Professor Anderson's research interests are in the area of social policy, labor market analysis, microenterprises, poverty and livelihood strategies, gender and parenting, and sexual risk-taking.

JESSICA BALL is a professor in the School of Child and Youth Care at the University of Victoria. Recent projects in her grant-funded program of interdisciplinary research have addressed early childhood policies and programs serving Indigenous and ethnic minority families in Canada and southeast Asia and the effects of transnational labor migration on father involvement and children's well-being. An internationally renowned scholar on these topics, Jessica is the recipient of many awards. She has published more than 100 articles, book chapters, monographs, and technical papers.

ANA M. A. CARVALHO (Ph.D., University of São Palo) is a retired professor and researcher in psychology at the University of São Paulo (USP) (1969–1993), Brazil. She did postdoctoral work at the University of Sheffield, UK, and at North Carolina and Duke Universities (USA). She received grants from the National Research Council (CNPQ) and FAPESP (State of São Paulo Agency for Research Support) for her work in early childhood development. She is a leading scholar in Brazil and maintains strong ties with the University of São Palo.

SUSAN S. CHUANG (Ph.D., University of Rochester) is an associate professor at the University of Guelph, Ontario, Canada. Her lines of research include parenting, fathering, parent–child relationships, and child development in various sociocultural contexts (e.g., Canada, China, Hong Kong, Paraguay, Taiwan, and the United States). She organized six international conferences on immigrant families. She is the series editor for Springer Science+Business Media on the *Advances on Immigrant Family Research*. She has coedited books and a textbook on human development with Worth Publishers.

CAMILLE DALEY is currently pursuing her Ph.D. in sociology at the University of the West Indies, Mona, Jamaica. She also teaches undergraduate courses in social policy and social research methods. Her research interests include parenting and the Caribbean family, social stratification, health, and education.

JAMES EARL DAVIS (Ph.D., Cornell University) is Bernard C. Watson endowed chair in urban education, teaching and learning at Temple University, where he serves as interim dean of the College of Education. His research focuses on gender and schooling outcomes; men, boys, and masculinity; sociology of higher education; and applied research methods. He has published extensively on African American males.

KIMBERLY DUTTON received her B.A. in child development from Mills College in Oakland, California, where she became interested in father–child interactions. She is currently enrolled in the graduate program in human development and family at the University of Delaware.

VIVIAN L. GADSDEN (Ed.D., University of Michigan) is William T. Carter professor in child development and education at the University of Pennsylvania. A former Spencer Foundation/National Academy of Education postdoctoral fellow, Dr. Gadsden served as associate director in the National Center on Adult Literacy and the director of the National Center on Fathers and Families, an interdisciplinary policy research center focused on child and family well-being. Her research interests focus on cultural and social factors affecting learning and literacy across the life course and within families, particularly those at the greatest risk for academic and social vulnerability. She has published extensively on vulnerable families and children across ethnic groups.

MINE GÖL-GÜVEN earned a undergraduate degree in counseling from Istanbul University, a master's degree from the Department of Child and Family Studies at Syracuse University, and a Ph.D. in early childhood education from Pennsylvania State University. She is an assistant professor of education at Boğaziçi University, Istanbul, Turkey, and is currently a visiting professor at Syracuse University. Her research interests are in early childhood education in cross-comparative perspective and children's play.

YUMI GOSSO received a master's degree from the Federal University of Pará and her Ph.D. from the University of São Paulo. She was awarded the CAPES (Coordination for the improvement of research and higher education) for her dissertation research. She has published in the areas of children's play among different cultural groups, including the Parakana Indians in Brazil.

ZIARAT HOSSAIN is an associate professor and regents' lecturer in the Department of Individual, Family and Community Education at the University of New Mexico. He received a Ph.D. in child and family studies from Syracuse University. His research documents patterns of fathers' involvement and early childhood development across understudied ethnic and cultural communities. He was a Fulbright scholar in Malaysia and president of the Society for Cross-Cultural Research.

JAMES HULL received his B.S. in human services and M.S. in human development and family studies (HDFS) from the University of Delaware and is currently in the process of completing his Ph.D. in HDFS, also from the University of Delaware. James has coauthored manuscripts on co-parenting and child well-being and father involvement and adolescent academic achievement.

CLEOPATRA JACOBS JOHNSON is a survey researcher at Mathematica Policy Research, where her research focuses on family well-being, early childhood, and education. Before joining Mathematica, Johnson was a research assistant at the National Center on Fathers and Families at the University of Pennsylvania. At both Mathematica and NCOFF, she has worked on private- and public-funded research studies on father involvement, parent–child engagement, and learning. Johnson holds a Ph.D. in applied psychology and human development from the University of Pennsylvania.

RUMAYA JUHARI earned a Ph.D. in family and child ecology from Michigan State University and currently is an associate professor in the faculty of human ecology at Universiti Putra Malaysia. She also heads the Family, Adolescent and Child Research Center at UPM. Her work focuses on marriage and family relationships, including fathering. Her professional endeavor is embedded in her personal duties of mothering four sons.

ZHANNA KRAVCHENKO received her Ph.D. in sociology from Stockholm University, with a dissertation on political, normative, and everyday frameworks for work and care reconciliation in Russia and Sweden. She currently works as a senior lecturer in the Department of Sociology at Uppsala University and as researcher at the School of Social Sciences at Södertörn University. Her research interests include sociological theory, comparative methodology, social policies, transition to adulthood, and social mobilization.

MICHAEL E. LAMB (Ph.D., Yale University) is professor of psychology at the University of Cambridge, is president-elect of Division 7 (Developmental Psychology) of the American Psychological Association and Editor of *Psychology, Public Policy and Law*. He is a premier researcher on fathering in the world and has researched and written extensively on fathering for four decades.

XUAN LI is a Ph.D. candidate at the University of Cambridge, where she conducts research on father–child interactions in contemporary Chinese families. She is particularly interested in parenting, child and youth development, and gender relations and has wide interests in issues pertaining to fatherhood, family studies, and cross-cultural research in general.

TAWANDA MAKUSHA is a post-doctoral fellow in the Human Sciences Research Council. He holds a Ph.D. in gender education and an M.A. in development studies from the University of KwaZulu-Natal. His doctoral studies focused on the determinants of father involvement in KwaZulu-Natal, drawing on the reports of men, women, and children. His areas of research interest are in parenting, families and fathers; the impact of poverty and HIV and AIDS on children and families. Tawanda has co-published peer reviewed journal articles and book chapters on child well-being, fatherhood, men, and masculinities in South Africa.

AYSEGUL METINDOGAN completed her undergraduate education in guidance and counseling in Turkey. She received a scholarship to pursue her graduate education at Syracuse University, where she received master's and doctoral degrees in the Department of Child and Family Studies. Upon returning to Turkey, she joined the faculty at Bogazici University, where she teaches courses on childhood development and research methods. Her research interests include parenting, fathering, gender role development, and marital relationships.

LUCIA V. C. MOREIRA received her Ph.D. in psychology from the University of São Paulo. She currently coordinates the graduate program on family in contemporary society at the Catholic University of Salvador (Bahia, Brazil). Her research projects focus on paternity, maternity, children's education, family, and human development.

ROBERT P. MORENO received his baccalaureate degree in psychology at UCLA and his Ph.D. in child and adolescent development from Stanford University. He is also a former recipient of the National Academy of Education/Spencer Fellowship. He is currently an associate professor and chair of the Department of Child and Family Studies at Syracuse University. His research examines familial and cultural influences on children's learning and academic achievement among Latinos.

SARAH MOSELLE is an independent scholar specializing in social policy research on topics of quality of life for families, social inclusion, and women's empowerment. She has published and presented on these topics. She holds an M.A. in religion and culture from Wilfred Laurier University. Currently based in southeast Asia, she is pursuing research and communication for international development agencies.

TERESA MWOMA (Ph.D.) is a lecturer in the Department of Early Childhood Studies, Kenyatta University, Kenya. While writing a chapter for this volume, Teresa was pursuing her post-doctoral research fellowship in education and care in childhood at the University of Johannesburg, South Africa. Her research interests lie in the areas of early childhood development and education, orphans and vulnerable children, and fatherhood. Teresa has mentored and successfully supervised several graduate students in early childhood studies.

JUN NAKAZAWA is a professor of developmental psychology with the faculty of education at Chiba University, Japan. He holds B.A., M.A., and Ph.D. degrees from Hiroshima University. He was a chief editor of the *Japanese Journal of Educational Psychology* and is now an associate editor of the *Japanese Journal of Psychology* and *Japanese Psychological Research*. He is also on the editorial board of *Fathering*. Nakazawa's research interests include child socialization (especially cognitive/emotional regulation), fathering, and comic reading literacy.

ROB PALKOVITZ (Ph.D., Rutgers University) is professor of human development and family studies at the University of Delaware. His research interests are in fathering and intergenerational relationships and development, with particular emphasis on the relationships between patterns of father involvement and developmental outcomes for men and their children. He is currently studying fathers' resources, transitions within fathering, and characteristics of resilient fathers in challenging circumstances.

LARS PLANTIN (Ph.D.) is a professor of social work with the faculty of health and society, Malmö University, Sweden. His main area of expertise is family sociology, with a special focus on fatherhood. He has published numerous articles on the subject focusing on various aspects such as class, ethnicity, and age. He has also published articles and books on such themes as parenthood and the Internet, reproductive health and migration, and work and family life.

LINDA RICHTER (Ph.D.) is director of the Department of Science and Technology (DST)–National Research Foundation (NRF) Centre of Excellence in Human Development at the University of the Witwatersrand and is a distinguished research fellow at the Human Sciences Research Council in South Africa. She is also an honorary professor in psychology and an elected fellow of the University of KwaZulu-Natal. She is an advisor to the World Health Organization in Geneva on early child development. Linda has conducted both basic and policy research in the fields of child, youth, and family development as applied to health, education, welfare and social development and has published more than 400 papers and chapters in the fields of child, adolescent and family development, infant and child assessment, protein–energy malnutrition, street and working children, and the effects of HIV and AIDS on children and families. She is the author of several books and monographs, including *Baba: Men and Fatherhood in South Africa* (HSRC Press, 2006).

MIHAELA ROBILA (Ph.D., Syracuse University) is professor of human development and family studies at Queens College, CUNY. Her research is on international migration, family relations and policies. She written extensively on families in other cultures and is the editor of *Handbook on Family Policies across the Globe* (Springer, 2014) and *Families in Eastern Europe* (Elsevier, 2004), and wrote a book on eastern European immigrant families (Routledge, 2010). She is a fellow of the American Psychological Association.

RONI STRIER (Ph.D.) is a senior lecturer in the School of Social Work at the University of Haifa, Israel. His areas of teaching and research are social exclusion, poverty, gender, and fatherhood. He is academic chair of the leadership and social change track at the master's social work program, head of the Interdisciplinary Center for the Study of Poverty and Social Exclusion, and academic chair of the University of Haifa Flagship program "Fighting Social Exclusion and Promoting Solidarity."

ALEJANDRA SALGUERO VELÁZQUEZ has a Ph.D. in sociology and is titular professor of psychology at the National Autonomous University of Mexico, Iztacala Campus. Her research interests include gender roles, family relationships, and masculinity and fatherhood. Her recent books are *Reproduction and Parenting: Learning Experiences of Men*, *Male Identity: Elements of Analysis in Process Construction*, and *Dilemmas and Conflicts in Motherhood and Fatherhood*. She is part of the meeting of experts on the issue of paternity organized by the Presidency of the Republic and the National Institute of Women y México.

KARIN WALL is a research professor at the Institute for Social Sciences at the University of Lisbon. Her main areas of expertise are sociology of families and comparative social policy. She coordinates the Observatory on Families and Family Policies and has worked since 1995 as an expert on family policies in Europe. Her research interests include family forms and interactions, work–family balance, men's roles in families, gendered divisions of labor, family and work–life policies, migrant families, and the life course.

Index